Fundamental Chess Openings

Paul van der Sterren

First published in English language in the UK by Gambit Publications Ltd 2009
Based on *De wereld van de schaakopeningen*, published in three volumes in Dutch language by Tirion Uitgevers BV
Copyright © Paul van der Sterren 2009
Reprinted 2011, 2012, 2015, 2016, 2018, 2020

ISBN-13: 978-1-906454-13-5
ISBN-10: 1-906454-13-2

DISTRIBUTION:

Worldwide (except USA): Central Books Ltd, 50 Freshwater Rd, Chadwell Heath, London RM8 1RX.
Tel +44 (0)20 8986 4854 Fax +44 (0)20 8533 5821. E-mail: orders@Centralbooks.com

Gambit Publications Ltd, 27 Queens Pine, Bracknell, Berks, RG12 0TL, England.
E-mail: info@gambitbooks.com
Website (regularly updated): www.gambitbooks.com

Edited by Graham Burgess
Typeset by Petra Nunn
Cover image by Wolff Morrow
Printed and bound by TJ International, Padstow, Cornwall, England

10 9 8 7 6

Gambit Publications Ltd
Directors: Dr John Nunn GM, Murray Chandler GM and Graham Burgess FM
German Editor: Petra Nunn WFM
Bookkeeper: Andrea Burgess

Contents

Symbols and Notation

x	capture	♔	king
+	check	♕	queen
++	double check	♖	rook
#	checkmate	♗	bishop
!!	brilliant move	♘	knight
!	good move		
!?	interesting move		
?!	dubious move		
?	bad move		
??	blunder		
0-0	castles kingside		
0-0-0	castles queenside		
(D)	see next diagram		

Algebraic Notation

Moves are shown by giving the piece symbol followed by the destination square. For instance, if a knight moves to the square marked in the diagram, this is written as ♘f3 in algebraic notation. If two pieces of the same type can move to the same square, more information is given. For instance, if there are knights on g1 and e5, then the one on e5 moving to f3 is written as ♘ef3.

For pawn moves, only the arrival square is given (for example, e4 means that a pawn moves to the e4-square). For pawn captures, the file the pawn is leaving is also given. Thus exf4 means that a pawn on the e-file makes a capture that brings it to the f4-square.

Introduction

In the colossal body of chess literature, no aspect of the game has been treated as extensively as the openings. In varying degrees of expertise, clarity and depth, thousands of books discuss every imaginable and unimaginable opening the game of chess has to offer. This is a process that will never stop. As long as a particular opening is being played, its variations will be worked out deeper and deeper and assessments will be modified on the basis of these new experiences. As long as chess is alive, its opening theory will also be alive and new books will be needed to document all of this new life.

This book intends to introduce the reader to this strange but fascinating world, the world of opening theory. There will be no long sequences of moves, no complicated analysis and no real attempt to keep up with the very latest developments. Instead I shall attempt to clarify the background, the genesis and the development of all major openings and try to show how they are much more interconnected and based on the same ideas and insights than many people think. This approach makes this book a very different one from the usual opening manuals. It could perhaps be said to precede them. If it has the effect on the reader that it whets his appetite for these 'usual' opening books, or at least makes him understand them a little bit better, this book will have fulfilled its purpose.

What is Opening Theory?

Everyone who devotes even the tiniest amount of thought to his first move not only makes a start with that particular game but also with the development of opening theory. From that moment on, every new game will confront him with the starting position again and therefore with his earlier thoughts on it. Also he will sooner or later find out that millions of other players have pondered exactly the same problems and, whether he wants to or not, he will to some extent start comparing his own ideas about how to start a game with theirs.

This means that opening theory arises quite naturally with the start of a game. No one can avoid it. It ends, equally naturally, with the end of a game. If we pursue our thinking about the opening position logically and systematically, while accepting only the highest possible degree of certainty as a satisfactory result, we cannot end our investigation unless we are sure we have reached either a winning or a drawn position. Seen in this light, thinking about the starting position involves a thorough examination of the middlegame and endgame as well.

It could be said then, that opening theory does not really exist, at least not as something separate from other aspects of the game. Ultimately, opening theory comprises *all* theory.

However, since the human brain and even the computer is still not capable of completely seeing through (and thereby destroying) chess as a whole, in practice opening theory does not end with an empty board but in positions where there is a certain consensus about how they should be assessed, for instance 'chances are equal' or 'White (or Black) has the advantage'.

Sometimes a question can be answered with total confidence. In the position after 1 e4 there is some room for discussion on how good or bad 1...g5 is (though not much), but if White continues 2 d4 here, there can be no question on the value of 2...f6 because 3 ♕h5# is then mate. End of game, end of theory.

But in most cases an assessment is merely a temporary stop. The moment somebody starts questioning it, the argument continues. Until the next temporary stop is reached.

And so, ever since the beginnings of chess, every single chess-player has contributed something to that gigantic construction called opening theory. This brings us to the next question.

How Much Theory Should a Player Know?

The most severe answer to this has to be 'everything', the softest 'as much as you like' and the profoundest 'nothing'. All three are correct.

Knowledge of opening theory is a double-edged sword. The player who knows a lot will undoubtedly profit by his knowledge, but he may also live in constant fear of meeting an opponent who knows even more. Everyone who has studied opening theory in depth will have learned that, no matter how well you do your work, there is always the possibility of having overlooked something or of not having looked deep enough. Trying to keep abreast of the latest developments, reading everything, keeping a close watch on the Internet, makes you very knowledgeable but also acutely aware of the possibility of missing something. In short, he who lives by the sword shall die by the sword.

It is therefore of the utmost importance for a chess-player to find his own personal balance between knowing too much and knowing too little. The purpose of studying opening theory should not be accumulating any set amount of knowledge, but being content with whatever knowledge one has. For someone with a natural flair for study, it may be perfect to work on openings all the time. For someone who is much less scientifically minded, even the slightest attempt to study openings may well be superfluous and even detrimental to his game.

But there is another aspect of studying opening theory to be mentioned. Anyone with even the slightest intellectual bent of mind (and which chess-player isn't?) may find getting to know a little bit about opening theory very interesting. Even without any ambition to improve your results and independent of your level of play, you may simply find the study of openings very enjoyable. You may also discover that this has absolutely nothing to do with memorizing variations or the need to occupy yourself with chess more than you want to.

This sheer fun is in my view an essential element of studying opening theory. It is my hope that this book will make some of this pleasure visible and perceptible. The book contains an overview of all major openings, how they have evolved through the years and how they are looked upon today, early in the 21st century. I shall be just sketching the outlines and will be very concise, but perhaps this is precisely the way to convey the fascination that opening theory has always had for me. Opening theory has been an almost inexhaustible source of pleasure for me throughout my active chess years. I sincerely hope it may be the same for you.

The First Move

The two most important opening moves by far are **1 e4** and **1 d4**. By playing either of these classical moves, White uses his right to open the game to occupy as large a portion of the centre as possible. He also opens lines and diagonals for his queen and one of his bishops and creates a possible square of development for one of his knights.

Slightly more modest, yet still very respectable, are **1 c4** and **1 ♘f3**. With these moves, White does not immediately occupy any of the centre squares (e4, d4, e5 and d5) but he controls them, which is strategically just as important. He does this from the side or, in military terms, on the flank. That is why these two opening moves are called Flank Openings.

It is mainly on these four moves that the grand structure of opening theory has been erected. Bordering on that structure (in the grounds so to speak) are the modest cottages of **1 g3**, **1 b3**, **1 f4** and **1 ♘c3**, while with other moves we gradually get bogged down in the marshlands surrounding the estate, lands which have hardly been made inhabitable and perhaps had better remain so.

We shall start our investigation with 1 d4.

1 d4

Speaking in very general terms, one might say this is the more strategically orientated of White's two main opening moves. If, on your classical opening move, the equally classical symmetrical reply is what you expect, then you know that after 1 e4 e5 you will immediately be able to attack an undefended pawn with 2 ♘f3 (or the much more radical 2 f4). White then has an obvious object of attack which makes the situation relatively clear and straightforward.

After 1 d4 d5 things are very different because Black's pawn on d5 is securely defended. Yet on closer inspection it turns out that White is able to attack Black's central stronghold, mainly because of the possibility of 2 c4. This attack has a different feel and is slower than White's plans in the equivalent position after 1 e4 e5. It is based on a long-term positional plan and therefore more of a strategic nature. That is why 1 d4 did not really flourish until the rise of positional play in the late 19th century. Until then 1 e4 was by far the most popular move.

This means that practically from the start, theory of the 1 d4 openings has been developed by players whose general outlook on chess was similar to ours today. That is why almost all of these openings are still very much alive, which can hardly be said of the 1 e4 complex. Especially in the 1 e4 e5, section quite a lot of the old theory has by now been shelved permanently.

1   d4 (D)

Black's most classical reply has already been mentioned: **1...d5**. Until about 1920, this was by far the most highly regarded and in some periods practically the only 'approved' move. The crucial position arises if White then plays **2 c4**, the **Queen's Gambit**. Black's principal defences to this set-up have grown into three major, independent openings: the **Queen's Gambit Declined (2...e6)**, the **Slav Defence (2...c6)** and the **Queen's Gambit Accepted (2...dxc4)**. These openings will be the subject of the first three

chapters of this book. In the fourth I shall give an overview of Black's less popular replies to 2 c4 and of White's alternatives to 2 c4.

Around 1920 the classical move 1...d5 began to be seriously challenged by the rise of an alternative: **1...♘f6**. Hesitant at first, suffering much scorn and sarcasm, then quickly gathering momentum and eventually quite triumphantly, this move has risen to the top of the bill.

Traditional theory had stated that 1...♘f6, although it does have the merit of controlling e4 and thus preventing 2 e4, had little more to offer against the logical **2 c4 (D)** than a hasty retreat to the safe ground of the Queen's Gambit with 2...e6 followed by 3...d5 and therefore had little independent significance.

In due course it became clear, however, that Black does not have just one, but several important possibilities. In fact, the position after 1 d4 ♘f6 2 c4 turned out a real goldmine of new openings. Most of these rose to prominence shortly after World War II and 1...♘f6 has been Black's most popular defence to 1 d4 ever since.

To begin with, it was discovered that Black has **2...e6 3 ♘c3 ♗b4**, the **Nimzo-Indian Defence**. Then it turned out that Black has two alternatives to 3...d5 if White plays **3 ♘f3** instead

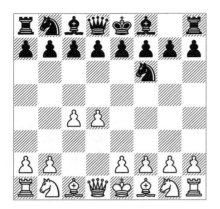

of 3 ♘c3, namely **3...b6**, the **Queen's Indian Defence**, and **3...♗b4+**, the **Bogoljubow Defence** or **Bogo-Indian**. All three have developed into very reliable openings, which are unlikely ever to disappear again.

Even more spectacular was the gradual acceptance of **2...g6**. No fewer than two new openings were introduced here, both equally important today and equally forceful: after **3 ♘c3** the move **3...♗g7** produces the **King's Indian Defence**, while **3...d5** is the **Grünfeld Defence**.

Finally, Black also has the possibility of **2...c5**, which is called the **Benoni**. This opening contains a surprisingly large number of subvariations, all offering Black an interesting game.

All of these openings will get a chapter of their own. We shall then consider some minor alternatives on Black's second move and we shall see what happens if White refrains from playing 2 c4.

Apart from 1...d5 and 1...♘f6, Black has several other replies, of which **1...f5**, the **Dutch Defence**, is the most important, at least in a historical sense. In the 19th century, this opening was considered the only reasonable alternative to the classical 1...d5. It was ranked far above

1...♘f6 until that move became popular around 1920. The rise of the Indian openings pushed the Dutch Defence into the background, but there it has held a respectable position ever since.

1...d5, 1...♘f6 and 1...f5 are moves that prevent the opponent from taking up the ideal central pawn-formation by playing 2 e4, which is what White would undoubtedly do if Black were to push his clock without making a move. And yet, the term 'ideal central pawn-formation' is perhaps a misleading one. It is not only a matter of *how* White (or Black) places his pawns in the centre, it is equally important (and perhaps even more so) what he can *do* with those centre pawns in any given situation. A broad pawn-centre can be strong, but it can also be vulnerable. It is strong if it cramps the enemy position or if it forms a base for an attack. It is vulnerable if it is *being* attacked, and it is weak when it crumbles as a result of that attack.

It is a perfectly legitimate opening strategy for Black to let White build up a central pawn-formation to his liking. If he does so without a plan and the necessary determination to fight back at the first opportunity, however, opening theory will regard this as a betrayal of its principles and turn its back on the offender. But if he acts with a plan and with determination, the result may be a fascinating opening struggle. In that case Black allows his opponent to form a broad pawn-centre only with the firm intention to annihilate it.

The major representatives of this category of openings are **1...e6**, **1...d6** and **1...g6**. A respectable body of theory has been developed around all three of these moves, especially in the last three decades, but to put this into perspective (for, after all, this is still only a fraction of the theory attached to the 'big' 1 d4 openings) I have condensed this into a single chapter.

Queen's Gambit Declined

1	d4	d5
2	c4	e6

The Queen's Gambit Declined is one of the oldest 1 d4 openings and has a long history. As long ago as the 19th century, when 1 e4 was still by far the most popular move, 1...d5 2 c4 e6 was the accepted reply to the far less respected 1 d4. With the rise of positional chess, attention shifted heavily to 1 d4 and the Queen's Gambit Declined automatically became the most important of all openings. In the 1927 match for the World Championship between Alekhine and Capablanca, for instance, the Queen's Gambit Declined was played in 32 of the 34 games (and 1 e4 only once). No doubt as a reaction to this one-sidedness, a much broader range of openings was developed after this, but the Queen's Gambit Declined has always remained important, simply because it is regarded as an intrinsically sound and trustworthy way of playing.

Black prepares to recapture on d5 with his e-pawn if necessary, while at the same time opening a diagonal for the king's bishop. He thus holds his ground in the centre and sets up a very natural plan of development for his pieces.

White now has two plausible moves, 3 ♘c3 and 3 ♘f3. The main significance of 3 ♘f3 lies in preparing the **Catalan Opening**, which arises after 3...♘f6 4 g3 and will be dealt with at the end of this chapter.

3 ♘c3 (D)

This is the most usual move, which brings us to our first major parting of the ways:

With **3...c5** Black claims an equal share of the centre at once. This is called the **Tarrasch Defence**.

He can also play **3...c6**. This move is based on a very clever idea and is much more aggressive than it looks. This is the **Noteboom (or Abrahams) Variation**.

B

Then we have the simple developing moves **3...♘f6** and **3...♗e7**. It is with either of these that the Queen's Gambit Declined proper is reached.

Finally, the move **3...♗b4** has been played on and off, especially in the 1990s. This is an attempt to combine two different openings, the Queen's Gambit Declined and the Nimzo-Indian Defence. Black keeps all options open to go either way depending on White's reply, a strategy that may well unsettle an opponent with a narrow opening repertoire. Theory has not yet managed to get a firm grip on this line, but one of White's best options seems to be 4 a3. By forcing his opponent's hand, White attempts to turn the situation around and use whatever Black plays (after 4...♗xc3+ 5 bxc3) to achieve a favourable variation of the Nimzo-Indian.

Tarrasch Defence

3 ... c5 (D)

This was regarded as the only correct move by Siegbert Tarrasch (1862-1934), one of the world's best players in his day and an extremely influential theoretician. His basic assertion was that White cannot very well take on d5 because

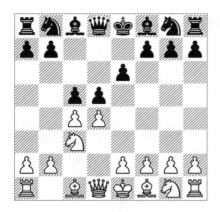

that would give Black "the advantage of an isolated d-pawn after 4 cxd5 exd5". Tarrasch valued open lines and freedom of movement for his pieces so highly that he considered it irresponsible for White to play like this and judged 4 e3 to be the best move, whereupon it was of course Black's turn to avoid making the same mistake by taking on d4. His view of the situation was that both players should wait for a favourable opportunity to break the tension in the centre.

Since then, the evaluation of the isolated queen's pawn has changed considerably. Pawns may become weak, especially when they are isolated. The judging of these positions could be said to have become a very personal affair and it is only natural that some famous grandmasters have often and successfully used the Tarrasch Defence (for example, Spassky and Kasparov) while others have never even tried it.

4   cxd5

4 e3 is hardly ever played nowadays, yet some positions resulting from this move are still relevant because they may also arise from very different openings. The position after 4...♘f6 5 ♘f3 ♘c6, for instance, is often reached via the Symmetrical English; e.g., 1 ♘f3 ♘f6 2 c4 c5 3 ♘c3 ♘c6 4 e3 e6 5 d4 d5. White then usually takes on d5 anyway but the subtle waiting move 6 a3 is popular as well, when Black often adopts the same strategy by playing 6...a6. In this position White has another useful waiting move in 7 b3 (in the best tradition of Tarrasch!) though this is also a good moment for releasing the

tension and developing the queenside with 7 dxc5 ♗xc5 8 b4 and 9 ♗b2.

4   ...   exd5

This recapture seems natural, yet Black has the option of trying to grab the initiative by sacrificing a pawn: **4...cxd4**. This is called the **Schara-Hennig Gambit** and its main line runs 5 ♕xd4 ♘c6 (I suspect being able to play this beautiful move is all the justification that quite a number of Schara-Hennig fans need) 6 ♕d1 exd5 7 ♕xd5 ♗d7 8 ♘f3 ♘f6 9 ♕d1 ♗c5 10 e3 ♕e7 11 ♗e2 0-0-0 12 0-0 g5. There is a sharp middlegame ahead which offers rather more scope for short-term tactical calculations than for considerations of a positional nature.

5   ♘f3   ♘c6 (D)

that would give Black "the advantage of an isolated d-pawn after 4 cxd5 exd5".

6   g3

Decades of practical experience have turned this into the main line of the Tarrasch Defence. The alternative **6 e3 ♘f6** is not unimportant, but it is usually reached via other openings. White's standard continuations are 7 ♗e2 and 7 ♗b5. These variations are not as sharp or as deeply worked out as the ones arising from 6 g3.

6   ...   ♘f6

The provocative move **6...c4**, which gives the game a totally different face, is an important and interesting alternative. This is called the **Swedish Variation**. Black takes a somewhat intimidating step forward on the queenside and tries to cramp his opponent's position. White has two standard strategies at his disposal to try to break up Black's pawn-formation: b3 and – even more forceful – a well-timed e4 and play is likely to revolve around either of these. After 7 ♗g2 ♗b4 8 0-0 ♘ge7 the thrust 9 e4 is already possible for White regains his pawn after 9...♗xc3 10 bxc3 dxe4 11 ♘d2.

7	**♗g2**	**♗e7**
8	**0-0**	**0-0** *(D)*

This is the most important starting position of the Tarrasch Defence. No other opening offers Black such free and easy development for his pieces. One might easily be led to believe that it was actually Black who started the game! In fact White's only chance lies in putting pressure on Black's d-pawn, but although this is White's *only* option it is also a very dangerous one, especially in the hands of a skilled positional player, so it would be wrong to assume that everything is going Black's way in this position. Whether one prefers White or Black is – at least to a certain extent – a matter of taste.

A large number of moves have grown into major variations here. **9 ♗e3**, **9 ♗f4**, **9 b3** and even the at first sight rather unimpressive **9 a3** are not bad, yet the outstanding main lines are **9 dxc5 ♗xc5 10 ♗g5** and **9 ♗g5**. After the latter move, Black has a choice of 9...♗e6, 9...c4 and 9...cxd4 10 ♘xd4 h6. Some of these lines have been analysed deep into the endgame, but this should not be as alarming as it sounds since play is of a very logical nature here which makes the variations fairly easy to understand.

Noteboom (or Abrahams) Variation

3	**...**	**c6** *(D)*

This innocent-looking little move is in fact the first step into one of the most exciting variations the world of chess openings has to offer.

4	**♘f3**	

By playing this natural move, flexible and aimed at a development of his pieces, White allows the Noteboom Variation, which is also known as the Abrahams Variation.

There are three major alternatives, the most popular one being **4 e3**. This normally leads to the Meran Variation of the Semi-Slav Defence (page 33) after 4...♘f6 5 ♘f3, but Black may also choose to go for a relatively favourable version of the Stonewall Variation of the Dutch Defence (page 175) by playing ...f5.

4 cxd5 is an attempt to reach the Exchange Variation (page 22), but White's options are limited here as compared to the 'regular' ways to reach this line. After 4...exd5 the move 5 ♗g5 is not possible while 5 ♗f4 allows 5...♗d6, giving Black a much easier game than in the Exchange Variation proper.

4 e4 is very interesting. This is a totally logical move, which has one disadvantage only, i.e. 4...dxe4 5 ♘xe4 ♗b4+. Now the retreat 6 ♘c3 offers little hope of an advantage because it gives Black the opportunity for a counter-thrust in the centre: 6...c5. The critical move is 6 ♗d2, sacrificing one or even two pawns after 6...♕xd4 7 ♗xb4 ♕xe4+ 8 ♗e2 (or 8 ♘e2). White has a sound lead in development, but Black's position has no real weaknesses. After some years of great popularity during the 1990s, White seems to have lost interest in this gambit.

4	**...**	**dxc4** *(D)*

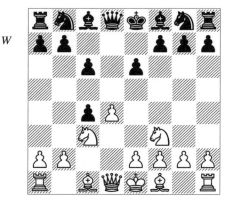

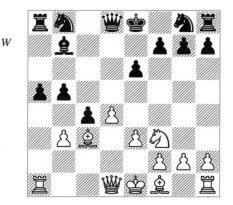

Taking on c4 is a major theme in many variations of the Queen's Gambit, its consequences being subtly different in almost every case.

5   e3

What makes this particular line so surprisingly uncontrollable is that this seemingly modest and reticent reply to Black's capture on c4, is in reality the starting point of the truly mind-boggling complications of the Noteboom Main Line. The seemingly more aggressive **5 e4** is less forcing (Black replies 5...b5 6 a4 ♗b4) and considerably less popular, as is **5 ♗g5**, though both these moves may well be worth some deeper investigation. **5 a4** has no independent significance after 5...♗b4 6 e3 (or 6 e4) 6...b5.

5   ...   b5
6   a4   ♗b4
7   ♗d2

White manages to win back the pawn because he still has the break b3 up his sleeve, but the real point of the Noteboom is that Black has a particularly venomous answer to this.

7   ...   ♗b7

7...a5, based on exactly the same idea, has also been played. Theory has not quite decided yet what the most accurate move is, but they usually lead to the same position, shown in the next diagram.

8   axb5   ♗xc3
9   ♗xc3   cxb5
10   b3   a5 (D)

This is the point and the reason why the Noteboom Variation has deserved its prominent place in chess theory. After 11 bxc4 b4 12 ♗b2 ♘f6 it turns out that Black has managed

to drop two connected passed pawns on the queenside behind the enemy lines, so to speak. These may well intimidate a *pessimistically* inclined player of the white pieces to a disastrous degree, yet the *optimistically* inclined will look at his mass of central pawns and judge the position quite differently. Whoever wants to play this line (with either colour) will need a good deal of theoretical knowledge or a lot of self-confidence and preferably both.

3...♘f6 / 3...♗e7

3   ...   ♘f6 (D)

This simple and natural developing move already constituted the main line of the Queen's Gambit Declined as far back as the 19th century and this situation has never really changed. A subtle modern variation on it is **3...♗e7**. This move is intended to limit the opponent's options. If White continues 4 ♘f3 then Black will simply play 4...♘f6 and return to the main lines. By preventing ♗g5, if only for one move, Black hopes to take the sting out of the Exchange Variation. It is precisely here, however, that the critical test for 3...♗e7 lies, for White can return the favour by playing 4 cxd5 exd5 5 ♗f4. Because Black has already put his bishop on e7, the natural reply 5...♗d6 is now slightly less attractive (though it is still not bad and actually played quite often) which means that Black is also limited in his choices. He will want to develop his queen's bishop to f5 but first 5...c6 6 e3 ♗f5 7 g4 and secondly 5...♘f6 6 e3 ♗f5 7 ♕b3 need to be properly evaluated.

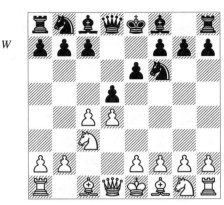

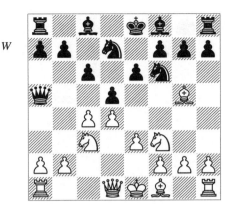

These lines are pretty sharp, but the amount of theory involved is moderate compared to the 'regular' Exchange Variation.

Three main lines have developed from this position. The oldest and most straightforward one is **4 ♗g5**, then there is the flexible **4 ♘f3** and finally we have **4 cxd5**, the **Exchange Variation**.

3...♘f6 4 ♗g5

4	♗g5

Many different variations have evolved from this position, especially in the first decades of the 20th century, when the Queen's Gambit Declined reigned supreme in the world of chess openings. Most of these lines have now been practically forgotten.

Black has, for instance, the possibility **4...c5 5 cxd5 cxd4**, called the **Dutch Gambit** (or the **Dutch-Peruvian Gambit**, due to the Peruvian player Canal's alternative idea 5...♕b6). This was still moderately popular as late as the 1950s, but has now been reduced to a footnote.

Then there is the older still **Cambridge Springs Variation**, which is less risky and fairly popular to this day. It can be reached either by playing **4...♘bd7** 5 e3 c6 6 ♘f3 ♕a5 (D) or by **4...c6** 5 e3 ♘bd7 6 ♘f3 ♕a5. Black unpins his king's knight and prepares the aggressive moves ...♗b4 and ...♘e4, both of which should not be underestimated.

White's most cautious reply is **7 ♘d2**, whereupon Black has two options: 7...dxc4 more or less forces the exchange 8 ♗xf6 ♘xf6 after

which many players, satisfied with this achievement, will be happy to withdraw their queen (9 ♘xc4 ♕c7), and 7...♗b4 8 ♕c2 0-0 9 ♗e2 and now either 9...c5 or 9...e5, continuing the attack.

A sharper reply is **7 cxd5 ♘xd5** (with the black queen on a5, 7...exd5 would produce an inferior version of the Exchange Variation) 8 ♕d2. White is prepared to sacrifice the pawn that will be lost after 8...♗b4 9 ♖c1 ♘7b6 (followed by 10...♘a4) in order to take over the initiative. This approach is perhaps the most feared nowadays although its consequences are far from clear. Black also has 8...♘7b6, immediately bringing the second knight into the assault on c3, when White also tends to sacrifice a pawn, by 9 ♗d3 ♘xc3 10 bxc3 ♘d5 11 0-0.

In practice many players avoid the Cambridge Springs by transposing to the Exchange Variation with cxd5 on move 5 or 6.

All other variations at Black's disposal start with...

4	...	♗e7

Just like 3...♘f6, this is a solid and natural move. Black is not in a hurry to try to take over the initiative, and simply develops his pieces instead.

5	e3	0-0
6	♘f3 (D)	

This is the starting point for all variations which are based on 4...♗e7. In the course of well over a century the following can be said to have evolved as the main lines: **6...♘bd7, 6...h6 7 ♗h4 ♘e4, 6...h6 7 ♗h4 b6** and **6...h6 7 ♗xf6**.

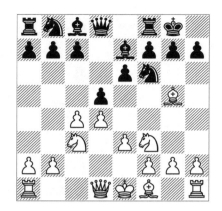

The oldest of these is **6...♘bd7**. After White's most common reply 7 ♖c1 Black may choose 7...c6 8 ♗d3 dxc4 9 ♗xc4 ♘d5, the **Capablanca Variation**. Here we touch upon some of the bedrock theory of the Queen's Gambit Declined. It has remained virtually unchanged since the 1920s yet it is still alive and very interesting. The point is that after the plausible 10 ♗xe7 ♕xe7 11 0-0 ♘xc3 12 ♖xc3 Black continues 12...e5, when he has reached a very acceptable position without any weaknesses. White has tried just about everything to hold on to at least a minimum of initiative. One option is the forcing 13 dxe5 ♘xe5 14 ♘xe5 ♕xe5 15 f4, which has been worked out very deeply. Theory's present favourite, however, seems to be 13 ♕c2 exd4 14 exd4.

Very closely related to the Capablanca Variation is **6...h6 7 ♗h4 ♘e4**, the **Lasker Variation**. Here too Black aims at a fairly uncomplicated middlegame by exchanging some minor pieces. In some cases the similarities with Capablanca's idea are astonishing; for instance, after 8 ♗xe7 ♕xe7 9 ♖c1 c6 10 ♗d3 ♘xc3 11 ♖xc3 dxc4 12 ♗xc4 ♘d7 13 0-0 e5 the only difference from the line given above is that Black's pawn is on h6 instead of h7. A good alternative plan is 13...b6. Perhaps the most principled approach is to play 9 cxd5 (instead of 9 ♖c1), forcing the exchange on c3. After 9...♘xc3 10 bxc3 exd5 White has a very sound strategy in 11 ♕b3 followed by c4 gaining a nice central pawn-majority. Black's reasons for allowing this are the open lines, which allow him an easy and active development of his pieces.

Both these variations are old and respectable *and* still quite fashionable, but the real main line of the Queen's Gambit Declined is now **6...h6 7 ♗h4 b6** *(D)*, the **Tartakower Variation**.

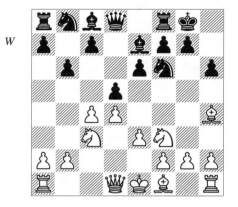

This gives rise to much more complex positions than both the Capablanca and the Lasker Variation have to offer while retaining about the same degree of reliability, a very fortunate combination of characteristics which makes the Tartakower very attractive indeed. In fact there is hardly a world-class player nowadays who has never played it.

White has tried a great number of ideas to gain at least a minimal opening advantage, often extremely subtle and sometimes involving a clever move-order to execute a standard plan in a new form.

Basically White has three different plans at his disposal. The first is to leave Black in peace and to concentrate instead on developing as actively as possible. This attitude may result in a variation like **8 ♗d3 ♗b7 9 0-0 ♘bd7 10 ♕e2 c5 11 ♖fd1**. The tension in the centre may be resolved at any moment, but how? This strategy is intrinsically sound but it does require some accuracy and good positional skills in order to be really effective.

The second plan is to do precisely the opposite: White fixes the central pawn-formation immediately by playing **8 cxd5**. This was the main line of the Tartakower until about 1970, but when it became increasingly clear that 8...♘xd5 9 ♗xe7 ♕xe7 10 ♘xd5 exd5 is entirely playable for Black, mainly because of the discovery that after 11 ♖c1 the somewhat surprising 11...♗e6 is much stronger than 11...♗b7, its popularity dwindled. 11...♗e6 leaves Black free to use the open b-file after 12 ♗e2 c5 13 dxc5 bxc5 14 0-0 ♘d7 for his rooks. Chances are considered equal here.

The third plan (and the most popular one nowadays), is actually a refinement of the second. White waits for 8...♗b7 to be played (this can be done in numerous ways, the most common ones being **8 ♗d3**, **8 ♗e2**, **8 ♖c1** and **8 ♕b3**), he then exchanges bishop for knight on f6 and only *then* does he take on d5. In this type of middlegame it is much more difficult for Black to free his position by means of ...c5 and if he does not achieve this pawn-break he runs the risk of ending up in a slightly passive, if still fairly solid position. Naturally by giving up the bishop-pair White does take a certain amount of long-term positional risk, so this strategy, popular though it is, does require a steady hand.

The reader may have noticed that both the Lasker and the Tartakower Variation are given here as starting with **6...h6**. This is played simply because in many of the resulting positions ...h6 turns out to be a useful move for Black. Inevitably the attempt to 'punish' Black for this insertion by not retreating the bishop and going for **7 ♗xf6** instead has also been investigated. Very similar to the above-mentioned third plan against the Tartakower, White gives up the bishop-pair in order to make it more difficult for Black to get ...c5 in. At the same time a ...b6 set-up (for instance 7...♗xf6 8 ♖c1 b6) is discouraged because White will then normally be just a tempo ahead of a regular Tartakower.

This means that Black will have to think of other methods of tackling the opening problems. Four main lines have been developed, all based on White's choice of move after **7...♗xf6** (D).

These lines are very subtle and need a good deal of positional understanding, but basically they all fit into the simple schedule: White chooses a move to make ...c5 as unattractive as possible, then Black reacts in such a way as to demonstrate that White has made the wrong choice.

After **8 ♖c1**, an enormously popular move around 1985, 8...c6 9 ♗d3 ♘d7 10 0-0 dxc4 11 ♗xc4 e5 is the main line.

On **8 ♕c2**, intended to make castling queenside possible, Black turns out to be able to play the much longed-for 8...c5 anyway, mainly because of the fearless pawn sacrifice 9 dxc5 ♘c6!.

Subtly different from this, **8 ♕d2**, also with a view to castling queenside, is met by 8...dxc4 9 ♗xc4 ♘d7 with 10...c5 to follow.

Perhaps White's most forceful move (though not necessarily the strongest!) is **8 ♕b3**, attacking Black's pawn on d5. In that case Black will have to look for a specific way to take advantage of the exposed position of the white queen: 8...c6 9 ♖d1 ♘d7 10 ♗d3 and now 10...♕b6, 10...a5 and 10...♖b8 (intending 11...b5) have all been played.

3...♘f6 4 ♘f3

4 ♘f3 (D)

This position very often occurs via 1 d4 ♘f6 2 c4 e6 ("A Nimzo-Indian – 3 ♘c3 ♗b4 – perhaps?") 3 ♘f3 ("No thank you, but I wouldn't mind a Queen's Indian – 3...b6 – or a Bogo – 3...♗b4+.") 3...d5 ("Well, now that you have put your knight on f3 I think I prefer a Queen's Gambit Declined.") 4 ♘c3.

Because 4 ♘f3 applies less direct pressure on Black's central position than 4 ♗g5, Black now has a very large choice. The main lines are **4...♗e7**, **4...♘bd7**, **4...c5**, **4...♗b4** and **4...dxc4**. **4...c6** is also important but this is one of several

move-orders to reach the Semi-Slav, and will be dealt with in the next chapter.

3...♘f6 4 ♘f3 ♗e7

4   ...   ♗e7

Black's most classical move. Now **5 ♗g5** will take us back to the 4 ♗g5 lines, but White has an important alternative which rose to great prominence in the 1990s.

5   ♗f4 *(D)*

On the face of it, this move is less aggressive than 5 ♗g5, but it has the great advantage of not overly encouraging standard simplifying manoeuvres like ...♘e4.

5   ...   0-0
6   e3

Now the 'normal' moves **6...♘bd7**, **6...c6** and **6...b6** have never really caught on. Most of the resulting middlegame positions are regarded as

just that little bit less attractive (from Black's point of view) than with a white bishop on g5. On the other hand Black now has a move that is simply bad with a bishop on g5, but is entirely feasible after 5 ♗f4.

6   ...   c5

Thus it is only natural that this has become the main line. With White's bishop on f4 instead of g5, Black's d5-pawn is safe.

7   dxc5   ♗xc5 *(D)*

White now has a choice of two fundamentally different plans. The first is to keep the position simple by exchanging on d5. The main line runs **8 cxd5 ♘xd5 9 ♘xd5 exd5** and now both 10 a3 and 10 ♗d3 have been played. 10 a3 stops Black from playing 10...♗b4+. After something like 10...♘c6 11 ♗d3 ♗b6 12 0-0 ♗g4 Black has developed his pieces satisfactorily, but White may still hope to besiege the isolated d-pawn. 10 ♗d3 ♗b4+ pursues the same strategy more fanatically, ignoring the somewhat precarious position of the white king and hoping to take advantage of the now rather loosely placed bishop on b4.

The other and far more popular plan is not to worry about a possible ...dxc4, play **8 a3** or **8 ♕c2**, develop the queenside and increase the pressure on d5 later on. A critical position arises after 8 a3 ♘c6 9 ♕c2 ♕a5 *(D)*.

Black's last move threatens ...♘e4 and forces White to react.

The oldest line in this position goes **10 ♖d1** ♗e7 11 ♘d2 allowing but also forcing Black (in view of the threat of 12 ♘b3) to lash out in

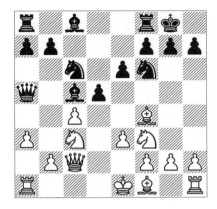

the centre with 11...e5 12 ♗g5 d4. This variation was thoroughly examined and considered acceptable for both sides.

Then, in 1988, **10 0-0-0** was introduced and this became extremely popular almost overnight. After 10...♗e7 both the ferocious attacking moves 11 g4 and 11 h4 *and* the more subtle 11 ♘d2 and 11 ♔b1 all turned out to be very dangerous for Black. It took a few years, but by now Black has managed to work out good defensive lines against all four of these moves and the Queen's Gambit Declined is back from the Intensive Care Unit, but it was mighty close!

3...♘f6 4 ♘f3 ♘bd7

4 ... ♘bd7 *(D)*

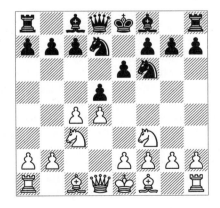

This move has not yet established itself sufficiently to get a name, but it is a sound and

flexible option which can be played with several ideas in mind.

To begin with, it may be used as an anti-5 ♗f4 weapon since on **5 ♗f4** Black now has the excellent reply 5...dxc4. The white bishop finds itself somewhat awkwardly placed after both 6 e4 ♗b4 and 6 e3 ♘d5, so this is usually avoided.

Against **5 ♗g5** Black has a choice between transposing to the 4 ♗g5 main lines by playing 5...♗e7 or 5...h6 6 ♗h4 ♗e7 (although he has of course committed himself to a ...♘bd7 line), the Ragozin Variation by 5...♗b4 (see page 21) or the Cambridge Springs by 5...c6 6 e3 ♕a5 (see page 15).

The critical test for 4...♘bd7 is **5 cxd5 exd5 6 ♗f4**. Again, as in the variation 3...♗e7 (see page 14), because there is a drawback to the natural reply ...♗d6 (in this case of course 6...♗d6 7 ♗xd6 cxd6 would be awkward) White is hoping to achieve a favourable version of the Exchange Variation.

The whole of the 4...♘bd7 line, although it has been known for quite some time, has somehow managed to stay clear of the theoretical steamrollers. This makes it an interesting choice for those who know their way about in the Queen's Gambit and can hope to lure their opponents into unknown territory.

3...♘f6 4 ♘f3 c5

4 ... c5

This is called the **Semi-Tarrasch Variation**, and it indeed bears a close superficial relationship with the line 3...c5. However, the name is at odds with the fact that Tarrasch was attracted to *his* opening, the Tarrasch Defence, by the point that Black is going to play ...exd5 if White ever takes on d5, while in the variation that we are discussing here, Black's aim is to *avoid* an isolated queen's pawn. Hardly a strategy that Tarrasch would have approved of, let alone given his name to! But of course chess opening nomenclature *is* not always logical and this is really a nice illustration of the fact.

However, the strategic idea behind the move 4...c5 is perfectly logical and that is what counts. Black attacks the white central formation in a very straightforward way.

5   cxd5   ♘xd5 *(D)*

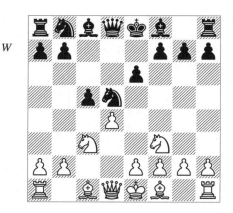

This is the idea. The whole variation has actually more in common with a Grünfeld Defence than with the Tarrasch. Black challenges his opponent to occupy the centre by playing **6 e4**. Such an aggressive attitude is not to everyone's taste, however, and the rather more reserved options **6 e3** and **6 g3** have also grown into proper variations.

After **6 e4 ♘xc3 7 bxc3 cxd4 8 cxd4 ♗b4+ 9 ♗d2 ♗xd2+ 10 ♕xd2 0-0** Black has developed very nicely and it is not clear how strong White's central position really is. The main line goes 11 ♗c4 ♘c6 12 0-0 b6 followed by 13...♗b7. The position seems to be asking for a d5 breakthrough, but its consequences are far from clear. A good variation for players with strong nerves!

Though outwardly less aggressive, **6 e3** also offers White some attacking prospects, but of a different nature. In fact he is inviting Black to play 6...cxd4, when 7 exd4 *(D)* now gives *White* an isolated queen's pawn with all the (latent) attacking chances on the kingside that go with it.

Theory recognizes two main lines here. One is easy development: **7...♗e7** 8 ♗d3 (or 8 ♗c4) 8...♘c6 9 0-0 0-0 10 ♖e1 and now, for instance, 10...♗f6. The other is more aggressive and rather tricky: **7...♗b4**. Now after the natural 8 ♕c2 ♘c6, White may fall into a 'trap' by 9 ♗d3 ♗a5 (threatening 10...♘db4) 10 a3 ♘xc3 11 bxc3 ♘xd4! losing a pawn, but then Black may find that this is actually rather unclear for after 12 ♘xd4 ♕xd4 13 0-0 White has a considerable lead in development which several players

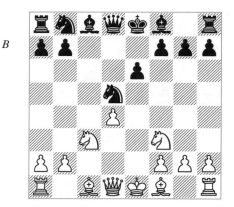

consider sufficient compensation for the material deficit. Nevertheless most people avoid this by developing their king's bishop in a slightly less active way, namely 9 ♗e2, avoiding the knight fork on b4. Also 8 ♗d2 (instead of 8 ♕c2) is often played.

The solid option is **6 g3** *(D)*.

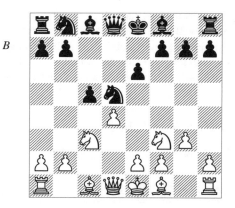

White follows a completely different strategy here. Instead of trying to establish some sort of central dominance, he aims for a symmetrical position with a tiny lead in development and some pressure against b7. After **6...cxd4**, for instance, 7 ♘xd5! ♕xd5 8 ♕xd4 ♕xd4 9 ♘xd4 is considered to be very slightly better for White. Theory at any rate prefers **6...♘c6** 7 ♗g2 and now 7...cxd4 (7...♗e7 8 0-0 brings us to a position discussed via the Keres-Parma Variation of the English Opening on page 210) whereupon 8 ♘xd4 (8 ♘xd5? ♕xd5 would now simply lose a pawn) 8...♘xc3 9 bxc3 ♘xd4 10

♕xd4 ♕xd4 11 cxd4 brings about an endgame with chances for both sides. White has some pressure against b7, but Black's pawn-majority on the queenside may eventually turn into a dangerous passed pawn.

3...♘f6 4 ♘f3 ♗b4

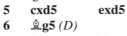

| 4 | ... | ♗b4 |

This is the **Ragozin Variation**, a near relative of the Nimzo-Indian (which is only one move away: **5 e3**). Black aims for counterplay by ...c5, ...♘e4 or ...dxc4. That is why White's best reply is thought to be...

| 5 | cxd5 | exd5 |
| 6 | ♗g5 *(D)* | |

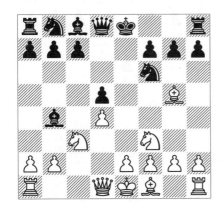

Now there are two main lines for Black, **6...♘bd7** and **6...h6**.

Against **6...♘bd7**, 7 e3 c5 8 ♗d3 constitutes White's most natural development. Black then lashes out on the queenside with 8...♕a5 9 ♕c2 c4. This leads, after 10 ♗f5 0-0 11 0-0 ♖e8, to a difficult position. White's ideal plan would be to play e4, preferably after ♘d2 and f3, but practice has shown that this is hard to achieve against an opponent who knows what he is doing. Still, this is White's most principled approach.

Very often, however, White avoids this type of middlegame altogether by playing 7 ♖c1 or 7 ♕c2. White plans to radically stop ...c5-c4 by taking on c5 should Black play ...c5. For instance, after 7 ♕c2 c5 8 dxc5 ♕a5 9 ♗d2! the game assumes a totally different character from the 7 e3 line. Though Black is certainly not

without his chances even here, these two moves have become quite fashionable of late.

6...h6 forces White to make a decision. Should he take on f6 or is 7 ♗h4 the stronger move? The latter invites the sharp response 7...g5 8 ♗g3 ♘e4, threatening 9...♘xc3 as well as 9...h5. White must deal firmly with this. The pawn sacrifice 9 ♘d2! ♘xc3 10 bxc3 ♗xc3 11 ♖c1 offers good attacking prospects (especially because 11...♗xd4? fails to 12 ♕a4+ ♘c6 13 ♖xc6), but exactly *how* good remains unclear.

What *is* clear is that in practice most players prefer 7 ♗xf6, leading to a much more sedate middlegame. The main line goes 7...♕xf6 8 ♕a4+ ♘c6 9 e3 0-0 10 ♗e2 ♗e6 11 0-0. In comparison with the Exchange Variation, Black's pieces are rather scattered all over the board so it may look as if White's opening play has been successful, yet a Ragozin expert usually manages to recoordinate them fairly quickly.

3...♘f6 4 ♘f3 dxc4

| 4 | ... | dxc4 |

This is one of the youngest variations of the Queen's Gambit Declined. It was hardly ever played before the 1990s. Black immediately forces his opponent to make a fundamental decision. He can win back the pawn very easily with 5 e3 or 5 ♕a4+ but both these moves transpose to another opening where White has then 'missed' a number of options. **5 e3** c5 6 ♗xc4 a6 is a Queen's Gambit Accepted and **5 ♕a4+** c6 6 ♕xc4 b5 is a variation of the Semi-Slav. Though neither of these lines is bad for White, he may not like the choice of variation that has been forced on him.

The more principled continuation is:

| 5 | e4 | ♗b4 |
| 6 | ♗g5 | c5 *(D)* |

This is called the **Vienna Variation**, a line that enjoyed a certain popularity in the 1930s, was completely forgotten for half a century but came back with a vengeance in 1987, when it was rejuvenated and analysed very deeply. It is a provocative way to handle the opening because at first sight White appears to have a great number of very attractive possibilities. Black's position turns out to be remarkably resilient,

however, and White's straightforward aggression may also create a few weaknesses in his own camp. At any rate it is a real tactician's variation.

The first move to catch the eye is **7 e5**. This was met in the 1930s by 7...cxd4, whereupon 8 ♕a4+ ♘c6 9 0-0-0 ♗d7 10 ♘e4 ♗e7 11 exf6 gxf6 leads to a highly complicated position where Black seems to have sufficient compensation for the sacrificed piece. The modern rejoinder to 7 e5 is 7...h6 8 exf6 hxg5 9 fxg7 ♖g8. This too has held up reasonably well in practice.

Then there is the alternative **7 ♗xc4**, seemingly simple and strong. White makes no immediate attempt to crush his opponent and instead relies on his lead in development to give him the initiative. Yet here too, things have turned out to be not that simple. The critical position arises after 7...cxd4 8 ♘xd4 ♗xc3+ 9 bxc3 ♕a5, when White has tried 10 ♘b5, 10 ♗xf6 ♕xc3+ 11 ♔f1 (the idea being to meet 11...♕xc4+ 12 ♔g1 gxf6? with 13 ♖c1), and 10 ♗b5+. Years of intensive research have not produced a clear main line.

3...♘f6 4 cxd5

4   cxd5
This is the **Exchange Variation** or, perhaps more accurately, the most important version of it. White can take on d5 in many positions of the Queen's Gambit Declined. By choosing this particular move-order, however, he optimizes the latent advantages of this exchange.

By taking on d5, White fixes the central pawn-formation and avoids the myriad variations that we have looked at on the previous pages. The strategic situation is now clear. Yet even here a great variety of plans and schemes of development have been tried and investigated, both for White and for Black.

4   ...   exd5 *(D)*
Analogous to the Semi-Tarrasch, **4...♘xd5** is sometimes played to avoid the typical Exchange Variation pawn-structure. A direct transposition is possible; e.g., 5 e4 ♘xc3 6 bxc3 c5 7 ♘f3 (page 20), but White may deviate with 7 a3!, preventing the simplifying check on b4.

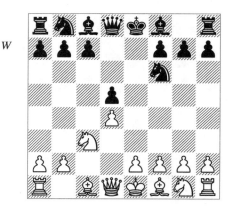

5   ♗g5
The best move and one of the reasons why this particular move-order constitutes the most accurate way of playing the Exchange Variation. If White plays an early ♘f3 he is normally unable to stop Black from playing ...♗f5, which practically solves all development problems Black may have in this line. For instance in the position after **5 ♘f3 c6**, which often arises from the Semi-Slav (1 d4 d5 2 c4 c6 3 ♘f3 ♘f6 4 ♘c3 e6 and now 5 cxd5 exd5), Black's opening problems are nowhere near to what he is facing in the main line: 6 ♗g5 ♗e7 (an immediate 6...♗f5 is also possible but leads to a more complicated middlegame after the disruptive 7 ♕b3) and now 7 e3 ♗f5 or 7 ♕c2 g6! 8 e3 ♗f5.

5   ...   c6 *(D)*
The alternative **5...♗e7** is likely to transpose after a few moves, but the text offers Black one or two interesting extras.

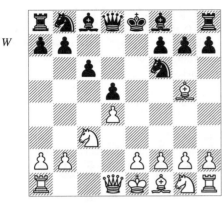

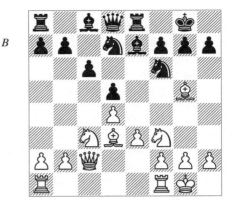

6 ♕c2

Preventing 6...♗f5. For a long time the more natural **6 e3** was also regarded as at least discouraging this move, but it appears that then 6...♗f5 7 ♕f3 (or 7 ♕b3 ♕b6) 7...♗g6 8 ♗xf6 ♕xf6 9 ♕xf6 gxf6 is quite playable for Black even though this may look a bit coarse. The deterioration of Black's pawn-formation on the kingside is compensated by active piece-play.

6	**...**	**♗e7**
7	**e3**	**♘bd7**
8	**♗d3**	**0-0**

This has been the main line for ages, but an important alternative has recently come to the fore which is probably just as good: **8...♘h5**. Black deflates the tension on the kingside even before White has shown any signs of aggression there. After 9 ♗xe7 ♕xe7 and now, for instance, 10 ♘ge2 Black continues 10...g6, intending ...♘g7, ...♘b6 and ...♗f5. He also retains the option of castling either side, the idea being to wait for White to castle and then go the same way.

It is difficult to say whether this is better than 8...0-0, but there is certainly far less theory to be studied.

After 8...0-0 White has to choose a plan. For most players this will be a matter of taste because the following variations differ considerably in their respective characters.

The classical method is to play **9 ♘f3** and, after Black's standard reply 9...♖e8, simply to castle kingside: **10 0-0** (D).

White then has several ways to implement the typical plan of a minority attack on the queenside, the most straightforward being 10...♘f8

11 ♖ab1 followed by b4-b5xc6. White creates a weakness in Black's pawn-structure (if all goes according to plan there will be a loose pawn either on c6 or on d5) which will be the object of further attacks. Black may try to stop this plan but he will eventually have to look for counterplay on the kingside. A possible continuation is 11...a5 12 a3 ♘g6 13 b4 axb4 14 axb4 ♘e4. Play may look a little slow in this line but it can actually become rather violent in the middlegame, especially when Black gets going on the kingside.

This is much more obvious if White decides to castle queenside, **10 0-0-0**. Now it will be White who attacks on the kingside (10...♘f8 11 h3 to be followed by g4).

The same plan is often executed in a slightly different version, starting with **9 ♘ge2** (D).

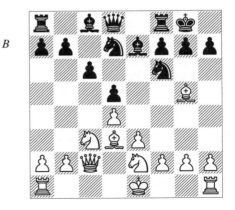

After 9...♖e8 **10 0-0-0** the general outlook is the same: White attacks on the kingside with

h3, g4 and perhaps ♘g3-f5, while Black tries his luck on the queenside. Both 10...a5 followed by ...b5 and ...a4 and 10...♘f8 followed by ...♗e6, ...♖c8 and ...c5 have been played.

In the late 1980s, a plan became popular which combines the development of White's king's knight to e2 with castling kingside: **10 0-0**. Of course this still allows White the more traditional plan of a minority attack on the queenside, but the modern idea is to continue 10...♘f8 11 f3 intending a frontal attack in the centre with e4. Thanks to some beautiful games by Kasparov, this line has become extremely popular. Play is very different from the more traditional Exchange Variation lines discussed above. White attacks in the centre and Black will have to think of a completely new strategy to adapt to the new situation. One important motif is the counter-thrust ...c5. Some typical problems are illustrated by the following sample line: 11...♗e6 12 ♖ae1 (it is still an open question whether this rook should go to d1 or e1) 12...♘6d7 13 ♗f4 (and here it is the choice between keeping the bishops on the board or not which leaves theoreticians baffled) 13...♖c8 and after 14 e4 dxe4 15 fxe4 c5! 16 d5 c4 17 dxe6 ♘xe6 Black regains the sacrificed piece and stands well. White should prepare e4 further by playing 14 ♔h1. If Black then goes 14...c5 anyway, White takes on c5 and plays against the isolated d-pawn.

We have now examined all major options for White of tackling the Queen's Gambit Declined with one exception. Technically speaking this is an independent opening which may arise in many different ways. Still, because the basic central formation is the one from the Queen's Gambit Declined, it seems to me that the best place for discussing this opening is in the present chapter.

We are talking about the **Catalan Opening**, in which White fianchettoes his king's bishop.

3 ♘f3: The Catalan

3 ♘f3

This is the most popular way of introducing the Catalan, although an immediate **3 g3** is also

not bad. On the other hand **3 ♘c3 ♘f6** and only now 4 g3 is considered less accurate because the possibility of playing ♘bd2 is very useful in the Catalan, so it seems rather a pity to give it away so early.

3 ... ♘f6
4 g3 *(D)*

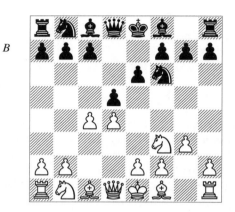

This, the basic position of the Catalan, is reached via many roads. Perhaps the most common one is 1 d4 ♘f6 2 c4 e6 3 g3 d5 4 ♘f3 (4 ♗g2 is equally sound and is likely to transpose after just a few more moves).

The fianchetto (meaning 'flank' development, i.e. to g2 rather than somewhere on the f1-a6 diagonal) development of the king's bishop is not intended to take immediate action in the centre nor is White aiming at any particular fixed pawn-formation. It is chosen with the long-term strategic goal of putting pressure on the long h1-a8 diagonal. This pressure is most likely to be felt when Black plays ...c5 or when he takes on c4 at some point. In the latter case White will in many cases regain the pawn with ♕a4+, but sometimes a gambit will also be an interesting option. White then allows his opponent to keep the pawn on c4, hoping to use whatever means Black employs to protect his booty to his own advantage. This could work along the lines of: Black plays ...b5 to protect his pawn on c4, White attacks b5 with a4, Black covers b5 with ...c6, White intensifies the pressure with ♘e5, Black blocks the h1-a8 diagonal with ...♘d5, White attacks in the centre with e4 and possibly d5.

Black's options against the Catalan can roughly be divided in three variations: notwithstanding the above he may try 4...c5 or 4...dxc4, because these moves are part of the fundamentally sound strategy of undermining White's central position no matter what reason White may have for allowing them. **4...c5** will normally transpose to a Tarrasch Defence after 5 cxd5 exd5, whereas **4...dxc4** has a great number of subvariations that will be examined below. The third option is simply to continue development: **4...♗e7**.

3 ♘f3 ♘f6 4 g3 dxc4

4   ...   **dxc4** *(D)*

This is called the **Open Catalan**. White can win back his pawn by playing **5 ♕a4+**. Black then has 5...♘bd7 6 ♕xc4 a6 preparing to meet 7 ♗g2 with 7...b5 8 ♕c2 ♗b7. By putting his bishop on b7 Black neutralizes any pressure the bishop on g2 may exert. Now all he needs to achieve full equality is to play ...♘bd7 and ...c5. To prevent this rather straightforward scheme from happening, White usually prefers a more pointed move:

5   **♗g2** *(D)*

In this position Black must lay his cards on the table. Those who feel like challenging the validity of White's last move will consider **5...b5**. Black walks into the scenario which I have outlined above, but if he is aware of the dangers awaiting him, this is a valid option. **5...a6** is a slightly more cautious move, based

B

on the same idea. Black delays the weakening ...b5 until White has castled, or – more cautious still – he may prefer (6 0-0) 6...♘c6, when perhaps ...b5 won't even be necessary.

5...♘c6 is often played with the same idea in mind. Now after 6 0-0 ♖b8 Black has simply economized on ...a6 which is very nice, but there is also a disadvantage. If White plays 6 ♕a4, Black is neither in a position to reply ...b5 nor can he achieve the freeing ...c5 very easily.

5...c5 is based on a totally different view of the situation. Black is not concerned with keeping his pawn on c4 at all; he is concerned with attacking White's last remaining stronghold in the centre: the pawn on d4. After 6 0-0 ♘c6 White has to play very aggressively in order to keep his chances of an opening advantage alive. Critical are 7 ♕a4 with the idea of 7...cxd4 8 ♘xd4! ♕xd4 9 ♗xc6+, and the pawn sacrifice 7 ♘e5.

5...♗d7 prevents 6 ♕a4(+) and aims at completing this bishop's development with 6...♗c6. The alert reaction 6 ♘e5 is probably critical.

3 ♘f3 ♘f6 4 g3 ♗e7

4   ...   **♗e7**

Priority is given to completing development of the kingside. Naturally, taking on c4 remains an option.

5   **♗g2**   **0-0**
6   **0-0** *(D)*

Black now faces the same choice again. **6...dxc4**, **6...c5** or **6...something else**; which is best?

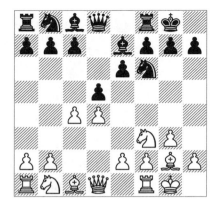

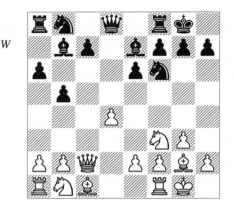

6...c5 is again very likely to transpose to a Tarrasch after 7 cxd5 exd5.

There is also the **Closed Catalan**, where Black develops his queenside without either taking on c4 or playing ...c5. This idea may be pursued with either **6...♘bd7** or **6...c6**. The two moves often transpose. An important scheme of development is to play ...b6 with an eye to developing the queen's bishop to b7 *or* a6 depending on where White puts his queen's knight (♘c3 leaves c4 undefended, which makes ...♗a6 an attractive option). After Black completes his development (for instance ...♗b7, ...♘bd7 and ...♖c8) the liberating ...c5 comes into view again. Another idea is to play ...c6 followed by ...b5. White's main plan is to open the centre by playing e4 at some point.

The Open Catalan approach is still available, although taking on c4 now is very different from taking on c4 two moves ago. In fact **6...dxc4** is one of *the* most popular ways of meeting the Catalan. The idea is to counter the plausible **7 ♕c2** with 7...a6. This leads, after **8 ♕xc4** b5 9 ♕c2 ♗b7 *(D)*, to a type of position that we have already encountered in the 4...dxc4 5 ♕a4+ variation.

Again Black is aiming at completing the development of his queenside by playing ...♘bd7

and ...c5. White has tried to prevent this or at least to make it as unattractive as possible in numerous ways, the most direct being 10 ♗f4 and 10 ♗d2 ♘bd7 11 ♗a5. Still, hundreds of games at the highest level have shown that White must be a supremely good positional player to squeeze any advantage from this line. Many players consider this sufficient reason for preferring the more robust **8 a4**. At the price of a certain loss of flexibility in his queenside pawn-formation, White stops ...b5 altogether. Black now has to look elsewhere for a way to develop his queen's bishop. The most popular solution is 8...♗d7, which is very solid. 9 ♕xc4 ♗c6 leaves Black with a little less space but well developed and 9 ♘e5 ♗c6 has also held up well in practice.

The same can be said about **7 ♘e5**. The surprising reply 7...♘c6 has taken the sting out of this seemingly very logical move. In a very unorthodox way Black gets some nice open files and diagonals for his pieces, both after 8 ♘xc6 bxc6 9 ♗xc6 ♖b8 and after 8 ♗xc6 bxc6 9 ♘xc6 ♕e8.

7 ♘c3 is the sharpest approach. White makes no attempt whatsoever to get his pawn back and simply intends to play 8 e4. This has been investigated far less deeply than the more cautious 7 ♕c2 and 7 ♘e5.

Slav and Semi-Slav

1	d4	d5
2	c4	c6 *(D)*

W

Though not as old as the Queen's Gambit Declined, the Slav has an excellent record of service and is considered a classical opening. It first became popular when it was extensively tested in the World Championship matches between Alekhine and Euwe in 1935 and 1937, with both players adopting it in turn. Since then it has always remained one of the most important 1 d4 openings with new variations being developed and refined all the time.

As in the Queen's Gambit Declined Black maintains a firm grip on d5, but the difference is an important one: he keeps the c8-h3 diagonal open for his queen's bishop where it can be aggressively developed to f5 or g4. Another point of 2...c6 is that now the threat of taking on c4 looms much larger over White's position than after 2...e6 since a black pawn on c4 can now be immediately protected by a pawn on b5 (...b5) which will itself be covered in advance by the pawn on c6. In fact 2...c6 forces White to take a fundamental decision: in comparison with 2...e6 he will either have to be more reticent in his natural development (moves like ♘f3, ♘c3 and ♗f4 or ♗g5 are less self-evident than in the

Queen's Gambit Declined) or he must be prepared to risk some fairly sharp variations where he may have to sacrifice a pawn.

The most radical way of eliminating ...dxc4 is **3 cxd5**, the **Exchange Variation**, yet the main lines of the Slav are to be reached with either **3 ♘f3** or **3 ♘c3**. These two 'natural developing moves' will often transpose, but of course there are a few important differences.

Exchange Variation

3	cxd5	cxd5 *(D)*

W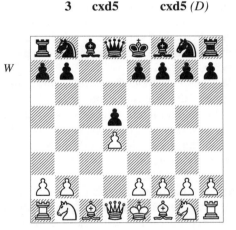

One of the great tragedies of the Slav Exchange Variation is that its reputation has been soiled in the past by the fact that is has been *the* most popular line for pre-arranged draws in tournament games.

Countless games have been 'played' along the lines of 4 ♘c3 ♘c6 5 ♘f3 ♘f6 6 ♗f4 ♗f5 7 e3 e6 8 ♗d3 ♗xd3 9 ♕xd3 ♗d6 10 ♗xd6 ♕xd6 11 0-0 0-0, followed by a random number of uninteresting moves and a draw before move twenty.

And yet the exchange on d5 is a perfectly legitimate and highly serious way of playing, a strategy that has been successfully employed by great champions like Botvinnik, Portisch and Kasparov! It is based on the assumption that it is precisely in a symmetrical position that the advantage of having the first move can be the most dangerous.

4 ♘c3   ♘f6

A somewhat puzzling feature of the Exchange Variation is that its theory does not really start before the position shown in the next diagram. In what way this position is best reached, however, is a sadly neglected question.

So much is certain that 4...♘f6 is played far more often than **4...♘c6** (with some aggressive ideas like 5 ♗f4 e5!?), yet the only move that could possibly prove the latter wrong or at least inaccurate is 5 e4 and almost nothing is known about this! Since 5...dxe4 6 d5 looks rather dangerous, 5...♘f6 seems a sensible reply. This produces a position from the Panov Attack of the Caro-Kann (see page 379) if White continues 6 exd5 ♘xd5 7 ♘f3, but 6 e5 ♘e4 7 ♗d3, for instance, leads us into totally unknown territory.

We should also note that **4...e5!?** transposes to a line of the Winawer Counter-Gambit (see page 38) and so totally changes the strategic picture. White can of course avoid this possibility by playing 4 ♘f3, or by inserting 3 ♘f3 ♘f6 before exchanging on d5.

5 ♘f3

At this point theory begins to be interested, if only vaguely. **5 ♘f3** and **5 ♗f4** are about equally popular with the latter move being considered slightly more flexible. Still, after 5 ♗f4 ♘c6 6 e3 the general picture is almost the same as after 5 ♘f3 ♘c6 6 ♗f4: 6...♗f5 and 6...e6 are the traditional moves and 6...a6 the cheeky newcomer.

5 ...   ♘c6
6 ♗f4 (D)

This is the most important point of departure for the Slav Exchange Variation. Black now has four moves, all giving the game a decided flavour of its own.

6...♗f5 is the most traditional option, preserving the symmetry and challenging White to show what his 'advantage' is worth. For this purpose 7 e3 e6 8 ♗b5 is the preferred choice.

B

White is threatening 9 ♘e5 and is hoping at least to saddle his opponent with a backward c-pawn after a future ♗xc6 bxc6. Black has to concede *some* ground here and 8...♘d7 is generally looked upon as the best defence. The main line then runs 9 ♕a4 ♖c8 10 0-0 a6 11 ♗xc6 ♖xc6 12 ♖fc1, when White has a tiny lead in development. However, it is very difficult to turn this into a more tangible advantage.

Another long-standing main line is **6...e6**, which is usually looked upon as perhaps a little bit on the passive side but very reliable. After 7 e3 ♗d6 (7...♗e7 is also a good move) White can simply take on d6 or he can keep a little more tension in the position by playing 8 ♗g3. This is aimed at making castling kingside less attractive for Black; e.g., 8...0-0 9 ♗d3 followed by 10 ♘e5 could become troublesome. A solid alternative is 8...♗xg3 9 hxg3 ♕d6, delaying castling and stopping White from playing ♘e5. Indeed Black could now take the initiative in the centre himself by playing ...e5 at some point.

Of far more recent origin is the attempt to pre-empt any possible aggression by White on the queenside by playing **6...a6 (D)**.

This has an added advantage in that it retains the possibility of ...♗g4, which would now be an excellent reply if White were to continue 7 e3. The immediate 6...♗g4 has a bad reputation because of 7 ♘e5, but if White does not have this reply (as after 6...a6 7 e3 ♗g4), this active development of the queen's bishop is perfectly playable. In fact this is why many players meet 6...a6 with 7 ♖c1 instead of 7 e3. Only if Black

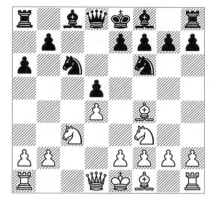

then 'commits' himself with 7...♗f5, is 8 e3 ventured. In practice, however, Black has experienced few difficulties in this line. Having a pawn on a6 has turned out to be simply quite useful. This ...a6 variation is especially important since those who play ...a6 in the standard Slav lines are committed to this line if White exchanges on d5 in a line like 3 ♘f3 ♘f6 4 ♘c3 a6 5 cxd5 cxd5.

Equally youthful and perhaps even more amazing is the bold sally **6...♘e4**. Black breaks the symmetry and intends to continue 7 e3 ♘xc3 8 bxc3 g6. This variation contains an element of risk but at least White must now really fight for the initiative and it therefore seems a very suitable choice against an opponent who had been looking forward to an easy draw.

3 ♘f3

3	♘f3 (D)

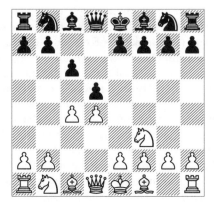

With this move we are entering main-line territory. White does not resolve the central tension and boldly develops a knight without being worried about a possible ...dxc4. It is interesting that this attitude was practically taken for granted for a very long period of time and was only brought up for discussion in the 1990s, when all of a sudden **3...dxc4** came to be taken very seriously indeed. Just like the Noteboom Variation (3...e6 4 ♘c3 dxc4; see page 13) Black aims for a sharp battle based on a very asymmetrical pawn-formation. Similar to the Noteboom, the main line runs 4 e3 b5 5 a4 e6 6 axb5 cxb5 7 b3 ♗b4+ 8 ♗d2 ♗xd2+ 9 ♘bxd2 a5 10 bxc4 b4. Black has 'saddled' his opponent with a strong pawn-centre while creating two dangerous-looking passed pawns for himself on the queenside. This has become accepted theory in recent years, although a name has not yet been given to this new branch of the Slav.

Nevertheless the traditional move firmly remains in place:

3	...	♘f6

White now has a choice of **4 cxd5**, going for the Exchange Variation after all, **4 e3**, which is cautious and not bad but considered relatively easy for Black after 4...♗f5 (while 4...a6 is also popular), or he may choose to ignore the threat of taking on c4 again by playing the most natural developing move:

4	♘c3 (D)

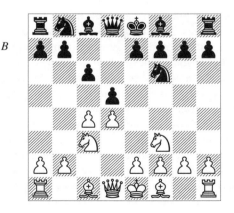

Traditionally, theory of the Slav splits up at this point into two main lines.

To begin with, **4...dxc4**, commonly called the **Slav Accepted**, is viewed by many as the only true way of playing this opening. It was this line which first drew serious attention to the Slav when it was played in the 1935 and 1937 World Championship matches between Alekhine and Euwe. Many famous grandmasters have used it since then, most notably perhaps World Champion Vasily Smyslov in the 1950s.

4...e6 is the other 'traditional' move. This position is often reached via other move-orders; e.g., 1 d4 ♘f6 2 c4 e6 3 ♘f3 d5 4 ♘c3 c6. It is called the **Semi-Slav** and it is the starting point for some of the most complicated variations the Queen's Gambit complex has to offer.

A list of 'other moves' has to start with **4...a6** (D).

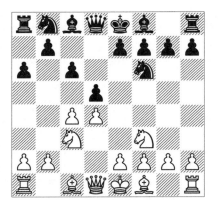

This move may look rather silly at first, yet it has been played by some of the world's best players since it started to become popular in the late 1980s and it is closing in on the two traditional main lines fast. It combines many of the characteristic traits of modern chess: it is provocative, flexible and it is based – although it may not look it at first sight – on sound positional principles. Black intends to meet the plausible **5 e3** with 5...b5 6 b3 and now 6...♗g4, an attractive developing move, which when played one move earlier would have been met by ♕b3, but is now perfectly satisfactory. Theory of this very young variation is growing fast, in recent years concentrating mainly (but by no means exclusively) on the logical rejoinder **5 c5**.

Immediate active development of the queen's bishop by means of **4...♗f5?!** is not good and is played very little because White then has 5 cxd5 cxd5 6 ♕b3, when the desirable answer 6...♕b6 can be met by 7 ♘xd5.

Finally, there is **4...g6** to be taken into account, but this variation is far less popular than its cousin 3 ♘c3 ♘f6 4 e3 g6, the Schlechter Variation (see page 39). Because White has not yet played e3, he has some aggressive options that are unavailable to him in the Schlechter proper. 5 cxd5 cxd5 6 ♗f4 in particular is considered quite good for White.

Slav Accepted

4	...	**dxc4** (D)

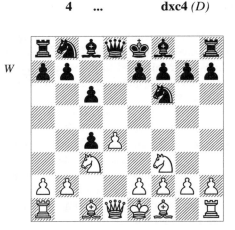

This variation has been very popular at all levels ever since its introduction in the 1930s.

5 a4

Not a useful developing move at all, yet this is by far the most common reply to the Slav Accepted. White prevents 5...b5, which is the reason why the alternatives **5 e4** and **5 e3** are not often played. Despite the loss of time involved and the obvious weakening of the queenside pawn-structure (Black's pieces will make good use of the b4-square in the future) 5 a4 has always been regarded as White's best chance for an opening advantage. Not that the other two moves have not had their loyal followers:

5 e4?! is a true gambit because Black remains a pawn up after 5...b5. This line has always attracted the bold and the impatient, but nobody has ever been successful enough to lure the more cautious away from 5 a4. The crucial position is reached after 5...b5 6 e5 ♘d5 7 a4 e6. White has more space on the kingside and may try to utilize this by playing 8 axb5 ♘xc3 9 bxc3 cxb5 10 ♘g5 ♗b7 11 ♕h5 g6 12 ♕g4 or an immediate 8 ♘g5. The problem with this type of approach is that although it *does* offer prospects of a quick and brilliant win, it also opens the door to a most drastic defeat.

The alternative **5 e3** is a very different cup of tea. In fact this is even more cautious than 5 a4 since White not only avoids having to play a gambit but he also avoids having to weaken his queenside. Here too 5...b5 is the critical reply but now White can play 6 a4 forcing 6...b4 *(D)* and thus robbing the pawn on c4 of its cover (6...a6 does not work on account of 7 axb5 cxb5 8 ♘xb5).

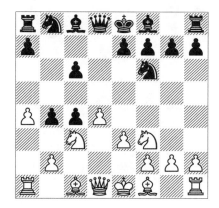

W

However, White will have to withdraw his knight from c3 and redevelop this piece, which means that he can put very little immediate pressure on his opponent's position. 7 ♘a2 e6 leaves the knight awkwardly stranded on a2 while after 7 ♘b1 ♗a6 White will have to invest additional time and effort in getting his pawn back. Black will be able to develop his pieces quite comfortably in both these lines. Nevertheless this line may be perfectly suitable for those wishing to reduce the element of risk to a minimum.

> **5 ... ♗f5**

This simple developing move has always been by far the most popular choice.

Black has a much more provocative alternative in **5...♗g4**, inviting 6 ♘e5, which is a main line after 5...♗f5 as well, so this looks totally stupid because now the knight on e5 attacks the black bishop and White gains a tempo. However, there is actually a very clever point to this: after 6...♗h5 7 f3 Black plays 7...♘fd7 8 ♘xc4 e5!, inviting White to lose a piece by playing 9 dxe5? ♕h4+ and – more importantly – creating a very complicated position after 9 ♘xe5 ♘xe5 10 dxe5 ♘d7. At the cost of a pawn, Black has managed to develop his pieces very nicely. Still, the reputation of 5...♗g4 is dubious at best. White has been fairly successful first with 9 ♘e4 and – more recently – with 9 e4 and 9 g3.

Black may also consider the non-committal **5...♘a6**, waiting for White to declare his intentions in the centre and intending to develop his queen's bishop accordingly; e.g., 6 e4 ♗g4. This move also has the advantage of allowing Black to answer 6 ♘e5 with 6...♘g4 7 ♘xc4 e5!, which is an improved version of the 5...♗g4 line. This variation has never been really popular, but it is not bad and by playing it Black avoids an enormous amount of theory.

We now return to 5...♗f5 *(D)*:

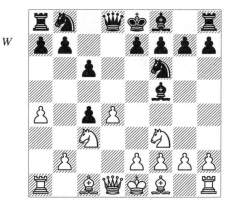

W

Starting from this position many thousands of games have been played, leaving behind layer after layer of theory. This never-ending process of improving, going deeper, refining and sometimes changing track abruptly, is likely to continue as long as chess will be played.

There are two main lines, **6 e3** and **6 ♘e5**, which are equally good but completely different in character.

6 e3 is the simple move. White calmly continues his development and does not commit himself yet to any middlegame strategy. It does *not*, however, lead to a simple type of position. A heavy positional struggle can be expected here, requiring great stamina from both players.

6 ♘e5 is the more ambitious choice. White's plan is to build a strong centre by means of f3 and e4. If this plan succeeds he will have won the opening battle, but Black has two possible reactions both leading to a hard-to-judge type of position.

The standard continuation after **6 e3** is 6...e6 7 ♗xc4 ♗b4 8 0-0 0-0 *(D)* (or 8...♘bd7). Here again White has two main lines, each with a distinct strategic idea.

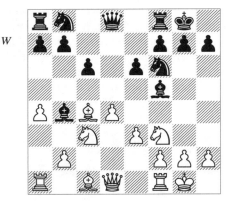

The older and more traditional one is **9 ♕e2**, intending to play e4. Black could try to obstruct this, e.g. by playing 9...♘e4, but most players just allow White to carry out his plan and continue 9...♘bd7 10 e4 ♗g6. This position is actually a very tense one with White controlling more space in the centre and Black exerting strong pressure *on* that centre, without there being a clear formula for either player how to continue. In this type of position the weakness of b4 makes itself felt: White has very little opportunity of creating attacking chances on the queenside.

The alternative **9 ♘h4** pursues a different idea: White wants to exchange the black bishop.

A lot now depends on how Black reacts to this plan. Initially 9 ♘h4 was most often met by 9...♗g4 intending to draw White's kingside pawns forward and hoping to exploit any weaknesses that might result from 10 f3 ♗h5 11 g4 ♗g6. In practice, however, this has proved to be no easy task for Black. Nowadays the laconic 9...♘bd7 is usually preferred (9...♗g6 is also possible). After 10 ♘xf5 exf5 White then has the two bishops, but the pawn on f5 forms a strong barrier against an attack both in the centre and on the kingside.

Against **6 ♘e5** there are also two main defences: 6...e6 and 6...♘bd7.

The crucial test of **6...e6** is 7 f3 ♗b4 8 e4, when the point of Black's opening play is to sacrifice a piece for three pawns by playing 8...♗xe4 9 fxe4 ♘xe4 *(D)*.

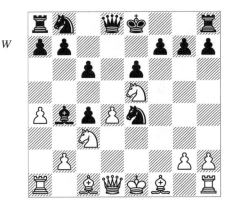

This sets the opponent some very concrete problems: 10 ♕f3 can be met by the cold-blooded 10...♕xd4 while the alternative 10 ♗d2 does not look particularly attractive either, also because of 10...♕xd4. Yet it is precisely this variation which suddenly became exceedingly popular in the 1990s and which is still being investigated to this day in ever-increasing detail. The crux of the matter is that most endgames after 11 ♘xe4 ♕xe4+ 12 ♕e2 ♗xd2+ 13 ♔xd2 have turned out to be much more difficult for Black (often to the point of being untenable) than older theory assumed. Black's problems were exacerbated by the fact that it also proved unexpectedly difficult to take any advantage of the exposed position of the white king.

The most important variations arise from 13...♕d5+ 14 ♔c2 ♘a6 15 ♘xc4. In this position Black may castle either side, with great complications to be anticipated in both cases. The whole variation is fascinating and may be particularly suited for lovers of unbalanced material *and* of course for the diligent and ambitious student.

For those who are scared off rather than attracted by this recommendation there is the alternative **6...♘bd7**, which has been the dominant choice in recent years, as Slav players have seemingly lost faith in the bishop sacrifice line discussed just above. This is a move with a totally different purpose. Black wants to meet 7 ♘xc4 with 7...♕c7, when he is threatening to take the initiative in the centre himself by playing 8...e5. White has only one effective antidote to this plan: 8 g3 e5 9 dxe5 ♘xe5 10 ♗f4 (D), forcing the opponent to slow down a little in order to neutralize the pin against his knight on e5.

B

This can be achieved by either **10...♖d8** 11 ♕c1 ♗d6 or **10...♘fd7**. The latter is the more popular choice. After 11 ♗g2, the traditional line is **11...f6** 12 0-0, when Black can choose between 12...♗e6 or the sharper and more modern 12...♘c5; in neither case has White found it easy to break down Black's firm hold on the centre. However, since 2000, **11...g5!?** has been a major alternative that White must take very seriously. Despite its shocking appearance, this move has a firm logical foundation as it breaks the pin on the e5-knight due to White's undefended knight on c4.

Semi-Slav

4 ... e6 *(D)*

The name Semi-Slav points at the hybrid character of this variation. With its distinctive move ...e6 it is in effect a cross between the Slav and the Queen's Gambit Declined.

W

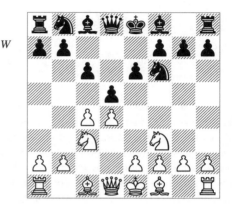

Again the threat of taking on c4 forces White to take a major decision. He cannot very well fall back on the Exchange Variation any more since **5 cxd5** exd5 is now relatively easy for Black (see page 22). Also **5 ♕b3**, though not of course a *bad* move, does not really make life very difficult for Black. Both Queen's Gambit Declined-inspired classical development like 5...♗e7 6 ♗g5 0-0 and a more Slav-orientated approach like 5...dxc4 6 ♕xc4 b5 should yield Black a satisfactory position. The latter variation might continue along the lines of 7 ♕d3 ♘bd7 8 e4 b4 9 ♘a4 ♕a5 10 b3 c5 with equal chances.

By far the most popular moves, which have grown into enormously theoretical main lines over the years, are **5 e3**, generally leading to the **Meran Variation**, and **5 ♗g5**, the **Anti-Meran Gambit**, daring Black to take on c4.

5 e3 and the Meran Variation

5 e3

Black now has a large choice of acceptable moves.

5 ... ♘bd7 *(D)*

This is the standard option, and also the main path to the Meran.

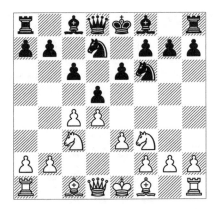

6   ♗d3

This is White's most natural move, allowing Black to head for the Meran by taking on c4. However, it says much about the respect in which Black's following moves are held that practically every legal move in this position has been tried to steer the game in a different direction. Still, even the most widely accepted of these alternatives, **6 ♕c2**, is not particularly dangerous for Black. It is true that taking on c4 is then inaccurate since after 6...dxc4 7 ♗xc4 White simply has a very useful extra move (♕c2) compared to the main line after 6 ♗d3, but the position after 6...♗d6 7 ♗d3 (or 7 ♗e2) 7...0-0 8 0-0 offers Black several possibilities of obtaining a good game; e.g., 8...dxc4 9 ♗xc4 and now either 9...b5 or 9...e5. Waiting moves too, at least the sensible ones like 8...♕e7, have been shown to be perfectly playable. The only theoretical problem seems to be the wild 7 g4 (instead of 7 ♗d3 or 7 ♗e2), creating unfathomable complications and steering the game in a totally different direction.

| 6 | ... | dxc4 |
| 7 | ♗xc4 | b5 *(D)* |

This build-up, introduced by Rubinstein in Meran 1924, bears a strong resemblance to the Queen's Gambit Accepted and has been extremely popular for at least half a century. Black relinquishes his stronghold on d5 in order to develop his queenside. Within just a few moves he will be ready to strike back against White's central position with ...c5. This is a very dynamic and flexible way of playing.

8   ♗d3

Again this seems to be the best square for the bishop. 8 ♗b3 and 8 ♗e2 have also been played but without a firm grip on e4 White will not be able to act quickly in the centre.

8   ...   a6

An inconspicuous move, yet this is the starting point for a truly magnificent complex of variations.

Black's strategic aim is to attack the pawn on d4 with ...c5. This will stop White from concentrating all his forces on the kingside where he would otherwise be able to build up a rather threatening initiative starting with e4.

This plan may be executed in several ways. Of these 8...a6 is only one, albeit the most important one.

The first alternative to be considered is **8...b4**. It *looks* as if this is not very good because after the logical continuation 9 ♘e4 ♗e7 10 0-0 0-0 11 ♘xf6+ ♘xf6 12 e4 White appears to have achieved his strategic goals while Black does not seem to have made a lot of progress. Yet on closer inspection it is revealed that Black has not done so badly because he will now simply play 12...♗b7, when ...c5 is unstoppable. Just how crucially important this advance of the c-pawn is, is shown by the fact that if White now plays 13 e5 Black will not move his knight to the superficially attractive central square d5, but to d7 from where it supports ...c5.

Black has another plausible and sound possibility in **8...♗b7** *(D)*.

If White then reacts by advancing in the centre immediately (9 e4) he will play 9...b4 10 ♘a4 c5 11 e5 ♘d5. This position has turned out

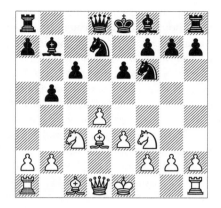

W

to be perfectly playable for Black, tactically because losing the right to castle after 12 ♘xc5 ♘xc5 13 dxc5 ♗xc5 14 ♗b5+ ♚e7 is not a problem, and strategically because other moves, such as 12 0-0 cxd4, always leave White with a somewhat isolated and vulnerable knight on a4 making it difficult for him to utilize his space advantage on the kingside.

After 8...a6 Black is ready to play 9...c5. If White really wants to test this variation he will have to respond without delay.

9   e4   c5 *(D)*

W

We have arrived at the most important starting position of the Meran Variation.

For almost a century White has been trying to refute Black's opening play outright. At first **10 e5** seemed the proper way to do this but it quickly transpired that Black has a very strong rejoinder to this advance in 10...cxd4. This exchange of hostilities creates a veritable jungle

of variations that is very hard to see through and is still in the process of being explored. White's best response is 11 ♘xb5, when Black has three major options: 11...♘g4, 11...axb5 and 11...♘xe5. The last move is based on the spectacular sequence 12 ♘xe5 axb5 13 ♗xb5+ ♗d7 14 ♘xd7 ♕a5+ 15 ♗d2 ♕xb5, leading to approximate equality. Anyone wishing to play one of these highly dynamic variations should be able to calculate very accurately. A single wrong step can be fatal.

Later it was thought that the more positional **10 d5** refutes Black's opening, especially because 10...exd5 is well met by 11 e5. This advance is much more awkward for Black now than a move earlier. Also keeping the position closed by playing 10...e5, although not *bad*, tends to favour White in the long run, provided he takes the precaution 11 b3 in order to impede further queenside expansion by Black.

That is why the immediate 10...c4 is considered Black's strongest reply to 10 d5 (Black can also play 10...♕c7 as a move-order subtlety, but he will need to play ...c4 in most lines quite soon). If White then simply retreats his bishop (11 ♗c2) closing the centre by means of 11...e5 becomes much more attractive. The critical test of 10...c4 is thought to be yet another vigorous move: 11 dxe6. Now 11...fxe6 12 ♗c2 leads to a sharp middlegame with chances for both sides. Black will be able to develop his pieces very aggressively (...♗c5 or ...♕c7, ...♗d6 and ...♘c5) while White has options like e5 and ♘g5 with possible attacking chances on the kingside. 11...cxd3 12 exd7+ ♕xd7 is also playable and perhaps more solid than 11...fxe6.

5 ♗g5 and the Anti-Meran Gambit

5   ♗g5 *(D)*

Not only is this a perfectly natural developing move, it is also a challenge. **5...dxc4** will now produce the ultra-sharp **Botvinnik Variation**, a line which has had the greatest of players baffled in the past, and which requires tremendous theoretical knowledge from anyone.

Of course Black is not forced to play this. He may prefer **5...♘bd7**, transposing to the

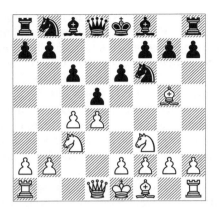

Cambridge Springs Variation of the Queen's Gambit Declined, or **5...♗e7**, which also avoids great complications.

But the most important alternative is **5...h6**, which is an important variation in its own right and is known as the **Moscow Variation**. Now if the bishop retreats (**6 ♗h4**) taking on c4 produces a very different sort of game from the Botvinnik Variation because after 6...dxc4 7 e4 Black will be able to throw in 7...g5 first and only after 8 ♗g3 will he defend his pawn on c4 by playing 8...b5 *(D)*.

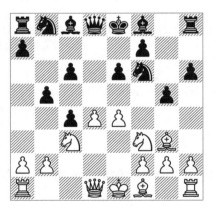

For a long time this was thought to be highly dubious for White at best, but recently this judgement has been queried. White simply continues 9 ♗e2 and turns out to have a surprising amount of compensation for the missing pawn in his strong pawn-centre and in potential attacking chances against the black king. In fact, this is one of the crucial variations of modern-day opening theory and can hardly be played without the most thorough preparation. To give but one example: after the deceptively normal continuation 9...♗b7 10 0-0 ♘bd7 11 ♘e5 ♗g7 the piece sacrifice 12 ♘xf7!? ♔xf7 13 e5 ♘d5 14 ♘e4 has caused no end of confusion ever since its introduction in January 2008.

Much more cautious and more traditional is **6 ♗xf6** ♕xf6. This is a positional variation which poses subtle problems, like what is the best plan for Black after 7 e3 (7 e4 is considered rash due to 7...dxe4 8 ♘xe4 ♗b4+) 7...♘d7 8 ♗d3? Perhaps the answer is 8...dxc4 9 ♗xc4 g6 10 0-0 ♗g7, when 11 e4 can be met by 11...e5.

| 5 | ... | dxc4 *(D)* |

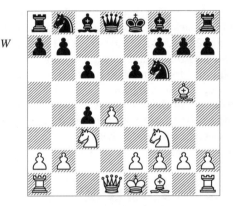

This variation, named after world champion Mikhail Botvinnik (1911-95), leads to a positionally unbalanced, even chaotic middlegame. In very many cases there is no question of material equality either, making it even harder to judge a position or to decide what is the best move. It really is a variation for specialists and lovers of thorough opening preparation with a good feel for the dynamic aspects of chess. A good memory is also recommended. Theory stretches its tentacles far into the middlegame, even into the endgame in this line.

| 6 | e4 | b5 |

Without this, Black's previous move would make little sense, but it would be far too simplistic a view of the Botvinnik Variation to assume that Black is just thinking of consolidating a material gain here. It is all about dynamics.

| 7 | e5 |

This is what makes the variation attractive to White. Black has only one response:

7	...	h6
8	♗h4	g5 (D)

9   ♘xg5

White too must be energetic. **9 ♗g3 ♘d5** would not get him anywhere (compared to the above-mentioned Moscow Variation White has conceded the d5-square). He does have a possible alternative though in **9 exf6 gxh4**, when 10 ♘e5 ♕xf6 11 a4 was popular for a while in the 1990s (without ever being able to replace 9 ♘xg5 though).

9	...	hxg5
10	♗xg5	♘bd7 (D)

10...♗e7 11 exf6 ♗xf6 has also been played, but the text-move is more aggressive. Black does not want to lose any time over the capture of the white pawn that is soon going to appear on f6.

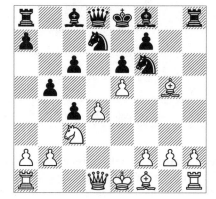

This is the most important starting point of the Botvinnik Variation. At first glance it seems impossible that this position should in any way be desirable for Black, but the hidden dynamics become obvious if one imagines Black continuing ...♗b7, ...♕b6, ...0-0-0 and ...c5, when all of a sudden his position springs to life. In fact the pressure against d4, the open files on the kingside and Black's pawn-mass on the queenside that may result from this set-up have unnerved many an unprepared and unsuspecting opponent in the past. White has to act decisively and fearlessly. It is, for instance, quite necessary after **11 exf6 ♗b7** to continue 12 g3, because this both defends the kingside against an attack on h2 via the b8-h2 diagonal and provides an excellent square on g2 for the bishop. White need not worry about the rejoinder 12...c5 because this allows 13 d5 (D), a bold advance that is usually of crucial importance whenever Black plays ...c5 in this variation.

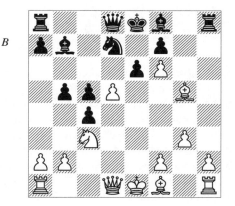

Just how explosive the situation is, becomes clear if Black now plays 13...b4?, when 14 ♗xc4! bxc3 15 dxe6 would win instantly. A much better idea is to play 13...♕b6 14 ♗g2 0-0-0 15 0-0 and only now 15...b4. This leads to a ferocious middlegame battle, demanding thorough theoretical preparation from both players.

Another variation that illustrates the level of difficulty of the Botvinnik Variation starts with **11 g3**. If Black now simply continues 11...♗b7 12 ♗g2 ♕b6 a transposition to the above-mentioned line with 13 exf6 0-0-0 14 0-0 c5 15 d5 is likely, but he may also consider 11...♖g8, provoking 12 h4, when 12...♖xg5 13 hxg5 ♘d5 leads to (another) totally unclear position. Theory gives 14 g6 fxg6 15 ♕g4 as the main line here, but will not tell you who is better.

3 ♘c3

I shall conclude this chapter by saying a few words about the differences between 3 ♘f3 and 3 ♘c3.

3   ♘c3 (D)

Black now has several alternatives to the 'normal' developing move 3...♘f6.

To begin with, **3...dxc4** needs to be considered. The implications of this move are slightly different from 3 ♘f3 dxc4. White's strongest reply is considered to be 4 e4, intending to meet 4...b5 with 5 a4, thus undermining the pawn on c4. If 5...b4 White plays 6 ♘a2, when both 6...e5 and 6...♘f6 have been tried. Theory has not come to any conclusions that are worth mentioning, but practice suggests that this line does not appear to be a problem for White.

The same holds true for **3...e5** (D), the **Wina-wer Counter-Gambit**.

Nevertheless a refutation of this old variation has never been found. The idea is to meet **4 dxe5** with 4...d4 5 ♘e4 ♕a5+, when both 6 ♗d2 ♕xe5 7 ♘g3 and 6 ♘d2 ♘d7 7 ♘f3 ♘xe5 8 ♘xd4 ♘xc4 allow Black to win back his pawn with a reasonable game. **4 cxd5 cxd5 5** ♘f3 e4 6 ♘e5 f6! 7 ♕a4+ ♘d7 is also considered playable for Black due to 8 ♘g4 ♔f7! 9 ♘xd5?! ♘b6!.

An important option of course is **3...e6**. This is the **Noteboom** (or **Abrahams**) **Variation**, which I have classified as part of the Queen's Gambit Declined in this book (see page 13) but which might equally reasonably be seen as a variation of the Slav or a form of the Semi-Slav.

Still, Black's most important move, just as it was against 3 ♘f3, is:

3   ...   ♘f6

Now **4 ♘f3** of course produces the main line that we have already looked at. Likewise **4 cxd5** cxd5 leads to a well-known position from the Exchange Variation. Many players who wish to avoid the Slav Accepted, however, now prefer...

4   e3 (D)

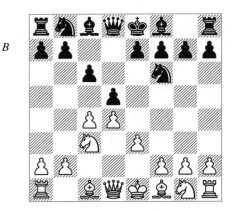

As we have seen before, Black has no problems after 3 ♘f3 ♘f6 4 e3, because he can then develop his queen's bishop very comfortably with 4...♗f5. With a knight on c3 instead of f3 this is a different matter altogether, because now **4...♗f5** can be met by 5 cxd5 cxd5 6 ♕b3!, when the plausible answer 6...♕b6 just drops a pawn to 7 ♘xd5.

If Black wishes to play a Semi-Slav (with White committed to the 5 e3 lines), then he can play **4...e6**, when 5 ♘f3 completes the transposition, but if he wishes to avoid the main lines Black often chooses either the modern move **4...a6**, with consequences very similar to 3 ♘f3 ♘f6 4 ♘c3 a6, or the more traditional...

4 ... g6 *(D)*

This is the **Schlechter Variation**, a hybrid of a Slav and a Grünfeld. Because White has already committed himself to e3 he does not have the means to react as sharply as in the case of a 'real' Grünfeld. This has given the Schlechter Variation a very solid reputation. Unlike many other Slav variations, play usually develops at a leisurely pace and is mainly of a positional nature.

5 ♘f3 ♗g7 *(D)*

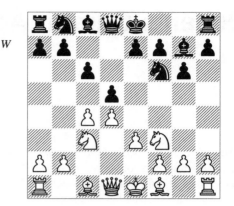

White's most natural move in this position is **6 ♗d3**. Black then usually plays to exchange his queen's bishop, a strategy which will leave him with a flexible position for the middlegame. The main line runs 6...0-0 7 0-0 ♗g4 (7...♗f5 is also sometimes played). If now 8 h3 ♗xf3 9 ♕xf3 Black may try to take over the initiative by playing 9...dxc4 10 ♗xc4 ♘bd7 to be followed by ...e5 or he may just play 9...e6 and 10...♘bd7, keeping his options open.

In order to avoid this, White sometimes plays **6 ♗e2**, when Black may still play 6...0-0 7 0-0 ♗g4 of course, but because f3 is now covered by his bishop White then has the sharp reply 8 cxd5 cxd5 9 ♕b3 without having to worry about taking on f3 (and getting saddled with doubled pawns as a consequence). In fact he more or less forces Black to weaken his queenside, if only very slightly, by 9...b6. With the white bishop on e2 though, the central advance e4 is no longer an issue, so Black may decide to try a less aggressive move than 7...♗g4. 7...a6 is an interesting alternative, intending to play 8...b5. 7...e6 too, with the idea of 8...♘bd7, 9...b6 and 10...♗b7, does not look bad.

Queen's Gambit Accepted

1	d4	d5
2	c4	dxc4 *(D)*

Having read the two previous chapters and noticed the multitude of variations where Black plays ...dxc4 at some point, the reader may have started wondering whether it is not much simpler to take on c4 straightaway.

The answer is a very simple yes, it is much simpler. By playing 2...dxc4 Black defines the outlines of the middlegame. White will have to regain the pawn which gives Black time to attack in the centre, usually with ...c5 or ...e5.

But whether it is a good idea to make this decision so early in the game is another matter. In fact *this* question is almost impossible to answer in a general way. It is very much a matter of choosing a type of middlegame. Are there positions that you prefer or that you wish to avoid? This is of course a very personal matter.

By playing the Queen's Gambit Accepted, Black really turns the logic of most of the ...dxc4 variations of the previous two chapters around. Instead of developing his pieces first and waiting for a suitable moment to capture on c4, he takes on c4 first and *then* adapts his development to the set-up chosen by White for recapturing the pawn.

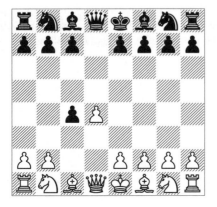

White now has to make up his mind. He may want to go all-out in the centre by playing **3 e4** or he may prefer to adopt a more flexible attitude and play **3 ♘f3**.

Two other moves, **3 e3** and **3 ♘c3**, were considered less accurate for a very long time because they allow the bold response 3...e5. The position after, say, **3 e3** e5 4 dxe5 ♕xd1+ 5 ♔xd1 ♗e6 is indeed fine for Black, but recent practice has shown that White can do much better: 4 ♗xc4! exd4 5 exd4 (or **3 ♘c3** e5 4 e3! exd4 5 exd4) when the resulting middlegame with an isolated pawn on d4 is perfectly playable for White.

If Black avoids this, play will usually transpose to a main-line 3 ♘f3 variation; e.g., **3 e3** ♘f6 4 ♗xc4 e6 5 ♘f3.

3 e4

3	e4 *(D)*

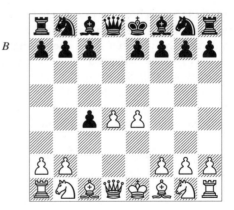

For a long time this very natural reaction to 2...dxc4 suffered the same fate as 3 e3 and 3 ♘c3: it was thought to be inaccurate because of **3...e5**. The difference is that in this case White has the promising pawn sacrifice 4 ♘f3! exd4 5 ♗xc4!, when his development is swift and aggressive and Black will have to take great care in getting his king into safety. This is in fact a lively variation with chances for both sides. Just one example of a critical line: 5...♘c6 6 0-0 ♗e6. Now 7 ♗xe6 fxe6 8 ♕b3 ♕d7 9 ♕xb7 wins back the pawn, but the remaining position is hard to judge. Black has secured his strong pawn on d4 and is catching up in development fast.

Another standard device for counterattacking against the white centre consists in **3...c5**. The d-pawn is drawn forward. White has of course the very quiet **4 ♘f3** cxd4 5 ♕xd4, but **4 d5** is the principal reaction, when the natural follow-up is 4...♘f6 5 ♘c3 and now **5...e6**, attacking the white pawn on d5. The position that then arises after **6 ♗xc4** exd5 7 ♘xd5 ♘xd5 8 ♗xd5 ♗e7 9 ♘f3 0-0 10 0-0 has turned out to be quite reasonable for Black *if* he attacks White's strong bishop on d5 without delay. This has been done with 10...♘a6 followed by 11...♘c7 (and in some cases 12...♗e6) and also with 10...♕b6 and 11...♗e6. Sharper (though not necessarily better) is **6 ♘f3**, intending to meet 6...exd5 with 7 e5. I shall discuss this position when we look at the variation 3 ♘f3 ♘f6 4 ♘c3 c5 below.

5...b5 *(D)* (instead of 5...e6) is an alternative.

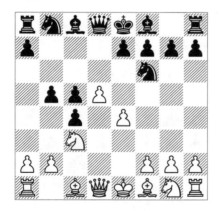

This is far more speculative and has as yet not been analysed very thoroughly. Black does not have to worry about 6 ♘xb5 ♕a5+ 7 ♘c3 ♘xe4 nor does 6 e5 b4 pose a serious threat, but a dangerous move seems to be 6 ♗f4.

Another way of drawing the enemy forward is **3...♘f6**, when 4 e5 (4 ♘c3 makes 4...e5 even more attractive than on the previous move) 4...♘d5 5 ♗xc4 offers White more space, but Black will have a solid position and a very useful square on d5 for his pieces. This variation has become very popular of late, with attention focusing mainly on 5...♘b6 6 ♗b3 ♘c6 7 ♘e2 ♗f5 8 0-0 e6 9 ♘bc3.

More provocative still is **3...♘c6** *(D)*, because this move blocks the pawn on c7 that would normally want to rush forward in this opening, at least in a classical interpretation of it.

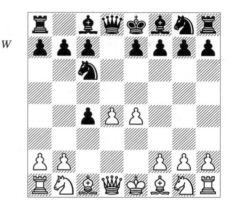

It comes as no surprise therefore that the playability of this variation largely depends on accurate calculations. Black has to know what he is doing, but if he does, this is a tricky variation also for White. Black intends to meet **4 d5** with 4...♘e5 and **4 ♘f3** with 4...♗g4. The main line goes **4 ♗e3** ♘f6 5 ♘c3 e5, when after 6 d5 Black has tried both the fairly solid 6...♘e7 7 ♗xc4 ♘g6 and the more bellicose 6...♘a5.

3 ♘f3

3   ♘f3 *(D)*

Throughout the history of the Queen's Gambit Accepted, this has been White's most popular move in this position. White does not hurry to win back the pawn that he has sacrificed. He calmly develops his pieces and offers his opponent as few targets for an immediate counterattack as possible.

| | 3 | ... | ♘f6 |

Alternatives to this natural move are mostly subtle attempts either to lure White into one of the variations discussed below or to avoid one of them.

3...a6, for instance, intends to steer clear of the sharp 3...♘f6 4 ♘c3 lines, hoping to transpose to the much quieter 3...♘f6 4 e3 variation after **4 e3** ♘f6 5 ♗xc4 e6 6 0-0 c5. The point of 3...a6 is to meet the straightforward **4 e4** with 4...b5, when the standard reply 5 a4 is not as powerful as White would like it to be because Black has 5...♗b7 attacking the pawn on e4. On **4 ♘c3** Black also has 4...b5, when 5 a4 can be met with 5...b4.

The same logic applies to **3...e6**. Black wants to meet 4 e4 with 4...b5 5 a4 ♗b7 (or 5...c6 6 axb5 cxb5 7 b3 ♗b7), when things are rather unclear. Here too 4 e3 will normally transpose to a 3...♘f6 4 e3 variation.

Theory of both these moves is still in the experimental stages.

3...c6 is again very similar. This move was discussed in the chapter on the Slav and Semi-Slav (see page 29). Here too Black tries to 'do something' with his pawn on c4 rather than follow the classical recipe of just giving it away and developing his pieces instead.

The most straightforward 'defence' of c4 of all, **3...b5**, is not to be recommended, however. In fact this move will give White the ideal opportunity to start an attack on all fronts by 4 a4 c6 5 axb5 cxb5 6 b3 cxb3 7 e4.

3...c5, a move that we have already seen as a possible reply to 3 e4, is based on a completely different idea. Black attacks the white centre straightaway. The most principled reply 4 d5 is met by 4...e6 and what makes this variation particularly interesting is that the quiet 4 e3 allows 4...cxd4 5 exd4 ♗e6, making it a little more difficult for White to get his pawn back.

We now return to the position after 3...♘f6 *(D)*:

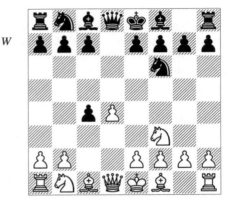

Now there are two main lines. The sharper is **4 ♘c3** intending to continue 5 e4. The older and more popular is **4 e3**.

A third option is **4 ♕a4+**, which is certainly not bad, but does not pose Black as many problems as the two main lines. A solid reply is 4...c6 5 ♕xc4 ♗f5, giving the game a distinctly Slav flavour.

3 ♘f3 ♘f6 4 ♘c3

| | 4 | ♘c3 *(D)* |

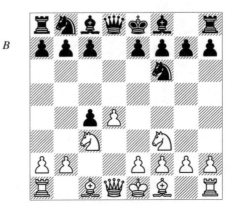

This aggressive move has caused many a devotee of the Queen's Gambit Accepted (including – I am sorry to have to admit – myself) some sleepless nights, especially in the 1970s when theory recommended **4...a6**. It is precisely this move which involves great risk for Black if White continues unflinchingly 5 e4 b5 6 e5 ♘d5 7 a4. Although this position may *look* attractive for Black, White's attacking chances are in fact very dangerous, particularly if White is a player with a natural flair for the initiative who is not afraid of sacrificing some material.

One example of what Black is in for in this line is provided by the variation **7...c6** 8 axb5 ♘xc3 9 bxc3 cxb5 10 ♘g5! f6 11 ♕f3 ♖a7 12 e6!. Although it is actually highly unclear how this position should be evaluated, it *is* clear that having one's kingside squashed is not to everyone's taste.

The most obvious defence runs **7...♘xc3** 8 bxc3 *(D)*.

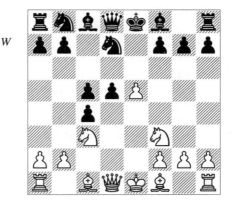

Now the natural **8...♗b7** is also not safe: once more 9 e6! gives White a very dangerous attack. During the 1980s it was established that **8...♕d5** is more solid, yet here too White turns out to have sufficient compensation for the pawn if he calmly plays 9 g3 ♗b7 10 ♗g2 ♕d7 11 ♗a3. Black is under pressure, though it is only fair to add that he is not without chances either. A gambit will always be a double-edged sword.

It was not until the very last years of the 20th century that a truly solid defence against this variation was unearthed at last. Much to everyone's surprise it turned out that **7...e6** 8 axb5,

and now the far from obvious 8...♘b6, really takes the sting out of White's attacking plans. The game takes on a positional character and the chances are more or less equal.

While this heavy theoretical battle raged through the 4...a6 line, the alternative **4...c5** was also explored in great depth. At first this move seemed unattractive because of the violent attack 5 d5 e6 6 e4 exd5 7 e5! but some staunch supporters of the black cause managed to establish a solid defence following 7...♘fd7 *(D)*.

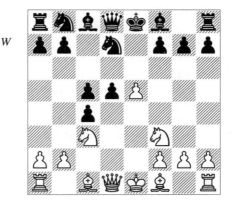

To begin with, it was discovered that after **8 ♕xd5** the surprising 8...♘b6 is perfectly satisfactory for Black and even the loss of tempo involved in 8 ♗g5 ♗e7 9 ♗xe7 ♕xe7 10 ♘xd5 ♕d8 turns out not to have any damaging effect on the black position provided he dislodges the knight on d5 as soon as possible. In fact the variation 11 ♗xc4 ♘c6 12 0-0 ♘b6! is considered about equal.

Black also has two fully acceptable transpositional moves at his disposal. **4...e6** produces a variation of the Queen's Gambit 'Declined' (1 d4 d5 2 c4 e6 3 ♘c3 ♘f6 4 ♘f3 dxc4) while after **4...c6** we suddenly find ourselves in a Slav Accepted!

3 ♘f3 ♘f6 4 e3

4 e3 *(D)*

This has always been *the* most popular way of meeting the Queen's Gambit Accepted. White wins back his pawn and calmly develops his kingside before taking any further action.

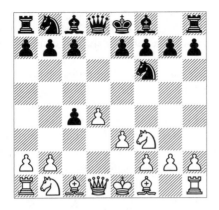

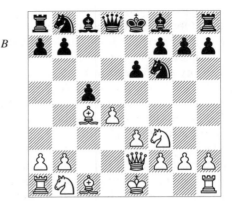

4 ... e6

Black also develops unhurriedly.

The attempt to hang on to the pawn on c4 by **4...b5** is ill-fated. White immediately demolishes the black pawn-phalanx with 5 a4 c6 6 axb5 cxb5 7 b3 and gets the upper hand.

4...♗g4 is more interesting. This active move poses White some concrete problems and is not easy to refute. In the early days it was thought that White could just win a pawn by 5 ♗xc4 e6 6 ♕b3 until it was demonstrated that Black gets an excellent game if he replies 6...♗xf3 7 gxf3 ♘bd7 8 ♕xb7 c5. White has an extra pawn but is lagging behind in development. A more careful approach is (5 ♗xc4 e6) 6 ♘c3 ♘bd7 7 h3 ♗h5 8 0-0 ♗d6 9 e4, but now the true point behind 4...♗g4 is revealed: Black will play 9...e5 and hold his ground in the centre. This makes 4...♗g4 a very lively variation with considerably less theoretical baggage to carry than 4...e6.

5 ♗xc4 c5
6 0-0

This is White's most natural move, but he has an interesting and very subtle alternative in **6 ♕e2** *(D)*.

Unafraid of the isolated queen's pawn that will result from an exchange on d4, he intends to take on c5 if Black continues 6...a6, parallel to the main line. The difference is that in this case 7 dxc5 will not allow an exchange of queens and this makes the position after 7...♗xc5 8 0-0 much more dynamic than in the parallel variation 6 0-0 a6 7 dxc5, which is discussed below. Remarkably enough perhaps, this position is full of danger for Black because it is precisely in an open position with a symmetrical pawn-structure that a slight lead in development will be felt the most acutely and that is precisely the advantage that White has here. The possibility of an advance in the centre (e4-e5) has to be carefully monitored. One of the many ways that theory has suggested of doing this is 8...♘c6 9 e4 b5 (not 9...e5?? immediately because of 10 ♗xf7+! ♔xf7 11 ♕c4+) 10 ♗b3 e5.

After 6 0-0 Black is faced with a far-reaching choice. The most obvious and also the simplest strategy is to take on d4 and play against the resulting isolated d-pawn. This may be done either at once, by playing **6...cxd4**, or in a slightly more subtle way by **6...♘c6**, waiting for 7 ♕e2 before taking on d4: 7...cxd4 8 ♖d1 ♗e7 9 exd4 0-0. If White then continues 10 ♘c3, which is the obvious move, 10...♘a5 11 ♗d3 b6 followed by 12...♗b7 is a standard manoeuvre for increasing control over d5.

This is a sound way of playing and theory *could* end here but, unfortunately perhaps, opening theory is never satisfied. It always looks further, it always wants to find something which is *even* better, *even* more accurate or *even* more difficult to handle for the opponent. That is why another move has become the uncontested main line in this position:

6 ... a6 *(D)*

Black waits for a more favourable opportunity to take on d4 and introduces the possibility of developing his queenside swiftly and comfortably with ...b5 followed by ...♗b7 and ...♘bd7.

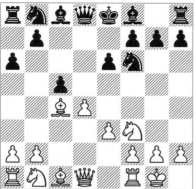

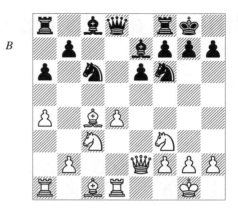

White has tried several ways of combating this scheme.

To begin with, **7 ♕e2** is important. White simply allows his opponent to carry out his plan and concentrates on his own chances: he wants to gain space in the centre by ♖d1 and e4. After 7...b5 8 ♗b3 ♗b7 9 ♖d1 ♘bd7 10 ♘c3 we arrive at a crucial position. Black now has to consider not only the e4 advance but d5 as well. These are dangerous plans, but by now theory has worked them out pretty thoroughly and it seems that Black will be able to cope with these threats. The most popular move nowadays is 10...♕b6.

Another idea altogether is to play **7 a4**, preventing Black's plan in a radical way at the cost of a slight weakening of the queenside. White abandons control over b4, a square which Black can now use for his knights or his king's bishop, especially if he now switches to the old plan of playing against the isolated queen's pawn: 7...♘c6 8 ♕e2 cxd4 9 ♖d1 ♗e7 10 exd4 0-0 11 ♘c3 (D).

This position is crucial for an evaluation of 7 a4 but, as in so many similar cases, here too the question of whether you want to play *with* or *against* the isolated queen's pawn is largely a matter of taste. It all boils down to weighing dynamic features against static ones, which is a difficult but also a very personal matter. Opening theory of course does not take a personal view of the matter and just tries to look at all the possibilities as accurately as possible. In this case a verdict has not yet been reached despite

decades of practical experience. Black's position is solid and he has good long-term prospects, but for the time being White has the freer piece-play and holds the initiative.

A much more flexible strategy that was popular during the 1990s is to anticipate ...b5 by retreating the bishop straightaway so as to be able to respond to ...b5 with an immediate a4, hoping to take over the initiative on the queenside. For this purpose both 7 ♗b3 and 7 ♗d3 have been played. Black's standard reaction to this plan is to switch to the strategy of playing against the isolated queen's pawn (7...cxd4), but there are a few interesting alternatives. Against **7 ♗b3** Black might consider 7...b5 anyway, while against **7 ♗d3** the subtle 7...♘bd7, sometimes followed by 8...b6, is an option.

A very radical solution to the problems of this opening is to play **7 dxc5**. Although this simplifies the position and looks totally harmless at first sight, world champions Boris Spassky and Vladimir Kramnik have successfully used this idea. After 7...♕xd1 8 ♖xd1 ♗xc5 White still has that minimal lead in development which a great champion may be able to use to his advantage even in the endgame.

Finally, White's sharpest move in this position is undoubtedly **7 e4**, yet strangely enough this is not particularly dangerous for Black. White's idea is to play 8 d5 if Black takes on e4 (7...♘xe4). Although it is far from clear if this poses any problems if Black simply continues 8...♗e7, most players prefer 7...b5 8 ♗d3 ♗b7, which has proved to be very reliable.

Other 1 d4 d5 Openings

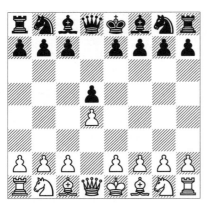

Most games that start like this continue with **2 c4**, the most aggressive move. White attacks the pawn on d5. This is the **Queen's Gambit**.

The next most popular move is **2 ♘f3**, which may either be played to steer away from the Queen's Gambit complex or to enter that complex through the back door by playing c4 later, usually with the aim of avoiding certain lines that are specific to the immediate 2 c4. For example, White may want to counter the Queen's Gambit Accepted (2...dxc4) with the variation 3 ♘f3 ♘f6 4 ♘c3, but he is worried about 2 c4 dxc4 3 ♘f3 a6. By choosing the move-order 2 ♘f3 ♘f6 3 c4 dxc4 4 ♘c3 he achieves his aim, provided of course that he is not worried even more about possible alternatives for Black in *this* line. In this case he is fairly safe, because the only possible way to get into the 3...a6 variation would be 2...a6, but this move makes a non-c4 set-up (3 ♗f4 or 3 g3 for instance) much more attractive, because ...a6 is practically a wasted move here.

Another reason why the position after 2 ♘f3 deserves some attention is that it is often reached via 1 ♘f3 d5 2 d4, so it is important for 1 ♘f3 players.

Those 2 ♘f3 lines where White refrains from (an early) c4 are collectively referred to as the **Queen's Pawn Game**.

The most emphatic way to do without c4 is **2 ♘c3**. This somewhat old-fashioned move is known as the **Richter-Veresov Opening**.

Much more modern is **2 ♗g5**, a move that has become popular in the wake of 1 d4 ♘f6 2 ♗g5, the **Trompowsky Attack**.

Other moves, like **2 ♗f4** or **2 e3**, are of course not illegal and are in fact quite often played, but not at the highest level where opening theory is forged and where every move has to be better than average. On these moves theory remains silent.

Quite the reverse can be said about **2 e4**, the **Blackmar-Diemer Gambit**. This is very rarely played at any level, but a small band of fanatical devotees have developed a considerable amount of theory on this pawn sacrifice. If Black takes up the challenge (2...dxe4) White will continue 3 ♘c3 ♘f6 4 f3 exf3 5 ♘xf3 and assume that his lead in development will compensate for the material deficit.

Queen's Gambit

2   c4 *(D)*

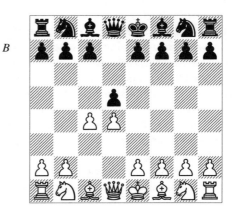

The most important alternative to **2...e6**, **2...c6** and **2...dxc4**, the three classical openings that we have investigated in the three previous chapters, is **2...♘c6**, the **Chigorin Defence**. This opening is perhaps not considered as solid as the 'Big Three', but it is still very respectable.

2...♗f5 is one step further away from the classical approach. This is a modern idea, which remains as yet unchristened, although the name **Baltic Defence** has been proposed.

Older and duly given a name, yet not fashionable at all, is the symmetrical reply **2...c5**, the **Austrian Defence**.

Finally, Black's most drastic option is **2...e5**, called the **Albin Counter-Gambit**.

Chigorin Defence

2   ...   ♘c6 *(D)*

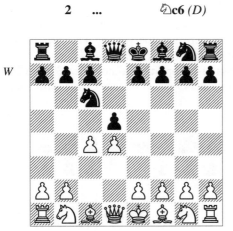

More than a century after its first bloom, this opening is making a remarkable comeback. With the steadily increasing stream of information and the possibility of computer-assisted analysis making opening preparation more concrete than ever before, general guidelines and considerations of a positional nature tend to be less authoritative (and less intimidating). Nowadays many players are fully prepared to take some positional risks in the opening in order to seize the initiative. The Chigorin Defence, named after the great Mikhail Chigorin (1850-1908) fits perfectly in this trend and the scepticism with which it was regarded throughout most of the 20th century has to a great extent been abandoned.

The principal test of the soundness of 2...♘c6 is **3 cxd5**, hoping after 3...♕xd5 to gain a tempo by playing ♘c3 after first protecting d4. Black has to act quickly. Both against 4 ♘f3 and 4 e3 it is of vital importance to play 4...e5. The main line is 4 e3 e5 5 ♘c3 ♗b4 6 ♗d2 ♗xc3 and now either 7 ♗xc3 or 7 bxc3 is good. The former is based on the possibility **7 ♗xc3** exd4 8 ♘e2! *(D)*.

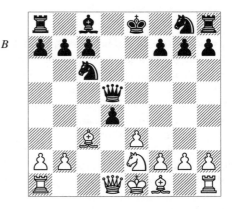

White intends to follow with 9 ♘xd4.

7 bxc3 intends to build a strong pawn-centre by means of f3 and e4. Both these lines are hotly debated and make for lively middlegame play.

Another important test of the Chigorin is the natural developing move **3 ♘c3**. Now the thematic 3...e5 is not considered very promising because of 4 cxd5 ♘xd4 5 e3 ♘f5, but both 3...dxc4 and 3...♘f6 are thought to be playable. Against 3...dxc4, the sharpest reply is 4 d5 ♘e5 5 f4 followed by 6 e4, but this is not played very often. The most popular move is 4 ♘f3, when 4...♘f6 produces a position that is also relevant to 3...♘f6 (4 ♘f3 dxc4). With 5 e4 ♗g4 6 ♗e3 and now either 6...e6 or 6...♗xf3 7 gxf3 e5 being the critical follow-up, this line is similar to the 3 e4 ♘c6 variation of the Queen's Gambit Accepted (page 41) and is likely to lead to a tense and double-edged middlegame.

3 ♘f3 is also a natural move. The main line here is 3...♗g4 4 cxd5 ♗xf3 5 gxf3 ♕xd5 6 e3 e5 7 ♘c3 ♗b4 8 ♗d2 ♗xc3 9 bxc3 *(D)*.

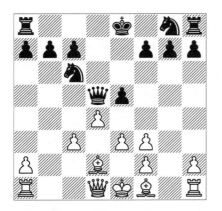

By now the reader will have understood that Black should not be afraid to give up his bishop-pair if he wants to play the Chigorin Defence. The very essence of this opening lies in the creation of unbalanced middlegame positions by introducing hard-to-judge positional elements, such as doubled pawns and bishop-against-knight situations.

Finally, against **3 e3** the characteristic 3...e5 4 dxe5 d4 is considered a strong reply. This is in effect the Albin Counter-Gambit in a more favourable version. The natural 5 ♘f3 runs into 5...♗b4+, while 5 exd4 ♕xd4 gives Black excellent compensation for the sacrificed pawn.

2 c4 ♗f5

2   ...   ♗f5 *(D)*

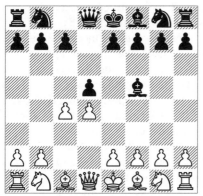

This move betrays an attitude very similar to the Chigorin Defence: Black is aiming for active piece-play. It is also a highly provocative move, perhaps even more so than 2...♘c6. This introduces a psychological element into the game: many a player behind the white pieces will feel that he *has* to punish such reckless opening play and perhaps becomes reckless himself. And in a way it is true that imaginative and aggressive play is required, for if White does no more than simply develop his pieces, he will not achieve any opening advantage (which may not be a problem for some, but terribly frustrating for others).

The first point of 2...♗f5 is that **3 cxd5** is met by 3...♗xb1. Now 4 ♕a4+ is a useful move to interpolate, forcing 4...c6, which gives White a choice between 5 ♖xb1 and 5 dxc6 ♘xc6 6 ♖xb1, when the sharp 6...e5 is thought to be best. Black regains his pawn and obtains what is usually called 'a reasonable position', meaning that theory has not yet examined this very deeply and is working on the primal hypothesis that until proved otherwise chances are considered more or less equal.

It is also important to note that **3 ♕b3** can (and probably must) be met by the ultra-sharp 3...e5 *(D)*.

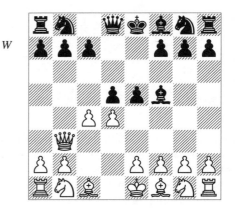

Theory has even less to say about this (although it should, as it is a possible refutation of 2...♗f5) than about 3 cxd5, but practice suggests that this is tricky since, although 3 ♕b3 is perfectly plausible, it is rarely played.

The sound developing move **3 ♘c3** is much more popular. This is usually met by 3...e6, when things start to slow down a bit. Attacking b7 by means of ♕b3 is still an important motif, but White usually protects his own pawn on d4 first by playing 4 ♘f3 *(D)*.

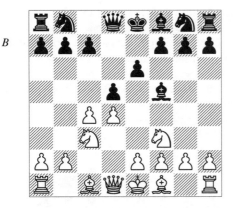

Black then usually replies 4...c6 in order to meet 5 ♕b3 with 5...♕b6. Perhaps rather surprisingly 6 c5 is then not met by exchanging queens, but by 6...♕c7 allowing White to gain yet another tempo by 7 ♗f4 (7...♕xf4 8 ♕xb7 is in White's favour). Still, the position after the modest retreat 7...♕c8 is not necessarily bad for Black. Because White has played c5, Black's central position is now safe. The position has become closed and fairly slow. White will try to exploit his space advantage on the queenside, but Black has the prospect of retaliating in the centre by means of ...e5.

3 ♘f3 is also a sound move, deserving careful consideration if only because this position often arises via 1 ♘f3 or 1 d4 d5 2 ♘f3. After 3...e6, 4 ♘c3 transposes to 3 ♘c3 e6 4 ♘f3, while 4 ♕b3 runs into the aggressive 4...♘c6!.

Austrian Defence

2 ... **c5** *(D)*

This interpretation of the Queen's Gambit (also known by the natural name, the **Symmetrical Queen's Gambit**) has never been fully trusted. Yet there probably is a lot to be discovered here and, being as unfashionable as it is, it could well make a wonderful surprise weapon for those who are prepared to put some work in it and perhaps lift our knowledge of this opening to a new level.

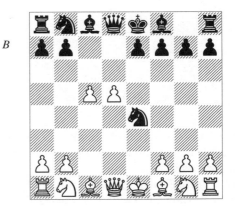

3 **cxd5** **♘f6**

Much more sophisticated than **3...♕xd5**, which allows White a comfortable lead in development after 4 ♘f3 cxd4 5 ♘c3 ♕a5 6 ♘xd4.

4 **e4**

It is this bold move which is responsible for the dubious reputation of the Austrian Defence. More conservative options like **4 ♘f3** cxd4 5 ♕xd4 ♕xd5 or **4 dxc5** ♕xd5 do not cause Black a lot of trouble.

4 ... **♘xe4**

5 **dxc5** *(D)*

White has managed to hold on to his pawn on d5, which gives him a space advantage and plenty of open lines for his pieces. A logical reaction by Black would be to play **5...♘xc5** 6 ♘f3 e6, eliminating the white pawn, but practice has shown that Black still has his work cut out for him after the simple 7 ♘c3 exd5 8

♛xd5, giving White a solid lead in development. **5...♛a5+** has been suggested as an improvement, but this has not been played very often. Here too Black will have to be very careful not to fall behind in development after 6 ♗d2 ♘xd2 7 ♛xd2 ♛xc5 8 ♘a3.

Albin Counter-Gambit

| 2 | ... | e5 |

Having called 2...♗f5 a provocative move, I am at a loss to find even stronger terms for this gambit. One may well stare in disbelief at this move and be quite unable to see the point. And yet it is by no means unfounded.

| 3 | dxe5 | d4 |

This is Black's idea: he gains a space advantage in the centre.

| 4 | ♘f3 | ♘c6 *(D)* |

We have arrived at the basic starting-point of this gambit.

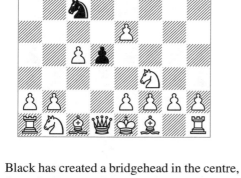

Black has created a bridgehead in the centre, he has all the open lines that he can possibly want for a quick development of his pieces and there is the realistic long-term prospect of surrounding White's pawn on e5, which will restore the material balance. Is it strange that this gambit has always held a strong attraction for the daring attacking player?

And what does White have to show for all this? Well, in the first place, by playing ...d4, Black has left the h1-a8 diagonal wide open, inviting a g3 set-up which may result in an attack on the queenside involving b4. Furthermore,

Black's pawn on d4 is not completely safe. It may be attacked with moves such as ♘bd2-b3 or b4 followed by ♗b2. Worries over the e5-pawn are misplaced. As long as it survives that is fine, but if it does fall, the strategic plans outlined above remain unaffected.

Strangely enough, despite the sharp nature of the position there are not a lot of clear-cut variations here. White's most popular move is **5 g3**, but **5 ♘bd2** and **5 a3** have also been played. Black usually continues 5...♗e6 or 5...♗g4. A plausible continuation (after 5 g3) is 5...♗e6 6 ♘bd2 ♛d7 7 ♗g2 *(D)*.

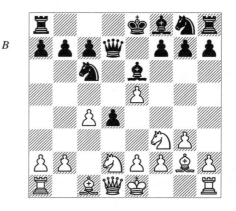

Now Black is able to regain his pawn by **7...♘ge7** 8 0-0 ♘g6. In practice, however, this has turned out to be quite good for White after 9 ♘g5 or 9 ♛b3 ♖b8 10 ♘g5. A more resolute approach is probably called for, for instance **7...♗h3** 8 0-0 0-0-0 followed by 9...h5.

Whoever wants to play this gambit does not need any thorough knowledge of variations, but a good eye for tactical chances and a feel for improvisation are indispensable.

Queen's Pawn Game

| 2 | ♘f3 *(D)* |

It could be said that, by not playing c4, White is trying to avoid a fight, but this is deceptive and, of course, ultimately impossible. In reality, White simply postpones c4 and waits for Black to show his hand first.

If White, for whatever reason, does indeed refrain from playing c4, opening play will

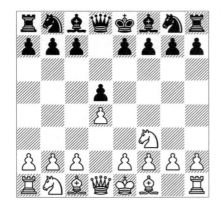

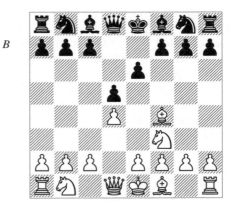

generally speaking be a bit slower than in the Queen's Gambit. In fact we then enter a dimly-lit area on the fringes of opening theory where it is still possible to discern general schemes of development, but where sharp and forcing variations are nowhere to be found.

As far as any roads can be said to exist in this border area, they are not highways, but lonely and rarely used footpaths. They may seem impassable and difficult to spot in some places, but this is never really a problem, because the experienced hiker can be depended upon to find an alternative path without any difficulty.

2 ... ♘f6

A useful, neutral reply, for which there are a great number of alternatives.

2...e6 is usually played in order to enter a specific variation of the Queen's Gambit, for instance **3 c4** dxc4 or 3...c5. It is also a useful preparation for 3...c5 in case White does not play 3 c4.

The most popular non-Queen's Gambit move against 2...e6 is **3 ♗f4** *(D)*.

This move introduces a scheme of development, known as the **London System**, that may be used against almost any black set-up, but it is more effective if Black has already played ...e6, as is the case here. The general idea is to play ♘f3, ♗f4, c3, e3, ♗d3 and ♘bd2, offering prospects of a successful attack on the kingside starting with ♘e5.

It is difficult to recommend a specific 'best reply' to this, but starting with 3...c5 4 e3 and then playing 4...♕b6, in order to induce White to play the slightly passive 5 ♕c1, is a good

idea. Classical development like 4...♘c6 5 c3 ♗d6 is also not bad.

If Black is thinking of a ...c5 set-up, he may want to consider the immediate **2...c5** *(D)*.

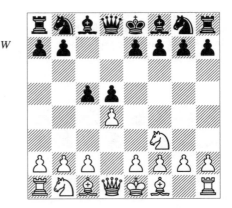

This is also an important move psychologically, because Black makes it clear that he is ready to take over the initiative, thus provoking a sharp reply or cowering White into submission. Moves like **3 e3** or **3 c3** cannot be said to be downright bad, but in this case they do clearly signal that White is not aiming for an opening advantage. If he finds this too meek, White has only two options. One is to force the opponent back into the realm of the Queen's Gambit by playing **3 c4** (Black may then opt for the Tarrasch Defence by 3...e6, or for the Queen's Gambit Accepted by 3...dxc4). The other is to take on c5 and enter relatively unknown territory. A possible continuation is **3 dxc5** e6 4 e4, a motif which we have already seen with colours reversed in the Queen's Gambit Accepted.

2...c6 is played with an eye to the Slav Defence if White goes 3 c4, while also keeping the active developing moves ...♗f5 and ...♗g4 in mind if White plays something else. If, for example, White chooses 3 ♗f4, then the resulting middlegame after 3...♗f5 4 e3 e6 5 ♗d3 ♗xd3 6 ♕xd3 ♘f6 will be somewhat easier for Black than the positions after the above-mentioned 2...e6 3 ♗f4. Perhaps in this case 3 ♗g5 is the more aggressive option.

Playing **2...♗f5** immediately is also perfectly sound, but it does of course allow White to transpose into a line of the 2...♗f5 Queen's Gambit with 3 c4. Other moves, like 3 ♗f4 e6, are again perfectly playable, but they do not make life difficult for Black in the opening. Perhaps this is the one line where I would advise even the most fanatical theory hater (who is of course unlikely to read this book) to go for a main line just this once and play 3 c4.

Quite the reverse can be said about **2...♘c6** (D).

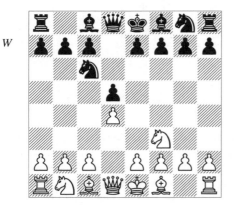

This is an invitation to enter a Chigorin Defence with 3 c4. Naturally **3 c4** is a perfectly valid option, yet in this particular case even the builders of highways consider two footpaths as just as reliable: 3 ♗f4 and 3 g3. These are not intended to avoid c4 altogether, but to play this move a little bit later so as to avoid a few standard Chigorin reactions.

3 ♗f4 is usually met by 3...♗g4, when the idea is to play 4 e3 e6 5 c4.

3 g3 is also often met by **3...♗g4**, in this case with 4 ♗g2 ♕d7 in mind, with a view to lashing out on the kingside with ...♗h3 and ...h5-h4. This may easily lead to chaotic situations where positional subtleties do not count for much.

Another, only slightly less radical, possibility is **3...♗f5** 4 ♗g2 ♘b4. This is not a rash attacking move but a clever ploy to clear the way for the c-pawn while at the same time making it more difficult for White to get c4 in. After 5 ♘a3 c6 6 c3 ♘a6 followed by ...e6, Black's position has turned out to be quite solid, much more so in fact than in a Chigorin proper.

We now return to 2...♘f6 (D):

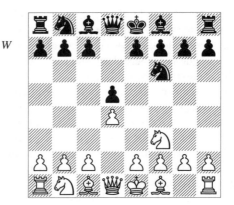

In fact the implications of 2...♘f6 are not so different from those of the moves we have just looked at. If White does not wish to return to the Queen's Gambit by playing **3 c4**, then **3 ♗f4** and **3 ♗g5** are his most plausible options. A third possibility, which may not look very impressive, but is nevertheless the starting point of a well-thought-out scheme of development, is **3 e3**.

Superficially modern and sophisticated, but in actual fact quite the opposite, is **3 g3**. After 3...♗f5 4 ♗g2 e6 or 3...c6 4 ♗g2 ♗f5 Black's position is much easier than in the Catalan Opening (page 24). In a situation where Black is able to develop his queen's bishop as comfortably as this, a g3 set-up is usually fairly innocuous.

2 ♘f3 ♘f6 3 ♗f4

3   ♗f4 (D)

B

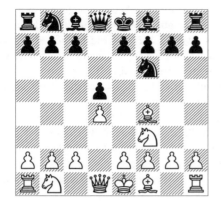

This is yet another form of the London System (and we shall be seeing quite a few more in the course of the book, as White can play these moves almost regardless of how Black replies). This variation is not a frequent guest in games at the highest level, because 3 ♗f4 does not exert any immediate pressure on Black's position, yet anyone not aspiring to world championship level may rest assured that 3 ♗f4 is a perfectly useful move. Pressure and ambition always work in two directions. Developing his pieces in this way, White also does not exert any pressure on his own position. Accidents are unlikely to happen here. White simply and soundly develops his pieces.

In the end, the intensity of a game of chess does not depend on the choice of opening, but on the effort and intensity that both players invest in it. An opening like this offers plenty of possibilities for a fierce middlegame, just as a sharp opening may fizzle out.

As I already mentioned when discussing 2...e6, a ♗f4 set-up is at its most effective when Black has already hemmed in his queen's bishop with ...e6. This means that Black has a fairly easy game here after **3...♗f5** or **3...c6**, intending to meet 4 e3 with 4...♗g4. **3...c5** is also a good move, producing a sort of Queen's Gambit with colours reversed after 4 e3. Black then has 4...♘c6 but also the more aggressive option of 4...♕b6. This move forces White to choose between the modest (but not bad) 5 ♕c1 and the more cheeky 5 ♘c3, when 5...♕xb2 6 ♘b5 is not exactly attractive for Black, but 5...c4 6 ♖b1 ♗g4 is a very good option.

2 ♘f3 ♘f6 3 ♗g5

3   ♗g5 *(D)*

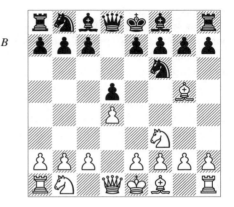

B

This method of development is slightly more aggressive than 3 ♗f4 because it raises some concrete, if not overly pressing, problems. In the first place the possibility of taking on f6, although it can hardly be called a threat, now looms over the position. As a consequence the sortie ...♘e4 needs to be considered: is this a welcome improvement of Black's chances or will this knight on e4 turn out to be a potential liability? These problems may not be world-shattering, yet a certain tension is palpable.

Black has several ways to react.

Undoubtedly the simplest reply is **3...e6**. Black continues in classical fashion and shows no inclination to try to wrest the initiative from his opponent immediately. White is allowed a return to the Queen's Gambit (4 c4), but the characteristic Queen's Pawn Game scheme e3, c3, ♘bd2, ♗d3 with a view to playing either e4 or ♘e5 and f4 is equally justifiable. Many games have continued 4 e3 ♗e7 5 ♘bd2 c5 6 c3 ♘bd7 7 ♗d3 b6 8 0-0 ♗b7 9 ♘e5 ♘xe5 10 dxe5 ♘d7 11 ♗xe7 ♕xe7 12 f4 with chances of a kingside attack for White.

Practically just as simple, yet a little more energetic, is **3...c5**. If White now takes on f6, Black intends to take back with his g-pawn, while against the quiet 4 e3 he has the aggressive options 4...♕b6 and 4...♘e4.

If Black is not worried about being saddled with doubled pawns on the f-file, he may freely play **3...g6**, **3...♗f5** or **3...c6**. In fact, players aiming for ♗xf6 are not likely to play this in combination with 2 ♘f3. They will usually prefer 2 ♗g5 (which will be discussed shortly), to allow themselves greater flexibility – moves like ♘e2 or ♕f3 may come in useful.

Finally, Black's most radical move is undoubtedly **3...♘e4**. Strangely enough though, theory has little to say on this. It is more or less agreed that, after 4 ♗h4, 4...c5 is the sharpest follow-up, when 5 e3 ♕b6 6 ♘c3 is considered 'interesting' and 5 dxc5 takes us into practically unknown territory, but basically we are left to work it out for ourselves.

2 ♘f3 ♘f6 3 e3

3   e3 *(D)*

Nowadays this modest little move will probably impress no one as deserving more than a cursory glance. Yet for the greater part of a century it was looked upon as the main line of the Queen's Pawn Game and some very strong grandmasters have used it to good effect in the past. But even though we see little of it in top-level tournaments any more and although it has been labelled 'solid but harmless' in the books, even today Black, especially if he suspects nothing, may find this ancient line surprisingly difficult to handle.

3   ...   e6

This reply was more or less standard during the first half of the 20th century, the heyday of this opening, but there are other moves.

The first move to become accepted as a legitimate alternative (this was sometime during the 1930s) was **3...♗f5**. The old-fashioned response is 4 ♗d3, hoping for 4...♗xd3 (4...e6 may well be a better idea) 5 cxd3 followed by e4, while 4 c4 (with either 4...e6 or 4...c6 the likely answer) is more modern.

This 'modern' reaction 4 c4 is also a good reply to **3...♗g4**, while if Black plays **3...g6** it even leads us straight into a modern main line of the Grünfeld Defence: 4 c4 ♗g7 5 ♘c3 (see page 132). Of course a set-up without c4 is also playable here. It always is.

3...c5 is also a good move. This may easily transpose to our main line, for instance after 4 c3 e6 5 ♗d3.

4   ♗d3   c5 *(D)*

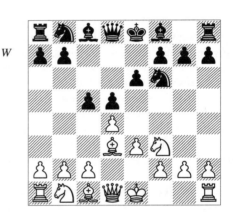

In this position there are two standard plans of development for White.

The older, favoured by Zukertort in the 19th century, starts with **5 b3**. After 5...♘c6 6 0-0 ♗d6 7 ♗b2 0-0 the traditional plan involves ♘e5 and f4 with an eye to a possible kingside attack. The modern alternative is to play 8 c4, which may give rise (after 8...cxd4 9 exd4 dxc4 10 bxc4, for instance) to a position with 'hanging pawns', a double-edged pawn-formation which tends to lead to a highly complex middlegame. Black will attack the centre pawns while White may (again) develop a dangerous attack on the kingside.

Compared to this, White's second option, **5 c3** *(D)*, is uncomplicated and pretty straightforward.

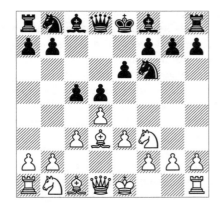

B

The plan is to play ♘bd2 and e4, sometimes preceded by capturing on c5. This is the **Colle System**, which was especially popular in the 1920s and 1930s. It is still an excellent choice for those who want to keep the opening as simple as possible.

Black's most plausible reaction is **5...♘c6** 6 0-0 ♗d6 7 ♘bd2 0-0, when 8 dxc5 ♗xc5 9 e4 produces what may be termed the starting point of this ancient opening. Black's best move here is considered to be 9...♕c7 to prevent 10 e5.

A slightly more subtle deployment of the queen's knight is **5...♘bd7** in order to capture on c5 with the knight. In this case White, after 6 0-0 ♗d6 7 ♘bd2 0-0, usually plays 8 e4 straightaway, though the preparatory move 8 ♖e1 is also moderately popular.

Richter-Veresov Opening

2	**♘c3** *(D)*

B

A positionally-inclined player will perhaps regard this move as somewhat unnatural. White blocks his own c-pawn and by so doing completely rules out the typical Queen's Gambit move c4. Nevertheless this strategy has always had its small band of devotees. After all, White does develop a piece and his strategic aim is sound enough: he wants to play e4.

This makes the Richter-Veresov an opening which is strongly related to the 1 e4 openings. It could even be said that this *is* a 1 e4 opening, but without the vast amount of theory which is attached to the 'real' 1 e4.

2	...	**♘f6**

The Richter-Veresov's close relationship to 1 e4 is made emphatically clear if Black plays either **2...c6** or **2...e6**, when 3 e4 will produce a Caro-Kann or a French Defence, respectively.

The sharp **2...c5** is not to be recommended if only because of 3 e4 dxe4 4 d5, an Albin Counter-Gambit with colours reversed and an extra tempo for White.

3	**♗g5**	**♘bd7** *(D)*

Other moves are not necessarily inferior, but allow White to complicate matters. If **3...c5**, for instance, 4 ♗xf6 gxf6 5 e3 produces a much more difficult position and if **3...c6**, both 4 ♗xf6 and 4 ♕d3 followed by 5 e4 are good alternatives to the 'normal' 4 e3 or 4 ♘f3. Similarly **3...♗f5** has been answered by both 4 ♗xf6 and 4 e3 e6 5 ♗d3, again intending to play e4.

3...e6 again allows a transposition to the French by 4 e4.

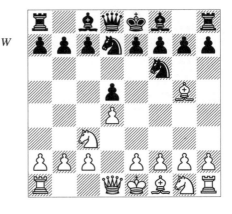

W

4	**♘f3**

This simple developing move has pushed the older **4 f3** into the background. Practice has shown that, although 4 f3 is a logical enough move (preparing an immediate e4), Black has too many good replies. The sharp 4...c5 and the waiting moves 4...c6 and 4...e6 have all done very well, as has interpolating 4...h6. In fact, although f3 is useful in *preparing* e4, it is a move which White would dearly like to retract *after* he has played e4, because it gets into the way of fast development (no ♘f3, no d1-h5 diagonal for queen and bishop). For this reason the modern Richter-Veresov player tries to get in e4 without f3.

After 4 ♘f3 Black has a solid scheme of development in **4...g6**, when a plausible continuation is 5 e3 ♗g7 6 ♗d3 0-0 7 0-0 c5 8 ♖e1, getting ready to play e4.

4...h6 5 ♗h4 e6 is a sharp alternative. Black dares his opponent to play 6 e4 at the cost of a pawn: 6...g5 7 ♗g3 ♘xe4, when 8 ♘xe4 dxe4 9 ♘d2 f5 10 h4 produces rather an obscure position. White is not without some compensation, certainly, but will it be enough?

2 ♗g5

2   ♗g5 *(D)*

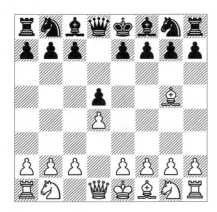

When during the 1980s the Trompowsky Attack, 1 d4 ♘f6 2 ♗g5, came into fashion and quickly gained acceptance as a serious opening, some of its pioneers started experimenting with this bishop sortie after 1...d5 as well.

While **2...♘f6** transposes to the Trompowsky proper (see page 171) a number of alternatives have been developed into a modest amount of independent theory.

Among moves like **2...c5** and **2...f6** (and many others), **2...c6** and **2...h6 3 ♗h4 c6** may be loosely called the main lines. They are based on a tactical finesse: after 2...h6 3 ♗h4 c6 4 e3 (or 2...c6 3 e3 h6 4 ♗h4) 4...♕b6 5 ♕c1 (or 5 b3) Black has the rather surprising 5...e5 *(D)*.

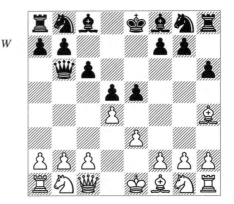

This is based on the fact that taking on e5 loses the bishop (6 dxe5?? ♕b4+). Strangely enough though, this has not unduly worried the 2 ♗g5 crowd. In the first place many of them simply play 6 ♘f3 instead of 6 dxe5 and continue as if nothing has happened (and they may have a point, proven in part by the fact that not everyone likes 5...e5; the quiet 5...♗f5 is often preferred). Secondly, White has tried 4 ♘f3 (instead of 4 e3) and this has also held up fairly well in practice. If now 4...♕b6, White intends to play 5 ♕c1 ♗f5 6 c4 e6 7 ♘c3. The battle for the initiative is in full progress.

Nimzo-Indian Defence

1	d4	♘f6
2	c4	e6
3	♘c3	♗b4 (D)

W

Named after its pioneer Aron Nimzowitsch (1886-1935), this opening has been one of Black's most popular defences to 1 d4 ever since its 'invention' (adoption really, because it had been played before) by Nimzowitsch during the 1910s.

Black prevents 4 e4, yet unlike the more classical approach that achieves this goal, 3...d5 (the Queen's Gambit Declined), he maintains maximal flexibility for his pawn-formation. Depending on White's reply, Black will be able to choose between a central formation based on ...d5, ...c5, ...b6 or ...d6 (and almost any combination of these).

This means that both players will have to assess the situation very carefully on practically every single move during the opening stage, not just tactically but strategically as well. This makes the Nimzo-Indian a demanding opening and it may explain why, no matter how highly regarded it may be, this opening is not popular with *everyone*.

Ever since Nimzowitsch, almost all top players have played the Nimzo-Indian at one time

or another and at times White has been so troubled by it that the move 3 ♘c3 all but disappeared for some years. Yet every single time this happened, after a while White managed to bounce back with new ideas and new insights. This constant to and fro of the theoretical battle has created a fascinating wealth of variations, a wealth that is not just at the disposal of players looking for a solid opening repertoire but also (and perhaps even more so) of the ardent student who wants to deepen his understanding of positions where flexibility and dynamic play are the key factors.

The first of these dynamic factors confronting us is the possible exchange of the Nimzo-Indian bishop for the knight on c3. This was the first question asked of 3...♗b4: does not the position after the straightforward **4 a3 ♗xc3+ 5 bxc3** simply favour White? Demonstrating where Black's chances lie in this type of position has perhaps been *the* great contribution by Nimzowitsch to the Nimzo-Indian. It meant that this simple reply to 3...♗b4, which later came to be called the **Sämisch Variation**, was not a refutation.

Then came the more subtle approach: **4 ♕c2**, intending to play 5 a3 ♗xc3+ 6 ♕xc3. White *does* want the pair of bishops, but not the doubled pawns. After initial success, this line fell out of favour because it was thought to be too slow until it was rehabilitated by Kasparov in the early 1990s. Today it is one of White's most dangerous weapons against the Nimzo-Indian.

The move which has been the most consistently popular one, however, is **4 e3**, the **Rubinstein Variation**. This may well be called a middle road between the two extremes 4 a3 and 4 ♕c2. White does not avoid the doubled pawns, but he is confident that the position after 4 e3 ♗xc3+ 5 bxc3 is so much better for him than the one arising from 4 a3 ♗xc3+ 5 bxc3 that he decides not to 'waste a move' on 4 ♕c2 and simply continues his development instead. And it is true that 4...♗xc3+ is completely unusual here, but the *threat* of taking on c3 remains and is executed in many subvariations a few moves later.

4 ♗g5 also allows the exchange on c3, yet this move poses a counter-threat: how is Black to react to the pin against *his* knight? This fairly sharp variation was popularized by Spassky and Timman in the 1970s and 1980s.

4 f3 is also a sharp move. It became uncommonly popular in the early 1990s, when White was extremely successful with it for a short time. All existing variations and assessments were completely overhauled, swept aside in fact, but soon things began to fall into place and new defences for Black were erected. Still 4 f3 remains a move to be reckoned with.

In comparison, the neutral developing move **4 ♘f3** may almost be called less ambitious although it is certainly not to be underestimated. It is strongly related not only to 4 e3, but also to **4 g3**. Both these moves have also been rehabilitated by Kasparov.

Lastly **4 ♕b3** must be mentioned, but the theoretical status of this line can be summarized briefly: the move dates back to the earliest times of the Nimzo-Indian, but although it seems sound enough, it fell out of favour for a very long time and to this day is rarely played. 4 ♕b3 is more forcing than 4 ♕c2 but less flexible. The reason it fell out of fashion is 4...c5 5 dxc5 ♘c6 6 ♘f3 ♘e4 (D).

This last move would obviously be impossible with the queen on c2 and gives Black a

fairly easy game after 7 ♗d2 ♘xd2 8 ♘xd2 ♗xc5.

Sämisch Variation

	4	a3	♗xc3+
	5	bxc3 (D)	

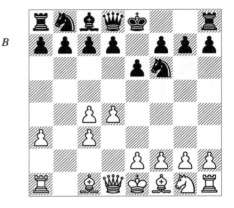

This is the fundamental test of 3...♗b4. White now has a great many pawns in the centre, giving him plenty of space. He also has the pair of bishops. These factors are not to be underestimated and in the hands of a skilful attacking player they may easily add up to a dangerous attack. But the downside is that, due to the doubled pawns on the c-file, White's pawn-formation is rigid and vulnerable. It is also still completely uncertain at this early stage whether the bishop-pair is going to turn out to be an asset or a liability.

In fact, these positional factors are extremely delicate and the slightest inaccuracy may tip the scales at any moment. Besides, many players are prejudiced in these matters one way or another. They simply *want* the Sämisch to be either good or bad, no matter what the books say.

	5	...	c5

This is perhaps the most popular move, both in practice and in theoretical investigations. Black takes a natural step forward in the centre and retains a certain amount of flexibility in his pawn-formation. For instance, the important decision whether to play ...d6 or ...d5, or whether to castle kingside or queenside, is left open.

On a more fundamental level, however, the choice is not between moves but between plans. How does Black intend to attack the white centre? Which pawn-formation does he have in mind? The range of these plans varies from classical to extremely provocative.

5...c5 may be called classical, while **5...b6** is perhaps Black's most provocative move, because while allowing his opponent a free hand in building a strong pawn-centre with 6 f3 ♗a6! 7 e4 Black concentrates fully on attacking the c4-pawn by 7...♘c6 (D).

Black intends 8...♘a5. Strangely enough, after many years of practice and research, theory is still not sure whether this strategy is sound. White has tried both 8 ♗g5 and 8 e5 ♘g8 9 ♘h3 without coming to firm conclusions.

Another interesting and slightly more modest idea is **5...d6** (D).

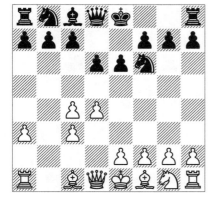

Here too theory refuses to give clear answers or even clear variations. After 6 f3, for instance, 6...e5 7 e4 c5 8 ♗d3 ♘c6 is a solid plan and one that we are going to see quite often in this chapter, yet Black has varied endlessly on this idea and it is very hard to say what is best. To start with, Black may throw in 6...♘h5 (threatening 7...♕h4+) 7 ♘h3 before he plays 7...e5. He may also play 6...c5 7 e4 ♘c6 first and leave his opponent guessing whether ...e5 is still to come.

We now return to 5...c5 (D):

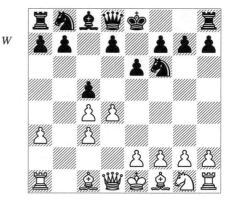

White now has two main lines: the ambitious **6 f3**, or the more cautious **6 e3**.

4 a3 ♗xc3+ 5 bxc3 c5 6 f3

6 f3

This is always the most aggressive approach; White is threatening to play 7 e4. Now Black can either allow this (we have just seen that **6...d6** 7 e4 ♘c6 is a valid option) or he can act directly against this plan by taking the initiative in the centre himself.

    6   **...**   **d5**
    7   **cxd5**

After this logical reply, the character of the middlegame will to a great extent be determined by Black's choice of how to recapture.

7...exd5 gives Black a firm foothold in the centre and prevents White from playing e4. This is a logical enough strategy, forcing White not only to change plans but also to slow down a little. In fact White has to start developing his kingside now, for which the standard scheme is 8 e3, 9 ♗d3, 10 ♘e2 and 11 0-0. When this is accomplished, he may return to the plan of playing e4. This scheme is fairly straightforward and although it is slow, it is difficult for Black to do any damage before White gets the e4 advance in.

That is why the alternative recapture **7...♘xd5** *(D)* has gradually replaced 7...exd5 as Black's most popular choice.

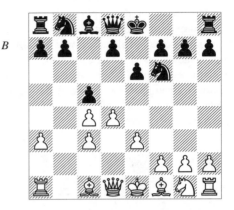

W

Black plays actively, trying to make use of a few concrete disadvantages of the move f3. To begin with, White cannot defend his c-pawn by the seemingly natural **8 ♗d2**, because this allows 8...cxd4 9 cxd4 ♕h4+, winning a pawn. This means that White does not have a really comfortable way of protecting c3 (**8 ♕d3** is relatively best in this respect, but then he must take 8...b6 9 e4 ♗a6 into account), which has caused White to look in an entirely different direction. The critical move is now thought to be **8 dxc5**. Abandoning the original idea of forming a strong pawn-centre (and indeed abandoning *any* idea of a solid pawn-formation), White opens as many diagonals as possible in order to maximize the positive effects of the bishop-pair. It is not the extra pawn that matters, and practice has shown that it is often a good idea for Black to subdue the white bishops by refusing to capture either of White's c-pawns too early. Many games have continued 8...♕a5 9 e4 ♘e7 10 ♗e3 0-0 11 ♕b3, when there are so many dynamic factors to be taken into account that it is almost impossible to say who is better.

4 a3 ♗xc3+ 5 bxc3 c5 6 e3

6 e3 *(D)*

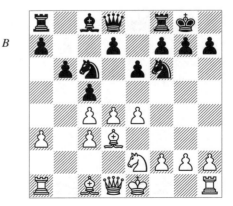

B

This is a more solid option than 6 f3, giving the opponent as little opportunity for counterplay as possible. White wants to play 7 ♗d3 followed by 8 ♘e2 and 9 0-0, when everything is ready for the central thrust e4.

The downside is that, compared to 6 f3, Black has one extra move with which to organize his defences.

6 ... ♘c6

This is perhaps Black's most flexible move, but not the only one. A sound alternative is **6...b6** 7 ♗d3 ♗b7 forcing his opponent to make one more preparatory move (f3) before he can play e4.

7	♗d3	0-0
8	♘e2	b6
9	e4 *(D)*	

This is one of the most critical positions of the entire Sämisch Variation. With minimal loss of time, White has managed to create the powerful central formation that he had in mind when playing 4 a3. Black now has to defend with the utmost accuracy, yet without letting himself be pushed into a passive position. His next move is far from obvious.

9 ... ♘e8

This move was first played by Capablanca and betrays the brilliant positional insight of the great Cuban world champion (1888-1942). By now it has become common property but it is still as vital to Black's plans as it ever was. Before he lashes out on the queenside with ...♗a6 and ...♘a5 (and ...♘e8-d6 if necessary!) Black prevents the pin ♗g5 and clears the path for his f-pawn.

Play now becomes very complicated. After 10 0-0 ♗a6 11 f4 f5 12 ♘g3 g6 13 ♗e3 ♘d6, for instance, nobody really knows who is better.

What *is* clear, however, is that whoever wants to play this variation (with either colour) should not feel half-hearted or worried about his chances. Total self-confidence is what is required here.

4 ♕c2

4 ♕c2 *(D)*

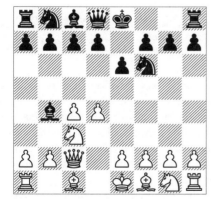

With this move we enter a world that is vastly different from the Sämisch. Whereas 4 a3 could be said to resolve the pin against the c3-knight quickly and radically, 4 ♕c2 does it

slowly and patiently. In most cases White will play a3 on one of the next moves and recapture on c3 with his queen, thus carefully guarding the integrity of his pawn-formation.

To our modern minds the soundness of this strategy seems commonplace, but this was not always the case. In the 1930s the reply **4...d5** was thought to bring about an improved version of the Queen's Gambit Declined (improved from Black's point of view, that is) because White's d-pawn comes under attack. For the same reason **4...♘c6** was thought to be a problem for White.

Later it was the move **4...c5** which kept the reputation of 4 ♕c2 at a moderately low level and later still the ultra-flexible **4...0-0** caused a lot of headaches.

But all these problems were solved when around 1990 4 ♕c2 suddenly became exceedingly popular. All theoretical assessments and variations were overhauled and renewed with great precision. Ever since that time 4 ♕c2 has been held in high esteem by all and sundry.

4 ♕c2 d5

4 ... d5 *(D)*

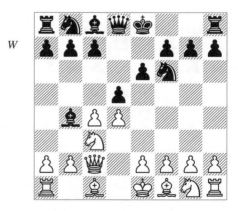

It is no coincidence that White had to find a satisfactory reply to this move before 4 ♕c2 could even begin to be taken seriously. Black attempts to take over the initiative at once.

5 cxd5

This is the most popular and certainly the most solid reply. The alternative **5 a3** is no less logical, but after 5...♗xc3+ 6 ♕xc3 ♘e4 White is made to feel that his plan, beautiful as it is, is also a trifle slow. Whether Black's initiative is really to be feared is in fact, despite a multitude of high-level games and much analysis, still a very moot point, but it is essential for White to be aware of the potential dangers that 5 a3 is sparking off. To give but a sample line: after 7 ♕c2 Black has 7...e5!?, intending 8 dxe5 ♗f5, and also 7...♘c6 8 e3 e5 with similar ideas, while the less intimidating 7...c5 8 dxc5 ♘c6 is in fact quite treacherous as well (as is revealed after 9 b4?? ♕f6!).

5   ...   ♕xd5 (D)

This perhaps somewhat surprising way of recapturing the pawn had an excellent reputation in the very first days of the Nimzo-Indian, then fell into oblivion for the better part of a century only to be fully rehabilitated in the 1990s.

The alternative **5...exd5** is also not bad, but a proper evaluation of this move is now thought to depend on (again) a rather sharp line: 6 ♗g5 h6 7 ♗h4 c5. If Black recoils from this and goes for something like 6...0-0 7 e3 c6 he will instead find himself in a slightly inferior version of the Exchange Variation of the Queen's Gambit Declined. His bishop on b4 does not fit into this scheme.

This position was already considered perfectly playable for Black in the 1930s, but this changed when it was discovered that White should perhaps not play **6 a3 ♗xc3+ 7 bxc3** or **6 e3** c5 7 ♗d2 ♗xc3 8 bxc3, recapturing on c3 with the b-pawn and hoping to create a strong central pawn-formation, but **6 ♘f3** c5 7 ♗d2 ♗xc3 8 ♗xc3, keeping the centre as open as possible in order to enhance the powers of his bishop-pair. Although Black is not under immediate pressure in this position, in the long term his prospects are no brighter than obtaining a hard-fought draw, which caused 5...♕xd5 to be practically abandoned. Then in 1993 Romanishin introduced the highly original move 6...♕f5 (instead of 6...c5) and this has caused the variation to make a full recovery. The endgame after 7 ♕xf5 exf5 is considered equal, while other moves (like 7 ♕b3 for instance) leave the black queen well positioned on f5.

4 ♕c2 ♘c6

4   ...   ♘c6

This move introduces a simple plan: Black wants to play ...d6 and ...e5.

5   ♘f3   d6 (D)

This is the key position. It may look as if White can now prevent Black from playing ...e5 very easily by **6 a3 ♗xc3+ 7 ♕xc3**, but in the long run this is impossible. Black will execute his plan by 7...0-0 8 e3 ♖e8, followed if necessary by 9...♕e7, when ...e5 can no longer be prevented.

For this reason White's main consideration should not be how to stop ...e5, but how to react when it happens. He has two fundamental options: either White decides to exchange pawns on e5 hoping that the bishop-pair will prove to be an advantage in the resulting semi-open position, or he plays d5 and relies on his space advantage. Both methods are basically sound and the choice between them is to a large extent a matter of taste.

Some players prefer **6 ♗d2** instead of 6 a3, intending to take back on c3 with the bishop (6...0-0 7 a3 ♗xc3 8 ♗xc3).

4 ♕c2 c5

> **4 ... c5**

This attack on d4 is so powerful that White is practically forced to abandon this central stronghold.

> **5 dxc5** *(D)*

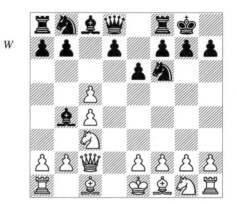

The theoretical assessment of this position has shifted very gradually over the years. For decades it was considered 'about equal', but this has changed almost imperceptibly to 'not quite as easy for Black as we thought it was'. Parallel to this, the ranking of 4...c5 dropped from '*the* answer to 4 ♕c2' to 'one of a multitude of possibilities'.

In the diagram position Black (again) has several options.

Perhaps the most ambitious move is **5...♘a6**. Black wants to regain his pawn without making even the smallest concession (like taking a step 'backwards' with ...♗xc5). The idea is to play ...♘xc5, followed by ...b6 and ...♗b7, gaining firm control over the important central square e4. White's most principled reaction is 6 a3 ♗xc3+ 7 ♕xc3 ♘xc5, and now either 8 b4 ♘ce4 9 ♕d4 threatening 10 f3, or 8 f3

threatening 9 b4. In both cases Black is forced to react very sharply. White is dangerously lagging behind in development, but if Black fails to capitalize on this fast, White will be able to create a strong pawn-centre *and* he will have the advantage of the bishop-pair in an open position.

For a long time the flexible **5...0-0** *(D)* was thought to be Black's best move.

This assessment was based mainly on the possibility of switching to the ...♘a6 plan after the neutral developing move **6 ♘f3**, when 6...♘a6 may be played without the potential drawbacks (outlined above) of the immediate 5...♘a6.

Here too the critical move is **6 a3**, practically forcing Black into a ...♗xc5 plan. Only then, after 6...♗xc5, does White start to develop his kingside: 7 ♘f3. Just like the position after 5 dxc5 itself, this line was also considered harmless for Black for a very long time because of 7...♘c6 8 ♗g5 ♘d4, based on the tactical point 9 ♘xd4 ♗xd4 10 e3 ♕a5. But when it was discovered that this too was 'not quite so easy for Black as we thought' because of 11 exd4 ♕xg5 12 ♕d2!, enthusiasm for 5...0-0 cooled down a bit and this line too could now be said to be just 'one of a multitude of possibilities'.

Considering the above, it may look rather illogical to play **5...♗xc5** *(D)* straightaway, without waiting for White to play a3.

Even so, this is played quite often, but with a very specific aim in mind: Black wants to reply to the natural 6 ♘f3 with the seemingly

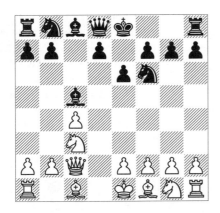

primitive 6...♕b6. Because 7 e4 ♘g4! would then be most unpleasant for White, he is forced to play 7 e3, blocking the c1-h6 diagonal for his bishop. Thus Black has avoided ♗g5, the move which caused all the trouble in the 5...0-0 line.

As an immediate 6 ♗g5? is out of the question because of 6...♗xf2+! 7 ♔xf2 ♘g4+, there is little White can do to avoid this. After 6 ♘f3 ♕b6 7 e3 Black calmly retreats his queen to a more civilized square (7...♕c7), fianchettoes his queen's bishop, and awaits further developments.

Whether this strategy is objectively good or not, this line undeniably allows Black to avoid a sharp and highly theoretical opening battle. In all probability a rather slow type of middle-game position will come about, in what is known as the hedgehog structure, which will be further discussed in the chapter on the Symmetrical English.

4 ♕c2 0-0

4	...	0-0

Strange as it may seem, this move is actually as stern a test of 4 ♕c2 as any of the more direct moves that we have just been looking at. Since **5 e4** is not to be feared (Black could then, for instance, strike back in the centre with 5...d5 6 e5 ♘e4 7 ♗d3 c5) and the neutral developing moves **5 ♘f3** and **5 ♗g5** can both be met by 5...c5 6 dxc5 ♘a6, giving Black a relatively favourable version of a 4...c5 line, White more or less has to 'carry out his threat', viz.:

5	a3	♗xc3+
6	♕xc3 (D)	

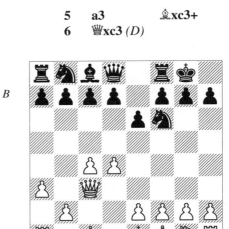

White has executed his plan. Without even the slightest weakening of his pawn-chain, he has acquired the pair of bishops.

But does this really mean anything? After all, Black can also claim a few 'theoretical' advantages, like having obtained a small lead in development and having preserved maximal flexibility for his own pawn-chain. It is not easy to answer this question and even less easy actually to play this line, but it pays to make a thorough study of it. It teaches you a few things about the subtleties of positional play.

6	...	b6

Roughly speaking, the outlines of the forthcoming battle have now been defined. But there is almost always *some* room for deviations from the main road and in this position **6...b5** has earned its rightful place in the books. Black sacrifices a pawn in order to open lines on the queenside so that his lead in development may make itself felt. On 7 cxb5 Black plays 7...c6, when 8 bxc6 ♘xc6 has held up very well in practice. Many players prefer to ignore this challenge, simply carrying on with their standard scheme of development: 8 ♗g5 cxb5 9 e3.

6...♘e4 is also an attempt to take the initiative. It is based on the tactical point that after 7 ♕c2 f5 (D) White is unable to chase back the knight immediately.

The reason is that **8 f3?** fails to 8...♕h4+. He will either have to accept the presence of the black knight on e4 for the time being and make

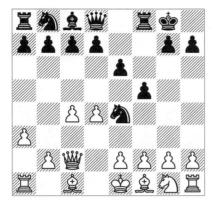

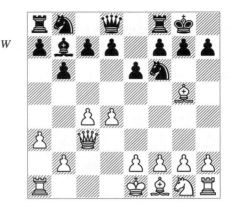

the battle for control over e4 a long-term one (for instance, **8 ♘f3** b6 9 g3 ♗b7 10 ♗g2) or make a concession like **8 ♘h3**, slightly misplacing the knight, in order to play a quick f3 anyway. In the latter case Black may reply 8...♘c6 9 e3 d6 10 f3 ♘f6, getting ready for ...e5, when it is not at all clear if White has gained anything by his swift reaction.

7 ♗g5

If White refrains from making this aggressive move and prefers the more modest **7 ♘f3** ♗b7 8 e3 instead, the position resembles the above line 6...♘e4 7 ♕c2 f5 8 ♘f3 and play will develop along similar lines. Black will be able to finish his development quite comfortably; e.g., 8...d6 9 ♗e2 ♘bd7 10 0-0 ♘e4 11 ♕c2 f5, taking a firm grip on e4. This makes it difficult for White to become active and he will have to be careful not to allow his opponent to build up an attack on the kingside.

7 ... ♗b7 *(D)*

This is the obvious move and it is certainly very logical, but it is not the only one. In the first place, Black may also consider directing his attention towards not the e4-square, but the c4-pawn, and thus play **7...♗a6**. After 8 e3 d6 9 ♗d3 ♘bd7 10 ♘e2 c5 followed by 11...♖c8 the white pawn comes under serious pressure.

Secondly, the immediate **7...c5** is also not bad. After 8 dxc5 bxc5 Black does not need to worry about ♗xf6. He can try to develop an attack along the b-file with moves like ...♘c6, ...♖b8 and ...♕b6 or ...♕a5.

It is from this position that most of the 4 ♕c2 0-0 variations start.

Theory's first impression was that **8 e3** d6 9 f3 is the best set-up, but in the early 1980s 9...♘bd7 10 ♗d3 c5 11 ♘e2 ♖c8 turned out to be a satisfactory answer. The threats against c4 hamper White's attempts to make his bishop-pair felt.

Because simple moves like **8 ♘f3** d6 9 e3 ♘bd7 10 ♗e2 were also unable to cause much damage, 4...0-0 was considered totally safe and sound in those days. But problems started when during the 1990s White, led by Kasparov, began to investigate the much sharper move **8 f3** *(D)*.

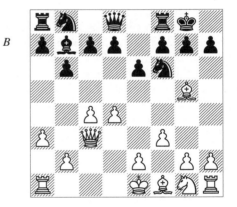

It soon transpired that White can permit himself the luxury of occupying the centre without completing his development first since after **8...d6** 9 e4 Black is unable to take advantage of his lead in development. An alternative would be to play **8...c5**, analogous to 7...c5, but with the bishop already committed to b7 this did not seem to be the perfect solution either.

Things were looking fairly bleak from Black's point of view until finally a narrow and only just passable path was discovered: **8...h6** 9 ♗h4 d5. White's most dangerous reaction to this turned out to be 10 e3 ♘bd7 11 cxd5 *(D)*.

Now **11...exd5** may look solid, but this puts very little pressure on White and allows him to complete his development with excellent prospects of turning his bishop-pair to good use in the long run (12 ♗d3). But the surprising move **11...♘xd5** saves the day. Suddenly Black's lead in development *does* make a difference. The endgame after 12 ♗xd8 ♘xc3 is about equal because **13 ♗xc7** is met by 13...♘d5, and now either 14 ♗d6 ♘xe3! or 14 ♗f4 ♖fd8 intending ...g5 (this is the reason why 8...h6 is an essential element of this plan). For these reasons White usually tries the modest **13 ♗h4** ♘d5 14 ♗f2, but practice has shown that Black's chances are not inferior here if he continues fearlessly with 14...c5.

Rubinstein Variation

    4   e3 *(D)*

Historically speaking, this is the main line of the Nimzo-Indian Defence. Over a period of more than half a century, dozens of variations have been developed from this position and found their way into the books.

The result is that, if you look at these books, the impression is created that theory is much more comprehensive here than it is in the 4 ♕c2 variations. But comprehensive does not mean

that it has become fixed. Evaluations will always remain open to modification, however subtle. A good variation is never finished and will always be influenced by new insights, new ideas, new experiments.

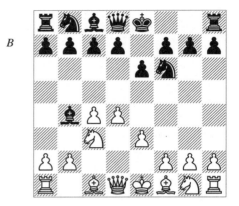

Now it is up to Black to define the further course of developments. He has a choice of several moves, which are all perfectly sound. The most important of these are **4...b6**, **4...c5** and **4...0-0**.

4 e3 b6

    4   ...   b6

A logical reaction to 4 e3. Now that White is clearly making no attempt to get the advance e4 in immediately, Black strengthens his grip on this important central square by developing his queen's bishop to b7.

    5   ♗d3

This looks like the natural developing move in this position and that is just what it is, but White has a major alternative in 5 ♘e2 *(D)*.

The idea is to play 6 a3 and, if Black then takes on c3, to take back with the knight. Thus after **5...♗b7** 6 a3, if Black replies 6...♗xc3+ 7 ♘xc3, White has solved the 'Nimzo-Indian Problem', the pin against the c3-knight, in the most elegant way imaginable. Black has tried several ways to try to thwart this plan, all producing unclear but lively play. To begin with, 6...♗e7 is an original idea, based on the assumption that White's knight is looking rather silly on e2 if it cannot proceed to c3 as planned.

But even more radical is **5...♗a6** 6 a3 ♗xc3+ 7 ♘xc3 d5. Black wants to expose the downside of the bishop-pair: if White now plays 8 cxd5 Black can be very satisfied after 8...♗xf1 9 ♔xf1 exd5. All that has remained from the two bishops is one unimpressive bishop on c1, hemmed in by its own pawns. Protecting c4 by 8 b3 is considered critical. Black then increases the pressure on c4 by playing 8...0-0 9 ♗e2 ♘c6 followed by ...♘a5, trying to force the exchange on d5 anyway.

> **5 ... ♗b7**
> **6 ♘f3 0-0**

Usually the opening battle in this variation is about control over e4. Besides the neutral 6...0-0 the more direct **6...♘e4** also serves this purpose. Black creates threats and frees the way for his f-pawn. A voluntary exchange on c3 (i.e. without waiting for White to play a3) fits into this plan. After 7 ♕c2 f5 8 0-0 ♗xc3 9 bxc3 0-0 a difficult strategic struggle lies ahead. White will have to make an effort to dislodge the knight from e4, starting, for instance, with 10 ♘d2 or 10 ♘e1 followed by f3. A trap to look out for is 10 ♘d2 ♕h4 11 g3?! (11 f3 is better) 11...♘g5! 12 gxh4?? ♘h3#!

> **7 0-0 (D)**

Now the road branches out.

Exchanging on c3 voluntarily is still possible, but not as popular (or as accurate) as in the 6...♘e4 line, mentioned above. After **7...♗xc3** 8 bxc3 ♘e4 White does not need to lose a tempo protecting his pawn on c3. Instead of 9 ♕c2 he can play 9 ♘e1 at once, when 9...♘xc3?? loses a piece to 10 ♕c2.

A much better idea is to play **7...c5**, when conventional moves like 8 a3 (8...♗xc3 9 bxc3 ♘e4) or 8 ♗d2 (8...cxd4 9 exd4 d5) yield White next to nothing. Only the unorthodox 8 ♘a4 has managed to pose Black some problems. The point of this knight sortie is that after 8...cxd4 9 exd4 d5 White now has 10 c5!, which not only creates a dangerous passed pawn but also embarrasses the Nimzo-Indian bishop. For this reason Black usually postpones ...d5 and voluntarily retreats the bishop first by playing either 9...♗e7 or 9...♖e8 10 a3 ♗f8. Now ...d5 is a positional threat which is difficult to assess and which gives this variation its distinct and rather tense character. Black often plays ...d6 (and perhaps ...♘bd7 and ...♖c8) before lashing out with ...d5 at a later stage, preferably in a situation where White no longer has the option of replying c5.

In comparison, Black's second main line, **7...d5 (D)**, is strategically uncomplicated.

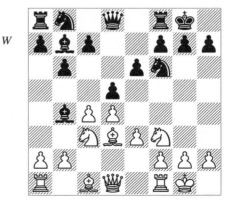

Black now has the option of retreating his bishop to d6 if necessary, for instance if White plays **8 a3**. After 8...♗d6 9 b4 Black has 9...dxc4 10 ♗xc4 a5 (or the immediate 10...♘bd7) 11 b5 ♘bd7, when he is ready to strike back in the centre with ...e5.

To avoid this, most players prefer to fix the central pawn-formation immediately by playing **8 cxd5**. After 8...exd5 White then has two fundamentally different plans:

One is to try to build up an attack on the kingside, starting with **9 ♘e5**. To this, Black's accepted reply is 9...♗d6 10 f4 c5, when a dynamic equilibrium is reached between White's attacking chances on the kingside and Black's in the centre and on the queenside.

The other plan is more modest and generally leads to quieter play: **9 a3 ♗d6 10 b4**. Nevertheless this too may well lead to a tense struggle eventually, especially if Black plays the intimidating ...♘e4 with an eye to taking the initiative on the kingside.

4 e3 c5

4   ...   c5 *(D)*

With this move, Black takes up the struggle for control of the centre in a very different way. Yet there are certain similarities between this move and 4...b6. For instance, White now faces the same choice between 5 ♗d3 and 5 ♘e2.

5   ♗d3

This move is aimed at natural, uncomplicated development. The alternative 5 ♘e2 is

sharper and is (usually) played with a more concrete aim in mind. Theory has always found it very hard to choose between these two moves and indeed most players seem to regard it as mainly a matter of taste. It could be said though, that with 5 ♘e2 White wants to dictate the course of the game *himself*, while with 5 ♗d3 he lets his opponent choose a type of middlegame.

The most important response to 5 ♘e2 is 5...cxd4. After 6 exd4 *(D)* Black then has two rather different options.

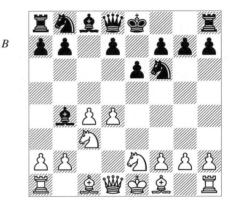

These are the straightforward **6...d5** and the more laid-back **6...0-0**. In both these lines, dropping the Nimzo-Indian bishop back to e7 if White plays 7 a3 has become a standard ploy (but not forced!) to saddle White with the same problem as we saw in the 4...b6 5 ♘e2 line: what should he do with the knight on e2 if the plan a3 ♗xc3+ ♘xc3 is side-stepped? The main lines start with 6...d5 7 c5 and 6...0-0 7 a3 ♗e7 8 d5. With his last move White stops his opponent from playing ...d5 (which could follow, for instance, after 8 ♘f4). After 8...exd5 9 cxd5 ♖e8 (or 9...♗c5) this leads to a hotly-debated key theoretical position.

5   ...   ♘c6 *(D)*

In connection with Black's next move, this gives the variation 4...c5 a face of its own. The alternatives **5...d5** and **5...0-0** are by no means bad, but they transpose to those variations that may also be reached via 4...0-0 and are treated under that heading.

6   ♘f3

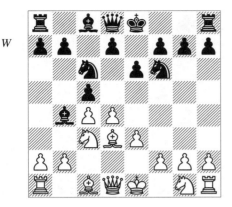

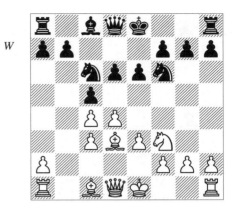

Many players prefer **6 ♘e2** here, in order to be better prepared for the forthcoming exchange on c3. The idea is not so much to take back on c3 with the knight (as is the idea of playing ♘e2 a move earlier!) should Black play 6...♗xc3+, because that would just leave the pawn on d4 undefended, but that the knight is better placed on e2 than on f3 in the position arising after 7 bxc3. In this type of middlegame it is of vital importance for White to be able to use his f-pawn, either by playing f3 or f4, which is of course much easier if there is no knight standing in the way.

But for another type of middlegame the knight is less well placed on e2: the typical Isolated Queen's Pawn position arising after 6 ♘e2 cxd4 7 exd4 d5 with the exchange ...dxc4 to follow. Of course, this position is perfectly playable for White (and indeed 6 ♘e2 was all the rage around 1990), but it is undeniable that a knight on e2 is less influential on the kingside than a knight on f3, and that it does not cover the important e5-square. This makes the choice between 6 ♘f3 and 6 ♘e2 (again) to a large extent a matter of taste. The question is: which central pawn-formation does White prefer?

6 ... ♗xc3+

This is the **Hübner Variation**, one of Black's most solid options against 4 e3 and one of the few lines where taking on c3 without waiting for White to play a3 first is completely accepted.

7 bxc3 d6 *(D)*

This is the same type of position that we have already seen in the Sämisch Variation. White

has economized on a3, but his knight on f3 blocks the f-pawn. As a result White experiences some difficulties in taking the initiative on the kingside as we saw him do in the Sämisch. In the meantime Black is ready to play ...e5, taking the initiative himself. The way in which White resolves to tackle these problems will define the further course of the opening.

The classical approach is **8 e4** e5 9 d5. White fixes the central pawn-formation and hopes to build up a slow-burning attack on the kingside. Practice has shown, however, that after 9...♘e7 Black's chances of doing just that for himself are by no means inferior. This has caused White to look for more subtle measures. Especially **8 0-0** has been investigated very deeply. If now 8...e5, instead of closing the centre immediately he plays either 9 ♘d2 or 9 ♘g5. White does not worry about the prospect of losing a pawn on d4 and plans f4 in both cases. The problems facing Black are of a more complex nature here than after 8 e4, yet in practice here too Black has done well.

4 e3 0-0

4 ... 0-0 *(D)*

The most flexible move, opening the door to a wide variety of variations.

5 ♗d3

Whereas the difference between 5 ♗d3 and 5 ♘e2 is more or less a matter of taste after both 4...b6 and 4...c5, **5 ♘e2** in this position is not nearly as popular. The difference is that Black now has the reply 5...d5 6 a3 ♗e7, turning the

opening into a kind of Queen's Gambit Declined where the moves e3 and ♘e2 compare rather poorly with the active moves ♗g5 and ♘f3 of the 'real' Queen's Gambit.

5   ...   d5

The alternative 5...c5 usually leads to the same position, especially if White simply continues 6 ♘f3. In case he prefers 6 ♘e2, then 6...cxd4 7 exd4 d5, a strategy that we have already seen in the 4...c5 5 ♗d3 ♘c6 6 ♘e2 variation, is a good reply.

6   ♘f3

Here too 6 ♘e2 is a perfectly valid alternative. Black then has two well-reasoned standard responses in 6...c5 and 6...dxc4 7 ♗xc4 c5, but in this particular case he could also try the much wilder 6...e5!?, based on the tactical point 7 dxe5 dxc4 8 ♗xc4 ♕xd1+ 9 ♔xd1 ♘g4.

6   ...   c5

This very natural move is by far the most popular one, but Black has also tried the unorthodox 6...♘c6. It may look rather crazy to block your own c-pawn in this variation, but there is a very sound idea behind it: Black is preparing to strike out in the centre with ...e5. After 7 0-0 he may set this plan in motion with 7...dxc4 8 ♗xc4 ♗d6, when he is just in time to meet 9 e4 with 9...e5. It is not at all easy for White to find an antidote against this original plan and 6...♘c6 has known several periods of popularity, especially in the 1950s and 1960s.

7   0-0 (D)

This is one of the most important and deeply analysed positions in the entire Nimzo-Indian. In practice it has occurred in thousands of games

and between about 1950 and 1970 the term Nimzo-Indian was almost synonymous with this position.

This huge popularity is based on a wealth of variations and subvariations, which are attractive for both sides. Careful study of these is certain to pay dividends, both in immediate practical results and in one's overall understanding of the game.

In fact almost every possible plan has been tried and each one of those has at one time or another been overhauled, refined and modernized.

First it is Black's move. Which type of middlegame does he choose?

The strategically simplest option is to define the central pawn-formation immediately with a double pawn exchange: **7...cxd4 8 exd4 dxc4 9 ♗xc4**. Black has chosen to play against the isolated queen's pawn. But *handling* this variation well is not so simple. 9...b6 (D) is considered the most reliable follow-up.

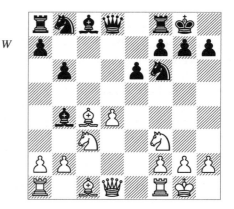

This is the **Karpov Variation**. Black puts his bishop on b7 and does not immediately decide between developing his queen's knight to d7 or to c6. Also the decision of what to do with the Nimzo-Indian bishop (taking on c3 or retreating?) is left open for the moment. White will have to make optimal use of the many open files and diagonals that the double exchange in the centre has given him. A good move is 10 ♗g5, followed (if Black plays 10...♗b7) by 11 ♖e1 or 11 ♖c1.

If Black is interested in this type of middle-game but does not want to allow ♗g5, he might consider taking on c4 only, postponing ...cxd4 until a more convenient moment. This brings us to the variation **7...dxc4 8 ♗xc4 b6** (D).

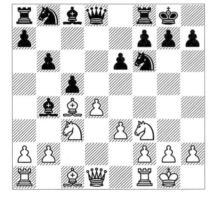

If White now plays **9 ♕e2**, for instance, a natural move preparing 10 ♖d1, Black can still opt for the Karpov Variation with 9...cxd4 or 9...♗b7 10 ♖d1 cxd4. Theoretically critical is the ultra-subtle **9 a3**, intending to meet 9...cxd4 with 10 axb4 dxc3 11 ♕xd8 ♖xd8 12 bxc3. Thanks to the pair of bishops this endgame is considered to favour White, if only slightly.

This brings us to the next variation, **7...dxc4 8 ♗xc4 ♘bd7** (D), which is basically an attempt to avoid even this little problem.

Now **9 a3** cxd4 10 axb4 dxc3 11 bxc3 may lead to the same pawn-structure, but with the queens still on the board the situation is totally different: Black gets counterplay on the queenside, starting with 11...♕c7.

Here it is **9 ♕e2** which has become the main line. After 9...b6 White will either just play 10

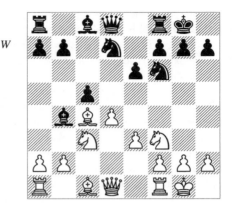

♖d1 allowing 10...cxd4 11 exd4 ♗b7 and a transposition to the Karpov Variation or he will try to refute Black's set-up with the sharp 10 d5. This move seems attractive because the meek 10...exd5 gives White an excellent position after 11 ♘xd5 ♘xd5 12 ♗xd5 ♖b8 13 e4, but it is actually very double-edged because Black has the much more critical reply 10...♗xc3 11 dxe6 ♘e5!, when 12 exf7+ ♔h8 13 bxc3 ♗g4 gives Black a dangerous initiative for the sacrificed pawns, though exactly *how* dangerous is a question still unanswered.

Finally, Black may decide to leave the central tension unresolved for the moment, for instance by playing **7...♘c6**. The only move which is then considered critical is 8 a3, when 8...♗xc3 9 bxc3 (D) brings about yet another key position of the Nimzo-Indian.

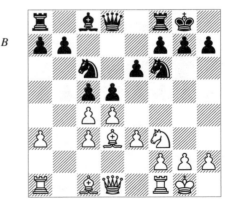

Looking at the static features of this position, one might be inclined to favour White. He has the bishop-pair and a pawn-majority in the centre. Taking on d4 is no longer attractive for Black as White will now be able to take back with a c-pawn, which only increases the strength of his pawn-centre.

But when we investigate the situation more carefully, we discover an excellent plan for Black, which highlights the more dynamic features of the position: **9...dxc4 10 ♗xc4 ♛c7!**. Black is ready to take over the initiative in the centre with ...e5, a move that will also awaken his only remaining dormant piece, the bishop on c8. How should White react to this threat and how should he awaken his own dormant bishop on c1? Many different answers have been suggested to these questions, but no definite conclusion has ever been reached, though in practice 11 ♗d3 e5 12 ♕c2 ♖e8 13 dxe5 ♘xe5 14 ♘xe5 ♕xe5 15 f3 has become something of a main line. White hopes to consolidate his position with e4 and ♗e3.

An attempt to refine this plan may be made by playing **9...♕c7** first, with the intention of exchanging on c4 one move later (for instance after 10 ♗b2). The only useful attempt to thwart this plan is to play 10 cxd5 exd5. This is in effect the same type of middlegame that we have seen in the Sämisch Variation, but with a knight on f3 White will not find it easy to achieve the essential e4 breakthrough; e.g., 11 a4 ♖e8 12 ♗a3 c4 13 ♗c2 ♘e4 with a firm grip on e4.

4 ♗g5

4   ♗g5 *(D)*

White meets the pin against his knight with a counter-pin. This seemingly calm approach runs into two concrete problems, which must be solved before White can *really* be confident.

4   ...   h6 *(D)*

One great advantage of 4 ♗g5 over 4 ♕c2 and 4 e3 is that Black has far fewer options. The only reaction to 4 ♗g5 which is considered fully acceptable is to play ...c5. Pushing the white bishop back to h4 is not essential but it is a useful little extra.

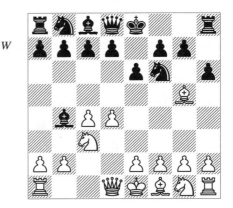

5   ♗h4

Black does not have to worry about **5 ♗xf6**. After 5...♕xf6 the advance ...c5 will have even greater impact.

5   ...   c5
6   d5 *(D)*

This advance is the point but also the necessary consequence of 4 ♗g5. After **6 e3 cxd4 7 exd4 ♕a5 8 ♕c2 ♘e4** White's bishop would only be sorely missed on the queenside.

In reply to 6 d5, Black has an aggressive tactical option and a solid positional one.

The tactical option is **6...b5**, an assault on White's pawn-centre based on the pawn sacrifice 7 dxe6 fxe6 8 cxb5 which gives Black a good many open files and a pawn-majority in the centre in return for his pawn. This is dangerous ground for both players requiring good calculating skills and a feeling for dynamic play.

The positional method is **6...♗xc3+ 7 bxc3 d6** or **6...d6 7 e3 ♗xc3+ 8 bxc3 e5**, aiming for the same pawn-structure as in the Hübner Variation. Black has no pawn weaknesses and no

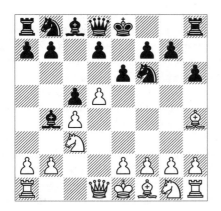

B

immediate tactical problems to worry about. Middlegame play will be practically restricted to the kingside, where neither player will find it easy to take the initiative.

So whoever wants to play 4 ♗g5 will have to feel comfortable both with the strategic difficulties of 6...♗xc3+ (or 6...d6 which is just a transposition of moves in most cases) and with the tactical turmoil of 6...b5. This makes 4 ♗g5 a variation for players with a truly universal style, which is exactly what the two great champions who have made this variation popular, Boris Spassky and Jan Timman, were renowned for.

4 f3

4   f3 (D)

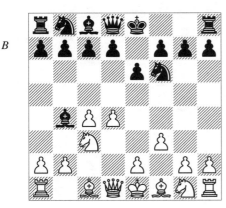

B

This is perhaps White's most radical way of meeting the Nimzo-Indian Defence. Without further ado he prepares to play 'the perfect move', e4. For decades this almost naïvely straightforward approach was looked upon with suspicion, especially because White robs himself of the natural square f3 for his king's knight. But during an outbreak of unheard-of popularity around 1990 all the pros and cons of 4 f3 were thoroughly investigated and by now the theoretical situation has cleared up.

In fact 4 f3 is now often used as a kind of parallel road to the Sämisch Variation by players who are aiming for one particular subvariation of the Sämisch and who prefer the side streets of the 4 f3 road to those of 4 a3.

4   ...   d5 (D)

Black does well to react to White's plans in the centre immediately. The main alternative to the text is **4...c5**, but it is precisely here that the 1990 thunderstorm has caused considerable damage. It was previously thought that after 5 d5 the sharp variations 5...♗xc3+ 6 bxc3 ♕a5 and 5...♘h5 were both quite well playable but they are now regarded as slightly dubious. A third option, 5...b5, has also turned out to be fairly innocuous because of the laconic reply 6 e4.

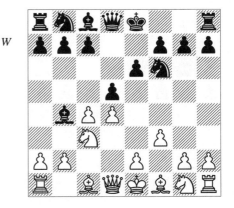

W

5   a3

Only this move can justify 4 f3. The struggle for e4 must be continued.

Now **5...♗xc3+** 6 bxc3 c5 transposes to a line of the Sämisch (see page 59). This is in fact the key test of 4 f3.

The alternative **5...♗e7** is provocative because it allows White to carry out his plan and play 6 e4. A proper assessment of this position depends on the sharp reply 6...dxe4 7 fxe4 e5 8 d5 *(D)*.

White has gained considerable space in the centre but he has had to make himself vulnerable to dangerous counterattacks to achieve this. Critical is 8...♗c5 9 ♘f3 ♘g4, but although White certainly needs nerves of steel here, this is considered rather dubious nowadays because of the bold 10 ♘a4.

4 ♘f3

4   ♘f3 *(D)*

This sound developing move may well be viewed with a sigh of relief by many readers after all the subtle and ambitious lines that we have looked at so far. Others may suffer from the opposite effect and look upon this move as strangely unpretentious.

4 ♘f3 was never a popular move until Kasparov rejuvenated it in his match for the world championship against Karpov in 1985. What their games clearly indicated is that all sorts of ambitious replies to 4 ♘f3 are risky. There is no refutation of this move, so Black does well to treat it with the same respect as the older variations of the Nimzo-Indian.

It then turns out that 4 ♘f3 has in fact little significance of its own because, depending on Black's reply, it is bound to transpose to other variations. This does of course demand a certain knowledge and appreciation *of* these other variations, which implies that 4 ♘f3 is an interesting option for those who want to play some particular variations of the 4 e3 or 4 g3 lines, while wishing to avoid others.

To begin with, **4...d5** takes us straight into the Ragozin Variation of the Queen's Gambit Declined (see page 21).

The Queen's Indian Defence is also just one move away: **4...b6**.

To complicate transpositional matters even further, both these options allow White to return to a 4 e3 Nimzo-Indian by playing 5 e3.

The only moderately popular independent reply to 4 ♘f3 is **4...0-0**, but this is not rated very highly because of 5 ♗g5 c5 6 e3 *(D)*, which is much better for White than the related variation 4 ♗g5 h6 5 ♗h4 c5 6 e3.

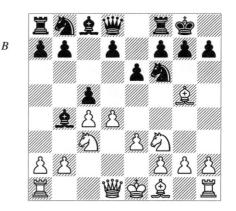

The difference is that 6...♕a5 can now be answered by the sharp 7 ♗xf6 ♗xc3+ 8 bxc3 ♕xc3+ 9 ♘d2 or even 7 ♗d3 ♗xc3+ 8 bxc3 ♕xc3+ 9 ♔f1, when in both cases White has excellent chances of launching an attack against the enemy king.

The most popular reply to 4 ♘f3 is **4...c5**, when 5 g3 will bring us to the next section, on the 4 g3 variation. White has then avoided the line 4 g3 0-0 5 ♗g2 d5 so he has reduced Black's options. For anyone appreciative of these subtleties, 4 ♘f3 may be a very useful move.

4 g3

4   g3 (D)

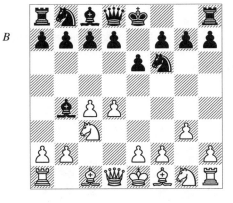

As mentioned before, this variation is closely interwoven with 4 ♘f3.

Black's main responses are **4...c5** and **4...0-0** 5 ♗g2 d5. The immediate **4...d5** is also possible (it is unusual but there seems to be no good reason for this), transposing to the 4...0-0 line after 5 ♗g2 0-0.

4 g3 c5

4   ...   c5

It is in this variation where the lines 4 ♘f3 and 4 g3 merge.

5   ♘f3 (D)

White has nothing better than this because **5 d5** is strongly met by 5...♘e4 (when 6 ♕c2? runs into 6...♕f6!).

We have now reached the same position as arises from 4 ♘f3 c5 5 g3.

5   ...   cxd4

At first sight **5...♘e4** appears a very attractive move here, but a game from the match

Kasparov-Karpov in 1985 confirmed that Romanishin's idea 6 ♕d3 is a good reply. After 6...♕a5 7 ♕xe4! ♗xc3+ 8 ♗d2 ♗xd2+ 9 ♘xd2 Black's initiative turns out to be short-lived.

Black has tried to refine this idea by playing **5...♘c6** first. If White then continues 6 ♗g2 (and what else could he possibly play?) the consequences of the knight sortie 6...♘e4 are much more complicated because **7 ♕d3** now runs into 7...cxd4 8 ♘xd4 ♘xc3 9 bxc3 ♘e5, while the alternative **7 ♗d2** also brings about a position which is not easy to judge following 7...♗xc3. Nevertheless Kasparov was successful against this line as well in 1985, and the theory of this line has more or less petered out into the modest variation 7...♘xd2 8 ♕xd2 cxd4, with perhaps a slight advantage to White but nothing very threatening.

Less adventurous is **5...b6** 6 ♗g2 ♗b7, when after 7 0-0 Black may either go for a Hedgehog type of position starting with 7...cxd4 (we shall look at the general aspects of the Hedgehog System in the chapter on the Symmetrical English) or he may prefer a solution in a more typical Nimzo-Indian style: 7...♗xc3 8 bxc3 d6.

6   ♘xd4 (D)

This is a key position not just for the 4 g3 Nimzo-Indian but for the Symmetrical English as well. It is often reached via 1 c4 c5 2 ♘f3 ♘f6 3 ♘c3 e6 4 d4 cxd4 5 ♘xd4 ♗b4 6 g3 or a similar move-order.

6   ...   0-0

If Black is eager to play ...♘e4 in this line this may be the best moment to do it. One reason why **6...♘e4** is so popular is the charming

B

little queen sacrifice 7 ♕d3 ♕a5 8 ♘b3 ♘xc3!, with the point that after 9 ♘xa5 ♘e4+ Black wins back the queen immediately. The critical line, however, is the calm 9 ♗d2, when Black still has to prove something.

7 ♗g2 d5 *(D)*

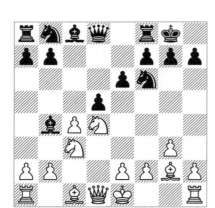

W

This position is crucial for the entire variation. The situation is tense. With his last move Black has taken the initiative in the centre but at the same time his queenside remains underdeveloped.

White has tried several moves, among which **8 ♕b3** and **8 0-0** have earned their places in the books, but the most principled approach is probably **8 cxd5 ♘xd5** and now either 9 ♗d2 or 9 ♕b3. White accepts an isolated pawn on c3 and relies on the open b-file and his strong

bishop on g2 to grant him good chances against Black's queenside. This is a hotly debated variation and one where every decision is based on extremely subtle positional nuances. After 9 ♗d2, for instance, it is not clear whether Black should take on c3 with the knight or with the bishop, while after 9 ♕b3 it is extremely unusual to take on c3 at all. In fact it has even become fairly standard for Black to accept an isolated c-pawn himself here by playing 9...♘c6 10 ♘xc6 bxc6.

4 g3 0-0

4 ... 0-0

Black refrains from any immediate action based on ...♕a5 and ...♘e4. He has a more classical strategy in mind.

5 ♗g2 d5 *(D)*

This move gives the opening a decidedly Catalan flavour (see page 24). **5...c5** 6 ♘f3 cxd4 7 ♘xd4 would transpose to the 4...c5 line.

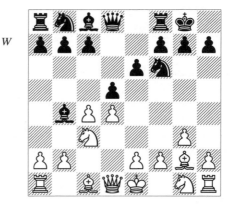

W

If White now plays the natural **6 ♘f3** he has to take 6...dxc4 into account because, unlike the Catalan Opening proper, winning back the pawn is not self-evident in this case. After 7 0-0 ♘c6 a fierce opening battle is to be expected.

6 cxd5 exd5 7 ♘f3 is the more prudent choice, but with the bishop on g2 this type of central pawn-formation is generally regarded as giving Black an easy game.

Queen's Indian Defence

1	d4	♘f6
2	c4	e6
3	♘f3	b6 (D)

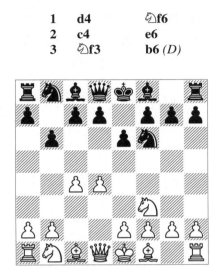

W

For a long time, playing the Queen's Indian with either colour was regarded as a sign of peacefulness. After all, by playing 3 ♘f3 White avoids the complications of the Nimzo-Indian Defence, whereas Black, by not transposing to the Queen's Gambit Declined via 3...d5, avoids a confrontation in the centre. In fact the term 'Queen's Indian' used to be almost synonymous with 'avoiding a fight'. In some books it has even been called a 'drawish' opening.

For those who only started playing chess after about 1980 and have consequently not lived through this 'anti-Queen's Indian' era, it will be hard to understand that such an attitude towards this opening ever existed. But it was only when Garry Kasparov made his way to the top in the early 1980s, using the move 3 ♘f3 to extremely good effect and creating a whole new world of variations in the Queen's Indian, that this attitude changed. Kasparov forged the variations 4 a3, 4 ♘c3 ♗b4 5 ♗g5 and (to a lesser extent) 4 g3 into new and very dangerous weapons and suddenly this became one of *the* most popular openings, superseding

3 ♘c3 and the Nimzo-Indian completely (for some time).

Since then, almost every top grandmaster has played the Queen's Indian, often with both colours, and they have all contributed something to the rapid development of dynamic and challenging variations offering rich potential rewards for both White and Black. As a result, theory of the Queen's Indian has become almost as complex as that of the Nimzo, and unlike forty years ago some knowledge of variations is now essential if you want to play this opening.

White's most important method was and still is **4 g3**. By putting his king's bishop on g2, White takes up the challenge of fighting for control over the important h1-a8 diagonal and over the central squares e4 and d5.

Although it may not look very to the point at first sight, **4 a3** takes up this challenge as well. White wants to play the natural developing move ♘c3 without being disturbed by the Nimzo-Indian pin ...♗b4. This amazingly laconic little move was first used by Tigran Petrosian and later by Kasparov to surprisingly good effect. The games of Kasparov in particular proved that, far from being a waste of time, 4 a3 is the vital starting move of an extremely aggressive strategy that caused Black quite a headache during the 1980s.

Strangely enough, **4 ♘c3**, although it is in fact *the* most natural move, was used by Kasparov as an even subtler starting move of this, 'his' aggressive strategy. By starting his plan with 4 ♘c3, White avoids the variation 4 a3 ♗a6, which became more and more of a problem for White during the 1980s. If Black simply replies 4...♗b7 White will play 5 a3 and against 4...♗b4 he has the sharp 5 ♗g5. This line is really a fusion of the Queen's and the Nimzo-Indian and it is a highly explosive mixture.

Completely different but no less important is **4 e3**. This quiet developing move does not spark off a fierce struggle right away, yet the resulting middlegame positions are often very tense and full of promise of a fascinating fight.

Finally there are the moves **4 ♗f4** and **4 ♗g5** to be mentioned, but these are relatively unburdened with theoretical baggage.

Although **4 ♗f4** caused quite a stir for a short period of time in the late 1970s it has become clear that this move does little to make life difficult for Black after 4...♗b7 5 e3 ♗e7 6 h3 (6 ♘c3 allows 6...♘h5, eliminating the bishop) 6...c5.

4 ♗g5 too has had its devotees, but it is generally regarded as equally harmless. The simple reply 4...♗b7 5 e3 ♗e7 (a crucial difference from the line 4 ♘c3 ♗b4 5 ♗g5, mentioned above) 6 ♘c3 ♘e4, leads to exchanges and a lessening of tension.

4 g3

4   g3 *(D)*

B

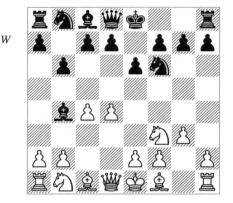

This move has constituted White's main line ever since the very first days of the Queen's Indian. During about three quarters of a century, it has been investigated in great detail, yet it still offers plenty of scope for new discoveries.

Just as in the Nimzo-Indian, Black has several plans at his disposal for tackling White's central position. Moreover, these plans can be executed in several different ways. White usually has a choice between a sharp and a more self-restrained approach to these variations. Which is objectively best is often impossible to say.

To begin with, Black has a choice between the natural **4...♗b7** and the more aggressive **4...♗a6**.

In fact he even has a third option: **4...♗b4+** *(D)*.

W

This Bogo-Indian check plays an important part in all variations of the 4 g3 line, a clear indication of how closely related the Nimzo-, Queen's and Bogo-Indian Defences really are, but at this moment it only has independent significance if Black wants to play the provocative and highly experimental line 4...♗b4+ 5 ♗d2 a5 6 ♗g2 ♗a6. In case of 5...♗xd2+ 6 ♕xd2 ♗b7 7 ♗g2 we enter the territory of the more 'civilized' variation 4...♗b7 5 ♗g2 ♗b4+, which we shall look at below.

4 g3 ♗b7

4	...	♗b7
5	♗g2	♗e7

This is the classical response to 4 g3, but **5...♗b4+** is a solid alternative. White then faces a fundamental choice between 6 ♘c3, 6 ♘bd2 and 6 ♗d2.

6 ♘c3 is a Nimzo-Indian variety that is generally regarded as less promising for White than the 'real' Nimzo-Indian and is not played very often.

6 ♘bd2 is also quite rare, but there seems to be no concrete reason for this lack of popularity, because Black has nothing better than a fairly neutral reply like 6...0-0 7 0-0 d5. In all probability, most players simply prefer their queen's knight to be on c3 in this type of position, where it exerts some pressure on d5. Also of course a knight on d2 always hinders the rapid development of the c1-bishop.

By far the best studied move is **6 ♗d2** *(D)*. Black then has a large number of variations at his disposal, all varying greatly in character.

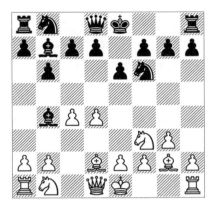

The oldest and simplest is **6...♗xd2+** 7 ♕xd2 (White again prefers the c3-square for this knight, so the perhaps rather more obvious move 7 ♘bxd2 is usually avoided) 7...0-0. Although this is a fairly quiet position, it is not without danger. For instance, White may opt for 8 ♘c3 ♘e4 9 ♕c2 with the treacherous point 9...♘xc3 10 ♘g5! winning the exchange. However, it is actually quite unclear whether this is good for White because Black gets fair compensation for the material deficit after both 10...♕xg5 11 ♗xb7 ♘xe2 12 ♕xe2 ♘c6 13 ♗xa8 ♖xa8 and 10...♘e4 11 ♗xe4 ♗xe4 12 ♕xe4 ♕xg5 13 ♕xa8 ♘c6. The latter variation was the subject of heated theoretical discussion back in the days of Capablanca and Euwe. It still is.

A totally different idea lies behind the modern move **6...a5**. Black is hoping for 7 ♗xb4 axb4, which would give him an open a-file for his rook and good control over the centre. White does well to avoid this. One critical line is 7 0-0 0-0 8 ♗f4, which practically forces Black to retreat his bishop because of the threat of 9 c5 followed by 10 a3. After 8...♗e7 9 ♘c3 ♘e4 10 ♕c2 a characteristic struggle for control over e4 breaks out. This fight for e4 is highly typical of the Queen's Indian and we are about to see it in several other variations.

Whereas 6...a5 is logical and quite understandable from a classical positional point of view, **6...c5** seemed very hard to swallow when it was first played around 1985. Here too Black accepts doubled pawns, but in this case (7 ♗xb4 cxb4) the capture is not *towards* the centre but *away* from it which, at first sight at least, seems totally wrong. Nevertheless this plan has served Black very well in practice and today it can be found in many different forms in both the Queen's and the Bogo-Indian. Black's position is very flexible. He can attack the white centre with ...d6 followed by ...e5 or with ...d5, while White cannot really do all that much with his central pawn-majority.

Finally, **6...♗e7** *(D)* is also a good move.

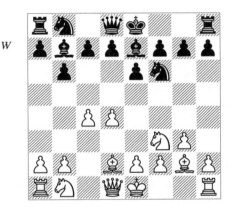

This bishop retreat is a recurring theme in this opening. Black lures the enemy bishop to d2 to prevent White from fianchettoing this bishop and to undermine a plan with the d5 advance, which is an important weapon against 5...♗e7, as we are about to see. With a bishop on d2, White's control over d5 is lessened, which makes 7 0-0 0-0 8 d5? exd5 rather pointless.

The d5 advance, which cuts off the 'Queen's Indian bishop' on b7 from the battle for e4, is in fact one of the major strategic motifs of the entire Queen's Indian. In most cases White will gain considerable space *if* he manages to consolidate this outpost.

Thus the value of **5...c5**, for instance, depends entirely on the question "how should one assess 6 d5?". The point is that 6...exd5 is met by 7 ♘h4, making use of the unprotected position of the bishop on b7 to regain the pawn. There are not too many players who have faith in this variation as Black.

We now return to 5...♗e7 (D):

6   0-0

6 ♘c3 is also often played, not with the idea of meeting **6...0-0** with 7 d5, because that would give Black the opportunity of undermining the outpost on d5 with 7...♗b4!, but in order to play 7 ♕c2 or 7 ♕d3, gaining control over e4.

The prudent reaction to this plan is **6...♘e4** which usually transposes to the line 6 0-0 0-0 7 ♘c3 ♘e4 discussed below, but there is one rather important way to turn this into an independent variation. If White responds to 6...♘e4 with 7 ♗d2 and Black then plays 7...f5, the characteristic push 8 d5 gains considerably in strength compared with the position where both sides have already castled, because White will not have to worry about 8...♗f6 9 ♕c2 ♗xc3 10 ♗xc3 exd5(?) now that Black's pawn on g7 is left undefended. These are of course rather subtle considerations which are for the really interested only and are best studied in connection with the main line 6 0-0 0-0 7 ♘c3 ♘e4 8 ♗d2.

6   ...   0-0 (D)
7   ♘c3

An interesting alternative, especially for players who like to sacrifice a pawn for the initiative, is **7 d5**. If 7...exd5 White (again) plays 8 ♘h4, when Black has nothing better than 8...c6,

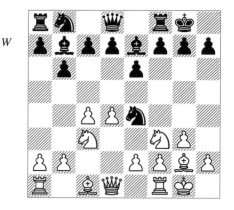

allowing White to build up a nice attacking position with 9 cxd5 ♘xd5 10 ♘f5 followed by e4.

7   ...   ♘e4 (D)

This characteristic knight move clears the way for the f-pawn before White is able to take control over e4 by playing 8 ♕c2 or 8 ♕d3. It also has the advantage of maintaining maximal pawn-structure flexibility.

The main alternative is to play **7...d5**, a frontal assault on White's pawn-centre which usually results in some heavy-weight positional manoeuvring. Black plans to play ...c5 and is holding ...♘e4 in reserve. White's most aggressive reaction is 8 ♘e5, when the perhaps slightly odd-looking 8...♘a6 is actually more accurate than the rather obvious 8...♘bd7, because 9 ♕a4 (with the positional threat of playing 10 ♘c6) is now neutralized by 9...♕e8.

This is one of *the* most important positions of the Queen's Indian Defence. It is also the main culprit for the somewhat dubious reputation this opening once 'enjoyed' as being dull or even downright drawish.

Innumerable games have been played where after **8 ♘xe4 ♗xe4 9 ♘e1 ♗xg2 10 ♘xg2** followed by a few more moves a draw was agreed (sometimes even a pre-arranged one). These games have done a great injustice to this position because apart from 8 ♘xe4 (which by the way *can* also be played with integrity) White has two 'real' main lines which have always been taken very seriously indeed by opening theory.

Of these two, **8 ♕c2** is the more cautious, but after 8...♘xc3 9 ♕xc3 White's control over the central squares e4 and d5 has been considerably reduced, which gives Black the chance finally to get 9...c5 in without having to worry about the standard reply d5. A more reserved approach, like 9...f5 followed by ...♗f6, ...d6 and ...♘d7, is also not bad.

8 ♗d2 *(D)* is a more aggressive and recently much more popular move.

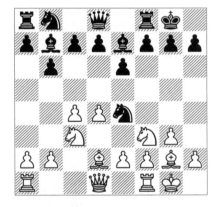

White concentrates on the battle for the central squares. His focus is on playing d5 in order to gain space, even if this is at the cost of the pair of bishops. This usually leads to tense and highly complex middlegame positions, especially if Black takes up the challenge and counters aggressively; for instance, **8...♗f6 9 ♖c1 c5 10 d5 exd5 11 cxd5 ♘xd2** or **8...f5 9 d5 ♗f6**. Strategically simpler and perhaps more cautious is **8...d5**. This has similar aims to the 7...d5 line. Here White usually fixes the pawn-structure immediately by 9 cxd5.

4 g3 ♗a6

| 4 | ... | | ♗a6 *(D)* |

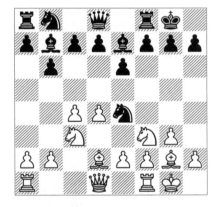

With the rise to fame of this funny-looking move, at first nicknamed the Slipped Bishop Variation but nowadays far too respectable to be treated as flippantly as that, began a transformation of the entire 4 g3 system in the late 1970s which would soon take hold of the classical 4...♗b7 as well.

Instead of following the classical strategy of aiming at a harmonious piece development while containing White's pawn-centre, Black seeks to take over the initiative, to attack the white centre pawns and generally to unbalance the position completely. This forces White to take some immediate and far-reaching decisions which are not at all easy to judge. When it transpired that this enormously increases the probability of something going wrong for White in the early stages of the game, 4...♗a6 quickly superseded 4...♗b7 as the main line.

5 b3

This is the least compromising way of protecting c4 but not the only one. At first **5 ♕a4** was thought to be a strong and aggressive way of meeting 4...♗a6, but it soon became clear that this is in fact not very forceful at all because it allows Black to reply 5...♗b7 6 ♗g2 c5 without having to worry about 7 d5 (a motif we have seen in the 4...♗b7 variation).

5 ♘bd2 *(D)*, on the other hand, has never been quite as popular as 5 b3 but it is certainly a move to be reckoned with.

Of course, a knight on d2 does not exert as much pressure against the centre as a knight on c3, but if White is prepared to play aggressively, this move may lead to interesting and complex middlegame positions.

The seemingly solid reply **5...♗b7 6 ♗g2 c5**, which is such a commendable choice against 5 ♕a4, now runs into the bold 7 e4! with the very nasty point 7...♘xe4 8 ♘e5, when 8...♘c3 loses a piece to 9 ♕h5! g6 10 ♕h3. 7...cxd4 8 e5 ♘e4 is a better choice, maintaining a state of dynamic equilibrium. It should be quite clear though that Black needs to play with the utmost accuracy in this line. Likewise, the value of an immediate **5...c5** also depends to a large extent upon the sharp 6 e4.

Black can steer away from these treacherous waters by playing **5...♗b4**. He renews the attack against c4 and lets further development depend upon White's reaction. 6 ♕a4 or 6 ♕b3 can be met by 6...c5 and on 6 ♕c2 he has a solid reply in 6...♗b7 7 ♗g2 ♗e4. By physically occupying e4 Black, for the time being at least, prevents White from playing e4. As a consequence of this plan he will have to give up the bishop-pair after 8 ♕b3, but this fits well into this Nimzo-oriented strategy. After 8...♗xd2+ 9 ♗xd2 0-0 10 0-0 d6 followed by 11...♘bd7 it will not be easy for White to find weaknesses in Black's compact position.

5	...	♗b4+

This check, which we have already seen in similar situations, is Black's most solid treatment of this line. The alternatives are sharper and tend to lead to extremely complex positions.

5...d5 is Black's most direct move. He intends to meet 6 ♗g2 with 6...dxc4 *(D)*.

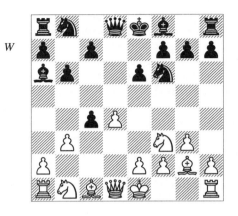

This allows the response 7 ♘e5 but forces White, if he so continues, to give up castling after 7...♗b4+, because 8 ♗d2?! is dubious in view of 8...cxb3!. After 8 ♔f1 White's position is sufficiently disorganized for Black either to prevent the imminent loss of material or to find satisfactory compensation for it with imaginative and very precise play, starting, for instance, with 8...♗d6 or 8...♘fd7. Black has to know exactly what he is doing though. 6 cxd5 is a more cautious but less dangerous reaction to 5...d5.

5...b5 *(D)* is an unorthodox move which equally upsets the balance of power in the centre but in a totally different way.

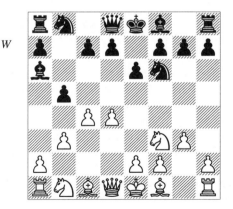

Rather than demanding a great capability for calculating and evaluating dangerous tactics as does 5...d5, this approach poses problems of a purely strategic nature. But these are no less difficult! What should we think, for instance, of the position after 6 cxb5 ♗xb5 7 ♗g2? Black leaves the h1-a8 diagonal unguarded and he will have to spend at least another move to remove his bishop from b5, yet in the meantime, by eliminating the pawn on c4, he has considerably weakened White's control over the centre while in the long run he will be able to strike back with both ...d5 and ...c5. This makes 5...b5, much more than the seemingly classical 5...d5, an ideal variation for the positional player, but *not* for the conventionally positional player.

The idea underlying **5...♗b7** is more subtle again. Black switches back to the 4...♗b7 variation and assumes (or hopes) that White's extra move b3 will actually work against him, an assumption which seems hardly realistic at first sight but which is based on the fact that after 6 ♗g2 ♗b4+ 7 ♗d2 a5 *(D)* the possibility of playing ...a4 becomes something of a positional threat.

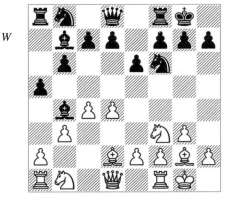

If 8 0-0 0-0 9 ♗f4, for instance, which I called a critical line in the analogous variation 4...♗b7 5 ♗g2 ♗b4+ 6 ♗d2 a5, Black now has 9...a4. This move not only saves the bishop from being ambushed on b4 but it also hurts White's pawn-formation on the queenside. The loss of a pawn after 10 bxa4 is irrelevant.

6 ♗d2 ♗e7 *(D)*

It is this characteristic manoeuvre, ...♗b4-e7, wrongfooting the white bishop, that has made the variation 4...♗a6 so very popular.

Nevertheless, the alternative **6...♗xd2+** is not bad either. After 7 ♕xd2 Black continues 7...c6 8 ♗g2 d5, the very same plan which we are about to see in combination with 6...♗e7. But 6...♗e7 is more ambitious: Black really wants to take advantage of the fact that White's bishop on d2 is standing in the way of his other pieces.

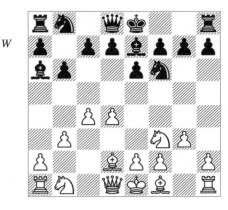

7 ♗g2 c6

Black can play **7...d5** at once if he wants to do so, but 7...c6 is just a little bit more profound, for Black can now recapture on d5 with the c-pawn if necessary. The symmetrical pawn-structure (after 8 ♘c3 d5 9 cxd5 cxd5 for instance) with the black bishop on a6 and its counterpart fairly powerless on g2 offers White almost no chances of obtaining an opening advantage. He will have to think of something else.

8 ♗c3

White frees d2 for his knight, so as to protect his pawn on c4. After the routine move **8 0-0**, the reply 8...d5 would more or less force White to adopt a set-up involving 9 ♕c2 which would allow Black to increase the pressure on c4 by playing 9...♘bd7 followed by ...♖c8 and ...c5.

8 ... d5 *(D)*

Now White has a choice of two main lines that have both been very deeply investigated over the years.

Perhaps the most obvious one is **9 ♘bd2**. After 9...♘bd7 10 0-0 0-0 Black will then have completed his development and he will be ready to play ...c5. In this situation it is of vital

importance for White to play his trump card as soon as possible: e4. This makes the position after 11 ☐e1 c5 12 e4 a veritable starting point, not just of this variation but of a sharp fight for the initiative in the centre.

The alternative is slightly more subtle: **9 ♘e5**. Since Black can hardly allow a white knight to stand unchallenged on this central square, he has to make a backward movement with 9...♘fd7. The knights are then exchanged and after 10 ♘xd7 ♘xd7 11 ♘d2 0-0 12 0-0 White is ready to play e4 while Black still needs another move to prepare ...c5. So it could be said that by playing 9 ♘e5 White has gained a tempo at the 'cost' of exchanging a pair of knights. Starting from this position, some very deep and precise variations have been developed.

4 a3

4	a3 (D)

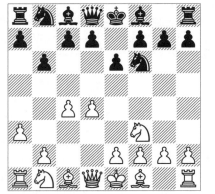

White prevents ...♗b4 and by so doing he prepares the 'perfect' developing move ♘c3. This variation did not really come under close scrutiny until the 1980s. The split of variations, however, is the same as after 4 g3. Black has the classical reply **4...♗b7** and the somewhat cheekier **4...♗a6**.

A third possibility is to change direction and play **4...c5**, giving the game a Benoni-like character. At first sight this may look attractive for Black since, after 5 d5, his 'extra' move ...b6 creates the impression of being more useful than White's a3, but this is not really the case and in practice the straightforward **5...exd5** 6 cxd5 g6 7 ♘c3 ♗g7, analogous to the Modern Benoni, is hardly ever played.

It is much more interesting for Black to return to the ...♗a6 motif by playing **5...♗a6**. After 6 ♕c2 a position is reached that we shall take a closer look at in the variation 4...♗a6, since the identical situation arises via 4...♗a6 5 ♕c2 c5 6 d5.

4 a3 ♗b7

4	...	♗b7
5	♘c3	d5

The strength of White's knight on c3 makes itself felt. Just as in many lines of the 4 g3 system, Black now has to take the advance d5 into account. This is why the simple developing move **5...♗e7?!** is hardly ever played at master level. White replies 6 d5 followed by 7 e4 and obtains a comfortable space advantage.

The alternative **5...g6** is more subtle because now Black will at least have his bishop actively placed on the long diagonal in case of 6 d5 ♗g7. This is an important and combative variation. Black challenges his opponent to execute his strategic threat and gets ready to fight against White's central position.

5...♘e4 is also quite popular but for a completely different reason: this variation is very solid. By exchanging a pair of knights (6 ♘xe4 ♗xe4) Black reduces the tension. If White wants to fight for an opening advantage he will have to sustain the struggle for control over e4. This is done either by the quiet 7 e3 followed by 8 ♗d3 or by the sharper 7 ♘d2.

We now return to 5...d5 *(D)*:

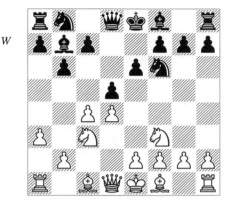

In this position the straightforward **6 cxd5** is White's most important option. Black is then faced with a fundamental choice between the robust **6...exd5** and the dynamic 6...♘xd5. In the former case White will try to put pressure on the enemy position by 7 ♗f4 or 7 g3, while Black will normally move forward in the centre with ...c5. This variation usually leads to a long-drawn-out struggle for small positional advantages.

The alternative **6...♘xd5** on the other hand is likely to ignite a fight for the initiative. White may play 7 ♕c2, for instance, aiming at an immediate occupation of the centre with 8 e4. This forces Black to react swiftly in order not to drift into a passive position, yet the situation is also potentially dangerous for White, for his broad pawn-front may turn out to be vulnerable if things go wrong. 7...♗e7 8 e4 ♘xc3 9 bxc3 0-0 10 ♗d3 c5 11 0-0 is a characteristic follow-up, when Black could try 11...♕c8, intending not only to play 12...cxd4 followed by an exchange of queens, but also to meet the plausible reaction 12 ♕e2 with 12...♗a6. Generally speaking, exchanges are to Black's advantage in this type of position, because White's attacking chances are lessened while Black's prospects of an advance on the queenside increase.

Less direct, but equally well-founded are **6 ♕c2** and **6 ♗g5 ♗e7 7 ♕a4+**. The latter variation aims at disorganizing Black's position: every single way of relieving the check has certain subtle positional disadvantages. These lines are

less thoroughly investigated than 6 cxd5 and require a talent for improvisation (from both players!).

4 a3 ♗a6

4 ... ♗a6 *(D)*

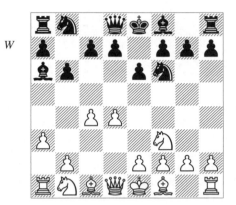

This unorthodox move has proved a great success against both 4 g3 and 4 a3. It makes it harder for White to 'easily' develop his pieces and it also poses some concrete problems without taking undue risks. Nevertheless, the choice between 4...♗b7 and 4...♗a6 is largely a matter of taste. Which type of position do you want to play or which do you want to avoid?

5 ♕c2

5 e3 is well met by both 5...c5 and 5...d5, while **5 ♘bd2** (which goes entirely against the spirit of 4 a3) is usually answered by 5...♗b7 6 ♕c2 d5. The knight is simply not well-placed on d2. **5 ♕b3** is more interesting, because it preserves the option of playing ♘c3, but 5 ♕c2 has the additional advantage of threatening 6 e4, which makes it the most popular move by far.

5 ... ♗b7

Should Black play **5...d5** in *this* position, White simply plays 6 cxd5 exd5 7 ♘c3, when the knight on c3 will exert considerably more pressure on Black's central position than in the above 5 ♘bd2 line.

Black usually builds his scheme of development around the advance ...c5. 5...♗b7 prepares this move, yet an immediate **5...c5** is also not bad. The critical reply to this is 6 d5 *(D)*.

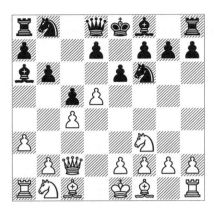

Black can now turn the opening into a kind of Modern Benoni by playing 6...exd5 7 cxd5 g6, a strategy which is much more promising now than in the event of 4...c5 5 d5 exd5 6 cxd5 g6 as mentioned above, since with a black bishop on a6 White cannot play e4 'for free'. He will have to give up the right to castle.

Another option for Black is to win material, for White's move 6 d5, natural as it is, does actually involve a pawn sacrifice. Though after 6...exd5 7 cxd5 Black cannot simply play 7...♘xd5??, because of 8 ♕e4+ winning a piece, following 7...♗b7 8 e4 ♕e7 the loss of either e4 or d5 becomes unavoidable. This greedy variation has never been very popular though. White plays 9 ♗d3 ♘xd5 10 0-0, when his lead in development promises full compensation for the lost pawn.

6   ♘c3 (D)

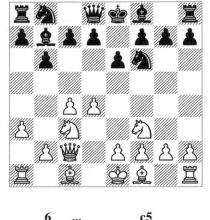

6   ...   c5

The point of Black's previous move becomes clear. Since **7 d5** is now a practically pointless pawn sacrifice, White has to find another plan.

7   e4   cxd4
8   ♘xd4 (D)

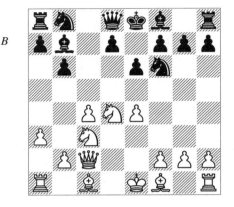

This is the fundamental starting position of most of the 4...♗a6 theory.

Though the position may look very good for White optically, it offers Black counter-chances which are not be underestimated. The moves **8...♘c6** and **8...♗c5** immediately reveal a weakness in White's position: his queen is not ideally placed on c2. **8...d6** is also not bad. Black will curl himself up into a Hedgehog-type of position and intends to show up the supposed clumsiness of both a3 and ♕c2 in this type of position at a later stage.

4 ♘c3

4   ♘c3

An unprejudiced observer will be likely to think this is the most natural move in the world. But to a player who has avoided the Nimzo-Indian just one move ago by playing 3 ♘f3 instead of 3 ♘c3, this is not self-evident at all. Nevertheless, White has a very good reason for playing this move. If Black now plays **4...♗b7**, 5 a3 will bring about the 4 a3 line without White having been bothered by 4...♗a6.

But what if Black plays the Nimzo-Indian move?

4   ...   ♗b4 (D)

W

White now has the opportunity of turning this into an independent variation by pinning the f6-knight.

5 &g5

Now that Black has committed himself to a ...b6 set-up, he will not be able to react to this pin in the same way as against 4 &g5 in the Nimzo-Indian proper (see page 72).

5 ... &b7
6 e3 h6
7 &h4 (D)

B

We have arrived at the key position in this line.

Black faces a crucial choice. White is practically challenging him to play **7...g5** 8 &g3 &e4, which breaks the pin against the f6-knight and at the same time looks like an attractive way to take over the initiative. But in reality this variation makes enormous demands on *both* players. After 9 ₩c2 &xc3+ 10 bxc3 d6 11

&d3 f5 a critical situation is reached. Black's initiative is very threatening indeed and White *has* to fight back quickly. The move that keeps him in business is 12 d5, a pawn sacrifice disrupting Black's pawn-formation. Now it is Black who has to be careful. Accepting the sacrifice is risky: 12...exd5 13 cxd5 &xd5 is met by 14 &d4 ₩f6 15 f3 and White takes over the initiative. Theory considers 12...&c5 or even the pawn sacrifice 12...&d7 to be a better choice. Black's chances in this very complicated position lie in his opponent's shattered pawn-formation on the queenside. White hopes to expose the vulnerability of the black king by attacking moves like &d4 and h4.

These complications are not to everyone's taste. Those who prefer a quieter game usually play **7...&xc3+** 8 bxc3 d6, a slower but much more solid variation. White will try to set up a strong pawn-centre by playing 9 &d2 and perhaps f3 followed by e4. Black will react with ...e5 at some point.

4 e3

4 e3 (D)

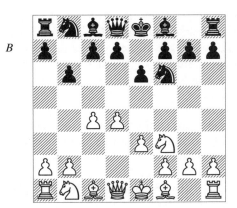

B

This variation is quite different from everything we have seen earlier in this chapter. White is in no hurry to start a battle for control over e4 and d5. Instead, he calmly completes his kingside development. This sober attitude forces Black into a similar role.

Such a treatment of the opening is of course a highly personal choice. White effectively postpones the start of the battle to the early middlegame, when complicated problems are bound to arise, for behind the following seemingly commonplace moves the tension is building. It should not come as a surprise then that 4 e3 has always been a relatively popular variation, even among top grandmasters, but that theory has remained somewhat rudimentary. In a way, the opening is skipped and the players head straight for the middlegame.

> **4 ... ♗b7**
> **5 ♗d3 (D)**

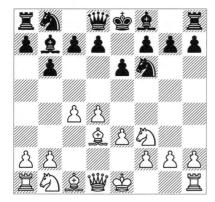

This is the starting point of the 4 e3 variation. Anyone making a study of this line will soon discover for himself one of the reasons why there are few clearly defined variations here: the order of moves is extremely vague. Both sides have certain standard schemes of development but within such a scheme there is hardly ever one particular move-order standing out as best. In the meantime all these uncertain move-orders *do* have their own particularities.

Perhaps Black's most solid plan is to play **5...♗e7** 6 0-0 0-0 7 ♘c3 d5 (or **5...d5** 6 0-0 ♗e7 7 ♘c3 0-0). A plausible continuation is then 8 b3 c5 9 ♗b2 ♘c6. This symmetrical position is very demanding of both players because there are so many different pawn exchanges, all leading to complex pawn-formations in the centre, most of which are hard to judge. It is this type of situation which is the most characteristic aspect of the 4 e3 line.

Black may also decide to head for this line by playing **5...c5 (D)** first.

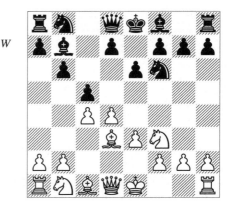

In that case he must be prepared for 6 0-0 ♗e7 7 ♘c3 though, when the simple 7...0-0?! is met very forcefully by 8 d5. The exchange 8...exd5 9 cxd5 ♘xd5 10 ♘xd5 ♗xd5 11 ♗xh7+ would then be positionally favourable for White. 7...cxd4 8 exd4 d5 is considered to be Black's best reply, but this too contains some problems. White could decide to start an attack on the kingside with 9 cxd5 ♘xd5 10 ♘e5 0-0 11 ♕h5 and although Black should be able, with accurate play, to maintain the balance, the mere fact that such accuracy is required is a factor which needs to be taken into account. A well-known trap, illustrating the danger, lies hidden in the position after 11...♘f6 12 ♕h4, when the seemingly natural 12...♘c6? 13 ♗g5 g6?? loses on the spot to 14 ♗a6!. A better way to develop this knight is 12...♘bd7, while 12...♘e4!? is also possible.

Bogo-Indian Defence

1	d4	♘f6
2	c4	e6
3	♘f3	♗b4+ *(D)*

This move was introduced at the highest level by Efim Bogoljubow (1889-1952) during the 1920s, but it was not until half a century later that it matured into a fully-fledged opening. Until then the laconic check on b4 was generally looked upon as a queer deviation from the Queen's Indian Defence and sort of hushed up in most opening manuals because it seemed to be lacking a clear strategic purpose.

From a modern point of view this seems almost incredible, for we now know that the Bogo-Indian contains not just one but a vast array of strategic ideas and purposes. To begin with, what may have looked like a lack of strategic purpose fifty years ago is now regarded as flexibility, which is an attractive feature in itself to many players. Black preserves the choice between no fewer than four different plans: a Queen's Gambit-oriented ...d5, a Queen's Indian-related ...b6, the Old Indian strategy of ...d6 and ...e5, and finally the Benoni move ...c5 in many different versions.

A second characteristic of the Bogo-Indian which is widely valued is its soundness. In the majority of cases the bishop on b4 will be exchanged on d2 and whether for a knight or a bishop, some of the pressure which Black often feels in the early stages of most other openings will be relieved. I think it is fair to say that *if* the opening does not go well for Black, this may lead to disaster in the sharper opening systems, but in the Bogo-Indian (as well as in some other solid openings) the worst that can happen is that Black finds himself in a somewhat passive position: long-term problems instead of short-term ones.

Whether this a actually an advantage of the Bogo-Indian is of course a matter of taste and temperament.

And if this all sounds as if the Bogo-Indian were unfit to play for a win with the black pieces: that would be a grave misunderstanding. There are quite a number of double-edged variations that offer White many opportunities to go wrong, especially in the area of making delicate positional evaluations.

A third feature which sets the Bogo-Indian apart is that, despite its recent popularity and the theoretical research this has involved, it still carries relatively little theoretical baggage.

In fact this aspect makes itself felt immediately for, apart from a return to the Nimzo-Indian with **4 ♘c3**, White has only two main lines: **4 ♗d2** and **4 ♘bd2**.

4 ♗d2

4	♗d2 *(D)*

The most natural reply. Unafraid of possible simplifications, White continues his development. Black now has several possibilities, differing greatly in character and intention.

By far the simplest move is **4...♗xd2+**, the preferred choice of Bogoljubow himself and the main line in the early years of the Bogo-Indian. White usually recaptures with the queen so as

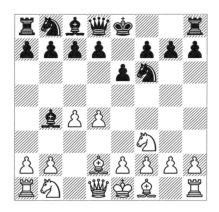

to develop the queen's knight to its ideal square c3. After 5 ♕xd2 d5 6 ♘c3 play strongly resembles a main line of the Queen's Gambit Declined (see page 16), while 6 g3 brings about a sort of Catalan (see page 24). Should White prefer 5 ♘bxd2, however, a plan based upon ...d6 in combination with ...e5 or ...c5 is best.

The alternative **4...♕e7** *(D)* is slightly more aggressive while also containing a subtle tactical point.

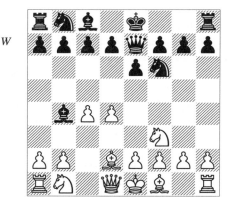

White's most popular reply 5 g3 can be met by 5...♘c6 preparing to meet **6 ♗g2** with 6...♗xd2+, when **7 ♕xd2?!** fails to 7...♘e4 8 ♕c2 ♕b4+ and now White must either give up the right to castle, offer a dubious pawn sacrifice or play an unattractive endgame with 9 ♘c3 ♘xc3 10 ♕xc3 ♕xc3+ 11 bxc3. White is thus more or less forced to play **7 ♘bxd2**, which is slightly less attractive on general grounds (as outlined above). Black then chooses the ...d6

plan where the white knight on d2 is at its weakest. 7...d6 8 0-0 0-0 9 e4 e5 10 d5 ♘b8 *(D)* is a characteristic follow-up.

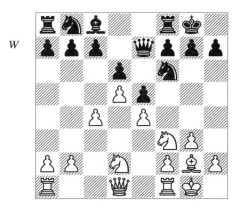

This promises a fundamental positional clash between White's space advantage and Black's 'better' bishop (meaning that it is not of the same colour as the fixed pawn-formation in the centre). Black can open hostilities both on the queenside (...c6) and on the kingside (...f5).

This is a very popular variation, illustrative of the fact that the Bogo-Indian is really all about subtle positional judgement. Lovers of wild tactical complications will not feel at ease here (at least not in the opening stage of the game) and for this reason many players use the Bogo as an occasional weapon, hoping to unbalance an opponent who they think might feel uncomfortable in this type of purely positional play.

White can opt for a different scenario by choosing **6 ♘c3**, pre-empting Black's idea of exchanging on d2. However, the nature of the position after 6...♗xc3 7 ♗xc3 ♘e4 8 ♖c1 0-0 9 ♗g2 d6, intending ...e5, is not fundamentally different.

4...a5 also leads to positions which are not easy to judge. We have seen this motif in the Queen's Indian Defence, to which a direct transposition is now possible with 5 g3 b6 6 ♗g2 ♗b7 (see page 79). Equally well-founded (and about equally popular) are 5...d5 and 5...d6 6 ♗g2 ♘bd7 7 0-0 e5 – another example of the perfect adaptability of the Bogo-Indian to a player's personal style and preferences.

Having read the chapter on the Queen's Indian, it will come as no surprise to the reader that **4...c5** *(D)* is also an important continuation.

W

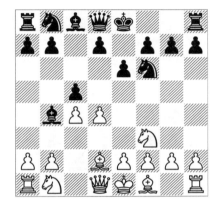

This provocative move is in fact one of Black's sharpest weapons in this opening, entirely in the typical Bogo-Indian way of always creating positional problems rather than tactical ones and of never taking undue risks.

After the natural 5 ♗xb4 cxb4 6 g3, a direct transposition to the Queen's Indian is again possible with **6...b6** 7 ♗g2 ♗b7, but practice has shown that a set-up based on **6...0-0** 7 ♗g2 d6 8 0-0 and now either 8...♘c6 or 8...♖e8, both with ...e5 in mind, may be an even better choice. In this type of position the bishop might well be more useful on the h3-c8 diagonal than on the Queen's Indian diagonal h1-a8.

4 ♘bd2

4 ♘bd2 *(D)*

This move betrays a totally different interpretation of the situation after 3...♗b4+. White wants to play 5 a3, forcing Black either to retreat his bishop or exchange it on d2 for a knight. In the latter case he will be the proud owner of a pair of bishops, without having had to worry about complications like doubled pawns (as would be so after 4 ♘c3). In the former case he will have gained a tempo (although of course a3 is not *that* spectacular an extra move) and he will have avoided the simplification of a bishop exchange on d2.

B

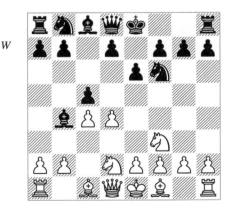

Clearly the positional problems involved in this dilemma are at least as difficult to judge as the ones we have just seen arising from 4 ♗d2. Under what circumstances is taking on d2 the right solution? When is it better to retreat the bishop and how important is it that the white knight will then be on d2 instead of c3?

Studying this line carefully and experimenting with it in practice will quickly acquaint you with these subtleties and give you an ever-increasing advantage over less-experienced players.

Just as in the 4 ♗d2 line, Black now has a major decision to make. He has several options.

To begin with, **4...c5** *(D)* is an important move if only because White cannot reply 5 d5.

W

Instead 5 a3 is both consistent and critical. After 5...♗xd2+, for instance 6 ♗xd2 cxd4 7 ♘xd4 ♘c6 leads to a position where White's two bishops cannot be said to yield him a clear advantage (yet), but they are still threatening and this may have an intimidating effect on Black, who will have to play accurately.

If Black has no objections to taking on d2 he might also consider **4...b6**. This is likely to produce a type of middlegame which is very similar to a well-known line of the Nimzo-Indian: 5 a3 ♗xd2+ 6 ♗xd2 ♗b7 7 ♗g5 (the Nimzo-Indian close relative being 3 ♘c3 ♗b4 4 ♕c2 0-0 5 a3 ♗xc3+ 6 ♕xc3 b6 – see page 64).

4...d5 *(D)* is based on a completely different idea.

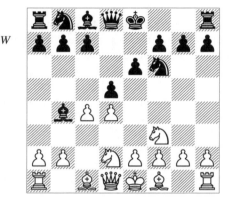

Black prepares to meet **5 a3** with 5...♗e7, without having to worry about 6 e4. This raises the fundamental question outlined above. Has White really gained a tempo or is this compensated for by his knight on d2 being less actively placed than it would be on c3? A clear answer is hard to give, which is of course exactly what

makes this variation so interesting. **5 ♕a4+** is a subtle attempt to improve on this line. Because the reply 5...♘c6 is forced, Black will not be able to play ...c5 for some time, which would otherwise be a very natural way to fight back in the centre. Still, whether this is actually an 'achievement' remains a matter of opinion.

4...0-0 takes this strategy one step further, for this laconic move allows White, after 5 a3 ♗e7, to play 6 e4 *(D)*.

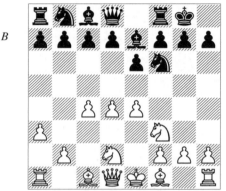

The idea is to strike back heavily against White's centre pawns, first with 6...d5 and if White replies 7 e5 ♘fd7 8 cxd5 exd5 9 ♗d3 again with 9...c5. Here Black is really trying to make use of the (relatively) passive position of White's knight, because if it were on c3 this would be completely impossible. Nevertheless, this too is an unclear and much-disputed variation.

King's Indian Defence

1	d4	♘f6
2	c4	g6 *(D)*

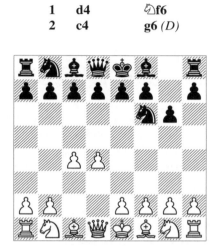

By playing 1...♘f6, Black approaches the opening in a way that is fundamentally different from 1...d5. While still turning his attention to the centre and taking control over some important squares, he as yet does not send his pawns forward. He maintains as flexible a pawn-structure as possible. Now by playing 2...g6 instead of 2...e6, Black takes this strategy one step further. Whereas 2...e6 prepares ...d5 and opens the way for ...♗b4, thus continuing the fight for control over e4, 2...g6 signals a complete lack of interest in preventing e4. Black allows his opponent a free hand in the centre, confident (or at least hopeful) that it is exactly this broad pawn-centre that will provide him later on with a beautiful target for a counterattack.

In fact, this is not an attempt to maintain equality, as a classical treatment of the opening could be said to be; it is a violent attempt to wrest the initiative from White. It is an unequivocal challenge – a challenge for a fight to the death.

In the early 20th century, the days of glory of the Queen's Gambit Declined, such an approach to the opening was unthinkable and what is now

a huge amount of deeply analysed opening theory was a mere footnote in the practically uncharted morass of what was called 'irregular openings' in those days. It was not until around 1920 that some promising young players started experimenting with it, most notably perhaps the future world champion Max Euwe. Little by little, the despised opening gained respectability and even a name: the King's Indian Defence. The decisive impetus came from the Soviet Union, reaching the international arena after World War II. Fantastic games from almost all the great Soviet players of that era (headed perhaps by Bronstein and Boleslavsky) brought to light an inexhaustible source of tactical and strategic new ideas. Both the King's Indian and the Grünfeld were lifted to the very top of the hit parade, where they have flourished ever since.

In this chapter we shall look at the King's Indian Defence, which is not really a name for a particular sequence of opening moves but rather for a scheme of development involving ...♘f6, ...g6 and ...♗g7, thus allowing White to play e4. One of the great attractions of this opening is in fact that it is not restricted to a particular sequence of moves and that it can be played against any first move except 1 e4 (although it could be said that the Pirc Defence represents the King's Indian against 1 e4).

The Grünfeld Defence, which we shall look at in the next chapter, though equally provocative, is very different in character, for here Black plays ...d5, starting the attack against White's pawn-centre immediately. Once these were just two variations of the same opening, but now they have grown far apart. It is even a rarity these days if a player has both these openings in his repertoire as Black, because they differ so greatly in character.

By far the most obvious continuation after 2...g6, is **3 ♘c3**, in order to prepare (or is it to threaten?) e4.

The second-most important move is **3 g3**.

Other moves are 3 ♘f3 and 3 f3. **3 ♘f3**, while a sound enough move in itself, has little independent significance because after 3...♗g7 White will still have to choose between a set-up involving 4 ♘c3 and one based on 4 g3. **3 f3** *(D)* is controversial.

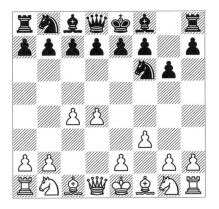

If Black replies **3...♗g7**, the continuation 4 e4 d6 5 ♘c3 will transpose into a Sämisch, a variation that we shall look at later on. If he plays **3...c5** the game turns into a Benoni after 4 d5 ♗g7 5 e4 d6 6 ♘c3 (see page 142). But if Black is not satisfied with either of these transpositions, if he feels he has to 'punish' the perhaps somewhat clumsy 3 f3, he may want to play **3...d5**. This is the Grünfeld approach that will be dealt with in the next chapter.

3 ♘c3

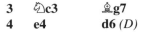

	3	♘c3	♗g7
	4	e4	d6 *(D)*

This is the most important starting position of the King's Indian Defence. White faces a fundamental choice on how to tackle the situation, a choice which is to a very large extent a matter of taste.

Outwardly the most intimidating, strategically a little primitive, yet all in all an important possibility is **5 f4**, the **Four Pawns Attack**.

Seemingly less aggressive, but on closer inspection very sharp indeed, is **5 f3**, the **Sämisch Variation**. White prepares a set-up involving ♗e3, ♕d2 and 0-0-0 followed by a pawn-storm

on the kingside, but he does not commit himself. He is keeping his options open.

Likewise, the natural developing move **5 ♘f3** *may* lead to unfathomable complications, but as yet no bridges are burned. Both sides may still steer the game into more navigable waters. In fact, this flexible and classical move must be considered *the* main line of the King's Indian Defence and probably constitutes the most severe test of its soundness.

5 ♗e2 0-0 6 ♗g5 is the subtlest approach, although like everywhere in this opening here too a sudden explosion into chaos is never far away. This is the **Averbakh Variation**.

Together with the g3 system, these are the main lines of the King's Indian Defence, but because of Black's initial reticence in this opening (meaning that no physical contact with the enemy forces is made during the first few moves) White has a great variety of moves in the early stage of the game. Practically all of them are good, playable, adequate or at least legal.

The moves 5 ♘ge2, 5 ♗d3 and 5 h3 in particular are really quite respectable variations with considerably more theoretical background than many a variation of a lesser opening, yet in the context of the hugely popular King's Indian they remain relatively small. **5 ♘ge2** is played with a view to 6 ♘g3, 7 ♗e2 and 8 0-0, **5 ♗d3** followed by 6 ♘ge2 is a variation on the Sämisch and **5 h3** prepares 6 ♗e3 (or 6 ♗g5 h6 7 ♗e3) by eliminating the annoying reply ...♘g4.

All of these moves are subtle attempts to improve on the main lines. When studying these variations it is essential always to keep in mind some typical responses for Black which are really standard King's Indian strategies. First and foremost Black has ...e5, possibly prepared by ...♘bd7 or ...♘c6. Secondly, White always has to take ...c5 into account when in most cases (though not all of them!) the d5 advance will be the crucial response, landing us into a Benoni.

There are many more schemes of development for Black, for instance ...c6 in combination with ...a6 intending to play ...b5, and of course it is always possible to find a very specific and non-standard reaction to almost any move by White.

All of these strategic motifs will recur in the variations below.

Four Pawns Attack

	5	f4	0-0
	6	♘f3 (D)	

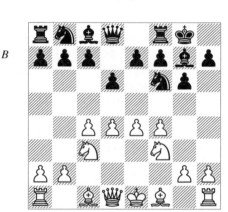

B

White has taken the greatest possible advantage of the freedom his opponent has allowed him in occupying the centre. Black is now under considerable pressure to launch a counterattack which must be swift, powerful and well-aimed. Decades of practical tests have established that only ...c5 and – to a slightly lesser degree – ...e5 are to be fully trusted in this respect. The ...c5 plan can be executed immediately: **6...c5**. The ...e5 plan needs some preparation. Curiously, it is not one of the obvious moves 6...♘bd7 or 6...♘c6 which has turned out to be ideal for this purpose, but the seemingly totally out-of-place **6...♘a6**.

5 f4 0-0 6 ♘f3 c5

	6	...	c5

Black's first five moves could be called reticent, but from this point onwards play will be very concrete. To begin with, White now has to take a decision with far-reaching consequences.

	7	dxc5 (D)

It is truly difficult to say what is best, but certainly White's sharpest and most principled move is **7 d5**, reaching a position which is of crucial importance for both the King's Indian and the Benoni. For reasons of systematic clarity, however, I shall discuss this and similar variations with the typical Benoni pawn-formation in the chapter on the Benoni, except the Averbakh which I regard as predominantly King's Indian.

A third option is **7 ♗e2** cxd4 8 ♘xd4 ♘c6 9 ♗e3. This continuation was popular in the early 1960s.

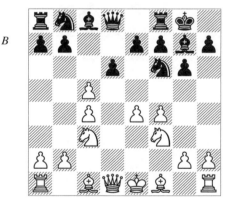

B

	7	...	♕a5

One cannot do full justice to the King's Indian without *always* – in each and every situation – looking for the most dynamic move. It may not always be the best, but it always deserves to be taken into consideration and more often than not, it should get the benefit of the doubt. In fact it is precisely this quality, this continuous tension between what is and what is not carrying imagination too far, which attracts so many players with a natural dynamic style to the King's Indian Defence.

The diagrammed position is a good case in point. Of course it is not illegal to play **7...dxc5**, but Black's position will be drained of all vitality and become rather static and perhaps slightly passive after 8 ♗d3 ♘c6 9 e5.

The text-move (7...♕a5), on the other hand, creates the threat of 8...♘xe4. Play might continue 8 ♗d3 ♕xc5 9 ♕e2 ♘c6 10 ♗e3, when Black has a choice between two squares for his queen. Superficially **10...♕h5** looks like the most active move, partly because it invites White to fall into the nasty trap 11 0-0? ♘g4 12 ♗d2?? ♘d4, but if White calmly responds 11 h3, the position of the queen on h5 is shaky. Most players prefer **10...♕a5**, when 11 0-0 can be met by 11...♗g4 and 12...♘d7, starting active play on the queenside.

5 f4 0-0 6 ♘f3 ♘a6

6   ...   ♘a6 *(D)*

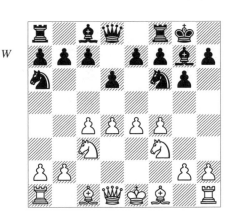

This move is likely to raise a few eyebrows, especially when one is told that the idea is not to prepare ...c5, but ...e5! We are now, indeed, entering hypermodern opening theory, where considerations of a general nature tend to get swept aside by concrete and precisely calculated variations. Black is planning a massive attack in the centre, hoping to take over the initiative at the cost of a pawn.

If White now simply replies **7 ♗e2**, allowing Black to carry out his plan by 7...e5, he will face a difficult choice. He can accept Black's pawn sacrifice in various ways, but a closer inspection

of these possibilities reveals that neither **8 fxe5** dxe5 9 ♘xe5 c5! nor **8 dxe5** dxe5 9 ♕xd8 ♖xd8 10 fxe5 ♘g4 is very attractive and that **8 dxe5** dxe5 **9 ♘xe5** *(D)* is really the only option that holds any promise.

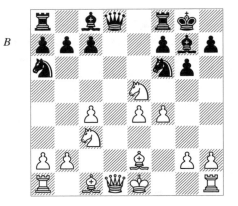

This, however, brings to light a very important point of 6...♘a6: 9...♘c5! increases the pressure on what is left of White's centre. If now, for instance, 10 ♕xd8 ♖xd8 11 ♗f3 ♗e6 followed by 12...♘fd7!, White is in danger of falling behind in development and Black will have more than sufficient compensation for the sacrificed pawn.

A more positionally oriented reaction to 7...e5 would be **8 fxe5** dxe5 **9 d5**. By refusing the sacrifice, White hopes to hold on to the initiative. But because this causes problems with the defence of e4 after 9...♘c5, attention has gradually shifted to the alternative **7 ♗d3**. This move is likely to produce, after 7...e5 8 fxe5 dxe5 9 d5 c6 (or 9...♘h5), a typical King's Indian battle, revolving around the question: is White's central formation a source of strength or is it the perfect target for Black's counterattack?

Finally, there is the aggressive reply **7 e5** *(D)*.

The consequences of this advance are hard to judge, but White should certainly not be working under the assumption that this simply refutes 6...♘a6 and that he is smashing his opponent easily. Black replies 7...♘d7, when he is ready to strike back with 8...c5. If White has nothing better in this position than completing

his development with 8 ♗e2 c5 9 exd6 exd6 10 0-0, he may not have a bad position but he would certainly like to put his f-pawn back on f2 again, which can hardly be what he intended when playing 5 f4.

Sämisch Variation

5   f3 *(D)*

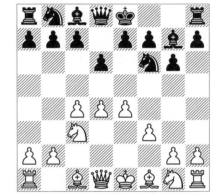

White consolidates his central position and prepares ♗e3. He is also laying the cornerstone for a kingside pawn-storm by g4 and h4-h5. Yet he does not commit himself to this plan. A queenside offensive remains just as realistic an option, when 5 f3 will serve as a precaution against an expected attack on the kingside by Black.

This versatility of 5 f3 has held a strong attraction over the years to players of varying style and personality. Almost all the world champions

and other top grandmasters since World War II have played the Sämisch. For decades, this was considered to be the ultimate weapon against the King's Indian Defence.

It was not until the 1990s that Black finally managed to come to terms with it and the Sämisch slowly began to give way to other variations, most notably 5 ♘f3.

The main objection that can be raised against 5 f3 is that it is not a developing move. White's pieces are a little slow in joining the battle and Black should try to take advantage of this. Over the years a wide variety of variations have been developed, based not just on the traditional stratagems of ...c5 and ...e5, but on some very original ideas as well.

5   ...   0-0

For almost all of these variations, castling has proved to be a useful preliminary, the only exception being the plan of playing ...c6 and ...a6, where the risk of an enemy attack is thought to outweigh the advantage of completing kingside development. This has made the position after **5...c6 6 ♗e3 a6** *(D)* the main starting position of this subvariation.

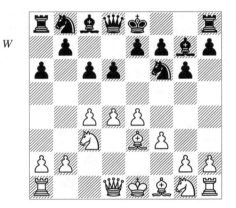

The Sämisch is one of only a few King's Indian variations where this plan has gained a solid reputation for itself, mainly because Black runs little risk of being pushed back by a swift central advance based on e5. The only situation where theory regards this as dangerous arises after **7 ♗d3**, if Black replies 7...b5. Then 8 e5! is thought to be annoying for Black and 7...♘bd7 (or even 7...0-0) is considered a better choice than the immediate 7...b5. The position after 7...0-0 8 ②ge2 b5 9 0-0 ②bd7 is characteristic for this line. White enjoys a space advantage but Black's position is both flexible and solid and it is far from clear how White should proceed.

White's most aggressive option is to play 7 ♕d2 b5 8 0-0-0, intending ♗h6 and h4-h5. It is precisely to take the sting out of this attacking scheme that Black does well to delay castling in this line. If he continues 8...♕a5, Black's attacking chances on the queenside will be no worse than White's on the opposite wing.

Finally, blocking Black's advance on the queenside by playing 7 a4 is also a valid option. Of course this means that White, hampered by his now sterile pawn-structure will no longer be able to make any serious headway on the queenside. A good reply is 7...a5, securing the 'hole' in White's pawn-structure, followed by ...②a6 and ...e5.

6   ♗e3

This is the classical interpretation of the Sämisch. In the last decade of the 20th century, however, when White was finding it increasingly difficult to cope with the many new problems that Black was posing, the search for alternatives, not just for this but for each and every 'self-evident' move in the Sämisch, became intense and **6 ♗g5** *(D)* came to the fore, though whether this move is really an improvement is still an open question.

Black has the same range of possible replies that he has against 6 ♗e3 except that he cannot play **6...e5?**, which is punished by 7 dxe5 dxe5 8 ♕xd8 ♖xd8 9 ②d5. In practice Black has usually replied with a ...c5 plan, which is very logical now that d4 is not as well protected as it is with a bishop on e3. **6...c5** 7 d5 is a direct transposition to the Benoni (see page 142), but there are subtle variations on this theme which are hard to evaluate properly, like **6...a6** 7 ♕d2 c5, when 8 d5 runs into the characteristic pawn sacrifice **8...b5**. This is a typical King's Indian/Benoni motif which will pop up in many different forms, culminating in the Benko Gambit (see page 153) where Black starts the game with this pawn sacrifice.

We now return to 6 ♗e3 *(D)*:

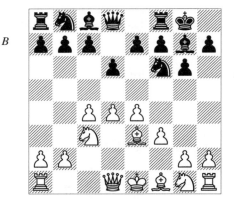

Starting from this position, an amazing diversity of variations has been developed, doing full credit to the pent-up strength hidden in Black's seemingly rather withdrawn position.

The classical approach is to play **6...e5**, when after White's principled reply 7 d5, Black again faces an important choice. His most obvious plan is to lash out on the kingside with **7...②h5** 8 ♕d2 f5. If, after 9 0-0-0, Black continues this strategy of gaining ground by playing 9...f4 10 ♗f2, the centre is closed and both sides will have to move forward with their pawns slowly and carefully, White on the queenside and Black on the kingside. It is more flexible (though not necessarily better) to play 9...②d7 10 ♗d3 ②df6, retaining the option of exchanging pawns on e4, though of course this also allows White to take the initiative himself by exchanging on f5.

The brave and the reckless may want to try their luck in one of the most famous (or should I say infamous?) variations of the entire world of opening theory: 7...♘h5 8 ♕d2 ♕h4+ 9 g3 ♘xg3!?. This is in effect a queen sacrifice since 10 ♕f2 will cut off the knight's retreat. Black then continues unflinchingly 10...♘xf1! 11 ♕xh4 ♘xe3, when after 12 ♔e2 ♘xc4 (D) a critical situation arises.

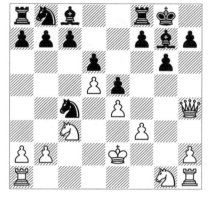

Black has only two minor pieces and two pawns to show for the queen, yet White's position has been damaged in such a vital way, in particular by the disappearance of his g-pawn and of his dark-squared bishop, that the positional compensation for this material deficit is thought to be sufficient. And this is not a passive variation either! Far from just banking on White being unable to break down his fortress, Black has hopes of taking the initiative himself by means of ...c6 or ...f5. What this variation requires – from *both* players – is not so much a good knowledge of opening theory but courage and, most of all, self-confidence.

In addition to 7...♘h5, Black has the possibility of playing **7...c6** (D), opening the c-file in anticipation of his opponent castling queenside.

If White now simply carries on with **8 ♕d2** cxd5 9 cxd5 a6 10 0-0-0, Black will get counterplay on the queenside, based on moves like ...♕a5, ...b5 and ...♘bd7-c5. For this reason, most players take 7...c6 as a signal for White to change plans and castle kingside instead. After **8 ♗d3** cxd5 9 cxd5 Black falls back on standard

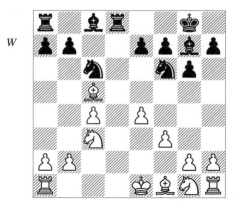

kingside aggression with 9...♘h5 10 ♘ge2 f5. In this position White must be careful not to give Black too much of a free hand on the kingside (11 0-0 f4). Therefore most players exchange pawns on f5 before castling (11 exf5 gxf5 12 0-0). The central pawn-formation is now less rigid than in the 7...♘h5 8 ♕d2 f5 line and Black will have to be on his guard for counter-aggression on the kingside, most notably based on the powerful thrust g4.

Another classical way to tackle the 'Sämisch problem' is to play ...c5. This plan can be executed in several ways.

To start with, the immediate **6...c5**, strange though it may look, has turned out to be eminently playable. At first sight Black's compensation is not obvious after **7 dxc5 dxc5 8 ♕xd8 ♖xd8 9 ♗xc5 ♘c6** (D), yet closer investigation reveals that this is actually a beautiful demonstration of the hidden powers of the King's Indian Defence.

White has difficulties in getting his pieces developed and he would dearly like to neutralize the pressure on the long diagonal (a1-h8) and plug the hole on d4 by putting his c-pawn back on c3. In fact, many players prefer a switch to the Benoni via **7 d5** or, perhaps slightly more accurate, **7 ②ge2 ②c6 8 d5 ②e5 9 ②g3**, which transposes to a critical line of the Modern Benoni after 9...e6 10 ②e2 exd5 11 cxd5 (see page 148).

It is partly this line which has caused White to take a closer look at 6 ②g5 because in this Benoni-type position, g5 is the more aggressive square for the bishop.

Although it is therefore not strictly necessary to make any preparations for ...c5, many players still prefer to do so. Especially **6...②bd7** *(D)* is a popular alternative to 6...c5.

This is mainly a matter of taste. Black avoids the exchange of queens (after 6...c5 7 dxc5) and is aiming for a complicated (probably Benoni-oriented) middlegame. For instance, now 7 ②ge2 c5 8 d5 ②e5 produces the same position as the above-mentioned 6...c5 7 ②ge2 ②c6 8 d5 ②e5. White may want to try to improve on this line by maintaining the tension in the centre with 8 ♕d2, or he may play 7 ②h3 (intending ②f2), making use of the fact that Black cannot play ...②xh3, ruining White's pawn-structure, with a knight on d7.

6...b6 is a rather old-fashioned way to prepare ...c5. This line was fairly popular in the 1960s but is now a rare bird. If White plays 7 ②d3 Black will have to make another preparatory

move because 7...c5? runs into 8 e5 followed by ②e4.

Finally, there is **6...②c6** *(D)*, a move based on an entirely different idea. Black's aim is to take the fullest possible advantage of the limitations of the Sämisch.

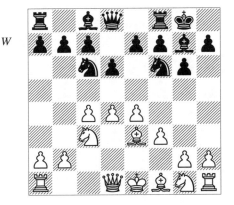

For a start, he does not need to worry about 7 d5 because he can simply reply 7...②e5, when White will begin to experience some difficulties in developing his kingside, while Black has an easy plan of action on the queenside, based on ...c6.

The idea behind 6...②c6 is to play 7...a6 and 8...♖b8, getting ready to play either ...b5 or ...e5 (and preferably both!), depending on which scheme of development White chooses. The ideal is to play ...e5 in a situation where d5 can be met by ...②d4, even if this involves a pawn sacrifice. The rook on b8 will support an attack on the queenside once the b-file is opened, for instance after ...b5 and ...bxc4.

This way of tackling the Sämisch is much more aggressive than ...a6 in combination with ...c6 and it has been one of the main lines of the Sämisch ever since its introduction in the 1960s. The most important starting position is reached after 7 ②ge2 a6 8 ♕d2 ♖b8 *(D)*.

If White now plays a calm move like **9 ②c1**, freeing the diagonal for his bishop on f1, the thematic reply is 9...e5 10 d5 ②d4. Then after **11 ②xd4?!** exd4, 12 ♕xd4? loses to 12...②xe4!, but even 12 ②3e2 allows Black excellent positional compensation. With all White's centre pawns fixed on light squares and the a1-h8

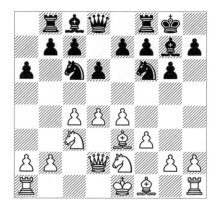

diagonal fully at the mercy of the black bishop, the absence of White's dark-squared bishop is making itself felt. But it may well come as a bit of a shock that White is not safe from aggression even if he plays the solid **11 ♘b3**, because Black then has another pawn sacrifice to add fuel to the fire: 11...c5 12 dxc6 bxc6! 13 ♘xd4 exd4 14 ♗xd4. Now after 14...♖e8 (or 14...♕a5, or even 14...d5) Black's plan is running like clockwork: he has open lines for his rooks and an open diagonal for his bishop on g7 and White has great difficulty in getting his pieces developed.

A much more aggressive approach is to play **9 h4** *(D)*.

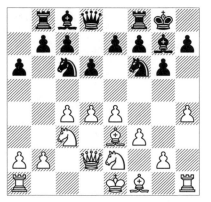

White is trying to get *his* attack in first. If Black plays **9...e5** now, the situation after 10 d5 is totally different. Because White has not moved his knight from e2, 10...♘d4 essentially just loses a pawn here, while if Black

plays 10...♘a5 11 ♘g3 c5 (a necessary move to prevent b4) 12 h5, White does indeed obtain excellent chances on the kingside. The alternative **9...b5** too, requires (at least) nerves of steel from Black in view of 10 h5. Black's most solid response to 9 h4 is **9...h5**. White then again faces a fundamental choice. He can either fall back on the ♘c1 plan or proceed with the attack; e.g., 10 0-0-0 b5 11 ♗h6.

5 ♘f3

5   ♘f3 *(D)*

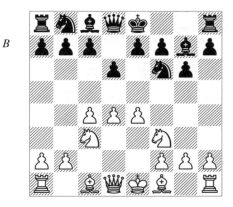

The fact that this position is often reached via a different move-order (e.g. 1 ♘f3 ♘f6 2 c4 g6 or 1 d4 ♘f6 2 ♘f3) would be more than sufficient reason in itself to regard this as a main line, but even in the move-order that we are using here, 5 ♘f3 is one of White's most important moves. He develops his king's knight and as yet does not commit himself to any particular pawn-formation.

5   ...   0-0
6   ♗e2

Again White makes a natural move, developing the bishop without committing himself, but the alternative **6 h3** (preparing ♗e3) is also quite popular. If Black responds in classical style with 6...e5, the idea is to play 7 d5, when after 7...♘bd7 8 ♗e3 ♘c5 White has 9 ♘d2 and if now 9...a5 (strengthening the position of the knight on c5 by preventing 10 b4), the bold 10 g4 reveals White's intentions: he is anticipating the thematic advance ...f5. If Black carries on with his standard plan of playing 10...♘e8 11 ♕c2 f5, the response 12 gxf5 gxf5 13 ♖g1 offers White chances of taking over the initiative on the kingside.

6   ...   e5

A major difference between this and the Sämisch Variation is that White's piece development is much more smooth after 5 ♘f3, making it harder for Black to use any of the 'non-classical' plans that are so useful against the Sämisch. For instance **6...♘c6** 7 d5 now offers poor prospects for Black and this is hardly ever played nowadays. The same goes for **6...c6** 7 0-0 a6.

6...c5 (D), on the other hand, is still a sound enough move.

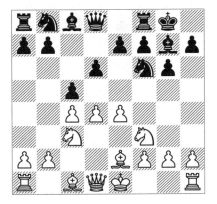

Black is seeking a transposition to the Benoni via **7 d5** (see page 142). However, he has to take another transposition into account, one that is much more surprising and which may not be entirely to his liking: after **7 0-0** cxd4 8 ♘xd4 ♘c6 9 ♗e3 we suddenly find ourselves in the Maroczy Bind, a line of the Sicilian Accelerated Dragon (see page 420)!

6...♗g4 (D), however, is an interesting and very specific attempt to take advantage of the downside of 5 ♘f3 and 6 ♗e2.

Black intends to put pressure on d4 with moves like ...♘c6 and ...♘fd7. In the meantime he leaves his opponent guessing whether he will play ...e5 or ...c5.

White's reaction to this aggressive plan has to be accurate. The logical 7 ♗e3, strengthening d4, is generally considered best. Now 7...♘fd7

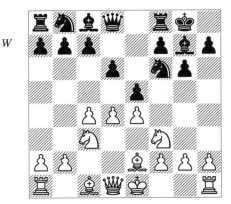

constitutes the main line of this variation, presenting White with a difficult choice. The casual **8 0-0** has the drawback that after 8...♘c6 9 d5 (if White does not play this, 9...e5 10 d5 ♗xf3 11 ♗xf3 ♘d4 will be annoying) 9...♗xf3 10 ♗xf3 ♘a5 a weakening of White's pawn-structure will be unavoidable. If, for instance, 11 ♗e2 ♗xc3 12 bxc3 e5! White's position has lost much of its dynamic power. Most players prefer to anticipate this attack by preventive measures like **8 ♖c1** or the surprising regrouping **8 ♘g1** ♗xe2 9 ♘gxe2.

We now return to 6...e5 (D):

constitutes the main line of this variation, presenting White with a difficult choice. The casual **8 0-0** has the drawback that after 8...♘c6 9 d5 (if White does not play this, 9...e5 10 d5 ♗xf3 11 ♗xf3 ♘d4 will be annoying) 9...♗xf3 10 ♗xf3 ♘a5 a weakening of White's pawn-structure will be unavoidable. If, for instance, 11 ♗e2 ♗xc3 12 bxc3 e5! White's position has lost much of its dynamic power. Most players prefer to anticipate this attack by preventive measures like **8 ♖c1** or the surprising regrouping **8 ♘g1** ♗xe2 9 ♘gxe2.

We now return to 6...e5 (D):

There are four main lines in this position, each with a clearly defined character of its own.

7 dxe5, the **Exchange Variation** is not just an exchange of pawns. White fixes the central pawn-formation immediately and is heading for a queenless middlegame.

Another way of fixing the central pawn-formation is **7 d5**, but unlike the Exchange Variation, White is closing the centre instead of opening it. This is the **Petrosian System**.

White's most popular and probably the most critical move is **7 0-0**, which can be called the **Classical Variation**. White keeps his options open as far as the pawn-formation in the centre is concerned, but he unhesitatingly commits himself to a place for his king.

The developing move **7 ♗e3** keeps even that option open. This is the **Gligorić Variation**.

Exchange Variation

7	**dxe5**	**dxe5**
8	**♕xd8**	**♖xd8**
9	**♗g5** *(D)*	

Taking on e5 is useless: 9 ♘xe5 ♘xe4! and Black wins back his pawn immediately.

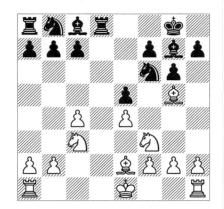

In the Exchange Variation, White is taking the long-term positional risk that d4, the tear in his pawn-formation, may become a problem. What is attractive in this line are the short-term advantages: a slight lead in development and some concrete threats.

For a long time **9...♖e8** was thought to be the best move and many players were tempted to try their hand with the tiny endgame advantage offered by 10 ♘d5 ♘xd5 11 cxd5.

But when **9...c6** came to the fore in the 1980s, White's interest in the Exchange Variation dropped sharply. Suddenly play becomes complicated and tricky. Black prevents ♘d5 at the cost of a pawn and although this may look rather dubious at first sight, Black does actually get some very good counterplay. If 10 ♘xe5 ♖e8 11 0-0-0 Black effortlessly regains the pawn in the case of 11...♘a6 12 f4 (12 ♖d6 is the main line) 12...h6 13 ♗h4 g5 14 ♗g3 ♘c5.

Petrosian System

7   d5 *(D)*

This move is more ambitious than 7 dxe5 and much more threatening for Black in the long run.

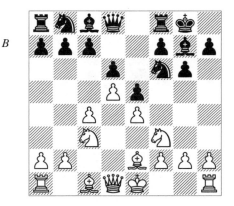

The type of middlegame that now arises is highly characteristic of the King's Indian Defence and very important in a general sense. White has a space advantage and, given the opportunity, he will take the initiative, most probably on the queenside where the natural plan of playing c5 presents itself. Black, on the other hand, will try to turn this very pawn-formation that gives White more space into a target for his own plan of attack. For him an advance on the kingside (and against e4!) is the natural plan: ...f5.

The point of the Petrosian System, as compared to 7 0-0, is of a strategic nature and becomes apparent if Black now carries out his ...f5 plan straightaway: because White has not yet committed his king to the kingside he can still take the initiative on that wing himself.

Thus **7...♘e8** is strongly met by 8 h4, while **7...♘h5** allows White to take advantage of the unsafe position of the knight: if he plays 8 g3, preventing Black from playing ...♘f4, the 'desirable' 8...f5 runs into 9 exf5 gxf5 10 ♘xe5!.

Therefore Black does better if he first develops his queenside. Traditionally this was done by **7...♘bd7**, intending to meet **8 0-0** with 8...♘c5 9 ♕c2 a5. By erecting a temporary blockade to White's ambitions on the queenside, Black hopes to be able to play ...f5 before White can take the initiative himself. The variation is named after Tigran Petrosian because this world champion introduced the strategic idea of postponing castling in order (again) to prevent or at least discourage ...f5. His plan starts with the move **8 ♗g5** *(D)*, pinning the knight.

If Black breaks the pin by 8...h6 9 ♗h4 g5 10 ♗g3 ♘h5, White has achieved two aims. First, he has taken some of the sting out of Black's plan because a future exf5 can now no longer be met by ...gxf5, a recapture which in many cases (though not always!) gives Black dangerous attacking chances on the kingside. Second, he can play 11 h4, again taking over the initiative on the kingside (or at least attempting to do so).

For this reason, subtler ways of achieving Black's plans were developed, which resulted in the following move gradually taking over as the main line:

> **7   ...   a5**

The modern key position is reached after...

> **8   ♗g5   h6**
> **9   ♗h4   ♘a6**
> **10   ♘d2   ♕e8** *(D)*

Both sides have developed their pieces actively while at the same time throwing as many obstacles in the way of their opponent's plans as possible.

Thanks to his last move, Black is now ready to play 11...♘h7 followed by ...f5, when he has retained the possibility of playing ...gxf5. White needs to tackle the queenside problem: he must find a way to play b4.

This line does not demand so much a willingness to throw everything forward in blind faith, as an ability to weigh carefully the consequences of each and every move. Characteristic finesse is demonstrated after **11 a3 ♗d7**, when the straightforward 12 ♖b1 (preparing to play 13 b4) is met with 12...a4!, considerably reducing White's flexibility on the queenside. White does well to prevent this by playing 12 b3 first.

Classical Variation

> **7   0-0** *(D)*

White maintains the tension in the centre. He is waiting for a better moment to play either dxe5 or d5.

But first it is up to Black now to decide whether *he* will use his chance to determine the central pawn-formation by playing **7...exd4** or if he too will maintain the tension and wait for a better moment. In the latter case he needs to find a move that fits in well with both the dxe5 and the d5 plan and which preferably increases the strength of a future ...exd4 as well.

All of these requirements are well met by the classical developing move **7...♘bd7** and it

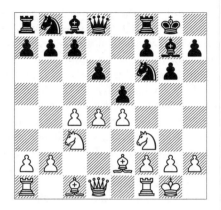

B

should come as no surprise that this was the first main line of the King's Indian Defence, reigning supreme until around 1950.

After that the much more provocative move **7...♘c6** took over, outgrowing the old main line in importance and even becoming one of the most difficult and complicated variations of the whole of opening theory.

Finally, in the late 1980s the possibility of playing **7...♘a6** was 'discovered'. Around that time, this way of developing the queen's knight, seemingly moving away from the centre but in reality eyeing the excellent square c5, began to pervade almost all variations of the King's Indian and this is one of the lines where it turned out to be eminently playable.

5 ♘f3 0-0 6 ♗e2 e5 7 0-0 exd4

7	...	exd4
8	♘xd4 *(D)*	

B

Black gives up his stronghold in the centre in return for open files and diagonals for his pieces.

8	...	♖e8
9	f3	

After this logical follow-up, there are two standard plans for opening the attack on White's stronghold in the centre.

The classical method is to play **9...c6**, envisaging the central advance ...d5. 10 ♔h1 is then a solid and typical reply, removing the king from the dangerous g1-a7 diagonal in order to pre-empt nasty moves like ...♕b6 and intending to meet 10...d5 with 11 cxd5 cxd5 12 ♗g5. Black usually avoids this, continuing his development with 10...♘bd7 instead.

9...♘c6 10 ♗e3 ♘h5 is an entirely different approach and one which was very popular in the 1990s. Black frees the way for ...f5 and forces his opponent to take drastic measures if he wants to preserve his central dominance. An important tactical point is that 11 f4 can be met by 11...♘f6 12 ♗f3 ♗g4!. The resulting exchanges (e.g. 13 ♘xc6 ♗xf3 14 ♕xf3 bxc6) are just what Black needs in order to solve what is really his only strategic problem in this line: a lack of space.

5 ♘f3 0-0 6 ♗e2 e5 7 0-0 ♘bd7

7	...	♘bd7 *(D)*

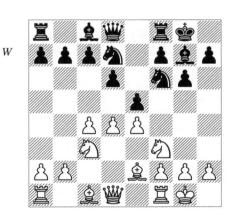

W

Although this is one of the oldest variations of the King's Indian Defence, it is also one of the most topical ones. After some 90 years of research, the theoretical problems are as fascinating as ever and we still do not even know what White's best next move is!

The essence of the problem lies in the fact that it is not a particularly good moment to resolve the tension in the centre. **8 d5** produces a position from the Petrosian System that we have just been looking at (7 d5 ♘bd7 8 0-0), while **8 dxe5** is really completely pointless here. All the books (and the players behind those books) agree that White should prefer a useful developing move, but which one?

The fact that it has proved to be almost impossible to answer this question with any degree of finality is of course precisely what makes this variation both difficult and attractive.

The classical move is **8 ♖e1** (D).

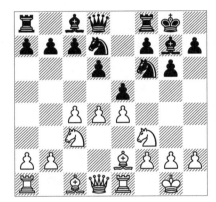

White assumes that Black will have to take on d4 sooner or later, when the rook will be well-placed on e1. But Black too is able to maintain his waiting policy, for instance by 8...c6 9 ♗f1, when one of the traditional lines continues **9...a5** 10 ♖b1 ♖e8. He may also want to consider an aggressive alternative: **9...exd4** 10 ♘xd4 ♘g4, intending to meet 11 h3 with 11...♕b6!. This is in effect an attempt to expose the downside of 8 ♖e1.

By playing **8 ♕c2**, White is thinking along d5 lines. If Black now plays 8...c6, this makes itself felt immediately since after 9 d5 the 'normal' 9...♘c5 is now useless. White's pawn on e4 is protected and he will be only too happy to play 10 b4. This implies that Black has to find

another antidote to the d5 plan. Closing the centre completely with 9...c5 is most players' preferred choice. We shall encounter several more examples of this pawn-structure in this book, culminating in the Czech Benoni: 1 d4 ♘f6 2 c4 c5 3 d5 e5 (see page 143). The circumstances for building such a wall are reasonably favourable in this variation because White has already castled kingside, which is not considered to be White's most dangerous strategy in this type of position. Also the move ♕c2 is not particularly useful here.

8 ♗e3 (D) can be said to be the modern move.

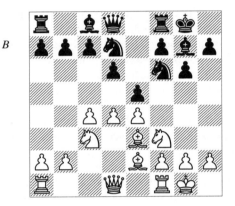

Here too the idea is to meet **8...c6** with 9 d5, when in case of 9...c5 the developing move ♗e3 is of more use to White than ♕c2. If **8...♘g4** then 9 ♗g5 f6 10 ♗d2 gives White a relatively favourable version of the Gligorić Variation (7 ♗e3; see page 110), because here Black no longer has the aggressive option ...♘c6.

5 ♘f3 0-0 6 ♗e2 e5 7 0-0 ♘c6

7	...	♘c6

This move forces White to lay his cards on the table. No longer can he maintain the tension in the centre, because the only move to do so, **8 ♗e3**, is not only troubled by the standard reaction 8...♘g4 9 ♗g5 f6, but also by the excellent 8...♖e8, when 9 d5 runs into 9...♘d4!. It is true that the situation is relatively favourable to try the dxe5 plan instead (8...♖e8 9 dxe5 dxe5), but practice has shown that even this does not really worry Black.

If White really wants to go for it, he has to accept the challenge:

8 d5 ♘e7 (D)

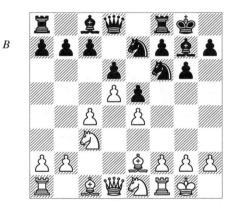

At first sight things seem to be going very well for White. Black has invested two moves in order to land his knight on what looks like an extremely unattractive square (e7), and the option of putting pressure on e4 with ...♘bd7-c5 (or ...♘a6-c5) is gone.

Yet a closer inspection of this intriguing position, one of the most important of the entire King's Indian Defence, reveals the positive sides of Black's play. With the central tension resolved, Black can fully concentrate on his kingside operations. He has no problems whatsoever in playing ...f5 and once this crucial advance is achieved, new prospects for the knight on e7 will open up automatically. In case his kingside pawns get rolling (...f4 and ...g5-g4, once White has been induced to play f3) an excellent square becomes available on g6, while if the game is opened by ...fxe4 (or exf5), then ...♘(x)f5 will be possible. What Black gives up in defensive strength on the queenside, he gets back in attacking power on the kingside.

It should come as no surprise then that this variation is an extremely popular choice with the uncompromising attacking player. It may easily come to a situation where White breaks through on the queenside and Black on the kingside, with *both* players having burned their bridges. Because Black's attack is directed at the enemy king, the danger for White may become very acute, but White's attack on the opposite wing is equally threatening and a single mistake may mean immediate disaster for both sides.

It is also a clash of opposing styles. There are very few players who play this variation with both colours. Almost everyone is either for White or for Black.

9 ♘e1, 9 ♘d2 and **9 b4** are the main lines, but if you look at these variations carefully you will find them to be closely related to each other. Many players study all three of them in order to get the fullest possible idea of where White's chances lie in this position.

9 ♘e1 (D) was the first of these moves to gain wide recognition.

White prevents ...♘h5, frees the way for his f-pawn (which can either move forward to f3, protecting e4, or more aggressively to f4) and prepares ♘d3, supporting the c5 advance. A well-established main line may serve as an example of how deeply attack on the one side and defence on the other are integrated in this variation: 9...♘d7 10 ♘d3 f5 11 ♗d2 ♘f6 12 f3 f4 13 c5 g5 14 cxd6 cxd6 15 ♖c1 ♘g6 16 ♘b5 ♖f7 17 ♕c2 (intending ♘c7) 17...♘e8 18 a4 h5 19 ♘f2 (D).

This variation has been studied down to the last detail, yet it is still as alive as it ever was. The sequence of moves given above may be varied at almost every moment; e.g., White may choose a completely different strategy by playing 11 exf5 (instead of 11 ♗d2) 11...gxf5

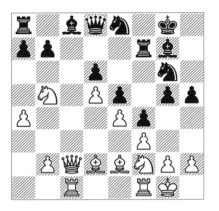

12 f4, shifting the battle to the kingside, or he may play 13 g4 (instead of 13 c5), hoping to achieve exactly the opposite, namely, to close off the kingside and reign supreme on the queenside afterwards.

9 ♘d2 *(D)* was a fantastically popular variation in the early 1990s.

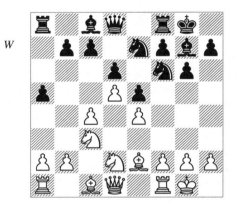

Here too White wants to play c5, but instead of preparing this pawn-break with ♘e1-d3, he chooses to prepare it with b4 so as to allow his knight to move to the truly splendid square c4 after he has played c5. This will enable him to put pressure on d6, which is the base and therefore the only really vulnerable point in Black's pawn-chain.

This variation too has been minutely analysed, with the emphasis on how Black should react to this plan on the queenside. Is ...c5 a wise precaution and if so, should White play dxc6 or is the patient a3 and b4 the better

choice? Is ...a5 a useful move, delaying White's attack, or will this turn out to be a weakening of the queenside in the long run? Is it better perhaps to forget about these nuances of positional play and go all-out on the kingside with **9...♘d7 10 b4 f5**, leaving the queenside to fend for itself?

These are very profound questions indeed and anyone who makes a thorough study of this line is likely not only to construct a solid opening repertoire but to discover a lot about the positional aspects of this type of position.

On a concrete level, theory seems to have decided that building a few defensive barriers on the queenside is a good idea. This has led to **9...a5** *(D)* becoming the main line.

Then there is a major division arising after the logical 10 a3, between 10...♘d7 11 ♖b1 f5 on the one side and 10...♗d7 11 b3 (11 ♖b1 allows Black to play 11...a4) 11...c5 or even the flexible 11...c6 on the other.

Troubled by this multitude of defensive possibilities, White then turned his attention to **9 b4** *(D)*, a move which until about 1995 had been relatively out of favour for two reasons.

First, 9...♘h5 was thought to be an annoying move because White must then either allow this knight to jump to f4 or he must play the weakening g3. Second, Black has 9...a5, disrupting White's pawn-phalanx on the queenside.

It is interesting to note that the recent history of this variation is at the same time a nice illustration of how opening theory works: ever more

B

detailed analysis uproots even the soundest general principles in the end (and thus creates new ones).

First it was shown that **9...♘h5** can be met by 10 ♖e1 ♘f4 11 ♗f1 *(D)*.

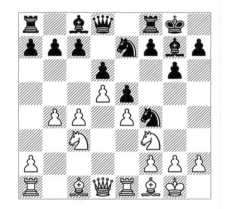

B

This manoeuvre had presumably been considered to be far too passive at first, but because Black's knight is not completely secure on f4, it is not so easy to proceed. 11...f5, for instance, runs into 12 ♗xf4 exf4 13 e5!.

Then it turned out that the damage done to White's pawn-phalanx by **9...a5** is not all that serious, because after 10 ♗a3 (10 bxa5 is also quite playable) 10...axb4 11 ♗xb4 ♘d7 12 a4 White will eventually press through c5 anyway with moves like a5 and ♘a4. Once this plan is successfully carried out, Black may well start to regret having started hostilities on the queenside with only his opponent having taken advantage of it in the end.

5 ♘f3 0-0 6 ♗e2 e5 7 0-0 ♘a6

7   ...   ♘a6 *(D)*

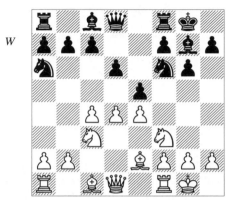

W

The rise to fame of this move during the last decade of the 20th century has radically changed the face of a good many variations of the King's Indian Defence. We have already seen how 6...♘a6 came to be accepted as an excellent way of meeting the Four Pawns Attack (see page 96). Here, in the Classical Variation, 7...♘a6 is really a subtle variation on the old main line 7...♘bd7. Black preserves the tension in the centre, while eyeing c5 as a future square for his knight, but without giving up the possibility of playing ...♗g4. This changes the character of the opening subtly but considerably.

Of course White can play **8 d5**, steering the game into the Petrosian System (8...♘c5 9 ♕c2 a5), just like he can against 7...♘bd7, but as we have seen, this does not really cause Black any headaches. Again, just as in the 7...♘bd7 line, the real test of 7...♘a6 is to play a useful developing move. The first difference is felt after **8 ♕c2**, which in this case is not useful at all since Black can play 8...♘b4 and if now 9 ♕b3 then 9...♘c6 10 d5 ♘d4! makes it very clear that the manoeuvre ♕c2-b3 is not something to be proud of.

The classical move is (again) **8 ♖e1**, when after 8...c6 9 ♗f1 a key position arises. On the one hand Black has the nimble **9...exd4** 10 ♘xd4 ♘g4, the idea being to meet 11 h3 with 11...♕b6 (or 11...♕f6); on the other hand he can play the rather more profound **9...♗g4** *(D)*.

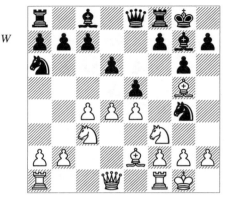

Profound because it now *looks* as if White can finally shut the a6-knight effectively out of play by 10 d5, now that **10...♘c5?!** is pointless (and will be met by 11 b4). However, Black has a highly original alternative to 10...♘c5 which keeps his position fully alive. By playing **10...♘b4!**, threatening 11...♗xf3, when 12 ♕xf3 ♘c2 costs White the exchange and 12 gxf3 disrupts his kingside pawn-formation, he more or less forces the reply 11 ♗e2. This gives Black just enough time to play 11...a5 so as to be able to retreat his knight *behind* the a-pawn instead of in front of it (12 a3 ♘a6). Suddenly, just because Black has managed to get ...a5 in, his knight on a6 is in the *middle* of the battlefield (namely, the battle for b4) instead of shut off from it. Perhaps I should add that Black has a good no-nonsense alternative to all this in the shape of the robust **10...c5**.

The second main line is **8 ♗e3**. Here too a variation has been developed to make good use of the position of Black's knight on a6: 8...♘g4 9 ♗g5 and now not the obvious 9...f6 but 9...♕e8 *(D)*.

This move is possible because 10 ♘d5, which would have been strong with the black knight on d7, makes no sense now that c7 is protected. There are a few nasty points to 9...♕e8, most notably the threat of 10...exd4 11 ♘xd4 ♘xh2! 12 ♔xh2 ♕e5+. Practical evidence seems to indicate that 10 dxe5 dxe5 11 h3 is White's best option in this line. This is in fact one of the few instances in the whole of the King's Indian Defence where the dxe5 strategy is really an excellent choice. Just like in the Exchange Variation

proper (see page 103) White hopes that his slightly more active piece development will yield dividends. The potential drawbacks are also the same: the d4-square remains the Achilles' Heel in White's pawn-formation.

Gligorić Variation

7   ♗e3 *(D)*

This move is even more flexible than 7 0-0. Not only does White retain the choice between d5 and dxe5, he also does not commit himself to a place for his king.

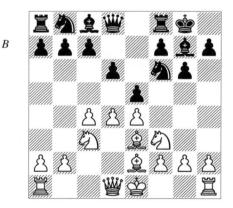

These advantages are demonstrated most clearly if Black now plays **7...♘c6**. White responds 8 d5 ♘e7 9 ♘d2, when he has in fact achieved a superior version of the variation 7 0-0 ♘c6 8 d5 ♘e7 9 ♘d2 because his knight on d2 is not obstructing his bishop on c1 and he is free to castle queenside should this be required.

Other developing moves, like **7...♞bd7** and **7...♞a6**, transpose directly to 7 0-0 lines after 8 0-0. This makes the Gligorić Variation especially popular with players who feel uncomfortable with the sharp 7 0-0 ♞c6, but who have no objection at all against the other 7 0-0 variations.

Therefore the immediate attack on the bishop is critical for the assessment of 7 ♗e3:

7	...	♞g4
8	♗g5	f6
9	♗h4 *(D)*	

We have reached the most important starting position of the Gligorić Variation.

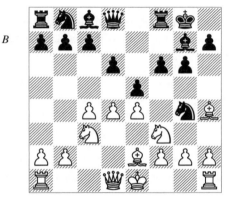

Has Black done well chasing the white bishop or has he just weakened his own position? This is a difficult question and one which has not been resolved so far. The usual continuation is:

9	...	♞c6
10	d5	♞e7
11	♞d2	♞h6

Strategically, the problems are the same as in the 7 0-0 ♞c6 line, but because White has not castled and his bishop is on h4, the solutions will have to be quite different.

A very important feature of the Gligorić Variation is that is has been analysed far less extensively than 7 0-0. Opening theory is not an obstacle if you wish to play this line, yet neither is it a support.

Averbakh Variation

5	♗e2	0-0

6	♗g5 *(D)*	

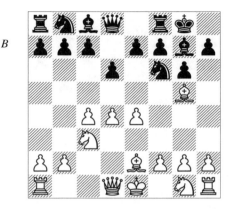

This variation was developed in the 1950s. It has always occupied a modest but not unimportant place in the King's Indian arsenal.

Just like in the Sämisch Variation, White keeps open the possibility of an attack on the kingside with moves like g4 and h4. Yet at the same time he reserves the f3-square for his knight so that he will also be able to play 'simply' with ♞f3 and 0-0.

Black faces a dilemma: should he tolerate White's bishop on g5 or should he chase it away with ...h6? He also has to make up his mind about which pawn-formation to choose in the centre.

At first a ...c5 formation was the most popular option, either by playing **6...c5** immediately or preceded by **6...h6**.

In recent years, attention has shifted to several ways of implementing the other standard plan: ...e5. In this case the immediate 6...e5?? is a bad blunder, losing to 7 dxe5 dxe5 8 ♕xd8 ♖xd8 9 ♞d5 (this line features prominently in several collections of opening traps), but both **6...♞bd7** and **6...♞a6** are useful moves, preparing this central advance.

5 ♗e2 0-0 6 ♗g5 c5

6	...	c5
7	d5 *(D)*	

This is the only ...c5 variation which I have decided not to move to the Benoni chapter. It is so generally known as belonging to the King's

Indian Defence that a breach of tradition is uncalled for.

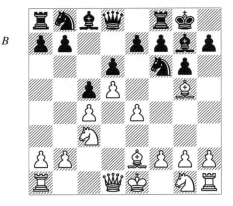

Black again faces a choice.

In the very first years of the Averbakh Variation, **7...a6** 8 a4 **Wa5** was the usual recipe for obtaining counterplay. Black intends to meet **9 Wd2** with the typical pawn sacrifice 9...b5! 10 cxb5 axb5 11 ♗xb5 ♗a6, obtaining a strong initiative against White's now slightly weakened pawn-formation on the queenside. But then the Soviet grandmaster Yuri Averbakh showed that **9 ♗d2** is much stronger than 9 Wd2 and that in fact Black's queen is rather misplaced on a5 after this move; e.g., 9...e6 10 ♘f3 exd5 11 exd5 and Black is not getting any counterplay at all.

This led to the emergence of **7...e6** *(D)* as the new main line.

But when after 8 **Wd2** exd5 here too recapturing on d5 with the e-pawn – 9 exd5 rather

than the traditional 9 cxd5 – turned out to leave Black with a slightly passive (if solid) position, the true King's Indian aficionado began to feel uneasy and started looking for other ways to deal with the Averbakh Variation. It is precisely this type of middlegame, by the way, that established the Averbakh's reputation as a line that does not allow Black to demonstrate his normal King's Indian aggression.

It is in this light that the pawn sacrifice **7...b5** 8 cxb5 a6 has to be judged. This is about the sharpest way of meeting the Averbakh that can be imagined, but although theory does not deny the latent dangers lying in store for White, it seriously doubts the correctness of this line. It is a variation 'for experts only'.

In the end it was really **7...h6**, intending to improve subtly on 7...e6, which carried the day. If White retreats his bishop to e3, Black will steer toward the same pawn-formation that we have seen in the 7...e6 variation with a small but vitally important difference: after **8 ♗e3** e6 9 **Wd2** exd5 10 exd5 ♔h7 there is no longer a white bishop on g5 to put pressure on Black's position. This tiny difference is enough to make theory (but not every King's Indian aficionado!) regard this line as satisfactory for Black. For this reason **8 ♗f4** has come to be looked upon as White's best move. This seems to prevent 8...e6 but strangely enough it is precisely this move which has become the main line: 8...e6! 9 dxe6 ♗xe6 10 ♗xd6 ♖e8 *(D)*.

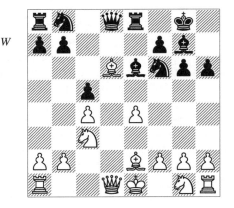

Black's lead in development gives him that typical King's Indian sort of compensation for the pawn, which seems almost invisible at first but very soon turns out to force White to play with great precision. This complicated position is one of the most theoretically critical of the entire Averbakh Variation.

5 ♗e2 0-0 6 ♗g5 h6

6   ...   h6

Black forces his opponent to choose a square for his bishop immediately.

If **7 ♗f4** Black has the clever reply 7...♘c6 8 d5 e5!. This holds little promise for White.

This makes **7 ♗e3** the main line, when Black has two options. First, he can play 7...c5, which after 8 d5 leads to a position that also arises from the 6...c5 variation (6...c5 7 d5 h6 8 ♗e3) and which we have seen to be satisfactory for Black. White may try to improve on this transposition by playing 8 e5 or 8 dxc5.

But 6...h6 can also be interpreted as a preparation for ...e5. In this case, 7 ♗e3 e5 8 d5 *(D)* brings about a second type of middlegame by which the Averbakh Variation is characterized.

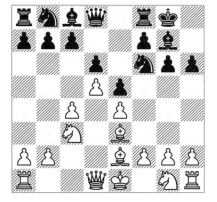

White's plan is to take the initiative on the kingside with g4 and/or h4. Black will try to counterattack on the queenside, using manoeuvres like ...♘bd7-c5, ...c6 and ...a5 or ...b5, yet it is vital that he does not remain entirely passive on the kingside either, because if White manages to seduce his opponent into answering h4-h5 with ...g5, chances are that it will be *White* who gets a free hand on the queenside. After all, he is the one with the natural space advantage on that wing.

So Black will have to perform a balancing act between being aggressive on the queenside and keeping open the possibility of lashing out on the kingside with ...f5. In this context, however, the move ...h6 began to be seen as a slight weakening of Black's chances. In due time attention shifted again, this time to Black's other ways of preparing ...e5: 6...♘bd7 and 6...♘a6.

5 ♗e2 0-0 6 ♗g5 ♘bd7

6   ...   ♘bd7

Black wants to play ...e5 without having to weaken his kingside first by playing ...h6.

7	♕d2	e5
8	d5	♘c5
9	f3	a5 *(D)*

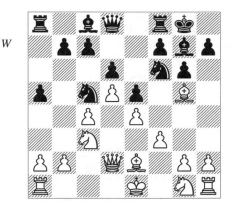

This is the key position. The question is: should White lash out with **10 h4** or should he try to suppress Black's queenside counterplay (...c6) with **10 0-0-0** first?

5 ♗e2 0-0 6 ♗g5 ♘a6

6   ...   ♘a6 *(D)*

This way of developing the knight was a godsend to players struggling with the older lines in the 1990s. It is now one of the most important lines of the Averbakh Variation.

6...♘a6 has the advantage over 6...♘bd7 in that it enables Black, after **7 ♕d2** e5 8 d5, to create immediate counterplay on the queenside

with 8...c6, because after 9 dxc6 bxc6 Black's pawn on d6 is now protected.

On the other hand, **7 f4** is stronger than after 6...♘bd7, because Black cannot reply 7...e5 in this case (7...e5?? 8 dxe5 dxe5 9 ♕xd8 ♖xd8 10 fxe5 and White is winning). Critical moves are **7...♕e8**, preparing 8...e5, and the unorthodox **7...c6** 8 ♘f3 ♘c7, with ideas including ...♘e6, ...♗g4 or sometimes even ...d5 or ...b5.

Fianchetto King's Indian

3   g3 *(D)*

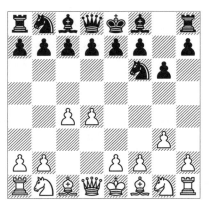

White refuses to be tempted into playing a quick e4. He is satisfied with what he has achieved (pawns on d4 and c4) and gives priority to developing his pieces without offering Black new targets for counterplay.

Developing the bishop on g2 fits well into this strategy. As long as the h1-a8 diagonal remains unblocked, the bishop will cover some vital squares in the centre and put pressure on Black's queenside. It also supports a later e4 (for this remains a move to be reckoned with) in a very natural manner.

A major difference between this and the 3 ♘c3/4 e4 scheme is that by playing 3 g3 White abandons any ideas of a swift kingside attack. Moves like h4 or g4 are not to be expected in this line. White concentrates on keeping Black's counterplay in check and maintains a flexible pawn-structure.

It should come as no surprise that the g3 system has always been particularly popular with those players who have a keen sense of positional play and a good technique in exploiting tiny advantages.

3   ...   ♗g7

With White unable to respond with 4 e4, Black has the option of playing **3...c6**, followed by ...d5, creating a mixture of Slav and Grünfeld motifs. This is a sound, but essentially non-King's Indian strategy and will be dealt with in the chapter on the Grünfeld.

4   ♗g2   0-0

By playing this move, Black lays his cards on the table: he wants to play a King's Indian Defence. **4...d5** is a Grünfeld.

5   ♘c3   d6
6   ♘f3 *(D)*

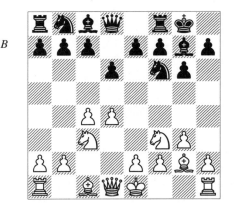

This is the starting point of all the important g3 variations.

A first difference from the 3 ♘c3 lines becomes visible: Black cannot play 6...e5 without any preparation since after 7 dxe5 dxe5 8 ♕xd8 ♖xd8 9 ♘xe5 he has simply dropped a pawn.

The classical move to prepare the advance ...e5 is **6...♘bd7**.

The more provocative **6...♘c6** also prepares ...e5, but this move also offers some completely different prospects.

6...c5 will transpose to a Benoni if White replies 7 d5 (see page 141), but if White plays 7 0-0 we remain in King's Indian territory. This is the **Yugoslav Variation**.

Finally, the flexible move **6...c6** also deserves a mention.

6...♘bd7

	6	...	♘bd7
	7	0-0	e5

This is Black's oldest reply to the g3 system. Over the last three quarters of a century, many alternatives have made their mark, but the wealth of resources offered by this classical strategy has not dried up in the least. It remains one of Black's most popular and most dynamic options.

8 e4 (D)

With this move, White brings about a key position.

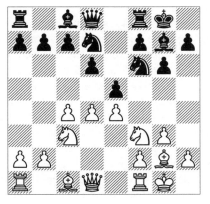

There is not really a lot of difference between this and the starting position of the Classical Variation with 7...♘bd7 (see page 105), only that White's bishop has been moved from e2 to g2. But eighty years of practical experience and intensive theoretical research have blown up this tiny difference to enormous proportions.

A first comparison between the two lines seems to favour the Classical Variation. Both the d5 and the dxe5 plans lose strength with a bishop on g2 because in the resulting rigid pawn-structure, this piece will no longer bring pressure to bear on he enemy queenside.

But the great advantage of the g3 system is that e4 is well-protected, which makes it difficult for Black to put pressure on White's centre pawns and this rules out some of the options Black used to good effect in the Classical Variation. Only by exchanging pawns on d4 at some point will he be able to complete his development. This does not mean that Black has no choice. It may make a great deal of difference *when* Black plays ...exd4 and even the mere threat of taking on d4 may be enough to determine the course of the opening.

Black's simplest option is to take on d4 straightaway and to develop some of his pieces to active posts; e.g., **8...exd4 9 ♘xd4 ♖e8 10 h3 ♘c5 11 ♖e1 c6** (D).

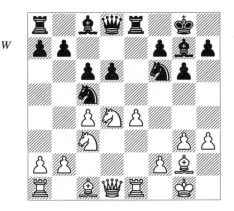

This is the classical treatment of the 6...♘bd7 variation. Black has less space, but his position has no weaknesses, his pieces are well-positioned and he has the prospect of continuing ...a5-a4 followed by ...♕a5. The manoeuvre ...♘fd7-e5 might also come in handy. White will have to be patient and careful. A good plan is to play ♖b1, b3 and a3 followed by b4, to chase away Black's knight and gain space on the queenside.

8...c6 *(D)* is a flexible alternative.

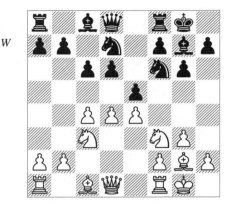

White then has a large number of sound moves; e.g., 9 ♖e1, 9 b3 and 9 ♗e3, but **9 h3**, preparing to play ♗e3 without being bothered by ...♘g4, has always been the most popular choice. Now the consequences of **9...exd4** are similar to 8...exd4, but maintaining the tension (e.g. **9...♕a5**) or even intensifying it by playing **9...♕b6** are no less interesting options. The latter move in particular presents White with a difficult decision, which decades of practical experience have failed to solve. What is he to do? Black is threatening to play 10...exd4 11 ♘xd4 ♘xe4 and the 'natural' reply 10 ♗e3 does not work because it leaves the pawn on b2 hanging. Taking on e5 is decidedly unattractive and **10 d5**, though not a bad move, does little to challenge the validity of 9...♕b6. After 10...♘c5 11 ♖e1 cxd5 12 cxd5 ♗d7 the queen is well-placed on b6.

In fact, the position after 9...♕b6 is a major parting of the ways. White can either preserve the tension with **10 ♖e1** or he can attempt a out-right refutation of Black's provocative queen move by means of the violent **10 c5** dxc5 11 dxe5, which, after 11...♘e8, will lead to a highly complicated position.

6...♘c6

6	...	♘c6

We have already seen this move as a reliable way of meeting the Sämisch Variation (see page 100). In this case Black intends to meet **7 d5** not

with 7...♘e5, but with 7...♘a5, attacking the pawn on c4.

Instead, White can simply continue his development:

7	0-0 *(D)*

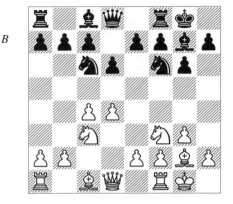

Black now has several options, all with their own specific idea.

With **7...e5** Black opts for the same classical strategy as 6...♘bd7, albeit in a more forceful manner.

7...a6 is more subtle. Black wants to play 8...♖b8 and 9...b5. This is the **Panno Variation**, one of Black's most popular options for more than half a century.

Other (more or less) respectable variations are 7...♗g4 and 7...♗f5, but these have never acquired the same following as the two main lines. **7...♗g4** is intended to put pressure on d4 with 8...♘d7, but since 8 d5 ♘a5 (after 8...♗xf3 9 exf3, White's play on the e-file is more important than the apparent weakening of his pawns) 9 ♘d2 produces the same pawn-formation as in the Panno Variation with the chances of ...♗g4 turning out less useful than ...a6 rather high, 7...♗g4 has never gained wide acceptance.

7...♗f5 is a way of seeking control over the important e4-square, but it is a highly provocative move, offering White a choice of attractive replies. Still, this move is played fairly often, perhaps *because* it is a rare opportunity for seriously provoking White in the otherwise very solid g3 system. After 8 d5 ♘a5 White can continue solidly enough with 9 ♘d2, but 9 ♘d4 is very tempting, intending to meet 9...♘xc4?!

(Black normally plays 9...♗d7) with 10 ♘xf5 gxf5 11 ♕b3. Another important option is 8 ♘e1, followed by 9 e4.

6...♘c6 7 0-0 e5

7   ...   e5 (D)

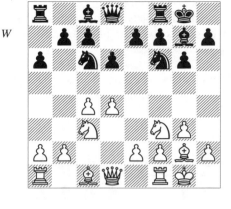

This is an attempt to bring about the well-known type of middlegame with a closed centre which we have already seen in several King's Indian variations, most notably in the Classical Variation.

In fact it is quite a forcing move since **8 dxe5** does not hold out any great promise for White even though the fact that he has omitted e4 means that taking on e5 does not involve the usual long-term positional risk of a 'hole' on d4. Therefore the ambitious player finds himself more or less forced to play **8 d5**, falling in with Black's plan. The critical position arises after 8...♘e7 9 e4 ♘e8 (or 9...♘d7). With his bishop on g2, White's prospects of making inroads on the queenside are reduced, but his defences on the kingside are strengthened. White can either play the aggressive 10 b4 or the prophylactic 10 ♘e1 f5 11 ♘d3, taking control of the important squares e4 and f4.

Panno Variation

7   ...   a6 (D)

This move seems less direct and less aggressive than 7...e5, but it is at least as ambitious and much more subtle.

Black wants to take the initiative on the queenside with 8...♖b8 and 9...b5, keeping ...e5 in reserve for future operations.

White has plenty of ways to meet this daring plan, but of course theory has always focused on the more aggressive ones.

8   d5

This is the traditional main line.

If White prefers a simple developing move instead, such as **8 b3**, Black will execute his plan undisturbed. After 8...♖b8 9 ♗b2 b5 10 cxb5 axb5 11 ♖c1 b4 12 ♘b1 ♘a7 chances are even. Far from being misplaced on a7, Black's knight is heading for a bright future on the active square b5.

The most important alternative to 8 d5 is a plan based on playing e4. Unfortunately for White, the immediate **8 e4** runs into 8...♗g4 9 ♗e3 ♘d7, intending 10...e5 11 d5 ♘d4 and putting considerable pressure on d4. White has to make a preparatory move: **8 h3** (D).

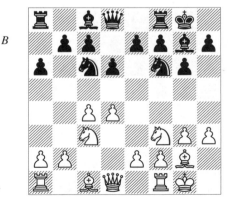

The position which then arises after 8...♖b8 9 e4 b5 contains many sharp variations, based on 10 e5 or 10 cxb5 axb5 11 e5, that have been investigated very deeply.

8   ...   ♘a5

By thus attacking the pawn on c4, Black puts his finger on the Achilles' Heel of the g3 system.

9   ♘d2   c5 *(D)*

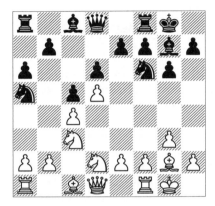

Safeguarding the knight on a5 against White's b4 advance. Black's plan remains unchanged: he wants to play ...♖b8 and ...b5. White's main line now is to anticipate this manoeuvre by preparing to play b3.

10   ♕c2

The immediate 10 b3?? is a blunder losing a pawn to 10...♘xd5.

10   ...   ♖b8
11   b3   b5
12   ♗b2 *(D)*

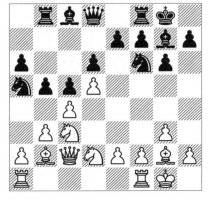

This position is the starting point for some subtle and deeply-analysed variations. Black can either take a natural step forward in the centre by playing **12...e6** or **12...e5** or he can play the more aggressive **12...bxc4** 13 bxc4 ♗h6. At first sight, Black's last move looks rather primitive but on closer inspection it turns out to contain quite a bit of poison. In the first place, White cannot parry the threat of 14...♗xd2 by the seemingly natural move **14 e3** because this runs into 14...♗f5!, when both 15 e4 ♗xd2 and 15 ♘ce4 ♘xe4 16 ♗xe4 ♗xe4 17 ♘xe4 ♘xc4! cost White a pawn. Therefore White must either take a (temporary) step backwards with **14 ♘cb1** or make a double-edged step forward by **14 f4**. The latter move in particular leads to a fierce battle (14...e5!) demanding great accuracy and cold-bloodedness (*and* some theoretical knowledge!) from both players.

Yugoslav Variation

6   ...   c5 *(D)*

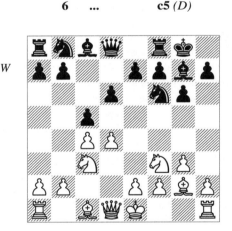

As we have seen, Black can use this move as an invitation to transpose to the Benoni (7 d5; see page 141) in every line of the King's Indian Defence. Independent lines arise only if White does not accept this invitation.

7   0-0   ♘c6

Increasing the pressure and inviting White, even more pressingly than before, to play **8 d5**. After 8...♘a5 9 ♘d2 a6 this would lead, perhaps somewhat surprisingly, to a position we have just seen as 'belonging' to the Panno Variation.

In fact 6...c5 can be said to be an alternative route toward this position. The choice between 6...c5 and 6...♘c6 will depend on which of the 'side effects' Black prefers. Choosing 6...♘c6 7 0-0 a6 means Black is not overly worried about White's alternatives to 8 d5. Choosing 6...c5 implies a readiness to play both the Benoni (7 d5) and the following more open position:

8 dxc5 dxc5 (D)

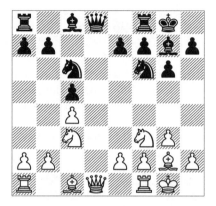

This variation had its heyday during the 1950s and 1960s but half a century later it is still popular and highly relevant for the entire g3 system. As so often in positions with a symmetrical pawn-formation, the rule of thumb is that if it is your move you have the advantage. The second rule is that once you have really fallen into a passive position, you will be condemned to a long and gruelling defence.

Nevertheless the choice between 8 d5 and 8 dxc5 is, to some extent at least, one of personal preference. One player may feel attracted by the long-term advantage of having more space, while the other may prefer the short-term advantage of having the initiative.

The first target that presents itself for using that initiative is the unprotected pawn on c5. In fact, the position after **9 ♗e3** is an excellent illustration of the general character of the entire variation. Both players will have to make subtle positional assessments, yet they also have to do some accurate calculating work. It is easy to see that the 'ideal' way of protecting c5, **9...b6?**, loses material to 10 ♘e5, but it is far more difficult to find an antidote to **9...♕a5**. The best

move theory has come up with is the modest 10 ♗d2. You cannot say 11 ♘d5 is actually a threat in this position but since it does prevent some of Black's natural moves (10...♖d8? for instance) it has become fairly normal to reply 10...♕d8, confronting White with the question if his extra move ♗d2 (as compared to the diagram above) has any real value. By playing 11 ♕c1 followed by 12 ♗h6 White can try to answer this question in the affirmative. Instead of protecting his pawn on c5, Black may want to counterattack against White's c4-pawn: **9...♗e6**. In that case it is up to White either to maintain the tension by 10 ♕a4 or to simplify with, e.g., 10 ♗xc5 ♕a5 11 ♗a3 ♗xc4.

9 ♗f4 is also a respectable move. White puts his queen's bishop on a good square without hurrying to create any direct threats.

6...c6

6 ... c6 (D)

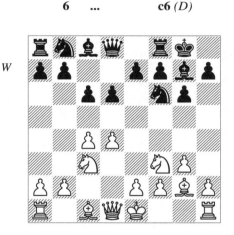

This is a move that fits into several plans.

7 0-0 ♕a5 (D)

This is the oldest and best accepted by theory of Black's many possibilities in this position.

7...a6 and 8...b5, although a normal enough plan in the King's Indian Defence, is not often played here, because White's bishop is well-nigh ideally posted on g2 for an immediate counterattack in the centre: 8 e4 b5 9 e5.

7...♗f5 is a much more common alternative and far less provocative and risky than when combined with 6...♘c6 (instead of 6...c6).

However, it is also slightly less aggressive, since a pawn on c6 is less influential in the centre than a knight on that square. 8 ♘e1 is a principled reply, but there are many players who prefer a calm development of their queenside with 8 b3 ♘e4 9 ♗b2.

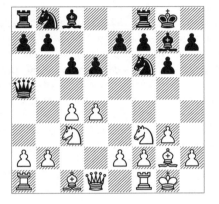

7...♕a5 is a move of an entirely different calibre, opening up the possibility of ...♕h5, which in turn enables Black to play ...♗h3 or ...♗g4. This is a fairly aggressive strategy.

        8   h3 *(D)*

The most cautious reply.

8 e4 has also been played, intending to meet 8...♕h5 with 9 e5, when a transition to an endgame after 9...dxe5 10 ♘xe5 ♕xd1 11 ♖xd1 is probably not very attractive to one who has just played ...♕a5-h5 in order to create attacking chances against White's king. 8...♗g4 and 8...e5 are more in keeping with such a view. The latter move transposes (after 9 h3) to a position that is also reached via 8 h3 e5 9 e4 and will be discussed below.

The positive side of 8 h3 is that it prevents Black from playing **8...♕h5?**, which would now run into 9 ♘g5!, followed by 10 ♗f3, trapping the queen.

The negative side is that it is a somewhat slow move, encouraging moves like **8...♗e6**, attacking c4. The critical test of this line is 9 ♕d3 ♕a6 10 b3 d5. Will Black be able to

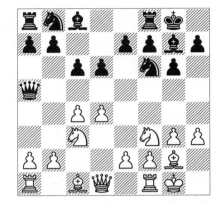

sustain the pressure against White's central formation or does Black's aggression not really bother White? The immediate **8...♕a6** has also been tried.

8...e5 *(D)* is a more classical approach.

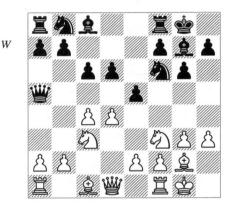

After 9 e4 Black has a direct transposition to the 6...♘bd7 variation by 9...♘bd7, but 9...exd4 10 ♘xd4 ♕c5 is an interesting alternative, the point being that 11 b3 (the natural way to protect c4) runs into 11...♘xe4!. It is true that White can simply play 11 ♘b3 ♕xc4 12 ♕xd6, exchanging c4 for d6, but whether this is actually a good idea is a moot point. White has solved his own problems, but by doing so he has also solved his opponent's problems for him.

Grünfeld Defence

1	d4	♘f6
2	c4	g6

As we have seen in the previous chapter, **3 ♘c3** is the first move to consider in this position, with **3 g3** (or **3 ♘f3 ♗g7 4 g3**) being the most important alternative.

A third move to have found its niche in opening theory is **3 f3**.

We shall now look at these moves not from a King's Indian, but from a Grünfeld perspective: before White is able to play e4, Black will counterattack in the centre with ...d5.

Timing is very important in this strategy. As an illustration of what Black should *not* do, let us first look at **3 ♘f3**. If Black wants to play a Grünfeld against this move, he is well-advised to play 3...♗g7 first and only throw in 4...d5 *after* White has played either 4 ♘c3 or 4 g3 (in the latter case Black can even wait a little longer; e.g., 4 g3 0-0 5 ♗g2 d5). Of course it is not illegal to play 3...d5?! at once, but this move allows the opponent an unnecessarily large freedom of choice in determining his reaction. After 4 cxd5 ♘xd5 5 e4 ♘b6 6 h3 (preventing the pin 6...♗g4) 6...♗g7 7 ♘c3 White's position is considerably more comfortable than in a 'regular' Grünfeld.

3 ♘c3

3	♘c3	d5 *(D)*

With this move Black gives the game a character which is totally different from the King's Indian Defence. One could even say that he is actually playing a Queen's Gambit Deferred, albeit a sharper version of it, focusing entirely on active piece-play and creating and utilizing as many open files and diagonals as possible. In most variations Black will play an early ...c5, giving his g7-bishop ample scope to join in the battle.

The opening is named after Ernst Grünfeld, who braved the scepticism of a totally classically

oriented chess world in the 1920s. His courage has since been richly rewarded, for many of the greatest chess-players after him have taken up his opening; e.g., world champions Botvinnik, Smyslov, Fischer and Kasparov. All of them have contributed towards the theoretical development of the Grünfeld Defence and most importantly they have all demonstrated the viability of its main strategic aim: the battle over the centre.

White has a choice of reacting ambitiously or cautiously. The most principled and therefore the most ambitious variation at his disposal is **4 cxd5**, the **Exchange Variation**.

The variations **4 ♗g5** and **4 ♗f4** are more cautious, yet not without venom. Both of these moves introduce concrete threats against d5 and c7, respectively.

4 ♘f3 is White's most neutral move. After the logical 4...♗g7 White then has several options, some of them cautious, one extremely ambitious.

Exchange Variation

4	cxd5	♘xd5
5	e4	♘xc3
6	bxc3	♗g7 *(D)*

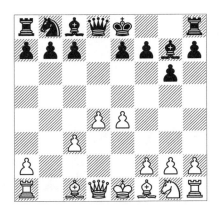

This is one of the fundamental positions of the Grünfeld. After more than eighty years of theoretical discussion, it is still not clear whether White's broad pawn-centre is strong or weak, unless we accept the philosophical conclusion that it is both.

On the one hand, White's centre pawns are a strong enough force that they can eventually suffocate the opponent, while on the other hand they do indeed provide Black with a beautiful target for a counterattack, starting with ...c5. It is true that the crucial link in White's pawn-formation, the pawn on d4, is well-protected by the pawn on c3, but it is also precisely this formation which lends a certain rigidity to White's position. Because the pawn on c3 is itself not protected, White will be unable to react to ...c5 with either d5 or dxc5, moves which would otherwise be very natural indeed. As a rule, White is thus condemned to defend his pawn on d4. Whether this is a good or a bad thing is entirely dependent on the specific circumstances.

So, the answer to the fundamental question remains open. This brings us to a much more important, and above all, a more practical question: who will make the most of his chances?

The main lines start with 7 ♘f3 and 7 ♗c4.

7 ♗a3 is also possible, but theory has never held this move in high regard, because it does not achieve what it pretends to achieve: to stop ...c5. With moves like ...♘d7 and ...b6, Black will have no trouble achieving this advance. Once he does, the positioning of the bishop on a3 is moot.

4 cxd5 ♘xd5 5 e4 ♘xc3 6 bxc3 ♗g7 7 ♘f3

7 ♘f3

This seemingly uncomplicated developing move had a bad reputation for over half a century until it was fully rehabilitated in the early 1980s thanks in part to the successes of Garry Kasparov with several of its variations. Today it is one of the most dangerous and thoroughly analysed variations of the entire Grünfeld.

7 ... c5 (D)

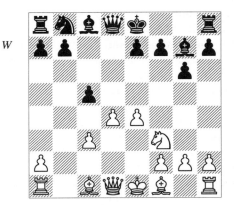

Now there are two main lines, the sound and logical move **8 ♗e3** and the profound **8 ♖b1**. The latter move in particular has been the subject of incredibly deep analysis.

The reason why 7 ♘f3 was out of grace for so long is that before the late 1970s, theory did not look deeper into the position than taking simple developing moves like **8 ♗e2** for granted. This causes problems with the defence of d4: after 8 ♗e2 ♘c6 9 ♗e3 ♗g4 White is practically forced to play 10 e5, which hands Black the d5-square on a plate and reduces the latent dynamics in White's position considerably.

It is exactly this sort of concession that White should try to avoid in the Exchange Variation. At the very least he should make the opponent pay a high price for it, not give it away for free.

7 ♘f3 c5 8 ♗e3

8 ♗e3 (D)

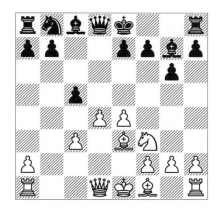

White anticipates the expected wave of attack against d4, which we have just seen bursting out over 8 ♗e2. Not only does he provide d4 with some extra cover beforehand, but he also prepares ♖c1, protecting c3 and thus enabling White to play d5.

Still, anyone wanting to play this line will have to agree to the simplification of the position that becomes unavoidable after Black's most natural reply:

8 ... ♛a5

This is not the only move – there is also **8...♗g4**, for instance – but it is a critical test of 8 ♗e3 and should be considered very carefully.

9 ♛d2 ♘c6
10 ♖c1 (D)

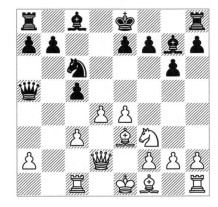

Threatening 11 d5, which would give White the initiative.

10 ... cxd4
11 cxd4 ♛xd2+

12 ♔xd2 0-0 (D)

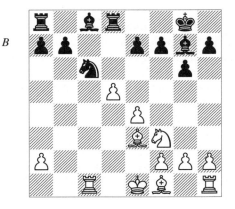

Now it is Black's turn to threaten to take the initiative by either 13...♖d8 or 13...f5.

13 d5

Another option is to play **13 ♗b5**, yet practice has shown that Black can simply give up the pawn and lash out with 13...f5 regardless. After 14 exf5 ♗xf5 15 ♗xc6 bxc6 16 ♖xc6 ♖ab8 Black has more than sufficient compensation for the pawn thanks to the insecure position of the white king.

13 ... ♖d8

Wringing as many concessions as he can from his opponent before finally moving the knight. Black now threatens both 14...e6 and 14...f5.

14 ♔e1 (D)

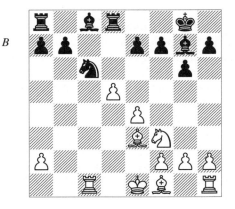

The theoretical status of this 'middlegame without queens' is much disputed. Has Black's initiative been brought to a halt or has it not? Can White finally start reaping the benefits of his spatial advantage?

Not only has White had to give up castling, but he has also been forced to move his king back to e1. Nevertheless, on the whole his strategy has proved justified. Those pieces that *have* been developed are well-positioned and the advance d5 is a sound method of putting pressure on Black's position.

Both the cautious **14...♞b4** and the more adventurous **14...♞a5** have been tried here with acceptable results, but **14...♞e5** has been shown to make it too easy for White to set his central pawns in motion.

7 ♞f3 c5 8 ♜b1

8   ♜b1 (D)

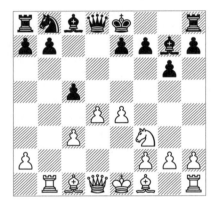

This subtle rook move leads us right into the heart of the modern-day Grünfeld. It is this variation, more than any other, which has given the opening a whole new face after 1980. Everybody who wants to play the Grünfeld has to have an answer – and a very good one – to *this* variation.

White is anticipating the ...♞c6 and ...♝g4 plan, but he does so in a less direct, and an apparently less aggressive, way than 8 ♝e3. For what is really the point of 8 ♜b1? It is easy enough to notice that ...♝g4 loses some of its attractions when a pawn on b7 is left behind unprotected, but what could possibly be the problem with **8...♞c6**?

The answer is as self-evident as it is unexpected. White plays the only move that *can* be a problem for ...♞c6, namely 9 d5!. Since there is no longer a rook on a1, White is sacrificing *only* a pawn (and not an exchange) after 9...♝xc3+ 10 ♝d2, and because Black is forced to exchange his powerful bishop, making his kingside vulnerable to attack, it turns out that White obtains excellent compensation after 10...♝xd2+ 11 ♛xd2, no matter to which square Black moves his knight.

The result of this is that Black must find a new plan, and this is what Grünfeld devotees have done with great enthusiasm ever since the 8 ♜b1 bomb exploded. This has resulted in two main lines, both starting from the next diagram.

8   ...   0-0
9   ♝e2 (D)

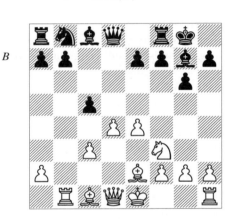

To begin with, notwithstanding the objections outlined above, the natural move **9...♞c6** was explored in great depth. This was the main line during the mid-1980s.

Then, in the last decade of the 20th century, attention shifted to **9...cxd4** 10 cxd4 ♛a5+. Black challenges his opponent to play 11 ♝d2, a particularly unclear pawn sacrifice. This is now seen by many as the main line of the entire Grünfeld Defence.

In the early days, the immediate **9...♛a5** was sometimes played, but when it became clear that a similar pawn sacrifice, 10 0-0, makes life much harder for Black than in the 9...cxd4 variation, this was largely abandoned. In case of 10...♛xa2 11 ♝g5 White has a full extra tempo as compared to 9...cxd4 10 cxd4 ♕a5+ 11 ♗d2 ♕xa2 12 0-0 followed by 13 ♗g5, while after 10...♕xc3 both 11 d5 and 11 ♗d2 ♕a3 12 ♕c2 look very promising for White indeed.

9...b6 is another early variation, but one which – unlike 9...♕a5 – has remained popular, if only moderately so. It is in fact the preferred choice of players who do not like long and forcing variations. Black simply accepts the fact that White has been able to consolidate his pawn-centre and moves on to the middlegame.

8 ♖b1 0-0 9 ♗e2 ♘c6

9   ...   ♘c6 (D)

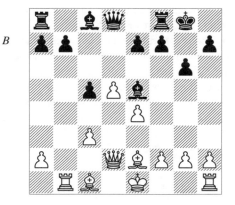

This is more accurate than 8...♘c6, which I have discussed above, because Black's 'extra move' 8...0-0 is likely to be more useful than White's 9 ♗e2.

10   d5   ♘e5

Accepting the sacrifice is rarely done and can only be recommended to those who have truly great confidence, not only in their position but also in themselves. After **10...♗xc3+ 11 ♗d2 ♗xd2+ 12 ♕xd2 ♘a5 13 h4!** Black will have to play with great accuracy to avoid going down in a kingside attack.

11   ♘xe5   ♗xe5
12   ♕d2 (D)

This is where the sharp and deeply analysed variations begin, which scare off some, and fascinate others.

12 ♕d2 may appear strange, but in this variation all theoretical moves have a profound

meaning. At first sight a middle-class move like **12 ♕c2** strikes one as a more plausible way of protecting c3, yet after 12...♕c7 13 h3 e6 it soon transpires that White's position lacks many of the dynamic possibilities which 12 ♕d2 offers.

Theoretical discussion of this line first concentrated on **12...e6** 13 f4, with the principled follow-up 13...♗g7 14 c4. Black tried just about everything to blow a hole in White's massive pawn-centre. Variations like 14...exd5 15 cxd5 ♗d4 16 ♗b2 and now either 16...♕b6 or 16...♕h4+ 17 g3 ♕e7 (intending to meet 18 ♗xd4 with 18...♕xe4) have been played in sometimes truly brilliant games. Eventually though, theory took a different route. The unconventional 13...♗c7 prevents White from supporting his stronghold on d5 with 14 c4?? because of 14...♗a5. All of a sudden, after 14 0-0 exd5 15 exd5, it is a fairly static position we are looking at. How should it be evaluated? Will White be able to take advantage of the absence of the Grünfeld bishop from g7 or will he not?

Also the slightly more cautious move **12...b6** has come to the fore. Black is waiting for 13 f4 ♗g7 14 0-0 before he opens the attack on White's pawn-centre with 14...e6, when most players choose between 15 dxe6 and 15 ♗c4.

Anyone who wishes to play this line, with either colour, will have to make a thorough study of these variations, which are not only difficult strategically, but are drenched in tactics as well.

8 ♖b1 0-0 9 ♗e2 cxd4

9	...	cxd4
10	cxd4	♕a5+
11	♗d2	

It took a long time for the chess world to realize that this pawn sacrifice is more than just an empty macho gesture. The initial response to 10...♕a5+ had been **11 ♕d2 ♕xd2+ 12 ♗xd2**, but by 1990 it had become clear that Black is doing well here, especially if he continues 12...b6. With this move, Black neutralizes the pressure along the b-file against his b-pawn while preparing to counterattack against e4 (13...♗b7).

11	...	♕xa2
12	0-0 *(D)*	

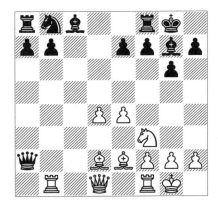

At first sight it may look almost incredible that White should have sufficient compensation for a pawn in this position, yet hundreds of games of the highest level have shown this to be the case.

Black's position has no apparent weaknesses, he has two connected passed pawns on the queenside *and* he has an extra pawn, but the pressure that is created by White's two centre pawns and his lead in development have proved to be intangible but telling factors time and time again.

In this focal point of modern opening theory, new ideas are being introduced, tried and discarded almost continuously, a dynamic process the end of which is not yet in sight. The most important variations are probably those starting

with **12...♘d7**, **12...b6**, **12...a5** and especially **12...♗g4**.

4 cxd5 ♘xd5 5 e4 ♘xc3 6 bxc3 ♗g7 7 ♗c4

7	♗c4 *(D)*

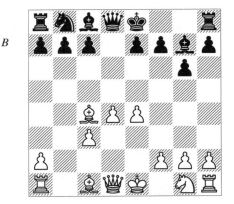

Until around 1980 this was *the* way of playing the Exchange Variation. It is still a very important line.

The point of 7 ♗c4 becomes visible after White's next move:

7	...	c5
8	♘e2	

By developing the knight to e2, White makes sure that the vital protection this piece provides for his pawn on d4 is not eliminated by ...♗g4. The knight also covers c3. Alas, there are some disadvantages as well. The first of these is shown up by Black's reply:

8	...	♘c6

Black does not need to worry about **9 d5**. Both 9...♘e5 and 9...♘a5 attack the white bishop, giving White no time to consolidate his central formation.

9	♗e3	0-0
10	0-0 *(D)*	

This is the key position for this variation. Two methods of obtaining counterplay have grown into main lines, **10...♕c7** and **10...♗g4**. Both intend to utilize the vulnerable position of the bishop on c4 to Black's advantage.

10...♕c7 was the favourite in the 1970s. Black hopes to make his opponent nervous by

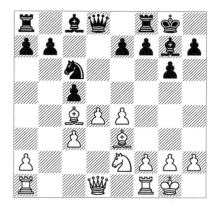

indirectly attacking the bishop on c4 (the possibility of playing 11...cxd4 12 cxd4 ♘xd4 is introduced, although this is not a real threat because by playing 13 ♗xf7+ White prevents the loss of a pawn). The real point of 10...♕c7 though, is that Black is going to play 11...♖d8, increasing the pressure on d4.

During the 1980s, attention shifted back to **10...♗g4**, which had been the main line several decades earlier. This is a more forcing move. White has to play 11 f3, whereupon Black has another aggressive move, 11...♘a5 *(D)*.

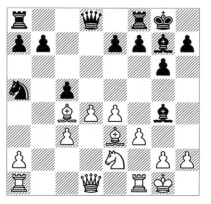

Now if the bishop drops back to d3 Black has managed to secure, after **12 ♗d3** cxd4! 13 cxd4 ♗e6, a good square for his bishop. As an immediate result he now has the unpleasant threat of 14...♘c4. White is a tempo short of a 'comfortable' way of parrying this threat and has to resort to aggressive options like the pawn sacrifice 14 ♖c1 ♗xa2 or even the exchange sacrifice 14 d5

♗xa1 15 ♕xa1. Although these are dangerous lines, with especially the latter one still hugely popular today, Black always seems to have sufficient defensive resources.

White has a major alternative in **12 ♗xf7+**. Until 1987, nobody took this acceptance of Black's pawn sacrifice (for that is what 11...♘a5 really is) seriously, but when Karpov used it to good effect in his match for the world championship against Kasparov in Seville, it became the height of fashion overnight. It was christened **Seville Variation** and analysed down to the last detail. Nevertheless, Black's position survived the onslaught and the popularity of 12 ♗xf7+ subsided. The starting position for all analysis arises after 12...♗xf7 13 fxg4 ♖xf1+ 14 ♔xf1. Black's initiative has turned out to be quite satisfactory, especially after the bold counter-thrust 14...cxd4 15 cxd4 e5 16 d5 ♘c4.

4 ♗g5

4   ♗g5 *(D)*

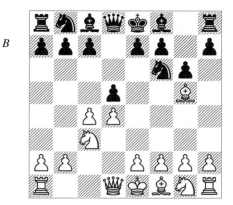

This move betrays a completely different mind-set, for strategically 4 ♗g5 is far less determined and less radical than 4 cxd5. Still, the problem confronting Black is real enough: how should the threat of 5 ♗xf6 be warded off?

4   ...   ♘e4

What White would really like to see is Black choosing either the 'easy' solution **4...dxc4**, presenting White with 5 e4 and a beautiful pawn-centre for free, or the passive option **4...c6**, which transposes to a sort of Schlechter

Variation of the Slav Defence (see page 39) with a white bishop actively placed on g5 instead of c1.

But any Grünfeld player who has a heart for his opening will probably not even consider these options. He will notice immediately that 4 ♗g5 not only poses a threat but also offers a target for a counterattack. It should come as no surprise then that 4...♘e4 is the classical reply.

And yet there is a fourth move, one that has only been noticed very recently: the ice-cold **4...♗g7** *(D)*.

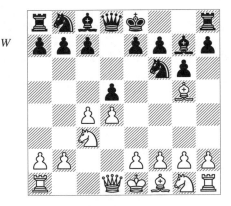

Black treats 4 ♗g5 with utter contempt, turning the variation into a gambit without so much as raising an eyebrow. After 5 ♗xf6 ♗xf6 **6 ♘xd5** he calmly retreats the bishop (6...♗g7), when he is ready to pounce on White's pawn-centre with 7...c6 or (in case of 7 e3) 7...c5. Taking on d5 with the pawn (**6 cxd5**) is more solid, but even here Black has a way of destroying White's centre and obtaining compensation for the pawn: 6...c6! and if now 7 dxc6 ♗xd4 8 cxb7 ♗xb7 Black has a substantial lead in development.

5   ♗f4 *(D)*

This retreat may look a bit confusing, but in fact the strategic idea behind 4 ♗g5 is already beginning to materialize. The threat against d5 is renewed and Black is invited to head for a pawn-formation which is similar to the Exchange Variation in so far as White does get a mass of centre pawns, but at the same time fundamentally different in that White can still play e3 instead of e4, thus giving full support to his

pawn on d4. In this way White hopes to slow things down a little bit and contain Black's counterplay.

The alternative **5 ♗h4** pursues the same idea.

In the early days of the Grünfeld White used to play the obvious move **5 ♘xe4** but this soon turned out to play into Black's hands. After 5...dxe4 and now, for instance, 6 f3 ♗g7 Black's control over the vital a1-h8 diagonal is a telling factor.

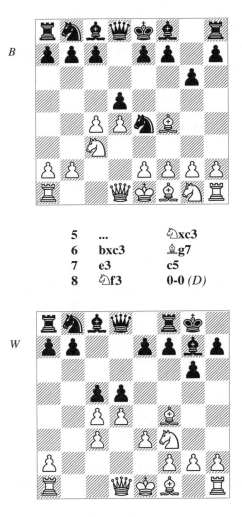

5	...	♘xc3
6	bxc3	♗g7
7	e3	c5
8	♘f3	0-0 *(D)*

This position is crucial for the 4 ♗g5 variation. White's plan to turn d4 into a fortress has succeeded, but at the price of relinquishing the pressure on Black's position that is so typical of the Exchange Variation. The whole line is tailor-made for players who prefer subtle manoeuvring to cut-throat aggression. A typical continuation is **9 cxd5** cxd4 10 cxd4 ♕xd5 11 ♗e2 ♘c6 12 0-0 ♗f5.

4 ♗f4

4 ♗f4

Just like 4 ♗g5, this has been a popular way of countering the Grünfeld ever since its inception. White combines a sound development of his pieces with controlled aggression.

4 ... ♗g7 (D)

There is not a wide variety of strategic motifs in this line, but the consequences of seemingly minimal differences in implementing them can be far-reaching. To begin with, the difference between **5 e3** and **5 ♘f3** is surprisingly large.

4 ♗f4 ♗g7 5 e3

5 e3

Strange as it may seem, this modest little move forces Black to sacrifice a pawn, or at the very least it challenges Black to do so. Of course there *is* the possibility of keeping everything protected with **5...c6**, just like 4...c6 against 4 ♗g5, but the real Grünfeld aficionado is unlikely to put a pawn on c6, whatever the circumstances.

5 ... c5

As in almost all variations of the Grünfeld, this move is the natural way of taking up the fight against White's pawn-centre, but of course

it is not only a matter of *what* to play. Accurate timing is at least as important.

For instance, in this position **5...0-0** is no less a natural move than 5...c5, intending to play this advance a little later, possibly after 6 ♘f3. Yet this move allows White to demonstrate a crucial point of his fourth move, namely 6 cxd5 ♘xd5 7 ♘xd5 ♕xd5 8 ♗xc7 *(D)*.

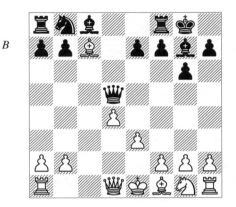

This pawn sacrifice has been hotly debated ever since it was first accepted. Black has tried several ways of taking advantage of White's now somewhat forlorn bishop on c7. Sharpest is 8...♘c6 9 ♘e2 ♗g4, yet modern theory considers this to be rather dubious. 8...♘a6 is a more solid option. Since hanging on to the extra pawn with 9 ♗g3 is risky because of 9...♗f5 threatening 10...♘b4, White has to exchange his material advantage for a positional one: 9 ♗xa6 ♕xg2 10 ♕f3 ♕xf3 11 ♘xf3 bxa6. The question then is whether the open files and diagonals fully compensate Black for the sacrifice of his queenside pawn-structure.

We now return to 5...c5 *(D)*:

6 dxc5

The great thing about the Grünfeld is that Black immediately takes over the initiative if White relaxes and starts avoiding the fight. For instance, Black would be very happy if White simply plays **6 ♘f3** in this position. Though a sound enough developing move in itself, this is just not sufficiently sharp to create any serious problems. After 6...cxd4 7 exd4 the opening skirmish is over already with Black having obtained a good position: no weaknesses and

W

the strategic prospect of putting pressure on d4.

6 dxc5 on the other hand, does put Black's opening play to the test. By opening the a1-h8 diagonal, White makes the bishop on g7 a very powerful piece, but he trusts his position to be sufficiently strong to withstand the pressure. His plan is to utilize the time that Black will need to regain the pawn on c5, to take the initiative.

6 ... ♕a5 (D)

W

This is a key position for the 4 ♗f4 system. Black does not have to worry about **7 cxd5**, because this allows 7...♘xd5!, based on 8 ♕xd5 ♗xc3+. There is in fact a forced draw in this line, a phenomenon not uncommon to sharp variations. If we take the above variation a little further with 9 bxc3 ♕xc3+ 10 ♔e2 ♕xa1, it looks like White is winning material because of 11 ♗e5. The trick is that Black then has

11...♕c1 12 ♗xh8 ♗e6! 13 ♕xb7 ♕c2+ 14 ♔f3 ♕f5+ and there is no escape from perpetual check.

'Real' theory works on the assumption that White's ambitions go further than this, and so concentrates on **7 ♕a4+** and **7 ♖c1**.

7 ♕a4+ breaks the pin against the c3-knight and protects the pawn on c5. After 7...♕xa4 8 ♘xa4 Black will need all the ingenuity he can muster if he is to find compensation for his missing pawn, but the offside position of the knight on a4 offers just enough of a target to maintain the balance. At first 8...♘e4 was thought to be the best move, intending to meet 9 f3 with 9...♗d7 10 fxe4 ♗xa4 which leads to a very murky and double-edged endgame. Later the laconic 8...0-0 also turned out to be playable and even the peremptory 8...♗d7 9 ♘c3 ♘e4!? 10 ♘xd5 ♘a6, winning one pawn back (on c5) and obtaining enough counterplay to compensate for the second.

7 ♖c1 is an attempt to keep the reins much tighter than this. Black can win his pawn back by playing **7...dxc4** 8 ♗xc4 0-0 9 ♘f3 (9 ♘e2 is an alternative that leads to sharp play, and makes use of the fact that White has not already committed this knight to f3) 9...♕xc5 (D).

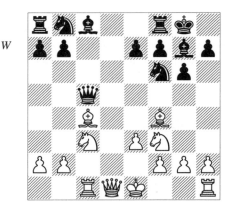

W

At first sight this position may look rather boring and devoid of tension, but this is deceptive. With all minor pieces actively developed on both sides, this line is more often than not the starting point for a fierce fight in the middlegame. Some players find this a little too simple and straightforward a solution, however, and prefer **7...②e4**. This leads to a position which is strategically more complex after 8 cxd5 ②xc3 9 ♕d2! ♕xa2 10 bxc3 ♕a5 (or 10...♕xd2+). It all depends on whether White's pawn on d5 will prove to be a strength, keeping Black's position under pressure, or a weakness, having given up control over the central squares e5 and c5.

4 ♗f4 ♗g7 5 ②f3

> 5   ②f3

The consequences of this move are subtly but substantially different from those of 5 e3.

> 5   ...   0-0 *(D)*

Here too, **5...c5** is sometimes played, but the difference from the variation 5 e3 c5 is that after 6 dxc5 ♕a5 7 cxd5 ②xd5 8 ♕xd5 ♗xc3+ White now has 9 ♗d2!, giving him a comfortable initiative if Black responds with the obvious 9...♗xd2+ 10 ♕xd2 ♕xc5 11 ♖c1. In an attempt to keep this variation alive, 9...♗e6!? 10 ♕xb7 ♗xd2+ 11 ②xd2 0-0 is sometimes played. Black is two pawns down and there is a rook *en prise* as well, but the point is that 12 ♕xa8?! ♖d8 13 ♖d1? loses the queen after 13...♗d5. Whether Black has sufficient compensation after the stronger 12 b4 is another question.

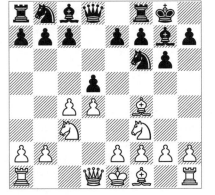

A second important difference from the 5 e3 variation is that accepting the pawn sacrifice with **6 cxd5 ②xd5 7 ②xd5 ♕xd5 8 ♗xc7** is now very risky because of 8...②c6 9 e3 ♗f5 with the fearsome threat of 10...②b4. Now that

his knight is already on f3, White is not in a position to consolidate his queenside by means of the manoeuvre ②e2-c3.

Instead White has two main lines. He can either head for a transposition to the 5 e3 variation with **6 e3** (6...c5 7 dxc5 ♕a5 8 ♖c1 dxc4 9 ♗xc4 ♕xc5) or he can play **6 ♖c1**. The latter move is intended to discourage Black from playing 6...c5 7 dxc5 ♕a5?, for in this case after 8 cxd5 there are no conjuring tricks based on 8...②xd5. A drawback of 6 ♖c1 is that it does nothing towards the development of White's kingside. This makes the 'easy' solutions 6...c6 and especially 6...dxc4, which Black has thus far scorned, relatively more attractive than before.

4 ②f3

> 4   ②f3 *(D)*

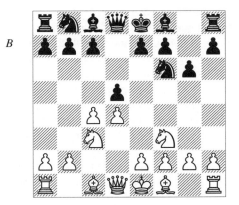

A solid developing move.

> 4   ...   ♗g7

Now, White can still go for the Exchange Variation by playing **5 cxd5 ②xd5 6 e4 ②xc3 7 bxc3**, or for the 4 ♗f4 variation, with **5 ♗f4**.

Likewise, White can steer for the 4 ♗g5 variation by playing **5 ♗g5**: 5...②e4 **6 ♗f4** ②xc3 7 bxc3 c5 8 e3 and we arrive at a position from 4 ♗g5. But, because with a knight on f3 the bishop on g5 is now protected (unlike after 4 ♗g5 ②e4), White may also consider meeting 5...②e4 with **6 cxd5**. If Black then plays **6...②xc3** 7 bxc3 ♕xd5 the position is almost identical to the one arising from 6 ♗f4 (or 6

♗h4) but with the important difference that White has an extra tempo, since he has saved himself the move ♗g5-f4/h4. The critical test of 6 cxd5 is **6...♘xg5** 7 ♘xg5 e6! *(D)*, regaining the pawn.

It is true that **8 ♕d2** exd5 9 ♕e3+ forces Black to give up castling (9...♔f8) but since White will need to spend a few moves on a regrouping of his queen and knight, this should not unduly worry Black. Players who like a fixed pawn-formation often prefer the quiet **8 ♘f3** exd5 9 e3. This is in fact one of just a few variations in the Grünfeld where the pawn-structure becomes static and although this line is not considered to be particularly dangerous for Black, it is regarded as a godsend by many players who have trouble coping with the dynamics and high-speed variations of the more popular lines.

Finally White can also play the really quiet move **5 e3**. Only in the early years was this line thought to be of theoretical importance, but it is still eminently playable if rather unambitious. If, after 5...0-0, White tries to prevent ...c5 by playing 6 b4, Black will simply prepare this advance with 6...b6.

But the most important way of turning 4 ♘f3 into an independent variation by far is...

> **5   ♕b3** *(D)*

This is the **Russian Variation**. Together with the Exchange Variation it is considered the sharpest and most ambitious way of countering the Grünfeld Defence.

> **5   ...   dxc4**

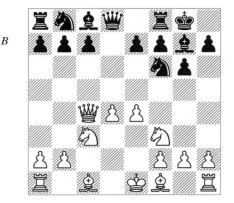

This move is more or less forced since most Grünfeld devotees are unlikely to scale down their dynamic ambitions to the level of playing **5...c6**.

> **6   ♕xc4   0-0**
> **7   e4** *(D)*

We have arrived at the starting point of this variation.

White has achieved quite a lot with his last three moves. He has the 'perfect' centre (pawns on e4 and d4), he has prevented ...c5 and he has managed to keep a tight rein on the knight on f6. It is almost enough to make one believe that White has won the opening battle already!

But if we go into the matter a little deeper and if we look at the vast amount of theory that has sprung into existence from this position over the years, we shall have to correct this optimistic viewpoint. The resilience of Black's position is in fact phenomenal. Black has a choice of no fewer than three plans (and perhaps more) to fight back against White's central formation, all of them based on the one weak spot that can be found in his position: the vulnerable position of the queen on c4.

The most direct way of showing up this vulnerability is **7...a6**, intending to play 8...b5. This is the **Hungarian Variation**.

Then there is **7...♞a6**, the **Prins Variation**. Black prepares to play 8...c5. Although not directly under attack, the white queen may well get into trouble once the fighting on the queenside gets underway.

7...♝g4 is the **Smyslov Variation**. Black tries to utilize the unstable position of the white queen to start an attack against d4, based on the ingenious manoeuvre ...♞fd7-b6.

A fourth possibility, **7...♞c6** *(D)*, is based on the same strategy.

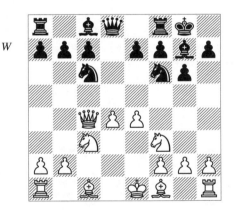

This move has not (yet) obtained quite the same rank in the hierarchy as the previous three moves, but it is perfectly playable nevertheless. The idea is to wait for 8 ♝e2 before playing the Smyslov move 8...♝g4 and to meet 8 d5 with 8...♞a5 9 ♕d3 c6!, attacking White's centre. White cannot afford to play 10 b4? here, because of the vicious reply 10...♞xe4!.

Hungarian Variation

7 ... a6 *(D)*

Black wants to chase the white queen away from c4 and then play ...c5. What makes this plan particularly venomous is that it cannot be

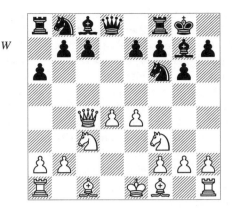

simply stopped by **8 a4?**. Not only does this move fail to fulfil its purpose, it even makes 8...b5! all the more attractive for Black. Since 9 axb5? axb5 loses material, White has to play 9 ♕b3, when after 9...c5! Black is firmly in the driving seat. If, for instance, 10 dxc5 ♝e6 11 ♕a3 b4! 12 ♕xb4 ♞c6 13 ♕a3? ♖b8, Black is already winning in view of the lethal threat 14...♖b3.

The real decision White has to take is whether he wants to continue calmly developing his kingside and allow Black to carry out his plan (**8 ♝e2**), or if he prefers to take the initiative by playing **8 e5**. This is not 'just' a question of what is best objectively, it is also to a large extent a matter of taste.

In case of **8 ♝e2**, the position after 8...b5 9 ♕b3 *(D)* is the starting point.

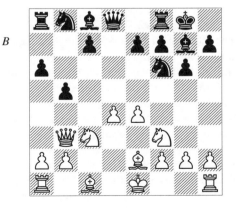

Black can either play 9...♝b7 or 9...c5. The latter variation splits again after the crucial reply

10 dxc5, when Black has a choice between 10...♗b7 and 10...♗e6. In most cases Black will win back his pawn without much trouble. The question then is how much power remains in what is left of White's centre.

If White plays **8 e5**, the game becomes very complicated. After 8...b5 9 ♕b3 ♘fd7 both 10 e6 and 10 h4 have been tried, moves that clearly intend to wipe out the enemy position fast. 10 ♗e3 is slightly more modest (though by no means boring) and also very popular.

Prins Variation

7   ...   ♘a6 *(D)*

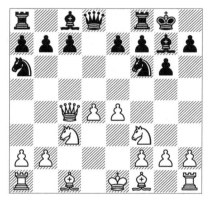

Black prepares ...c5, when a sharp fight in the centre and on the queenside is likely to flare up, leaving White's queen dangerously trapped in the middle of the battlefield.

8   ♗e2

The fact that Black is developing his pieces faster than in the Hungarian Variation has discouraged most players from trying the aggressive **8 e5**, although on and off this has been played, with the follow-up 8...♘d7 9 e6.

8 ♕b3 is an entirely different idea. White creates the possibility of taking on a6, ruining Black's pawn-formation on the queenside. This 'threat' has done little to deter Grünfeld devotees from playing 8...c5 though. After 9 d5 (the immediate 9 ♗xa6 is met by 9...cxd4!) 9...e6 10 ♗xa6 bxa6, the pair of bishops and the open b-file more than compensate Black for the doubled pawns.

8   ...   c5 *(D)*

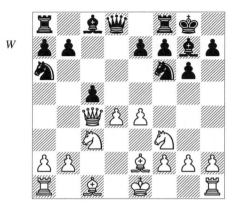

9   d5

9 dxc5 ♗e6, and now, for instance, 10 ♕b5 ♖c8 11 ♕xb7 ♘xc5, would reveal Black's strategy in its full splendour. The text-move is stronger and takes the question of the correctness of 7...♘a6 to a deeper level. Does Black's position have the resources to attack White's central formation effectively?

9   ...   e6
10   0-0   exd5
11   exd5   ♗f5 *(D)*

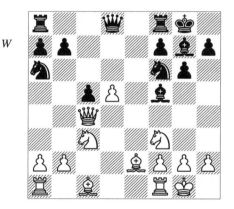

This is a key position in the Prins Variation. Positionally speaking, the situation is very tense. The crucial factor is White's d-pawn. Will this turn out to be a powerful passed pawn or a source of worry for White? The position of the knight on a6 is also hard to evaluate. On the one hand this piece stands offside; on the other it performs the useful task of protecting c5. Besides, in many variations White has to take ...♘b4 into account.

Smyslov Variation

7	...	♗g4 *(D)*

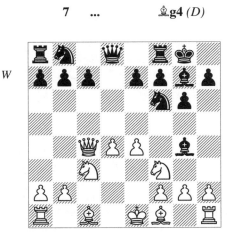

A classical developing move with a venomous point. By attacking the knight on f3, Black is undermining White's d-pawn. Besides, the 'threat' of taking on f3 adds some extra tension to the position. How should this exchange be judged?

8 ♗e3

White can radically solve the question of the exchange on f3 by playing **8 ♘e5**, but because this knight sortie gives Black new targets for a counterattack, it has never been very popular. Black draws White's d-pawn forward by playing 8...♗e6 and after 9 d5 retreats the bishop to its original square (9...♗c8). Although the manoeuvre ...♗g4-e6-c8 has resulted in no fewer than three extra moves for White, Black has every reason to be satisfied. He is ready to pounce on the white centre pawns with ...e6 and it will not be easy to prove that e5 is actually a good square for the knight.

The simple developing move **8 ♗e2**, although by no means bad, has never enjoyed great popularity either. Most of those who study the Smyslov Variation come to the conclusion that, generally speaking, White does not have to be afraid of meeting ...♗xf3 with gxf3 and that if he is, he had better give up the idea of playing 5

♕b3 altogether. After 8...♘fd7, supporting the d-pawn with 9 ♗e3 is necessary. Now if Black continues 9...♘b6, White's choice of a square for his queen is limited compared with the position after 8 ♗e3 ♘fd7 9 ♖d1, because the pawn on d4 is in need of protection. After 10 ♕d3 ♘c6 11 ♖d1 (or 11 0-0-0), for instance, Black has the characteristic action 11...♗xf3 12 ♗xf3 e5 13 d5 ♘d4.

8	...	♘fd7 *(D)*

This is the point of the Smyslov Variation. By manoeuvring his knight from f6 to b6, Black chases the queen away from c4 while at the same time opening the diagonal of the bishop on g7. All of a sudden White's pawn on d4, that was looking unassailable a mere two moves ago, finds itself under heavy pressure.

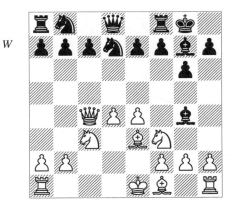

The classical way to protect d4 is **9 ♖d1**. Putting a rook on the d-file discourages an attack based on ...e5, as we saw in the 8 ♗e2 line. 9...♘b6 10 ♕b3 ♘c6 then intensifies the pressure on d4 to a point where it becomes necessary to play 11 d5. This advance leads to an extremely complicated position after 11...♘e5 12 ♗e2 ♘xf3+ 13 gxf3 ♗h5, which is critical for a proper evaluation of the Smyslov Variation. Black plans to attack the white centre pawns with ...c6, ...e6 or ...f5, or a combination of these moves. White has the option of launching an attack on the kingside with h4 and f4, but he will also have to react accurately to whatever scheme of counterattack his opponent chooses. This situation is further complicated by the uncertain position of White's king and with an eye to this problem, the alternative **9 0-0-0** has been suggested (and played). Yet this move too has its disadvantages. For one thing, with the white king committed to the queenside, the plan of playing 9...♘b6 10 ♕b3 a5, followed by ...a4-a3, becomes much more attractive.

Fianchetto Grünfeld

3   g3 *(D)*

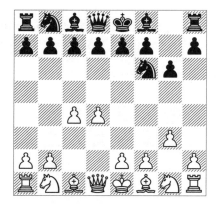

I have already discussed the relative merits of this move and 3 ♘c3 in the chapter on the King's Indian Defence. In general, White's approach in the g3 system is slightly more measured. Rather than rushing forward to occupy the centre with a quick e4, White completes his development without giving his opponent undue targets for a counterattack.

Now, if Black wants to play a Grünfeld rather than a King's Indian, he has a choice between **3...♗g7** 4 ♗g2 d5 and **3...c6**.

3 g3 ♗g7 4 ♗g2 d5

3   ...   ♗g7
4   ♗g2   d5 *(D)*

Black does not let the absence of a white knight on c3 – which implies that he won't be able to respond to 5 cxd5 ♘xd5 6 e4 with ...♘xc3 followed by ...c5 (as in the Exchange Variation) – discourage him from carrying out his aggressive plan.

5   cxd5

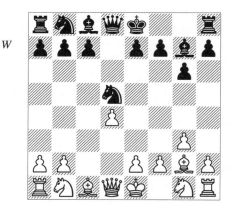

5 ♘f3 is a major alternative. Now if 5...0-0 6 0-0, Black can switch to the solid 3...c6 line with 6...c6 or he can pursue his active strategy by playing 6...dxc4. The usual response to this is 7 ♘a3, when Black has two important schemes of putting pressure on White's central formation. Both 7...♘c6 8 ♘xc4 ♗e6, intending to meet the plausible 9 b3 with 9...♗d5 10 ♗b2 a5, and 7...c3 8 bxc3 c5, creating a pawn-formation which is similar to the Exchange Variation, have left their mark on opening theory.

5   ...   ♘xd5 *(D)*

Again White faces a fundamental decision. Should he accept the challenge and play **6 e4** or should he prefer the quiet developing move **6 ♘f3**?

The answer to this question has been steadily rocking to and fro over the years and this is not because spectacular theoretical discoveries were knocking out one move or the other, but simply because the g3 system has been enjoying an unbroken run of popularity among positional players. There has been a continuous process of ever more detailed and deeper analysis and ever more accurate assessments, which is continuing to this very day.

6 e4 is of course the sharpest move. The reply **6...♘b4** then forces the d-pawn to move forward because 7 ♘e2? would run into the fork 7...♗xd4! 8 ♘xd4? ♕xd4 9 ♕xd4 ♘c2+. The advance 7 d5 allows 7...c6, opening lines for counterplay. On the other hand, the knight from b4 is likely to end up on the somewhat disappointing square a6.

An alternative possibility is to play **6...♘b6**, when after 7 ♘e2 both 7...c5 8 d5 e6 and 7...e5 8 d5 c6 have been tested. In both cases Black's pieces circle freely around White's pawn on d5, which itself, however, is firmly protected and poses a latent threat. These positions are difficult to evaluate.

By playing **6 ♘f3**, White pursues his strategy of sound development and ignoring Black's provocations. In fact, this position is doubly important because it often arises if White plays ♘f3 much earlier; e.g., 1 ♘f3 or 1 d4 ♘f6 2 ♘f3. The basic starting position is reached after 6...0-0 7 0-0 ♘b6 8 ♘c3 ♘c6 *(D)*.

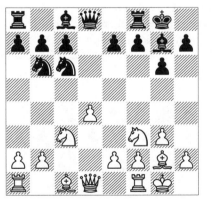

If White now plays **9 d5**, the reply 9...♘a5 is considered Black's best move. The knight is not standing offside on a5. Upon 10 e4 Black has the standard method 10...c6, opening files and diagonals on the queenside and allowing the

knight to join in the fight quite naturally via c4 and perhaps d6.

Whether 9 d5 is best is a much-debated question. The alternative is to play **9 e3**, again preferring self-restraint to action. In fact, Black faces the same dilemma in this position. Both an immediate attack against the centre (9...e5) and the preparatory move 9...♖e8 are well-respected possibilities and nobody knows which one is better.

3 g3 c6

3   ...   **c6** *(D)*

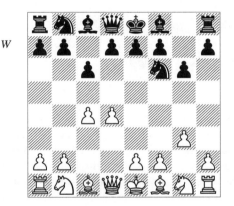

This line was specifically designed as an attempt to neutralize 3 g3. Black intends to play ...d5, but only when he can recapture on d5 with his c-pawn. The resulting position will be rather static, which is unusual for a Grünfeld. Nevertheless it is a very important option for every Grünfeld player for, in its own modest way, it constitutes a critical test of the g3 system.

Does White have a constructive plan against this solid plan? And even if the answer is 'yes', is this the type of middlegame that he really wants? Is he not sorry to have lost the chance for playing one of the much more aggressive and dynamic lines starting with 3 ♘c3? For many players who like the g3 variations against both the King's Indian and the Grünfeld Defence, these are pertinent questions.

Of course Black may be troubled by similar pangs of conscience. Do I go all-out for my usual Grünfeld or King's Indian or am I (secretly perhaps) quite happy with the much quieter and safer positions after 3...c6?

As is so often the case, the answer is entirely up to you.

> **4   ♗g2   d5**
>
> **5   ♘f3** *(D)*

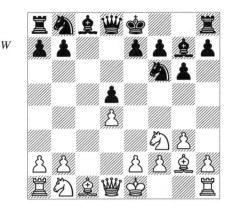

> **5   ...   ♗g7**

It is a bit too early yet to take on c4, because White will win back his pawn very easily following 5...dxc4 6 ♘e5, but after 5...♗g7 White needs to consider this possibility very carefully. If he absentmindedly continues **6 0-0**, he will now find it much harder to find a satisfactory reply to 6...dxc4, because 7 ♘e5 is met by 7...♘g4!, indirectly attacking d4.

If White protects his c-pawn, for instance by **6 ♘bd2** or **6 b3**, Black will have an easy scheme of development: 6...0-0, 7...♗f5 and 8...♘e4. This is playable of course, but practice has shown that the real test of Black's set-up lies in the only concrete solution to the problem that is available to White:

> **6   cxd5   cxd5** *(D)*

Now, is this symmetrical position really White's best chance against 3...c6 or is it just plain boring?

Unfortunately, and perhaps not surprisingly, there is no more honest answer to this question than 'both'. This is in fact White's dilemma in a nutshell. If he wants to play the theoretically most critical strategy against Black's ...c6 plan, he must have the motivation *and* the technical skills to play a 'boring' position, that is a position which is all about small advantages, subtle

judgements and, perhaps more than anything else, stamina.

Timing is of the utmost importance in this line. It all started with players calmly continuing **7 0-0** 0-0 8 ♘c3, when after **8...♘c6**, 9 ♘e5 introduces the first starting point of this variation. 9...♗f5 was the main line in the 1960s. Confident that his position is sufficiently solid, Black allows his opponent to saddle him with a backward c-pawn by 10 ♘xc6 bxc6 11 ♘a4. Then **8...♘e4** became popular. Black wants to be a step ahead of his opponent, introducing the possibility of taking on c3 instead of allowing White to do the same on c6. Theory concentrated on 9 ♘xe4 dxe4 10 ♘e5 and on the immediate 9 ♘e5, showing clearly how important a good feel for the initiative is (and for the aggressive moves ♘e5 and ...♘e4 in particular), even in this quiet variation.

Later still, **7 ♘c3** 0-0 8 ♘e5 *(D)* became the main line.

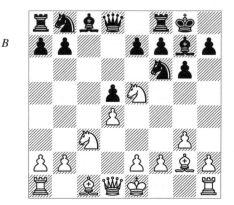

The subtle 8...e6 9 0-0 ♘fd7, intending to play ...♘c6 only after White has weakened his pawn-structure by playing 10 f4, has come to the fore as the modern interpretation of this variation.

3 f3

3   **f3** *(D)*

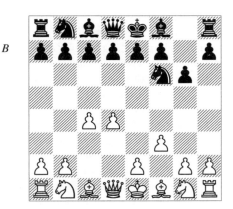

This unsophisticated little move has a very odd status.

If Black plays 1...♘f6 and 2...g6 with the idea of playing a King's Indian, he has no problem whatsoever. He will simply play **3...♗g7**, when 4 e4 d6 5 ♘c3 brings about a Sämisch Variation (see page 97) as if nothing has happened.

Another transpositional possibility is to play **3...c5**. This reply to 3 f3 is likely to come naturally to the Benoni expert.

It is only when Black wants to play a Grünfeld, that 3 f3 is the starting point of an independent opening variation. This makes it in effect an anti-Grünfeld move: White does nothing to avoid a King's Indian, but he specifically steers clear of the 'normal' main lines of the Grünfeld Defence. Paradoxically though, the Grünfeld move **3...d5** is also the real test of the soundness of 3 f3, for unless we consider the Sämisch as a second-rate choice against the King's Indian and the f3 system as harmless in the Benoni, this is the only way to try to prove that 3 f3 is too slow and that White really needs the f3-square for his knight.

3   ...   **d5**

The point of 3 f3 is that White can now build up his broad pawn-centre without allowing his opponent the plan of exchanging knights on c3 and play ...c5. We have seen this strategy in other variations as well; e.g., the g3 system.

4	cxd5	♘xd5
5	e4	♘b6
6	♘c3	♗g7
7	♗e3	0-0 *(D)*

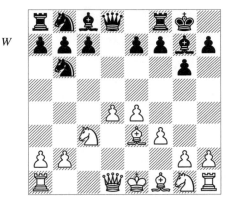

This is the critical position of the 3 f3 variation.

White has an aggressive and natural scheme of development in **8 ♕d2**, followed by 0-0-0 and an attack on the kingside (h4 and ♗h6). Black will have to be careful not to fall in with this plan. Swift counterplay against White's centre is needed; e.g., 8...♘c6 9 0-0-0 e5 10 d5 ♘d4.

8 f4 is an important alternative. While 'correcting' his pawn-formation, he frees f3 for the knight and strengthens control over e5. Now 8...♘c6 forces the d-pawn forward (if 9 ♘f3 the reply 9...♗g4 will force 10 d5 anyway) when after 9 d5 ♘a5 or even 9...♘b8, Black is ready to play 10...c6, attacking White's outpost on d5. This variation is generally considered the most critical test of 3 f3.

Benoni and Benko

	1	d4	♘f6
	2	c4	c5 *(D)*

W

The chapter on the King's Indian Defence has already taught us that this move constitutes a standard way of attacking White's pawn-centre. The Benoni is closely related to the King's Indian, especially if Black develops his bishop on g7, as he does in most Benoni variations. The main difference is that by playing 2...g6 Black keeps his pawn-formation as flexible as possible, while 2...c5 is a choice in favour of the immediate clarification of the central pawn-structure.

But clarity is not the same as simplicity. The Benoni often leads to enormous complications, perhaps because it *is* in fact already a sacrifice to play 2...c5: a positional sacrifice of space. Since the simple reply d5 gives White a stable spatial advantage in the centre, Black takes upon himself the obligation to play the opening and middlegame with the utmost vigour, especially in the more modern variations. He will have to seize every opportunity to take the initiative, often at the cost of material sacrifices. In short, the Benoni is a very combative opening, tailor-made for the truly uncompromising fighter.

The Benoni is characterized by ...c5, a move that may be played in many different positions. It started in the 19th century with 1 d4 c5 and the most modern version is to play ...c5 only after White has committed himself to a particular scheme of development; e.g., 1 d4 ♘f6 2 c4 e6 3 g3 and now 3...c5. The move-order adopted in this chapter is the most universal one, keeping as many strategic options open as possible.

The name Benoni is somewhat ominous, for it is Hebrew for 'child of sorrow'. Far from being a cry of despair by a player who has just lost his third game in a row with this opening, however, this name is the result of a bizarre little twist of history. 'Ben-oni' is the first word of a much longer title of a general book on chess openings which was published in 1825. Among many other things, this book dealt with the consequences of 1 d4 c5. For some totally obscure reason the word Benoni then got stuck to this particular opening, eventually becoming its official name which was later extended to include the more modern version of 1 d4 ♘f6 2 c4 c5.

3 d5 *(D)*

The most principled approach. White accepts the challenge and occupies a large portion of terrain in the centre. It is only with this move that we enter the Benoni proper, for the alternatives **3 ♘f3** and **3 e3** take us into a different kind of position and even into a different opening altogether.

3 ♘f3 is a direct transposition to a line of the Symmetrical English (see page 212), while **3 e3** may transpose to a Panov Caro-Kann after 3...cxd4 4 exd4 d5 (see page 378) or to a Queen's Gambit after 3...d5 or 3...e6 4 ♘f3 d5. 3...g6 is another good reply and one that is more Benoni-oriented.

3 dxc5 is rarely played. Whatever 2...c5 is, it is not a pawn sacrifice. Black wins back the pawn quite effortlessly by playing 3...e6.

In this position Black has no fewer than four variations at his disposal, all with a totally different strategic background.

The oldest interpretation of the Benoni is to play **3...g6** (or **3...d6** 4 ♘c3 g6). Of all Benoni variations, this is the one that is the most closely related to the King's Indian Defence. Though dating from the early 19th century, it is still a highly topical line.

During the 1920s and 1930s it was considered more modern and stronger to close the centre with ...e5. This resulted in the variation **3...e5** being developed, which is now called the Czech Benoni, whereas the Modern Benoni refers to the much more dynamic approach **3...e6**. The latter very sharp and double-edged interpretation of the Benoni rose to fame in the 1950s and 1960s, mainly due to the brilliant successes of world champion Mikhail Tal (1936-92). With his exceptionally dynamic style, he proved to be the perfect ambassador for this opening. It is hardly an exaggeration to say that it was Tal who taught the world to play the Benoni.

But in the meantime, an even more modern variation has sprung up: the pawn sacrifice **3...b5**. When this line was in its infancy it was seen as an obscure and dubious side branch and it was called Volga Gambit. It reached maturity when around 1970 the Hungarian-American grandmaster Pal Benko came up with a new and much more profound interpretation. Nowadays it is usually called the Benko Gambit, and rightly so, because Benko's ideas have turned it into a sound opening that offers Black unusually good winning chances.

3...g6

3 ... g6 (D)

An uncomplicated developing move, delaying the decision of what to do about White's spatial advantage to a later stage. Black will let his choice between ...e6, ...e5 or ...b5 depend on White's scheme of development.

With the same idea in mind, **3...d6** is sometimes played. This will usually transpose; e.g., after 4 ♘c3 g6 5 e4 ♗g7.

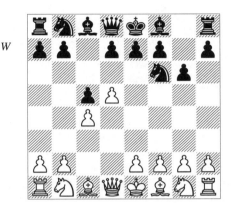

4 ♘c3

What makes this variation a difficult one from White's point of view is that he has to anticipate all three of the above-mentioned plans. A transposition to the Modern Benoni with ...e6 in particular is something which has to be carefully weighed and the first (and perhaps most crucial) aspect of such an evaluation is whether a transposition is acceptable to White or whether there is a chance for something better.

An interesting option to make ...e6 possibly less attractive is to fianchetto the king's bishop, when ...e6 (and also ...e5 for that matter) can be met by taking on e6, opening a beautiful diagonal for the bishop on g2. Now, an important finesse of this plan is that an early ♘c3 is best avoided. After 4 ♘c3 ♗g7 5 g3 0-0 6 ♗g2 d6 7 ♘f3 e6 (or 7...e5), for example, 8 0-0 exd5 9 cxd5 will simply transpose to the Fianchetto Variation of the Modern Benoni (see page 151) but if 8 dxe6 ♗xe6 9 ♘g5, the exchange sacrifice 9...♗xc4! 10 ♗xb7 ♘bd7 11 ♗xa8 ♕xa8 is considered very promising for Black. But if

White delays ♘c3 in this set-up; e.g., **4 g3 ♗g7 5 ♗g2 d6 6 ♘f3 0-0 7 0-0 e6**, *then* **8 dxe6 ♗xe6 9 ♘g5 ♗xc4?! 10 ♗xb7 ♘bd7 11 ♘a3!** (D) is very good for White.

But then again, and just to show how complicated such a choice of variation really is: playing 4 g3 also requires a willingness to play the Fianchetto Variation against the Benko Gambit, for if, after 4 g3 ♗g7 5 ♗g2 d6 6 ♘f3, Black plays 6...b5, there is nothing for White but to accept the gambit and transpose to this line with 7 cxb5 a6 8 bxa6 ♗xa6 (see page 157). And *this* transposition, in its turn, is ruled out by 4 ♘c3.

4	...	♗g7
5	e4	d6 (D)

6 ♘f3

This healthy developing move offers the best chances for a specific anti-3...g6 strategy.

Alternatives are usually played with a transposition to the Modern Benoni in mind.

For instance, most players who prefer **6 f4** will be counting on 6...0-0 7 ♘f3, when **7...e6** 8 ♗e2 exd5 9 cxd5 transposes to the Four Pawns Attack of the Modern Benoni (note that Black has thus avoided the dangerous Taimanov Attack – see page 147). However, Black has an important alternative in **7...b5** 8 cxb5 a6. This pawn sacrifice is similar to the Benko Gambit but there is no literal transposition. Still, a general knowledge of that opening will help to cope with the specific problem of this line. After 9 bxa6 ♕a5 10 ♗d2 ♗xa6 White should not underestimate the difficulties; 9 a4 is better.

6 f3 also allows a transposition to the Modern Benoni, for instance with 6...0-0 7 ♗e3 e6 8 ♘ge2 exd5 9 cxd5. Here 7 ♗g5 is slightly more aggressive, but it will not prevent 7...e6. It is true that White can then play 8 ♕d2 exd5 9 ♘xd5, which perhaps *looks* very promising, but the pin on the f6-knight turns out to be a problem for Black if he just continues 9...♗e6 10 ♘e2 ♗xd5. For this reason most players prefer the 'orthodox' 9 cxd5.

Another possibility is **6 ♗e2 0-0 7 ♗g5**, which is a direct transposition to the Averbakh Variation of the King's Indian Defence (see page 111).

6	...	0-0 (D)

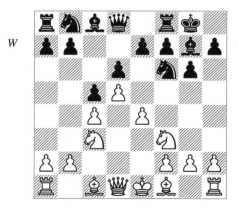

7 h3

One of the advantages of 3...g6 over 3...e6 is that after **7 ♗e2** White's development runs less smoothly here. The point is that, after 7...e6 8

0-0, Black is in absolutely no hurry to take on d5 (8...exd5 9 cxd5 would take us straight into the Classical Variation of the Modern Benoni; see page 149), since he has an excellent waiting and preparatory move in 8...♖e8. It then becomes difficult for White to keep on anticipating a transposition to the Modern Benoni, while at the same time he has no obvious alternatives. If (by analogy with the Modern Benoni) he plays 9 ♘d2, Black increases the tension with 9...♘a6. If he plays the natural developing move 9 ♗f4, he will have to recapture on d5 with his e-pawn (9...exd5 10 exd5), when 10...♘e4 leads to a fairly quiet position with few problems for Black.

The idea of 7 h3 is to get precisely this type of position (with White having played exd5 instead of cxd5) in a more favourable version.

| 7 | ... | e6 |
| 8 | ♗d3 *(D)* | |

White's piece development is directed towards minimizing the impact of some of Black's standard options in the pawn-formation that arises after **8...exd5 9 exd5**. 8 ♗d3 is intended to prevent the simplifying manoeuvre ...♖e8 followed by ...♘e4 (which we have just seen in the 7 ♗e2 variation) and to discourage ...♗f5. The alternative active development ...♗g4 has already been ruled out by 7 h3.

On the face of it, this set-up seems to offer Black one particularly attractive possibility, namely 9...♖e8+ 10 ♗e3 ♗h6 *(D)*.

But closer inspection reveals that White can turn this into a promising pawn sacrifice: 11

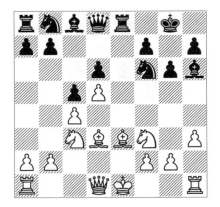

0-0! ♗xe3 12 fxe3, and after **12...♖xe3** 13 ♕d2 ♖e8 14 ♕h6 White is already close to winning. Black does better not to accept the sacrifice and to play **12...♘bd7**, but even then the open f-file and the weakened dark squares on the kingside are ample compensation for the backward e-pawn. Black's dark-squared bishop is badly missed.

This does not mean that there is anything wrong with 'the other capture' **9 cxd5**. In fact, this is played quite often because it transposes to a highly popular line against the Modern Benoni. The choice between 9 exd5 and 9 cxd5 is to a large extent a matter of taste. Opening theory can be useful though in helping a player to make up his mind and in determining which particular circumstances favour the one pawn-formation and which favour the other.

Czech Benoni

| 3 | ... | e5 |

Black barricades the centre, leaving only the flanks open for future action.

| 4 | ♘c3 | d6 |
| 5 | e4 | ♗e7 *(D)* |

This brings us to the most important starting position of the Czech Benoni. Of course **5...g6** is also a good move. Play then assumes a King's Indian character.

But by playing 5...♗e7 Black pursues a different goal, one that is more specifically attuned to the blocked central pawn-formation. He intends to play ...0-0 and ...♘e8. While ...g6, to prepare ...f5, remains fully possible,

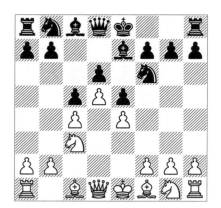

Black also creates the option of playing ...♗g5, exchanging the dark-squared bishops, which will make his slightly cramped position more comfortable.

Strategically, the situation is perfectly clear. While Black will concentrate on the advance ...f5 (and in some cases ...b5), White will start an attack against the enemy fortress with b4 or f4.

But it is not always easy to execute even a clear enough plan satisfactorily. In fact White faces something of a dilemma in this variation: should he concentrate his forces entirely on the queenside or should he first try to neutralize Black's attack on the kingside? And if he decides to allow Black to play ...f5, how should he react to this move?

The most classical piece development is **6 ♘f3** 0-0 **7 ♗e2**, when 7...♘e8 8 0-0 ♘d7 (or 8...g6) 9 a3 (preparing b4) 9...g6 10 ♗h6 ♘g7 11 ♕d2 *(D)* is a characteristic (though by no means forced) continuation.

White's last move anticipates 11...f5, which can now be met with the annoying 12 ♘g5. Things usually develop at a leisurely pace in this type of position. Black can calmly play ...♔h8 followed by ...♘df6-g8 to drive away the bishop from h6, before turning his attention to playing ...f5. In the meantime White will play b4 and open a file on the queenside.

Nevertheless, once the battle gets started, this may lead to sharp play, especially on the kingside.

If White prefers to try to smother Black's attack on the kingside before it even gets started, he may consider a scheme of development like ♗d3, h3, g4 and perhaps 0-0-0, starting, for instance, with **6 ♗d3** 0-0 7 h3 ♘e8 8 ♘f3 (to stop 8...♗g5) 8...g6 9 g4 *(D)*.

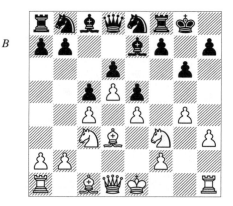

Although a quick ...f5 is not physically impossible, it is decidedly less attractive now that White may well be the one who profits from an opening of the g-file.

But this strategy makes high demands on White. In the long run it is far from easy to combine anticipating ...f5 on the one side and making the desired amount of progress on the queenside on the other. At any rate this set-up too usually results in a very complicated middlegame.

Modern Benoni

3   ...   e6 *(D)*

With this move Black is heading for the exchange 4...exd5 5 cxd5. This is an extremely

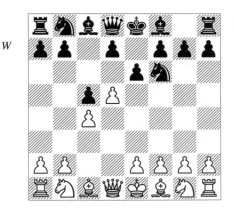

sharp plan because what Black is doing here is in effect raising the positional stakes, which were already quite high after 2...c5.

After the exchange on d5, White will not only have a spatial advantage but also a pawn-majority in the centre, something he can only dream of in many other openings. And this does not even come at the price of immediate tactical complications, as is the case in many gambits. White will have no problems in completing his development whatsoever.

So what is it that makes this opening worthwhile for Black? For we *are* talking about a respected opening here, not to everyone's taste certainly, but in the hands of an expert as fully playable as the more classical defences against 1 d4.

It is hard to find words to describe the power and dynamism of Black's strategy. The best way to discover them is to study a number of classic Modern Benoni games in their entirety, for instance the games of world champions Mikhail Tal and Garry Kasparov. Again and again in these games White's pawn-centre turns out to be not only strong and potentially very dangerous for Black but also vulnerable, sometimes rigid, sometimes no more than a sitting target.

Moreover, Black's pawn-majority on the queenside plays an important role in this opening. The advance ...b5, often in combination with ...c4, can be very threatening, especially when supported by the powerful bishop on g7. White may easily come under heavy pressure on the queenside, which will automatically lessen

his control over the centre, for instance by his knight being chased away from c3 (...b5-b4).

And even on the kingside Black does not have to restrict himself to passivity. Both ...f5, ...h5-h4 and even ...g5-g4 can be very useful plans under the right circumstances.

Move-order is an important aspect of playing the Modern Benoni. Many players prefer 2...e6 to 2...c5, choosing to play a Benoni only if White plays 3 ♘f3 or 3 g3 (3...c5), when White's choice of variation is restricted (after 3 ♘f3 he will be unable to play a f4 or f3 variation, while after 3 g3 White is committed to the Fianchetto Variation). Against 3 ♘c3, which does keep all options open in case of a Benoni (3...c5 4 d5), they then play either a Nimzo-Indian (3...♗b4) or a Queen's Gambit Declined (3...d5).

But there is also a variation of the Benoni that is specific to 2...e6 3 ♘f3: the **Blumenfeld Gambit**. After 2...e6 3 ♘f3, Black plays 3...c5 and if White accepts the challenge to play a Benoni (4 d5), he lashes out on the queenside with **4...b5** *(D)*. Black is sacrificing a pawn, hoping to gain a pawn-majority in the centre himself.

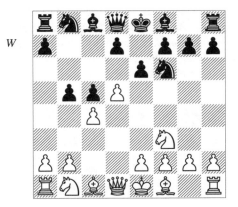

Although this gambit has never reached the pinnacle of respectability, it has always had its loyal devotees and it should not be underestimated.

White faces a fundamental decision. If he accepts the gambit by playing **5 dxe6 fxe6 6 cxb5** he will be in for a dangerous fight against a shadowy and intangible enemy initiative. But if he maintains the Benoni pawn-structure the situation is equally unclear. The most popular move is **5 ♗g5**, hoping for the meek reply 5...bxc4, when 6 ♘c3 or 6 e4 will consolidate the centre, but Black has stronger moves in 5...h6 and 5...♕a5+. In fact opening theory has little grip on the Blumenfeld Gambit. This makes it an attractive opening for some and unattractive for others. In any case the Blumenfeld requires some independent thinking from both sides.

4	♘c3	exd5
5	cxd5	d6 (D)

This is the main starting position of the Modern Benoni. In the course of half a century, many variations have sprung up from this position (and many have disappeared again).

The most obvious move is to play **6 e4** (D).

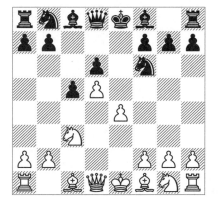

After the thematic 6...g6 White then has a choice between the sharp **7 f4**, the **Four Pawns**

Attack, **7 f3**, which is more of a consolidating move, and **7 ♘f3**, the most classical set-up, which keeps a fair amount of options open and which is considered by many to be the main line of the Modern Benoni.

6 ♘f3 is slightly more subtle, but of extra importance because this position is often reached via an earlier ♘f3; e.g., 2...e6 3 ♘f3 c5 4 d5 exd5 5 cxd5 d6 6 ♘c3. After 6...g6 White can still play 7 e4, but he also has **7 g3**, the **Fianchetto Variation**, and **7 ♗f4**, which is a very concrete attempt at disorganizing Black's plans.

Four Pawns Attack

6	e4	g6
7	f4	♗g7 (D)

The fact that this has been called the Four Pawns **Attack** makes it sufficiently clear that this is not a variation for the insecure and the hesitant. Yet it is not just the bold and the aggressive who like this variation, it is even more the domain of those who simply feel at home in deeply analysed opening variations, where there is relatively little room for surprises and where good preparation offers potentially rich rewards.

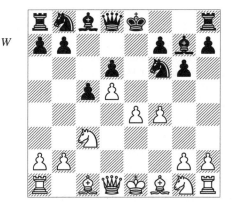

White has three possibilities in this position.

The sharpest move is **8 e5**. This is the **Mikenas Attack**. After 8...dxe5 9 fxe5 ♘fd7 10 e6 Black will have to be very careful not to get smashed, but the immediate 8...♘fd7 is considered a solid reply. Without the exchange of pawns on e5, the thrust 9 e6 loses its edge

(Black simply replies 9...fxe6 10 dxe6 ♘b6) while 9 exd6 0-0 cannot possibly be a justification for White's aggressive opening play. Much more to the point is the pawn sacrifice 9 ♘b5, yet even here Black's defences appear to be strong enough after 9...dxe5 10 ♘d6+ ♔e7 11 ♘xc8+ ♕xc8, in spite of the exposed position of Black's king.

Slightly more self-restraint is shown by **8 ♘f3**, a line that is particularly important as it often arises from the King's Indian Four Pawns Attack (the 8 e5 and 8 ♗b5+ lines are unique to the Modern Benoni move-order). The starting point of this popular variation arises after 8...0-0 9 ♗e2 *(D)*.

Black now has the fairly solid **9...♗g4** 10 0-0 ♘bd7, keeping the advance e5 in check, but he also has the more direct **9...♖e8**, attacking e4. It is then White's turn to choose between the respectable **10 ♘d2** on the one hand and the sharp **10 e5** on the other. The latter boils down to a pawn sacrifice after 10...dxe5 11 fxe5 ♘g4, because White cannot protect his pawn on e5. After 12 ♗g5 ♕b6 13 0-0 *(D)* the utmost will be asked of both players' talent for coping with dynamic and highly tactical situations (and a certain amount of theoretical knowledge will also come in handy!).

For example, 13...♘xe5 14 d6 or 14 ♘xe5 ♗xe5 15 ♗c4, when White's attacking chances against the enemy king and his powerful d-pawn compensate for the material deficit.

An even sharper option is to play **9...b5**, based on the tactical point **10 ♗xb5 ♘xe4!** 11

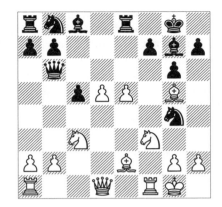

♘xe4 ♕a5+. Here too the consequences of **10 e5** dxe5 11 fxe5 ♘g4 are critical.

But White's most dangerous weapon is probably the **Taimanov Attack: 8 ♗b5+** *(D)*.

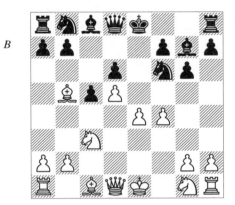

The point of this check is not obvious at first sight, but if we investigate a little deeper, it is not hard to understand why this line is thought to constitute the perfect middle way between the aggression of 8 e5 and the sound piece development of 8 ♘f3.

The point is that the two most plausible replies, 8...♘bd7 and **8...♗d7**, are now met very strongly indeed by 9 e5. Black is thus more or less forced to play the anti-developing move 8...♘fd7 (though it must be said that die-hard fans of 8...♘bd7 fanatically maintain that the position after **8...♘bd7** 9 e5 dxe5 10 fxe5 ♘h5 11 e6 is playable because of 11...♕h4+ 12 g3 ♘xg3 13 hxg3 ♕xh1). After **8...♘fd7** play slows down a bit. 9 a4 prevents a counter-attack on the queenside based on ...a6 and ...b5 and prepares a smooth development of White's kingside. One critical position arises after 9...0-0 10 ♘f3 ♘a6 11 0-0 ♘b4 12 ♖e1.

The Taimanov Attack came into fashion some thirty years ago and it is now generally viewed as one of the very strongest lines against the Modern Benoni. Many players prefer to avoid it by seeking refuge in 2...e6, playing the Benoni only in case of 3 ♘f3 or 3 g3.

6 e4 g6 7 f3

| 6 | e4 | g6 |
| 7 | f3 (D) | |

Just as in the Sämisch Variation of the King's Indian Defence, White consolidates his central position and prepares to play either ♗e3 or ♗g5. There is no immediate confrontation here, yet in the long run play can easily become just as complicated and sharp as in the Four Pawns Attack.

Because of this slightly more relaxed attitude (Black has in effect complete freedom to develop as he pleases), move-order in this line is not all that important.

| 7 | ... | ♗g7 |
| 8 | ♗g5 | |

This way of developing the bishop contains a little more venom than 8 ♗e3, although there is nothing wrong with that move either. In fact, there are even one or two lines where 8 ♗g5 and 8 ♗e3 converge to the same position!

After 8 ♗e3 0-0 9 ♘ge2 ♘bd7 10 ♘g3 ♘e5 11 ♗e2 we arrive at a position that is equally

relevant to the Sämisch Variation of the King's Indian Defence (see page 100). This is one of those instances where Black is justified in taking the initiative on the kingside: he can play 11...h5 (or 11...a6 12 a4 h5). After 12 0-0 ♘h7! the way is freed for the f-pawn and play becomes very sharp indeed; e.g., 13 ♕d2 h4 14 ♘h1 f5.

| 8 | ... | 0-0 (D) |

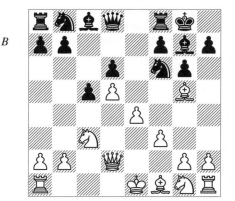

| 9 | ♕d2 (D) | |

Theory has not yet decided whether this move is stronger than 9 ♘ge2. The knight move develops the kingside a little faster but by playing 9 ♘ge2 White does forfeit the manoeuvre ♘h3-f2, which is useful in case an early ...♘bd7 by Black should temporarily prevent him from playing ...♗xh3.

9 ♘ge2 h6 10 ♗e3 ♘bd7 11 ♘g3 ♘e5 12 ♗e2 h5 leads to the same position that we have seen above as arising from 8 ♗e3.

9 ... h6

If White's intention in playing 9 ♕d2 was to prevent this move, he will be disappointed. Because of the 'weakening' move f3, **10 ♗xh6** can now be met by 10...♘xe4! 11 ♘xe4 ♕h4+. Although White remains a pawn up after 12 g3 ♕xh6 13 ♕xh6 ♗xh6 14 ♘xd6, his position is weakened by the demise of his dark-squared bishop and a manoeuvre like ...♘d7-b6 followed by ...♖d8 is likely to give Black ample compensation.

By far the more usual reply to 9...h6 is **10 ♗e3**, when 10...a6 11 a4 ♖e8 12 ♘ge2 ♘bd7 13 ♘g3 h5 will produce positions which are similar (and in some cases even identical) to the ones that we have seen arising from 8 ♗e3.

6 e4 g6 7 ♘f3

6 e4 g6 *(D)*

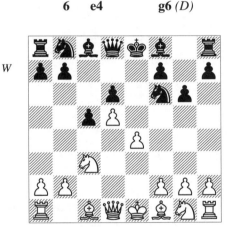

7 ♘f3

This is probably White's most natural developing move. White seizes the opportunity to play e4, but the emphasis of his opening play is on completing his kingside development.

Strangely enough, even though theory has worked its way far into the middlegame in this line, it has as yet failed to establish what the most accurate move to *start* this variation is! Apart from the move-order given here, the candidates are **7 ♗d3**, **7 h3** and **6 ♘f3** g6 7 h3 or 7 ♘d2, depending on which of the two main lines (as outlined below) White intends to play. The idea of all these moves is to avoid ...♗g4, but

whether this is really something to worry about is moot.

7 ... ♗g7 *(D)*

The discussion about the most precise move-order centres around the question of how strong **7...a6** 8 a4 ♗g4 is. The point is that this will enable Black to force a certain type of position which I shall discuss below, namely the one arising after 9 ♗e2 ♗xf3. In this particular move-order, White is not given the chance to prevent the exchange on f3 by a timely ♘d2.

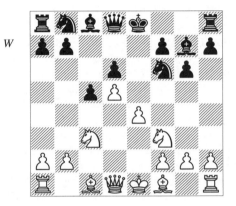

This is where the classical and the modern main lines of the Modern Benoni divide.

The former starts with **8 ♗e2**, the latter with **8 h3** to be followed by 9 ♗d3.

Classical Variation

8 ♗e2

White develops his kingside rapidly and simply. The most important starting position arises after...

8 ... 0-0
9 0-0 *(D)*

9...♖e8 is the classical move in this position. White then plays 10 ♘d2, not just to protect e4 but also (and this is the main strategic point of White's plan) to manoeuvre this knight to c4 in due course, where it will occupy an excellent post, exerting strong pressure against d6.

Black has two ways of developing his queen's knight, **10...♘a6** and **10...♘bd7**, which are equally important but very different in character.

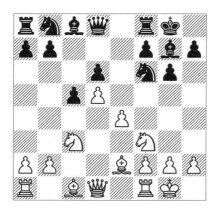

After **10...♘a6** 11 f3 ♘c7 the battle revolves around the advance ...b5. There are many intricacies to consider. If White continues 12 a4, then the straightforward 12...a6 allows White to carry out his basic strategic plan: 13 ♘c4 with a very good position. Much more subtle (and stronger!) is 12...b6, planning to meet 13 ♘c4 with 13...♗a6. A characteristic follow-up is 14 ♗g5 h6 15 ♗e3 ♗xc4 16 ♗xc4 and only now does Black play 16...a6 (followed by 17...♕d7). Thanks to the exchange ...♗xc4, White will now find it much harder to prevent ...b5.

With **10...♘bd7** *(D)* Black chooses a strategically much more complicated plan, envisaging to make a forward move not on the queenside but on the kingside.

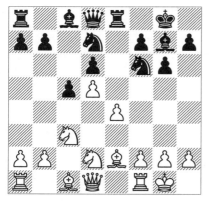

After 11 a4, for instance, Black has the provocative 11...♘e5. White would then like to play 12 f4, but this would cause a major traffic-jam after 12...♘eg4. White needs a preparatory

move, like 12 ♕c2, but this allows Black to stop 13 f4 by boldly playing 12...g5. It then becomes a matter of carefully manoeuvring and waiting for a favourable opportunity for both sides. White will be looking at moves like ♘d1-e3 or ♖e1 followed by ♘f1-e3 to keep control over f5. Black will be interested in further kingside expansion with ...g4 or ...♘h5-f4.

More recently, the idea of playing ...♗g4, already mentioned above, has come to the fore as an important alternative. This plan is normally preceded by **9...a6**, a move which, without being strictly necessary, usually comes in handy for Black. Like in most cases where Black plays ...a6, the reply 10 a4 (to stop 10...b5) is practically forced. Now Black plays 10...♗g4 *(D)*.

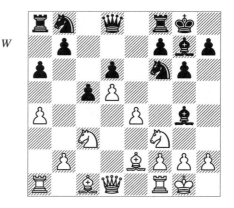

Black is aiming for a strategically uncomplicated middlegame. If White plays **11 ♘d2** he will reply 11...♗xe2 12 ♕xe2 ♘bd7, when his position is easier to play (compared to the 9...♖e8 lines) thanks to the exchange of a minor piece. Most players prefer **11 ♗f4**, when **11...♖e8** 12 ♘d2 ♗xe2 13 ♕xe2 leads to the same type of position but with White's dark-squared bishop already on a good square. But this gives Black the opportunity to exchange on f3 instead. After **11...♗xf3** 12 ♗xf3 ♕e7, **13 ♖e1** ♘bd7 brings us to a crucial position. Black is keeping White's centre pawns in check and even has chances of taking the initiative on the kingside with a manoeuvre like ...h5 followed by ...♘h7-g5. The only violent way to break open the position, **13 e5** dxe5 14 d6 ♕e6 15 ♖e1 (this is where an advantage of having played ...a6 becomes tangible: without this move 15 ♗xb7 would have been winning), has not been very convincing in practice. Black simply plays 15...♘bd7, when his position is solid.

Modern Variation

8	h3	0-0
9	♗d3 *(D)*	

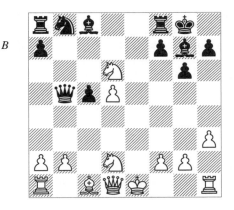

This line came into fashion around 1990. It grew up very quickly and is now one of the most important lines of the Modern Benoni.

Whereas in the Classical Variation, White's play centres around the manoeuvre ♘d2-c4, the Modern Variation is based on taking optimal advantage of the position of the knight on f3, where it is excellently placed to control both the e5-square and the kingside. That is why h3 is essential (to prevent ...♗g4 and also the manoeuvre ...♘g4-e5 in combination with ...♘d7) and why the bishop goes to d3, where it covers e4 so that ♘d2 is not necessary.

Black has tried all sorts of plans.

He can simply play a few developing moves, like **9...a6** 10 a4 ♘bd7 11 0-0 ♖e8, but the downside of this relaxed attitude is that it also allows White to complete his development at his leisure, for instance by 12 ♖e1 or 12 ♗f4.

9...♖e8 10 0-0 c4 is an attempt to hinder this easy plan of development. White now has to make up his mind whether to take on c4 and try to prove that he has an advantage after 11 ♗xc4 ♘xe4 12 ♘xe4 ♖xe4 (and now 13 ♗g5 or 13

♗d3) or to maintain the tension and play 11 ♗c2, allowing 11...b5. This position is hard to assess. The advance ...c4 gives Black chances for an attack on the queenside but it relinquishes control over d4.

9...b5 is even sharper and more concrete. It is also the most popular move, but Black needs to be aware of the latest theoretical developments here (as does White of course).

The pawn on b5 may be captured in two different ways. **10 ♗xb5** is met by 10...♘xe4! 11 ♘xe4 ♕a5+ 12 ♘fd2 ♕xb5, when 13 ♘xd6 *(D)* brings about a critical position.

White is a pawn up but Black has the initiative and there are good prospects of regaining the pawn, for instance after 13...♕a6 14 ♘2c4 ♘d7 15 0-0 ♘b6.

10 ♘xb5 was initially met by the ultra-sharp **10...♘xe4** 11 ♗xe4 ♖e8 but once the vicious 12 ♘g5 was discovered (the point being 12...h6 13 ♘e6!) the somewhat calmer **10...♖e8** became the new main line. If then 11 ♘c3 there is no objection to 11...♘xe4 12 ♘xe4 f5 while 11 ♘d2 allows 11...♘xd5. Most players have preferred the uncomplicated 11 0-0, returning the pawn immediately and hoping for a slight advantage after 11...♘xe4 12 ♖e1.

Fianchetto Variation

6	♘f3	g6
7	g3 *(D)*	

This scheme of development radiates modesty, yet in the long run it will be just as effective

as some of the sharper variations. In most cases White will play e4 anyway, but at a later stage and in a situation where the pawn will be safely protected by the bishop on g2. This strategy gives Black few targets for a swift counterattack.

The Fianchetto Variation is also important for adherents of the Catalan Opening, who like to meet 1 d4 ♘f6 2 c4 e6 with 3 g3 and who need an answer to 3...c5. They have a choice of 4 ♘f3 cxd4 5 ♘xd4, transposing to a variation of the Symmetrical English (see page 213) and 4 d5, which brings about the Modern Benoni after 4...exd5 5 cxd5 d6 6 ♗g2 g6 7 ♘c3 ♗g7 8 ♘f3.

7	...	♗g7
8	♗g2	0-0
9	0-0 (D)	

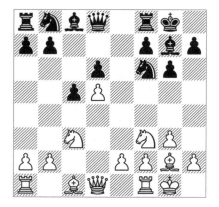

This is the starting point.

Black has several plans at his disposal, yet the most popular one has always been a set-up based on ...♘bd7; e.g., **9...a6** 10 a4 ♘bd7. In this position White has played 11 e4, 11 ♗f4 and the classical 11 ♘d2. This last move in particular has been heavily analysed, and leads to surprisingly sharp play. After 11...♖e8 12 h3 ♖b8 13 ♘c4 Black has two ways of combining the defence of d6 with an attack against the well-placed knight on c4: 13...♘b6 and 13...♘e5. This latter move creates enormous complications if White responds ambitiously with 14 ♘a3, threatening 15 f4 followed by a return of the knight to c4. Now 14...♘h5 turns the position into a highly explosive one. Black plans to meet 15 f4 with 15...♘xg3! and, even sharper and very surprisingly, 15 g4 by a piece sacrifice: 15...♕h4!. Both lines are very dangerous for White and it is probably wise to play the solid 15 e4 (D) instead.

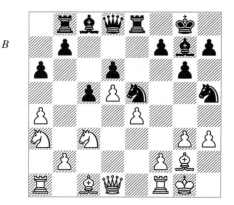

This extremely complicated variation requires very good preparation from both sides and, more than anything else, an excellent feel for the dynamics of the position.

6 ♘f3 g6 7 ♗f4

6	♘f3	g6
7	♗f4 (D)	

We have seen the move ♗f4 popping up in several of the variations that we have examined so far. It is a natural method of putting a finger on Black's weakest spot: the pawn on d6.

In this particular case, there is a very concrete motive behind 7 ♗f4, namely to meet

7...♗g7 with 8 ♕a4+. This check practically forces the reply 8...♗d7, when after 9 ♕b3 *(D)* a critical position is reached.

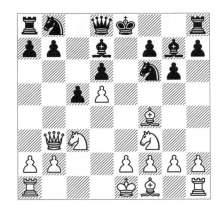

The initial reaction by Black was to play **9...♕c7**, protecting both d6 and b7. However, White then has plenty of time to develop his pieces very actively. Especially after 10 e4 0-0 11 ♘d2 it is not easy for Black to get rid of the pressure.

But in 1986 the Belgian player Luc Winants introduced a much more aggressive reply to White's opening idea, namely **9...b5**, which is a pawn sacrifice in two ways. If **10 ♗xd6**, Black takes over the initiative by playing 10...♕b6 11 ♗e5 0-0 12 e3 c4. If **10 ♘xb5**, play becomes even more complicated, especially if Black chooses to sacrifice another pawn by 10...♗xb5 11 ♕xb5+ ♘bd7 12 ♗xd6 ♘e4 13 ♗e5 0-0. White is lagging behind in development and has to be extremely careful.

Anyone not wishing to enter (or to study!) these sharp lines will probably be more interested in **7...a6**, which avoids such complications. Now the routine reply 8 a4 (the alternative is to play 8 e4, allowing 8...b5, which is looked upon as rather unclear) gives Black the opportunity to play 8...♗g7 without being troubled by a check on a4. This is likely to transpose (or be very similar) to the Classical Variation after, for instance, 9 e4 ♗g4.

Benko (or Volga) Gambit

3 ... b5 *(D)*

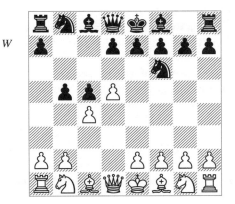

The two different names for this gambit not only reflect its historical background. They also express a fundamental difference in interpretation of this surprising pawn sacrifice.

'Volga Gambit' is the older name. It dates from a time when 3...b5 was played with the intention of following up with ...e6, trying to break down White's pawn-centre. This idea bears a strong resemblance to the Blumenfeld Gambit, which I briefly discussed earlier in this chapter.

But around 1970, Pal Benko demonstrated a totally different way of looking at the position after 4 cxb5. It was then (or, to be more precise: a few years later, when his ideas were duly recognized and appreciated) that 3...b5 was promoted from 'a dubious gambit' to a fully-fledged opening and that it was renamed the Benko Gambit.

Strictly speaking, we are talking about two different openings here, but the Benko version is completely predominant these days. Nevertheless, the spirit of the old Volga Gambit still lingers in the shadows. The breaking-down of White's pawn on d5 by means of ...e6 remains an important strategic motif. Especially in those lines where White does not take on a6 after 4 cxb5 a6, the earlier version of this opening is still recognizable.

The Benko Gambit occupies a place of its own within the Benoni complex. It is a pure sacrifice. Black is not giving up a pawn in the hope or even the certainty that he will regain his lost material; his sole intent is to take advantage of the positional pluses that compensate for the missing pawn. Remarkably, these pluses are of an almost entirely positional nature. Despite the fact that the game starts with a pawn sacrifice, play does not usually become unduly sharp or tactical.

What is asked of Black, then, is mainly a psychological quality: he should not feel uncomfortable with his slight material deficit.

4 cxb5

Over the years many attempts have been made to avoid this move and steer the game in a different direction, but without success.

4 ♘f3 *(D)* is probably the best of these alternatives.

It is a sound enough move, but not very powerful. White is hoping for 4...bxc4, when 5 ♘c3 followed by 6 e4 leads to a more 'normal' Benoni-type position, but Black has some excellent alternatives. He can either play 4...b4, depriving the queen's knight of its natural square

c3, or he can maintain the tension by 4...g6 or 4...♗b7. There is also 4...e6, transposing to the Blumenfeld Gambit (see page 145).

4 a4 has also been tried. While refusing to accept Black's pawn sacrifice, White does insist on clarifying the situation. Here too 4...b4 is a good reply, but 4...bxc4 also becomes more attractive now that White has weakened his pawn-structure on the queenside (having given up control over b3 and b4).

4 ... a6
5 bxa6

In this position, however, White does have some fully acceptable alternatives.

To begin with, refusing the gambit by playing **5 b6** *(D)* is an option.

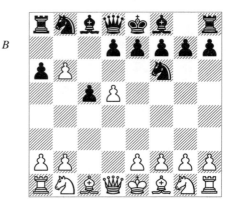

At first sight it may look a bit sheepish to return the pawn in such a blunt way and in a position where it seems so natural to take on a6, but one who has been made to feel the strength of the Benko Gambit may well appreciate the fact that there will be no bishop on a6 and that the a-file remains closed. In fact, White often takes the initiative on the queenside himself in this line. After **5...♕xb6** 6 ♘c3 d6 7 e4 g6, for instance, 8 a4 is a popular move, forcing Black to decide whether he wants to allow 9 a5, seriously cramping his queenside, or to play 8...a5, giving up the b5-square. Either way Black will not be able to get the kind of active play on the queenside that he is expecting in a Benko Gambit. An alternative is to play **5...e6**, in the spirit of the old Volga Gambit that we shall consider later on.

5 e3 is another important alternative. This too may seem a bit clumsy at first sight, but it is a far more profound move than it looks. While accepting the sacrifice, White concentrates on neutralizing Black's initiative on the queenside, rather than going for a quick ♘c3 and e4. This line was particularly popular in the 1980s and it can easily lead to very complicated positions indeed, especially if Black decides to put himself in 'refutation mode' by launching an all-out attack against d5: **5...axb5** 6 ♗xb5 ♕a5+ 7 ♘c3 ♗b7 *(D)*.

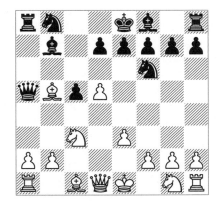

Now, if **8 ♗d2 ♕b6 9 ♕b3** Black has the powerful 9...e6, when the obvious reply 10 e4 runs into 10...♘xe4! 11 ♘xe4 ♗xd5. In this position 12 ♕d3 is the only move to keep everything protected but Black then has not only **12...f5** but also **12...♕b7** (the idea being to meet 13 f3 with 13...c4! 14 ♗xc4 ♗xc4 15 ♕xc4 d5 and Black regains the piece), with tremendous complications in both cases. In order to avoid this chaotic situation, **8 ♘e2** has been tried, giving up d5 without a fight but hoping to take advantage of White's slight lead in development.

If Black plays **5...g6**, things are less confusing. Black makes no attempt to refute 5 e3 and simply adopts a normal Benko strategy. After 6 ♘c3 ♗g7 7 ♘f3 0-0, for instance, 8 a4 is a characteristic move. White is hoping to prevent his opponent's usual counterplay on the queenside by keeping a firm grip on the b5-square. In the long run, however, this plan is not without risk, because the weakness of b3 and b4 may make itself felt in the end.

When theoretical developments in the 5 e3 line finally slowed down a little around 1990, another variation became popular: the sharp **5 f3** *(D)*.

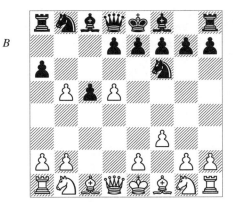

White returns the pawn to build up a strong pawn-centre. One critical position arises after **5...axb5** 6 e4 ♕a5+ 7 ♗d2 b4 8 ♘a3! intending ♘c4. Another principled reaction is **5...e6**, the original Volga Gambit theme, which leads to very difficult and highly dynamic positions, especially if White takes up the gauntlet and plays 6 e4 exd5 7 e5. It is more in line with standard Benko Gambit strategy simply to play **5...g6** 6 e4 d6, without worrying whether this is perhaps relatively better for White than the 5 bxa6 main lines, a difference which is very hard to assess in any case.

5   ...   ♗xa6

The decisive factor in understanding the Benko Gambit, which it has been Pal Benko's outstanding merit to unearth, is that there is absolutely no need for Black to hurry. By opening the a- and b-files, his counterplay on the queenside has already started, unnoticed by anyone!

The original idea of the Volga Gambit was to eliminate d5 by playing **5...e6**, hoping in due course to play ...d5, so that it would in the end be Black who occupies the centre. However, this plan is less likely to succeed here than in the Blumenfeld Gambit, because after 6 ♘c3 exd5 7 ♘xd5 ♘xd5 8 ♕xd5 ♘c6 9 e3 White has no trouble in completing his kingside development.

It is important to note that 5...♗xa6 is the original Benko move-order, which is given as the main line here for the sake of systematic clarity, but that **5...g6** is in fact the most popular move nowadays. The idea is to avoid the variation 5...♗xa6 6 g3 d6 7 ♗g2 g6 8 b3. By playing 5...g6, the bishop arrives on g7 a move earlier, which makes 6 g3 d6 7 ♗g2 ♗g7 8 b3? unplayable due to 8...♘fd7. In practically all other cases, 5...g6 will simply transpose to the 5...♗xa6 lines.

We now return to 5...♗xa6 *(D)*:

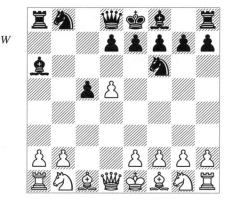

Now what does Black have for his pawn?

This question had a sceptical ring to it before 1970, a troubling and urgent one when Pal Benko and his fellow pioneers started scoring point after point from this position in the 1970s, until it finally became an existential question when players on the white side started to become really desperate. Many of them simply could not understand why and how things went wrong for them time and time again.

It is perhaps the Benko Gambit's greatest strength that it is so extraordinarily difficult for White to get a grip on it by means of concrete variations. That is why the alternatives 5 b6, 5 e3 and 5 f3 have become so important. They change the character of the game.

As I have said before, the advantages of Black's opening play are of a positional nature. In the first place he has a lead in development, enlarged by the fact that the rook on a8 no longer needs to be developed, its position on a8 already being the best possible one. Secondly, the two open files on the queenside form an excellent attacking base. Black's standard plan is: bishop to g7, rooks to a8 and b8, queen to b6 or a5 and perhaps a knight manoeuvre to c4 (e.g. ...♘bd7-b6-c4), or – in case White plays e4 – to d3 (...♘a6-b4 or ...♘g4-e5).

The latter aspect is already a clear indication that White's pawn-centre has lost a great deal of its usual strength now that the pawn on c4 has disappeared, and that it may even become a weakness. Not only is the d3-square a most unpleasant Achilles' Heel in many cases, but the standard Benoni advance e4-e5 also loses much of its power now that the pawn on d5 is no longer protected by a neighbour on c4. This means that Black has created attacking chances for himself on the queenside and reduced his opponent's chances on the kingside and in the centre at the same time!

Besides, and this is perhaps the strangest aspect of the Benko Gambit, an exchange of pieces, normally a standard method of capitalizing on a material advantage, does not necessarily have the desired effect in this case. The structural advantages of Black's position do not fade away in the endgame. If anything, in many cases their importance only increases. Paradoxically, this makes the Benko Gambit one of Black's safest openings not only of the Benoni complex, but of the entire range of 1 d4 openings.

White has two main lines. The most popular one is to play **6 ♘c3** followed by 7 e4.

There is, however, no consensus as to the value of exchanging of bishops on f1. Many players prefer the **Fianchetto Variation (6 g3)**, whereby White avoids the exchange and delays e4.

3...b5 4 cxb5 a6 5 bxa6 ♗xa6 6 ♘c3

    6   **♘c3** *(D)*

In spite of all the alternatives that have been developed over the years, this natural developing move has always been White's most principled reaction.

    6   **...**   **g6**
    7   **e4**

White does not worry about giving up the right to castle 'regularly' since it requires very little effort to castle 'by hand' in this position.

7	...	♗xf1
8	♔xf1	d6
9	g3	♗g7
10	♔g2	0-0
11	♘f3	♘bd7 (D)

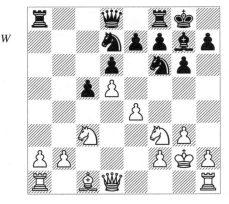

This is the most important starting position of this main line. Black is ready to execute the standard plan of playing 12...♕b6 or 12...♕a5, followed by 13...♖fb8. A modern variation on this theme is to play 12...♖a6 (or 12...♖a7) and 13...♕a8. With a queen on a8, a pawn-break in the centre with ...e6 becomes interesting. It will at least make the white king feel uneasy on g2.

White's standard moves are **12 ♖e1** and **12 h3** (preventing ...♘g4-e5). He will have to try to develop his queenside very cautiously.

Fianchetto Variation

6 g3 *(D)*

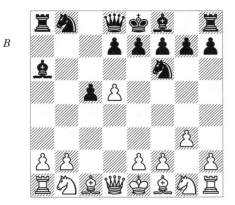

White postpones e4 and avoids an exchange of bishops. The underlying idea is that with all his pieces still in play, Black will have some slight coordination problems. White is in effect trying to use his traditional Benoni space advantage even in this position.

| 6 | ... | d6 |
| 7 | ♗g2 | g6 (D) |

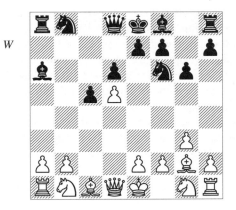

8 ♘c3

When discussing the relative merits of 5...g6 and 5...♗xa6, I already mentioned the subtle alternative **8 b3**, which is the reason why most players prefer 5...g6 these days. 8 b3 neutralizes the dangerous bishop on g7. After 8...♗g7 9 ♗b2 0-0 White will have to develop his king's knight via h3, because 10 ♘f3 ♗b7 would leave the d-pawn very vulnerable (11 ♘c3 ♘xd5 being obviously not what White intended when he played 8 b3), but this should not be a problem since there is an excellent square for this knight on f4.

| | 8 | ... | ♗g7 |
| | 9 | ♘f3 | ♘bd7 *(D)* |

This is the most important starting position for the Fianchetto Variation.

Strategically the problems are the same as in the 6 ♘c3 line, but tactically there are some major differences.

Initially **10 0-0** was played almost unanimously, with Black replying equally casually **10...0-0**. For decades no one knew how White should develop his pieces in this position until it finally became clear that 11 ♕c2 followed by 12 ♖d1 is probably best. White plans to consolidate his queenside with ♖b1, b3 and perhaps ♗b2. With this conclusion firmly established, the immediate 11 ♖b1 followed by b3 turned out to be an equally sound way of carrying out this plan.

To prevent these manoeuvres, the idea was developed to play **10...♘b6** instead of 10...0-0. Not only does this prevent 11 ♕c2, but also 11 ♖b1 is now dubious because of 11...♗c4! attacking both a2 and d5. This was rather disappointing from White's point of view because it meant that he would have to fall back on other schemes of development, like 11 ♖e1 0-0 12 e4, for which enthusiasm had never been overwhelming.

At the start of the 21st century, however, the ingenious **10 ♖b1** *(D)* was discovered.

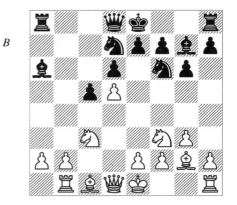

Now White is just in time to meet 10...♘b6 with the simple 11 b3, preventing 11...♗c4. If 11...♗b7, White does not play 12 e4, which would be problematic after 12...♗a6, but 12 ♘h4. This protects d5 and allows White gradually to develop his queenside. An easing of the pressure on his position then finally comes in sight. Of course the knight is not well placed on h4, but if all goes well, this is a temporary drawback only.

Other 1 d4 ♘f6 Openings

| 1 | d4 | ♘f6 *(D)* |

W

Generally speaking, the situation regarding White's 2nd-move options is much the same as in the position after 1 d4 d5. In the majority of games **2 c4** is played, intending to take complete control over the centre with 3 ♘c3 and 4 e4.

Second place in the hierarchy is occupied by **2 ♘f3**, which may be intended either as the first part of a scheme of development which does *not* include c4, or as a simple postponement of c4. In the latter case it is used as a clever ploy to avoid certain openings that are feasible only after an immediate 2 c4, like the Benko Gambit and the Budapest Gambit.

2 ♗g5, the Trompowsky Attack, is a wholly different move. This relatively young opening has been particularly popular in Great Britain during the last three decades. Instead of juggling with ultra-subtle moves to reach a slightly more favourable version of this opening or to avoid a slightly inferior version of that variation, White radically enters new territory.

Other moves also leave the well-trodden paths of opening theory behind. Moves like **2 e3**, **2 c3** or **2 ♗f4** are certainly playable, but there is nothing to know about them. Because

they do not put any immediate pressure on the opponent, there are no problems to be solved.

Things are different if White plays **2 ♘c3**, which is really like saying "I would like to play an 1 e4 opening after all, if you do not mind". If Black does mind and plays the most logical reply 2...d5 to prevent 3 e4, we find ourselves in the Richter-Veresov Opening (see page 55).

2 c4

| 2 | c4 *(D)* |

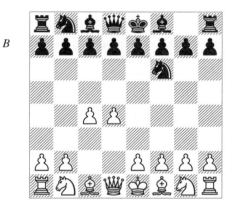

B

In the previous chapters we have discussed the consequences of **2...e6**, **2...g6** and **2...c5**. There are a few other possibilities which are not as popular as these 'major' openings, but which are quite interesting nevertheless.

The soundest of these alternatives is **2...d6**, the Old Indian Defence. Black wants to play ...e5, a solid positional motif which we have already encountered in the King's Indian Defence.

Strictly speaking though, it is not necessary to make any preparations for ...e5, as is shown by the existence of the Budapest Gambit: **2...e5**. Anyone happening to notice that this pawn is actually *en prise* will understand, however, that this radical opening is far from self-evident. Still, it is an attempt to grab the initiative that is not to be underestimated. It is in fact quite a favourite with some players who like to provoke their opponents.

2...♘c6 *(D)* is also provocative, but in a different way.

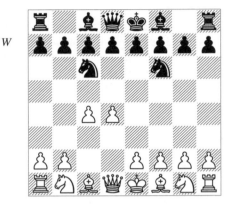

This opening is of recent origin, and has been dubbed the **Black Knights Tango** although the name is not universally used, but it can boast a steadily growing number of devotees. Here too, the idea is to play 3...e5 (after 3 ♘c3 for instance) but it also challenges White to play 3 d5. The idea is to reply 3...♘e5 followed by 4...e6, hoping to develop some serious counterplay by attacking the enemy centre pawns.

2...b6 is nameless yet this is a far older opening than 2...♘c6. It is actually a rudimentary form of the Queen's Indian Defence, developed in the 1920s, but recently taken up again by some as a way to throw the opponent out of the theory books. After 3 ♘c3 ♗b7, 4 ♘f3 will transpose to a regular Queen's Indian following 4...e6, but White can take up the challenge by playing 4 d5 or 4 ♕c2.

Old Indian Defence

    2   **...**   **d6** *(D)*

As is suggested by the name, this is one of the oldest interpretations of the opening move 1...♘f6. Black allows his opponent to build up a broad pawn-centre with 3 ♘c3 and 4 e4, a strategy which was revolutionary a century ago,

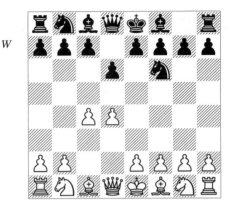

but his plan to create a foothold in the centre by playing ...e5 is based on classical principles.

The Old Indian Defence has acted as a precursor of the more dynamic King's Indian, where Black fianchettoes his bishop first and makes a decision about playing ...e5 later, depending on White's scheme of development. The Old Indian Defence is characterized by a more modest development of the dark-squared bishop: ...♗e7, which is why many theory books have labelled the Old Indian a passive opening. As usual such a label is inaccurate. It conceals a complex and fascinating reality. It must also be borne in mind that Black can still switch to a King's Indian by playing ...g6 in the next few moves, so White needs to take this into account when choosing his reply.

    3   **♘c3**

White can temporarily prevent ...e5 by playing 3 ♘f3, reaching a position which also occurs quite frequently via 1 ♘f3 or 1 d4 ♘f6 2 ♘f3.

Though not a bad move, 3 ♘f3 gives Black a few extra options that he does not have after 3 ♘c3. Developing the bishop to f5 (**3...♗f5**) becomes slightly more attractive now that White can no longer prepare a quick e4 with moves like f3 or g3 and ♗g2, but **3...♗g4** is also quite interesting. **3...♘bd7** is the way to stick to the classical plan of playing ...e5. And of course, **3...g6** leads to King's Indian terrain with White committed to an early ♘f3.

    3   **...**   **e5** *(D)*

This straightforward move does not really have what can be called a disadvantage objectively, but some players do prefer to play the preparatory move **3...♘bd7** in order to avoid the possible exchange of queens after 4 dxe5.

3...♗f5 is a much sharper variation which came into fashion around 1985. On the face of it, preventing e4 in this way seems totally pointless because what is Black to do now after the simple reply 4 f3? The point is that if Black *now* plays 4...e5, White is committed to 5 e4, which can be met with 5...exd4 6 ♕xd4 ♘c6, followed by 7...♗e6. The tempo lost with ...♗f5-e6 is compensated for by the attack on the white queen and an open, lively struggle, quite unlike the classical Old Indian variations, lies ahead. Another critical reaction to 3...♗f5 though, is to prepare e4 by 4 g3 and 5 ♗g2.

It is also not too late to transpose to a King's Indian Defence by playing **3...g6**.

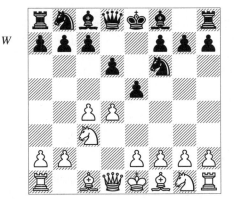

4   ♘f3

This move keeps the tension in the centre intact, while attacking the pawn on e5.

The main alternative is to play the endgame after **4 dxe5** dxe5 5 ♕xd8+ ♔xd8 6 ♘f3, hoping to take advantage of the somewhat shaky position of Black's king on d8.

Closing the centre with **4 d5**, though certainly not bad, is not likely to worry an opponent who feels at home in the King's Indian Defence. After 4...g6 most players will feel that White has limited his options by having committed himself to d5 so early.

4   ...   ♘bd7 (D)

The advance **4...e4** is critical for an evaluation of 4 ♘f3, but this is not often seen in tournament practice. It usually leads to a much

more chaotic type of position than 4...♘bd7. The crucial reply is 5 ♘g5 ♗f5 6 g4. White eliminates the potential bridgehead on e4 at the cost of his g-pawn.

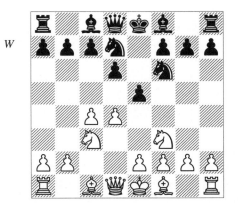

This is the most important starting position of the Old Indian Defence. Three different ways for White to develop his position have grown into main lines.

5 e4 is undoubtedly the most natural move. After 5...♗e7 White plays 6 ♗e2 0-0 7 0-0, when 7...c6 followed by 8...a6, preparing ...b5, is the traditional plan for Black. It is not easy to start an attack against Black's very solid position. White's main weapon is to play d5 at some point. Some players prefer to adopt a King's Indian set-up by 5...g6, seeking a transposition to a ...♘bd7 Classical (see page 105).

Contrary to the situation in the King's Indian Defence, a fianchetto of the light-squared bishop does not fundamentally alter the character of the game in this case. If White plays **5 g3**, the critical situation also arises after 5...♗e7 6 ♗g2 0-0 7 0-0 c6 8 e4 a6.

On the other hand, **5 ♗g5** *does* alter the situation. White radically prevents a belated switch to the King's Indian (5...g6? runs into 6 dxe5 dxe5 7 ♘xe5!) while 5...♗e7 can now be met aggressively by 6 e3 0-0 7 ♕c2, when Black has to take a possible kingside attack, based on 0-0-0 and g4, into account.

Budapest Gambit

2   ...   e5 (D)

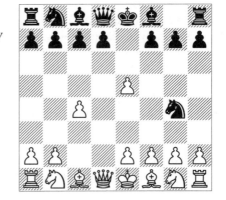

What a contrast with the Old Indian move 2...d6 that we have just seen! Still, there is one similarity between these two diametrically opposed openings: they are of the same age. The Budapest Gambit was brought to the attention of the chess world around 1917, when several Hungarian players started using it to good effect. Although occupying a relatively modest place in the opening books, it has always had its loyal devotees.

Black is disturbing the positional balance and is looking to complicate the game by creating tactical problems. However, these tactical complications will only arise if White goes for an all-out refutation of the gambit, especially if he decides to hang on to the extra pawn. If he behaves as if nothing has happened, returns the pawn and develops his pieces, the position will 'normalize' and White may be justified in counting on a small positional advantage. Anyone wishing to play the Budapest Gambit must be prepared (technically, but also mentally) for either of these approaches.

3   dxe5   ♘g4 *(D)*

Even sharper (and weirder!) is **3...♘e4**, the **Fajarowicz Gambit**. Black is not concerned with winning back the gambit pawn and tries to unnerve his opponent by creating vague threats along the e1-a5 diagonal instead. 4 ♕c2 ♗b4+ 5 ♘d2 d5! 6 exd6 ♗f5 7 dxc7 ♕xc7 would be a dream scenario for Black, transforming the vague threats into an attack with the force of a hurricane. 4 ♘f3 ♗b4+ 5 ♗d2 ♘xd2 6 ♘bxd2 ♘c6 7 a3 ♗xd2+ 8 ♕xd2, 'normalizing' the position, is much more solid.

4   ♗f4

The most level-headed way of temporarily hanging on to the extra pawn.

The rather impulsive **4 f4**, though providing radical protection for e5, does a lot of damage to White's pawn-structure and is probably exactly what Black would be hoping for. After 4...♗c5 5 ♘h3 d6 there can be no doubt that Black has sufficient compensation for the small material deficit.

4 ♕d4 is less draconian, yet this too, like 4 f4, is a relatively rare bird in tournament practice. Black's best answer is the uncompromising 4...d6, giving top priority to fast piece development.

Rather more important are two other moves that are based on a totally different strategy: White does not worry about defending his pawn on e5 and concentrates on developing his position quickly and harmoniously.

Of these, **4 e4** *(D)* is certainly the sharper.

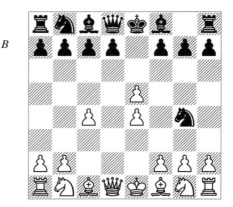

After 4...♘xe5 White continues 5 f4, when 5...♘ec6 (or 5...♘g6) leads to a position where it is unclear whether White's centre will turn out to be weak or strong in the end.

4 ♘f3 is a much more modest move. Black regains the pawn very easily with 4...♗c5 5 e3 ♘c6. Now 6 ♘c3 ♘gxe5 7 ♗e2 0-0 8 0-0, for instance, leads to a situation where Black will not find it so easy to get his teeth into his opponent's position as after 4 e4, but he also has far less to worry about.

4	**...**	**♘c6**

The crazy-looking **4...g5** is a move very much in the spirit of the Budapest Gambit, but while this move makes it easier for Black to regain his pawn, the resulting gash in his kingside pawn-formation puts off all but the boldest or most reckless players.

5	**♘f3**	**♗b4+** *(D)*

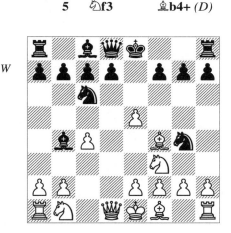

This is the most important starting position of the Budapest Gambit.

White faces a fundamental decision, reflecting his personal style and temperament. Black will have to feel at ease with either possibility.

6 ♘c3 is the most ambitious move. White safeguards his extra pawn, because 6...♗xc3+ 7 bxc3 ♕e7 can be met with 8 ♕d5. Amazingly, although this is one of the oldest variations of the Budapest Gambit, there is still very little theoretical clarity about this position. Black continues 8...f6 9 exf6 ♘xf6 10 ♕d3 d6 *(D)*.

White's weakened pawn-structure on the queenside and the many open lines for Black's pieces definitely compensate to a certain extent

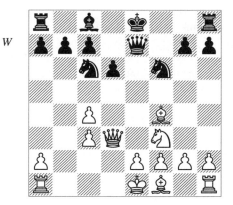

for the missing pawn, but to what extent exactly?

But if you are looking forward to trying your hand at this double-edged variation, the alternative **6 ♘bd2** may come as a cold shower. White does not want to risk a doubling of his pawns and sticks to a strategy of simple and sound development. 6...♕e7 7 e3 ♘gxe5 8 ♘xe5 ♘xe5 9 ♗e2 will give him an improved version of the 4 ♘f3 ♗c5 5 e3 line, because his dark-squared bishop is actively placed on f4, while its counterpart is not really being very useful on b4.

2 ♘f3

2	**♘f3** *(D)*

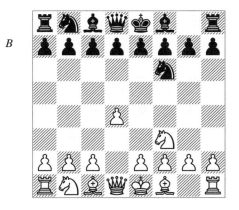

Most players will react to this move in the same way as they would to 2 c4. If you want to play a King's Indian or a Grünfeld, you will play **2...g6**. If it is a Nimzo- or Queen's Indian you are thinking about, it will be **2...e6**.

But if you want to play a Benoni, things are different. If he so wishes, Black can play **2...c5** and turn this into an independent way of countering 2 ♘f3. In other words: this *could* be an attempt to 'punish' White for not playing 2 c4, because after 2 ♘f3 c5 3 d5 Black has a few possibilities that are not available after 2 c4 c5 3 d5. But if Black plays 2...c5, thinking that this is just another way of playing the Benoni, he may be in for an unpleasant surprise, because in that case White also has an important possibility which is not available after 2 c4 c5. Very confusing of course, so both players will have to know exactly what they are doing.

Another possibility for Black is to say goodbye to the 1...♘f6 openings and play **2...d5**, heading for a Queen's Gambit. This move-order (1 d4 ♘f6 2 ♘f3 d5 rather than 1 d4 d5) may be attractive to those who would like to play a Queen's Gambit, but who have a problem with certain variations that are only available to White after 1...d5 and not if the game starts 1 d4 ♘f6 2 ♘f3 d5. For instance, if 3 c4 e6 4 ♘c3 ♗e7 White no longer has the option of playing the strongest subvariation of the Exchange Variation of the Queen's Gambit Declined (see page 22), or, in the Queen's Gambit Accepted (3 c4 dxc4), the variation 3 e4 (see page 40) is not available in this move-order.

2 ♘f3 g6

2   ...   **g6** (D)

Now it is White's turn to lay his cards on the table. If he still does not want to play **3 c4**, without excluding the possibility of transposing to either the King's Indian or the Grünfeld Defence by playing c4 on one his next moves, he might want to consider **3 g3**.

If White has made up his mind to steer clear of these 'major' openings, he has **3 ♗f4, 3 ♗g5**, or – excluding an early c4 rather emphatically – **3 ♘c3**.

2 ♘f3 g6 3 g3

3   **g3** (D)

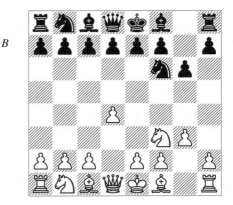

This is a modern and subtle variation, which is mainly intended to confuse an opponent who wants to play a King's Indian Defence. White leaves his opponent guessing whether he will play c4.

The most important starting position arises after 3...♗g7 4 ♗g2 0-0 5 0-0. Now, if Black plays **5...d5**, White does not really have a fully fledged alternative to 6 c4, which is a Grünfeld (see page 136), although 6 ♘bd2 is sometimes played. But against **5...d6**, the King's Indian set-up, there are a few alternatives to 6 c4 (see page 114) that need to be taken very seriously. For instance, White can play 6 ♘c3, intending to transpose to a line of the Pirc Defence with 7 e4, or he can play 6 b3, choosing a set-up which does not give Black the usual King's Indian targets for a counterattack, but without entirely giving up the option of playing c4 at a later moment.

2 ♘f3 g6 3 ♗f4

3   ♗f4 *(D)*

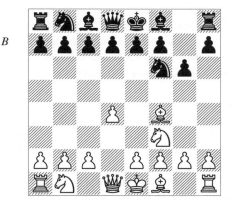

This is a set-up that we have already considered in the chapter on 1 d4 d5 2 ♘f3. White leaves the well-trodden paths of opening theory and chooses a simple and sound scheme of development for his pieces. It is a variation *par excellence* for those who do not have the time or the inclination to study opening theory. But this does not imply that this is a low-level variation! In fact it is popular at all levels. Even a top player sometimes feels the need for a day without heavy opening preparation.

Black can react in several ways. The first thing that comes to mind is to play a quick ...e5 in order to make the bishop feel unwelcome on f4. For instance, after the natural continuation 3...♗g7 4 e3 0-0 5 ♗e2 d6 6 0-0, Black can play 6...♘bd7 7 h3 (to prepare a retreat-square for the bishop) 7...♕e8, when 8...e5 is unstoppable. Another healthy idea is to play ...c5; for example, 6...c5 7 c3 b6 8 ♘bd2 ♗b7 and Black develops his kingside first before committing himself to any form of action in the centre.

2 ♘f3 g6 3 ♗g5

3   ♗g5 *(D)*

The same can be said about the difference between this move and 3 ♗f4 as I already did in the coverage of 1 d4 d5 2 ♘f3. A development of the dark-squared bishop to g5 is slightly more

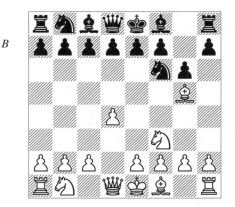

aggressive because it introduces the possibility of ♗xf6 and because it challenges Black to reply with sharp moves like ...♘e4 or ...h6.

With a bishop on g5, many players feel that they can do better than a quiet set-up based on e3. After 3...♗g7 4 ♘bd2, with possible ideas of e4, Black can prevent this advance altogether with the solid **4...d5**, or he can try **4...0-0**. Then the straightforward **5 e4** can be met by 5...d6 6 c3, when 6...♘bd7 7 ♗c4 e5 and 6...c5 are both ways to attack White's centre in true King's Indian spirit. He can also seek to show up White's central advance as premature by playing 5...d5!?, meeting 6 e5 with 6...♘e4. Therefore White often plays the slower **5 c3**, when Black can again choose between 5...d5 or 5...d6.

2 ♘f3 g6 3 ♘c3

3   ♘c3 *(D)*

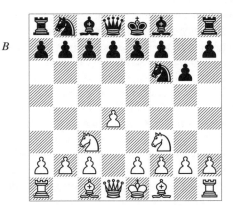

White is confronting his opponent with the same decision as in the variation 3 ♗g5 ♗g7 4 ♘bd2 above: should he allow e4?

Naturally, with a knight on c3 blocking its own c-pawn, playing **3...d5** becomes much more self-evident. This brings about a kind of Richter-Veresov Opening (see page 55). White's scheme of development is 4 ♗f4 ♗g7 5 e3 0-0 6 ♗e2, often followed by a timely ♘e5.

3...d6 4 e4 ♗g7 is a choice in favour of a Pirc Defence.

2 ♘f3 e6

2   **e6** (D)

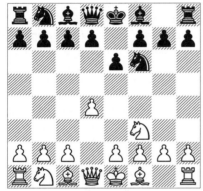

Again, White has a choice of several alternatives to **3 c4**.

The longest standing of these is **3 ♗g5**, the **Torre Attack**. Unlike most of the 2...g6 variations given above, this line has been researched and charted fairly well.

3 ♗f4 is a more reserved move, emphatically avoiding any sort of mainstream theory.

3 g3 is of much more recent origin than these two bishop moves. As in the variation 2...g6 3 g3, White plays a subtle game of 'threatening' to play c4 at some point, transposing to other openings, most notably in this case the g3 variation of the Queen's Indian Defence and the Catalan.

Last but not least, the deceptively modest little move **3 e3** combines elements of the other three variations. It is solid, yet not without poison and there are several transpositional subtleties that need to be taken into account.

Torre Attack

3   ♗g5

To begin with, this move forces Black to think about a possible e4. It is not easy to judge whether a variation like **3...h6** 4 ♗xf6 ♕xf6 5 e4 is good for White because of his perfect pawn-centre or for Black thanks to his pair of bishops. The same goes for **3...b6** 4 e4 h6, forcing 5 ♗xf6.

Though of a different nature, the problem of how to assess **3...d5** is also quite difficult, as we have seen in the section on 1 d4 d5 2 ♘f3 ♘f6 where this position was reached via 3 ♗g5 e6 (see page 53).

All these variations occupy their legitimate place in the books (and in practice), yet the most popular move has always been the flexible and aggressive...

3   **c5**

White cannot treat this as a Benoni, because **4 d5** is not an option. Nor is **4 e4** a serious move, now that Black can simply reply 4...cxd4, meeting 5 e5 with 5...h6 6 ♗h4 g5.

4   **e3** (D)

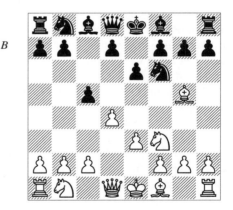

This is the starting position of the Torre Attack.

The variation is named after the Mexican player Carlos Torre, who celebrated many triumphs with it in the 1920s, including a famous win over world champion Emanuel Lasker in 1925, which continued **4...cxd4** 5 exd4 ♗e7 6 ♘bd2 d6 7 c3 ♘bd7 8 ♗d3 b6 9 ♘c4 ♗b7 10 ♕e2 ♕c7 11 0-0 0-0 12 ♖fe1 ♖fe8 13 ♖ad1 and ended in the total annihilation of Black's kingside. This unmistakable attacking potential in combination with the natural simplicity of White's opening play made the variation quite popular.

It is not easy to disturb the execution of this scheme of development. **4...♕b6** is the sharpest attempt, resulting in a rather murky position after 5 ♘bd2 ♕xb2 6 ♗d3 *(D)*.

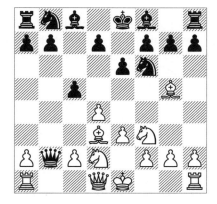

It is absolutely unclear if White has enough compensation, but so many black players have fallen victim to this pawn sacrifice that it has become a variation 'for specialists only'. Most of the less well-prepared prefer a quieter move, like **4...♗e7**, postponing the choice between a ...d6 and a ...d5 set-up. The light-squared bishop may be developed on b7, as Lasker did in the above game, but an immediate fianchetto with **4...b6?!** is not to be recommended because of the very surprising 5 d5! *(D)*.

The point is that if 5...exd5 White simply continues 6 ♘c3, winning back the pawn, when White can be very satisfied about having created a nasty crack in Black's pawn-structure on d5. Black can play 6...♗b7, but after the continuation 7 ♗xf6 ♕xf6 8 ♘xd5 he cannot strike back with 8...♗xd5 9 ♕xd5 ♕xb2? because this would simply lose a rook after 10 ♖d1.

2 ♘f3 e6 3 ♗f4

3   ♗f4 *(D)*

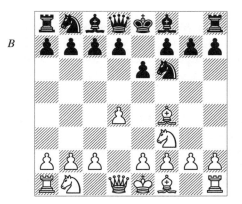

Unlike 3 ♗g5, this is a move which leaves the opponent a practically free hand. Here too the most popular reply is **3...c5**, when 4 e3 ♕b6 again leads to enormous complications, but almost any other scheme of development is equally feasible.

Those who have no objections to a transposition to the 4 ♗f4 variation of the Queen's Indian (see page 78) may want to play 3...c5 4 e3 b6 or **3...b6**.

2 ♘f3 e6 3 g3

3   g3 *(D)*

This can be an annoying move for players with a limited opening repertoire. Without an early c4, the possibility of a Bogo-Indian is ruled out, as are a number of Queen's Indian variations. To illustrate this, let us consider the implications of **3...b6** 4 ♗g2 ♗b7 5 c4 (or 5 0-0 ♗e7 6 c4). A standard position of the Queen's Indian has arisen, but only those who like to

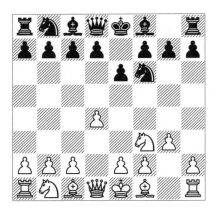

play the 4 g3 ♗b7 lines of that opening as Black will be happy about this. The 4 g3 ♗a6 variation, arguably the most important part of modern-day Queen's Indian theory, has been bypassed.

The same goes for **3...d5**, inviting a direct transposition to the Catalan Opening with 4 c4. If White plays 4 ♗g2, delaying c4 for just a few moves, e.g. 4...♗e7 5 0-0 0-0 6 c4, then a player who feels at home in the 4...♗e7 line of the Catalan (see page 25) does not have a problem, but someone who only has a 4...dxc4 variation (see page 25) in his repertoire will be in trouble.

Less clear in this respect are the consequences of **3...c5** *(D)*, a move which we have come to recognize as being tailor-made for any situation where White cannot reply d5.

In this case the juggling with transpositions to other openings continues, requiring a broad

opening knowledge of both players. If White responds with **4 c4**, the situation is relatively simple: 4...cxd4 5 ♘xd4 will transpose to a line of the Symmetrical English (see page 213). The implications of **4 ♗g2** are more complicated. If Black then plays 4...♘c6 5 0-0 cxd4 6 ♘xd4 ♛b6, for instance, the situation strongly resembles the same line of the Symmetrical English, but because White has not (yet) played c4, the two are not identical and therefore difficult to compare.

If Black plays 5...d5 (instead of 5...cxd4 in the previous variation), transpositions literally abound. To name just a few: 6 c4 dxc4 is a Catalan (see page 25), while 6...♗e7 7 cxd5 exd5 is a Tarrasch Defence (see page 11).

Finally, those who are not happy with any of these transpositions or who want to give the opening a face of its own may want to consider the 'improved Queen's Indian': **3...b5** *(D)*.

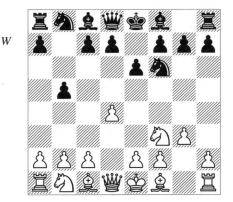

Had Black ventured this bold advance on his first or second move, he would have had to face a quick e4 (or e3) with the bishop on f1 opening the attack against b5 at once. Now that White has played 3 g3, practically committing himself to a fianchetto, it is not so risky to play ...b5. A similar idea can be seen in the variation 1 ♘f3 ♘f6 2 g3 b5 (see page 260).

2 ♘f3 e6 3 e3

    3   **e3** *(D)*

This line is closely related to the Queen's Pawn Game: 1 d4 d5 2 ♘f3 ♘f6 3 e3 (see page

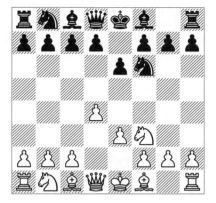

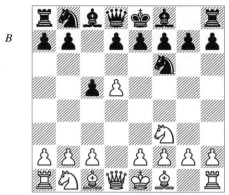

54). White's idea looks very modest, yet in the long run he is not at all intending to avoid a sharp fight. His plan is to continue 4 ♗d3, when he has a choice between c3 and ♘bd2, eyeing a possible advance in the centre based on e4, and a fianchetto of his queen's bishop.

An interesting and possibly attractive feature of this line is that Black does not have a whole lot of choice. **3...c5** is certainly a good start, but after 4 ♗d3 his only realistic options are a set-up with ...d5 and one with ...b6. In the former case (an immediate 4...d5 for instance) the game transposes to the above-mentioned line of the Queen's Pawn Game. In the latter case, 4...b6 5 0-0 ♗b7 gives White a choice between an immediate transition to the 4 e3 variation of the Queen's Indian Defence with 6 c4 (see page 88) or playing 6 ♘bd2 or 6 b3 with a possible c4 continuing to hover over the board.

2 ♘f3 c5

	2	...	c5

As I explained in the previous chapter, the name Benoni has always been used rather loosely. In the majority of cases it refers to variations arising from 1 d4 ♘f6 2 c4 c5 3 d5, but there is a strong argument for calling any defence against 1 d4 which is based on ...c5 a Benoni.

Be that as it may, 2 ♘f3 c5 is the starting point for several interesting variations, some ancient and some modern, which cannot be reached via 2 c4.

	3	**d5** *(D)*

Apart from 3...e5??, which is clearly inadvisable here, Black now has the same candidate moves as in the analogous position after 2 c4 c5 3 d5, namely **3...e6**, **3...g6** and **3...b5**. Only the consequences are different.

2 ♘f3 c5 3 d5 e6

	3	...	**e6** *(D)*

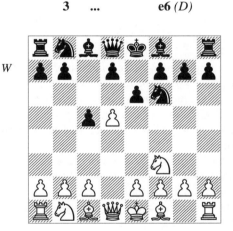

Now **4 c4** transposes to the Modern Benoni (or a Blumenfeld if Black chooses 4...b5), but it is generally agreed that the critical test of this variation is **4 ♘c3**. White wants to take back on d5 with a piece, not with a pawn. This will result, after 4...exd5 5 ♘xd5 ♘xd5 6 ♕xd5 and now, for instance, 6...♗e7 7 e4 0-0 8 ♗c4, in a position where White may hope for a positional advantage thanks to his firm control over d5, the weak point in Black's pawn-formation. The whole variation would not be of theoretical interest though if it were simply to White's advantage. What makes it potentially attractive for Black is that there is no white pawn on d5 cramping his position, as is the case in a 'regular' Benoni. With moves like ...♘c6 and ...♗e6 freely available, Black enjoys free and easy development for his minor pieces.

2 ♘f3 c5 3 d5 g6

3 ... g6 *(D)*

A comparison with 2 c4 variations shows approximately the same result as did 3...e6. While **4 c4** is a direct transposition to the Benoni, **4 ♘c3 ♗g7 5 e4** is seen as the most critical test of Black's opening. This is often called the **Schmid Benoni**.

White is hoping that not having played c4 will offer him benefits like greater mobility for his light-squared bishop and a calmer situation on the queenside, where the enemy now lacks a target for ...b5 operations.

Black is hoping that there will be less pressure on his position without a white pawn on c4, so that he will be able to develop his pieces comfortably and perhaps play ...e6 (or ...b5 anyway) at a later stage.

A major starting position arises after **5...d6 6 ♗e2 0-0 7 0-0 ♘a6**. If White now plays the natural move 8 ♗f4 Black will develop his queenside along the lines of 8...♘c7 9 a4 b6 and 10...♗b7. Curiously though, the theoretical problems do not just lie in this position, as the road towards it is equally uncertain and open for debate.

White may attempt to disorganize Black's position by inserting 6 ♗b5+. If Black tries to avoid this problem by playing **5...0-0**, he needs to consider 6 e5.

2 ♘f3 c5 3 d5 b5

3 ... b5 *(D)*

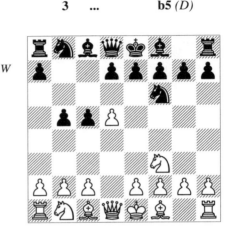

This is in effect an attempt to punish White for not having played 2 c4. All the 2 ♘f3 variations that we have seen so far allow White, if he so chooses, to return to 'major' 1 d4 openings by playing c4 at a later stage. After 3...b5 such a return is considerably less self-evident, because although **4 c4** is certainly possible, it brings about a mere side-line of the Benko Gambit (see page 154). If White has nothing better than this, then 3...b5 is to a certain extent an argument against 2 ♘f3.

But White does have a good alternative. By playing **4 ♗g5**, he threatens to regain control over the crucial e4-square. If **4...♗b7**, then 5 ♗xf6 exf6 6 e4 consolidates White's central position and Black's pawn on b5 will become an object of attack; e.g., 6...a6 7 a4. Black faces a dilemma here: should he protect his pawn on b5 where it will remain a target, or should he play 7...b4, giving White a beautiful square for his pieces (especially a knight) on c4?

The same can be said about **4...♕b6**: White replies 5 ♗xf6 ♕xf6 6 c3, to be followed by 7 e4.

4...♘e4 is definitely the sharpest and probably the most critical move. This takes the game into virtually unknown territory, where both players will be facing unfamiliar problems. A position like the one arising after 5 ♗h4 ♗b7 6 ♕d3 f5 is totally unlike 'regular' Benoni positions and requires ingenuity and a high degree of alertness from both players.

Trompowsky Attack

2   ♗g5 (D)

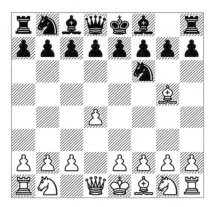

This move has been known for a long time. It was named after the Brazilian player Trompowsky, who experimented with it during the 1930s and 1940s. But for about half a century all that could be said about 2 ♗g5 was that it had a name but lacked a reputation (let alone a following). Until about 1980 the general idea was that Black needs no more than a few sound moves to show up the rashness of such an early development of the bishop.

But during the 1980s the Trompowsky suddenly gained an unheard-of popularity, first in Great Britain, then in the rest of the world. Little by little, vague positional judgements became more precise, clearly defined variations were developed and one by one all these 'sound moves' that Black had at his disposal turned out to be not quite so sound as had been thought. After about three decades of intense practical experience, the Trompowsky might now be described as on the one hand an opening like any other with a full-grown theoretical standing, while on the other it has retained something of that freshness and sparkle that is

the true mark of a rebel opening. And it is still nothing like as overgrown with theory as the 2 c4 openings!

Black's most important options are the solid **2...d5**, the sharp **2...♘e4** and the avant-garde move **2...e6**.

Other moves, like **2...c5** and **2...g6**, for instance, are definitely playable, but do not figure as prominently in practice (any more) as these three main lines.

2...c5 transposes to a position that we shall consider under 2...♘e4 if White replies 3 d5 ♘e4 4 ♗f4, but 3 ♗xf6 is also a critical test. After 3...gxf6 4 d5 ♕b6 5 ♕c1 we find ourselves in a typical Trompowsky middlegame, full of tension, where it is quite unclear which is the more influential factor: Black's bishop-pair or the damage to his pawn-structure, which makes it harder for Black to become active in the centre than in a 'regular' Benoni.

2...g6 3 ♗xf6 exf6 4 e3 and now, for example, 4...f5 5 c4 ♗g7 6 ♘c3 raises the same question, albeit in a slightly different form.

In both cases it is very difficult to provide an answer, but what *is* clearly noticeable is that it is exactly in this evaluation that something has changed over the last thirty years. It used to be the players who dared to take up these variations with the white pieces who were regarded as somewhat eccentric, whereas now playing them with Black is thought to be a bit strange.

2 ♗g5 d5

2   ...   d5 (D)

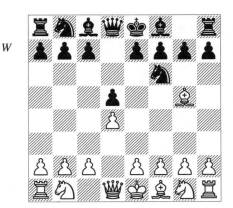

While accepting a possible doubling of his f-pawns, Black refuses to give up any territory in the centre. Now, although White may equally well play the neutral move **3 e3**, the most important starting point of this line arises after the principled reply:

3   &xf6   exf6

Although **3...gxf6** is also perfectly playable, the open e-file and the compact mass of pawns on the kingside make Black's position very solid after 3...exf6. Apparently this is what most players expect of 2...d5, because this is by far the most popular choice.

4   e3 *(D)*

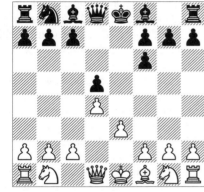

In this position **4...&d6** is usually played. If White then chooses the classical Queen's Gambit strategy of playing **5 c4**, the reply 5...dxc4 6 &xc4 0-0 7 &c3 again confronts us with the question of what is more important: Black's bishop-pair or White's central pawn-majority? In this case the position is fairly open, which in principle favours the two bishops, but on the other hand White's pawn on d4 gives him a strong hold on the centre. Again, it is hard to decide which is the more important of these two factors. Some players prefer a more modest approach, like **5 g3** c6 6 &g2 f5 7 &d2 &d7 8 &e2, keeping c4 in reserve.

2 &g5 &e4

2   ...   &e4

A logical and aggressive reply to White's second move, but it does put Black under an obligation. Unlike 1 d4 d5 2 &f3 &f6 3 &g5 &e4, for instance, White will be in a position to chase back the knight with f3 after he has retreated the bishop. Playing 2...&e4 has to be part of a plan.

3   &f4 *(D)*

This is a safer square for the bishop than h4. In fact, **3 &h4** has a few very unexpected drawbacks. To begin with: after **3...c5** 4 f3 Black has the surprising rejoinder 4...g5. Since 5 &g3 &xg3 6 hxg3 would now leave White with a rather miserable position after a move like 6...&b6, he is more or less forced to go for 5 fxe4 gxh4, when White's pawn-formation is just as badly damaged as Black's.

Another way to bring about this type of position is **3...g5**, when after 4 f3 gxh4 5 fxe4 Black not only has 5...c5 (transposing to the previous variation) but also 5...e5.

Finally Black also has a more cautious plan for attacking the bishop on h4: **3...d5** 4 f3 &d6 with 5...&f5 to follow.

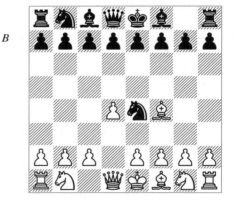

Now Black has to lay his cards on the table.

The most solid move is undoubtedly **3...d5**, but if White is willing to sacrifice a pawn with 4 f3 &f6 5 e4, even this will lead to sharp play. White is in effect playing a Blackmar-Diemer Gambit (see page 46) with the extra move &f4 thrown in for encouragement. If White leaves the chance of playing f3 unused, the game will take a much quieter course; e.g., 4 e3 &f5 5 &d3 e6 6 &d2 &xd2 with few complications.

Generally speaking, the positions arising from **3...c5** are much harder to evaluate, let alone to play. If **4 d5** Black has the sharp reply 4...♕b6, forcing his opponent to choose between a passive defence of b2 and an unclear pawn sacrifice (5 ♘d2). If **4 f3** Black could try to disrupt White's pawn-formation even further by inserting a check on a5. The idea is that after 4...♕a5+ 5 c3 ♘f6 6 d5 the surprising 6...♕b6 *(D)* again forces White to make a tricky decision, this time with the added attraction of a hidden trap.

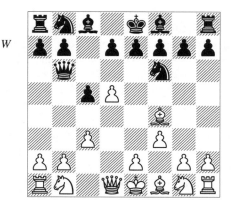

The aforementioned trap is **7 ♕d2?** ♘xd5! 8 ♕xd5 ♕xb2, winning material. Nevertheless, White can still hope for a 'normal' opening advantage if he quietly defends his b-pawn with **7 b3** or even **7 ♗c1**. In fact, this bizarre anti-development move very nicely illustrates the central idea of 2 ♗g5: White provokes his opponent and challenges him to think for himself at an unusually early stage of the game. Even if White is forced to retreat his bishop to c1 within just a few moves, the resulting position may well be very hard to evaluate. Has White simply lost time or has he provoked Black into some useless moves with his queen and knight?

2 ♗g5 e6

2	...		e6

A modern move, combining the soundness of 2...d5 with the dynamism of 2...♘e4. In fact Black is giving his opponent a taste of his own medicine here, for White is now confronted with a radical choice between a quiet move like 3 e3 or 3 ♘d2, or the principled reply:

3	e4	h6
4	♗xf6	♕xf6 *(D)*

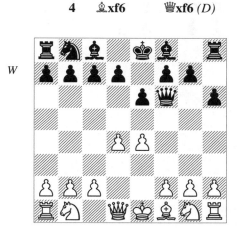

Again a perfect pawn-centre is facing battle with a pair of bishops. Black has managed to keep his pawn-structure intact (no doubled pawns), but for the time being at least he has no influence in the centre whatsoever.

This too is a variation that makes high demands on both players. Theory offers very little support. After **5 ♘f3** a position arises that is also of relevance to the Torre Attack, where it is reached via 1 d4 ♘f6 2 ♘f3 e6 3 ♗g5 h6 4 ♗xf6 ♕xf6 5 e4. However, many Trompowsky players prefer the more aggressive **5 ♘c3**, leaving the f-pawn free to advance.

Dutch Defence

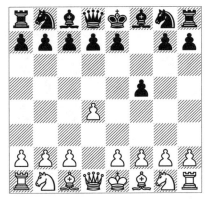

W

In a way, the Dutch Defence is the equivalent of 1 e4 c5, the Sicilian. Whereas 1...c5 is the natural alternative to 1...e5 as a reply to 1 e4, in that both moves prevent the formation of the ideal pawn-centre with 2 d4, 1...f5 is the 'other' way of preventing 2 e4 if White plays 1 d4 and has been so since times immemorial (or at least long before 1...♘f6 was taken seriously).

Both the Dutch and the Sicilian can be said to avoid a direct confrontation in the centre, i.e. in the one case 1 e4 e5 2 f4 and in the other 1 d4 d5 2 c4. But while giving White a free hand on one flank, Black, in return for this generosity, emphatically claims domination on the other flank.

This is a bold approach and just like the Sicilian, the Dutch Defence is considered a sharp opening. Black avoids symmetry and rapid exchanges and he makes no attempt to maintain a positional balance. Without worrying too much about what the opponent is doing, Black goes for his own chances. In short, this is an opening for the true fighter.

The origins of the name Dutch Defence are shrouded in mystery, but they probably go back to a book by Elias Stein that was published in

the Dutch city of The Hague in 1789, in which 1...f5 as a reply to 1 d4 is warmly recommended.

During the whole of the 19th century, the Dutch was considered to be *the* alternative to 1...d5, until Steinitz and Tarrasch started teaching the basic elements of modern-day positional chess to the world and the Queen's Gambit Declined became the one and only correct opening. The Dutch Defence, along with many others, was taken up to the attic, from where, in the course of the 20th century, it found its way back to the tournament halls only with great difficulty. Many antiquated variations had to be removed or cleaned up thoroughly before the Dutch was presentable again and able to compete with modern alternatives, like the 1 d4 ♘f6 openings. Special credit should go to Botvinnik and Bronstein, who both made a decisive contribution to the revival of the Dutch Defence. In their match for the world championship in 1951 it even was the most important opening!

Since then a new and dangerous weapon has been added to Black's arsenal: the Leningrad Variation, in which Black fianchettoes his king's bishop. This line became popular around 1980 and it has yielded some excellent results.

2   g3

Fianchettoing the bishop has become the most popular way of developing the kingside over the years. This makes the Dutch Defence the only 1 d4 opening where a set-up based on 2 c4 (and in many cases 3 ♘c3) is not the main line. This is to a large extent a matter of flexibility. By playing 1...f5 Black makes it clear that he is not going to challenge White's superiority in the centre (at least not immediately) and therefore it is not necessary for White to strengthen that central position by playing 2 c4. The problems confronting White are more of a long-term nature: how do I develop my position in such a way as to be optimally prepared for all possible plans that Black has at his disposal? The fianchetto of the light-squared bishop has proved its worth in this respect. From g2 the bishop will strengthen White's control over the important squares e4 and d5 and it will put pressure on the enemy queenside. It will also protect the white king if he decides to castle kingside, which is the most plausible choice in most variations. White will proceed to develop his queenside depending on Black's plan. In the Stonewall, for instance, it definitely has its advantages to keep the queen's knight on b1 for a while, while in the Leningrad Variation, the move c4 is often postponed or even not played at all.

Notwithstanding all this, **2 c4** ♘f6 **3** ♘c3 *(D)* remains a sound option.

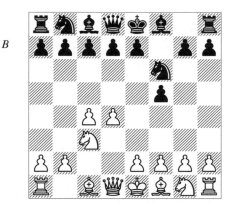

As is the case after 2 g3 ♘f6 3 ♗g2, Black then has to make a fundamental decision as to how to structure his position.

If Black is thinking about a Leningrad set-up, he faces the question of how dangerous the sharp attack **3...g6** 4 h4!? is. The idea is to meet 4...♗g7 with 5 h5 ♘xh5 6 e4. Theory is still largely undecided on this line. Black may try to avoid the problem by playing **3...d6**, waiting for a neutral move like 4 ♘f3 before committing himself to 4...g6.

If Black is envisaging a ...e6 set-up, he can play **3...e6** straightaway without any fear. Now **4 e3** d5 (with positions that are often reached via the Queen's Gambit; e.g., 1 d4 d5 2 c4 e6 3 ♘c3 c6 4 e3 f5) produces a relatively favourable version of the Stonewall Variation because White

has denied himself both an aggressive development of his dark-squared bishop to f4 or g5 and the subtle ♗a3. If White plays **4** ♘f3, the Nimzo-Indian move 4...♗b4 becomes slightly more attractive because White can no longer play ♘e2.

A completely different treatment of the Dutch (if not a maltreatment) is to open the centre right away by playing **2 e4** *(D)*, the **Staunton Gambit**.

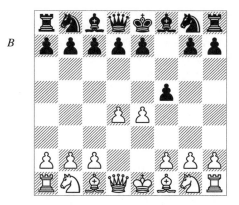

This radical strategy, sacrificing a pawn to try to obtain the initiative, was popular in the 19th and early 20th centuries but since then it has faded into the background. Still, Black has to be prepared for this approach. The situation is far more dangerous than in the Blackmar-Diemer Gambit, because the absence of a pawn on f7 makes the position of Black's king rather insecure.

If, for instance, after 2...fxe4 3 ♘c3 ♘f6, White plays the straightforward **4 f3**, defending e4 with 4...d5 5 fxe4 dxe4 6 ♗g5 ♗f5, no matter how insignificant that pawn on e4 might seem, is considered much more solid than the fearless 4...exf3, unreservedly accepting the extra pawn but allowing White fast and easy development for his pieces.

In order to eliminate this defence, **4 ♗g5** is a more common move. Black will then have to say goodbye to his pawn on e4 because 4...d5? 5 ♗xf6 exf6 6 ♕h5+ would be decidedly counterproductive. Instead, the provocative 4...♘c6, intending to meet 5 f3 boldly with 5...e5 and 5 d5 calmly with 5...♘e5 6 ♕d4 ♘f7, has a good reputation. The simple 4...e6 5 ♘xe4 ♗e7 is also considered reliable.

The preparatory move **2 ♘c3** started its career as a by-product of some one and a half centuries of analytical attempts to improve the results of the Staunton Gambit, but nowadays this sideline is considered the more important of the two. It is also a way of forcing Black to show his intentions. If he wants to stop e4, he will either have to play 2...d5 or 2...♘f6 3 ♗g5 d5, but this characteristic pawn-structure (which we shall discuss more fully in the section on the Stonewall Variation) is not to everyone's liking. The alternative is simply to allow e4, for instance by playing 2...♘f6 3 ♗g5 e6, when 4 e4 fxe4 5 ♘xe4 ♗e7 produces the same position with which we rounded off our discussion of the Staunton Gambit above.

| 2 | ... | ♘f6 |
| 3 | ♗g2 (D) | |

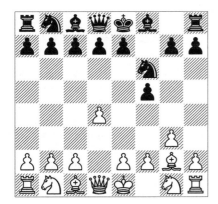

In this position Black faces a fundamental decision.

3...e6 is the oldest move. Black can then build up a central position with ...d6 or with ...d5. His dark-squared bishop is likely to find a place on the a3-f8 diagonal. **3...g6** is of more recent origin. Black develops his bishop on g7 and prepares to attack White's central bastion with ...e5. This is the **Leningrad Variation**.

2 g3 ♘f6 3 ♗g2 e6

| 3 | ... | e6 |
| 4 | ♘f3 | |

Although the Dutch Defence could well be called a robust opening, the earliest stage of the game is marked, to a surprisingly high degree, by positional subtleties and perhaps even more so by profound move-orders.

For instance, in this position it is totally unclear whether **4 ♘f3** or **4 c4** is the more accurate move, while even the rather eccentric **4 ♘h3** (D) is a serious option.

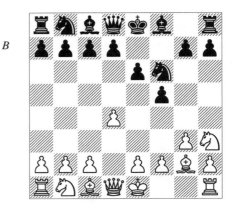

It all revolves around the question of how White is going to tackle both ...d6 and ...d5 in the best possible way. Black's oldest plan, not surprisingly called the **Classical Dutch**, is a scheme based on ...d6 and ...e5, similar to the Leningrad Variation. The sturdy ...d5 is called the **Stonewall Variation**. This system first became popular in the days of Botvinnik (the middle of the 20th century) and enjoyed a remarkable revival during the 1980s, very largely based on the idea of putting the bishop on d6 rather than e7, and with some new ideas of playing on the queenside and in the centre. Thus some positional judgements of the Botvinnik era were changed or altered. A development of the king's knight via h3 and f4 (and perhaps d3), for instance, used to be thought highly of against the Stonewall but to present-day Stonewall adepts it is little more than a minor inconvenience. That is why the old books strongly recommend 4...d6 against an immediate 4 ♘h3, and it is indeed a useful idea, but today some players prefer to reply 4...d5 anyway.

For the same reason Black used to approach **4 c4** (D) with waiting tactics (except of course when he intended to play 4...d6 all along), keeping the option of playing ...d5 open until White had committed himself to a square for his king's knight.

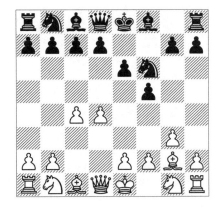

For instance, he might first developing the kingside: **4...♗e7 5 ♘c3 0-0**. In this way Black preserves the possibility of meeting ♘h3 with ...d6 and other knight moves with ...d5. However, this also means putting the bishop on e7, rather than on d6, and so does not fit in with the modern Stonewall. So if Black does delay ...d5, then it is likely to be by **4...c6**, with ...d5 and ...♗d6 normally to follow, hoping to have encouraged White to commit himself to a less-than-ideal move in the meantime. However, these are relatively minor questions of move-order to the modern Stonewall player, whose motto seems to be "you do whatever you like; I play the Stonewall".

We now return to 4 ♘f3 *(D)*:

There are now two main lines.

By playing **4...d5** Black goes straight for the **Stonewall Variation**, while **4...♗e7** postpones the choice between ...d6 and ...d5. According to the latest insights, however, d6 is a better square for the dark-squared bishop than e7, so although 4...♗e7 may well result in a Stonewall, I use this move in this book as a preliminary step for a set-up with ...d6 only. This is called the **Classical Dutch**.

Stonewall Variation

4 ... d5 *(D)*

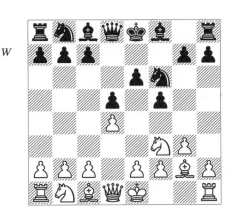

The term 'Stonewall' is not so much used for a particular move-order, but for the pawn-formation as it now (almost) stands: pawns on d5 and f5, supported by pawns on e6 and c6.

This formation can hardly be called flexible, but it is strong, very strong. In almost all of the 1 d4 openings, the central advance e4 plays an important part, either as a way of occupying the centre or in order to open a second front, for instance after first having started an attack on the queenside. But against pawns on d5 and f5 this plan is well-nigh impossible to achieve.

Because of this, the battle assumes a wholly different character. In general White will have to manoeuvre very patiently before he gets a chance of becoming really aggressive. In these manoeuvres the e5-square plays a pivotal role. Black has voluntarily conceded pawn control over this square; that is the price he has paid for stopping e4. But what use is this to White? A random knight jump ♘e5 will be neutralized by a move like ...♘bd7. Is 'control' over e5 no more than control over a few square inches of air?

It is here that patience and positional understanding play a crucial part. White must cautiously take the initiative somewhere, most likely on the queenside, and by **threatening** to plant a knight on e5 in connection with this initiative, he may finally be able to put effective pressure on the enemy position. This is a case where the old wisdom 'the threat is stronger than its execution' is fully applicable.

And what will Black be doing in the meantime, sitting safely behind his medieval fortress walls?

In the 19th century the answer would have been: Black leaves his opponent to do whatever he likes on the queenside, while he himself plays for mate on the kingside with moves like ...♕e8-h5, ...♘e4, ...♖f6-h6 and ...g5. This plan should not be underestimated even today, but if things were really that simple then probably 1 d4 would have gone out of business a long time ago.

Later the manoeuvre ...♗d7-e8-h5 came into fashion. This is a slow but sound way to make the bishop useful in the struggle for e5, creating the positional threat of ...♗xf3.

The most modern plan, and the real reason for the Stonewall's renewed popularity, is to fianchetto this bishop. After Black has played ...♗d6, ...b6, ...♗b7 and ...♘bd7, White has to reckon with the counterattack ...c5. Black is *not* remaining passive on the queenside any more, and his 'stonewall' actually turns out to have some flexibility.

A good understanding of these general strategic aspects of the Stonewall is really much more important than knowledge of concrete variations.

5	c4	c6
6	0-0	♗d6 *(D)*

This position may well be called the (modern) starting point of this opening system.

White now has all kinds of healthy moves, like **7 ♘bd2**, **7 ♘c3** and **7 ♕c2**, for instance, yet the most popular one is **7 b3**. If Black then simply plays 7...0-0, White will continue 8 ♗a3.

An exchange of dark-squared bishops lessens Black's control over e5 and must be considered to be to White's advantage even when the effects will only be felt later on in the game. 7...♕e7 is widely regarded as Black's best move. This is a very natural way of preventing ♗a3. After 8 ♗b2 0-0 9 ♘bd2 a typical situation is reached by 9...b6 10 ♘e5 ♗b7, where the subtle manoeuvring begins. Will White be able to find an opening somewhere? Is Black going to play ...c5? But a plan based on 9...♗d7 is still equally feasible.

Another idea is to play **7 ♗f4**. This way of exchanging bishops is more forcing but also riskier, because the doubled pawns resulting from 7...♗xf4 8 gxf4 *(D)* make White's kingside position less flexible and slightly vulnerable as well.

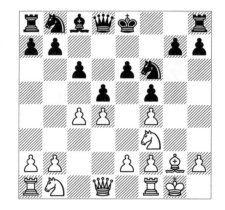

In fact, it was the discovery that this type of position is quite playable for Black that caused

...♗d6 to become popular in the first place, thereby freeing the way for a lasting revival of the Stonewall.

Classical Dutch

4	...	♗e7
5	0-0	0-0
6	c4	**d6** *(D)*

Here too **6...d5** is perfectly possible. This was in fact the standard way of reaching the Stonewall until about 1985. On the whole, all strategic considerations and evaluations are the same as when Black plays 4...d5 and 6...♗d6, but the dark-squared bishop is simply less active on e7. This becomes visible, for instance, if White plays 7 b3. With a bishop on e7, Black does not have ...♕e7 and is unable to prevent 8 ♗a3.

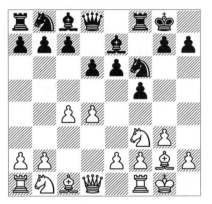

W

By playing 6...d6, Black keeps his pawn-structure flexible. After due preparation, ...e5 might be played. The plan of starting an attack on the kingside by means of ...♕e8-h5 (as in the Stonewall) is another option.

The crucial difference from the Stonewall is that without ...d5, White has the opportunity of breaking through in the centre. The opening stage is thus likely to revolve around White threatening to play e4 and Black threatening to play ...e5. At the same time Black must keep an eye on another possible breakthrough: d5, especially in positions where he does not have the chance of replying ...e5.

Tactical subtleties play a major role in this line, much more so than in the rather static

Stonewall Variation. Consequently the Classical Dutch has always been a favourite of players who like dynamic positions with plenty of concrete variations to calculate.

7	♘c3	**♕e8** *(D)*

This is a standard move in the Classical Dutch. During the 1970s, **7...a5** used to be popular, paying attention to the queenside first, before trying to take the initiative on the other side of the board. Unfortunately, this allows White rather a free hand in the centre. Against 8 ♖e1, threatening to play 9 e4, Black has little better than 8...♘e4, when 9 ♕c2 forces Black either to take on c3 (which will not stop e4) or to sacrifice a pawn with 9...♘c6!? 10 ♘xe4 ♘b4 11 ♕b1 fxe4 12 ♕xe4 and now the equally spectacular and logical 12...e5, based on the idea that after 13 dxe5 ♗f5 the white queen is in some trouble. Whether this variation is correct or not (theory does not think so), it is an excellent illustration of the character of the Classical Dutch, which tends to lead to some very sharp fighting.

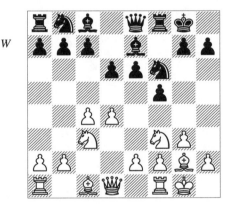

W

This is the most important starting position of the Classical Dutch.

Here too, a straightforward approach with **8 ♖e1** is considered critical for a correct assessment of both sides' chances, but Black can now play 8...♘e4 9 ♕c2 ♕g6, which is not possible in the 7...a5 line. The immediate 8...♕g6 may also look good, but it does not stop 9 e4, because after 9...fxe4 10 ♘xe4 ♘xe4 11 ♖xe4! ♕xe4? 12 ♘h4! Black loses his queen. Instead of 11...♕xe4, however, Black has the simple developing move 11...♘c6, when it is uncertain if White has actually achieved anything.

The alternative method of preparing e4, **8 ♕c2**, also runs into an interesting tactical surprise: if Black continues 8...♕h5 he will be able to meet 9 e4 with 9...e5 because of 10 dxe5 dxe5 11 ♘xe5 fxe4, when the white knight on e5 comes under attack.

8 b3 is the most flexible approach. White creates two excellent squares for his dark-squared bishop (b2 and a3) before embarking on an e4 plan. A characteristic point of this line is that after 8...♕h5 9 ♗a3 a move like 9...a5, though logical enough in itself, is strongly met by 10 d5. This is the perfect moment for this advance because the 'desired' reply 10...e5 unexpectedly loses a pawn to 11 ♘xe5!.

Leningrad Variation

3   ...   **g6** (D)

The Leningrad Variation can be said to be the natural successor of the Classical Dutch. In both variations, achieving the advance ...e5 is Black's most important plan. Around 1900, developing the bishop to e7 was thought of as self-evident, but around 1950 it gradually became clear that fianchettoing the bishop might well be a better way of executing this classical plan. Not only does the bishop support the advance ...e5 much better from g7, but the move ...e5 itself also supports the bishop, because it is very likely to result in the disappearance of White's pawn on d4, when a bishop on g7 will

exert strong pressure against White's queen-side.

The name 'Leningrad Variation' contains a little bit of political history for the development of this variation started in the Soviet Union, in particular in Leningrad, the city which is now St Petersburg.

4   **♘f3**

Here too, developing the knight to h3 is a perfectly viable alternative to the rather more classical ♘f3.

White can either play **4 ♘h3** immediately or **4 c4 ♗g7 5 ♘c3 0-0 6 ♘h3** (D).

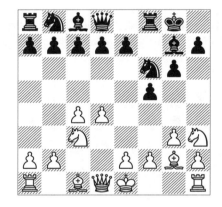

The idea is to meet the thematic 6...d6 with the equally thematic 7 d5, offering White's king's knight the prospect of jumping to f4, from where it will eye Black's weak point e6 very menacingly. But, however logical this plan may be, it has never really seemed to worry Black. By plainly showing his hand at such an early stage, White gives his opponent a clear plan of counterattack, based on utilizing the squares e5 and c5 for his knight. Black can simply play ...e5 regardless, if necessary in connection with ...c6; e.g., **7...♘a6** 8 0-0 ♘c5 9 ♘f4 e5 10 dxe6 c6 covering b7, when White is unable to keep his pawn on e6. Another characteristic reply is **7...c6** 8 ♘f4 e5 9 dxe6 ♕e7.

Another, somewhat more sneaky and very specific anti-Leningrad build-up starts with **4 c3**. After 4...♗g7 5 ♕b3 White prevents his opponent from castling and attacks b7. This variation has not been deeply examined yet. Black has tried 5...♘c6 followed by 6...e6 and 5...c6 with the idea of playing 6...♕b6. And someone who feels equally at home in a Stonewall will probably have few scruples in playing 5...d5.

| 4 | ... | ♗g7 |
| 5 | 0-0 | 0-0 *(D)* |

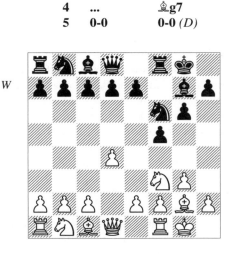

W

6 c4

This is the classical approach to every 1 d4 opening. White gains space on the queenside and reinforces his hold on the centre. But in this case it is not a bad idea at all to postpone c4 or even to do without it. In fact, by playing **6 b3** d6 **7 ♗b2** *(D)* White is following another specific anti-Leningrad strategy: he attempts to neutralize the effects of the powerful g7-bishop.

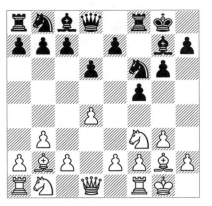

B

This is a very flexible system and it is difficult to distinguish anything resembling a clear-cut 'main variation' here. White can 'simply' develop his queen's knight on c3, but also on d2, where it does not obstruct the working of the

b2-bishop. He can play c4 at whatever moment he sees fit, but he can also manoeuvre his knight to c4 (♘bd2-c4). Black has many different ways of coping with this system, varying mainly in how fast he tries to get ...e5 in. **7...c6** is always a healthy move and **7...♕e8** is very popular. The latter move not only supports ...e5 but has a few other points as well. After 8 ♘bd2 ♘c6 9 ♖e1, for instance, Black could try 9...h6 10 e4 fxe4 11 ♘xe4 ♘xe4 12 ♖xe4 g5, followed by 13...♕h5, launching an attack against White's kingside in the same way as in the 3...e6 variations. The relationship between the Leningrad Variation and the Classical Dutch is plainly visible here.

7...♘e4 is another way of preparing ...e5; e.g., 8 ♘bd2 ♘c6 9 c4 e5, when White has to make up his mind: is it best to close the centre with 10 d5 or should he open the position with 10 dxe5 ♘xd2 11 ♕xd2 dxe5?

| 6 | ... | d6 |
| 7 | ♘c3 *(D)* | |

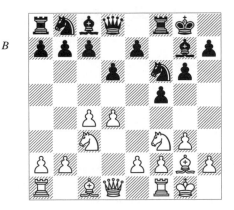

B

This is the most important starting point of the Leningrad Variation.

7...c6 is the classical move and the provocative **7...♘c6** has also been around for a long time, but the most popular variation is **7...♕e8**, a move that has long been standard in the 3...e6 variations but is relatively new in the Leningrad.

7...c6

| 7 | ... | c6 |

We find this little pawn move in almost all subvariations of the Leningrad. The positional advantages are evident: Black safeguards his pawn on b7 against the constant threat of the white bishop, the d8-a5 diagonal becomes available to the queen and in many cases control over the d5-square turns out to be of vital importance.

8   d5

Throughout the years, this advance in the centre has been considered the critical reaction to 7...c6. It shows up one of the darker sides of the Leningrad Variation: the combination of pawn moves ...f5 and ...d6 has left behind a latent weakness at e6. It should come as no surprise that the standard reaction to White's d5 advance is...

8   ...   e5
9   dxe6   ♗xe6 (D)

 W

This position is critical for an evaluation of 7...c6. It also illustrates the pros and cons of ...f5 very nicely. On the one hand, the open a2-g8 diagonal makes Black's position somewhat vulnerable, while on the other hand having a pawn on f5 gives Black a firm grip on e4. It is difficult for White to play e4 and perhaps Black will be able to manoeuvre a knight to this vital square.

A second important factor in the diagrammed position is the pawn on d6. Will White be able to force his opponent on the defensive by turning this pawn into a target or will Black develop active piece-play and perhaps even be able to play ...d5?

In a strategic sense this is a fairly uncomplicated type of position, but if we look at the concrete, tactical problems it becomes obvious that both sides have to tread carefully.

For instance, **10 b3** is often played, a move which may look ordinary but which is actually an exchange sacrifice since Black has the aggressive reply **10...♘e4**. The idea is to meet this knight sortie very prosaically with 11 ♘xe4 ♗xa1 12 ♕xd6 ♕xd6 13 ♘xd6. White is hoping that his initiative and the two pawns more than compensate for the exchange and most players on the black side seem to agree with this assessment, because in practice **10...♘a6** is by far the more popular option.

10 ♕d3, the alternative way of protecting c4, also involves some complicated tactics. The radical attempt to solve all strategic problems by playing **10...d5** does not work because of 11 ♘g5!, but **10...♘a6** 11 ♗f4 ♘e8 is quite playable. Black also has the ingenious little move **10...♖e8**, intending to meet 11 ♗f4 with 11...♘e4!, when 12 ♘xe4? fxe4 13 ♕xe4 ♗f5 unexpectedly costs White his queen.

7...♘c6

7   ...   ♘c6 (D)

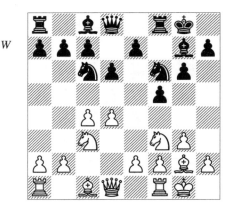

W

Black is making it plain that he intends to play 8...e5. He also emphatically challenges White to thwart this plan by replying 8 d5. The whole idea looks rather foolish at first sight, because we have just seen that, in general, d5 is an attractive move in any case. Nevertheless, Black has two different ways of trying to justify 7...♘c6. In both cases, play is likely to become much more complicated than in the 7...c6 variation.

8　d5

8...♘a5 is the more solid of the two options at Black's disposal. If White covers his c-pawn with 9 ♘d2, Black plays 9...c5 (D), warding off the threat of 10 b4 and bringing about the typical middlegame structure that is best known from the Panno Variation of the King's Indian Defence (see page 117).

The difference is that in the Dutch Defence Black has (obviously) already played ...f5. The opening battle will revolve around this small, but strategically important factor. Which side will be able to take advantage of it? Just by way of an example: after 10 ♕c2 e5 there are two differences in the evaluation of 11 dxe6, that make this exchange more logical here than in the analogous situation in the King's Indian. In the first place Black will not be able to recapture on e6 with his f-pawn, which he would like to do on principle. Secondly, not taking on e6 is not really an option here as having a pawn on f5 will then be a bonus for Black, something he will have got for free and which he would have had to work for in every comparable King's Indian variation.

If 8...♘a5 requires some subtle strategic thinking, the alternative **8...♘e5 9 ♘xe5 dxe5** (D) leads to a position where one's prospects will depend almost entirely on one's ability to calculate concrete variations.

If 10 e4, for instance, Black has the surprising rejoinder 10...f4!?, a pawn sacrifice the

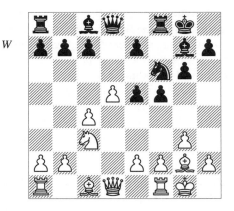

consequences of which have not been cleared up despite decades of research and practical evidence. The idea is to meet 11 gxf4 with 11...♘h5! 12 fxe5 ♗xe5 13 ♘e2 ♕d6, when the prospect of an attack against White's king and control over the dark squares on the kingside are very real. The critical test is probably 14 f4, returning the pawn. In the resulting simplified position, White may hope to have retained some initiative.

7...♕e8

7　...　♕e8 (D)

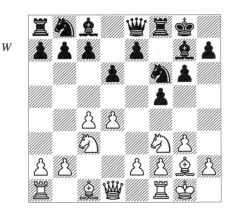

This move caused a major revival of the Leningrad Variation (and indeed of the whole Dutch) around 1985. Initial scepticism dwindled when again and again new ideas were found that made it clear that 7...♕e8 is much more than just a one-dimensional preparation for ...e5. Tournament practice also showed that it is remarkably difficult for White to avoid getting involved in an all-out battle, the outcome of which is totally unclear in most cases, making this an ideal variation to 'play for a win' with the black pieces. This uncompromising character is perfectly in line with the general spirit of 1...f5. It is not a coincidence then, that this variation has quickly become one of *the* main lines of the modern Dutch Defence.

8   d5

This advance comes equally naturally here as it did after 7...c6 and 7...♘c6. But in this case there are a number of major alternatives, all of which aim to prevent or discourage ...e5.

To begin with, **8 ♖e1** is an interesting little move. White intends to meet 8...e5 with 9 dxe5 dxe5 10 e4, when the presence of an enemy rook on the same file suddenly makes the black queen feel rather awkward on e8 (a subtle but vitally important difference from the position after **8 ♕c2** e5 9 dxe5 dxe5 10 e4, where Black can just continue 10...♘c6 without any problems). On closer inspection, however, it transpires that Black can turn the situation around with the sly 8...♕f7. If White now protects his pawn on c4 with the natural move 9 b3, Black will play 9...♘e4, to which White finds himself unable to respond with 10 ♘xe4 fxe4 11 ♘g5, because all of a sudden f2 has come under attack.

A very different, but no less interesting idea is to play **8 ♘d5**. White is hoping that after 8...♘xd5 9 cxd5 his doubled pawns will cramp the enemy position sufficiently to prevent him from becoming aggressive. And it is true that the straightforward **9...e5** 10 dxe6 ♗xe6 11 ♘g5 now looks very good for White. But White's rigid pawn-formation has its weak spots as well. To begin with there is the ingenious **9...♕b5**, attacking d5, while the modest **9...c6** also seems perfectly reasonable.

8 b3 is also quite popular. White does not prevent 8...e5, but he prepares to attack Black's central formation immediately by means of 9 dxe5 dxe5 10 e4. Tactically this is justified by **10...fxe4** 11 ♘xe4 ♘xe4 12 ♕d5+, winning back the piece. If, however, Black calmly responds by developing with **10...♘c6**, a fierce

battle is likely to ensue, starting with 11 ♗a3 ♖f7 12 ♖e1 or 11 ♘d5.

8   ...   ♘a6 *(D)*

Black calmly continues his development without committing himself immediately to any particular pawn-formation. He will play ...c6, ...c5 or ...e5, depending on White's further play.

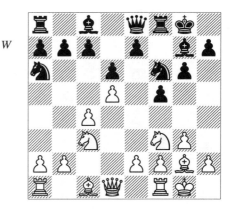

In the early days of the 7...♕e8 variation, **9 ♘d4** was the main line, intending to take the initiative with a quick e4. However, logical though this plan is, Black's position turned out to be well equipped to deal with it. After 9...♗d7 10 e4 fxe4 11 ♘xe4 ♘xe4 12 ♗xe4 and now, for instance, 12...c6, followed by 13...♘c7, chances are about equal.

The discovery that a plan based on e4 did not automatically yield a superior position was in fact the first indication that 7...♕e8 is a really solid line. Suddenly it became clear that it is not at all easy to find a good plan for White.

After several years of confusion, a plan involving a queenside attack finally proved to be White's best chance. This led to **9 ♖b1** becoming the most popular move and to the type of position arising after 9...c6 10 dxc6 bxc6 11 b4 becoming critical for the evaluation of the entire 7...♕e8 system. The result of this plan is a heavy battle between Black's central pawn-mass and White's queenside majority. White's chances are based mainly on the advance b5, often in connection with the knight manoeuvre ♘d4-c6.

Both sides need a healthy dose of vigorousness here and preferably they should be **absolutely** convinced of being in the right.

Other 1 d4 Openings

1   **d4** *(D)*

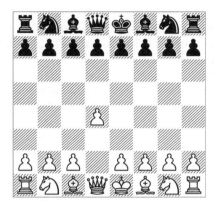

B

Having looked at 1...d5, 1...♘f6 and 1...f5, we now have a clear picture of Black's most popular and most important replies to 1 d4. These are the moves on which the vast majority of 1 d4 theory is based. They are also the three moves that take up the fight for central dominance right from the start. All of them prevent White from playing 2 e4.

Depending on his opening repertoire against 1 e4, Black could also follow a different strategy. By playing either **1...e6**, **1...d6** or **1...g6**, he offers his opponent a chance of 'correcting' his first move, for if White responds with 2 e4, the players find themselves in 1 e4 territory after all. In that case 1 d4 theory has nothing to say but goodbye (except in the case of 1...g6 2 e4 ♗g7 3 c4). Not every 1 d4 player will be happy to do this though, some because they do not know any 1 e4 theory, others because they think there are better moves than 2 e4. Whatever the reason, by not playing 2 e4 White steers the game into new territory and this has resulted in three independent 1 d4 openings.

In this chapter we shall take a closer look at these three openings, which are all of fairly recent origin. There are a few other options for

Black on his first move, but these have as yet caused considerably less theoretical turmoil and I shall treat them only very briefly here:

1...c5 is really a primeval form of Benoni, that has long been superseded by the modern move-order 1 d4 ♘f6 2 c4 c5. Black could try to prove that some of the well-known Benoni plans are equally playable without ...♘f6; e.g., 1 d4 c5 2 d5 e5 *(D)*.

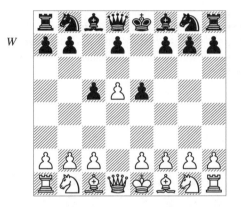

W

However, this idea has never really caught on.

1...♘c6 is a highly provocative move, analogous to 1 d4 ♘f6 2 c4 ♘c6. On the one hand Black allows a transposition to the Nimzowitsch Defence by 2 e4 (see page 461), on the other he challenges his opponent to play 2 d5. And as if these possibilities are not confusing enough, both players also have to consider the consequences of 2 c4, when 2...e5 is the intended reaction. With an opening move like this, Black is really stretching his resources to the limit as well as those of opening theory and (perhaps) those of his opponent. 2 ♘f3 is a frustratingly solid reply, when Black must either return to civilized theory (2...d5) or stick out his neck even further; e.g., with the risky 2...d6 3 d5 ♘e5 4 ♘xe5 dxe5.

1...b5 is taking this provocative attitude one step further. This is the **Polish Defence**. Instead of stopping the opponent from playing 2 e4, Black prevents 2 c4. Paradoxically, this leads to a 1 e4 opening that does not exist against 1 e4! For, unless White prefers to be ultra-cautious, he will play 2 e4, which creates a true 1 e4 type of position, albeit one that cannot be reached via 1 e4 (assuming that after 1 e4 b5? White does not overlook his chance of winning a pawn by 2 ♗xb5). Strangely enough, this opening does have a name, but hardly any fans and not a good reputation either. After 2...♗b7 White can play 3 f3, but 3 ♘d2 and 3 ♗d3 are equally strong. In any case, by playing 1...b5 Black appears to have imposed a slight(?) handicap upon himself.

1...b6 is a more cautious, but also a more passive move than 1...b5. Here too 2 e4 is both the most straightforward and the strongest reply, which in this case does indeed land us into 1 e4 theory.

1...e6

1   ...   e6 *(D)*

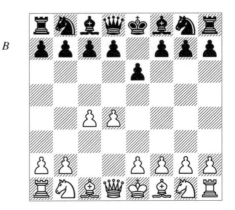

Any player who is not afraid of a transposition to the French Defence by 2 e4, will find that this is an interesting and flexible reply to 1 d4. It has attracted players renowned for their bold and imaginative play in the past, like Paul Keres and Jonathan Speelman. Playing 1...e6 requires a certain knowledge of a few other 1 d4 openings, for one of the strong points of this

move is that Black 'threatens' to transpose to other 1 d4 openings, so the more of these openings a player has available to him, the more he can take advantage of this transpositional aspect of 1...e6.

2   c4

For those who have no wish to venture 2 e4, this move is the most important possibility, but even those whose repertoire does include 2 e4 may find 2 c4 an interesting option. In fact, trying to say which of these two moves is objectively better is as impossible as saying 1 d4 is better than 1 e4 or vice versa.

A third option is the neutral move **2 ♘f3**. White avoids the two lines that make 1 d4 e6 2 c4 an independent opening, for 2...♗b4+ makes little sense when White's c-pawn is still on c2 and 2...b6 3 e4 does not offer Black the same powerful counterplay as does 2 c4 b6 (it will more closely resemble 1...b6). To make a choice between 2 c4 and 2 ♘f3 White needs to consider whether 2...d5, 2...♘f6 and 2...f5 transpose to the 'right' variations for him and whether he does not mind 2 ♘f3 c5. Since the standard Benoni reply 3 d5 is not particularly attractive in this case, 2...c5 is an important move, but it can only be played by those who are prepared to defend the black side of a Sicilian, which arises – perhaps surprisingly – after 3 e4.

We now return to 2 c4 *(D)*:

After 2 c4 Black has three transpositional possibilities. **2...d5** is a Queen's Gambit Declined, **2...♘f6** is the Nimzo/Queen's/Bogo-Indian complex and **2...f5** is a Dutch Defence.

Of these, only the last, 2...f5, gives Black's move-order some practical importance. Many devotees of the Dutch use 1...e6 as their first move in order to restrict White's options. After 1 d4 e6 2 c4 f5 White is committed to a variation with c4.

But 1...e6 gets its independent significance from two other moves: **2...♗b4+** and **2...b6**, the **English Defence**.

1...e6 2 c4 ♗b4+

2 ... ♗b4+ *(D)*

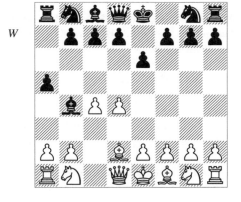

This variation is a close relative of the Bogo-Indian Defence. But what may look like a microscopic difference only (the moves ♘f3 and ...♘f6 have not yet been played) makes the position much more dynamic. In several variations Black allows his opponent to play e4 and immediately starts an attack against White's centre pawns.

3 ♗d2

Probably White's most natural way of relieving the check.

In case of **3 ♘d2**, the differences from the Bogo-Indian Defence are rather smaller. Both 3...c5 and 3...d5 often cause a transposition to the Bogo; e.g., 3...d5 4 ♕a4+ ♘c6 5 ♘f3 ♘f6. 3...f5 would be the main alternative, giving the game a decidedly Dutch flavour without directly transposing.

If **3 ♘c3** White allows a transposition to the Nimzo-Indian Defence (3...♘f6). Here too, 3...f5 must be considered the main alternative.

3 ... a5 *(D)*

Unlike the analogous variation of the Bogo-Indian Defence, this move has become the main line here, but the alternatives **3...♗xd2+** and **3...♕e7** are equally playable. An original interpretation of 3...♗xd2+ was suggested by Tony Miles, when he played 4 ♕xd2 b6 5 ♘c3 ♗b7 6 e4 ♘h6 several times during the early 1990s. Black plans to attack the enemy centre pawns with ...f5. The strategic idea of the Dutch Defence is in fact turned around here. Instead of playing ...f5 to prevent e4, Black even invites his opponent to play e4 and only then, when it is really powerful, does he play ...f5. As we shall see below, this idea is closely related to the English Defence.

Is this not a strange opening? Black does not even seem to notice that the board has a centre, let alone that he should be trying to occupy it.

That it is taken very seriously indeed, however, is amply proven by the fact that few players take 'advantage' of the opportunity to play **4 e4**, even when there is not really any concrete reason why this move should not be good. Black may react in a self-controlled way with 4...d6, followed by ...e5, or he may lash out by 4...d5, with 5 cxd5 exd5 6 e5 ♘e7 the most likely continuation.

4 ♘f3 is the more popular choice, inviting Black to transpose to the Bogo-Indian proper with 4...♘f6. Black has several alternatives, of which 4...d6 5 g3 ♘c6 6 ♗g2 e5 is the most important.

English Defence

2 ... b6 (D)

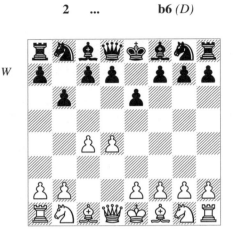

W

Black is stretching the laws of classical opening play to the very limit. He allows his opponent to form a pawn-centre from e4 to c4 in order to attack this formation with truly breathtaking ferocity. This is a strategy that demands total commitment, an open mind and an unusual capacity for independent thinking. Most of all, it requires the mentality of the uncompromising fighter. No quarter asked, no quarter given.

The English Defence first became popular in Great Britain during the 1970s. Since then, games by Grandmasters Speelman, Miles and Short and many others have brought its dynamic possibilities to the attention of the international chess world.

3 e4

This principled move constitutes the natural main line of this opening, but the cautious **3 a3** is also taken very seriously by both players and theoreticians. White eliminates the possibility of ...♗b4 and prepares to meet 3...♗b7 with 4 ♘c3. He should not be averse to playing the 4 a3 variation of the Queen's Indian Defence, because if Black replies 4...♘f6 there does not seem to be anything better than 5 ♘f3 with a direct transposition. Instead of 4...♘f6, many prefer the sharper 4...f5, giving the game a Dutch flavour.

3 ♘c3 ♗b7 4 ♘f3 and **3 ♘f3 ♗b7** 4 g3 are also not bad, but since both these lines offer

Black the chance of 'going back' to a respected line of the Queen's Indian Defence by playing 4...♘f6 (4...♗b4(+) is a good and more combative alternative in both cases) they can hardly be called an attempt at refutation, and that – of course – is what the English Defence is really begging for.

3 ... ♗b7 (D)

W

Now what is it that makes this position more attractive for Black than the one after 1...b6 2 e4 ♗b7, which I treated so briefly (and perhaps a trifle disparagingly) in the introduction to this chapter?

The difference is the extra move c4. With pawns on e4 and d4 only, it is very hard for Black to make any real impact with his counterattack, but with a pawn on c4 White lacks the possibility of strengthening d4 with c3. White has also had to invest an extra tempo so that he is a developing move behind on the 1...b6 line.

Nevertheless the move c4 is intrinsically sound. It will only serve to make White's central position even stronger in the long run, that is *if* White is given the time to consolidate his position. Thus it is really 'time' which is the key factor in this opening, which explains why its variations are so very highly charged with dynamics.

To begin with, it is not at all clear how White should protect e4.

A first impression of what White is in for may be formed by looking at **4 ♕c2**. Black can then afford to intensify the attack against e4 with a move which in practically every other opening is completely out of the question: the extremely aggressive 4...♕h4. If then 5 ♘c3 or 5 ♘d2 Black continues 5...♗b4 6 ♗d3 f5. The outcome of this early charge may be unclear, but White certainly has to be very careful if his centre pawns are not to be reduced to a row of targets.

4 ♗d3 *(D)* is equally double-edged.

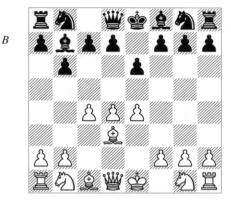

The reason is that it allows the characteristic counter **4...f5!?**. At first this was played with the idea of simply taking on g2, should White play 5 exf5, but this was soon found to be too dangerous. After **5...♗xg2** 6 ♕h5+ Black is forced to play 6...g6 7 fxg6 ♗g7 (7...♘f6? loses to 8 g7+!) 8 gxh7+ ♔f8. The loss of some material is now unavoidable for White, but Black's king is in great danger. After the rook sacrifice 9 ♘e2 ♗xh1 10 ♗g5 ♘f6 11 ♕h4 (threatening 12 ♘f4) had been successful for White a number of times around 1980, this variation was largely abandoned and a search for a new defence to 4 ♗d3 began.

The first discovery was that there is an alternative interpretation of 4...f5: after 5 exf5 Black has the sneaky zwischenzug **5...♗b4+**. If White then simply plays **6 ♘c3**, taking on g2 becomes much more attractive, because Black now has 6...♗xg2 7 ♕h5+ ♔f8!, when all of a sudden the imminent loss of a rook becomes a very dubious investment for White. This means that White is in fact forced to meet 5...♗b4+ with **6 ♔f1** *(D)*.

But this changes the character of the position completely. Black now turns his opening plan

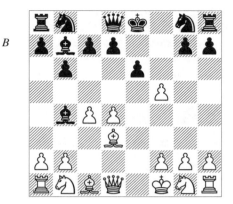

into a pawn sacrifice and after 6...♘f6, followed if possible by castling kingside, *he* will be the one who has the initiative and it will be White who will have to cope with an attack against his king.

It is remarkable and characteristic for the flexibility of the English Defence that Black also has a solid (but not passive!) alternative, namely **4...♘c6** *(D)*.

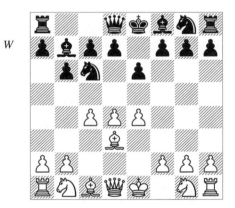

Now it is the pawn on d4 that needs to be defended, but both 5 ♘f3 and 5 ♘e2 allow 5...♘b4, when White has to give up the bishop-pair. Of course he will have some compensation in the shape of a lead in development and a central pawn-formation which is now really strong, but this too is an interesting and lively position which contains chances for both sides.

Even **4 f3** is less safe than it looks, and again this is because of the typical counter-thrust ...f5. Back in 1979, Tony Miles introduced the astonishingly bold reply 4...f5!?, based on the miraculous point 5 exf5 ♘h6!?. At the time this idea caused a sensation, but now it is a standard device, known to every 2...b6 player. After 6 fxe6 Black calmly continues 6...♘f5 (D).

White has two extra pawns, but the holes in his position seem to increase in size with every move and Black's lead in development is becoming very menacing indeed (the immediate threat is 7...♛h4+).

Finally, there is the sound developing move 4 ♘c3, but this only postpones the problem until after 4...♗b4 (D).

In this position 5 ♛c2 and 5 f3 are the most popular moves, the consequences being very similar to the variations given above. 5 ♛c2 ♛h4 and 5 f3 f5 are considered critical. The alternative 5 ♗d3 is less common than on the previous move, because (as we have seen) White

will now not be able to go for 5...f5 6 exf5 ♗xg2.

In all of these lines, theory has not come to any firm conclusions yet. There is still much to analyse and to refine. What is clear though is that this is an opening not for followers but for creators of fashion and that it is tailor-made for players with a good feel for the dynamics of the game.

1...d6

| 1 | ... | **d6** (D) |

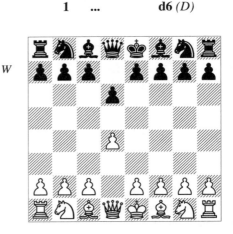

In a strategic sense, 1...d6 is very different from 1...e6. Black introduces the possibility of playing ...e5, rather like the Old Indian Defence. Yet there are some remarkable similarities between the two moves. In the first place Black has to be prepared for **2 e4**, which in this case transposes to a Pirc Defence. Secondly, it is very hard to say whether 2 e4 is actually the best move and, finally, the main alternatives are the same: if White is not sure about 2 e4 he will want to consider **2 c4** and **2 ♘f3**.

1...d6 2 c4

| 2 | **c4** |

This is perhaps the move that comes most naturally to a 1 d4 player.

Black now has **2...♘f6**, transposing to the Old Indian proper, and **2...f5**, transposing to the Dutch Defence. Just like 1...e6 2 c4 f5, this move-order is popular with players who like the Dutch but prefer to avoid some non-c4 lines. After 2...f5 3 g3 ♘f6 4 ♗g2 g6, for example, Black has taken a shortcut to the Leningrad Variation.

But the main reason why 1...d6 is an important opening move is...

2   ...   **e5** *(D)*

Now the two ways of resolving the tension immediately, **3 d5** and **3 dxe5** dxe5 4 ♕xd8+ ♔xd8 (just as in the corresponding situation in the Old Indian, after 1 d4 ♘f6 2 c4 d6 3 ♘c3 e5), are not really bad, but definitely not overly attractive either. White would much rather maintain the tension with either **3 ♘c3** or **3 ♘f3**. But unfortunately he cannot play both moves, so he has to choose between them and it so happens that they both have a specific drawback. It is on these two drawbacks that the variation 2...e5 is based.

3 ♘c3 is met by **3...exd4**. This immediate capture forces White to take back on d4 with the queen (4 ♕xd4), when Black has 4...♘c6 with gain of tempo. Although this does not mean that Black's opening problems are automatically solved, it must be regarded as a concession by White, if only a minor one.

This brings us to the alternative **3 ♘f3**, covering d4 but provoking 3...e4, an advance which is now relatively more attractive than in the comparable situation in the Old Indian Defence (1 d4 ♘f6 2 c4 d6 3 ♘c3 e5 4 ♘f3), because after 3...e4 4 ♘g5 Black has the option of providing solid support for his e-pawn by playing 4...f5 *(D)*.

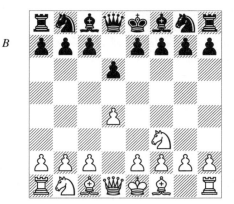

This too does not imply that Black has already won the opening battle, but it certainly does test the opponent's nerves. Not every player likes to be facing an enemy pawn on e4 as White so early in the game.

1...d6 2 ♘f3

2   ♘f3 *(D)*

When studying the consequences of 2 c4 e5, it is only natural to start wondering: is it not far simpler to prevent 2...e5 altogether? Admittedly, by playing 2 ♘f3 White makes the (minimal) concession of committing himself to a ♘f3 variation in the Old Indian (**2...♘f6** 3 c4), the Modern (**2...g6**) and the Dutch Defence (**2...f5**), but, if that is the whole extent of the problem, does not 2 ♘f3 make life a lot easier for White?

Unfortunately, life is *never* easy in the world of opening theory. Even a neutral move such as 2 ♘f3 gives Black a target for a counterattack.

2   ...   ♗g4 *(D)*

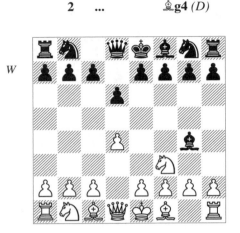

As is the case with so many new ideas, this move met with initial scepticism but gained wide acceptance once people got used to it. In fact, 1...d6 owes its current popularity mainly to 2...♗g4, which raises problems of a rather unusual and positional nature.

The most important variations are **3 e4** and **3 c4**.

Other moves, like **3 e3** or **3 ♘bd2**, for instance, to prevent a possible doubling of pawns by ...♗xf3, are unnecessarily timid.

1...d6 2 ♘f3 ♗g4 3 e4

3   e4

A natural move, giving the position a distinctly 1 e4 character. It is like asking the opponent "Well then, what do you want?" The answer is as simple as it is sobering.

3   ...   ♘f6
4   ♘c3   e6 *(D)*

Black is preparing to play ...d5, a somewhat surprising, but very logical follow-up to his opening move 1...d6. He is aiming to create a pawn-structure that is typical of the French Defence (1 e4 e6 2 d4 d5), but with one small yet extremely important positional improvement: the bishop from c8 has been developed 'through' the impassable barrier which is formed by Black's own pawn-chain in the French Defence proper.

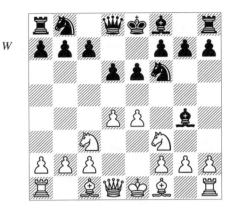

If the typical French pawn-formation of white pawns on e5 and d4 against black pawns on d5 and e6 arises, Black will have solved the one big problem of that opening in advance: the development of his light-squared bishop. This means that White will have to think of something better than 5 ♗e2 d5 6 e5, or a similar routine reaction. But what?

That is not an easy question. There are three directions in which White has been looking for an answer.

In the first place, White may radically prevent ...d5 by putting a pawn on d5 himself: **5 d5**.

Secondly, he could consider allowing ...d5 and then try to take advantage of the loss of time entailed in Black playing ...d6-d5 rather than ...d5, for instance by playing **5 ♗e2** d5 6 exd5 or 5...♗e7 6 0-0 0-0 7 ♗e3 d5 8 exd5.

Thirdly, White can try to take the initiative right from the start. It is mainly the sharp reaction **5 h3** ♗h5 6 ♕e2 (anticipating a future ...♗g6 and creating the possible threat of ♕b5+) 6...c6 7 g4 ♗g6 8 h4 that has come to be seen as the critical test of the entire 2...♗g4 system. White is threatening to trap the bishop with 9 h5. A plausible continuation is 8...h5 9 g5 ♘fd7. White has considerably more space, but Black's position is solid and still very flexible.

1...d6 2 ♘f3 ♗g4 3 c4

3   c4 *(D)*

Most 1 d4 players will feel more at home with this move than with 3 e4. Nevertheless, if

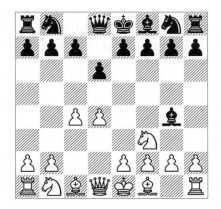

Black now plays **3...♗xf3**, a very unusual position arises, for which 'regular' 1 d4 openings offer little or no guidelines. If White recaptures with his g-pawn (**4 gxf3**), he will have a large but somewhat unwieldy mass of central pawns. Black's position is much more flexible. It is hard to say which side has the better chances here, but not everyone will feel comfortable in this kind of double-edged situation.

The alternative **4 exf3** keeps a tighter rein on things. White is hoping to utilize the open e-file to put pressure on the enemy position and to give the opponent no targets, but Black's position remains solid.

If Black played 2...♗g4 more in order to unnerve the opponent than actually to take on f3, he may want to return to a regular Old Indian Defence with **3...♘f6**, but another option is to play **3...♘d7**. The prospect of being able to meet 4 e4 e5 5 ♗e2 with 5...♗e7 6 ♘c3 ♗xf3 7 ♗xf3 ♗g5 may be tempting to a player who likes to think in positional terms. Black loses quite a few tempi, but if he succeeds in keeping the centre closed he may well profit from these exchanges in the long run.

1...g6

1   ...   g6 *(D)*

Surely this is the most casual reaction to 1 d4 that one can possibly think of. It could in fact be called the ultimate non-reaction. Black does not lift a finger to prevent his opponent from forming a broad pawn-centre or from developing his pieces in whatever way he likes. Nor does

Black make a secret of what his next move is going to be. With the possible exception of 2 ♗h6, any second move by White will be met by 2...♗g7. But can Black really afford such a laid-back attitude?

For a very long time the official answer to this question was a loud and clear 'no'. In a book by Carl Jaenisch from 1843, 1...g6 gets a place in the chapter on 'Various incorrect openings'. Nearly a century later Alexander Alekhine repeatedly condemned 1...g6 in his game commentaries.

It was not until the mid-20th century that the tide began to turn. The rise to fame of the King's Indian Defence stimulated interest and a renewed appraisal of related openings such as the Pirc Defence and 1...g6. When during the 1960s great champions like Tigran Petrosian, Mikhail Botvinnik and Vasily Smyslov experimented with 1...g6, the result was a breakthrough. Finally 1...g6 had become a fully respectable opening. It has been given several names, of which the **Modern Defence** is the most widely used. But whatever its name, the opening 1...g6 firmly stands nowadays, supported by the same strategic pillars that carry the weight of the King's Indian and the Pirc Defence.

Black's position is elastic, offering a large number of possible ways in which to attack White's central position. A practical advantage of 1...g6 is that it can be played against both 1 e4 and 1 d4. In fact it cannot even be said to belong to either 1 e4 or 1 d4 theory; it is part of both!

In an attempt to do justice to this aspect of universality of 1...g6, I shall split this opening into two parts. All the typical 1 e4 variations (i.e. those lines where White plays e4, but not c4) will be dealt with in the section on 1 e4 g6 in the last chapter of this book. All variations where White does play c4 (either in combination with e4 or not) will be discussed below.

2   c4

As is the case after 1...e6 and 1...d6, the choice between 2 c4 and 2 e4 is largely a matter of taste. One could say though, that by playing 2 e4 White retains the greater number of options. After all, 2 c4, the characteristic 1 d4 approach, does allow Black an immediate transposition to a 'major' opening, namely the King's Indian Defence. It is true that after **2 e4** White could also allow a transposition – in this case to the Pirc Defence, for instance via 2...♗g7 3 ♘c3 d6 followed by 4...♘f6 – but this is not forced and White may well choose a set-up with c3 instead, to avoid a Pirc. He could also change tack and go for the 1 d4 solution after all, by playing 2 e4 ♗g7 3 c4.

2   ...   ♗g7 *(D)*

If Black wants to be sure of a King's Indian he could play **2...♘f6** right away, although in that case there does not seem to be any point in having opened 1...g6. In any case, 2...♗g7 is the more flexible move.

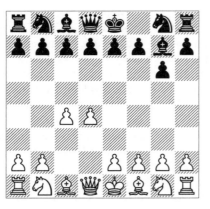

White now faces a major decision. He has to take several transpositions to other openings into account.

3   e4

This principled move constitutes the main line, but there may be good reasons why a player might prefer a slightly more cautious approach, like **3 ♘c3** or **3 ♘f3**.

In the first place Black has a few interesting moves against 3 e4, that White may well wish to avoid. Secondly, some players may want to play the g3 system against a King's Indian Defence and in that case the logical move would be **3 ♘f3**. Apart from an actual transposition to the King's Indian with **3...♘f6**, Black then has **3...f5**, transposing to the Dutch, and **3...c5**, provoking a transposition to the Benoni (4 d5) or to the Sicilian Defence (which may come as a surprise to some) by 4 e4 cxd4 5 ♘xd4.

If Black wants to steer clear of all these 'other' openings, **3...d6** 4 g3 ♘d7 5 ♗g2 e5 6 ♘c3 and now, for instance, 6...♘e7 is a solid option.

Black also has a few independent options against the alternative **3 ♘c3**, the most important one being 3...c5. This is quite an awkward move for White, because **4 d5** does not necessarily result in the desired transposition to the Benoni now that Black can reply 4...♗xc3+ 5 bxc3 f5 *(D)*.

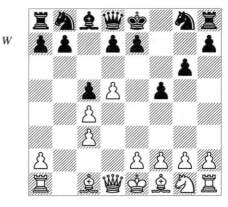

This hypermodern variation, which combines elements from the Nimzo-Indian Defence (the exchange on c3) and the Dutch (the prevention of e4 by ...f5), has not yet been wholly assimilated by opening theory and, perhaps because of this, many players do not feel comfortable with it. Unfortunately for White, the alternative **4 ♘f3** is also problematic, because this leads to a line of the Symmetrical English that is thought to be relatively unfavourable for White, after 4...cxd4 5 ♘xd4 ♘c6 (see page 207).

3   ...   d6

Here too Black can play the Benoni move **3...c5** if he so desires, but in this case there are no specific problems with either 4 d5 or 4 ♘f3.

4   ♘c3 *(D)*

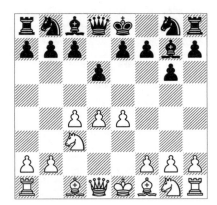

B

This is the most important starting position of this opening. The crucial question is: does Black have anything better than a transposition to the King's Indian Defence with **4...♘f6** (or at least something which is equally playable)?

The main attempts to answer this question in the affirmative are **4...♘c6** and **4...e5**, two moves that immediately attack d4, exploiting the fact that without a knight on f6, the diagonal of Black's g7-bishop is still open.

A third option is to prepare ...e5 by playing **4...♘d7**. This was a fairly common move in the early years of 1...g6, but nowadays such preparation is considered superfluous.

1...g6 2 c4 ♗g7 3 e4 d6 4 ♘c3 ♘c6

4   ...   ♘c6 *(D)*

This move poses a very concrete problem. Should White let himself be provoked into playing 5 d5 or is it more sensible to protect d4, and if so, how should he do this? Theory does not offer a clear answer to these questions but it does provide some lively and original variations.

W

Especially after **5 d5** tensions may run high. A critical position is reached after 5...♘d4 6 ♗e3 c5 7 ♘ge2. If Black now simply takes on e2, his knight manoeuvre has not brought him any great benefits. After 7...♘xe2 8 ♗xe2 we have a Benoni pawn-structure in a relatively favourable version for White because his pieces are better developed than Black's. But the real point of the 4...♘c6 line is the much more ambitious move 7...♕b6 *(D)*.

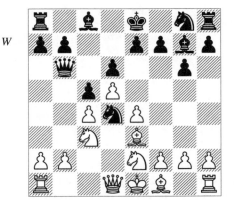

W

Black keeps his knight on d4 as long as possible, while attacking b2. Against the obvious reply **8 ♕d2** he has 8...♘f6 9 ♘xd4 cxd4, with the idea of meeting 10 ♗xd4 very powerfully with 10...♘xe4!, while after 10 ♕xd4, he maintains the material balance by 10...♕xb2. The immediate **8 ♘xd4** cxd4 9 ♘a4 is considered more dangerous for Black, especially if, after 9...♕a5+ 10 ♗d2 ♕c7, White sacrifices a pawn with 11 c5. The idea is that 11...dxc5 12 ♗b5+

disorganizes Black's position, while giving White a substantial lead in development. Yet even this sharp reaction has not been able to refute 4...♘c6. Black's most solid defence seems to be 11...♘f6. **8 ♘a4 ♕a5+ 9 ♗d2** is a more cautious approach by White.

If White has no wish to enter these complications, he has two obvious alternatives: **5 ♗e3** and **5 ♘ge2**. A third option, **5 ♘f3**, is less plausible because it gives Black an easy way of intensifying the pressure against d4 with 5...♗g4.

Against **5 ♗e3** the main line is 5...e5 6 d5 and now 6...♘ce7 instead of the perhaps more obvious 6...♘d4. This is because after **6...♘d4 7 ♘ge2** Black is unable to maintain his knight on d4, with 7...♘xe2 8 ♗xe2 and 7...c5 8 dxc6 as two rather unattractive prospects. After **6...♘ce7** (D) the position resembles a King's Indian Defence, while containing a few original extra options for both sides.

In case of a 'normal' move like 7 ♕d2, Black can lash out on the kingside immediately with 7...f5, an advance he usually has to work a bit harder for in a regular King's Indian. On the other hand, White has the option of playing 7 g4, anticipating ...f5. He also has 7 c5, which in principle is always a sound plan in the King's Indian but often difficult to achieve.

Similar problems arise after **5 ♘ge2** e5. Against 6 d5 Black again plays 6...♘ce7, while against 6 ♗e3 (a position that may also result from 5 ♗e3, if White continues 5...e5 6 ♘ge2) Black has some rather aggressive options in 6...f5 and 6...♘h6 7 f3 f5. Another possibility

is to play 6...exd4, which – after 7 ♘xd4 ♘ge7 – transposes to a line that we shall look at next: 4...e5.

1...g6 2 c4 ♗g7 3 e4 d6 4 ♘c3 e5

    4   **...**   **e5** (D)

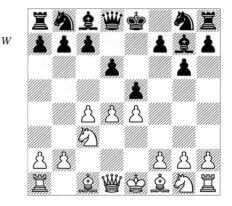

We have seen how important this central advance is in the 4...♘c6 variation. White now faces the same strategic problem that confronts him in the King's Indian Defence. How should he react to this attack against the heart of his pawn-formation?

In principle this is always a choice between playing d5 and dxe5, but the really important question is: when? What is the best moment for either of these options?

    5   **♘f3**

This neutral developing move postpones the decision. Whether this is best is uncertain. The immediate relieving of the tension, either way, also has its supporters.

If White is thinking of exchanging on e5, any further delay is unwise. Only by playing **5 dxe5** immediately can he seriously hope that this approach will work. After 5...dxe5 6 ♕xd8+ ♔xd8 White will open the position further with 7 f4. He will then try to take advantage of the position of Black's king, for whom there is no easy escape-route (like castling) from the oncoming struggle in the centre. This variation may lead to a lively confrontation between two fundamentally different styles of play: White's initiative against Black's long-term prospects of controlling d4. Who will make the most of his chances?

The immediate **5 d5** is also not bad, but it does give Black complete freedom to adapt his piece development as well as he can to this particular pawn-formation. The bold 5...f5 6 exf5 gxf5 is a critical variation. Perhaps somewhat surprisingly, Black invites his opponent to play 7 ♕h5+. He is counting on the solidity of his position after 7...♔f8 and believes that gaining a tempo by playing 8...♘f6 will provide sufficient compensation for the loss of the right to castle.

5 ... exd4

This is the crucial test of 5 ♘f3. If White refuses to choose between dxe5 and d5, it is only logical that Black will try to 'punish' him by taking on d4.

5...♗g4, **5...♘c6** and **5...♘d7** are the alternatives.

Against **5...♗g4** the usual reply is 6 d5.

After **5...♘c6** White can also play 6 d5, but another possibility is to make good use of the fact that he has played ♘f3 and throw in 6 ♗g5 (D), just to annoy Black.

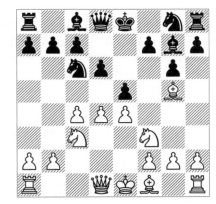

If 6...f6, White drops his bishop back to e3 and has his pawn on d4 firmly protected.

Finally, **5...♘d7** is a solid move but not exactly difficult to handle for White. After 6 ♗e2 ♘gf6 7 0-0 0-0 we are in a variation of the King's Indian Defence (see page 105). 6...♘e7 would be a way of avoiding such transpositions.

6 ♘xd4 ♘c6

Just as in the King's Indian Defence, Black should never just take on d4 at random. In this position he has a definite plan in mind.

7 ♗e3 ♘ge7 (D)

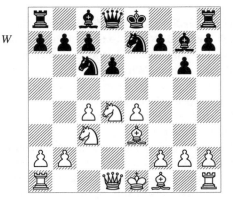

This is one of the most critical positions of the entire Modern Defence.

Black develops his king's knight on e7 in order to use his f-pawn as a battering-ram against White's central position. After **8 ♗e2** 0-0 9 0-0 he will play 9...f5, threatening 10...f4 and forcing his opponent to play with great precision. The obvious solution **10 exf5**, for instance, meets with the treacherous reply 10...♗xd4! 11 ♗xd4 ♘xf5, when White is reduced to playing the rather miserable 12 ♗e3 ♘xe3 13 fxe3, leaving him with a deplorable isolated little pawn on e3. **10 ♕d2** is a better move, which is usually met by 10...fxe4 11 ♘xe4 ♘f5. Another option is to play **10 ♘xc6**. Most players then prefer 10...bxc6 to 10...♘xc6. Although the latter move is certainly not bad, doubling the c-pawns strengthens Black's control over some important central squares and makes his position more dynamic.

A possible drawback of the development of the knight to e7 (as opposed to ...♘f6) is that it leaves Black's kingside vulnerable to a flank attack: **8 h4**. Nevertheless, Black has done pretty well in practice with moves like 8...f5 and 8...h5.

Flank Openings

Now we shall look at the flank openings, of which **1 c4** and **1 ♘f3** are the most important. These opening moves betray a rather more moderate attitude. While not as yet physically occupying any central squares, White does start taking control over them. White prepares for a fight in the centre but he does not want to be the one to take the first step.

1 c4 has been called the **English Opening** ever since Howard Staunton (1810-74), one of the strongest players in the world in the mid-19th century, played this opening move in a time when 1 e4 was still regarded as practically a matter of course. But it was not widely accepted as a serious opening until around 1920, a time when many obsolete theories and dogmas were looked at in a new light and often cast aside as a result.

Around the same time, 1 ♘f3 came to the fore as being the natural counterpart of 1 c4. One of the pioneers of this revolutionary new approach to openings in general (called **Hypermodern** at the time) was Richard **Réti** (1889-1929), after whom 1 ♘f3 was eventually named. It is mainly thanks to his efforts that the new phenomenon of a flank opening, as a fully legitimate alternative to the classical opening moves 1 d4 and 1 e4, was brought to the attention of both the general public and the world's elite of top players.

In fact, 1 c4 and 1 ♘f3 are so closely related that they could well be regarded as a single opening system. They are both based on the same principles and many variations may arise equally well from either move. This has resulted in this section of opening theory literally abounding in transpositional possibilities, not just between 1 c4 and 1 ♘f3, but involving 1 d4 and even (though to a lesser extent) 1 e4 openings as well. Especially the type of position

where *both* players move their c-pawn forward is a veritable melting pot. This system, the largest in the entire complex of flank openings, is reached via 1 c4 c5 or via 1 ♘f3 ♘f6 2 c4 c5. It is called the **Symmetrical English** and we shall start our journey through the flank openings from there.

There is, however, one major difference between 1 c4 and 1 ♘f3. By playing **1 c4** White allows his opponent to play 1...e5, a move which gives rise to a Sicilian (1 e4 c5) position with colours reversed. Because the Sicilian is both Black's most popular and his most controversial defence to 1 e4, it stands to reason that the reversed version is equally conducive to markedly diverging opinions. Some players have great trust in White's position after 1 c4 e5, some have equally great faith in Black's chances, while many do not know what to think of it and do not like it with either colour. This opening is often called the **Reversed Sicilian**.

1 ♘f3 prevents 1...e5. It also allows White, if he so chooses, to bail out of the flank openings after 1...d5, by playing 2 d4. Naturally, real flank strategy offers a totally different perspective on 1...d5. As was first shown by Réti, White can either attack the pawn straightaway with 2 c4 or he can delay a frontal attack until he has further strengthened his control over important central squares with 2 g3 or 2 b3.

Finally, there are moves like **1 g3**, **1 b3**, **1 f4** and **1 ♘c3** to consider. By choosing one of these openings, White distances himself from the heavy traffic on the highways that have been built by opening theoreticians. In all of these openings White (*and* Black for that matter) is doing a balancing act between opening theory (meaning the whole body of known and accepted theoretical variations) and pure improvisation.

Symmetrical English

1	**c4**	**c5**	*(D)*

The Symmetrical English occupies a central place in the area of the flank openings, not only because the symmetrical 1...c5 is as logical and sound a reply to 1 c4 as 1...d5 to 1 d4 and 1...e5 to 1 e4, but also because the same applies for 1 ♘f3. Against that opening move too the symmetrical reply 1...♘f6 is one of the most critical and the symmetry even continues here, because against 2 c4 (White's most popular continuation) the symmetrical reply 2...c5 is again of crucial importance. The Symmetrical English is really what binds the opening moves 1 c4 and 1 ♘f3 together.

By responding in a symmetrical way Black is really saying to his opponent "The ball is in your court again". By opening 1 c4, White has decided not to occupy the centre immediately. Black does the same. What now?

Fundamentally, there are two options.

The first is to carry on with a consistent flank strategy: increase control over the central square d5 before undertaking any kind of positive action in the centre. The standard method of implementing this plan is **2 ♘c3**, followed by 3 g3 and 4 ♗g2. This is the classical way of playing the Symmetrical English and it was the main

line from the time of origin (say the 1930s) until around 1980.

The second option is to do exactly the opposite: open the centre by playing d4. This plan is logically introduced by **2 ♘f3**, when White is ready to play 3 d4. But he is not committed! He *could* also continue 3 ♘c3, perhaps even 4 g3, before lashing out in the centre. He will choose the moment which he considers the most favourable for himself and this will largely depend on Black's opening play. This is the modern interpretation of the Symmetrical English.

2 ♘c3

2	**♘c3**	*(D)*

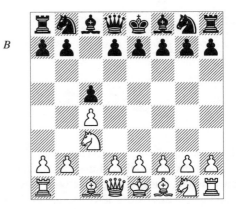

Now it is Black's turn to face the fundamental decision between a plan with or without an advance in the centre. By playing **2...♘c6** Black copies his opponent's strategy. With **2...♘f6** he prepares ...d5.

2 ♘c3 ♘c6

2	**...**	**♘c6**
3	**g3**	

If a flank strategy (first maximize your influence in the centre, then – perhaps – open it) is indeed what White has in mind, this is the logical move, but there are two other possibilities: **3 ♘f3** and **3 e3**.

3 ♘f3 will be discussed under 2 ♘f3 (see page 207).

3 e3 is a totally different way of preparing d4. White wants to be able to recapture on d4 with a pawn. Most players prefer to meet this plan by playing ...d5, an eye for an eye. This line is very likely to transpose to other openings. After 3...♘f6 4 d4 cxd4 5 exd4 d5 we find ourselves in a Panov Attack of the Caro-Kann (see page 378), while 3...e6 4 d4 d5 transposes to a line of the Tarrasch Defence of the Queen's Gambit Declined (see page 12).

3	...	g6
4	♗g2	♗g7 (D)

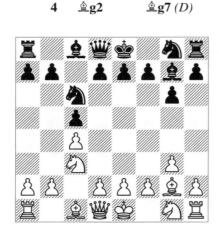

This, a key position in the Symmetrical English, is a pretty illustration of the consequences of the classical flank strategy that both players have adopted. Both sides have increased their influence in the centre to a degree where it has become difficult for the opponent to play d4 or ...d5 with any hope of success. But this does not mean that the opening struggle has reached a deadlock! White has several plans at his disposal and, because of the symmetry, Black has exactly the same options.

The first question that is confronting White is: how to develop the king's knight?

The first answer that comes to mind is **5 ♘f3**.

If Black then continues to reply symmetrically by playing **5...♘f6**, he in fact quite suddenly allows White to play 6 d4. This transposes to the 2 ♘f3 variation (see page 210).

5...e6 (D) is a more flexible move and this has always been one of Black's most popular defences against 5 ♘f3.

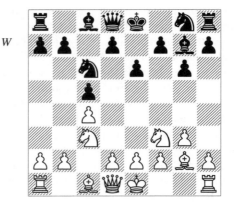

After, for instance, **6 0-0 ♘ge7 7 d3 0-0**, Black will later play ...d5 and reach a satisfactory position. Unfortunately this somewhat sleepy variation has been unpleasantly startled of late by the shocking pawn sacrifice **6 d4!?**. White is trying to take advantage of the weakening of the d6-square in a tactical manner; e.g., 6...cxd4 7 ♘b5. Whether this is actually dangerous for Black remains to be seen, but it certainly shows that even in a sheltered place like this, venomous tactical tricks are always possible.

More reliable tactically, but double-edged in a strategic sense, is **5...e5** (D).

Black takes an iron grip on the d4-square while creating space for future expansion on the kingside; e.g., ...f5-f4. White is given control over d5, but just like in the Stonewall Variation of the Dutch Defence (see page 177) it is unclear just how important this is. A characteristic manoeuvre is (after 6 0-0 ♘ge7) 7 ♘e1, intending to further strengthen control over d5 with ♘c2-e3. The plan of a3, ♖b1 and b4 constitutes another major trump card for White.

White's second option is to play **5 e3**, with the idea of now finally advancing in the centre with ♘ge2 and d4. This is a sound enough plan in itself, but it has a major drawback in that the position becomes drawish if Black continues to play symmetrically: **5...e6** 6 ♘ge2 ♘ge7, and now, for instance, 7 d4 cxd4 8 ♘xd4 d5 9 cxd5 ♘xd4 10 exd4 ♘xd5. Few players have managed to create serious winning chances from this position. If Black finds this too dry, the alternative **5...e5** 6 ♘ge2 ♘ge7 might be useful. **5...♘f6** is less logical here, because it does nothing to stop White from executing his plan with 6 ♘ge2 0-0 7 d4.

Finally, White can adopt the plan that we have just seen as a serious possibility for Black in both the above variations: **5 e4** *(D)*.

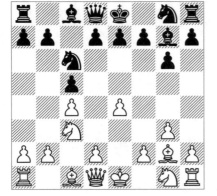

This particular pawn-formation is often called the **Botvinnik System**. White has prospects of expansion on both wings. An attack on the queenside with a3 and b4 is just as feasible as an attack on the kingside with f4-f5. In the meantime, a counterattack in the centre with ...d5 is firmly ruled out. This means that Black

will have to play 'around' the centre (as will White). A characteristic continuation is 5...♘f6 6 ♘ge2 d6 7 0-0 0-0 8 d3 ♘e8, analogous to the manoeuvre ♘e1-c2 in the 5 ♘f3 e5 line. 5...e6 is also a common response.

Anyone studying these variations carefully will start wondering at some point whether it is perhaps worthwhile to postpone this crucial decision about a central pawn-formation. This has given rise to a fourth possibility: **5 a3** *(D)*.

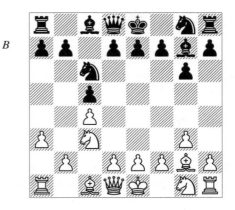

In fact, this little move has grown into one of White's most popular options. White starts an attack on the flank *before* developing his kingside any further, which is a complete turning around of the approach of the three previous variations. Against **5...♘f6** or **5...e6** White will play 6 ♖b1, when Black will have to decide whether to allow b4 or to prevent it with ...a5 at the cost of a weakening of his queenside (the b5-square). Against **5...e5** he can even play 6 b4 at once for the acceptance of the pawn sacrifice, 6...cxb4 7 axb4 ♘xb4, gives White rather a dangerous initiative, starting with 8 ♗a3 (for instance 8...♘c6 9 ♘b5!). This gambit is also possible after 5...e6, although less clear.

It is interesting that this is a variation where Black is able to continue playing symmetrically for an almost absurdly long period of time. One of the critical replies to 5 a3 is **5...a6** 6 ♖b1 ♖b8 with the idea of meeting 7 b4 with 7...cxb4 8 axb4 b5 9 cxb5 axb5 *(D)*.

Isn't it beautiful?

Both sides have carried out their flank strategy to its extreme. Now that they have cleared

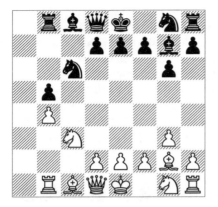

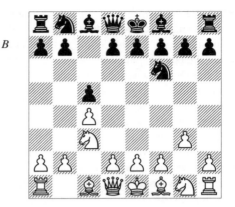

each other's c-pawns out of the way, the road is finally free for a clash in the centre, starting, for instance, with 10 ♘f3.

2 ♘c3 ♘f6

> 2   ...   ♘f6

Black breaks the symmetry. He intends to meet White's classical flank strategy with a classical advance in the centre: ...d5.

> 3   g3 *(D)*

Just like after 2...♘c6, it is this move which is the most consistent if White wants to pursue a classical flank strategy. But in this case, 3 g3 implies that White does indeed allow his opponent to take the initiative in the centre by playing 3...d5. If White feels uncomfortable with this, he should consider returning to the 2 ♘f3 variation by playing **3 ♘f3**. The difference from 3 g3 is that after 3 ♘f3 White will always be in a position to meet ...d5 with d4, if he so wishes.

3 e4, which is the only move that really prevents 3...d5, has never been particularly popular, though it cannot be said to be bad. After 3...♘c6 4 ♘f3 a position from the 2 ♘f3 variation is reached (see page 208), while 3...e6 transposes to the Flohr-Mikenas Attack (see page 237).

> 3   ...   d5

This is Black's most ambitious interpretation of the Symmetrical English. He in fact takes over from White his natural role of aggressor in the centre. This is precisely why many players do not like this variation as White. They feel that they are being thrown on the defensive, as if they are really playing Black instead of White.

But the true 1 c4 player does not know any such doubts or fears. He knows where his chances lie and he will wait for the right moment to take over the initiative. As a result, this variation often leads to exciting and dynamic chess. Both players are fighting for the initiative and are prepared to take some positional risks.

However, there is an alternative method of playing ...d5 which is also not without venom: **3...e6** *(D)*.

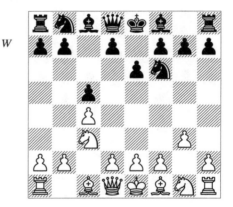

If White now goes for the 'automatic' **4 ♗g2**, he will have a problem after 4...d5 5 cxd5 exd5. The unpleasant advance 6...d4 is a positional threat and 6 d4 is not the perfect solution, because White will have to recapture with the queen (6...cxd4 7 ♕xd4), when 7...♘c6 gives Black a nice and easy extra tempo for his development. **4 ♘f3** is more accurate, when after 4...d5 5 cxd5, **5...exd5** 6 d4 transposes to the

Tarrasch Defence (page 12) and **5...♘xd5** 6 ♗g2 ♘c6 to the Keres-Parma Variation (page 209).

If Black decides to opt for a ...g6 scheme after all, e.g. **3...g6** or **3...♘c6** 4 ♗g2 g6, we are back in the 2 ♘c3 ♘c6 variation (or something akin to it), with Black having committed himself to a ...♘f6 plan.

4	cxd5	♘xd5
5	♗g2	

Now that Black has executed his plan, it also becomes clear where White's chances lie. The pressure exerted by the g2-bishop is palpable. The d5-knight is attacked and behind the knight lies a vulnerable spot at b7. Black has to tread carefully. The obvious move **5...e6?**, for instance, loses a pawn to 6 ♘xd5 exd5 7 ♕b3!. Nor is the 'easy' solution **5...♘xc3** really that easy for, if anything, it is White who is given an easy plan of attack against the queenside: 6 bxc3 g6 7 ♖b1 ♘c6 8 ♕a4, etc.

But Black's opening plan in this variation is based on a wholly different idea, less obvious and much more ambitious.

5	...	♘c7 (D)

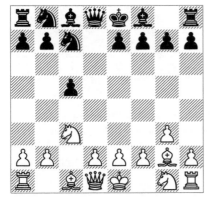

This is the **Rubinstein Variation**, named after the famous Polish grandmaster Akiba Rubinstein (1882-1961).

By retreating his knight, Black emphasizes his control over the crucial d4-square, which can be strengthened by ...e5 in the near future. If White does not do something special now, he will indeed be playing Black soon or, to be more precise: he will find himself in a Maroczy

Bind of the Sicilian Defence with colours reversed.

The key position of this line arises after the following moves.

6	♘f3	♘c6
7	0-0	e5
8	d3	♗e7 (D)

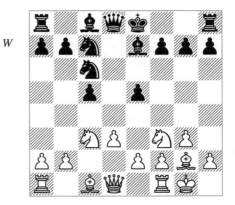

Black is now well on his way to completing a healthy development of his pieces. White needs to act quickly and with a clear aim in mind in order to utilize the tiny lead in development that he has. By far the most popular method of doing so is **9 ♘d2**. If Black then nonchalantly castles (**9...0-0**) White will exchange on c6 (10 ♗xc6 bxc6) when a highly characteristic middlegame arises. Practice has shown that Black's doubled pawns are an enduring liability and that it is not easy to divert attention from this weakness by an attack against White's kingside (although this may look a realistic prospect at first sight). For this reason **9...♗d7** has become the main line. White then continues his plan with 10 ♘c4 (D).

This forces Black to make a fundamental decision. If he protects his pawn on e5 with **10...f6**, White will intensify the pressure by playing 11 f4. This will result in a full-scale battle, where a sharp eye for tactical solutions is as much a prerequisite (for both players!) as subtle positional judgement. The alternative is to sacrifice a pawn with the surprising **10...0-0**. After 11 ♗xc6 ♗xc6 12 ♘xe5 Black calmly retreats his bishop (12...♗e8), intending simply to chase away the knight from e5 and put the bishop back on c6 again. This powerful bishop

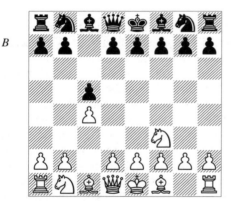

and his central predominance promise Black adequate compensation for the missing pawn.

2 ♘f3

2   ♘f3 *(D)*

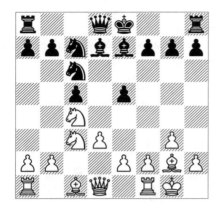

After this move, Black faces more complicated problems than after 2 ♘c3. Not only does he have to decide on a strategy of his own (for instance, whether he wants to play a quick ...d5), but he also has to anticipate a possible d4 by White.

Let us see just how subtle these problems are by considering what Black should do if he wants to play ...g6. It looks completely natural to play **2...g6** immediately and this is indeed not a bad move at all, but Black should be well aware of the fact that 3 d4 will then land him in a Maroczy Bind of the Sicilian Defence: 3...cxd4 4 ♘xd4 ♗g7 5 e4.

With this in mind, many players prefer **2...♘c6**, when 3 d4 leaves Black with more options than just a Maroczy Bind, while if White does not play 3 d4, a plan with ...g6 remains fully possible. 2...♘c6 is in fact one of the two main lines in this position.

The other one is **2...♘f6**. This again gives Black a wide range of options for how to deal with 3 d4. It is also a preparation to take the initiative in the centre himself by playing ...d5, in case White does not play d4. Finally, 2...♘f6 also prepares to play ...b6 in some lines, without a knight on c6 blocking the diagonal of the bishop that will appear on b7.

2 ♘f3 ♘c6

2   ...   ♘c6 *(D)*

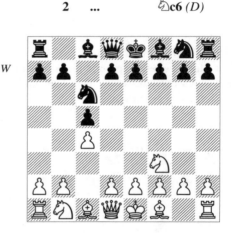

The dance around the d4-square begins. Will White play **3 d4** or will he postpone this crucial advance? In the latter case, **3 ♘c3** is both the most flexible and the most popular option.

2 ♘f3 ♘c6 3 d4

3	d4	cxd4
4	♘xd4	♘f6
5	♘c3 *(D)*	

It is clear that by playing d4 White has chosen a completely different type of plan from the pure flank strategy that we have seen in the 2 ♘c3 variation. It could well be argued that this variation is actually much closer to a 1 d4 or a 1 e4 opening than to the flank openings!

This is in fact an excellent illustration of the modern interpretation of both 1 ♘f3 and 1 c4. These moves *may* be used to introduce a flank strategy, but they are equally useful for adopting a classical central strategy after all. Being able to use both these options is a great asset for any white player, giving him maximum flexibility in choosing the right plan for any specific match situation and any specific opponent.

5   ...   e6 *(D)*

5...g6 6 e4 again transposes to a Maroczy Bind of the Sicilian Defence. Although this variation is eminently playable (in spite of the slightly ominous term 'Bind' in its name), not everyone feels at ease in this type of position, where Black has little manoeuvring space and needs to play with great accuracy if he is not to be reduced to passive defence.

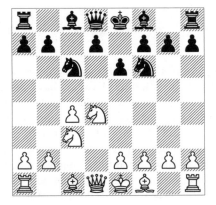

5...e6 also allows a transposition to the Sicilian Defence with **6 e4**, but in this case it is a

position from the Taimanov Variation that arises which is considered to be completely harmless for Black because of the powerful reply 6...♗b4 (see page 422), so this is rarely played.

The really important variations are **6 a3**, **6 g3** and **6 ♘db5**.

6 a3 is an odd-looking little move that might appear to have no merit other than preventing ...♗b4. However, that merit is a considerable one, and poses Black the problem of precisely what he *is* going to do, knowing that White can tailor his response accordingly (6...d5 7 cxd5 exd5 8 ♗g5 with play against the isolated pawn, or 6...♗e7 7 e4 0-0 8 ♘f3 with a kind of hedgehog). The move a3 can also prove of some use in a variety of contexts, as at a later point a b4 advance may become possible. A much more subtle point is that compared with 6 g3, the line 6 a3 ♕b6 7 ♘b3 ♘e5 does not threaten ...♕c6 with an attack on the h1-rook! White can also meet 6...♕b6 with 7 ♘db5, intending 8 ♗e3, a line in which the move a3 proves very useful.

6 g3 *(D)* and the subsequent fianchetto of the light-squared bishop is a common scheme in this type of position.

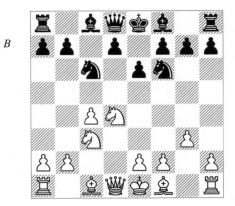

White strengthens his grip on the centre without sticking his neck out as he does with 6 e4. The bishop will also hinder Black's queenside development and support a future attack on that wing.

Strangely enough, however, this quiet approach usually leads to a very sharp battle, because it invites Black to counterattack with 6...♕b6. Then **7 ♘db5** ♘e5 8 ♗f4 ♘fg4 9

♕a4!? is a remarkable pawn sacrifice that leads to great complications. Against the plausible reply 7 ♘b3 Black has 7...♘e5, attacking the c-pawn and threatening 8...♕c6. White is then practically forced to play 8 e4 after all, inviting yet another sharp rejoinder: 8...♗b4, threatening 9...♘xe4. Again White has little choice: 9 ♕e2 *(D)* is practically forced. This brings us to the most critical position of this variation.

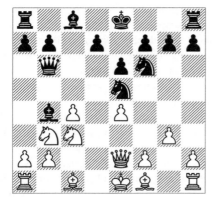

If White had hoped that 6 g3 would promise him a calm opening, he will be disappointed. He has been forced to play the aggressive and somewhat compromising e4 and in order to chase away the annoying knight from e5 the equally bold f4 will also be necessary. Besides, the double-edged exchange on c3 is in the making and the pawn on c4 is weak. Fortunately for him, the situation does have its positives as well, for Black's attacking play is not without risk. 9...d6 10 f4 ♘c6 11 ♗e3 ♗xc3+ 12 bxc3 ♕c7 is a characteristic follow-up. White is looking to launch an attack on the kingside, while Black will be eyeing the doubled c-pawns.

6 ♘db5 *(D)* is a very different sort of move.

By threatening to play 7 ♘d6+ and 7 ♗f4, White is hoping to bully his opponent into passivity. Again, a bold counterattack is critical, introduced by 6...d5 in this case, a move which is both a pawn sacrifice and a challenge to play 7 ♗f4.

The pawn sacrifice is **7 cxd5** ♘xd5 8 ♘xd5 exd5 9 ♕xd5, based on the fork 9...♕xd5 10 ♘c7+. But this is not as strong as it looks, for

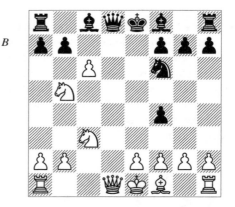

instead Black has 9...♗b4+ 10 ♗d2 ♕e7, which reveals the one big benefit of **all** pawn sacrifices: they always clear a file or a diagonal! White has to be very careful here.

Instead, **7 ♗f4** is considered the critical reply. White provokes 7...e5, which seemingly allows White a very favourable tactical exchange: 8 cxd5 exf4 9 dxc6 *(D)*.

This was a fashionable position back in the 1980s. Many high-level games have demonstrated that Black is doing fine after 9...bxc6 10 ♕xd8+ ♔xd8 in spite of his fractured pawn-structure and the loss of the right to castle. Again, it is fast and easy development, the result of the many open files, which is the compensating factor. After, for instance, 11 ♖d1+ ♗d7 12 ♘d6 ♗xd6 13 ♖xd6 ♖b8 14 ♖d2 ♖e8 White is a long way away from creating pressure in leisurely fashion against the isolated pawn on c6.

2 ♘f3 ♘c6 3 ♘c3

3   ♘c3 (D)

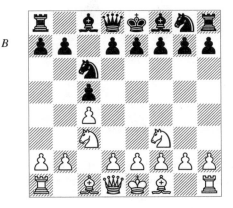

A natural developing move. White will decide whether to play d4, depending on Black's reaction. He also consciously gives Black the opportunity of playing ...d5.

3   ...   ♘f6

Black is returning the favour. He too calmly continues to develop his pieces, without posting his plan of action. This is the most popular approach, but by no means the only one. Black has at least three alternatives, all directed at obstructing the advance d4.

To begin with, there is the straightforward **3...e5** *(D)*.

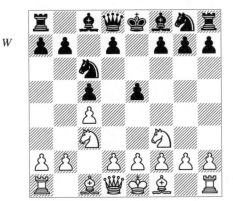

This usually leads to a line of the 2 ♘c3 ♘c6 variation; e.g., 4 g3 g6 5 ♗g2 ♗g7 (see page 200). An attempt to force d4 by playing the preparatory 4 e3 is possible, but not considered very promising because of the sharp reply 4...♘f6 5 d4 cxd4 6 exd4 e4 and now, for instance, 7 ♘g5 ♗b4.

3...g6 is a much more subtle way to discourage d4. White is not stopped from playing **4 d4**, but a serious problem awaits him in the position after 4...cxd4 5 ♘xd4 ♗g7. The situation is almost identical to the variation 2 ♘c3 ♘f6 3 g3 d5 4 cxd5 ♘xd5 5 ♗g2 (see page 203), with colours reversed. The difference is that White has played the extra move ♘c3, which turns out – very remarkably – to be not necessarily in his favour. The problem is that 6 ♘c2 allows Black to take on c3, a strategic motif which is also important in the reversed variation. After 6...♗xc3+ 7 bxc3 d6 it is by no means certain that White's bishop-pair will be sufficient compensation for his badly damaged pawn-structure.

Even so, 3...g6 is not regarded as a particularly good move. This is because 3...g6 creates the ideal situation for White to switch to a e3 plan with **4 e3** *(D)*.

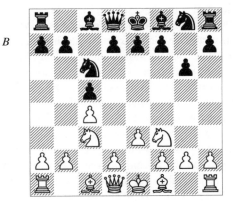

Then if Black simply continues **4...♗g7** 5 d4, he will be unable to stop his opponent from playing the strategically vital d5 advance with a gain of tempo. But because Black has already played 3...g6, it is not easy to find an alternative to 4...♗g7. The standard reaction to any e3 plan, **4...♘f6** 5 d4 cxd4 6 exd4 d5, can be met very forcefully by 7 ♗g5. White is threatening to take on f6 and d5, while 7...dxc4 8 ♗xc4 ♗g7 (again) allows the powerful advance 9 d5.

The third option is **3...♘d4** *(D)*.

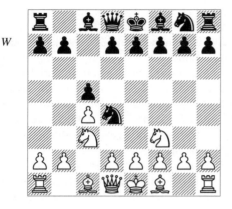

This is a highly unorthodox but undeniably solid way of preventing 4 d4. It was introduced in 1988 and has been popular ever since. The point is that **4 ♘xd4** is unattractive because after 4...cxd4 the knight on c3 is attacked. Stoically continuing normal development with **4 g3** is also not self-evidently sound, because of the doubling of pawns that 4...♘xf3+ 5 exf3 involves, although this is in fact quite playable – White will continue with ♗g2 and d4.

The standard reaction is **4 e3 ♘xf3+ 5 ♕xf3**, but it would be a mistake to think that this reduces Black's knight manoeuvre to a silly loss of time, because the white queen is not well-placed on f3. This is brought home by the fact that, after 5...g6 6 d4 ♗g7, the only sound way of protecting d4 is 7 ♕d1. For this reason most players prefer 6 b3 ♗g7 7 ♗b2. Black then has a flexible position with prospects of a possible initiative on the queenside, based on ...a6 and ...b5. A plausible continuation is 7...d6 8 g3 ♖b8 9 ♗g2 ♘f6. White should not overlook a nasty threat in this position: 10...♗g4.

We now return to the position after 3...♘f6 *(D)*:

4   g3

This is one of the most popular variations of the entire Symmetrical English. White tenaciously continues his strategy of postponing d4. This is in effect an alternative version of the pure flank strategy that we have seen in the 2 ♘c3 ♘c6 variation. The crucial difference is that the 'threat' of playing d4 and ...d5 now

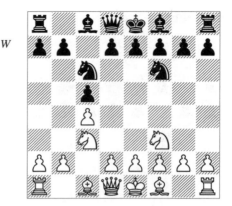

constantly hangs over the position and needs to be carefully evaluated at almost every turn.

The main alternative to 4 g3 is in fact the immediate **4 d4**, leading (after 4...cxd4 5 ♘xd4) to a position that I have discussed as part of the 3 d4 variation (see page 204). It is typical of the Symmetrical English and of flank openings in general that they do not necessarily arise via one logical or forced move-order only. Most variations can be accessed from several directions and this is something to be well aware of.

Another possibility is to play **4 e4** *(D)* first (to stop Black from playing 4...d5) and follow up with d4 as soon as possible.

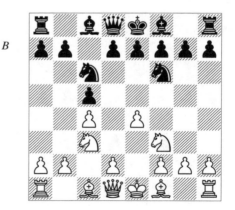

This is usually met by 4...e6. We already know from our survey of the 3 d4 variation (see page 205) that the position that arises if White now plays 5 d4 cxd4 6 ♘xd4 forms part of the Sicilian Defence and is considered innocuous. It is slightly more subtle to postpone d4 further with a move like 5 ♗e2. A key position then arises after 5...d5 6 exd5 exd5 7 d4. The question is: can White transform his minimal lead in development into something more tangible?

We now return to 4 g3 (D):

There are now two main lines: **4...d5** and **4...g6**.

4...e6 5 ♗g2 d5 is also perfectly sound, but following 6 cxd5 this will normally transpose, either to a position from the Tarrasch Defence of the Queen's Gambit Declined after 6...exd5, or to the Keres-Parma Variation after 6...♘xd5. The latter option will also be available to Black if he plays 4...d5.

2 ♘f3 ♘c6 3 ♘c3 ♘f6 4 g3 d5

4	...	d5
5	cxd5	♘xd5
6	♗g2 (D)	

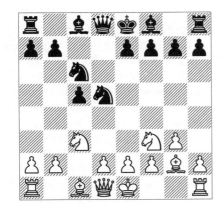

This position is almost identical to the one arising after 2 ♘c3 ♘f6 3 g3 d5 4 cxd5 ♘xd5 5 ♗g2 (see page 203). The difference is the presence of knights on f3 and c6, which slightly reduces the influence of the bishop on g2. Black should be careful though. If he thinks he can lash out now with **6...e5?**, the unpleasant 7 ♘xe5! will teach him a lesson.

Three moves have grown into important variations. The most ambitious one is **6...♘c7**. Black prevents d4 and prepares to play ...e5. This is the Rubinstein Variation, which I discussed above via the move-order 2 ♘c3 ♘f6 3 g3 d5 (see page 203).

If Black likes the sort of position that is typical for the Rubinstein, but wants to keep things a little bit more solid, **6...g6** (D) is an interesting alternative.

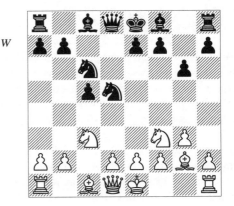

Black does not hurry with ...e5 and fianchettoes his dark-squared bishop first. He does not need to worry about 7 d4, because this only gets White into trouble after the calm 7...♗g7, when 8...♘xc3 9 bxc3 cxd4 is already a nasty threat. The most important starting position of this variation is reached after 7 0-0 ♗g7 8 ♘xd5 ♕xd5 9 d3 0-0 10 ♗e3. White's last move introduces the threat of 11 ♘d4. White is banking on his tender lead in development. That is why he is not afraid of 10...♗xb2, which would just play into his hands: after 11 ♖b1 ♗g7 12 ♕a4 White's initiative is already very threatening.

The third possibility (and a very important one) is **6...e6**. This is the **Keres-Parma Variation**, a line that can be reached in a multitude of ways. Black's idea here is totally different from the one underlying the two previous variations. Instead of preventing d4, Black assumes that this advance will not be dangerous. If White captures on d5, Black will, as a rule, take back with the e-pawn. The basic position arises after 7 0-0 ♗e7 8 d4 0-0 *(D)*.

W

White now has two plans that are fundamentally different, but about equally important. The sharpest and most dynamic approach is to play **9 e4**. White is hoping to obtain a strong central position here; e.g., 9...♘xc3 10 bxc3 or 9...♘b6 10 d5.

The alternative **9 ♘xd5** exd5 10 dxc5 ♗xc5 on the other hand, stresses the static aspects of the position. White intends to play against the isolated queen's pawn. Compared to the Tarrasch Variation (the difference being that a pair of knights has been exchanged), White lacks the possibility of intensifying the pressure against d5 by playing ♗g5.

2 ♘f3 ♘c6 3 ♘c3 ♘f6 4 g3 g6

4   ...   **g6** *(D)*

Black continues to imitate White's play. As we have seen in the 2 ♘c3 ♘c6 variation, this tactic can sometimes be sustained for a very long time.

5   ♗g2   ♗g7
6   d4

This move is the critical test of Black's opening play. White is the first to break the symmetry.

W

6   ...   cxd4
7   ♘xd4   0-0
8   0-0 *(D)*

B

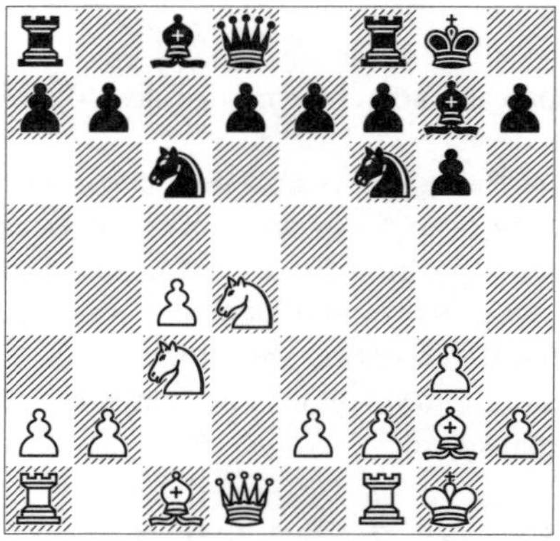

Anyone who has been reading this chapter from the start will probably have begun to feel that everything is interconnected in this opening, that every single variation is closely related to each and every other variation. This is indeed a distinguishing feature of the Symmetrical English and one that can have both a clarifying and a bewildering effect upon the student. This opening is not so much about concrete and forcing move-orders as about general strategic motifs and characteristic plans. These plans and motifs keep coming back, sometimes slightly modified, in different variations. And what makes things really confusing is that they are the same for both sides!

In this position, for instance, we are in effect looking at a situation we have already seen with colours reversed, via 4...d5 5 cxd5 ♘xd5 6 ♗g2 g6 7 0-0 ♗g7.

Does the simple fact that it is now 'the other side' to move alter the assessment of this line? Does the extra tempo mean that White suddenly has chances of an opening advantage in a situation where – with colours reversed – we have just been wondering whether he can equalize?

It all depends on just how accurate we want the answer to be. No, generally speaking it does not make a lot of difference and the position can be viewed as about equal. Yes, the one whose move it is will always be in a position to achieve his own characteristic plans first, forcing the opponent to respond, which may entail that the opponent will have to drop 'his' characteristic plans.

Now what does this all mean concretely? The following three plans have come to the fore in this position.

The simplest and most obvious solution is to play **8...♘xd4 9 ♕xd4 d6** (D), the same as we saw White play in the 'mirrored' version of this variation.

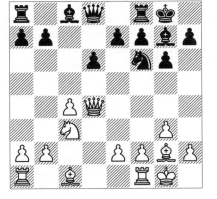

A good reply to this is 10 ♕d3, taking the sting out of the pawn sacrifice 10...♗e6 (as in the mirror variation), because Black now does not have the threat of ...♘d5 to follow this up. This is why 10...♗f5 is much more common. Black provokes 11 e4 and only then does he play 11...♗e6. Also 10...a6, planning an advance on the queenside (...♖b8 and ...b5) is a popular plan.

8...♘g4 is a surprising alternative. At first sight it seems unlikely that a primitive knight sortie like this could possibly solve Black's problems, but there are a number of good reasons why it can. In case of the logical reply 9 e3, the pawn sacrifice 9...d6 (D) is very promising.

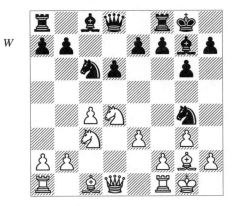

If White accepts, **10 ♘xc6** bxc6 11 ♗xc6 ♖b8 will give Black a substantial initiative against the white queenside thanks to the beautiful open diagonal of the g7-bishop and the open b- and c-files. If White declines he sacrifice and plays a natural developing move like **10 b3** instead, Black has the far from obvious rejoinder 10...♘xd4 11 exd4 ♘h6, followed by ...♘f5, attacking d4. Both these lines are likely to result in a heavy middlegame struggle with chances for both sides.

The same pawn sacrifice can be offered immediately by playing **8...d6**. Again Black is counting on (or hoping for) compensation in the shape of open files and diagonals, a lead in development and attacking chances on the queenside after 9 ♘xc6 bxc6 10 ♗xc6 ♖b8 (or 10...♗h3).

The choice between these three variations is mainly a matter of taste, although it must be added that the last (8...d6) is by far the most experimental of the three.

2 ♘f3 ♘f6

2 ... ♘f6 (D)

This is one of the most common positions of the entire Symmetrical English. It is of vital

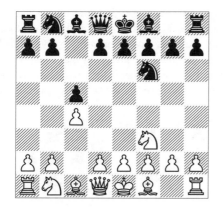

importance to both 1 c4 and 1 ♘f3 (1...♘f6 2 c4 c5).

Again, the main variations start with **3 d4** and **3 ♘c3**, but in this case **3 g3** too has some independent significance.

2 ♘f3 ♘f6 3 d4

3	**d4**	**cxd4**
4	**♘xd4** *(D)*	

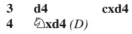

This line is a good illustration of how closely interconnected the whole body of opening theory really is, for a certain basic knowledge of both 1 d4 and 1 e4 openings is needed if we are to understand this position properly. To begin with: the position itself might very well arise out of a 1 d4 opening, namely 1 d4 ♘f6 2 c4 c5 3 ♘f3 cxd4 4 ♘xd4. It could even be regarded as part of the Benoni rather than the Symmetrical English!

The point of contact with 1 e4 theory is the Maroczy Bind of the Sicilian Defence (1 e4 c5 2 ♘f3 ♘c6 3 d4 cxd4 4 ♘xd4 g6 5 c4), which has already been mentioned a few times in this chapter. This would arise if Black plays **4...g6** and White were to reply 5 ♘c3 and 6 e4.

4	...	**e6**

This classical developing move is the main alternative to the equally classical **4...♘c6**, which would lead to a variation that I have discussed under 2...♘c6 (3 d4 cxd4 4 ♘xd4 ♘f6; see page 204). The two moves are closely related and may easily transpose. The main difference is that by playing 4...♘c6 Black concentrates on attempts to undermine the knight on d4 by the sharp ...♕b6, while 4...e6 is geared to moves like ...d5 and ...♗b4(+).

The immediate **4...d5** is also possible, but the timing is unfortunate since after 5 cxd5, both 5...♘xd5 6 e4 and 5...♕xd5 6 ♘c3 give White an extra developing tempo for free.

4...b6 and **4...e5** are more serious. Both of these variations are of recent origin.

A ...b6 set-up was long thought to be strategically dubious in any situation where White can respond with a quick e4, as is the case here, where White can meet **4...b6** with 5 ♘c3 ♗b7 6 f3 to be followed by e4. With the rise of the Hedgehog Variation and the resulting upgrading of this particular pawn-formation, 4...b6 also came to be accepted as a reasonable line, although it is still considered a somewhat cheeky imitation of the 'official' Hedgehog Variation, 3 ♘c3 e6 4 g3 b6, which I shall discuss later (see page 216).

4...e5 is a good deal more cheeky still. Black is in effect trying to add more power to the central advance ...d5. The idea is to meet the critical reply 5 ♘b5 with a pawn sacrifice: 5...d5 6 cxd5 and now, rather than blundering a piece with 6...♘xd5?? 7 ♕xd5!, Black plays 6...♗c5 *(D)*.

At first sight it may seem unlikely that Black should have anything even resembling sufficient compensation for the pawn. But practice has shown that Black's chances, based on fast development and the space that ...e5 has given him on the kingside, are not to be underestimated. Two immediate problems for White are

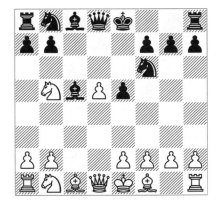

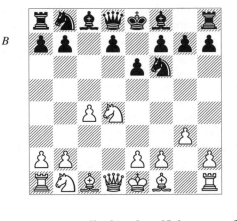

the insecure position of his knight on b5 and the vulnerability of f2. Most games have seen the modest continuation 7 ♘5c3 0-0 8 e3 (8 e4? ♘g4! would be awkward), when 8...♕e7 9 ♗e2 e4 reveals the long-term problem: Black has managed to isolate White's pawn on d5, which he will now start to lay siege to with moves like ...♖d8 and ...♘bd7-b6. This is in fact one of the sharpest and most interesting variations of the entire area of flank openings.

5 g3 (D)

Again, we find ourselves at a crossroads between queen's pawn and flank opening theory. Anyone wanting to meet 1 d4 ♘f6 2 c4 e6 with 3 g3 will have to have an answer to 3...c5. His main options are 4 d5, a Benoni, and 4 ♘f3, which, after 4...cxd4 5 ♘xd4, brings about the very position that we are looking at here, as part of the Symmetrical English.

The same can be said about 5 ♘c3, for if Black then plays 5...♗b4 and White replies 6 g3, the opening has transposed to a variation of the Nimzo-Indian Defence: 1 d4 ♘f6 2 c4 e6 3 ♘c3 ♗b4 4 g3 c5 5 ♘f3 cxd4 6 ♘xd4, although this Nimzo-Indian move-order could equally well be said to be leading to a variation of the Symmetrical English. The habit of labelling and categorizing opening variations is made to look rather futile here, but the interconnectedness of all opening theory becomes perfectly clear.

After 5 g3, Black has a great many reasonable moves, but there are three main lines: **5...d5**, **5...♗b4+** and **5...♕c7**.

5...d5 is the most classical move. It shows up a slight disadvantage of White's last move: he cannot very well play 6 cxd5 because after 6...♕xd5 his rook is attacked and 7 ♗g2 is prevented. This means that 6 ♗g2 is practically forced, but this again allows Black to make use of the specific features of the position and play 6...e5 7 ♘f3 d4. Because 8 ♘xe5?? fails to 8...♕a5+, Black is able to make a giant step forward in the centre and in effect take over his opponent's natural role of first aggressor. The key position arises after 8 0-0 ♘c6 9 e3, with the opening battle mainly revolving around the question of whether Black's pawn on d4 is going to be weak or strong after, for instance, 9...♘c5 10 exd4 exd4.

5...♗b4+ (D) could also explode into sharp play very easily.

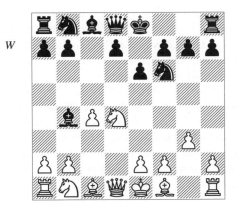

If White thinks he can keep the position simple by playing the solid 6 ♗d2 (instead of 6 ♘c3, which again transposes to the abovementioned line of the Nimzo-Indian), the sharp reply 6...♕b6 will come as a shock. Suddenly there are pawn sacrifices and difficult decisions all over the place. Against **7 ♗g2** the unexpected 7...♗c5 forces the reply 8 e3 (8 ♗c3 runs into 8...e5!), which, after 8...♗xd4 9 exd4 ♕xd4 10 0-0, leads to a sharp and principled fight between Black's material advantage (he can even take a second pawn on c4) and White's lead in development. In case of **7 ♗xb4 ♕xb4+** White is also forced to sacrifice a pawn. His most solid option (but also the least intimidating one) is to play **7 e3**.

Likewise, **5...♕c7** *(D)* also challenges White to a principled fight between the forces of mind and matter.

The first question is: is it necessary to protect c4? Opinions seem to be evenly divided on this, because 6 ♘d2 and 6 ♘c3 are about equally popular. 6 ♗g2 is played less frequently, because this does not pose any concrete obstacles in the way of Black taking on c4. After the more subtle 6 ♘c3, 6...♕xc4 is risky because of 7 e4, attacking the queen. In this case Black usually plays 6...a6, when 7 ♗g2 ♕xc4 again leads to this sharp, difficult-to-judge type of position where White has the short-term advantage of the lead in development and Black has the long-term advantage of the extra pawn.

2 ♘f3 ♘f6 3 ♘c3

3   ♘c3 *(D)*

I guess that by now most readers will be able to spot the most obvious transpositions

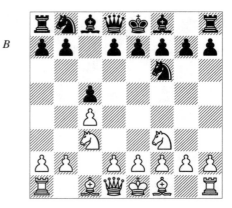

for themselves. If **3...♘c6** we reach a position that we have already looked at on page 208, while **3...g6** 4 d4 cxd4 5 ♘xd4 ♗g7 (or 4 e4 ♗g7 5 d4) is the Maroczy Bind Sicilian again.

The alternatives **3...d5** and **3...e6** also offer possible transpositions to variations that we have already seen, but these two moves have independent significance as well. In fact these are two of the most important variations of the Symmetrical English.

2 ♘f3 ♘f6 3 ♘c3 d5

3	...	d5
4	cxd5	♘xd5 *(D)*

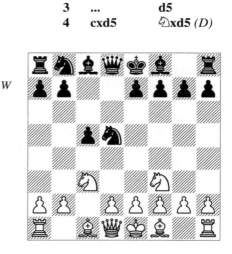

If White now plays **5 g3**, the reply 5...♘c6 will bring us back to the well-known territory of the ...d5 variations we have already looked at (see page 209), but because Black has played ...d5 here *before* White has played g3, there are a couple of interesting alternatives. Instead of the standard flank strategy (the cornerstone of 5 g3), White can make a U-turn: both **5 d4** and **5 e4** are moves that aim at a classical confrontation in the centre.

In fact **5 d4** *(D)* offers Black a choice of transposing to two different 1 d4 openings:

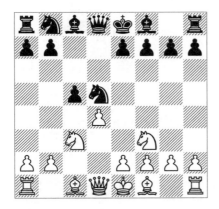

B

5...e6 is a Semi-Tarrasch Variation of the Queen's Gambit Declined (see page 19) and **5...g6** 6 e4 ♘xc3 7 bxc3 is a Grünfeld (see page 122). Most players who choose 3...d5 will have one of these transpositions in mind, but there is one other possibility: **5...cxd4**. This move leads to a somewhat dry position after 6 ♕xd4 ♘xc3 7 ♕xc3 ♘c6 8 e4 e6 with a tiny lead in development and an equally tiny space advantage for White. He has to watch out for 9...♗b4 though. The main lines start with 9 ♗b5 and 9 a3. Black's position is solid and if he is happy with a draw, this variation is quite playable.

The same two transpositions are feasible after **5 e4** *(D)*, but there are a couple of major differences from 5 d4.

If Black were to play **5...♘xc3**, then **6 bxc3** would indeed transpose to either the Semi-Tarrasch (6...e6 7 d4) or the Grünfeld (6...g6 7 d4). But in this specific situation the 'other recapture' is an excellent option: **6 dxc3**. This move may in fact come as a cold shower to many who, having played 3...d5, are mentally tuned to a dynamic Grünfeld battle. Queens are exchanged and the position becomes rather static. Providing he feels confident in this type of position, White may be satisfied. After 6...♕xd1+

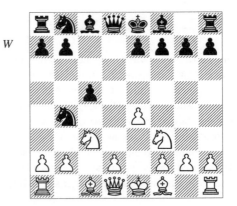

B

7 ♔xd1 White's pawn move e4 is more useful than Black's ...c5 and his king will find a comfortable square on c2.

But the most critical reply to 5 e4 is not 5...♘xc3, but the sharp **5...♘b4** *(D)*.

W

White now either has to get in d4 or do something useful with his small lead in development, and preferably both.

The immediate **6 d4** cxd4 7 ♘xd4? is not an option because this runs into 7...♕xd4!, winning a piece.

The main lines are **6 ♗b5+** and **6 ♗c4**. Both moves lead to highly original positions which are difficult to assess.

The point of **6 ♗b5+** is to meet 6...♘8c6 with 7 d4 cxd4 8 a3!, when 8...dxc3 9 ♕xd8+ ♔xd8 10 axb4 cxb2 11 ♗xb2 produces an endgame where his lead in development and the unsafe position of Black's king promise White enough compensation for the pawn he has sacrificed.

If this is already a fairly complicated variation, the difficulties involved in judging **6 ♗c4** are even more complex. To begin with, this move virtually gives up the right to castle, for if Black now plays 6...♘d3+, it would be an outrage to reply with the meek 7 ♗xd3. The key position arises after 7 ♔e2 ♘f4+ 8 ♔f1 ♘e6 (D).

W

One of the main variations here is the pawn sacrifice 9 b4!?, meeting 9...cxb4 with 10 ♘e2. White is poised to play d4, taking control over the centre and pushing Black onto the defensive. The loss of the right to castle does not seem to diminish his chances. The king's rook is often brought into play by h4-h5 followed by ♖h4. This line rose to prominence around 1980, but theory has never managed to get a firm hold on it. It is clear though that both sides have to be mentally prepared for a gruelling battle.

2 ♘f3 ♘f6 3 ♘c3 e6

<table>
<tr><td>3</td><td>...</td><td>e6 (D)</td></tr>
<tr><td>4</td><td>g3</td><td></td></tr>
</table>

4 d4 cxd4 5 ♘xd4 transposes to one of the by now familiar d4 variations (see page 213). The position after **4 e4 ♘c6** has also been discussed before, on page 208.

<table>
<tr><td>4</td><td>...</td><td>b6</td></tr>
</table>

This move introduces the **Hedgehog System**.

The alternative **4...♘c6** has been treated on page 209. **4...d5** 5 cxd5 also offers a familiar picture: after 5...exd5 6 d4 we are in a Tarrasch

W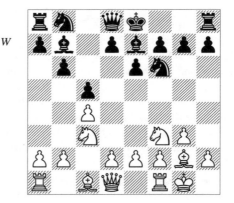

Defence (see page 12), while 5...♘xd5 is the Keres-Parma Variation (see page 209).

<table>
<tr><td>5</td><td>♗g2</td><td>♗b7</td></tr>
<tr><td>6</td><td>0-0</td><td>♗e7 (D)</td></tr>
</table>

Black is in effect playing a Queen's Indian Defence, the only difference being that White has not played d4 (yet). Strategically, this is a very delicate situation. After all, playing d4 is widely regarded as White's most powerful plan, but the question is how?

The classical recipe is to play **7 d4** without any more ado. The modern variation starts with the seemingly slow, but actually very ambitious **7 ♖e1**.

3...e6 4 g3 b6 5 ♗g2 ♗b7 6 0-0 ♗e7 7 d4

<table>
<tr><td>7</td><td>d4</td><td>cxd4</td></tr>
<tr><td>8</td><td>♕xd4 (D)</td><td></td></tr>
</table>

Even though the white queen is obviously vulnerable to an attack on d4, this recapture is widely regarded as the best way of creating pressure. After **8 ♘xd4 ♗xg2 9 ♔xg2** the exchange of bishops lessens the tension and Black is given more freedom to develop his queenside properly; e.g., 9...♕c8 10 ♕d3 ♘c6.

B

8   ...   d6 *(D)*

The obvious move **8...♘c6** is well met by 9 ♕f4. In fact, it was the discovery that Black's queen's knight is better developed on d7 that was the main reason for the Hedgehog's rise to great popularity during the 1970s. On d7 the knight does not obstruct the diagonal of the b7-bishop nor the c-file and it can jump to c5, from where it will attack a white pawn on e4. In this type of position, the gain of tempo involved in playing 8...♘c6 is of little importance. The white queen is not very well placed on d4 anyway and will usually step back voluntarily.

W

It is not so much this specific position as this *type* of position which became extremely popular in the 1970s and 1980s and which became known during that era as the **Hedgehog System**. The name is appropriate, for Black is in effect curling up on his back three ranks and anyone trying to tackle the Hedgehog without a pair of really thick gloves is likely to get himself pricked.

According to classical positional thinking, Black's pawn on d6 is simply weak and, providing he manages to keep possible breakouts with ...d5 or ...b5 in check, White should gradually be able to demolish Black's position. But innumerable games by Hedgehog pioneers from the 1970s (among whom Ulf Andersson deserves a special mention) have shown that this view underestimates Black's chances. Preventing every possible form of counterplay is such a hugely demanding task that very few players even get to the stage where any sort of demolition work can be contemplated.

I would advise anyone interested in studying this opening scheme to concentrate on the strategy first. There are a number of variations which require some accuracy and theoretical knowledge, but in general understanding the characteristic plans and ideas is far more important.

Well then, what are these ways of attacking d6 and how should Black defend himself against them? What is Black's ideal piece deployment if White does not force him to respond to any particular threat immediately? It is this type of question that has to be asked again and again in this line and which a student becomes more and more familiar with as his insight into the secrets of the Hedgehog grows.

One direct (some would even say primitive) way of attacking d6 is to play **9 b3** 0-0 and now simply 10 ♗a3. Black then blocks off the diagonal of this bishop by 10...♘a6 11 ♖fd1 ♘c5, when after 12 ♘b5 ♘fe4 he has got everything covered. Developing the queen's bishop not at a3 but at b2 is more of a long-term plan. After 10 ♗b2 a6 11 ♖fd1 ♘bd7 12 e4 ♕c7 13 ♕e3 *(D)* a key position is reached that may be achieved by a multitude of different move-orders.

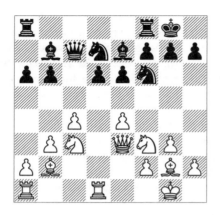

B

A good plan here is to play 13...♖fe8 14 ♖ac1 ♗f8. Black may continue with ...♖ac8 (or ...♖ad8), possibly followed by ...♕b8 and ...♗a8, supporting a possible advance ...b5, while removing the queen from the reach of the rook that is likely to appear on c1. Black could follow up with moves like ...♕a8 and ...♘c5, attacking the pawn on e4. As long as the white queen remains on e3 there is also the possibility of playing ...d5 when an exchange of e-pawns (exd5 exd5) is unpleasant for White. In the meantime the f8-bishop covers d6, with prospects of rather more active service on g7.

9 ♗g5 *(D)*, intending to exchange on f6, is a way of keeping things a bit simpler.

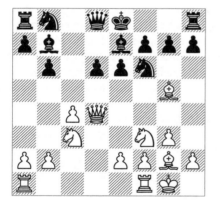

B

Anyone not accustomed with the Hedgehog will probably find this a strange plan at first, but on closer inspection a variation like 9...a6 10 ♗xf6 ♗xf6 11 ♕f4 will reveal its merits. Black's control over the crucial e4-square has been diminished and the defence of d6 is weakened. After 11...0-0 12 ♖fd1 Black has to play 12...♗e7, when 13 ♘e4 more or less forces him to surrender his bishop-pair and play 13...♗xe4. A further implication is that after 14 ♕xe4 Black is reduced to playing 14...♖a7, because in view of the dangerous knight manoeuvre ♘d4-c6, Black's knight will have to stay on b8 for the time being. The rook's prospects are not that bad in fact, with both c7 and d7 as useful possible destinations. In general the position remains much more static than in the 9 b3 variation. Black has hardly any influence in the centre but his position is solid.

Another characteristic way of attacking d6 is by manoeuvring a knight to e4; e.g., **9 ♖d1** a6 **10 ♘g5** *(D)*.

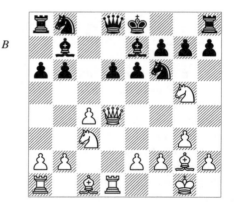

B

Like 9 ♗g5, this is a relatively simple plan which demands a certain precision from both players. It seems strange that White suddenly allows the exchange of light-squared bishops which he avoided only two moves ago (by playing 8 ♕xd4 instead of 8 ♘xd4). But although it is true that in principle this makes Black's position easier to play, the threat against d6 is very real. After 10...♗xg2 11 ♔xg2 Black must defend himself against ♘ge4, followed (if necessary) by b3 and ♗a3. 11...♘c6 12 ♕f4 ♖a7 13 ♘ge4 ♖d7 is considered a reliable solution.

3...e6 4 g3 b6 5 ♗g2 ♗b7 6 0-0 ♗e7 7 ♖e1

7   ♖e1 *(D)*

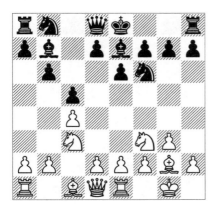

White intends to play d4 only after he has thrown in 8 e4 first. He can then recapture on d4 with the knight without having his king's bishop exchanged. This is a much more aggressive scheme of development than anything we have just seen in the 7 d4 variation. Black now has to decide whether he wants to prevent this plan.

7   ...   d6

The true Hedgehog fanatic will never be disturbed by anything White comes up with and curl up in his Hedgehog position regardless, but Black does in fact have two solid alternatives: **7...♘e4** and **7...d5**. In the latter case he must be prepared to play a totally different type of middlegame though, for after 8 cxd5, a position arises from 8...exd5 9 d4 that resembles a variation of the Queen's Indian Defence (see page 80), while 8...♘xd5 9 e4 ♘xc3 10 bxc3 0-0 11 d4 creates the sort of position that we know from the Keres-Parma Variation (see page 210).

8   e4 (D)

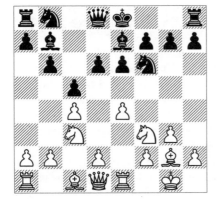

8   ...   a6

Another way to prevent White's plan is to play **8...e5** in this position. However, White's pieces are probably better placed to deal with this symmetrical pawn-formation than Black's. He can take the initiative right away with 9 ♘h4, followed by ♘f5 and/or f4.

9   d4   cxd4
10   ♘xd4   ♕c7

Black has to be on his guard. If he carelessly plays 10...♘bd7?, White gets the upper hand immediately with the simple 11 e5!.

11   ♗e3   ♘bd7

Taking on c4 is too risky: after 11...♕xc4? 12 ♖c1 Black has not so much won a pawn as ruined his position.

12   ♖c1   0-0
13   f4 (D)

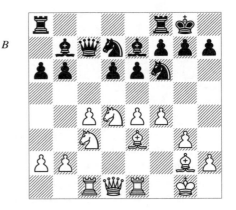

This is a key position for the 7 ♖e1 variation. Thanks to the small investment of a single preparatory move (7 ♖e1) White has been able to take up a position that is both solid and aggressive. White is not concerned with attacking the pawn on d6; he wants to gain space on the kingside with g4. A Hedgehog position is always solid, but in this case Black has to be very careful not to be pushed off the board. An illustration of what might happen in this potentially violent line is provided by the sample variation **13...♖fe8** 14 g4 ♘c5 15 ♗f2 g6 (in order to play ...e5, creating counterplay in the centre, without having to worry about ♘f5) 16 b4 ♘cd7 and now the spectacular 17 ♘d5!? exd5 18 cxd5. This positional piece sacrifice has been played a number of times and with great success. After 18...♛d8 White simply carries on with his bulldozer strategy: 19 ♘c6 ♝xc6 20 dxc6.

Black has tried to improve on this line in many different ways (for instance by playing **13...h5**), but the battle will always be fierce and highly complicated.

2 ♘f3 ♘f6 3 g3

3   g3 (D)

B

If White does not want to play 3 d4 (yet), 3 ♘c3 is the most flexible alternative, but there is also an argument to be made for 3 g3. Against a ...d5 set-up in particular, this move offers some new prospects since, without a knight on c3, the sometimes annoying exchange ...♘xc3 (after cxd5 ♘xd5) is ruled out. This may well make a d4 advance (in response to ...d5) more attractive.

The immediate **3...d5** is the move most affected by this subtle difference, for White can now avoid both the Rubinstein Variation and the ...g6 line (see pages 203 and 209 respectively). If, after 4 cxd5 ♘xd5 5 ♝g2, Black plays **5...g6**, the moment is right for 6 d4 *(D)*.

This is because **6...cxd4** 7 ♛xd4 is awkward for Black, his rook being attacked and 7...♝g7 prevented. This means that he would have to make a small concession and play either 7...♘f6 or 7...f6. It is probably a better idea to play **6...♝g7**, but this leads to Grünfeld-related positions after 7 e4 or 7 dxc5, which may not be to Black's liking.

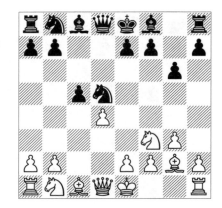

B

The alternative **5...♘c6** can also be met by 6 d4, preventing a possible Rubinstein set-up (6...♘c7 and ...e5) and forcing a type of position upon the opponent which he (possibly) was not counting on.

But you cannot expect something for nothing. 3 g3 gives Black a chance to choose a variation which he cannot expect to reach without White's cooperation via any other Symmetrical English move-order (like 3 ♘c3):

3   ...   b6 (D)

W

If White had played 3 ♘c3 he would now have the powerful reply 4 e4. Having played 3 g3, there is nothing better than...

4   ♝g2   ♝b7 (D)

This position has all the characteristics of the Symmetrical English. But the decision to regard it as part of that opening is a random one for it is equally relevant (to say the least) to the opening 1 ♘f3 ♘f6 2 c4 b6 (see page 246). As

we shall see, 3 g3 is then one of White's major options, with the reply 3...c5 or 3...♗b7 4 ♗g2 c5 leading to the very position that we are labelling here as a line of the Symmetrical English.

This is in fact another example of how interconnected all openings and variations really are (and how arbitrary any attempt at categorization is in the end).

5   0-0

Now if Black were to play **5...e6** we would be back in a 'regular' Hedgehog after 6 ♘c3. There is, however, an interesting possibility to play this system in a subtly different way.

5   ...   g6
6   ♘c3   ♗g7 (D)

In almost all of the ...g6 variations that we have seen in this chapter, its value depended to a large extent upon the reply d4. How should the situation after an exchange on d4 be assessed? In terms of opening theory, this is the first question that needs to be asked. If White chooses a different plan, a ...g6 set-up is usually vindicated.

In this case, after **7 d4** cxd4, the natural recapture **8 ♘xd4** has the same drawback as in the Hedgehog Variation, namely that there is little tension left in the position after 8...♗xg2 9 ♔xg2. Of course White's position is sound, but so is Black's after 9...0-0 10 e4 ♕c7.

That is why here too **8 ♕xd4** is regarded as the critical move. Without a weakness on d6 (for Black's e-pawn has not left its original square yet), Black's position is more solid than in the Hedgehog, while the g7-bishop does offer some prospects of active piece-play. For instance, after 8...0-0 there is already the threat of 9...♘e4.

The alternative **7 ♖e1**, although not bad, is probably less effective here than in the ...e6 variation. With a bishop on g7, both 7...d5 and 7...d6 8 e4 e5 are easier to play, while 7...♘e4 is also quite solid.

Reversed Sicilian

1 c4 e5 (D)

This move constitutes both the least complicated and the most radical reply to the English Opening. It is carefree and it is formidable. It shows up the beauty of 1 c4 and its ugliness. For some it is *the* reason to play 1 c4, for others it is why they will never even contemplate it. It is the heart of the English Opening.

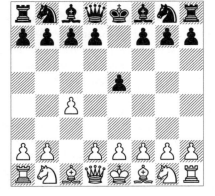

W

White now has to face the consequences of his first move. Black has occupied the centre and White will attack from the flank. If he does this feebly or not at all, the traditional roles will soon be reversed, for if Black can freely develop his pieces, he will take over the initiative.

2 ♘c3

For those who are familiar with the wealth of variations of the Sicilian Defence, it may come as a surprise to find that alternatives to 2 ♘c3 are rare and of little theoretical significance. The only other move that has any importance at all is **2 g3** and even this can hardly be called an independent variation. Moves like **2 d3** or **2 e3** are practically never seen.

If we compare the situation to the position after 1 e4 c5 2 ♘f3 it is important to note that in that case Black has to anticipate White's impending central advance, 3 d4. But after 1 c4

e5, White does not have to *react*, he must *act*. It is not a matter of finding the best way to cope with the opponent's initiative, it is a matter of ensuring that the opponent does not get any initiative in the first place!

Anyone who deliberately 'missed' the opportunity of playing 1 d4 just one move earlier, is unlikely to try to prepare the same advance with **2 e3** in this position, which will yield him no more than a rather unglamorous line of the French Defence (2 e3 ♘f6 3 d4 exd4 4 exd4 d5 results in the same position as 1 e4 e6 2 d4 d5 3 exd5 exd5 4 c4 ♘f6).

After 2 ♘c3, Black too lacks the wide range of choice that White has on his second move in the Sicilian Defence. Moves like **2...g6** and **2...f5** are considered slightly inaccurate because of the firm reply 3 d4. In both cases 3...exd4 4 ♕xd4 produces a position where the white queen is not badly placed on d4.

A more sophisticated way of anticipating 3 d4 is **2...d6** (D), the **Smyslov Variation**.

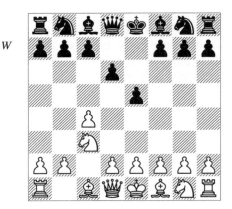

W

We are again faced with a curious entanglement of two different openings here, in this case the English Opening and 1 d4 d6. Both 3 d4 and 3 ♘f3 f5 4 d4 e4 5 ♘g5 transpose to variations that can also be reached via 1 d4 d6 2 c4 e5 (see page 191). A third option, 3 g3, is similar to the Closed Variation and could easily transpose.

2...♗b4 *(D)*, on the other hand, is a move of a different calibre altogether.

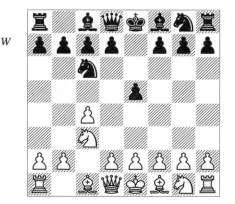

This is the youngest variation of the Reversed Sicilian, nameless as yet, but very popular already. It is a provocative move, for 3 ♘d5 looks like a plausible and strong reply. Why should Black give his opponent an aggressive move like that for free? The point is that the knight is not safe on d5. Black simply withdraws the bishop and chases away the knight with ...c6. This can lead to a fierce opening struggle. Black can play 3...♗a5 4 b4 c6!, or 3...♗c5 or even 3...♗e7. In the latter case, Black assumes that after an exchange on e7 (e.g., 4 d4 d6 5 e4 ♘f6 6 ♘xe7 ♕xe7) his lead in development will compensate for the loss of the bishop-pair. Here too, **3 g3** is a calmer reply.

The traditional main lines start with **2...♘c6**, the **Closed Variation**, and **2...♘f6**, which generally leads to the **Four Knights Variation**.

Closed Variation

> 2 ... ♘c6 *(D)*

By analogy with the Closed Sicilian (1 e4 c5 2 ♘c3), this move is called the Closed Variation. Black is more concerned with preventing a possible d4 than with making a move in the centre of his own (...d5). If White now plays **3 ♘f3**, the reply 3...♘f6 will transpose to the

Four Knights Variation, but he also has to take 3...f5 into account, when 4 d4 e4 leads to the same type of position as 2...d6 3 ♘f3 f5 4 d4 e4, a line we have just looked at. Basically, an ...f5 set-up, though always possible, only becomes truly attractive if White has already played ♘f3, for this will allow Black to meet d4, the most principled reply, by ...e4 with gain of tempo.

> 3 g3

Now **3...f5** is slightly less accurate (although it should be stressed that even here this advance is not what you call bad). White continues 4 ♗g2 ♘f6 5 e3 followed by d4 and if Black then replies ...e4, White can immediately eliminate Black's intimidating outpost at e4 by playing f3.

> 3 ... g6
> 4 ♗g2 ♗g7 *(D)*

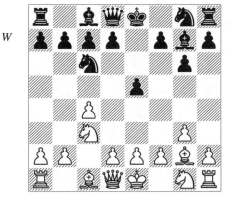

This is the main starting point of the Closed Variation. In the course of almost a century, many games have been played from this position, making it one of the oldest in the entire English Opening. Perhaps somewhat surprisingly though, there are hardly any clearly defined variations. For the time being there is little or no direct contact between the opposing armies. In a situation like this there is usually little need for concrete and precise move-orders. It is all about long-term strategic planning.

Speaking very generally, one could say that White has two standard plans: he can become aggressive on the queenside or in the centre, in which case his attack will be directed at e5.

The most common form of an attack on the queenside is to play ♖b1, followed by b4-b5. This is often (but not always) combined with d3 and ♘f3. White allows his opponent a free hand on the kingside.

A plan of action in the centre will normally be based either on e3 in combination with ♘ge2, or on e4. The latter move creates the opportunity of attacking e5 from the flank with f4.

If we translate these abstract considerations into concrete variations, White has the following moves:

First of all, he can decide to develop his kingside first, starting with **5 ♘f3**, and concentrate on the queenside later. After 5...d6 6 d3 ♘f6 7 0-0 0-0 for example, he could play 8 ♖b1 *(D)*, preparing 9 b4. This position, which can be reached in a multitude of different move-orders, is in fact one of the most popular in the entire range of flank openings.

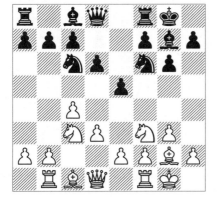

B

White now fully concentrates his forces on the queenside and Black will have to find counterplay on the kingside. A characteristic (though by no means forced) continuation is 8...a5 9 a3 h6 (in order to play ...♗e6 without being troubled by ♘g5) 10 b4 axb4 11 axb4 ♗e6 12 b5 ♘e7 13 ♗b2 ♕d7, intending 14...♗h3.

White could also start by playing **5 ♖b1**, postponing ♘f3 to a later stage and keeping the options of a development with e3 or e4 open.

By playing **5 e3**, White emphatically creates the possibility of an advance in the centre (d4), yet he does not commit himself to such a plan. On the contrary, the whole point of this variation is to *threaten* to play d4, not necessarily to play it. Black must constantly be on his guard for this advance, which requires some subtle assessments. If **5...d6** 6 ♘ge2 ♘f6, for instance, 7 d4 is a perfectly sound move and very annoying for Black. If Black plays 6...♘ge7 (instead of 6...♘f6), the situation is different: now, after 7 d4 exd4 8 exd4 0-0, Black is well-placed to attack the enemy centre with moves like ...♗g4 and ...♘f5. This explains why 6...♘ge7 is usually met by 7 0-0 0-0 8 d3 or 8 ♖b1, not by 7 d4.

An interesting reply to 5 e3 is a swift advance on the kingside: **5...h5**. By introducing the threat of ...h4, Black is testing the strength of his opponent's kingside defences (and his nerves). This provocative line came into fashion around 1980 and is still quite popular.

Finally, White may choose the same pawn-formation that we have seen in the chapter on the Symmetrical English under the name of the Botvinnik Variation (see page 201): **5 e4**. White concentrates on neutralizing any possible enemy initiative on the kingside. The standard scheme of development comprises moves like ♘ge2, d3, 0-0, ♗e3 and ♕d2. White has the long-term prospect of playing either b4 or f4, or both.

Four Knights Variation

> 2   ...   ♘f6 *(D)*

By playing this move, Black makes it clear that he does not resign himself to White's domination of the central square d5, which so markedly defines play in the Closed Variation. Black

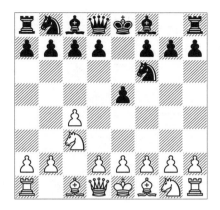

intends to diminish that domination by playing ...♗b4 or even to neutralize it completely with ...d5, the very strategy that is regarded as critical (with colours reversed) in the Sicilian Defence.

He does not have to be afraid of **3 d4**, a move that is crucial (or at least highly relevant) after 2...g6, 2...f5 and even the much stronger 2...d6, for in this case the position after 3...exd4 4 ♛xd4 ♘c6 is (even) easier for Black than after 2...d6 3 d4 exd4 4 ♛xd4, his dark-squared bishop still having prospects of getting developed very actively at c5 or b4. If White wants to play this type of position it is much better to throw in 3 ♘f3 ♘c6 first, when 4 d4 exd4 5 ♘xd4 keeps the white queen safely out of reach of Black's queen's knight.

3   ♘f3

3 g3 is also played fairly often. This move is intended to give White some extra options for dealing with 3...♗b4 (as compared to 3 ♘f3 ♘c6 4 g3 ♗b4). With his king's knight still on g1, he can meet this move with 4 e4, followed by ♘ge2. If Black chooses 3...d5, then White's choice of third move has little independent significance. The plausible 4 cxd5 ♘xd5 5 ♗g2 ♘b6 6 ♘f3 ♘c6 will lead to the position that we shall encounter under the heading of 3 ♘f3 ♘c6 4 g3 d5.

3   ...   ♘c6 *(D)*

Since about 1900, this position has been the starting point for most of the theoretical discussions of the Reversed Sicilian. With his carefree and aggressive opening play, Black has made optimal use of the freedom of movement

that White has given him by opening 1 c4. Now the moment has come for White to justify his first move.

The various ways in which White has tried to do this form an excellent illustration of the evolution of opening theory over more than a century. For a very long time, until around 1970, **4 d4** was regarded as the main line. White takes the initiative in the centre, a classical strategy.

After that, **4 e3** held the limelight for about a decade. This is much more flexible, although still based on the same view of the situation. White introduces the possibility of taking back on d4 with a pawn, but, more importantly, he prepares to deal with the aggressive ...♗b4, which is the main problem after 4 d4, in an altogether different way.

But in the mid-1980s it was **4 g3** that rose to ever greater popularity until it finally overshadowed its two predecessors completely and became the 'self-evident' main line. White does not hurry with d4 and increases his influence in the centre instead by putting a bishop on g2. This is the pure flank strategy that we know so well from the Symmetrical English. It is very tempting to call this the most logical move in the opening scheme that was started with 1 c4, but just to illustrate the relative value of this epithet I would like to mention that various theoretical works from every period of the 20th century have emphatically given 4 d4 and 4 e3 that honour...

Naturally, in a calm position like this there are many playable moves. Especially the waiting moves **4 a3** and **4 d3** and the rather wooden

4 e4 are played fairly often, but there is little to say on these moves in a theoretical sense and perhaps that is precisely their strength (or weakness). Moves like this should not be seen as ways to create or advance opening theory, but as attempts to avoid it.

2 ♘c3 ♘f6 3 ♘f3 ♘c6 4 d4

4   **d4** *(D)*

White immediately attacks Black's central outpost at e5 and stops his opponent from increasing his influence in the centre by means of ...d5. It could be said that by playing 4 d4 White decides to go for a 1 d4 opening after all. The theoretical assessment of this approach has seen great changes over the years. Nowadays it is regarded as sound, but not particularly threatening for Black.

There are two fundamental replies, **4...e4** and **4...exd4**.

After **4...e4** 5 ♘d2 Black has a choice between the open type of position resulting from 5...♘xd4 6 ♘dxe4 and the more complex position after 5...♗b4.

The alternative **4...exd4** combines these two qualities, for the position after 5 ♘xd4 ♗b4 *(D)* is at the same time open and complicated. This is in fact a fairly treacherous and double-edged variation. White will have to accept some damage to his pawn-formation in return for obtaining a firm grip on the centre.

A characteristic (though by no means forced) continuation is 6 ♗g5 h6 7 ♗h4 ♗xc3+ 8 bxc3

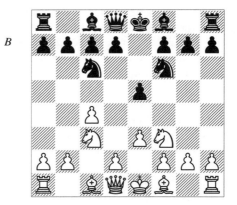

d6 9 f3. White will build up a strong pawn-centre with e4, and Black will break the nasty pin against the f6-knight with the manoeuvre ...♘e5-g6. Both sides will have to make an effort to let the positives of their respective positions prevail over the negatives after, for instance, 9...♘e5 10 e4 ♘g6 11 ♗f2 0-0.

2 ♘c3 ♘f6 3 ♘f3 ♘c6 4 e3

4   **e3** *(D)*

This little move has been known since the beginnings of the English Opening, but for a long time it led a very modest existence in the shadow of 4 d4. And then, quite suddenly, in the mid-1970s, *everybody* started to play it. Almost overnight, 4 e3 turned from a wallflower into the star variation of the Reversed Sicilian. Nowadays, although 4 g3 has taken over the top position, it remains a move to be reckoned with.

The problem for Black is that the bold reply **4...d5** is strongly met by 5 cxd5 ♘xd5 6 ♗b5, followed if necessary by d4.

Meekly waiting for White to decide whether to play d4 is also not to everyone's liking, although **4...♗e7** does in fact have a solid enough reputation. Because after 5 d4 exd4 the aggressive 6 exd4 is well-countered by 6...d5, White has to be a little more prudent and play 6 ♘xd4 instead. We then have almost the same position as after 4 d4 exd4 5 ♘xd4 ♗b4, with the extra moves e3 and ...♗e7 taking the edge off the tension. ...♗e7 is less aggressive than ...♗b4, while e3 hems in the queen's bishop.

But no matter how good or bad these alternatives are, the crucial reply to 4 e3 has been since times immemorial a move which combines the aggression of 4...d5 with the soundness of 4...♗e7, yet is totally different from either of them:

4 ... ♗b4

Introducing the possibility of an exchange on c3, which will reduce White's control over the central squares considerably.

5 ♕c2 (D)

An important point of 4...♗b4 is that **5 ♘d5** e4 leaves White without a good square for the knight. 6 ♘g1 is unimpressive, while after 6 ♘xb4 ♘xb4 7 ♘d4 c5 Black is already taking over the initiative.

The first move to be played in this position was **5...0-0**. This allows 6 ♘d5, but it was thought that after the cold-blooded 6...♖e8, threatening 7...e4 and freeing the f8-square for

the bishop, Black would have no problems. It is this position which harbours the secret of the enormous popularity of 4 e3 during the 1970s, for it was the discovery of the highly unorthodox move 7 ♕f5!? which caused all the problems for Black. The idea is a purely positional one: White wants to saddle his opponent with doubled f-pawns. The fact that 7...♘xd5 8 cxd5 loses a pawn is of vital importance, for this means that Black has no 'easy' answer to 7 ♕f5. The critical line is 7...d6 8 ♘xf6+, when Black can choose between the sharp 8...gxf6!? 9 ♕h5 d5 and the rather more cautious 8...♕xf6 9 ♕xf6 gxf6.

After a while, the alternative **5...♗xc3 6 ♕xc3 ♕e7** was developed, mainly by players who did not like being forced into these double-edged lines. At the cost of his bishop-pair, Black neutralizes his opponent's influence in the centre. Black can hope to take over the initiative by playing ...d5.

2 ♘c3 ♘f6 3 ♘f3 ♘c6 4 g3

4 g3 (D)

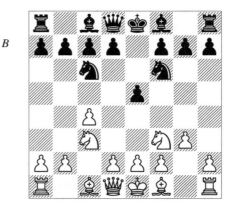

With this move we are walking onto the Centre Court of the Reversed Sicilian. This is the arena where for the past twenty-odd years most of the theoretical discussions have been held, most of the gladiator fights have been fought and most of the theoretical progress has been made.

Unlike 4 d4 and 4 e3, 4 g3 makes no attempt to prevent Black from playing ...d5. The first move to be considered then, must be **4...d5**.

Another plausible and powerful move is **4...♗b4**, yet the consequences of this are totally different from 4 e3 ♗b4.

Then there is the straightforward developing move **4...♗c5**, quite a popular move in fact, as is the tricky **4...♘d4**.

Other moves, like **4...g6** *(D)* for instance, are relatively unexplored.

Allowing White to play d4 is generally regarded as a minor concession and is not overly popular. Theory does not go much deeper than claiming that if play continues 5 d4 exd4 6 ♘xd4 ♗g7, then exchanging on c6 is critical and that after 7 ♘xc6 bxc6 8 ♗g2 Black will have some trouble getting his queen's bishop developed.

4 g3 d5

4	...	d5
5	cxd5	♘xd5
6	♗g2 *(D)*	

This is a position from the Dragon Variation of the Sicilian Defence with colours reversed. But what does this mean? Is it just a matter of a can of paint, with White now playing with black pieces and vice versa? What is it really that justifies White in playing the opening 'as if he is playing Black'?

The answer to these questions and the secret of all 'reversed' openings is the extra tempo. In every position where it would 'normally' be Black's move it is now White's. This invisible and difficult-to-evaluate difference from the

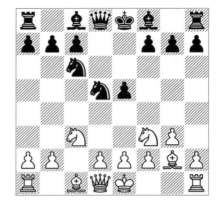

normal Dragon Variation defuses what would 'normally' be the most powerful anti-Dragon scheme: ...♗e6, ...f6, ...♕d7 and ...0-0-0 followed by a storm on the flank with ...h5-h4. If **6...♗e6** 7 0-0 f6, then 8 d4 will break open the centre and disrupt Black's plan.

Another aggressive idea, **6...♘xc3** 7 bxc3 e4, is also not dangerous for White. After the simple 8 ♘g1 Black will have trouble protecting his e4-pawn. 8...♗f5?! is met strongly by 9 ♕a4, when 9...♕e7 10 ♖b1 0-0-0 loses to 11 ♕b5, and if, e.g., 8...f5 9 d3 exd3 10 exd3, Black would probably dearly love to consolidate the vulnerable a2-g8 diagonal with the impossible move ...f5-f7.

In order to avoid these problems, Black is obliged to choose a much more conservative plan.

| 6 | ... | ♘b6 |

This prevents 7 d4.

| 7 | 0-0 | ♗e7 *(D)* |

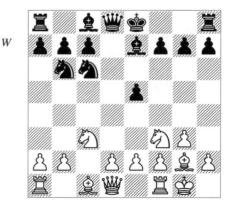

This is the most important starting point of this variation. Black has consolidated his spatial advantage in the centre. For the time being this situation is not particularly threatening for White, but given time Black will eventually start a potentially dangerous attack on the kingside with ...f5 and perhaps ...g5-g4. Another sound plan for Black is to strengthen his grip on the centre with ...f6, ...♗e6 and ...♕d7, perhaps followed by ...♘d4. White's chances lie on the queenside. A plausible plan is to advance the a- and b-pawns, gaining space and indirectly threatening the e5-pawn. Another standard manoeuvre is ♘d2-b3-c5 or ♘a4/e4-c5, bringing considerable pressure to bear on Black's queenside pawns.

Understanding the positional aspects of this position and the various characteristic plans of action is in fact much more important than knowledge of concrete variations.

To begin with, White can play **8 a4**, intending to carve a hole in Black's queenside immediately with a5-a6. But although this is quite an attractive prospect in itself, 8 a4 is not held in high regard because the simple reply 8...a5 gives Black control over the important square b4, making it more difficult for White to create inroads on the queenside.

8 d3 0-0 9 ♗e3 *(D)* is less compromising and for a long time this was the main line of this variation.

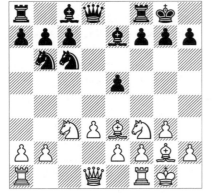

Illustrative of this position's volatility is **9...f5** 10 b4!?, when after 10...♗xb4?! 11 ♕b3+ ♔h8 12 ♘xe5 White can be satisfied about having eliminated Black's central pawn. A safer reply to 9 ♗e3 is **9...♗e6**.

But nowadays the most popular plan is to gain space on the queenside with b4.

The most common way of implementing this idea is to play **8 a3**. Although here too Black can play **8...a5**, this is now less painful for White than if he had played 8 a4, for now it is not White who gives up control over an important square (b4), but Black (b5). White will switch to another plan, 9 d3 0-0 10 ♗e3 for instance, and be happy. For this reason most players on the black side just allow b4. After **8...0-0** 9 b4 ♗e6 (9...♖e8 is also viable, as 10 b5?! ♘d4 11 ♘xe5 ♗f6 is good for Black), for instance, the threat of 10 b5 is elegantly parried by 10...♘d4, when 11 ♘xe5?? would lose to 11...♗b3. Instead, 10 ♖b1 renews the threat. After 10...f6 11 d3 *(D)* this leads to a position which is of crucial importance for the entire opening.

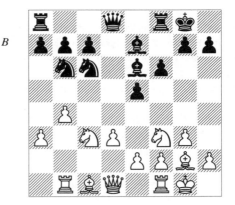

Black has tried both 11...♘d4 and 11...a5 12 b5 ♘d4 here. The point of inserting ...a5 is that in some cases ...a4 will clamp down White's queenside and allow Black to take over the initiative on that wing; e.g., 13 ♘xd4 exd4 14 ♘e4 a4, when both b5 and a3 become vulnerable. White should probably play a move like 13 ♘d2 instead, activating the g2-bishop.

The modern way of preparing b4 is to play **8 ♖b1**. Now, after 8...0-0, White can play 9 b4 without any further preparation, as 9...♗xb4?! is met by 10 ♘xe5!, winning back the pawn, in the process eliminating Black's central stronghold.

4 g3 ♗b4

4   ...   ♗b4 *(D)*

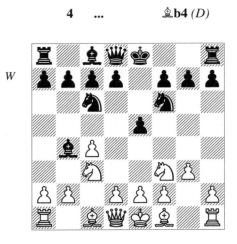

This move creates a totally different sort of tension. The position remains flexible, but fairly closed and the struggle is more about long-term positional problems. Much more than 4...d5, a move which is popular at all levels, this is a variation for the heavyweights. Top players have always found this variation to their liking, while the average club player has stayed aloof. But whether this is a recommendation is for the reader to decide!

The first problem now confronting White is the possible exchange of minor pieces on c3. Is this a threat – and if not, how should White recapture?

5   ♗g2

The main alternative to this natural developing move is **5 ♘d5** *(D)*.

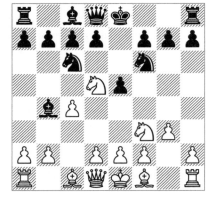

This move is now more appropriate than after 4 e3 ♗b4, because the aggressive reply **5...e4** does not force 6 ♘g1: White can play 6 ♘h4. Of course h4 is not the ideal square for a knight, but White's development is not hindered and Black will have to take care not to lose his e-pawn.

Another critical reply is **5...♘xd5** 6 cxd5 ♘d4 7 ♘xd4 exd4. The presence of no fewer than four d-pawns makes this a mysterious position. Both sides are facing some fundamental and bewildering problems concerning pawn-formations. How, for instance, should Black respond to a possible e3 or e4? And if he decides to take on e3 (...dxe3), should White recapture with his d- or with his f-pawn?

The least committal reply to 5 ♘d5 is to retreat the bishop: **5...♗c5**. Black refuses to be drawn into complications and maintains a flexible position. The crucial question after 5...♗c5 is whether d5 is actually a better square for the knight than c3, for this is by no means certain. After, e.g., 6 ♗g2 0-0 7 0-0 d6 and now either 8 d3 (intending to play 9 ♗g5) or 8 e3 (intending to play 9 d4) a delicate situation has arisen. Whom is a possible exchange of knights on d5 going to favour? The answer will be slightly different in every slightly different position.

5   ...   0-0

Another difference from the variation 4 e3 ♗b4 is that **5...♗xc3** can now be excellently met by 6 bxc3 in combination with 0-0, d3, e4, followed by ♘h4 and f4. If he can achieve this plan without disturbance, White will get a firm grip on the centre, enabling him to start an attack on the kingside at his leisure.

Taking back on c3 with the d-pawn is also not bad, but decidedly less aggressive. This is usually played in positions where the standard plan after bxc3 is not feasible.

6   0-0   e4 *(D)*

Black takes the initiative in determining the type of middlegame. Alternatives like **6...♗xc3**, **6...♖e8** and **6...d6** are not bad, but they have always been less popular than 6...e4. The latter two lines depend mainly on how good (or bad) the reply ♘d5 is. Taking on c3 is only advisable if Black has a concrete plan to throw a spanner in the works of White's standard plan, as outlined above. He could, for instance, follow **6...♗xc3** 7 bxc3 up with 7...♖e8 8 d3 e4.

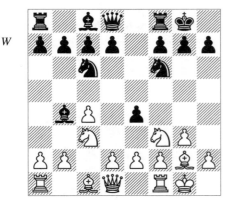

There are two fundamentally different moves in this position.

For a long time **7 ♘e1**, intending to meet 7...♗xc3 with 8 dxc3, was the main line. Black continues 8...h6, preventing 9 ♗g5, when a rather static position arises, where both sides will have to manoeuvre very patiently.

7 ♘g5 is riskier and more aggressive. Now the plan is to meet 7...♗xc3 with 8 bxc3, when after 8...♖e8 White has two ways of attacking the pawn on e4: 9 d3 and 9 f3. Two games from the 1987 match for the world championship between Kasparov and Karpov have demonstrated how extremely difficult these positions are, especially after 9 f3. White is hoping that Black will meekly play 9...exf3, when 10 ♘xf3 followed by d3 and e4 gives White a strong central position, but Black can play 10...d5, taking the initiative in the centre himself. Even more double-edged is the positional pawn sacrifice 9...e3!?. If White accepts by 10 dxe3, Black can calmly start attacking the hopelessly weak c4-pawn with moves like ...♘a5 (or ...♘e5), ...b6 and ...♗a6, or even ...♕e7-c5.

4 g3 ♗c5

| 4 | ... | ♗c5 *(D)* |

After being overshadowed by 4...♗b4 for a very long time, this old and sound developing move experienced a veritable renaissance in the 1990s.

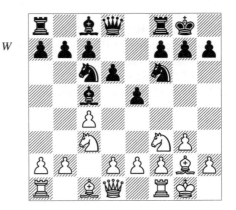

| 5 | ♗g2 |

For a long time most opening manuals gave **5 ♘xe5** as the critical reply, but in practice this has never been a popular choice. The point, of course, is 5...♘xe5 6 d4, when White gets his piece back with a good position, but 5...♗xf2+ 6 ♔xf2 ♘xe5 is stronger and enthusiasm for this somewhat odd position has never been great. In the long run White's central pawn-majority may become a positive factor, but for the time being White will need all the energy he can muster for a successful reintegration of his king.

| 5 | ... | d6 |
| 6 | 0-0 | 0-0 *(D)* |

This is the most important starting point of the 4...♗c5 variation. Remarkably, it differs from a position of the 4...♗b4 5 ♘d5 ♗c5 line in one respect only: White's queen's knight is on not d5, but c3. It is not clear who benefits from this tiny difference. Perhaps White's position is a little more flexible with his knight still on c3. He can try to take the initiative with a3 and b4 or with e3 and d4. Black has a solid and well-developed position with prospects of counterplay on the kingside. **7 d3** h6 (to prevent 8 ♗g5) 8 a3 a6 9 b4 ♗a7 10 ♗b2 ♗e6, intending 11...♕d7 followed by 12...♗h3, would be characteristic follow-up.

4 g3 ♘d4

4	...	♘d4 (D)

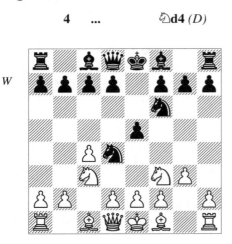

Although this move is based on a nasty opening trap, it is actually an exchange of knights and a consequent simplification of the position that Black is after. Paradoxically then, it is in fact the most defensive of Black's fourth-move options. As such, it enjoys a good reputation.

5	♗g2

Black is hoping that his opponent, after playing **5 ♘xe5** and facing the reply 5...♕e7, will get so confused as to allow 6 ♘d3?? ♘f3#! Instead, White has 6 f4 d6 7 ♘d3, maintaining an extra pawn, but nobody has ever shown great interest in trying to prove that this material advantage compensates for White's rather crumpled-up position.

5	...	♘xf3+
6	♗xf3	♗b4 (D)

6...♗c5 has also been played.

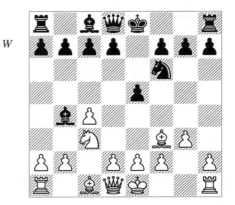

This position does not contain the weighty and far-reaching strategic problems of the 4...♗b4 variation. **7 d4** is not particularly strong because of 7...e4. The most popular move is **7 ♕b3**, when Black's most light-footed reply is 7...♗c5. White's queen is then (perhaps) less well placed on b3 than it was on d1, because on b3 it is blocking the flank advance b4-b5 and not supporting the central advance d4. After 8 0-0 0-0 9 ♘a4 ♗e7 10 ♖d1 the struggle is slowly heating up. White has more space, but Black has a solid position without any weaknesses.

1 c4 ♘f6 and Other English Lines

1 c4 (D)

1 c4 *(D)*

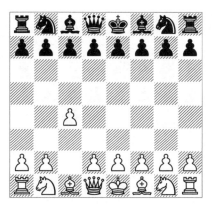

1...c5 and 1...e5, the two moves we have looked at so far, deserve to be called the most important moves in this position, because these are the two ways in which Black can immediately dictate the course of the opening. They are the two most ambitious and the most principled moves. After 1...c5 or 1...e5 there is no way back for White, nor for Black. The stage for the opening struggle is set.

But Black can also react in a totally different way, or perhaps I should say: it is also possible not to react at all. In that case, the most obvious and the most popular reply to 1 c4 is...

1 ... ♘f6

Black simply develops a piece, without making any announcements concerning his plans for the future. He allows his opponent to 'correct' his opening move by playing 2 d4 and in fact challenges him to show that 1 c4 really is a move which can look after itself. So, in a more indirect way, this is as good a test of the merits of 1 c4 as are 1...c5 and 1...e5.

There are a few other moves as well, which are by no means bad, but which lack the extended set of variations of 1...♘f6. Most of them are specifically designed for a transposition to

another opening. I shall just briefly outline these alternatives here:

1...e6 is played almost exclusively for meeting 2 ♘c3 with 2...d5, when the threat of 3...d4 practically forces White to play 3 d4, which transposes to the Queen's Gambit Declined. If White does not relish this prospect he will normally play 2 ♘f3 d5 3 g3 ♘f6, a Réti-like set-up discussed on page 243. 2 e4, which may look like a powerful advance in the centre at first glance, actually transposes to an innocuous sideline of the French Defence (see page 349).

1...c6 has a similar background. Here too, the idea is to transpose, after 2 ♘c3 d5 3 d4, to a Queen's Gambit, in this case the Slav (or an Exchange Slav after 3 cxd5 cxd5 4 d4). Likewise, 2 ♘f3 d5 3 g3 (or 3 b3), with a transposition to the Réti Opening (see page 251), is a major alternative. But an important difference from 1...e6 is that in this case 2 e4 *is* a move to be reckoned with, for this transposes to one of the more testing lines against the Caro-Kann (see page 376).

By playing **1...g6** *(D)*, Black is thinking along King's Indian lines.

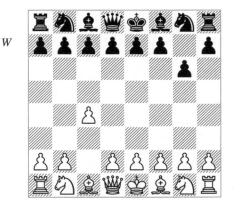

2 d4 and 2 e4 ♗g7 3 d4 transpose to a variation from 1 d4 g6, with a possible further

transposition to a 'real' King's Indian Defence. If White avoids this and persists in a pure flank strategy, e.g. by playing 2 ♘c3 ♗g7 3 g3, the opening will sooner or later take on the features of another English variation. An ...e5 set-up will lead to positions similar (or identical) to the Closed Variation of the Reversed Sicilian, while ...c5 will transpose to a line of the Symmetrical English. A transposition to the Leningrad Variation of the Dutch also remains an option.

If the Dutch Defence is what Black is thinking of, he can of course play **1...f5** *(D)* straight-away.

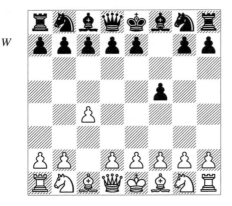

If White then refuses the invitation for a trans-position, either immediately (2 d4) or on one of his next moves, he will in the first place have to consider the consequences of ...e5 at some point. For instance, someone who has just studied the previous chapter of this book, will (perhaps) play 2 ♘c3 and not be afraid of 2...e5, because in that case 3 d4 has a good reputation (see page 222). But after 2...♘f6 3 ♘f3 g6 4 g3 ♗g7 5 ♗g2 0-0 6 0-0 d6, he will have to make a choice between a main-line Leningrad Dutch with 7 d4 (see page 181) and something more modest, like 7 d3 e5 8 ♖b1, which will then be similar to a Reversed Sicilian. If he chooses the latter, he will be leaving the safe(?) and well-charted terri-tory of the 'official' opening theory behind, yet anyone playing this regularly is likely to develop his own set of variations very quickly.

Finally, **1...b6** is a move to be reckoned with. After 2 d4, a transposition to the English

Defence with 2...e6 or 2...♗b7 followed by 3...e6 is critical, but many players will want to avoid this double-edged opening by playing 2 ♘f3 ♗b7 3 g3 instead. In that case 3...♘f6 transposes to a position that we shall return to later in this chapter. For those who prefer the fringes of opening theory, there is the adven-turous alternative 3...♗xf3. At the cost of his bishop-pair, Black saddles his opponent with doubled pawns.

We now return to 1...♘f6 *(D)*:

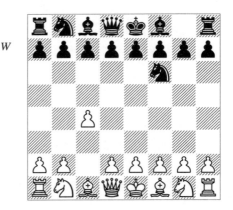

There are two main lines from this position (not counting 2 d4): **2 ♘c3** and **2 ♘f3**.

At first glance this may not look like an im-portant division. Is it not completely arbitrary in which order these sound developing moves are made?

But behind these two moves lie two totally different ways of anticipating the wide range of possible opening strategies that Black has at his disposal. Obviously, the first difference between the two knight moves is that **2 ♘c3** again allows both 2...e5 and 2...c5, and **2 ♘f3** only the latter, but this is not something that will unduly worry the 1 c4 player. The real decision at stake is about the great issues that also dominate the 1 d4 openings. How is White going to respond to a King's Indian set-up, to a Grünfeld, or to a Nimzo/Queen's Indian scheme? And what hap-pens if Black were to switch to a Queen's Gam-bit with 2...e6 or 2...c6, followed by 3...d5?

This subtle 'move-order game' is in fact one of the most prominent features of modern open-ing play. Many players with a 1 d4-oriented opening repertoire use the flank opening moves 1 c4 and 1 ♘f3 as side doors to their favourite 1 d4 openings, some to avoid a Benoni, some to avoid a Queen's Gambit Accepted, some perhaps to simplify the complexity of the Grünfeld or the Nimzo-Indian Defence. In fact, everyone who plays 1 c4 or 1 ♘f3 with a purpose like this will have reasons of his own and will develop a clearly defined footpath of his own to lead him through the jungle of variations.

Then of course there are those who cannot be bothered with subtleties like this and who just want to play a flank opening. For those players any division between **2 ♘c3** and **2 ♘f3** is indeed artificial and completely superfluous.

2 ♘c3

2   ♘c3 *(D)*

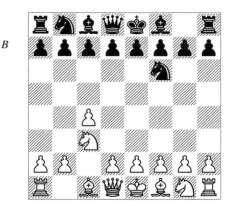

The most important moves in this position (apart from 2...c5 and 2...e5 of course) are **2...e6**, **2...g6** and **2...d5**.

An attempt to reach a Slav Defence with **2...c6** has never been particularly popular, probably because the reply 3 e4 makes life relatively more difficult for Black here than in the comparable variation 2...e6 3 e4.

For the same reason, **2...b6** has also never quite 'made it'. The problem again is 3 e4, when 3...♗b7 4 e5 ♘e4 is not the safe reply it is in the variation 2...e6 3 ♘f3 b6 4 e4 ♗b7 5 e5 (see page 240), because of the annoying 5 ♕f3.

2 ♘c3 e6

2   ...   e6 *(D)*

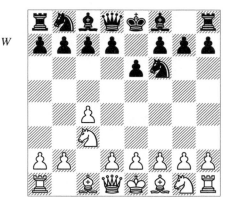

A natural choice for lovers of the Nimzo-Indian Defence, who are probably looking forward to seeing **3 d4** now. However, White has two major alternatives. First, there is **3 e4**, the **Flohr-Mikenas Attack**, an aggressive variation requiring considerable alertness from Black. Second, there is the sober developing move **3 ♘f3**. The real Nimzo-fanatic will perhaps regard this as just as 'good' as 3 d4 and play 3...♗b4, but the absence of a pawn at d4 makes this a totally different type of position.

3 g3 is less accurate in this position, because after 3...d5 Black is threatening 4...d4. White parries the threat quite easily with 4 d4, but the problem is that he then finds himself in a specific version of the Catalan Opening where c3 is not often the best square for his queen's knight.

Flohr-Mikenas Attack

3   e4 *(D)*

This move poses a concrete problem. A timid reaction like 3...d6, which allows White to play 4 d4, is not really an option, at least not according to the high standards of opening theory. Black will either have to strike back in the centre immediately, by playing **3...d5**, or he will have to try to expose a fundamental weakness of White's third move: the d4-square. This may be attempted with the provocative **3...c5**.

2 ♘c3 e6 3 e4 d5

| 3 | ... | d5 |
| 4 | e5 | |

The point of Black's last move is that after this there is no longer any need to withdraw the knight. Black can just imitate White's fourth move:

| 4 | ... | d4 |

This advance leads to a rather curious position.

| 5 | exf6 | dxc3 |
| 6 | bxc3 | ♛xf6 (D) |

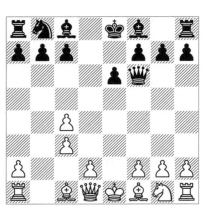

The result of the complicated exchange of pieces is that White now has doubled pawns on the c-file and that Black's queen is on an unusual square. This position is not easy to judge. Do the doubled pawns support White's central position or are they a liability? Is the black queen actively placed at f6 or vulnerable to an attack? These problems have resulted in some intriguing variations.

White's oldest move in this position is the natural **7 d4** and Black's first reply to this was 7...c5. White then plays 8 ♘f3, introducing the annoying possibility of harassing the black queen with ♗g5. Around 1990 the sharper 7...e5 became popular. Like 7...c5, this move immediately attacks White's central formation, but it has the added advantage that the diagonal of the light-squared bishop is cleared, the development of which is one of Black's fundamental problems in the 7...c5 variation. It is true that after 7...e5, 8 ♛e2 wins a pawn, but, surprisingly perhaps, it appears that 8...♗e7 gives Black fully sufficient counterplay after 9 dxe5 ♛g6 or 9 ♛xe5 ♛xe5+ 10 dxe5 ♘c6 11 ♘f3 ♗g4. Black's pieces are much more actively placed than White's, underlining the vulnerability of the doubled pawns.

For this reason, most players have changed their preference from 7 d4 to **7 ♘f3** over the years. The idea of this move is simply to transpose after 7...c5 8 d4 and to meet 7...e5 with a totally different plan, starting with the highly unorthodox 8 ♗d3 *(D)*.

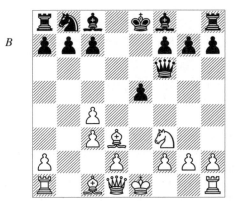

With this seemingly anti-positional move, White is banking not on the formation of a broad pawn-centre but on a fast development of his pieces, using both open files as bases of attack. Theory of this variation is still fairly embryonic. A sample of how play could develop: 8...♗d6 9 0-0 0-0 10 ♗e4 ♘c6 11 ♛c2 h6 12 ♖b1.

2 ♘c3 e6 3 e4 c5

| 3 | ... | c5 |

If White now plays the rather indifferent developing move **4 ♘f3**, a position is reached that I have given as part of the Symmetrical English (see page 216). But White has a much more critical and sharper reply:

| 4 | e5 |

Black is now forced to retreat his knight.

| 4 | ... | ♘g8 *(D)* |

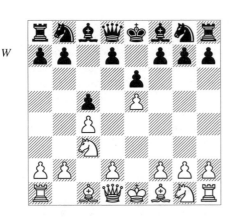

At first glance, Black's opening play makes a somewhat curious impression, but anyone studying the position a little deeper will soon realize that things are not that simple. Black has not developed a single piece, yet he can hardly be said to be lagging too far behind in development, since White has developed only one piece himself. Besides, White's pawn on e5 is exposed to attack, not only by ...♘c6 but also by ...d6, when a pawn exchange on d6 may leave White with a nasty hole in his pawn-formation at d4. To prevent this, White will have to play d4 at some point, but when?

The simplest solution is to play **5 d4** at once, but this has the drawback of White having to take back on d4 with the queen (5...cxd4 6 ♕xd4), allowing Black to play 6...♘c6 with gain of tempo. Although this variation is pretty solid for White (he will simply reply 7 ♕e4), the popularity of the Flohr-Mikenas Attack is mainly due to a much sharper idea: **5 ♘f3 ♘c6** and only now 6 d4. Again, this looks very strange at first sight, for does this not simply

give away a pawn by 6...cxd4 7 ♘xd4 ♘xe5? Indeed it does, but it turns out that White obtains excellent compensation for this small material loss if he continues 8 ♘db5. To begin with, the seemingly safe reply 8...d6? gets brutally crushed by 9 c5!, when after 9...dxc5? 10 ♗f4 Black is already lost. Black should probably play 8...a6 9 ♘d6+ ♗xd6 10 ♕xd6 f6 *(D)*.

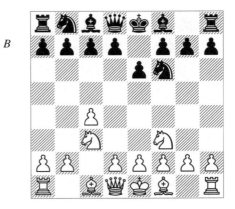

This fascinating position, where White has the bishop-pair, a space advantage and the initiative, while Black has an extra pawn, is one of the most theoretically critical of the entire Flohr-Mikenas Attack.

2 ♘c3 e6 3 ♘f3

| 3 | ♘f3 *(D)* |

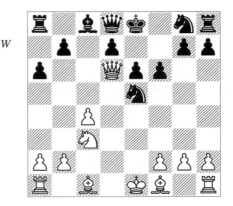

This position is a meeting point of three different move-orders. It is of vital importance for

1 ♘f3, for 1 c4 ♘f6 2 ♘f3 and for 1 c4 ♘f6 2 ♘c3 e6 3 ♘f3.

Black has four options. The first is the uncomplicated **3...d5**. Since White can hardly allow his knight to be chased back by 4...d4, he has practically no choice but to play 4 d4 (with 4 e3 being a very modest, but theoretically possible alternative). This transposes to a Queen's Gambit Declined (see page 17).

Then there is **3...c5**, a slightly more modest but equally solid move, with which Black is also bringing a central square under his direct control. This transposes to a variation of the Symmetrical English (see page 216).

A third possibility is to play **3...♗b4**, sometimes called the **Nimzo-English**. Black chooses the Nimzo-Indian game plan and challenges his opponent to find something better than 4 d4 (which would directly transpose).

Substituting the Queen's Indian for the Nimzo, the same can be said about Black's fourth option: **3...b6**.

Nimzo-English

| 3 | ... | ♗b4 *(D)* |

Just like the 'real' Nimzo-Indian (that would arise after **4 d4**), this variation offers a wealth of different types of middlegame. It requires confidence, good positional judgement and a wide knowledge of opening theory.

To begin with, White has to decide how to deal with a possible exchange on c3.

| 4 | ♕c2 |

With this, the most popular move for almost half a century now, White wants to recapture on c3 as 'cleanly' as possible and does not mind investing a considerable amount of time in this plan.

4 ♕b3 is an obvious alternative, seemingly more forcing than 4 ♕c2, because 4...♗xc3 5 ♕xc3 is unattractive for Black compared to the main 4 ♕c2 line, where White needs the extra move a3. The drawback of 4 ♕b3 is that after 4...c5 5 a3 ♗a5, the queen is less well placed on b3 than on c2. Nevertheless, this is a perfectly viable variation.

Another important option is to stoically continue developing the kingside, using the classical flank opening scheme **4 g3**. The main line here is 4...0-0 5 ♗g2 d5, though the Queen's Indian move 4...b6 is also quite popular.

The late 1990s, however, saw the introduction of a move of a wholly different calibre, if not from another planet: **4 g4** *(D)*.

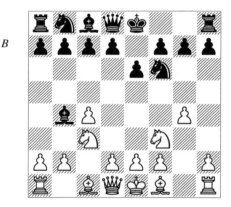

This has been played with great enthusiasm by many a top player and it shows how unpredictable and adventurous life is, even in the flank openings. 1 c4 and 1 ♘f3 may look like slow moves, but there can be a lot of pent-up energy behind them. If 4...♘xg4, White simply wins back the pawn with 5 ♖g1, while against other moves the g5 advance will disrupt Black's 'normal' game plan.

| 4 | ... | 0-0 *(D)* |

In the early days of the Nimzo-English, the 1960s and 1970s, **4...c5** 5 a3 ♗a5 was the main line, giving rise to a sort of Symmetrical English with the curious difference of a black bishop on a5, which you would normally expect to be at g7. Although this line has by no means been refuted, the preferred choice of modern players is the more typically Nimzo-Indian strategy of capturing on c3.

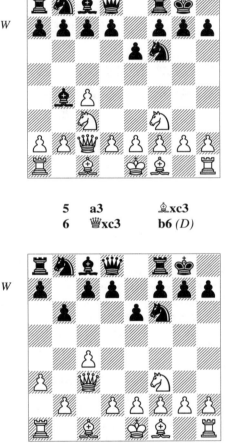

| 5 | a3 | ♗xc3 |
| 6 | ♕xc3 | b6 *(D)* |

This position is closely related to the 4 ♕c2 0-0 variation of the Nimzo-Indian Defence and anyone desiring to unravel its secrets will have to be aware of the many transpositional possibilities. The immediate **7 d4** is a realistic option, but many other moves, like **7 e3 ♗b7 8 ♗e2** for instance, emphatically keep the door to the Nimzo-Indian open as well.

Other important moves are **7 g3** and **7 b4**. Both moves leave Black the choice between a very flexible position, based on ...d6 and ...♘bd7

(often in combination with either ...e5, ...c5 or both), and an immediate counter-thrust in the centre with ...d5. After, for instance, **7 g3 ♗b7 8 ♗g2 d5 9 cxd5 ♘xd5 10 ♕c2 c5** Black has a solid position, having given up the bishop-pair in exchange for a firm grip on the centre. The alternative **7 b4** makes this strategy less attractive for Black, most notably in the variation 7...♗b7 8 ♗b2 d5 9 cxd5, when 9...♘xd5 is now strictly prohibited on account of 10 ♕xg7#! In this case, a plan based on ...d6 and ...e5, giving the bishop on b2 as little scope as possible, seems the most natural option.

2 ♘c3 e6 3 ♘f3 b6

| 3 | ... | **b6** *(D)* |

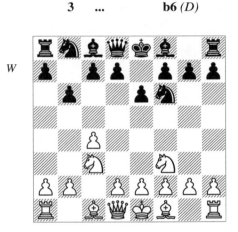

This was a popular variation in the 1970s and 1980s. Black chooses the Queen's Indian model for his development. **4 d4** would be a direct transposition, but this is unlikely to worry the average 3...b6 player unduly. A more critical test of 3...b6 is...

4 e4

Another option is the much quieter **4 g3**, giving rise, after 4...♗b7 5 ♗g2 ♗e7 6 0-0 0-0, to a position that is more often reached via other move-orders, in particular 1 ♘f3 ♘f6 2 c4 b6 or 1 c4 ♘f6 2 ♘f3 b6. I have assigned it to 2 ♘f3 b6 in this chapter (see page 247). Black may also seek a transposition to a Hedgehog Variation of the Symmetrical English with 4...c5 or ...c5 at a later stage.

| 4 | ... | ♗b7 |

Unlike after 2...b6 3 e4 (see page 235), there is no need to be afraid of **5 e5**, because there is no problem with 5...♘e4 now.

Generally speaking, one can say that the critical test of 3...b6 is a plan consisting of maintaining the pawn on e4 (thus ruling out Black's usual 'Queen's Indian' control over e4) and then playing d4, creating a broad pawn-centre. But achieving such a plan is far from easy. White has to be constantly on his guard for possible counterattacks in the centre with ...d5 and ...c5. Paradoxically perhaps, White's most successful move has been...

5   ♗d3 *(D)*

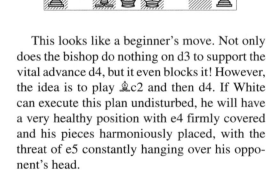

This looks like a beginner's move. Not only does the bishop do nothing on d3 to support the vital advance d4, but it even blocks it! However, the idea is to play ♗c2 and then d4. If White can execute this plan undisturbed, he will have a very healthy position with e4 firmly covered and his pieces harmoniously placed, with the threat of e5 constantly hanging over his opponent's head.

Black faces a fundamental decision. Lovers of the Hedgehog System will probably feel at home in the position after **5...d6** 6 ♗c2 c5 7 d4 cxd4 8 ♘xd4, but they must realize that White's attacking chances on the kingside are considerably enhanced by his bishop standing on c2 rather than its 'normal' square g2. An attempt to reach the same position with **5...c5** is slightly riskier, because it allows the aggressive 6 e5.

Another idea is to strike back in the centre at once: **5...d5**, but this strategy is also not free

from potential danger. The critical line is 6 cxd5 exd5 7 e5 ♘e4 (or 7...♘fd7), when Black has indeed created a stronghold in the centre, but he has also given his opponent a pawn on e5, which may generate potentially dangerous attacking chances against his kingside.

2 ♘c3 g6

2   ...   g6 *(D)*

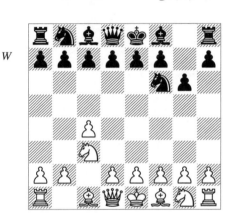

This is the move for someone who wants to play the King's Indian Defence.

White has to make up his mind. **3 d4** is of course a direct transposition to 1 d4 theory, but it does leave it up to Black to choose between a King's Indian (3...♗g7) and a Grünfeld (3...d5). Rather more incisive is **3 e4**, avoiding the Grünfeld and steering towards a King's Indian (3...d6 4 d4). But if White has a different variation of the King's Indian in mind, or if he does not want a 1 d4 opening at all, these options are not particularly attractive. In that case White is likely to prefer **3 ♘f3** or **3 g3**.

Although **3 ♘f3** is a perfectly valid option, it leads to a position that is far more often reached via 1 ♘f3 or 1 c4 ♘f6 2 ♘f3 g6 3 ♘c3, which is why I have decided to classify it as such (see page 245).

By playing **3 g3** *(D)*, White sticks to classical flank strategy.

As always, this gives the opponent almost total freedom of choice. The position is literally crawling with transpositions, so some knowledge of the openings concerned is certainly

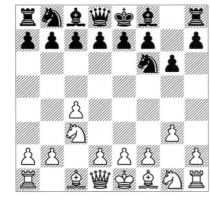

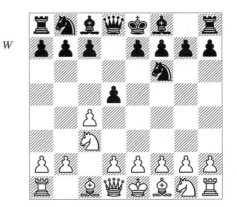

useful. There is a wide range of transpositions (primarily to a King's Indian or a Grünfeld Defence, but there are also variations of the Reversed Sicilian or the Symmetrical English involved) for Black to choose from, but each time it is up to White whether to 'finalize' the transposition by playing d4.

It is impossible to give a complete picture of these transpositions. I shall just name a few of the more important ones: if **3...d5** 4 cxd5 ⟶xd5 we have reached a position that we examine in the next section via 2...d5, after **3...c5** we find ourselves in a Symmetrical English and after **3...⟶g7** 4 ⟶g2 0-0 White can either transpose to a King's Indian immediately with **5 d4**, or play the 'neutral' **5 ⟶f3**, when it is again up to Black to choose between 5...d6 (and possibly 6 0-0 e5 7 d3 ⟶c6, transposing to a line of the Reversed Sicilian; see page 224), 5...c5 and the Grünfeld-related 5...d5.

2 ⟶c3 d5

> **2   ...   d5** *(D)*

While 2...e6 is the move for lovers of Nimzo- and Queen's Indian variations and 2...g6 is the best choice for the King's Indian players, 2...d5 is the way to remain within reach of the Grünfeld Defence. It is true that after 2...g6, transpositions to the Grünfeld are possible, but there is no guarantee that this will happen, because White may choose to play 3 e4, thus preventing ...d5 altogether. Of course there is no such thing as a 'guarantee' after 2...d5 either, but at least Black cannot be forced into a King's Indian! By

playing 2...d5, Black sets up a Grünfeld-related position. Eventually, it is always up to White to make it a real Grünfeld – by playing d4 – or not.

> **3   cxd5**

After **3 d4**, 3...g6 transposes to the starting position of the Grünfeld Defence. Black could also turn it into a Queen's Gambit, Declined, Slav or Accepted, with 3...e6, 3...c6 or 3...dxc4, respectively.

> **3   ...   ⟶xd5**
> **4   g3** *(D)*

By fianchettoing his king's bishop, White goes for a true flank opening. **4 d4** g6 transposes to the Grünfeld, as does **4 e4** ⟶xc3 5 bxc3 g6 6 d4.

4 ⟶f3 g6 will be discussed in the section on 2 ⟶f3 g6 3 ⟶c3 d5 4 cxd5 ⟶xd5, later in this chapter (see page 245).

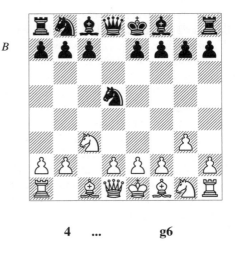

> **4   ...   g6**

The final decision in favour of a Grünfeld. Naturally, **4...e5** and **4...c5**, transposing to the Reversed Sicilian and the Symmetrical English respectively, are perfectly sound alternatives.

5   ♗g2

In this position Black has two options that both fit well into his Grünfeld-oriented strategy: **5...♘xc3** and **5...♘b6**.

After **5...♘xc3** 6 bxc3 ♗g7 *(D)* we have reached a position where Black has made all the typical Grünfeld moves. White on the other hand has stubbornly refused to play that most typical of queen's pawn opening moves, namely d4 itself.

This variation provides a beautiful example of the essence of flank strategy. By keeping his pawns back, White gives his opponent no targets for a counterattack. His plan is first to put maximum pressure on the enemy position from the flanks and only then throw in (if still needed) the infantry, preferably at a moment when Black is unable to strike back. This general idea often gives rise to some highly original play. For instance, a veritable 1 c4 player will not even dream of meekly playing **7 d4** in this position, transposing to an innocuous variation of the Grünfeld (7...c5). An approach like **7 ♘f3** 0-0 8 0-0 c5 9 ♖b1 ♘c6 10 ♕a4 is much more difficult for Black to handle. While attacking Black's queenside, White is at the same time preparing a surprise attack against Black's king with ♕h4 and ♗h6 *and* he is looking for a favourable opportunity to play d4.

The immediate **7 ♖b1** is also a popular move. This introduces two rather tricky tactical points. One is that 7...0-0? is not only a clever idea to tempt White into 8 ♗xb7?? ♗xb7 9 ♖xb7 ♕d5!, attacking both rooks, but also a blunder: after 8 ♖xb7! it is Black who has been tricked. The subtler and more sensible version of this idea is to play 7...♘d7, when 8 ♗xb7? ♗xb7 9 ♖xb7 ♘b6! traps the rook.

Another widely accepted plan of attack is the very direct **7 h4**.

All this does not mean that this is a bad variation for Black. His position is intrinsically sound, but the resulting type of middlegame is different from a 'real' Grünfeld and this requires some adaptation.

The alternative **5...♘b6** *(D)* is more cautious.

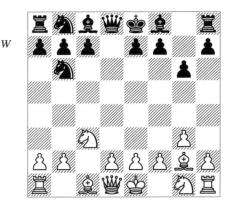

In this case a transposition to the Grünfeld with **6 d4** ♗g7 7 ♘f3 0-0 8 0-0 (see page 137) is a fully acceptable option. But persisting in a pure flank strategy is equally realistic. The sharp **6 h4**, for instance, is quite often played, as is the less drastic **6 ♘f3** ♗g7 7 0-0 0-0 8 d3, when after 8...♘c6 White has an excellent plan in 9 ♗e3, followed by ♕c1 and ♗h6. By eliminating Black's dark-squared bishop, White reduces the pressure against his queenside and makes the position of Black's king slightly more vulnerable. **6 d3** ♗g7 7 ♗e3 follows the same idea. By keeping the knight on g1, White retains a few aggressive options, like playing h4, should Black castle too quickly, or ♗xc6 in case Black plays ...♘c6.

2 ♘f3

2   ♘f3 *(D)*

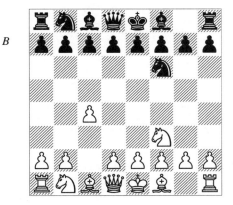

This position is of vital importance for two reasons. In the first place, as I have elaborated before, there is a great difference between 2 ♘c3 and 2 ♘f3 in the way both moves anticipate Black's characteristic plans in this opening. How is White going to respond to a King's Indian set-up, to a Grünfeld, to a Nimzo- or Queen's Indian, etc.?

Secondly, this position belongs to 1 ♘f3 theory as much as to 1 c4. Many a would-be 1 c4 player lets himself be frightened by the daunting prospect of having to face 1 c4 e5 and uses 1 ♘f3 as a side door. This avoids the Reversed Sicilian and after 1...♘f6 2 c4 White has got what he wanted!

Now, what are Black's options in this position?

To begin with, there is of course **2...c5**, with a transposition to the Symmetrical English. Then there is **2...c6**, which usually transposes, either to a Slav Defence after 3 d4 d5 or 3 ♘c3 d5 4 d4, or to a Réti Opening after 3 g3 d5 (see page 251).

The potentially independent variations start with **2...e6**, **2...g6** and **2...b6**. The queenside fianchetto is now much more solid than after 2 ♘c3, because White does not have 3 e4.

Another difference from 2 ♘c3 is that in this case **2...d5?!** is not very well timed. After 3 cxd5 ♘xd5 4 d4 g6 5 e4 we have reached a position that was mentioned in the chapter on the

Grünfeld Defence (see page 121). Since there is nothing on c3 to justify ...♘xc3, Black will have to retreat the knight to b6 or f6. The result is a rather poor imitation of a Grünfeld, with Black exerting far less pressure against White's pawn-centre than in the real Grünfeld.

2 ♘f3 e6

2   ...   e6 *(D)*

Unlike after 2 ♘c3 e6, Black won't be thinking of a Nimzo-Indian set-up here, for without ♘c3 there is no point in playing ...♗b4. The main reason (but not the only one!) for playing 2...e6 in this position is to continue 3...d5, in the spirit of the Queen's Gambit Declined.

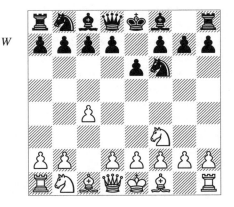

3   g3

By playing this move, White turns 2 ♘f3 into an independent variation. Naturally, **3 ♘c3** (see 2 ♘c3 e6 3 ♘f3) and **3 d4** are perfectly sound alternatives.

3 b3 d5 4 ♗b2 is also not bad, but much more experimental. Playing like this is leaving mainstream opening theory rather than following it. White will normally fianchetto his king's bishop at a later stage, but in some cases a scheme involving e3 and a bishop move along the f1-a6 diagonal is equally playable. This line is closely related to 1 ♘f3 d5 2 b3, an opening we shall be looking at in the next chapter.

3   ...   d5

This is the classical approach. Black occupies the centre and accepts a possible transposition to a Catalan.

3...c5 is a Symmetrical English again. **3...b6** 4 ♗g2 ♗b7 will be discussed under 2...b6.

An adventurous variation on the latter theme is to play **3...a6** *(D)*.

W

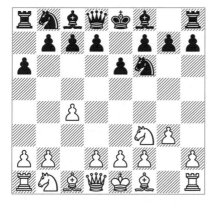

The idea is to continue **4 ♗g2 b5**, not only creating a square at b7 for the light-squared bishop, but immediately starting hostilities on the queenside as well. Oleg Romanishin started pioneering this line around 1975 and a decade or so later it suddenly became all the rage. Although this looks risky (and is obviously rather provocative), it is in fact remarkably solid. An attempt to win a pawn by 5 ♘d4 c6 6 cxb5 axb5 7 ♘xb5 would be dubious at best in any case, since the white knight is in trouble after 7...d5, but with 7...cxb5 8 ♗xa8 d5! trapping the bishop, White is clearly ill-advised to try this. The main line runs 5 b3 ♗b7 and now, for instance, 6 0-0 c5 7 ♘c3.

A subtle, but very important point of 3...a6 is that the plausible **4 ♘c3**, to prevent 4...b5, is not as strong as it looks, because Black now switches to 4...d5. With 5...d4 a serious threat, White would like to reply 5 d4, but this transposes to a somewhat problematic version of the Catalan Opening (5...dxc4). As a rule (though there are exceptions!) White's queen's knight should not be developed at c3 too early in this opening. This is the same problem that White has to deal with if he plays 2 ♘c3 e6 3 g3 (see page 235).

We now return to 3...d5 *(D)*:

This position is also relevant to the Réti Opening, for instance via 1 ♘f3 d5 2 c4 e6 3 g3 ♘f6.

W

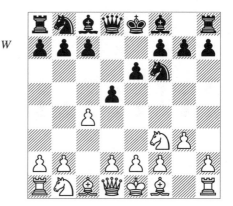

Now, if White does not want to transpose to the Catalan Opening immediately with **4 d4**, he has two well-established main lines: **4 ♗g2** and **4 b3**.

4 ♗g2 is often played with the idea of transposing to the Catalan a few moves later, for instance after 4...♗e7 5 0-0 0-0 6 d4. This avoids some variations, most notably the 4...dxc4 complex, thus narrowing Black's options. This is another example of White using a flank opening in effect to play a 1 d4 opening on his own terms, a phenomenon which runs like a common thread throughout 1 c4 and 1 ♘f3 theory. The critical test of 4 ♗g2 could be said to be 4...dxc4. If then 5 ♕a4+ ♘bd7 6 ♕xc4 c5, for instance, the opening struggle will revolve around the question: will Black find a comfortable way to develop his queen's bishop?

4 b3 avoids this problem. Black is given as little opportunity for creating counterplay as possible. This usually leads to a rather slow build-up. Eruptions of violent action (if any) are not to be expected before the middlegame. Black is left free to develop his position as it pleases him. Classical plans are 4...♗e7 5 ♗g2 0-0 6 0-0 and now 6...c5 7 ♗b2 ♘c6 or 6...b6 7 ♗b2 ♗b7. More cheeky (and more modern) is 4...a5, making the opponent worry about the possible advance 5...a4.

2 ♘f3 g6

> **2   ...   g6** *(D)*

This move introduces either a King's Indian or a Grünfeld set-up. As regards the latter, the

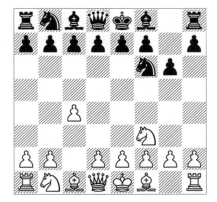

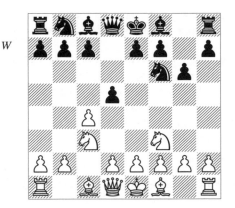

situation is exactly the opposite of 2 ♘c3, where 2...d5 is the Grünfeld-oriented move, not 2...g6.

3   ♘c3

This creates the possibility of 4 e4 and forces Black to lay his cards on the table.

Anyone intending to meet the King's Indian or the Grünfeld with the g3 system will probably prefer **3 g3**. In that case the picture is similar to the one presented by 2 ♘c3 g6 3 g3 (see page 240): Black can go for a King's Indian set-up with ...d6 and ...e5, he has ...c5 with a possible transposition to the Symmetrical English or he can play the Grünfeld move ...d5 at some point. In all of these cases it is up to White to decide whether (and if so, when) to play d4, which usually results in a transposition to a King's Indian or Grünfeld.

3   ...   d5 *(D)*

This is an invitation to a Grünfeld and theoretically the most interesting move. If **3...♗g7**, 4 e4 d6 5 d4 transposes to a King's Indian without any subtleties. After 3...d5, White has a number of ways of refusing the invitation.

After 3...d5, how realistic is it to try to find something better than (or at least as good as) **4 d4**, with an immediate transposition to the Grünfeld?

This is in fact a very difficult question. It is partly a matter of personal preferences (White has a few options of defining the middlegame in a very concrete way) and partly a matter of exact calculations, for there are a few variations that depend largely upon very precise evaluation.

At any rate, Black will have to be prepared for a great variety of possible types of play.

4   cxd5

Most variations start with this exchange of pawns, but **4 ♕a4+** is another important test of the soundness of 3...d5. White makes an attempt to disorganize Black's position. First he provokes 4...♗d7, making it impossible for Black to meet 5 ♕b3 with 5...d4. Then, after 5...dxc4 6 ♕xc4 ♗g7, he has the energetic 7 e4, intending to counter 7...0-0 with 8 e5. Only then, after 8...♘e8 for instance, White finally plays 9 d4. In comparison with the Russian Variation of the Grünfeld Defence (see page 132), Black's position is now an unusually passive one. A true Grünfeld devotee will probably try to find something better – something more active. Theory has not determined any 'best line' yet, but Black has been experimenting with 7...♗c6 (instead of 7...0-0) and with 6...a6 (instead of 6...♗g7), intending to play a quick ...b5.

4   ...   ♘xd5 *(D)*

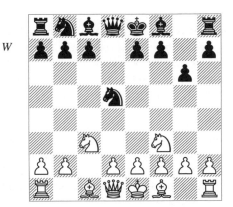

Now **5 d4** is an 'honest' Grünfeld again. The many attempts to improve on this are of a varied nature.

Sharpest (again) is the destabilizing **5 ♕a4+**, especially when after 5...♗d7 White continues 6 ♕h4. If Black then retreats the knight by 6...♘f6, White again has 7 e4, while 6...♘xc3 7 dxc3 offers prospects of fast and aggressive development. Black will have to play with some accuracy here.

Another major option for White is to continue **5 e4**. This transposes to a Grünfeld if, after 5...♘xc3, White recaptures with the b-pawn (6 bxc3 ♗g7 7 d4), but most players who go for 5 e4 have something else in mind: 6 dxc3 ♕xd1+ 7 ♔xd1 (D).

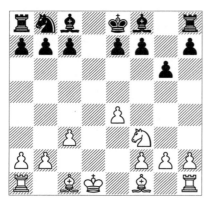

White is working on the assumption that this queenless middlegame offers him slightly the better chances on account of his small lead in development. His king is likely to find refuge at c2. Much will depend, of course, on the quality of White's endgame technique and it is by no means certain that White *does* stand better, but the most important thing about this position is that many a Grünfeld player who was counting on a sharp opening battle will be disagreeably surprised by this sudden turn of events.

Finally, **5 g3** is often played in this position. This quiet developing move introduces a typical plan, which we have by now encountered in many different forms. After 5...♗g7 6 ♗g2 Black is not forced to withdraw his knight from d5 (as he is in case of 2 ♘c3 d5 3 cxd5 ♘xd5 4

g3 g6 5 ♗g2), so he can calmly play 6...0-0, when after 7 0-0 he has a choice of 7...c5, with a transposition to the Symmetrical English (see page 209), and 7...♘c6, when White can finally decide to turn it into a proper Grünfeld after all by playing 8 d4.

2 ♘f3 b6

| 2 | ... | **b6** (D) |

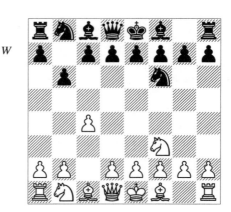

With this move Black makes it clear that he would like to transpose to a Queen's Indian Defence, more so than if he plays 2...e6 3 ♘c3 b6, which allows the sharp 4 e4 (see page 239). After 2...b6, there is in fact very little room for White to avoid a Queen's Indian. However, many 1 c4 and 1 ♘f3 players are not trying to avoid this transposition completely; they are just trying to avoid certain variations of the Queen's Indian.

3 g3

White is hoping to reach the 4 g3 variation of the Queen's Indian without having to worry about the troublesome 4 g3 ♗a6.

In a similar way, White can try to reach the 4 a3 variation without the parallel line 4 a3 ♗a6, by playing **3 ♘c3** here. If Black refuses to cooperate (i.e. 3...♗b7 4 d4 e6 5 a3), he has little choice but to play 3...e6, which of course allows 4 e4 again.

| 3 | ... | **♗b7** |

3...c5 is an important alternative. I have classified this move as a line of the Symmetrical English (see page 220).

4 ♗g2 *(D)*

If White is already satisfied with what he has achieved (the elimination of ...♗a6), he could also play **4 d4** straightaway, with a view to 4...e6 5 ♗g2, transposing to a 4 g3 ♗b7 Queen's Indian. However, he has to take the sharp retort 4...c5 5 d5 b5!? into account. So far, this has hardly been tested.

B

4 ... e6 *(D)*

Black chooses a purely Queen's Indian set-up. **4...c5** or **4...g6** 5 0-0 ♗g7 6 ♘c3 c5 transposes to the variation that he could already have chosen on move three (3...c5).

W

5 0-0

There is, of course, no objection at all to playing **5 d4**, but for those who are not worried about a transposition to the Symmetrical English (which is available to Black at any moment just by playing ...c5) there is no need to rush with this advance.

5 ... ♗e7
6 ♘c3 0-0 *(D)*

In this position it is not too late to play **7 d4**, but, in a similar way as we have seen in the Hedgehog Variation (see page 219), White also has the chance of confronting his opponent with more complicated problems than this simple transposition to a well-known variation of the Queen's Indian. By playing **7 ♖e1**, White 'threatens' to play 8 e4 first and d4 afterwards. A logical reply to this idea is to play 7...d5. After 8 cxd5, **8...exd5** 9 d4 leads to a type of position that is specific to the Queen's Indian Defence, comparable to the variation 4 g3 ♗b7 5 ♗g2 ♗e7 6 0-0 0-0 7 ♘c3 d5 (see page 80). The alternative **8...♘xd5** 9 e4 ♘xc3 10 bxc3 c5 11 d4 is also quite playable. In fact, we have seen this very position before: in the 7 ♖e1 variation against the Hedgehog (see page 219).

And perhaps it is only fitting that we should end our investigation of the English Opening with a complicated maze of interconnected variations like this.

Réti Opening

1   ♘f3 (D)

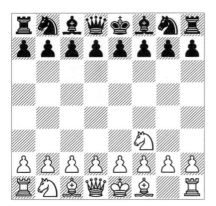

B

Nowadays, it seems almost incomprehensible that there ever was a time when this solid and natural opening move was not taken seriously at all. And yet this was the consensus view until Richard Réti (1889-1929) was hugely successful with it in 1923 and 1924 and published several theoretical articles to support his views. Only then did 1 ♘f3 manage slowly (and in the face of a great deal of resistance from conservative theoreticians) to emerge from the marshland of what was once called the 'Irregular Openings'. Little by little, Réti's ideas gained acceptance and his name began to be attached to 'his' opening.

What Réti so brilliantly conceived was not just a certain move-order or a single variation, but an entire concept, the strategic concept of a flank opening. Not only did he examine the consequences of 1 ♘f3, he also reinterpreted the older 1 c4 in the light of his (then) revolutionary idea that one need not immediately start **occupying** the centre squares from the first moves, but that it is possible to **control** them from the flank. Many of the positional ideas that we have seen in the three chapters on the English Opening were devised by him. Practically all world champions

and other top grandmasters after him have used his ideas and his opening. Now, in the early years of the 21st century, a world without 1 ♘f3 seems unthinkable.

Still, it is important to realize that this opening can be used in two different ways, the same as I outlined for 1 c4. The first one is to use 1 ♘f3 as the starting move of a pure flank strategy, no matter how Black reacts to it. The second is to use 1 ♘f3 as a side door to 1 d4. In this case White will try to reach his favourite 1 d4 variations (or avoid those of his opponent!), depending on how Black reacts to 1 ♘f3. Both interpretations of 1 ♘f3 are perfectly legitimate and do not exclude each other. Most 1 ♘f3 players will combine them, thus creating a tailor-made, highly personal 1 ♘f3 repertoire.

The classical reactions to 1 ♘f3 are of course **1...d5** and **1...♘f6**.

Many other moves are equally sound, but most of them are in effect an invitation to transpose to a different opening.

1...c5, for instance, is a clear invitation to a Sicilian Defence (2 e4). Of course Black also has to take 2 c4 into account, a transposition to the Symmetrical English. On the other hand, Black's choice makes it much harder for White to direct the game into a main-line 1 d4 opening system.

And anyone playing **1...f5** *(D)* naturally expects a transposition to the Dutch Defence, for which White only needs to play d4, now or later.

But Black has to be aware of **2 e4**, the **Lisitsyn Gambit**. This is an attempt to take advantage of the vulnerability of Black's kingside, an unavoidable consequence of 1...f5. White is hoping for a blitzkrieg and indeed things can develop very quickly in this position. After 2...fxe4 3 ♘g5 ♘f6 4 d3! exd3 5 ♗xd3, Black is already staring a mating idea in the face: 6 ♘xh7! ♘xh7 7 ♗g6#! Fortunately, there is no need for

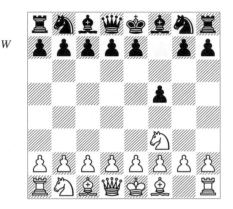

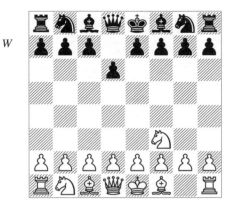

Black to self-destruct. Instead of 4...exd3, he has several more solid moves, like returning the pawn with 4...e3 or 4...e5, or on the previous move, 3...e5 4 d3 e3. There is also the sharp option 3...d5!? 4 d3 ♕d6 5 dxe4 h6, if Black wishes for a more lively fight. However, White has a related option in **2 d3**, intending to play e4 next move (e.g. 2...♘f6 3 e4 fxe4 4 dxe4 ♘xe4 5 ♗d3 ♘f6 6 ♘g5 transposes to the dangerous line mentioned above). Black should probably decline this form of the gambit.

As a more general point, Black must be careful in all these Dutch vs Réti/English lines that White cannot make an advantageous e4 advance at a slightly later stage. Thus, a rather more subtle reaction to 1...f5 is to play **2 g3**, postponing a decision about d4 until Black has made his intentions clearer. If Black chooses a Stonewall set-up, it may be worthwhile to play d3 and e4 instead of d4, if only to annoy the opponent, who in a 'real' Stonewall (with White having played d4) has probably never faced an e4 breakthrough in his entire life. Stonewall players need to plan out their specific move-orders very carefully here.

Parallel to the growing popularity of 1 d4 d6 (see page 190), **1...d6** *(D)* has developed from an insipid opening move (with intentions unknown) to an assertive reaction to 1 ♘f3.

Black challenges his opponent to prevent the 'threatened' 2...e5 by playing 2 d4, and indeed this does seem to be the theoretically critical reply. Players who prefer a pure flank opening will have to go for 2 c4 e5 3 ♘c3, a transposition to the Reversed Sicilian (see page 222), or a King's Indian Attack: 2 g3 e5 3 ♗g2.

Finally, **1...g6** *(D)* is a move to be reckoned with.

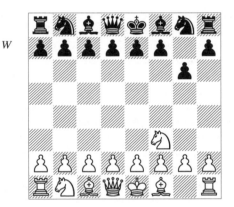

Here too, White can stoically continue 2 c4 or 2 g3, but in this case it is really tempting to change tack and play 2 e4 or 2 d4, accepting the freely offered central territory. This must be considered the critical test of 1...g6. Note that this is a significant difference between 1 c4 and 1 ♘f3: King's Indian players can comfortably meet 1 c4 with 1...g6, but cannot do so after 1 ♘f3 unless they are also happy playing the Modern Defence. We shall look at the position after 1 ♘f3 g6 2 e4 ♗g7 3 d4 in the section on 1 e4 g6 (see page 462).

1...d5

1   ...   **d5** *(D)*

W

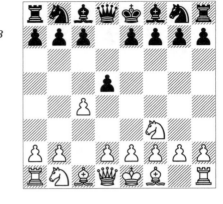

B

In the 1920s, a time when classical positional dogma did not tolerate heretical views and the central squares **had** to be occupied by pawns, this was the self-evident reason why 1 ♘f3 was an unimportant move. After all, according to orthodox dogma, White now *has* to play 2 d4 to avoid a disadvantage. So why not simply play 1 d4 instead?

It is chiefly thanks to Réti that the chess world saw the breakthrough in positional thinking that has allowed the alternatives **2 c4** and **2 g3** to come to the fore. Even **2 b3** has become an accepted way of playing, mainly because of the efforts of Nimzowitsch.

It is these three moves that we shall be looking at in this chapter, but it is interesting to note that – ironically – **2 d4** has recently become very popular again. Many of the modern generation of 1 ♘f3 players are satisfied with Black having committed himself to a Queen's Gambit by playing 1...d5. A large part of 1 d4 theory has been side-stepped, so 1 ♘f3 has done its job, and back to business.

1...d5 2 c4

> 2   **c4** *(D)*

It is mainly thanks to this move that Réti and his fellow pioneers managed to get 1 ♘f3 going in the 1920s. Nevertheless, 2 c4 has remained a controversial move to this day. The critical reply is **2...d4**, accepting the challenge to play a Benoni with colours reversed. This line has been alternately called good and bad ever since the days of Réti himself.

The alternatives **2...e6**, **2...c6** and **2...dxc4** are a little more cautious, though in their own way they also ask White the question: what is the point of your opening?

Of these three moves I shall only discuss the latter two here, because **2...e6** will normally (i.e. after the 'normal' 3 g3 ♘f6) transpose to a variation that we have already looked at in the previous chapter (1 c4 ♘f6 2 ♘f3 e6 3 g3 d5; see page 243). 3 d4 is of course a Queen's Gambit Declined (or a Catalan).

2...♘f6?! is not to be recommended. This line was also (briefly) discussed in the previous chapter (via 1 c4 ♘f6 2 ♘f3 d5?!; see page 243).

1...d5 2 c4 d4

> 2   **d4** *(D)*

Just as the 'regular' Benoni is one of the most controversial defences to 1 d4, this line (which is in effect a Benoni Reversed) has always been assessed in strong, almost emotional terms. What is most remarkable perhaps, is that 'the books' have always been fairly sceptical about 2...d4, but in practice there are few players who have had the courage to play this line *as White*! 2 d4 and 2 g3 are far more popular than 2 c4.

After 2...d4, White has three rather different methods of play, all of which are easily recognizable as originating from the Benoni.

To begin with, there is **3 e3**, attacking Black's far-advanced d-pawn at once. The most important theoretical starting position of this line arises after 3...♘c6 4 exd4 ♘xd4 5 ♘xd4 ♕xd4 6 ♘c3 e5 7 d3. White is aiming at a complete

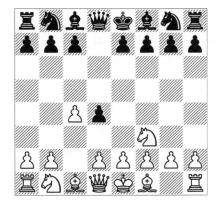

opening of the centre by 8 ♗e3 and 9 d4. The more ambitious 3...c5 is not all that popular, probably because players are worried about the unclear consequences of a Reversed Blumenfeld Gambit: 4 b4.

A second option is to surround the d4-pawn, by playing **3 b4** followed by 4 ♗b2. Black has various ways of defending his outpost; e.g., the solid 3...g6 4 ♗b2 ♗g7 or the sharp 3...f6 4 e3 e5 (intending 5 exd4 e4!).

The most flexible option is **3 g3**. White starts by developing his light-squared bishop on g2 and keeps the options of playing either e3 or b4 open. This allows Black considerable freedom in choosing a scheme of development for his pieces. The most popular plan is to play 3...♘c6 4 ♗g2 e5 5 d3 ♘f6. If now 6 0-0, Black must be on his guard against 6...♗e7 7 b4!, when 7...♗xb4 runs into 8 ♘xe5 ♘xe5 9 ♕a4+, regaining the piece. Moves like 6...a5 or 6...♘d7 are more prudent. White will then be looking at e3 to try to take the initiative in the centre.

1...d5 2 c4 c6

> **2 ... c6** (D)

Naturally, anyone playing this move will have to be prepared for a Slav Defence after **3 d4**. In fact, by playing 2...c6 Black signals his intention to play a Slav-related opening scheme anyway, whether White plays d4 or not, for he is preparing to play ...♗f5 or ...♗g4.

> **3 b3**

More than 2...e6, 2...c6 urges White to do something about a possible ...dxc4, since an easy recapture by ♕a4+ and ♕xc4 is now out of the question. For this reason 3 b3 is safest and simplest.

Nevertheless, **3 g3** is not a bad move. This is more aggressive than 3 b3, for if Black now takes on c4, White is counting on different ways to get his pawn back or he might even sacrifice the pawn and play for the attack. And if Black does not take on c4, White will still be free to play b3. A few example lines after 3 g3 (D):

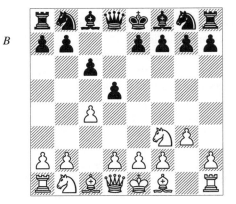

a) **3...dxc4** 4 ♗g2 b5 5 a4 ♗b7 6 b3 cxb3 7 ♕xb3. Both sides have got what they wanted: Black is a pawn up and White has a big lead in development.

b) **3...♘f6** 4 ♗g2 and now:

b1) **4...dxc4** 5 ♘a3 b5 6 ♘e5 ♕c7 7 d4. Again, a principled battle between mind and matter is taking shape. The outcome will be impossible to predict.

b2) **4...♗f5** 5 cxd5 cxd5 6 ♕b3. White's position is more flexible than in the Exchange Slav (see page 27), because he has not played d4. If 6...♕c8 7 ♘c3 e6, for instance, White can start an attack in the centre with 8 d3 followed by e4.

3   ...   ♘f6
4   g3 *(D)*

Naturally, **4 ♗b2** is perfectly sound, but in some cases the possibility of playing ♗a3 will be useful. Therefore 4 g3 is the more popular move.

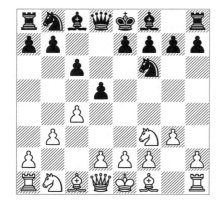

B

There are two main lines from this position: **4...♗f5** and **4...♗g4**.

A ...♗f5 build-up is called the **Lasker** or **New York Variation**, because this was first played by Lasker in the famous New York tournament of 1924, against no less an opponent than Réti himself. There are no forced or preferred move-orders here, but a characteristic continuation would be **4...♗f5** 5 ♗g2 e6 6 0-0 ♘bd7 7 ♗b2 ♗e7 and now 8 d3 h6 (to be able to retreat the bishop safely to h7) 9 ♘bd2 0-0 10 a3 a5 (to stop b4) 11 ♕c2. White has made a central break with e4 a realistic prospect, but he is equally ready to support the b4 advance and increase the pressure along the a1-h8 diagonal with moves like ♗c3 and ♕b2. Black on the other hand has a solid position without any weaknesses. This variation often starts with a lot of manoeuvring before unravelling (if at all) into a concrete fight. Patience is a virtue here.

The alternative ...♗g4, introduced in 1925 by Capablanca, anticipates a possible d3 and

e4, an advance which is obviously more powerful with a bishop to be attacked at f5. If **4...♗g4** 5 ♗g2 *(D)*, Black should not let himself be tempted by the prospect of material gains.

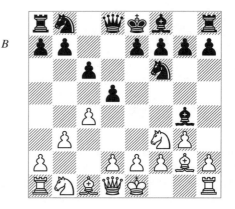

B

Thus after **5...dxc4** 6 bxc4 ♗xf3 7 ♗xf3 ♕d4, the reply 8 ♕b3! will disillusion him (8...♕xa1? 9 ♕xb7 and White regains the sacrificed material with a lot of interest). Correct is **5...e6** 6 ♗b2 ♘bd7 7 0-0 ♗e7. In this position, the traditional Réti approach is to play 8 d3 and 9 ♘bd2, but nowadays 8 d4 is a popular alternative. The plan is to play 9 ♘bd2, 10 ♖e1 and 11 e4, which would not be possible with the black bishop at f5. This modern variation shows that even in the Réti Opening, where the game often develops slowly and in rather stereotyped fashion, it is still possible to find room for a precise and subtle treatment of the opening.

1...d5 2 c4 dxc4

2   ...   dxc4 *(D)*

This is the natural choice of the Queen's Gambit Accepted player. Black resolves the central tension in an uncomplicated way. In most cases, the idea is not so much to keep the extra pawn, but to achieve maximum flexibility. Black will adapt his plan of development to the way in which White regains the pawn.

The most direct way of doing so is to play **3 ♕a4+**. If then 3...♘d7, the most popular move is 4 g3. There is no hurry to take on c4, and fianchettoing the light-squared bishop is a logical

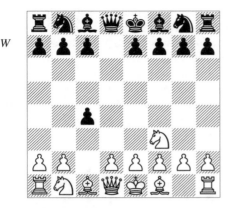

plan now that the h1-a8 diagonal is lying wide open.

3 ♘a3 is equally plausible. This move combines recapturing the pawn with manoeuvring a knight to c4, where it will assume control over e5. Black has many plans here, the most assertive being 3...c5 4 ♘xc4 ♘c6, with perhaps ...f6 and ...e5 to follow. The more reserved 3...♘f6 4 ♘xc4 g6 also makes a very natural impression.

3 e3 often transposes to the Queen's Gambit Accepted; e.g., 3...♘f6 4 ♗xc4 e6 5 d4. An attempt to maintain the extra pawn with 3...b5 will fail to 4 a4. After 4...c6 5 axb5 cxb5 the characteristic break 6 b3!? wins back the pawn and yields White the initiative.

1...d5 2 g3

2   g3 *(D)*

For most people who are familiar with 1 d4 or 1 e4 theory only, and who perhaps just leaf through these chapters on the flank openings, this move may come as a shock. If 1 ♘f3 d5 2 c4 is still vaguely acceptable because of the direct attack against d5, 2 g3 must look like the ultimate bore. No action at all!

Well, in fact this is a very narrow view which does not do justice to 2 g3. White's opening plan is not intended to avoid a fight. Actually, 2 c4 and 2 g3 are really very similar and Réti used both moves with the same idea in mind. 2 g3 is not slower, it is more flexible than 2 c4. Depending on how Black reacts to 2 g3, White can decide to play c4 after all (which is what Réti

did) or he can choose an entirely different plan: d3 and e4, the **King's Indian Attack**.

During the 1950s, when the King's Indian Defence against 1 d4 rose to great heights, 1 ♘f3 in combination with 2 g3 became extremely popular as well. It was played by the strongest players of that time: Botvinnik, Smyslov, Petrosian and – a decade later – Bobby Fischer all were successful with this opening scheme.

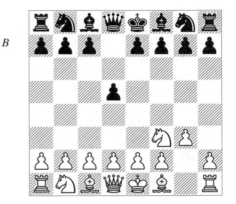

The reason why 2 g3 may look a little slow is that Black is left completely free to develop as he sees fit. He can really do as he pleases. But when studied more deeply, the situation is not all that easy for Black, since he has to take three different plans for White into account: c4, d4 and d3 followed by e4. In some cases White will even fianchetto his queen's bishop first, before making a choice. This means that for the time being Black does not have a clue as to his opponent's intentions, a situation that may well get on his nerves.

Now, what are the normal moves in this position where everything is possible? Without discussing every single move individually, we can distinguish four different strategies for Black.

The most assertive option must be to play **2...c5**. As if colours really have been switched, Black assumes the role of a 1 d4 player, preparing to play 3...♘c6 and 4...e5.

The neutral developing move **2...♘f6** is a major alternative. Black keeps (almost) all options open, but after 3 ♗g2 he will have to show his hand after all.

2...♞c6 is based on a different idea and this move is far less complex than the previous two. Black is looking for clarity. By introducing the possibility of playing 3...e5 he forces White to make a decision.

The same can be said about **2...g6**. Does White, after 3 ♗g2 ♗g7, allow 4...e5 or not? And if not, will he choose a plan based on c4 or d4?

1...d5 2 g3 c5

    2   ...   c5
    3   ♗g2   ♞c6 *(D)*

The slightly more cautious **3...♞f6** will be discussed under the heading 2...♞f6.

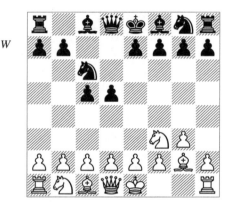

After 3...♞c6 the moment of truth has come. What is White going to do about 4...e5?

    4   d4

This move, which in effect creates a **Reversed Grünfeld**, comes naturally to a modern player, especially if he knows something about 1 d4 theory. Ultimately though, the choice is a matter of taste.

4 0-0 e5 5 d3 is a **Reversed King's Indian**, in a version that is now regarded as relatively favourable for Black. Of course, a true lover of this opening scheme will not object to (and probably not even agree with) this judgement and in fact this was a popular line in the 1950s and 1960s. But in recent years, many players have become a little more fastidious, preferring to reserve the Reversed King's Indian for situations where Black has developed in the rather

less assertive ways, that we shall be looking at later in this chapter.

4 c4 d4 transposes to a position that can also be reached via 2 c4 d4. Alternatives for Black are 4...♞f6 5 cxd5 ♞xd5, transposing to a line of the Symmetrical English (see page 220), and 4...e6 5 cxd5 exd5 6 d4, transposing to the Tarrasch Defence (see page 12).

We now return to 4 d4 *(D)*:

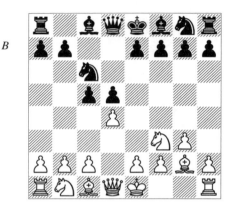

On the face of it, Black now has the same wide range of possibilities that White has in the starting position of the Grünfeld proper, but a closer examination reveals that he had better be careful. It is precisely in a sharp opening like this, that White's extra move (♗g2) is a telling factor. If **4...cxd4** 5 ♞xd4 e5 6 ♞xc6 bxc6 7 c4, for instance, Black is already in some trouble.

4...♞f6 5 0-0 e6 (or **4...e6** 5 0-0 ♞f6) is more cautious. Following 6 c4, this transposes to a line of the Catalan Opening after 6...dxc4 (see page 25) or to the Tarrasch Defence after 6...♗e7 7 cxd5 exd5 (see page 13).

1...d5 2 g3 ♞f6

    2   ...   ♞f6
    3   ♗g2 *(D)*

In this position, which in practice often arises after 1 ♞f3 ♞f6 2 g3 d5 3 ♗g2, Black has to choose a game plan.

Naturally, it is still quite possible to play the assertive **3...c5**. After the plausible continuation 4 0-0 ♞c6 White then faces the same choice as after 2...c5 3 ♗g2 ♞c6. But precisely

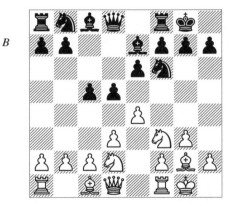

because of the Grünfeld-inspired 5 d4, many players prefer to delay ...♘c6 and play 4...g6 instead. If then 5 d4 cxd4 6 ♘xd4 ♗g7, we have the g3 system against the Grünfeld (with colours reversed), where White lacks the obvious target for an immediate attack: without a knight on c6, ♘xc6 followed by c4 is not possible.

If 5 c4, Black (again) has a choice between the ambitious 5...d4 and the quiet 5...♗g7.

The King's Indian plan (5 d3 ♗g7 6 ♘bd2, followed by 7 e4) is perhaps slightly more incisive in this case than after 2...c5 3 ♗g2 ♘c6. White's extra move (extra compared to the 'real' King's Indian) may well carry some extra weight in the dynamic type of play that characterizes the Fianchetto Variation.

The same scheme of development may be achieved with **3...g6**. Black allows his opponent greater freedom in choosing an appropriate d4 plan (in fact he is even opening the door to a possible transposition to the Grünfeld Defence with 4 d4 ♗g7 5 c4), but he is also reserving for himself the option of a plan without ...c5. If 4 0-0 ♗g7 5 d3 0-0 6 ♘bd2, for instance, Black may well do without ...c5 and play 6...♘c6 7 e4 e5 instead.

Similar considerations apply to **3...e6** *(D)*.

Every player behind the black pieces will make his choice in this opening on the basis of the contents of his entire personal opening repertoire. For someone who likes to play the Grünfeld against 1 d4, the move 3...g6 will probably come naturally, but someone who prefers the Queen's Gambit Declined will think of

3...e6 first, especially because a transposition to the Catalan with 4 0-0 ♗e7 **5 d4** 0-0 6 c4 is unlikely to worry him.

But an important criterion for determining the value of 3...e6 is the King's Indian option, for this is one of those situations where the King's Indian Attack gains in strength. After 4 0-0 ♗e7 **5 d3** and now, for instance, 5...0-0 6 ♘bd2 c5 7 e4 *(D)* the e5 advance is looming darkly over Black's position.

The resulting spatial advantage for White on the kingside may easily lead to a dangerous situation for the black king. In many cases White can even afford almost to neglect whatever is happening on the queenside and concentrate his forces entirely on the opposite wing. A characteristic (though by no means forced) continuation is 7...♘c6 8 ♖e1 b5 9 e5 ♘d7 10 ♘f1 a5 11 h4 b4 12 ♘1h2. While Black is moving his army forward on the queenside, White is preparing to blow a few holes in Black's kingside defences, for instance by playing ♘g4 and h5-h6 or ♗f4 in combination with ♘g5 and ♕h5. The diagrammed position was in fact a very fashionable and hotly debated one in the 1960s.

It is also a remarkable crossroads between 1 ♘f3 theory and 1 e4, for it belongs equally to the Réti Opening, the French Defence (1 e4 e6 2 d3 d5 3 ♘d2, etc.) and the Sicilian (1 e4 c5 2 ♘f3 e6 3 d3 d5 4 ♘bd2, etc.).

An entirely different plan for Black is to play **3...♗f5** or **3...c6** 4 0-0 ♗f5, analogous to the Lasker Variation (2 c4 c6 3 b3 ♘f6 4 g3 ♗f5). The decision on whether to preface ...♗f5 with ...c6 depends on how Black evaluates a possible c4. Is he afraid of 3...♗f5 4 c4 c6 5 cxd5 cxd5 6 ♕b3 (see page 252), for instance? If not (or if he is putting his trust in 4...e6 instead of 4...c6), he might prefer 3...♗f5 and perhaps save a tempo (...c6) if White does not play 4 c4. Unfortunately, even though this is quite a popular variation, theory does not seem to give a clear answer to these questions. Both sides will have to rely on their own judgement.

But a major difference from the 2 c4 lines is that White still has the King's Indian option. If, for example, **3...c6** 4 0-0 ♗f5, then **5 d3** e6 6 ♘bd2 h6 7 ♕e1 (this is a rather more effective way of preparing e4 than the perhaps more obvious 7 ♖e1, for after 7 ♖e1 ♗e7 the intended 8 e4? will simply lose a pawn to 8...dxe4 9 dxe4 ♘xe4!) 7...♗e7 8 e4 ♗h7 *(D)* is the starting point of an exciting and double-edged variation.

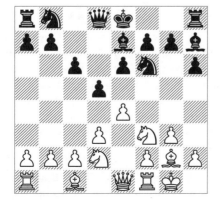

It is of course useful for White to have gained a tempo by attacking the black bishop on f5. On the other hand, the bishop is now an important defender of the black king. Another idea is to play **5 b3** e6 6 ♗b2 first and start hostilities in the centre afterwards.

If Black is thinking of playing along the lines of Capablanca's method (2 c4 c6 3 b3 ♘f6 4 g3 ♗g4) with **3...♗g4** or **3...c6** 4 0-0 ♗g4, he has to come to terms with the same problems. 4 c4 is the critical reply to the immediate 3...♗g4 and if he prefers 3...c6 4 0-0 ♗g4, then 5 b3 ♘bd7 6 ♗b2 e6 7 d3 and 5 d3 ♘bd7 6 ♘bd2, followed by 7 e4, are major tests of Black's opening play.

1...d5 2 g3 ♘c6

2	...	♘c6 *(D)*

More than anything else, this move is an invitation to the Chigorin Defence to the Queen's Gambit (**3 d4**; see page 52). If White does not care for this transposition, he has a choice of **3 ♗g2** e5 4 d3, which I shall treat as a variation of 1 g3 in the next chapter, and **3 c4**, giving Black the option of playing a Benoni with colours reversed again (3...d4; see 2 c4 d4).

1...d5 2 g3 g6

2	...	g6
3	♗g2	♗g7 *(D)*

Again, White has to make a decision as to how to deal with ...e5. If he plays **4 d4**, then a

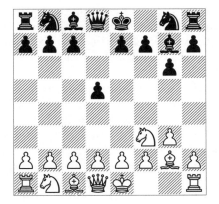

W

transposition to the g3 system against the Grün-feld, 4...♘f6 5 c4, is not far away (see page 136).

If he plays **4 0-0**, allowing 4...e5, then after 5 d3 we find ourselves in one of those shadowy versions of the King's Indian Attack, where theory has little or no access. White's position is perfectly sound, of course, but so is Black's. There are almost no variations or even theoretical guidelines to be distinguished here.

A third option is to play **4 c4**, when, as always in a situation like this, 4...d4 is the critical reply.

1...d5 2 b3

2   b3 *(D)*

B

This move came to the fore in the 1920s as an alternative to a classical (central) opening strategy, together with 2 c4 and 2 g3. But unlike these brothers in arms, 2 b3 has always remained an outsider, a non-member, an avant-garde opening *pur sang*.

However, this does not mean that the correctness of 2 b3 is in any sort of doubt; on the contrary, 2 c4 is much more controversial (because of the possible reply 2...d4) than 2 b3. The difference between 2 c4 and 2 g3 on the one hand and 2 b3 on the other, is that the former are very flexible moves, that combine well with a 1 d4 repertoire, while 2 b3 is based on one scheme of development only and is a pure flank opening. This implies that the modern 2 c4 and 2 g3 player requires a certain understanding of possible transpositions to (and knowledge of) other openings. No such theoretical baggage is necessary for the 2 b3 player. There is plenty of scope for creativity here. Such variations as there are in this opening, are not too clearly-defined and are constantly in a state of flux.

Which then, are these ill-defined variations?

In the first place the assertive **2...c5** must be mentioned, a move that clearly signals Black's attitude: "if you are not prepared to occupy the centre, I shall".

Equally sound and a little more flexible is **2...♘f6**.

2...f6 is an alternative that has never become really popular. Though logical enough in itself, this move is a bit one-dimensional and it is too easy for White to stop 3...e5 by playing 3 d4. As we are about to see though, the *idea* of occupying the centre with ...f6 and ...e5 is a not uncommon theme in this opening.

1...d5 2 b3 c5

2   ...   c5 *(D)*
3   e3

The unsuspecting **3 ♗b2** runs into 3...f6!, when all of a sudden ...e5 really is unstoppable, because 4 d4 is now met by 4...cxd4 and 5...e5. The emergency measure 4 e3 e5 5 d4 is no great success either: after 5...cxd4 6 exd4 e4 Black can be satisfied.

3   ...   ♘f6

Now **3...f6** would again be met by 4 d4, when ...e5 is prevented.

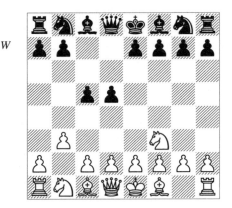

3...♘f6 in effect creates a Queen's Indian Reversed, although that name fell out of use long ago. But the crucial problem of the opening 1 d4 ♘f6 2 c4 e6 remains the same: does Black want to play ...♘c6, allowing his knight to be pinned by ♗b5, or not? And if yes, what is the best moment for doing so?

Some players prefer **3...a6** in order to 'safeguard' their knight on c6, while others play **3...♘c6**, in order to meet 4 ♗b5 very subtly with 4...e6, followed by 5...♘e7. The truly laconic, however, play ...♘c6 and ...♘f6 without worrying about move-order or any such subtleties.

> **4   ♗b2** *(D)*

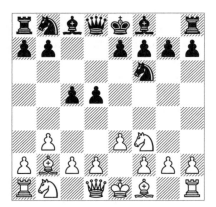

If now **4...♘c6**, pinning the knight with 5 ♗b5 is certainly critical. A plausible continuation then is 5...♗d7 6 0-0 e6 7 d3 ♗e7 8 ♘bd2 0-0 9 ♗xc6 ♗xc6 10 ♘e5. This position was a favourite of Nimzowitsch, the great pioneer of

2 b3 in the 1920s. If Black is not careful he may easily find himself under severe pressure. With moves like f4 and ♖f3-g3 coming up, the black king might be starting to feel the heat very soon.

4...e6 is a little more cautious, preparing to meet 5 ♗b5+ with 5...♗d7 and 5 ♘e5 with 5...♘bd7. This makes it harder for White to initiate an attack on the kingside, which is why most players switch to another plan here, viz. 5 c4 or 5 d4 and a direct confrontation in the centre.

Analogous to the g3 system against the Queen's Indian Defence, **4...g6** also looks quite healthy, yet this move is strangely unpopular in practice. Perhaps potential 4...g6 players just do not like being unable to recapture immediately on d5 in case of 5 c4 ♗g7 6 cxd5. Anyway, we are so deeply into uncharted territory here, that theory simply stops asking questions, let alone providing answers.

1...d5 2 b3 ♘f6

> **2   ...   ♘f6**
> **3   ♗b2** *(D)*

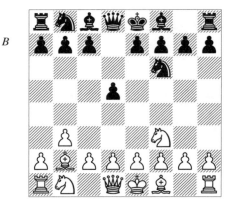

Black now has a large number of alternatives to **3...c5** (which after 4 e3 would take us back to the 2...c5 line). **3...e6** and **3...g6** produce roughly the same type of play as when combined with 2...c5. Black could also consider **3...♗f5** and **3...♗g4**, two moves that have earned a solid reputation against 2 c4 and 2 g3.

A major difference between these bishop moves is that **3...♗f5** allows White to switch to a 2 g3 line by playing 4 g3. This would be tricky after **3...♗g4**, since 4 g3 would then be inviting Black to take on f3, which may not be a refutation of 4 g3, but it does create a totally different type of play from what White was probably looking for. At any rate, 4 e3 is the much more common reply to 3...♗g4, with 4...♘bd7 5 ♗e2 e6 6 c4 a thematic follow-up. This variation is considered one of Black's most solid replies to 2 b3. Unlike the lines 3...e6 or 2...c5 3 e3 ♘f6 4 ♗b2 e6, where Black postpones development of his light-squared bishop, Black now enjoys easy and sound development for all of his pieces. At the same time White is given just a minimum of leeway to implement his flank strategy.

1...♘f6

1 ... ♘f6 *(D)*

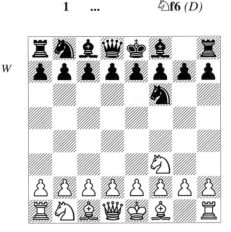

When choosing his first move, Black always has to calculate on 1 ♘f3 being no more than a feint. By continuing 2 d4, White *could* turn the opening into a queen's pawn opening against any possible reply, except 1...c5, but then of course Black has to be prepared for a Sicilian Defence in case of 2 e4. Just like Black makes it clear that he has no objections against a Queen's Gambit by playing 1...d5, he keeps access to that other major group of 1 d4 openings by playing 1...♘f6. If White now plays **2 d4**, Black is free to choose any 1 d4 ♘f6 opening he likes.

2 g3

2 c4 is of course a major alternative and in fact the most popular move in this position. I have included this in the previous chapter as it is really a variation of the English (1 c4 ♘f6 2 ♘f3). Many players who are afraid of opening 1 c4 because of 1...e5, but who do want to play a flank opening, go for 1 ♘f3 ♘f6 2 c4 instead. In this move-order, some lines of the English Opening are not available to White, since he has committed himself to an early ♘f3, but this need not be a problem.

2 b3 is by no means bad, but has less independent significance here than after 1...d5. As an alternative to 2...d5 (which transposes to 1 ♘f3 d5 2 b3 ♘f6) Black has the King's Indian-oriented 2...g6 and 2...d6, intending to play 3...e5. After 2...g6 3 ♗b2 ♗g7 4 g3 we reach a variation that I shall discuss via 2 g3 and, strangely enough, 2...d6 3 d4 g6 4 ♗b2 ♗g7 5 g3 transposes to the very same line!

We now return to 2 g3 *(D)*:

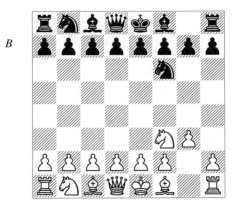

Most of the many possible moves in this position lead to variations we have already seen via a different move-order. And even if there is no immediate transposition, the well-known paths are never far away.

2...d5 is the first move to be considered. I have treated this position as part of the 1...d5 complex, but the present move-order, 1 ♘f3 ♘f6 2 g3 d5, is in fact an important one, because many players do not want to play 1...d5 because of the possible transposition to the Queen's Gambit with 2 d4. By playing 1...♘f6

2 g3 and only now 2...d5, they do not have to worry about this, since 3 d4 would now result in a fairly innocuous sideline of the Queen's Pawn Game (see page 52).

All other moves leave White free to switch to the English or to a 1 d4 opening by playing 3 c4 or 3 d4. The important thing here is to investigate possible alternatives to such a transposition.

The most popular move in this category is probably **2...g6** *(D)*.

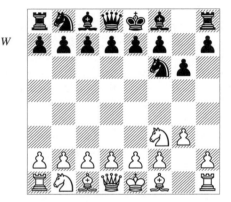

Now, if both players persist in their refusal to advance their d- and c-pawns more than a single square, a symmetrical continuation like **3 ♗g2 ♗g7 4 0-0 0-0 5 d3 d6 6 e4 e5** might result. Both players are playing the King's Indian! In fact, many players prefer to break the symmetry at the very last moment by choosing 6...c5 instead of 6...e5. Now the opening looks more like a Sicilian Defence.

For those who prefer to stay closer to the world of 1 d4, but do not want a direct transposition to the main lines with 3 d4, there is the alternative **3 b3 ♗g7 4 ♗b2 0-0 5 ♗g2**. The idea is to meet 5...d6 with 6 d4, making the central advance ...e5 more difficult to achieve than in the 'regular' g3 system in the King's Indian Defence. The result is a variation that can also be reached via 1 d4 ♘f6 2 ♘f3 g6 3 g3 ♗g7 4 ♗g2 0-0 5 0-0 d6 6 b3 (see page 164).

2...b6 has an equally good reputation. Again, if White does not care for a transposition to the

English or the Queen's Indian with a quick c4 and/or d4, he has the option of playing the King's Indian Attack: 3 ♗g2 ♗b7 4 0-0 and now, for instance, 4...e6 5 d3. Most players will then put an obstacle in White's way of playing 6 e4 by choosing 5...d5.

Another good move is **2...c5**, but this is extremely likely to result in a transposition; e.g., 3 c4 (Symmetrical English) or 3 ♗g2 ♘c6 4 0-0 e5 5 d3 d5 (see page 254).

Apart from all these transpositions (or attempts at transposition) there is one move for Black to give the opening a face of its own: **2...b5** *(D)*, the **Spassky Variation**.

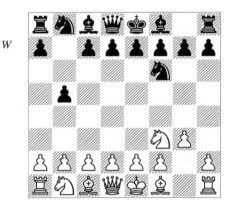

We have seen this idea of an 'extended' fianchetto before, viz. in the variation 1 d4 ♘f6 2 ♘f3 e6 3 g3 b5 (see page 168). Black is in effect playing an aggressive version of the 2...b6 variation. Now that White has played g3, he will need an extremely good reason *not* to develop his bishop to g2, so Black does not need to worry so much about a frontal attack against his pawn on b5 with e3 or even e4. Just like in the 2...b6 line, Black will have to make up his mind after 3 ♗g2 ♗b7 4 0-0 e6 5 d3 whether he is going to allow 6 e4 (and simply develop with 5...d6 6 e4 ♗e7 for instance) or whether he will accept the challenge to a fight for the centre with 5...d5. In both cases ...b5 will give Black more elbow room on the queenside than he would have had after 2...b6.

Other Flank Openings

To round off this section on the flank openings, we shall now take a brief look at what used to be called the 'Irregular Openings': everything other than 1 e4, 1 d4, 1 c4 and 1 ♘f3.

Some of these openings deserve better than to be bundled into a single chapter like this, for the quality and the nature of the openings in this chapter vary enormously. 1 g3 in particular is just marginally more 'irregular' than 1 ♘f3. These two moves could just as easily have been treated in the same chapter.

So a word of apology is due here, but in order to present all openings more or less in proportion to their relative importance (after all, the amount of theory involved in 'the big four' is immeasurably greater) I have decided that a single chapter for 'the rest' will have to do.

There are no fewer than twenty legal opening moves for White to choose from. All of them have been given a name at some time or another, but it would be a mistake to think that this implies they are all important. For behind the facade of a name, some of these 'openings' consist of a small but well maintained and respectable building, but others are no more than a ramshackle cottage, and behind some of the names there is just nothing at all.

Now, what does this all mean?

As I have already said, **1 g3** ties in very neatly with the previous chapters.

To a somewhat lesser degree, the same goes for **1 b3**. This move introduces a scheme of development that we know from the Réti Opening.

If 1...f5 is an acceptable reply to 1 d4, then surely **1 f4** must be an acceptable move as well. This is called the **Bird Opening**.

Finally, although it is a rare move in top-level tournaments, **1 ♘c3** *(D)* is also accepted as a reasonable way of starting the opening battle. This is an opening of many names, but being Dutch I prefer the relatively new name **Van Geet Opening**.

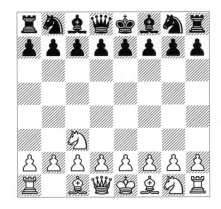

B

These four moves will form the bulk of the contents of this chapter.

The remaining twelve possible first moves can be roughly divided into three categories. To begin with, there are moves like **1 e3** (**Van 't Kruys Opening**) and **1 d3** (**Mieses Opening**), which are of course fully playable, but lack the necessary strategic backbone to really worry Black. White is fully entitled to like **1 e3** e5 2 d4, for instance, but a transposition to the Exchange Variation of the French Defence (2...exd4 3 exd4 d5; see page 349) is a meagre result in the eye of a theoretician (and of most practitioners too). There is also nothing wrong with 2 c4 (instead of 2 d4), yet the greatest merit of this move is undoubtedly that it may suggest ideas of trying 1 c4 on another occasion.

Then there are those moves with which White really tries to shoot himself in the foot, like **1 f3** or **1 g4**. Out of loyalty to those unfortunates who have occasionally indulged in these strange moves in their youth, I shall not even give you the names of these 'openings'.

Finally, there is one move that maintains a perfect balance between the extremes of tediousness and foolishness: **1 b4** *(D)*.

This very provocative opening was first named after **Englisch** (1851-97), then after

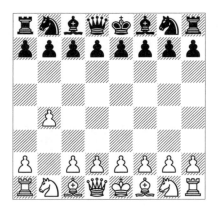

Sokolsky (1908-69), but ever since Tartakower invented the name **Orang Utan Opening** for it, there have been few players willing to have their name attached to this move.

Black has a wide choice of possible responses, but in so far as we can talk of a theoretical discussion in this opening, it concentrates on the position after 1...e5 2 ♗b2. Should Black now play a solid move like 2...d6 or 2...f6, or should he simply develop his pieces quickly and easily with 2...♗xb4 3 ♗xe5 ♘f6?

1 g3

1   g3 *(D)*

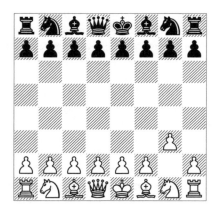

At the start of the chapter on the Réti Opening, I have already paid tribute to the pioneering work of Richard Réti for 1 ♘f3 in particular and for the concept of a flank opening in general. This concept includes 1 g3, and Réti played this

opening move quite often. In fact several older books name 1 g3 after him. It was only when 1 ♘f3 turned out to be the more important of the two, that his name became firmly attached to that move.

Just like it could be argued that 1 ♘f3 and 1 c4 are more flexible than 1 e4 and 1 d4, and that 1 ♘f3 d5 2 g3 is more flexible again than 1 ♘f3 d5 2 c4, it is also not unreasonable to state that this thinking in terms of flexibility reaches its peak in 1 g3. White develops his bishop on g2, but otherwise he preserves all options for a future game plan. Of course, the downside of this attitude is that Black is given exactly the same freedom. Nevertheless, 1 g3 is a move that has to be taken seriously and which has been adopted by many a top player.

One thing about 1 g3 that makes this move rather special is that it can be played with widely varying intentions. It may be played to create new and original situations, drawing the opponent out of his comfort zone of well-known openings and into the unknown: the art of unsettling the opponent. This was, for instance, how Bent Larsen used 1 g3 around 1960, and very successfully too (although it might be added that he achieved much the same effect with almost every opening he played!).

But 1 g3 may equally well be the starting point of very traditional variations from the English or Réti Opening, or at least lead to completely 'normal' positions. This interpretation of 1 g3 is more modest, but in the hands of somebody who knows his way around the flank openings, it can be just as effective.

Finally, it must be remembered that 1 g3 can also come across as a provocation, thus raising great psychological tension right from the start. Black is challenged to occupy the centre as if he were White. The idea of course, is to hit back at the right moment, hoping that the extra tempo will make a difference after all.

1   ...   e5

If Black intends to accept the challenge, either this move or **1...d5** is the obvious choice. In determining which of these two moves is better, it is important to realize that White *could* still prevent the formation of a classical central formation with pawns on e5 and d5, by answering

1...e5 with 2 c4 (which is a Reversed Sicilian) and 1...d5 with 2 ♘f3 (which is a Réti).

Other first moves too, always offer White a chance to switch to another opening. After **1...c5** 2 ♗g2 ♘c6, for instance, 3 e4 produces a Sicilian, while 3 c4 is a Symmetrical English. Lovers of the Dutch Defence will have to decide whether, after **1...f5**, a possible set-up with 2 ♗g2 g6 3 d3, followed by e4, is a nuisance.

Nor is it self-evident that Black can reach a King's Indian Defence, for after **1...g6** 2 ♗g2 ♗g7 or **1...♘f6** 2 ♗g2 g6 White can avoid this opening by playing 3 e4. This creates a type of position which is similar to the Pirc Defence and might even transpose, for instance after 3...d6 4 d4 ♗g7 5 ♘c3 (see page 459).

2 ♗g2 d5 *(D)*

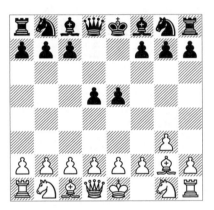

In this position Bent Larsen used to harass his opponents with **3 ♘f3**. After 3...e4 4 ♘d4 a kind of Alekhine Defence (1 e4 ♘f6) with colours reversed arises, while 3...♘c6 4 d3 is a Pirc reversed. Instead of the somewhat conventional 4 d3, however, Larsen went as far as to play 4 0-0, again provoking 4...e4, which now forces the reply 5 ♘e1.

The more popular choice is to play **3 d3**. This prevents a possible ...e4 (thus preparing ♘f3), but does not put as much pressure on Black as 3 ♘f3 does. After 3...♘f6 4 ♘f3 ♘c6 5 0-0 ♗e7 a standard position of the Pirc Defence is reached (see page 457), with colours reversed and an extra tempo for White. White's most important options are 6 c3 (which introduces the possibility of playing b4) and 6 ♗g5

(in order to attack d5 with 7 ♘c3 and then perhaps ♘d2 and e4 at some point).

A third option is to play **3 c4**, inviting ...d4 and a reversed Benoni, very similar to 1 ♘f3 d5 2 c4.

1 b3

1 b3 *(D)*

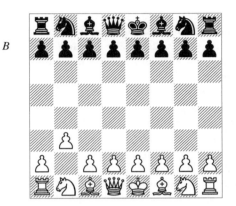

This seemingly modest move strikes a balance between the provocative 1 b4 and the solid 1 ♘f3 d5 2 b3 (see page 257). It was in fact first introduced alongside 1 ♘f3 d5 2 b3 by Nimzowitsch, who analysed, played and propagated both lines during the 1920s and 1930s. After him it was mainly Bent Larsen who ventured 1 b3 in the days when he was one of the strongest players in the world, the 1960s. Both these great players and pioneers have had their names attached to 1 b3. Indeed, the name **Nimzowitsch-Larsen Attack** has been widely used. Larsen himself jokingly called 1 b3 the **Baby Orang Utan**, thus not only showing a sense of humour but also making it clear that he saw 1 b3 and 1 b4 as being closely related.

A comparison with 1 ♘f3 d5 2 b3 is also of interest. From a classical viewpoint, one would be inclined to think 1 ♘f3 must be the more logical move, because this stops Black from playing 1...e5. But looking at the theory and the practical evidence of 1 b3, one can only conclude that it is precisely because White has so many ways of attacking a black pawn on e5 that

1 b3 is a popular opening move. So it is the 'logical' drawback of 1 b3 (the allowing of 1...e5) that seems to be its greatest attraction!

1 ... e5

Black is completely free in his choice of opening scheme, but he has to be aware of a few possible transpositions. A King's Indian set-up, for instance, **1...♘f6 2 ♗b2 g6**, allows 3 e4, which gives the game rather a 1 e4 look. And if **1...d5 2 ♗b2 ♘f6**, White not only has 3 ♘f3 (which transposes to 1 ♘f3 d5 2 b3), but also 3 e3 followed by f4, which is a Bird Opening.

2 ♗b2 ♘c6 (D)

After 1 b4 e5 2 ♗b2 this would run into 3 b5, but in this position there is no objection to this robust developing move and it is in fact Black's most popular choice here. Still, the alternative **2...d6** is also perfectly sound. Black renounces any intentions of playing ...d5 and follows a King's Indian scheme of development. Roughly speaking, White then has two possible plans. The characteristic flank strategy is to play 3 g3 ♘f6 4 ♗g2 g6 5 c4, creating a kind of Reversed Sicilian. The more direct approach is to challenge Black's domination of the centre by playing 3 d4, or something like 3 e3 ♘f6 4 c4 g6 5 ♘f3 ♗g7 6 d4.

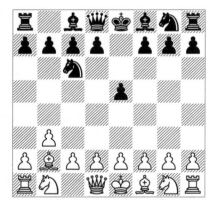

3 e3

This may look very modest (just like 1 b3 in fact) but a closer examination reveals that it is both a courageous and ambitious move. After all, it allows Black to play 3...d5.

The seemingly more aggressive **3 c4** is really much more cautious and conventional, since White remains within the relatively safe bounds of the Reversed Sicilian (that is to say: c4 and ...e5 have been played – there is no question of an actual transposition here). Nevertheless, this too is a controversial variation, the critical line being 3...♘f6 4 e3 d5 5 cxd5 ♘xd5.

3 ... d5

Taking up the challenge. Of course there is nothing wrong with a move like **3...♘f6** either. 4 ♗b5 can then be met by 4...d6, so Black is effectively following the same plan as with 2...d6. A possible continuation would be 5 ♘e2, followed by d4 or f4, thus starting an attack against e5.

4 ♗b5 ♗d6 (D)

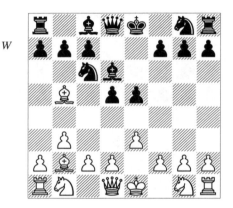

From the point of view of opening theory, this is the crucial position of this opening. Black has occupied the centre and it is now up to White to show his intentions. Still, there is remarkably little 'accepted' theory on how to proceed. The sharpest and the most uncompromising move is undoubtedly **5 f4**. The books do not agree on how good (or bad) this is. Should Black play 5...♕e7, for instance, or is 5...♕h4+ 6 g3 ♕e7 more accurate? And in the latter variation, how good is 7 ♘f3 f6?

Showing a little more self-restraint (and quite as logical as 5 f4) are the alternatives **5 c4** and **5 ♘f3** f6 6 c4.

Bird Opening

1 f4 (D)

Opening with the king's bishop's pawn has been an accepted phenomenon for centuries,

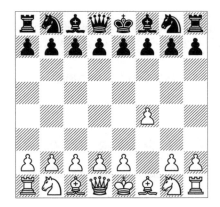

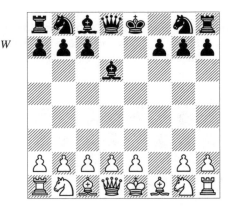

but when the English player Henry Bird (1830-1908) began to play 1 f4 regularly, according to himself "because he had forgotten the more familiar openings after a six years' absence from chess", the opening came to be named after him. It has also been called the Dutch Attack.

The Bird Opening has always been the domain of 'ordinary' club players rather than grandmasters, but just as with 1 g3 and 1 b3, the Danish world-class player Bent Larsen deserves a special mention in this respect. He admitted that his colleagues did not think much of 1 f4, but "precisely for this reason they do not play it and have no knowledge of it". Larsen himself on the other hand knew the possibilities of this opening very well and he had some shrewd and original ideas about it. He often used it as a surprise weapon or to test his opponents. Well, if they think 1 f4 is not a good move, let them show it! So in a way he was subjecting his opponents to an examination, which of course always added a certain psychological tension to the opening phase.

1   ...   d5

1 f4 can be played for all sorts of reasons but – remarkably! – preventing 1...e5 is not one of them, for the pawn sacrifice **1...e5 2 fxe5 d6** is in fact the most radical attempt to try to refute 1 f4. It is called the **From Gambit**. After 3 exd6 ♗xd6 *(D)* White is threatened with mate in three (starting with 4...♕h4+) and although this threat can easily be warded off, the fact remains that the situation is tricky and that it will demand a lot of *sangfroid* and inventiveness from both players to handle these complications.

After 4 ♘f3, for instance, Black has two serious variations: the uncompromising 4...g5 and the slightly more conventional 4...♘f6.

But Black has to be aware of a countersurprise: **2 e4** transposes to a King's Gambit. Instead of accepting the adversary's pawn sacrifice, White is offering one himself!

To offer a gambit like 1...e5 is first and foremost a matter of taste. Many a positionally oriented player will not care much for such wild and unruly positions. Instead of considering whether and how to play ...e5, he will probably be thinking the same thoughts about ...d5.

If Black plays neither 1...d5 nor 1...e5, he will have to take 2 e4 into account. After **1...c5**, for instance, 2 e4 or 2 ♘f3 g6 (or 2...♘c6) 3 e4 transposes to a line of the Sicilian Defence, while **1...♘f6** 2 ♘f3 g6 is also likely to raise questions of e4 sooner or later; e.g., after 3 g3 ♗g7 4 ♗g2 0-0 5 0-0 c5 6 d3.

If Black chooses to play ...d5 at some point (which I shall consider the main line) we have, in effect, the typical pawn-structure of the Dutch Defence, with colours reversed.

2   ♘f3

Although colours are reversed and White is a tempo ahead of Black in the normal Dutch Defence, positional themes remain largely the same. Probably the greatest difference is that, owing to a scarcity of top-level games, there is far less theory about 1 f4 than there is about 1 d4 f5. So there is plenty of room for experiments here!

Instead of 2 ♘f3, for instance, it might be an interesting idea to play **2 b3**, preventing 2...g6.

2   ...   ♘f6 *(D)*

An uncomplicated and neutral developing move. Whether it is also the best move objectively is moot. **2...c5** and **2...g6** look like logical alternatives.

Just like in the 'regular' Dutch, White now faces a fundamental choice between a plan based on g3 and one that is built around e3, with the latter option being subdivided into several variations.

3 g3 is of course the Leningrad Variation reversed. Here, the position after 3...g6 4 ♗g2 ♗g7 5 0-0 0-0 6 d3 c5 is the most important starting point, with 7 ♘c3, 7 c3 and 7 ♕e1 being the main options.

3 e3 is usually played not so much intending a Stonewall formation (pawns on d4 and f4), which would perhaps be unnecessarily defensive with White, but with a rather more aggressive scheme in mind, trying to take advantage of the extra tempo. The choice is mainly between the plan of the Classical Dutch; e.g., 3...g6 4 ♗e2 ♗g7 5 0-0 0-0 6 d3 c5 7 ♕e1, and a plan based on b3. The latter possibility is rarely a serious option in the Dutch Defence, mainly because White usually takes control of the h1-a8 diagonal himself by playing (1 d4 f5) 2 g3. But strategically it is perfectly logical to put a bishop on b2, for this increases White's influence in the centre in a very natural way. After 3...g6, a plausible continuation is **4 b3** ♗g7 5 ♗b2 0-0 6 ♗e2 c5 7 0-0 ♘c6, but Larsen (of course!) has had the original idea of playing **4 b4**, thus preventing Black's standard

development ...c5 and ...♘c6 and intensifying the fight for control over the centre. This is in effect an improved version of the Orang Utan.

1 ♘c3 (Van Geet Opening)

1   ♘c3 *(D)*

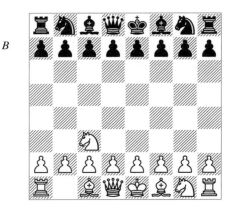

At first glance this move may create the impression of being the logical counterpart of 1 ♘f3, the Réti Opening. But this impression is very deceptive indeed. In fact the two knight moves have nothing in common whatsoever.

By playing 1 ♘f3, White prevents 1...e5 and prepares to meet 1...d5 with 2 c4, attacking Black's central position from the flank, a plan that we have come to know as a classical example of flank strategy. What a contrast with 1 ♘c3, which not only does nothing to prevent the corresponding advance 1...d5, it even asks for it! What is more, White does not intend to counterattack from the flank, but right through the middle with 2 e4, making it not a fight *for* control over the centre, but a fight *in* the centre. Even if Black does not play 1...d5, preferring, for instance, **1...e5**, **1...c5** or **1...♘f6**, the opening struggle will revolve around moves like e4 and d4, which open the centre rather than play around it. It would therefore be misleading to call the Van Geet Opening a flank opening, for it is nothing of the kind. It is a 1 e4 opening in disguise.

1 ♘c3 has been lying around in a corner of opening theory's attic for a very long time, for lack of a champion and a clear interpretation.

But since the Dutch master Dick van Geet has used it with great success, both in over-the-board and in correspondence chess, driving innumerable opponents to despair in the process, 1 ♘c3 has finally aroused public interest. Its merits have recently been hotly debated and many assessments have been overturned.

1   ...   d5

This and 1...e5 are of course the first moves to be considered, at least if Black intends to deal firmly with 1 ♘c3. Both moves allow a transposition to an entirely different opening, but Van Geet's idea is certainly not simply to make use of these possible transpositions as soon as they are available. He wants to toy with them, that is to keep them within reach, to make use of them if the moment is right, but above all: to try to find something which is even better.

If **1...e5**, for instance, his idea is not to play **2 e4**, which would transpose to the Vienna Game, but to start a fight in the centre with **2 ♘f3 ♘c6 3 d4 exd4 4 ♘xd4** (D).

Black then not only has to take another transposition into account, viz. to the Scotch, he also has to guard against a few far more venomous options. For example, **4...g6** is very risky because of 5 ♘d5, threatening 6 ♘b5. Nor does **4...♘f6** reach the 'safe haven' of the Scotch (5 e4), for White has the alternative 5 ♗g5. And the variation **4...d5 5 e4** is another beautiful illustration of the very high 1 e4 content of the Van Geet Opening.

It is all about fast piece development and keeping an eye out for tactical opportunities.

There is no deep strategy involved, but these positions require a high degree of alertness and a capacity for independent and original thinking.

If Black plays **1...c5**, he can expect similar treatment. **2 e4** transposes to the Closed Sicilian (see page 391), but true Van Geet strategy is to play **2 ♘f3**, followed, for example, by 2...♘c6 3 d4 cxd4 4 ♘xd4 (D).

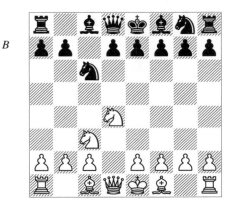

While Black then has to remain alert to a possible transposition to the Sicilian Defence (with e4), he also has more vicious threats to cope with. Playing in the spirit of the Sveshnikov Variation (see page 411), for instance, with 4...e5 5 ♘db5 d6?, fails miserably to 6 ♘d5! and Black gets squashed as he cannot defend c7.

If Black wants to be entirely safe from treacherous ambushes like the above, his best bet is probably to play **1...♘f6** (D).

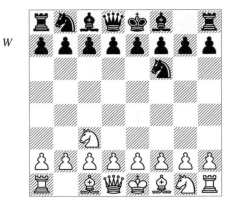

Now, if White does not want to take the emergency exit of playing 2 d4 or 2 e4 (which are perfectly sound options) he will really have to create his own footpaths. With 2 ♘f3 d5 3 e3, for instance, White is turning his back on established opening theory for good.

2   e4 *(D)*

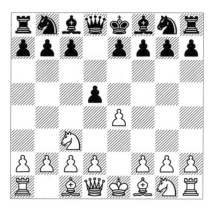

This is the main starting point of the Van Geet Opening. Again, there are a great many possible transpositions to 1 e4 openings to be aware of. **2...♘f6**, for instance, is a minor variation of the Alekhine Defence, **2...c6** a Caro-Kann and **2...e6** a French Defence.

But anyone interested in really testing the strength of the Van Geet Opening is likely to prefer either **2...d4** or **2...dxe4**. Both moves are logical and attractive, but it would be unwise to underestimate White's chances.

After **2...d4** 3 ♘ce2 e5 4 ♘g3 *(D)*, a crucial position is reached.

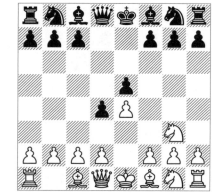

White wants to develop his light-squared bishop to c4 and create attacking chances on the kingside. If Black prevents this by 4...♗e6, White has an alternative method of development in 5 c3 c5 6 ♗b5+ ♘d7 (or 6...♘c6) 7 ♘f3.

A deceptive position arises after **2...dxe4** 3 ♘xe4 *(D)*.

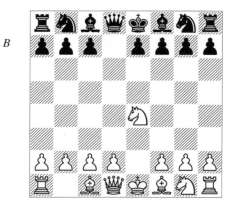

One would say that it should be very easy to find something more useful than **3...e6** or **3...c6** (when 4 d4 would produce a French Defence or a Caro-Kann respectively). Still, there does not seem to be any consensus on what that 'easy' improvement should be. Both 3...e5 and 3...♘d7 are met by 4 ♗c4, pricking Black's Achilles' Heel f7 rather annoyingly. Black must tread carefully. A few examples: after **3...♘d7** 4 ♗c4 ♘gf6 (4...♘df6 is more solid) he has to take the sacrifice 5 ♗xf7+!? into account. After 5...♔xf7 6 ♘g5+ ♔g8 7 ♘e6 White is already winning back some material. And if **3...e5** 4 ♗c4, the plausible 4...♘f6 is risky due to 5 ♘g5 while the seemingly more prudent 4...♗e7? is even worse (5 ♕h5!). Perhaps the most reliable move is 4...♘c6.

3...♗f5, analogous to the 4...♗f5 variation of the Caro-Kann, is a sound option, but even here an interesting point of 1 ♘c3 is revealed: White does not have to hurry with d4. After 4 ♘g3 ♗g6 5 ♘f3 ♘d7 there is the possibility of playing 6 ♗c4 e6 7 d3. This reduces the sphere of influence of Black's g6-bishop, which is now not as actively placed as it is in the more common version of this type of position with White's pawn on d4.

1 e4

By opening the game with his king's pawn, White enters into an ancient and venerable tradition. Our oldest sources, books from the 15th century, make it emphatically clear that **1 e4** *(D)* was *the* opening move even in those days.

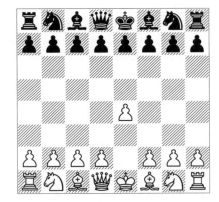

B

This situation remained basically unchanged for centuries. It was not until the rise of modern, positional chess at the end of the 19th century that **1 d4** rose to the fore and then it took another half century or so for **1 c4** and **1 ♘f3** to achieve similar recognition.

Nowadays, the choice of a first move is largely a matter of taste. Every one of these opening moves has its own specific consequences, brings about certain typical positions and creates its own specific problems. It is not enough to compare these consequences objectively (if such a comparison is possible); individual preferences and differences in playing style are at least as important when it comes to deciding how to open a chess game.

This historic development of opening theory is mirrored by the individual learning process of most chess-players. Almost everyone starts out with 1 e4 and does not learn or practise other moves until later.

Why is it then, that 1 e4 is the birthplace of all opening theory, both individually and globally?

Is there something special about this move, something mysterious?

The answer is paradoxical. If there is such a thing as a secret of 1 e4, then it must be its complete lack of mystery. The lucidity, the directness and the almost naïve sweetness of it are staring one in the face. White takes a healthy step forward, opens the way for his bishop and queen (perhaps already thinking of a Scholar's Mate: ♗c4 followed by ♕h5 and ♕xf7#) and is threatening (on a higher level of strategic thinking) to take full control of the centre with 2 d4. It is this noble simplicity that makes 1 e4 such a wonderful move for beginner and grandmaster alike.

The next question that the chess world has had to answer, and which every individual player will face, is of course how to respond to such a demonstration of power.

For centuries this was in fact as much of a non-issue as the question regarding White's first move. It was a matter of course that Black was thinking in exactly the same terms as his opponent. A respectable game of chess between two respectable people could only start in one respectable way: **1 e4 e5** *(D)*.

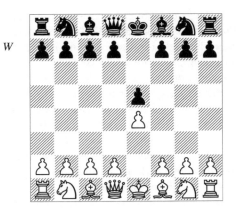

W

Only here, on the second move, did the roads in antiquity diverge. White's most obvious continuation was (and still is) the powerful developing move **2 ♘f3**, by which, in a very natural, almost casual, way he attacks e5. It is from this move that some of the oldest and most important openings in chess literature have sprung.

In the first place – from a modern perspective at least – there is the **Ruy Lopez** (also called the **Spanish Opening**): **2...♘c6 3 ♗b5**. This is a very ancient opening, but it was not until the middle of the 19th century that it – gradually yet irresistibly – emerged as the most critical test of 1...e5, a position it has held to this day. White introduces the possibility of taking on c6, thus indirectly threatening Black's e5-pawn.

About the same age as the Ruy Lopez is the **Italian Game**, **2...♘c6 3 ♗c4**. By putting his king's bishop on c4, White is creating threats that at first glance seem much more dangerous than 3 ♗b5, because they are directed at Black's most vulnerable spot, f7. For many beginners this is the most attractive opening and historically 3 ♗c4 was the first move to develop a serious body of opening theory. Today, there are quite a number of forcing variations in this opening, so a certain knowledge of those is recommended.

Equally forceful, yet wholly different in nature, is **2...♘c6 3 d4**, the **Scotch Opening**. White opens the centre, eliminates Black's e-pawn and prepares the way for some fast and aggressive development.

Finally, there is the **Four Knights Game**, introduced with **2...♘c6 3 ♘c3 ♘f6**. This ancient opening has stood the test of time just as the other openings mentioned. Like the Scotch, it has recently enjoyed a veritable revival.

So far we have only considered 2...♘c6 as a reply to 2 ♘f3, but this is not Black's only option. **2...♘f6** in particular is a major alternative. Instead of defending his pawn on e5, Black counterattacks against e4. This is the **Petroff** or **Russian Defence**. It rivals the four 2...♘c6 openings above in ancientness and surpasses most of them in importance. Today, in the early years of the 21st century, this move is extremely popular with players at the very highest level. As a result, it is more relevant to the theoretical status of 1 e4 now than it has ever been in the past.

Nowadays, 2 ♘f3 may look not just natural but completely self-evident, to the beginner and the experienced tournament player alike. How could White possibly do better than this? But this outlook has not always been the universally accepted one. In the first half of the 19th century in particular, the position after 1 e4 e5 was viewed in a totally different light. In those days players were not concerned with the difficult strategic problem of how best to attack *Black's e5-pawn* in such a way as to obtain *long-term* prospects of building up *a solid initiative*. They were looking for ways of *annihilating Black's king, right now*. Seen from this perspective, the knight is not very well placed on f3 at all; on the contrary, it is standing in the way. That f-file needs to be opened! **2 f4** has to be played first, and only after 2...exf4 can the knight be developed: 3 ♘f3. Bishop to c4, pawn to d4, castles, and wow! What could possibly come between White and a brilliant victory?

This is the **King's Gambit**, an opening that symbolizes power, courage and elegance for some, and utter madness to others. White gives away a pawn and weakens his own king's position, but he firmly takes the initiative and opens files and diagonals that are meant to lead not to his own but to Black's king. Although it seems an anachronism in today's world of ever more accurately calculating computers, the King's Gambit remains a living opening to this day.

Back to 1 e4. No matter how dominant the reply 1...e5 may have been, even in ancient times alternative moves were known and examined, though they were usually considered inferior. This situation began to change around 1800, when the first of these alternatives to gain recognition was **1...e6**. Black follows a completely different strategy here. He allows White to play 2 d4, only to hit back immediately with 2...d5. This opening came to be known as the **French Defence** and it has been considered safe and sound now for some two hundred years.

With the acceptance of the French Defence, the ground was prepared for other openings that deviated even further from classical principles. In the second half of the 19th century, the move **1...c6** was given a face and a name:

the **Caro-Kann Defence**. Just as in the French, Black intends to play 2...d5. What makes 1...c6 much harder to swallow from a classical point of view though, is that it is not a developing move. No diagonal is opened for the king's bishop (as with 1...e6) and the 'natural' square c6 is made unavailable to the queen's knight. Nevertheless, this treatment of the opening has shown itself to be effective. Compared to the French, the great advantage of 1...c6 is that the other black bishop, the one on c8, now has much better prospects.

A third move to gain some (modest) recognition in the 19th century was **1...c5**, the **Sicilian Defence**. This move is easier to accept from a classical viewpoint in one way, namely that it stops White from occupying the centre with 2 d4, but since it does nothing for quick piece development (just like 1...c6) it was mistrusted for a very long time. It does not even do anything to attack White's e4-pawn, as 1...e6 and 1...c6 do.

A fundamental reassessment of one very important type of middlegame was needed before the Sicilian could be viewed in a more positive light. At first it was thought that 2 ♘f3, followed by 3 d4 and an exchange of pawns in the centre, would give White a very comfortable position indeed. Shielded by his stronghold on e4, White will easily find some good squares for his pieces, not to mention the impressive spatial advantage that White enjoys in this kind of position. The advantages of Black's position are less obvious, yet very slowly – and this is a process that has spanned the entire 20th century – they have come to the fore. It is precisely here that a wealth of new possibilities has come to light. It turned out that Black's seemingly cramped position contains enormous power that is only waiting to be released.

By now many different schemes of development have been discovered for Black, each one of them based on solid strategic considerations and each with its own specific advantages. A chess-player from the 21st century looks at these positions in a way that is completely different from the outlook of his predecessor of one or two centuries ago. Nowadays, even the enormous amount of variations available to Black is enough to intimidate many a player

behind the white pieces into avoiding the main lines based on 2 ♘f3 and 3 d4.

The search for possible alternatives to the classical 1...e5 reached its peak in the 1920s, 1921 to be exact, when Alexander Alekhine, one of the most famous grandmasters in the history of chess, started experimenting with the shocking **1...♘f6**. This move is nothing less than a provocation, not just addressed at White's e-pawn, but at White himself. If White accepts the challenge by 2 e5, Black will respond 2...♘d5 and start attacking White's pawn in earnest with ...d6. Black freely allows his opponent to play d4 and to chase his knight away a second time (with c4). In fact the whole idea of this opening is to provoke White into occupying too much of the centre. This will almost always lead to a sharp fight, for it is true that although White is taking a natural, aggressive step forward by playing 2 e5, he is also sticking his neck out. This opening is now known as the **Alekhine Defence** (even though there is little defensive about it).

Superficially, to play **1...d6** is to take a step backwards on this rising scale of ever more daring replies to 1 e4. After all, this move prepares 2...♘f6 by eliminating the advance e5. Is not that an outdated viewpoint? But what 1...d6 sacrifices in speed, it gains in depth. 1...d6 is not a slow or a passive opening move. Black allows his opponent to form a 'perfect' pawn-centre with 2 d4, but he is doing so on the assumption that there is no real danger in this. This attitude is based either on a naïve lack of understanding or on a very profound understanding indeed. This is the **Pirc Defence**, that was not drawn out of the marshlands of that much-distrusted category of 'irregular' openings until after 1950. It is (more or less) the final destination of our survey of 1 e4.

All of these openings, ranging from the frank 1...e5 to the profound 1...d6, have their own ideas, their own 'speed' and their own peculiar strategic colouring. They are all playable. Choosing between them is a matter of personal style and perhaps a question of how much study material one is able to deal with. It is my hope that this book may help the reader to form his own judgement of these and related aspects of the game of chess.

Ruy Lopez

1	e4	e5
2	♘f3	♘c6
3	♗b5 *(D)*	

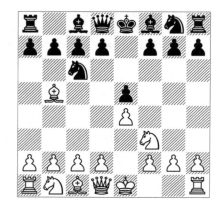

This ancient opening owes its name to the Spaniard Ruy Lopez de Segura (c. 1530-80), who recommended 3 ♗b5 in a book published in 1561. This did not greatly impress his contemporaries, however, and for a very long time the Italian Game (3 ♗c4) was far more popular. It was in fact not until the 1840s that the time was ripe for a proper appreciation of 3 ♗b5. From this time onwards, the Ruy Lopez became increasingly popular, not only gradually surpassing the Italian, but also pushing *all* alternatives to 2 ♘f3, most notably the King's Gambit, into the background. The Ruy Lopez became *the* opening against 1...e5, a position it has not lost in over a century and a half of ever-changing positional insights.

This steadfast reputation of 3 ♗b5 is almost equalled by the status of **3...a6** as the most popular reply. What justifies this little yet significant move is the fact that 4 ♗xc6 dxc6 5 ♘xe5 does not win a pawn (yet), because of 5...♕d4, but a much deeper point of 3...a6 is revealed after 4 ♗a4: from now on Black has the opportunity of breaking the pin of the c6-knight by

playing ...b5 at a moment of his own choosing. It is from this position that the great main lines of the Ruy Lopez have germinated, some of them more than twenty moves deep and with innumerable subvariations.

Nevertheless, around 2000 the natural and simple move **3...♘f6** enjoyed a wave of enormous popularity. This is the **Berlin Defence**, which is much older than 3...a6, but seemed to have all but disappeared in the 20th century, when it was thought that on general grounds the insertion of 3...a6 4 ♗a4 could only be to Black's advantage. But the present popularity of 3...♘f6 is based on a highly specific way of making use of White's bishop standing on b5 rather than at a4.

3...f5 is a move of a totally different calibre. This is in fact a variation on the theme of the King's Gambit and it has caused many a 3 ♗b5 player a headache over the years. Although always looked upon with distrust at the very highest level, this bold pawn sacrifice has always had a large following among the masses. It is called the **Jaenisch Gambit** or **Schliemann Defence** and it is only recommended for lovers of sharp and concrete variations who are not afraid of taking risks.

I shall treat these three moves as main lines in this book. But in a truly great opening like the Ruy Lopez, almost all legal moves have been investigated at one time or another and have been given a name, an assessment and a set of variations in chess literature. The best of these 'alternative' lines are undoubtedly quite playable and each of them has its own (modest) circle of adherents.

3...d6 *(D)*, for example, the **Steinitz Defence**, certainly deserves our respect, if only because it is named after the first world champion, Wilhelm Steinitz (1836-1900).

Black defends his pawn on e5 and prepares ...♗d7, neutralizing the pin of the c6-knight.

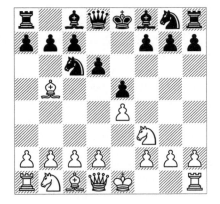

This is a solid plan, with a single drawback only, namely that it allows White to carry on with his development undisturbed. A characteristic type of middlegame arises after 4 d4 exd4 5 ♘xd4 ♗d7 (or 4...♗d7 5 ♘c3 exd4 6 ♘xd4). White enjoys a space advantage and easy development for his pieces, but Black's position has no weaknesses and is intrinsically sound, if – for the moment – a little passive. Though this is not necessarily a problem, it has caused top players to prefer the Neo-Steinitz (3...a6 4 ♗a4 d6; see page 277), where it is not so easy for White to achieve this type of position.

Likewise **3...♗c5** *(D)*, the **Cordel Variation**, can hardly be put down as an obscure sideline.

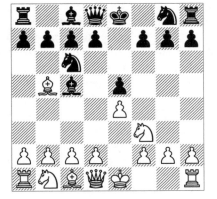

This is a sharper approach than 3...d6, especially if Black is intending to meet 4 c3 (in preparation of 5 d4) with the gambit variation

4...f5 (4...♘f6 is a more solid alternative). Another point of 3...♗c5, one of a strategic nature, comes to light after 4 0-0 (which takes the edge off 4...f5, for this move can now simply be met by 5 exf5 e4 6 ♖e1). Black exchanges a pair of knights with 4...♘d4 5 ♘xd4 ♗xd4, which allows White to build up his desired central pawn-formation by 6 c3 ♗b6 7 d4, but gives Black the opportunity to consolidate his own central stronghold with 7...c6, followed by 8...d6. Unlike 4 c3 f5, this variation offers quiet, positional play where White needs the ability to make the most of a small lead in development and a tiny space advantage.

The same idea can be implemented rather more drastically by playing **3...♘d4** *(D)*, the **Bird Defence**.

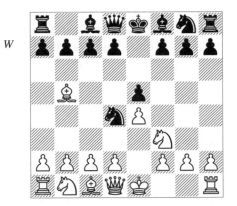

In this case, however, Black has to recapture on d4 with his e-pawn, which makes quite a difference. This unorthodox approach dates back to the 19th century but enjoyed a revival around 1980. After 4 ♘xd4 exd4 the pawn on d4 makes it impossible for White to make a quick d4 advance, so he needs another plan. The obvious solution is to play 0-0, d3 and f4. Black will be looking at ...c6 and ...d5 for counterplay.

3...a6

3   ...   **a6** *(D)*

This move is called the Morphy Defence, but it is now so firmly established as the main line that this name is rarely used.

As I have already indicated, there is nothing to be gained now by playing the greedy **4 ♗xc6** dxc6 5 ♘xe5, as Black wins back his pawn immediately. But White has more profound moves than 5 ♘xe5 and these are of sufficient interest to turn this into an important system. This is the **Exchange Variation**, which occupies a very special place in the Ruy Lopez.

The alternative of course, and the most common move by far, is to play **4 ♗a4**, when Black is facing the same problems as on move three.

Exchange Variation

4   ♗xc6   dxc6 *(D)*

By exchanging on c6, White has chosen a type of middlegame that differs considerably from the majority of Ruy Lopez variations. For a long time it was thought that this was completely harmless for Black, but when Bobby

Fischer turned it into a dangerous weapon in the 1960s it suddenly became very popular, with quite a number of players going so far as to specialize in this line.

White has two main trumps. In the short term he has a lead in development, while in the long run he can build on his superior pawn-structure. And of course 4 ♗xc6 has the added practical advantage of avoiding the enormous mass of theory involved in the Ruy Lopez main lines (all starting with 4 ♗a4).

Looking from Black's perspective, there is no choice. If Black wants to play one of the main lines of the Ruy Lopez, he will have to reconcile himself to the Exchange Variation and its unique character. Fortunately, there are plenty of reasons for such a reconciliation. For one thing, Black's lag in development is not as bad as it looks. By recapturing with his d-pawn, he has opened a diagonal for his light-squared bishop and a file for the queen, which means that even without making a move, these two pieces are half-developed already. On the whole it can be said that Black enjoys an unusually great freedom of movement in the Exchange Variation.

5   0-0

This is White's most flexible move and ever since the days of Bobby Fischer this has been the main line. But in order to get a first impression of the positional make-up of the Exchange Variation, it may be useful to take a brief look at the older move **5 d4**. With this move White simplifies the position considerably. He is hoping that the endgame after 5...exd4 6 ♕xd4 ♕xd4 7 ♘xd4 *(D)* will be in his favour, because of the simple fact that White has a sound pawn-majority on the kingside (meaning that this majority will logically result in a passed pawn), while Black's majority on the opposite wing, handicapped in this respect by the doubled pawns, cannot hope to achieve the same result (at least not without a little help from White).

Unfortunately for White (and luckily for Black) there are some downsides too to this beautifully straightforward plan. Because the move d4 has opened the position even further, Black's bishop-pair will gain in strength and his

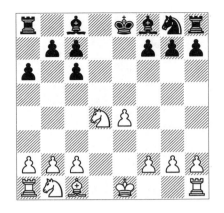

rooks will find dominant positions on the two central files. After queenside castling in particular (7...♗d7 followed by 8...0-0-0 for instance) Black has good prospects of attacking the e4-pawn and taking over the initiative with moves like ...c5, ...♖e8 and ...f5.

However, as we are about to see, White does not reject this plan by playing 5 0-0 *(D)*. Rather, he is hoping to execute it under more favourable circumstances. And this, of course, is the essence of opening theory. It is not just a matter of finding the right plan, it is at least as important to implement the plan as advantageously as possible. Opening theory is a never-ending search for the optimal solution.

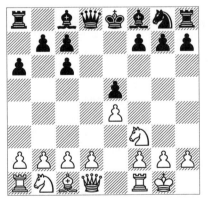

Now Black has to concern himself with the defence of the e5-pawn. For years it was thought that **5...♗g4** 6 h3 h5!? was the perfect answer to this problem, but even before Fischer, the Dutch master Johan Barendregt demonstrated that this

spectacular idea is by no means a refutation of 5 0-0. It is true that there is the opportunity for White to self-destruct with something silly like 7 hxg4 hxg4 8 ♘xe5?? ♕h4, but if White proceeds with a little more caution than this, there is no reason why he should have any particular problems completing a healthy development. A critical position arises after 7 d3 ♕f6 8 ♘bd2 (if 8 hxg4 hxg4 9 ♘g5, Black has 9...♕h6) 8...♘e7 9 ♖e1 ♘g6 10 d4 ♗d6 *(D)*.

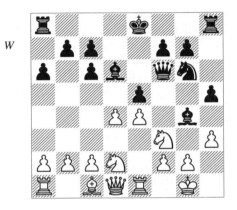

Black has positioned his pieces very threateningly, but the cold-blooded 11 hxg4 hxg4 12 ♘h2 ♖xh2! (12...♕h4? fails to 13 ♘df1) 13 ♕xg4! (13 ♔xh2? ♕xf2 would be very dangerous indeed) and now, for instance, 13...♖h4 14 ♕f5 neutralizes Black's initiative. After the storm has died down, the game finally takes on the desired Exchange Variation features.

The simple **5...f6** *(D)* is less pretentious than 5...♗g4 and has always had a solid reputation.

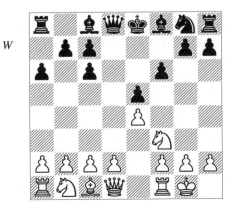

In fact there is only one drawback to this move, namely that the standard plan of 6 d4 exd4 7 ♘xd4 c5 8 ♘b3 (or 8 ♘e2) 8...♕xd1 9 ♖xd1 now produces the desired result of being relatively favourable to White as compared to 5 d4, since castling has been very useful for White, while Black's 'extra' move ...f6 is of virtually no use at all in this type of position. Nevertheless, this is an important starting position for a great many deeply-analysed variations. Black does have one major alternative, which is to play 6...♗g4 instead of 6...exd4. This too usually results in an endgame: 7 dxe5 ♕xd1 8 ♖xd1 fxe5. Black has maintained a pawn on e5, but whether this is something to be proud of remains to be seen. It is true that this pawn keeps White's pawn-majority on the kingside in check, but it is also quite vulnerable. Still, this is an important variation which has enjoyed spells of popularity at the highest level.

Another way of protecting e5, **5...♗d6**, has never enjoyed the same popularity, probably because after 6 d4 Black will have to give up his stronghold anyway, since 6...f6?! 7 dxe5 fxe5?! would now be refuted by 8 ♘xe5! ♗xe5 9 ♕h5+. The alternative 6...exd4 7 ♕xd4 also looks a bit gloomy at first sight since White is threatening to take on g7, but it is precisely this position, with 7...f6 as the critical move, which makes 5...♗d6 a very interesting possibility. Black has avoided an exchange of queens and provided he succeeds in completing his development, he has every reason to be satisfied with the opening.

Modern opening theory does not care much for general considerations and is based to a great extent on concrete and exact calculations. This computer-like attitude has brought **5...♕d6** *(D)* to the fore, an ugly move at first sight, but probably the main line nowadays alongside 5...f6.

If **6 d4** exd4 7 ♕xd4, Black does not worry about having lost a tempo and simply plays 7...♕xd4 8 ♘xd4 ♗d7. If 7 ♘xd4 instead, Black has a very aggressive reply in 7...♗d7, followed by 8...0-0-0 and in some cases ...♕g6.

A subtler attempt to harass the black queen is to play **6 d3**, with the idea ♘bd2-c4, yet Black has plenty of time to prepare himself for this

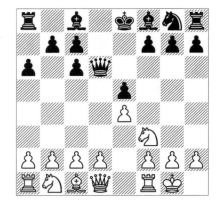

W

simultaneous attack against his queen and his pawn on e5, for instance with 6...♘e7 7 ♘bd2 ♘g6.

The same idea, executed in a subtler way, underlies **6 ♘a3**. White preserves the option of opening the centre quickly and efficiently with d4. Should Black reply 6...b5, White has 7 c3, preparing d4 and bringing the knight back into play via c2. If 6...♗e6, White has both 7 ♘g5 and 7 ♕e2 followed by 8 ♘c4 or 8 ♖d1 and d4.

In the position after 5...♕d6 6 ♘a3, which has been very popular since the 1990s, the Exchange Variation shows its tactical, explosive side. This variation has two faces. Players who feel at home both in the dry, technical positions of 5...f6 6 d4 exd4 *and* in the dangerous, double-edged tactical melee of 5...♕d6 6 ♘a3 are the ones for whom the Exchange Variation is tailor-made.

4 ♗a4

4   ♗a4 *(D)*

If this move had a motto, it would probably be 'the threat is stronger than its execution'. White does not let himself be tempted by the exchange on c6 and maintains the tension.

This gives Black the opportunity of immediately chasing the bishop off the a4-e8 diagonal by playing **4...b5**, the **Taimanov Variation**.

Another plausible reply is to play **4...d6**, the **Neo-Steinitz Variation**.

But the most popular move by far is **4...♘f6**. It is on this natural developing move that the lion's share of the theory of the Ruy Lopez has been built.

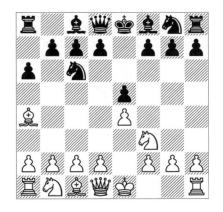

Conspicuously absent from this list is the gambit move **4...f5**, which was considered a main line just one move earlier (3...f5). The reason for this is that with the bishop on a4, the reply 5 d4 is now very dangerous for Black. Since **5...fxe4** 6 ♘xe5 ♘xe5 7 dxe5 c6 no longer makes sense (which it does after 3...f5 4 d4; see page 299), Black has little choice but to play **5...exd4**. But now comes a surprising yet typical positional pawn sacrifice, revealing the darker sides of ...f5: 6 e5. While obstructing Black's natural kingside development (no f6-square for the knight), White is hoping to obtain a tangible initiative. After 6...♗c5 7 0-0 ♘ge7 8 ♗b3, for instance, Black's king has trouble getting away from the centre.

Taimanov Variation

4	...	b5
5	♗b3	♘a5 (D)

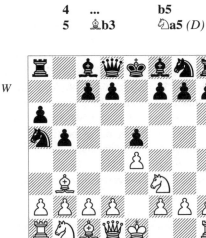

It is this daring knight sortie which gives 4...b5 a face of its own. Black jumps at the opportunity not just to chase away the white bishop, but to eliminate it.

6	0-0

Black's plan is positionally motivated, but it is made possible by two tactical points. In the first place, White cannot just win a pawn by taking on e5, because **6 ♘xe5 ♘xb3 7 axb3 ♛g5** wins back the pawn immediately. Secondly, the tempting piece sacrifice **6 ♗xf7+ ♚xf7 7 ♘xe5+** does not refute 5...♘a5. After the calm 7...♚e7 8 ♘c3 ♗b7 Black should be able to hold his own.

6	...	d6
7	d4	♘xb3
8	axb3	f6 (D)

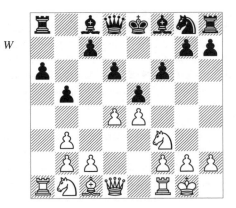

This is the strategic idea of the Taimanov Variation. Black maintains his stronghold on e5 in an unorthodox yet extremely solid way. Because White no longer has a light-squared bishop, Black need not worry about opening the a2-g8 diagonal, which would otherwise be a risky undertaking (as we have just seen in the 4...f5 variation).

White has a considerable lead in development, but he will have to proceed with patience and accuracy if he is to make an impact on Black's sturdy position. He may aim for ♘h4 and f4 to try and break Black's grip on e5.

Neo-Steinitz Variation

4	...	d6 (D)

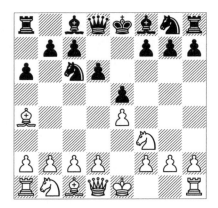

This variation is sometimes called the Improved Steinitz Variation because by inserting 3...a6 4 &a4 Black has defused **5 d4** (which is the main drawback of 3...d6), for this would now run into 5...b5 6 &b3 ♘xd4 7 ♘xd4 exd4, when 8 ♕xd4?? loses a piece to 8...c5! followed by 9...c4, an opening trap typical of the Ruy Lopez, and so old that it is known as the **Noah's Ark Trap**. 9 ♕d5, with a double attack against a8 and f7, does not help because of 9...&e6 10 ♕c6+ &d7 11 ♕d5 c4 and the bishop is lost in any case.

5 &xc6+ is a subtler attempt to bring about that typical Steinitz Defence type of middlegame. When compared to the Exchange Variation, it seems a weird loss of time to play &a4 first and &xc6+ immediately afterwards, but in fact the consequences are entirely different, because Black now has to recapture with his b-pawn. After 5...bxc6 6 d4 *(D)* there are two variations:

If Black plays **6...exd4**, he gives White what he was looking for, but it is moot to whose advantage this is, for Black's freedom of movement is considerably greater than in the position after 3...d6 4 d4 exd4 5 ♘xd4 &d7.

Black also has **6...f6**, defending his central outpost in much the same way as in the Taimanov Variation. This is hardly a move to promote a speedy development (since f6 is made unavailable to the knight and the f8-bishop will have to remain dormant for the time being), but it does give Black a very solid position.

White's most important moves, however, are **5 c3** and **5 0-0**.

5 c3

5　　c3 *(D)*

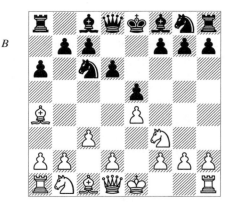

This is a move that we are going to see very often in the Ruy Lopez. White prepares to play d4, while creating an escape-route for his king's bishop via c2 so that he no longer has to worry about Black exchanging off his bishop with ...b5 followed by ...♘a5. The obvious drawback to this plan is that development of the queenside is being held up and even made rather difficult. The knight on b1 in particular will now not be able to join in the fight as easily and naturally as would have been the case if ♘c3 were still possible. Nevertheless, the plan of playing c3 in this type of position is one of the cornerstones of the success of the Ruy Lopez. Tournament practice has shown that White usually manages to get away with its relative slowness, mainly because exchanging pawns on d4 is normally very unattractive for Black in a situation where White can recapture with his c-pawn and maintain a strong central formation with pawns on e4 and d4. Effectively screened by these two pawns, White calmly develops his pieces, the queen's knight typically following the route ♘bd2-f1, when both e3 and g3 are attractive squares.

Generally speaking, Black has two fundamentally different ways in which to react. He can either let the opponent do whatever he likes and make optimal use of the opportunity to develop his own position as well as he can, or he can start a fight in the centre at once, before White is ready for it. In most cases the choice is a matter of opinion and personal style. This position is no exception. Black can either proceed with his development or make an attempt to punish 5 c3 with the aggressive **5...f5**.

If Black chooses the former plan, then his most flexible option is to play **5...♗d7** for the alternative **5...♘f6** can simply be met by 6 d4, when 6...♘xe4?? loses a piece to 7 d5 b5 8 ♗c2.

In the position after **5...♗d7** 6 d4, three main lines have been developed over the years. The oldest and most straightforward is to play **6...♘f6** 7 0-0 ♗e7 8 ♖e1 0-0. Slightly more subtle is **6...♘ge7**, intending 7 0-0 ♘g6, when the king's knight supports e5 and may be employed aggressively on the kingside (ideas like ...♘h4 and ...♗e7-g5 spring to mind). This line can lead to sharp play, especially if White responds with 7 ♗e3 (to meet 7...♘g6 with 8 h4) or 7 ♗b3, which threatens 8 ♘g5 and forces Black to play 7...h6. A third option is to play **6...g6** 7 0-0 ♗g7, postponing the decision whether to play ...♘f6 or ...♘ge7. All these plans offer Black a solid position, but no prospects of quick counterplay.

This cannot be said about **5...f5** (*D*).

This move has been given the rather strange name of **Siësta Variation**, even though it is obvious that neither player will be able to afford a little nap in this position. It is an excellent moment for playing ...f5, since White has no aggressive reply. The critical position arises after 6 exf5 ♗xf5 7 0-0 (if 7 d4, in order to prevent

Black's next move, 7...e4 gives Black a comfortable position) 7...♗d3 8 ♖e1 ♗e7. Black's d3-bishop paralyses White's entire queenside and has to be removed at once, but an important point of Black's plan is that **9 ♖e3** can be met by 9...e4, when 10 ♘e1 ♗g5 11 ♖h3 ♘f6 12 ♘xd3 exd3 13 ♖xd3 0-0 gives Black excellent compensation for the lost pawn in the shape of a huge lead in development. **9 ♗c2** is a more cautious approach. Now 9...e4 10 ♗xd3 exd3 11 ♕b3 is risky for Black and most players prefer 9...♗xc2 10 ♕xc2 ♘f6.

5 0-0

5	0-0

This is a plausible move. White avoids the complications of the Siësta Variation (**5...f5** 6 exf5 ♗xf5 is rather pointless with White having substituted the useful move 0-0 for the weakening c3), while moves like **5...♗d7** and **5...♘f6** can be met in much the same way as before. If 5...♘f6, for instance, 6 ♖e1 ♗e7 7 c3 0-0 8 d4 ♗d7 transposes to a variation that we have just seen as part of the 5 c3 complex.

But there is one problem with 5 0-0, a theoretical as well as a practical one: White is walking into a minefield. *If* Black has a lot of self-confidence, *if* he has a great flair for tactics and *if* he is armed to the teeth with theoretical knowledge, he can now set the game on fire in a way which pales the complications of the Siësta Variation into insignificance.

5	...	♗g4
6	h3	h5 (*D*)

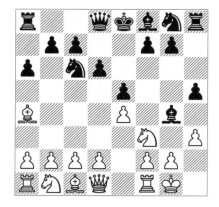

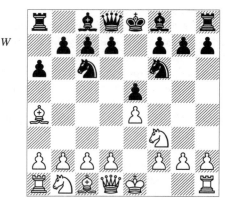

We have seen this tactical motif before in the Exchange Variation (see page 275). Taking on g4 is useless, but contrary to the situation in the Exchange Variation White now has a very sharp reply: **7 d4**. At first sight this seems ludicrous, because Black is invited to play 7...b5 8 ♗b3 ♘xd4. But *now* White accepts the piece sacrifice and after 9 hxg4 hxg4 he has 10 ♘g5, blocking the black queen's way to h4. This leaves us, after the calm reply 10...♘h6 (protecting f7), with an extremely double-edged position, for on the one hand the knight is excellently placed on g5, but on the other hand it will be attacked and has no escape-route. Decades of analysis have failed to come up with a final assessment of this line. What is quite clear, though, is that if White wants to go in for this, he too will need self-confidence, tactical flair and some very solid preparation.

4...♘f6

4 ... ♘f6 *(D)*

Black still does nothing to defend e5. Instead he attacks e4. White now faces the important decision about whether to protect this pawn.

5 0-0

This is unquestionably the critical move as well as the most flexible one. The only drawback is that it is this very move which carries the heaviest burden of theoretical baggage and for this – essentially practical – reason many players prefer a different move after all. In fact, White has a number of alternatives, all of them quite reasonable but all of them taking away

some of the positional tension. White is making life a little bit easier for himself (which is nice) but for his opponent as well (which is a pity).

But in fact play does not really become easy at all. Each one of these alternatives has been minutely examined, just like every other variation of the Ruy Lopez. I shall outline them very briefly.

To begin with, White has **5 d3** *(D)*.

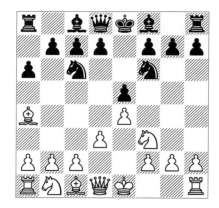

Now 6 ♗xc6 followed by 7 ♘xe5 is finally a real threat and Black should not forget this. **5...b5** 6 ♗b3 and now either 6...♗e7 or 6...♗c5 is a good reply, as is **5...d6**, analogous to the Neo-Steinitz Variation. But the move d3 in general is not as harmless as it may look and there are very many positions in the Ruy Lopez where this move is a perfectly valid option. In most of these cases White continues c3, sometimes followed by d4 at a later stage, and concentrates his forces mainly on the kingside. In such a strategy it could prove useful to delay castling and play ♘bd2-f1-e3 (or g3) first.

5 ♘c3 is also a move that *could* be more than just a one-dimensional protection of e4. After 5...b5 6 ♗b3 ♗e7, for instance, White may try to take the initiative with 7 d3 d6 8 ♘d5 or (sharper) 7 0-0 d6 8 ♘d5, retaining the option of playing d4 without the loss of tempo d3. White need not worry about 8...♘xe4 since the reply 9 d4 followed by 10 ♖e1 would then give him a strong initiative.

5 ♕e2 is the alternative which stays closest to the sort of play that is typical of the main line 5 0-0, because White usually continues in the same vein: c3 followed by d4, possibly in combination with ♖d1. Apart from 5...♘xe4 of course, Black has the same range of possible replies. After 5...b5 6 ♗b3 he can play 6...♗c5, giving his king's bishop an active role in the struggle for the centre; he also has the simple 6...♗e7 7 0-0 d6 8 c3 0-0 analogous to the Closed Variation, or he can offer the same pawn sacrifice as in the Marshall Attack: 7...0-0 8 c3 d5.

Finally, White has a move that we have seen him play in several variations before, viz. **5 d4** *(D)*.

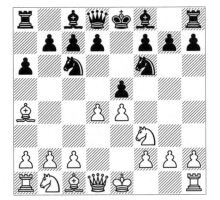

This is called the **Centre Attack** or the **Centre Gambit**, even though there is no sacrifice involved (as the term 'gambit' would suggest). After 5...exd4, White regains the pawn by playing 6 e5 ♘e4 7 0-0 ♗e7 8 ♘xd4. This position may look promising for White at first glance, but closer inspection reveals that a well-timed

...d5 or ...d6 usually neutralizes the danger. If 8...0-0, for instance, the pseudo-aggressive 9 ♘f5 is harmless because of 9...d5, making it impossible for White to maintain his knight on this beautiful square.

We now return to the position after 5 0-0 *(D)*:

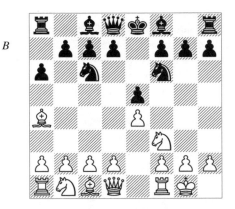

It is from this position that the great main lines of the Ruy Lopez start.

To begin with, Black has **5...♘xe4**, the **Open Variation** (or the **Open Spanish**). This is a critical test of 5 0-0, though not in the sense of making White look stupid for forgetting to protect e4, because White regains the pawn without any trouble. By taking on e4, Black opts for a direct confrontation and a relatively open type of position.

Then there is **5...♗e7**, the **Closed Variation** (or the **Closed Spanish**). This move does not as yet define the character of the middlegame. Black may choose to keep the position closed, but he also has one extremely violent and aggressive possibility a few moves later.

A third option and one that has become extremely popular since the mid-1990s is **5...b5**, introducing the **Arkhangelsk Variation** and the **Neo-Arkhangelsk**. In the wake of this, the much older move **5...♗c5** has also come to the fore again, but with a re-interpretation that makes it a close relative of the Neo-Arkhangelsk.

Open Variation

5   ...   ♘xe4

No player behind the black pieces will be under the illusion of winning a pawn here, for White need only take on c6 and e5 to level the material. But a deeper meaning behind 5...♘xe4 is revealed once it becomes clear that such a simple and straightforward recapture does not promise White any opening advantage whatsoever. From the lofty viewpoint of opening theory (which is never satisfied with anything less than maximum dividends), 6 ♗xc6 and 6 ♖e1 ♘c5 7 ♗xc6 dxc6 8 ♘xe5 ♗e7 leave White with empty hands. He has achieved nothing but a reduction of tension and material, leaving Black with easy development for his remaining pieces.

But things look different when White chooses the one move that really puts 5...♘xe4 to the test:

6   d4 *(D)*

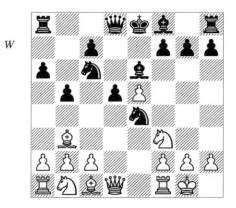

Now Black has to be careful. For instance, **6...♗e7** is met by 7 ♖e1 (or 7 ♕e2), when 7...d5 8 ♘xe5 gets Black into trouble. Nor is 7...f5 8 dxe5 0-0 9 ♗b3+ very attractive.

6...exd4 7 ♖e1 d5 8 ♘xd4 looks at first even riskier for Black, yet strangely enough this is a 'real' variation with a name, a point and the required theoretical uncertainties. The name is the **Riga Variation** and the point is 8...♗d6, whereupon 9 ♘xc6 ♗xh2+! 10 ♔xh2 ♕h4+ 11 ♔g1 ♕xf2+ is a draw by perpetual check. However, when the legendary Jose Raul Capablanca won an impressive game with 10 ♔h1 ♕h4 11 ♖xe4+ dxe4 12 ♕d8+ ♕xd8 13 ♘xd8+ ♔xd8 14 ♔xh2 in 1915, the variation was almost

forgotten. Only at the end of the 20th century was this endgame analysed in depth and then it turned out to be not so easy for White after all. At the moment the position after 7...d5 is undergoing some drastic theoretical renovation. Perhaps White should not play the obvious 8 ♘xd4 at all but try to unhinge Black's position with 8 c4!? instead. In any case, this is a beautiful example of a variation that has been gathering dust for decades and then suddenly turns out to be still fully alive!

But the classical reply to 6 d4 remains...

6	...	b5
7	♗b3	d5
8	dxe5	♗e6 *(D)*

We have now reached the basic position of the Open Ruy Lopez.

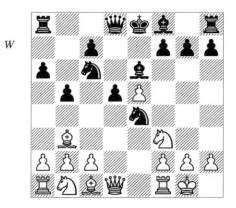

With his pawn on d5, Black has gained a solid foothold in the centre, he has open diagonals for both bishops and he has a knight aggressively posted at e4. White has a strong pawn on e5, potentially offering him attacking chances on the kingside. Who holds the advantage?

It is only natural that this question should have caused a major division of minds. The Open Ruy Lopez has always had staunch supporters and equally fervent critics. Tarrasch, Lasker and Euwe considered it the main line of the Ruy Lopez and in more recent times Korchnoi and Yusupov have made a living out of it. As is usually the case in these sharp variations, playing them successfully requires a good deal of theoretical knowledge and a readiness (an eagerness even) to keep on solving theoretical problems again and again.

At first these problems centred mainly around **9 c3**, but from 1981 onwards **9 ♘bd2** has become increasingly popular and this move now rivals 9 c3 as White's most dangerous line.

Nor have other moves been overlooked. Until 1981 it was **9 ♕e2** which was given as the main alternative to 9 c3 in opening manuals, but this move has receded into the background. Nowadays it is **9 ♗e3** that can be said to be 'the alternative line'. However, this move is based on ideas very similar to 9 c3 and 9 ♘bd2 and will not be elaborated in this book.

9 c3

9   c3 *(D)*

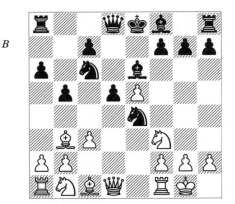

The classical approach to the Open Variation. White provides his king's bishop with an escape-route against a possible exchange with ...♘a5 or ...♘c5 and prepares an attack against Black's aggressively-posted knight with ♘bd2 and ♗c2.

9   ...   ♗c5

This way of developing the bishop has superseded the old main line **9...♗e7** ever since Viktor Korchnoi was successful with it in the 1970s and 1980s. Not that there is anything wrong with the old move, but Open Ruy Lopez devotees are simply no longer interested in it, now that the new main line is holding up so well. Theory of 9...♗e7 gives 10 ♘bd2 0-0 11 ♗c2 f5 as the main line, and the position after

12 ♘b3 ♕d7 13 ♘bd4 ♘xd4 14 ♘xd4 c5 15 ♘xe6 ♕xe6 16 f3 ♘g5 *(D)* as one of the most critical.

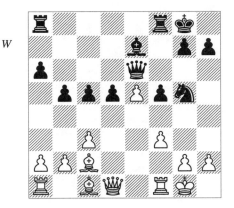

The situation has changed dramatically in the last eight moves. Thanks to the pawn on f5, Black does not for the moment have to worry about a kingside attack. He also has an impressive pawn-phalanx on the queenside. This latter factor is critical for an evaluation of the position. White's standard plan is to play 17 a4, starting an attack against these pawns and hoping that they will turn into a row of targets rather than be a threat.

10   ♘bd2   0-0
11   ♗c2

Now Black faces a fundamental decision. How should he deal with the attack on his knight? The range of possible answers varies from very simple to extremely complex.

It is of course simplest to play **11...♘xd2**, yet this is remarkably unpopular probably because it does not really put up a fight. After the subtle recapture 12 ♕xd2! (intending to move the queen to d3 as quickly as possible – after 12 ♗xd2 f6 13 exf6 ♕xf6 the bishop would be standing in the way on d2), followed, for example, by 12...f6 13 exf6 ♕xf6 14 ♕d3 g6 15 ♗h6 ♖fe8 16 ♖ae1, Black has completed not only his own development but also that of his opponent.

The first alternative that comes to mind is **11...f5** *(D)*.

This is sharper and therefore both riskier and more attractive than 11...♘xd2. If White goes

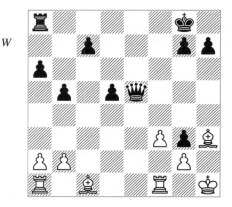

for the same type of position as in the line given above by playing **12 exf6**, Black is relatively better off after 12...♘xf6 13 ♘b3 ♗b6. The critical response to 11...f5 is thought to be **12 ♘b3 ♗b6 13 ♘fd4**. Ever since the 19th century, each and every new generation has made an effort trying to assess and calculate this position afresh. After 13...♘xd4 14 ♘xd4 ♗xd4 15 cxd4 it looks like White has won the opening battle, for he is threatening to play 16 f3, driving away the knight, after which the open c-file and the hole in Black's pawn-formation on c5 promise White a positional advantage. But Black has the diabolical reply 15...f4 16 f3 ♘g3!, when after 17 hxg3 fxg3 all of a sudden a threat of mate in the shape of 18...♕h4 is looming over White's king. White in his turn has the clever response 18 ♕d3, with the double idea of neutralizing 18...♕h4 with 19 ♕xh7+ ♕xh7 20 ♗xh7+ ♔xh7 (when ♗d2-e1 will pick up Black's pawn on g3 quickly and efficiently) and of meeting the zwischenzug 18...♗f5 with a queen sacrifice: 19 ♕xf5! ♖xf5 20 ♗xf5 ♕h4 21 ♗h3. The attack has been halted, White's king is safe and, with rook and two bishops, White has ample material compensation for the queen. The problem is that Black eliminates an unfortunate number of white pawns: 21...♕xd4+ 22 ♔h1 ♕xe5 *(D)*.

To give the reader an idea of how deep opening theory is capable of extending its tentacles into the middlegame (and even the endgame): this is not the final but the **starting** point of the theoretical discussion in this line. It is true that the theoretical assessment does

not greatly differ from what every reader's first impression probably is (namely that the position is unclear with chances for both sides), but the amount of variations developed from this position is impressive. White starts by giving away yet another pawn for the sake of a quick development of his queenside: 23 ♗d2.

But no matter how spectacular and fascinating these lines are, the highly specialized nature of them caused public interest in the Open Ruy Lopez to dwindle alarmingly between about 1950 and the late 1970s. Then in 1978 Viktor Korchnoi gave the whole variation a new lease on life. He chose the Open Ruy Lopez as his main defence against 1 e4 in two matches for the world championship against Anatoly Karpov, in 1978 and 1981, demonstrating a wealth of new ideas. For instance, he showed **11...♗f5** *(D)* to have been a grossly underestimated move.

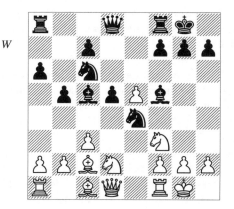

If 12 ♘b3, Black should not play the obvious 12...♗b6, but the surprising and very effective 12...♗g6. Taking on c5 and g6 does not harm Black, for after **13 ♘xc5 ♘xc5 14 ♗xg6 fxg6** his position is fine, nor is **13 ♗xe4** a problem due to 13...dxe4 14 ♘xc5 ♕xd1 15 ♖xd1 exf3. And a deeper point of 12...♗g6 is revealed after **13 ♘fd4**, for this gives Black the chance to play 13...♗xd4 without having lost a tempo first by playing ...♗b6. This gives him just enough time to meet 14 cxd4 with 14...a5!, continuing 15 f3 a4. If White instead plays 15 ♗e3, and meets 15...a4 with 16 ♘c1, Black has a highly promising piece sacrifice: 16...a3 17 b3 f6 18 f3 fxe5!.

This variation clearly shows that a true devotee of the Open Ruy Lopez almost never retreats if there is still even the faintest hope of moving forward. Always look for the most aggressive solution to each and every problem in this variation! In fact, this attitude may be said to reach its peak in Black's fourth option after 11 ♗c2: **11...♘xf2**, the **Dilworth Attack**. This line was very popular in the 1940s, then for a long time retreated to the world of correspondence chess, only to gain wide acceptance as a full-blown variation in recent years. Black not just exchanges two minor pieces for rook and pawn (which would be enough to create an unbalanced position in itself), he also destroys the natural cover of White's king. The main starting point of this line arises after 12 ♖xf2 f6 13 exf6 ♗xf2+ 14 ♔xf2 ♕xf6 *(D)*.

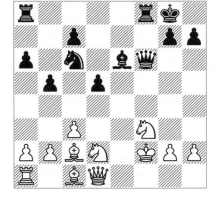

W

Black has a huge lead in development and is threatening to intensify the pressure with moves

like ...♘e5, ...♗g4 and ...♖ae8. With the material balance destroyed, this variation requires cold-bloodedness and a sense for the dynamic aspects of chess from both players.

9 ♘bd2

9 ♘bd2 *(D)*

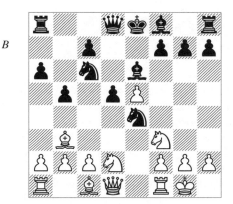

B

This move was thought to be completely harmless for a very long time. Although ordinary developing moves like **9...♗e7** and **9...♗c5** were always recognized as a little bit risky because of 10 ♘xe4 (though in fact recent attempts to turn 9...♗c5 10 ♘xe4 into a playable variation have been fairly successful), traditional theory maintained that Black has one totally reliable reply to 9 ♘bd2:

9 ... ♘c5
10 c3 d4 *(D)*

With this fearless advance, Black opens up the centre and seeks to take the initiative. This prevents White from playing ♘d4, a blockading move that featured so prominently in the 9 c3 variation. By way of comparison: after **10...♘xb3** 11 ♘xb3 it is White who has the initiative *and* a firm grip on the vital squares c5 and d4.

An alternative that is much stronger than 10...♘xb3 and of approximately the same value as 10...d4 is **10...♗g4**, which *does* take up the fight for control over d4 and which hinders White's natural development.

In 1981, during the second of the aforementioned matches for the world championship,

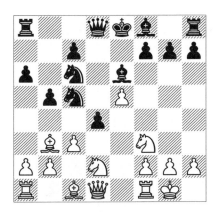

Karpov scored two resounding victories from the position after 10...d4. As a result, 9 ♘bd2 became enormously popular. First, it was Karpov's strictly positional approach from 1981, starting with **11 ♗xe6**, that attracted people. Remarkably, and perhaps as a result of the ever-increasing calculating powers of the computer (which began to play a serious role in opening preparation in the mid-1990s), it was only *after* this first wave of popularity died down that the far sharper move which had been played by Karpov in his *first* world championship match (in 1978), finally managed to catch the public eye, viz. the incredible **11 ♘g5**. It is this move that now constitutes one of the biggest problems for lovers of the Open Ruy Lopez and which provides theoreticians with one of their greatest challenges.

After **11 ♗xe6** ♘xe6 12 cxd4 ♘cxd4, everything looks fine for Black. His knights are actively posted and there are hardly any weaknesses in his pawn-chain. But in 1981 Karpov, with his characteristic merciless accuracy, demonstrated that White's tiny lead in development and his space advantage on the kingside do promise him chances of obtaining the initiative. Both 13 a4 and 13 ♘e4 ♗e7 14 ♗e3 brought him success.

But in the years following this match Black's defences were strengthened and after a while it became clear that there was no real danger for Black in this line, provided he knows his theory. For instance, in the latter variation (after 14 ♗e3) 14...♘f5 turned out to be much stronger than Korchnoi's move 14...♘xf3+. The entire 9

♘bd2 seemed about to be abandoned, until it gradually became clear where the real problem with 10...d4 lies.

When Karpov played the astounding **11 ♘g5** *(D)* against Korchnoi in 1978, he naturally had the world shell-shocked for a while (not to mention his opponent!).

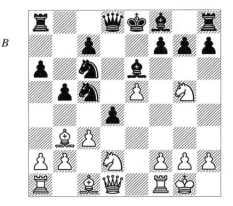

But although the correctness of this move was immediately recognized, surprisingly it failed to attract the huge following that one would be inclined to expect. The reason may have been that Karpov did not in the end win this game, or perhaps the world was not ready yet for a revolution of the kind that such a move entails.

The point of 11 ♘g5 is that after **11...♕xg5** White plays 12 ♕f3!, when the most obvious way to protect the knight on c6 fails to achieve its purpose: after 12...♔d7? 13 ♗d5! Black is in serious trouble. 12...♗d7 13 ♗xf7+ ♔e7 is less clear but obviously risky. The best-established line is the cunning 12...0-0-0 13 ♗xe6+ fxe6 14 ♕xc6 ♕xe5. This position is regarded as critical for a correct evaluation of 11...♕xg5. The resolute 15 b4 in particular has been the subject of detailed analysis extending many moves ahead.

Black also faces a practical problem after 11 ♘g5 in that there is no emergency exit, no way to avoid these unfathomable complications. For a long time it was thought the way in which Korchnoi had managed to rescue himself in 1978 was such an escape-route: **11...dxc3** 12 ♘xe6 fxe6 13 bxc3 ♕d3 *(D)*.

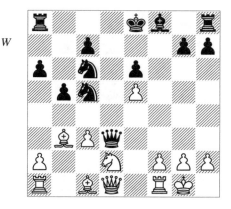

In fact it needed another historic game from a world championship match to show that here too Black is walking into a minefield. In 1995, Kasparov played 14 &c2 ♕xc3 15 ♘b3! in this position against Anand. This is the sort of move that shocks a human being into silence but makes a computer run even faster. White sacrifices a whole rook (15...♘xb3 16 &xb3 ♕xa1) in order to keep Black's king trapped in the centre. And whether Black accepts the sacrifice or not, he suddenly finds himself in an extremely dangerous situation. Ever since this game, anyone interested in playing this variation must really know what he is doing.

Closed Variation

     5   **...**   **&e7** *(D)*

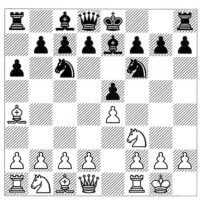

A simple developing move, yet it is the starting point for some of the most complex and challenging variations in the whole of opening theory.

To begin with, White again has to decide how to protect e4. The implications of **6 d3**, **6 ♘c3**, **6 ♕e2** and **6 d4** are all very similar to 5 d3, 5 ♘c3, etc., which I discussed briefly on pages 280-2. Strictly speaking, all of these moves could be said to be slightly more precise at move six, because Black has already committed himself to a ...&e7 plan, but this advantage is only marginal at best and most people who play these lines do so on move five in order to avoid the Open Ruy Lopez.

But compared to the situation on move five, White has two extra options:

The first of these is the strange-looking **6 &xc6**, the **Steenwijk Variation**. Again, the idea is *not* to meet 6...dxc6 with 7 ♘xe5, for in that case 7...♘xe4 solves all Black's opening problems. The paradoxical point of this belated exchange is to play 7 d3 *(D)*, when despite having made two extra – and normally very useful – developing moves (4...♘f6 and 5...&e7), Black has more problems protecting e5 than in the Exchange Variation.

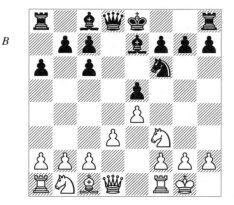

If **7...&g4**, for instance, the reply 8 h3 forces Black to take on f3, because after 8...&h5 9 g4 he simply loses a pawn. But after 8...&xf3 9 ♕xf3 Black has given up his bishop-pair, which is one of his main trumps in almost any variation where White takes on c6.

7...♕d6 too becomes decidedly less attractive now that 8 ♘bd2 immediately confronts Black with the threat of 9 ♘c4.

Therefore by far the most accepted reply to 7 d3 is **7...♘d7**, which though solid enough in itself, does have the disadvantage of making Black's further piece development a bit difficult. Theory concentrates mainly on the position after 8 ♘bd2 0-0 9 ♘c4 f6, with 10 ♘h4 ♘c5 as one of the main lines.

The second is a move that was not possible before:

6   ♖e1

It is this highly flexible move which causes most of the theoretical problems in the Ruy Lopez. To begin with, Black now finally has to do something about the threat of taking on c6 and e5.

6   ...   b5

The logical follow-up to 3...a6. Black plays the trump card that he has been holding up his sleeve for two moves. **6...d6** transposes to the Neo-Steinitz (page 277).

7   ♗b3 *(D)*

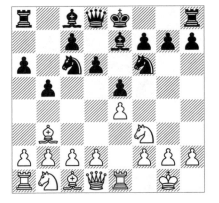

There are two main lines in this position. By playing **7...d6**, Black finally indicates that he *is* heading for a closed type of position. **7...0-0**, on the other hand, is a necessary preliminary to the renowned **Marshall Attack**.

7...d6

7   ...   d6 *(D)*

Black chooses the same type of defensive formation as in the Neo-Steinitz, the insertion of ...b5 being the only difference. Insignificant though this addition may seem, it changes the

position fundamentally, not just because the possibility of ♗xc6+ is disabled, but because Black has gained space on the queenside – space that can be used for a developing move like ...♗b7 or for further aggression with ...♘a5 followed by ...c5. Black has made it clear that he has no wish to leave the initiative on the queenside to his opponent.

As a rule, the Closed Variation leads to a positionally complex middlegame.

8   c3

I have already explained some of the implications of this move in the section on the Neo-Steinitz (see page 278). White makes sure that his bishop is not going to be exchanged by ...♘a5 and is preparing to advance in the centre with d4. The immediate **8 d4** would run into 8...♘xd4 9 ♘xd4 exd4 10 ♕xd4?? c5!, when 11...c4 traps the bishop.

If White is looking for an alternative to 8 c3, he has a much sounder option in **8 a4**. This is an attempt to take immediate advantage of the one (potential) drawback of ...b5. This line became popular around 1990, though it never managed to surpass 8 c3 as the main line. As a positional motif, a4 plays a crucial role in the Closed Ruy Lopez: it is White's chief method of fighting back on the queenside. However, most players do not wish to play this trump card so early in the game. The critical replies are 8...b4 and 8...♗g4.

8   ...   0-0 *(D)*

9   h3

This move looks very slow at first sight, almost irresponsibly so in fact. Black has practically completed his development, while White's

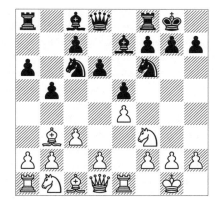

entire queenside has not even begun to get started, but instead of hurrying up a bit, White calmly makes another preparatory move for d4 (eliminating the reply ...♗g4). However, this little move turns out to be a golden investment. White's position is like a sleeping giant. Well and truly awakened, it will be a tremendous force, but when clumsily trying to get up too soon, it will be vulnerable to a sharp counterattack (which is what variations like the Marshall Attack are based on). As we shall see, once the giant awakens, it is very difficult for Black to hold him in check and this is really the fundamental problem of the Closed Ruy Lopez: how to develop counterplay once White has 'safely' played d4. It has been said that a player has not truly mastered the game until he knows how to handle this opening as Black.

Notwithstanding all this, the immediate **9 d4** is a perfectly legitimate alternative to 9 h3, especially for those with a dynamic and aggressive style and with little patience for the subtleties involved in 9 h3. After 9...♗g4 there are two main lines (not counting 10 h3 ♗xf3, when White must choose between the rather speculative pawn sacrifice 11 ♕xf3 exd4 and the positionally suspect 11 gxf3).

The first is to protect d4 with **10 ♗e3**, which is possible because 10...♘xe4?? loses a piece to 11 ♗d5. After 10...exd4 11 cxd4, Black will attempt to take the initiative, for instance with 11...d5 12 e5 ♘e4 or 11...♘a5 12 ♗c2 c5 (or 12...♘c4).

The second is to close the centre with **10 d5** ♘a5 11 ♗c2. Here too Black will want to

counterattack as fast as possible, starting, for instance, with 11...c6.

We now return to 9 h3 *(D)*:

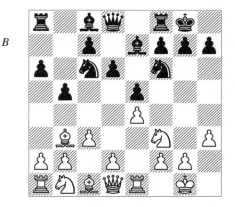

This is the starting position for a great number of well-analysed variations. I shall elaborate three of them, starting with Black's oldest move, **9...♘a5**, the **Chigorin Defence**. Then comes **9...♘b8**, the **Breyer Defence**, which was tremendously popular in the 1960s and 1970s and is still considered critical today. The third is **9...♗b7**, the **Zaitsev Variation**, which completely dominated the tournament arena in the 1980s.

Of Black's remaining options, I shall just briefly mention the three most important ones: **9...h6**, **9...♘d7** and **9...♗e6**.

9...h6, the **Smyslov Variation**, prepares 10...♖e8 by preventing ♘g5. This variation had its heyday before the rise of the Zaitsev Variation, which showed that Black does not have to worry about this knight sortie.

The idea of **9...♘d7** is to regroup with moves like ...♘b6 and ...♗f6. This variation has no generally accepted name (though those of Keres and Karpov have been associated with it) but it does have a good reputation (which is of course much more important).

9...♗e6 also goes through life without a proper name, even though it has a good reputation and was favoured by world champion Botvinnik, amongst others. Critical is 10 d4 ♗xb3 11 axb3 exd4 12 cxd4 d5 13 e5 ♘e4 14 ♘c3, and in particular the pawn sacrifice 14...f5 15 exf6 ♗xf6!? 16 ♘xe4 dxe4 17 ♖xe4 ♕d5. Does

Black's active play compensate for the missing pawn or not? That is the question.

Chigorin Defence

9   ...   ♘a5

Unlike 5...♘a5 in the Taimanov Variation (see page 277), this move is not intended to exchange the bishop (for White is almost certain to reply 10 ♗c2), but to make way for the c-pawn.

10   ♗c2   c5
11   d4 *(D)*

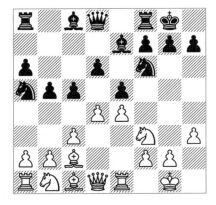

At last the opposing pawn armies make contact. From now on, the fundamental problem for White will be whether to exchange on e5 (or c5) or to close the centre with d5, and for Black whether to take on d4. In the majority of cases this is an extremely subtle evaluation, which usually depends on personal preference as much as on objective positional factors. Speaking in a general sense, one could make the following observations though:

- Exchanging on e5 becomes a serious option if there is any way in which White can make use of the d5-square, for instance with the manoeuvre ♘bd2-f1-e3-d5. This was thought to be White's principal strategy in the 1950s and 1960s.
- After about 1970 the (older) plan of playing d5 received a lot of attention. White closes the centre, hoping that this will free his hands for an attack on the kingside.
- With the above in mind, it may seem logical for Black to play ...cxd4, opening the c-file

as a base for counterplay. But in that case Black has to be aware of a possible boomerang effect, for if White manages to neutralize any short-term threats, he has every chance of taking over control of the c-file with good prospects of even taking over the initiative on the queenside in the longer run.

11   ...   ♕c7

The classical move in this position, yet there are some trustworthy alternatives, most notably **11...♘d7** and **11...♗b7**. The latter move is made possible by the tactical blow 12 dxe5 dxe5 13 ♕xd8 ♖axd8 14 ♘xe5 ♗xe4!. After 15 ♗xe4 ♘xe4, 16 ♖xe4? is bad due to 16...♖d1+, when Black wins back the sacrificed piece.

12   ♘bd2 *(D)*

Players with a marked preference for a closed centre will want to play **12 d5** right away. Although this is certainly not bad (even quite popular in fact), 'official' opening theory will never approve of immediately carrying out a plan, however good, without giving very careful consideration to the matter of timing. Always wait for the best possible moment! By playing 12 ♘bd2 White wants to develop his queenside first, beginning with the knight, for which ♘f1 and then either to e3 or g3 is clearly indicated.

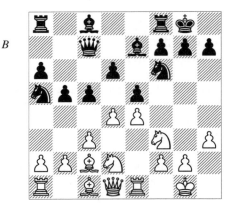

A veritable wealth of variations has been developed from this position. They are all very much alike, and in order to understand them properly, one will have to study them all!

Let us first look at Black's most radical option: **12...cxd4**. Black cuts the Gordian Knot by opening the c-file immediately. After 13 cxd4 he has several ways to try to take the initiative on the queenside.

The most obvious is perhaps to play **13...♗b7**, but if one studies the Chigorin deeply it will become clear that there is a downside even to this seemingly natural developing move. As long as its diagonal remains open, this bishop is very well placed indeed, but if White plays d5 the situation changes dramatically. Now, the variation 12...cxd4 13 cxd4 ♗b7 is not without some finer points. In the first place: if **14 ♘f1**, the advance ...d5 becomes an option. Black will reply 14...♖ac8, whereupon 15 ♘e3 fails to 15...♘xe4! and every other move – 15 ♗b1, 15 ♗d3 and 15 ♖e2 – can be met by 15...d5!? with great complications that need to be examined very thoroughly. Theory has been working on this since 1908(!) and still has not come up with a clear judgement. Secondly, if **14 d5** Black has the sharp 14...♖ac8 15 ♗d3 ♘d7 16 ♘f1 f5. By opening a second front on the kingside and attacking e4, Black undermines the d5-pawn and keeps his queen's bishop in play.

A second way of justifying the exchange on d4 with active play starts with **13...♘c6** *(D)*.

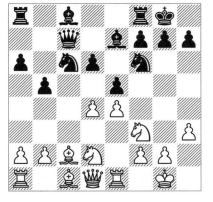

W

If then **14 ♘f1**, White will not be able to meet 14...♘xd4 15 ♘xd4 exd4 with 16 ♕xd4?? because the c2-bishop is left *en prise*. The advance **14 d5** is also quite different now that Black can reply 14...♘b4 15 ♗b1 a5 16 a3 ♘a6. Black will develop his queen's bishop to d7, when his piece deployment on the queenside (bishop on d7 and knight on a6) is in much better harmony with the central pawn-structure

than with the bishop at b7 and the knight stranded on a5.

The main line is **14 ♘b3**. This rather provokes 14...a5, but White has just enough time to develop his bishop (15 ♗e3) so as to meet 15...a4 with 16 ♘bd2 *(D)*. This is the main starting point of this variation.

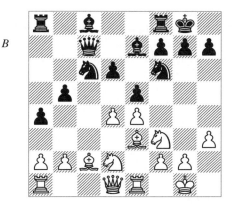

B

Black has gained space on the queenside, but White has managed to consolidate his centre and complete his development. From all of the subvariations of the Chigorin, this is both one of the oldest and one of the most topical.

Finally, the flexible **13...♗d7** is often played. In this case 14 ♘f1 ♖ac8 15 ♘e3 and *now* 15...♘c6 is considered critical.

So much for 12...cxd4. Let us see now if there is any sense in carrying out the above plans without capturing on d4 first.

The immediate **12...♘c6** actually was one of the most important variations of the entire Ruy Lopez until about 1970. Since 13 ♘b3 is hardly attractive with a black pawn on c5 and 13 ♘f1 is (again) met by 13...cxd4 14 cxd4 ♘xd4, it was assumed for decades that *this* was a position where **13 dxc5** dxc5 14 ♘f1 is White's best plan. This variation was analysed very deeply, with the position after 14...♗e6 15 ♘e3 ♖ad8 16 ♕e2 c4 taking most of the limelight.

Then, around 1970 a reassessment of the old **13 d5** plan took place. It turned out that White's chances in this type of position had been rather underestimated. Not only does White have prospects of an attack on the kingside, based on g4 and ♘f1-g3, but he might even take the initiative on the queenside with a4. Although Black's position will always be very solid, enthusiasm for 12...♘c6 cooled down somewhat and nowadays this variation is seen very little.

The same can be said about **12...♗b7**. This line was thought to be practically identical to its twin variation 12...cxd4 13 cxd4 ♗b7 for a very long time, but here too the renaissance of 13 d5 has taken its toll. In this type of position, b7 is simply not a good square for Black's bishop.

Nowadays, it is **12...♗d7** that is the most important non-12...cxd4 variation. With the bishop on d7, 13 d5 is not particularly to be feared (a good reply being 13...c4 14 ♘f1 ♘b7 followed by ...♘c5). If 13 ♘f1 on the other hand, Black has a choice between 13...cxd4 after all and maintaining the tension with 13...♘c4 14 b3 ♘b6. Black's knight is well placed at b6, whether White plays d5 or not.

Breyer Defence

9 ... ♘b8 (D)

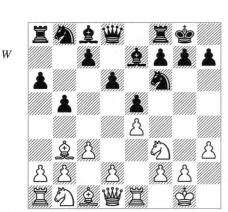

Anyone seeing this move for the first time might well get the impression that Black is actually setting up the pieces for a new game. What else can be the point of a seemingly totally useless move like this?

Nevertheless, the Breyer is one of Black's very best options in this position. The underlying motifs are not easy to spot, yet a comparison with the Chigorin Defence may be revealing:

• It is true that 9...♘a5 gains a tempo, but in itself a5 is not a very good square for the knight. We have already seen that Black always continues with manoeuvres like ...♘c6, ...♘c4-b6 or ...c5-c4 followed by ...♗b7. Compared to these, a regrouping involving ...♘b8-d7 does not at all look bad. Black's knight will be useful and flexible on d7.

• The advance ...c5, which is another characteristic of the Chigorin Defence, also has its cons as well as its pros. It is a useful territorial expansion on the queenside but it does allow White to establish a very stable space advantage by playing d5 at some point. By keeping the c-pawn back for the time being, Black retains the chance of meeting d5 with ...c6, attacking White's central pawn-formation.

The question remains of course whether 9...♘b8 does not cause more problems than it solves, but this does not appear to be the case.

10 d4 ♘bd7
11 ♘bd2 ♗b7 (D)

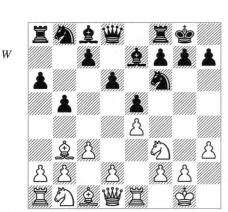

The first positive effects of 9...♘b8 make themselves felt. To begin with, **12 d5** does not make much sense in this position, since 12...c6 (or 12...♘c5 13 ♗c2 c6) forces White to exchange pawns on c6, when Black's pieces are very actively posted.

Another strong point of Black's opening scheme is that the much-desired manoeuvre ♘f1-g3 is not so easy to carry out, because e4 has to be protected.

12 ♗c2

Once we begin to understand that White has nothing better than this voluntary retreat (that is, without being forced to do so by ...♘a5), it becomes clear that the apparent uselessness of 9...♘b8 is only on the surface. The paradox of White being forced to play ♗c2 without being prompted by ...♘a5 reveals the hidden strength of the Breyer Defence.

12	**...**	**♖e8**

Preparing ...♗f8 in order to increase the pressure on e4.

13	**♘f1**	**♗f8**
14	**♘g3**	**g6** *(D)*

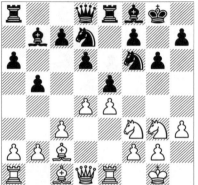

This is a key position of the Breyer. Black's last move is intended to prevent a future ♘f5 and introduces the possibility of playing ...♗g7. **15 d5** is still not to be feared because of 15...c6. Not only does White now have to take a possible ...c5 into account, but he also has to be wary of a frontal attack in the centre with ...d5. What should he do?

The classical answer to this question is **15 a4**. This is a subtle and logical move. White takes advantage of the opportunity offered by Black's apparent lack of interest in queenside expansion by taking the initiative on that wing himself. If 15...♗g7, the idea is to play 16 ♗d3, inducing the small but important concession 16...c6, which blocks the diagonal of Black's queen's bishop and in consequence relieves the pressure on e4. But the downside of 15 a4 is that it makes 15...c5 attractive again, for 16 d5 c4 now offers Black an unassailable strongpoint for his knight on c5. If, for instance, 17 ♗e3 ♘c5 taking on c5 is unattractive, while – having played a4 – White is no longer in a position to drive away the knight with 18 b4 cxb3 19 axb3 followed by b4.

Nowadays, White is searching for alternative methods. The most popular of the new variations is **15 b3**. White simply wants to carry out the classical plan of playing d5. By preparing to meet ...c6 with the supportive c4, he avoids having to exchange on c6.

Zaitsev Variation

9	**...**	**♗b7** *(D)*

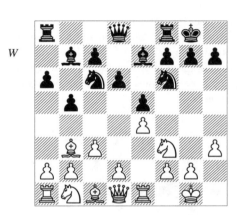

This move became exceedingly popular after World Champion Anatoly Karpov 'inherited' it from his long-time coach and second Igor Zaitsev in the late 1970s, scoring some magnificent victories. It is a sort of restyling of the idea behind the Breyer Defence. The knight on c6 remains in place, but the pressure on e4 is increased all the same. There is, however, one very odd thing about the Zaitsev which makes it unfit to be used on all occasions.

10	**d4**	**♖e8**

This is the point of Black's previous move. Surprisingly, Black does not need to worry about **11 ♘g5**, since after the laconic reply 11...♖f8 White appears to have no way of backing up the aggressive knight sortie. Naturally, however, White may retreat the knight (12 ♘f3) and in so doing invite Black to repeat moves (12...♖e8 13 ♘g5, etc.). Paradoxically then, this line, which is one of the most complex and dynamic of the entire Ruy Lopez, can only be played by someone who is prepared to accept a most ignominious draw by repetition in the opening.

11	**a4** *(D)*

If White simply develops according to the well-known pattern of **11 ♘bd2 ♗f8 12 ♗c2 g6**, he faces a problem: the standard continuation 13 ♘f1 would be too slow, for it allows Black to play 13...exd4 14 cxd4 ♘b4, forcing the exchange of this knight for the 'Spanish' bishop on c2, thus decidedly lessening White's attacking chances. For this reason, 13 d5 is usually played. After 13...♘e7 or 13...♘b8 White then has 14 b3 c6 15 c4, consolidating his stronghold at d5.

This line illustrates the pros and cons of the Zaitsev rather well. Black puts pressure on e4 without having to play ...♘b8-d7, but the crucial plan of playing d5 (supported by b3 and c4 if necessary) becomes more attractive with a knight on c6.

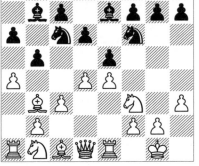

By playing 11 a4, White hopes to carry out this plan in its most effective form. He first softens up Black's pawn on b5.

11   ...   h6

A subtle anticipatory move. It is not ♘g5 that Black is worried about, but ♗g5. The idea of 11 a4 is to play 12 d5 followed by an attack against b5 (with ♘a3, for example). This will force Black to play ...c6, when a battle for control of the crucial square d5 is likely to ensue. At that moment ♗g5 would be an excellent move. A sample line: if Black plays the unsuspecting **11...♗f8**, then after 12 d5 ♘b8 13 axb5 axb5 14 ♖xa8 ♗xa8 15 ♘a3 c6 16 dxc6 ♗xc6 17 ♗g5! ♘bd7 18 ♘c2 White gets firm control over d5 and can be very satisfied with the outcome of the opening.

12   ♘bd2

Now **12 d5** would be less effective. Black's best reply is probably 12...♘a5 13 ♗c2 c6. The fact that White cannot play ♗g5 seriously hampers him in his struggle for d5.

By playing 12 ♘bd2, White falls back on the traditional development scheme, but always with an eye on attacking b5.

12   ...   ♗f8
13   ♗c2 (D)

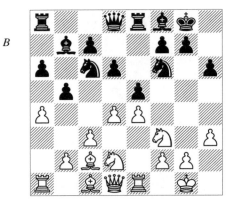

This is a crucial position strategically. White is poised to take the initiative on the queenside with moves like ♗d3 or d5 in combination with b3 and c4. Black has several ways to counter this plan, but he can also alter the position dramatically by making use of the one drawback of a4:

13   ...   exd4
14   cxd4   ♘b4

We have seen this knight move before, viz. in the variation 11 ♘bd2 ♗f8 12 ♗c2 g6 13 ♘f1. Then, it was a tactical stroke intended to eliminate White's bishop-pair. Here, the idea is a strategic one. Now that White can no longer play a3, Black's b4-knight is unassailable. The crucial question is: is this really the right moment for an all-out attack against White's centre pawns, or is giving up the central stronghold at e5 too high a price?

The critical position arises after the following moves:

15   ♗b1   c5
16   d5   ♘d7 (D)

With this knight retreat, Black prepares two assaults that are potentially lethal and *must* be

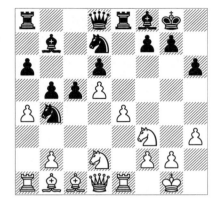

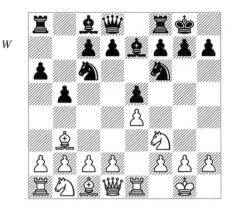

countered with extreme vigilance. The threat of ...c4 followed by ...♘c5 and an invasion by the knights on d3 looms large over White's queenside, and on the kingside a well-timed ...f5 might destroy White's entire pawn-centre.

This is an extremely explosive situation, asking the utmost of both players. Some unbelievably complicated games have been played with this line, with sometimes White showing true virtuosity in making use of his attacking chances on the kingside, and sometimes Black wiping out the enemy position without any problems.

White's best move is thought to be **17 ♖a3**. The idea is to transfer the rook to the kingside via e3, f3 or g3. If 17...c4 White intends to play 18 ♘d4 or 18 axb5 axb5 19 ♘d4. If 17...f5 both 18 exf5 and 18 ♘h2 (freeing the way for the rook to f3 or g3) have been played. In the latter variation White concentrates all his forces against Black's king.

Marshall Attack

7 ... 0-0 *(D)*

This seemingly innocuous move is in fact the preliminary to a pawn sacrifice which completely changes the hitherto closed character of the position.

8 c3

White continues with the same plan as against 7...d6. Black must now either revert to standard main lines of the Closed Ruy Lopez that we have just examined by playing 8...d6, or else make the characteristic pawn sacrifice of the Marshall Attack.

In order to prevent Black's next move, alternatives to 8 c3 have been thoroughly examined, much more so than after 7...d6. Perhaps the most important one is **8 a4** (other possibilities are **8 d3** and **8 h3**), which is more pointed after 7...0-0 (as compared to 7...d6), because Black cannot reply with the aggressive 8...♗g4. This move often leads to a rather slow opening phase with White playing d3 rather than d4. This can be frustrating to a player who is mentally geared for the totally different type of play arising in the Marshall Attack. An important starting position for this line arises after 8...♗b7 9 d3 d6.

8 ... d5 *(D)*

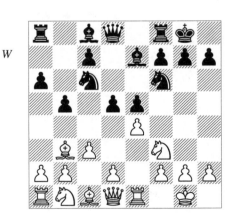

A perfectly logical way of taking the initiative in the centre, especially now that White has played 8 c3, making a fast mobilization of this queenside forces rather difficult. The only drawback is that it loses a pawn.

It is the great merit of Frank Marshall (1877-1944), one of the best players in the world during the first half of the 20th century, to have discovered how powerful this courageous treatment of the opening really is, but his gambit did not become truly popular until after World War II. Nowadays it is one of the most heavily analysed opening variations in chess and accurate theoretical knowledge is an absolute requirement if one is to play this gambit with any degree of success. But it is by no means a matter of just learning variations by heart. Theory of the Marshall is very much alive and is being refined and enriched with new ideas almost every day. The bulk of these variations start with...

9	exd5	♘xd5
10	♘xe5	♘xe5
11	♖xe5	c6 (D)

11...♘f6 and 11...♗b7 are major alternatives, but 11...c6 is the main line. Black is ready to start an attack against White's king with ...♗d6 and ...♛h4. White will have to defend against this, while at the same time making sure that his queenside forces wake up before it is too late.

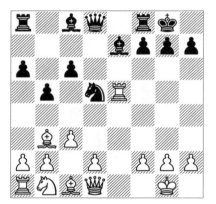

12 d4

The most natural move and also the main line, but there are several alternatives, some of them very subtle indeed, for instance **12 d3**, **12 ♖e1** and **12 ♗xd5**.

12	...	♗d6
13	♖e1	♛h4
14	g3	♛h3 (D)

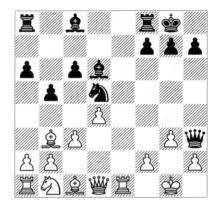

This position illustrates the character of the Marshall Attack very well. White's position is not exactly bad, but he will have to work hard to catch up on his piece development and for the moment his extra pawn has no significance. An opponent with a good eye for attacking chances is likely to put no end of obstacles in his way.

15 ♗e3 is the traditional move. Black then continues 15...♗g4 and after 16 ♛d3 he has 16...♖ae8 17 ♘d2 and now 17...f5 or 17...♖e6, to name just a few of the more characteristic ideas.

In order to prevent this easy attacking plan, the ingenious **15 ♖e4** has been tried. This prevents Black from playing 15...♗g4 and gives him the opportunity of blundering his queen by 15...♗f5?? 16 ♖h4. After the equally ingenious 15...g5 (based on 16 ♗xg5?? ♛f5) this too leads to a fierce and unpredictable battle.

Arkhangelsk Variation

5	...	b5

We have seen this move being played in different circumstances and for various reasons. In this case the idea is to carry out a plan that we have not seen before, one that is relatively new, at least in a 'Ruy Lopez' context. Before 1970 it was hardly ever seen in grandmaster games. Nowadays, it is one of the main lines and it has produced some offspring of its own, the Neo-Arkhangelsk (which we shall be looking at shortly). Even the much older and almost forgotten 5...♗c5 has been dug out and given a new lease on life. This used to be called **Møller**

Variation, but now that it is being played with a wholly different idea, a name like **Ultra-Neo-Arkhangelsk** or **Turbo-Arkhangelsk** would perhaps be more appropriate. After 5...♗c5 6 c3, Black intends to continue 6...b5 (the old Møller idea was to play 6...♗a7), when 7 ♗b3 d6 brings about a Neo-Arkhangelsk. By choosing this subtle move-order Black has avoided the tricky line 5...b5 6 ♗b3 ♗c5 7 a4 ♗b7 8 d3 followed by 9 ♘c3.

Those who want to contest the soundness of this Turbo-Arkhangelsk Variation will probably want to meet 5...♗c5 6 c3 b5 with **7 ♗c2** instead of 7 ♗b3.

      6   ♗b3 *(D)*

B

The 'classical' **Arkhangelsk Variation** now continues with **6...♗b7**. The **Neo-Arkhangelsk**, which has been very popular since 1994, starts with **6...♗c5**.

The older move, **6...♗b7**, is the sharper of the two. Even the solid reply **7 ♖e1** leads to a highly complex middlegame after 7...♗c5 8 c3 d6 9 d4 ♗b6 and now, for instance, 10 ♗g5 (a logical move in itself, now that Black's king's bishop is not at its usual post e7, but risky nevertheless) 10...h6 11 ♗h4 ♕d7!? 12 a4 0-0-0, followed by ...g5 and ...h5. Even more unfathomable are the consequences of **7 c3**. This move gives Black no time to play both ...♗c5 *and* ...d6, so 7...♗c5 8 d4 is good for White. But Black does have the cold-blooded, materialistic 7...♘xe4 8 d4 ♘a5 9 ♗c2 exd4. This is a true all-or-nothing variation and it requires some theoretical knowledge from both sides.

Ironically, the success of **6...♗c5** *(D)*, the **Neo-Arkhangelsk**, is due to it being much more solid and less dependent on razor-sharp variations that need to be calculated extremely accurately.

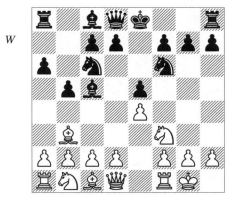

W

By delaying ...♗b7, Black gives himself just enough time to meet **7 c3** with 7...d6 8 d4 ♗b6, consolidating his central pawn-formation. This has the added advantage that Black can now play the aggressive ...♗g4 in some positions, instead of the 'traditional' Arkhangelsk move ...♗b7.

Tactically, the Neo-Arkhangelsk is made possible by the fact that **7 ♘xe5 ♘xe5 8 d4** is not as promising for White as it may look. Black cold-bloodedly replies 8...♗xd4 9 ♕xd4 d6 (threatening to win a piece by 10...c5 and 11...c4), when after 10 c3 0-0 followed by ...♗b7 and ...c5 Black achieves a satisfactory position.

Two lines have shown themselves as critical tests for the soundness of the Neo-Arkhangelsk, both of them involving an attack against b5. The first is **7 c3 d6 8 a4**; the second is **7 a4**. In the latter case, 7...♗b7 8 d3 d6 9 ♘c3 brings about the position that the Turbo-Arkhangelsk, 5...♗c5, is designed to avoid.

Berlin Defence

      3   ...   ♘f6 *(D)*

This natural move is less flexible than 3...a6 4 ♗a4 ♘f6, but has one specific point which has aroused a great deal of enthusiasm in recent years.

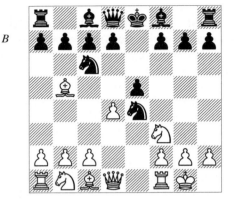

4　0-0

Castling is by far the most popular move and theoretically the critical reply. White has the same range of options that he has after 3...a6 4 ♗a4 ♘f6, viz. **4 d3**, **4 d4**, **4 ♕e2** and **4 ♘c3** (which in this case is a direct transposition to the Four Knights Game; see page 319) and even **4 ♗xc6** has been played, but theory has little to say on any of these.

4　...　　　♘xe4

Another option is to steer the opening toward a Steinitz Variation with **4...d6**; for instance, 5 d4 ♗d7 6 ♘c3 exd4 7 ♘xd4 ♗e7 (see page 272). In fact, this may well be a more accurate move-order than the traditional 3...d6, since White has already castled kingside, while in the Steinitz proper, castling queenside is often a powerful move.

4...♗e7 and **4...♗c5** are perfectly legal as well, but they are far less popular (and consequently less heavily analysed) than their 3...a6 4 ♗a4 counterparts. Critical for 4...♗c5 is the position after 5 c3 0-0 6 d4 ♗b6.

5　d4 *(D)*

Just like in the Open Ruy Lopez, other ways of recapturing the pawn, like **5 ♗xc6** or **5 ♖e1** ♘d6 6 ♘xe5 ♗e7, are too modest to trouble Black. By playing 5 d4, White aims to develop his pieces as aggressively as possible. However, frustrating this aggression is precisely what Black's opening play in this line is all about.

5　...　　　♘d6

If the moves 3...a6 4 ♗a4 had been inserted, Black would not have this attack on the bishop.

The opening now takes on a rather unique character. Not only in the Ruy Lopez, but in the whole of opening theory there is no parallel for what happens next.

6　♗xc6　　　dxc6
7　dxe5　　　♘f5
8　♕xd8+

Exchanging queens seems logical since Black now loses the right to castle, but the downside is that it does relieve the pressure on Black's rather cramped position. In fact **8 ♕e2**, to keep the queens on the board, would be a major option *if* Black did not have the tactical reply 8...♘d4! 9 ♘xd4 ♕xd4 10 ♖d1 ♗g4!, which solves all his problems neatly and efficiently.

8　...　　　♔xd8 *(D)*

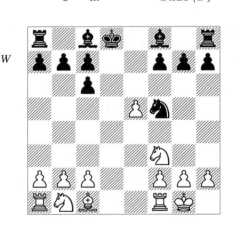

In a period of just a few years, this position has turned into a nightmare for the true 1 e4 player, that is the healthy and energetic player who was hoping for an honest, straightforward attacking game. The variation is actually very old, but until recently it was hardly ever played. Opening manuals usually repeated the intimidating (but utterly meaningless) remark that White has a slight advantage. The problem is that it is very difficult to say what White should **do** in this position. And if you do not have a good plan, then the theoretical assessment that you are supposed to stand slightly better is just a source of frustration.

For this reason the variation has often been referred to as the **Berlin Wall** in recent years. Black's position is a little cramped, but is without weaknesses and in the long run his pair of bishops might start dictating the course of events. Black cannot castle but it turns out that this is not much of a problem. His king may move to c8 or e8 and without queens on the board, creating anything even vaguely resembling an attack on the king is going to be a tall order for White.

9 ♘c3

After this standard developing move, Black has tried a number of plans. **9...♗e6** looks natural but has the drawback of inviting 10 ♘g5, which eliminates the bishop-pair. As a preparatory move, both **9...h6** and **9...♔e8** have been tried. After these variations had been popular a few years, it became clear that **9...♗d7**, enabling Black to play ...♔c8, is also a serious option. Even the unbelievably artificial **9...♘e7** is an important option. Black manoeuvres the knight to g6 and opens the way for his queen's bishop to f5 or g4.

In almost all of these cases, White will have to start a long-term offensive on the kingside sooner or later. By advancing his f- and g-pawns (f4 and g4) he gains space, but Black will be on the lookout to strike back with a well-timed ...h5.

This is a variation that requires positional insight and a lot of patience from both players. The single-minded attacking player is likely to feel extremely unhappy here.

Schliemann Defence (or Jaenisch Gambit)

3 ... f5 (D)

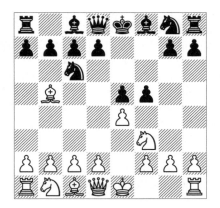

W

This variation is intended to create a direct and highly tactical confrontation in the centre. It has shown itself to be attractive not just to good tacticians, but also to lovers of thorough and exact opening preparation – good analysts. It is not a coincidence that it is (co-)named after Carl Jaenisch (1813-72), who was the first to publish an extensive analysis of this line, but who never was a great player.

4 ♘c3

The first point of 3...f5 is that **4 exf5** is met by 4...e4, when White does not really have a good square for his knight. 5 ♕e2 ♕e7 6 ♗xc6 dxc6 7 ♘d4 ♕e5 cannot exactly be called a refutation of Black's gambit.

A second and much more treacherous point is revealed if White ventures the energetic **4 d4** (D).

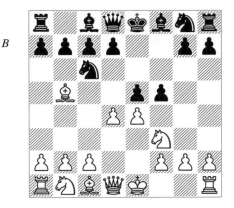

B

Although a logical enough move in itself, this runs into the nasty 4...fxe4 5 ♘xe5 ♘xe5 6 dxe5 c6!, when any move by the bishop loses a pawn to 7...♕a5+.

The solid **4 d3** is also a perfectly logical reply to 3...f5, but not really enough to worry Black. After 4...fxe4 5 dxe4 ♘f6 6 0-0 Black used to play 6...d6, protecting e5, but nowadays the aggressive 6...♗c5 is the main line. If White accepts the pawn sacrifice, Black gets plenty of counterplay after 7 ♗xc6 bxc6 8 ♘xe5 0-0, thanks to his lead in development.

It turns out then to be not so easy to find a weak spot in the Schliemann Defence. By playing 4 ♘c3, White accepts the challenge to a fierce struggle. Black is forced to commit himself even further.

    4   **...**   **fxe4**
    5   **♘xe4** *(D)*

    5   **...**   **d5**

5...♘f6 is a little more cautious. After 6 ♕e2 d5 7 ♘xf6+ gxf6 8 d4, play is less complicated than in the main line.

    6   **♘xe5**

This surprising move is a clear sign that White is not going to be intimidated by Black's early aggression. On the contrary, the text-move is the one and only attempt to refute the Schliemann Defence outright.

    6   **...**   **dxe4**
    7   **♘xc6** *(D)*

7 ♕h5+ g6 8 ♘xg6 would be over-enthusiastic but the text-move looks really excellent, for what is Black to do now?

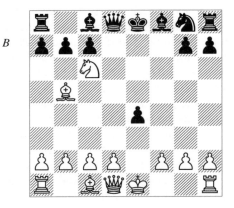

If **7...bxc6?**, then 8 ♗xc6+ ♗d7 9 ♕h5+ would force him to play 9...♔e7, when 10 ♕e5+ ♗e6 11 ♗xa8 ♕xa8 12 ♕xc7+ ♔e8 13 0-0 is very good for White. And what options does Black have? He is already a pawn down and about to be hit by a catastrophic discovered check.

It is remarkable that Black has two moves that both ward off the threats *and* practically take over the initiative: **7...♕d5** and **7...♕g5**. Both moves have been heavily analysed and have grown into independent variations.

By playing **7...♕d5**, Black forces the reply 8 c4, which constitutes a considerable weakening of White's position. After 8...♕d6 9 ♘xa7+ ♗d7 10 ♗xd7+ ♕xd7 11 ♘b5 ♘f6 12 0-0 ♗c5, for instance, White has two extra pawns but Black's position is dangerously active.

With **7...♕g5** Black is setting his sights on g2. After 8 ♕e2 ♘f6 (the immediate 8...♕xg2 is weaker because of 9 ♕h5+) a critical position is reached. The tricky 9 f4 is thought to be White's best move here. White sacrifices his f-pawn in order to save his g-pawn. After 9...♕xf4, both 10 ♘e5+ c6 11 d4 ♕h4+ 12 g3 ♕h3 13 ♗c4 and 10 ♘xa7+ have been tried.

Italian Game

1	e4	e5
2	♘f3	♘c6
3	♗c4 *(D)*	

B

For centuries, 3 ♗c4 was so self-evident a move that it was not thought necessary to give it a name, like 1 e4 also has no name. Names were only given *after* 3 ♗c4, in order to distinguish between Black's major replies. **3...♗c5** was called the **Giuoco Piano** and **3...♘f6** the **Two Knights Defence**.

The mere fact that in this book I follow the modern trend by lumping them together and calling 3 ♗c4 the Italian Game, is sadly illustrative of the diminished importance of this opening. Ever since the second half of the 19th century, the Ruy Lopez has been *the* dominant opening against 1...e5. Very little fresh energy was invested in the alternatives and opening books were inclined to condense what once was a veritable jungle of deeply-analysed variations into a few shallow standard lines. As a result, much of the old 1 e4 e5 theory has been fossilized. Many variations were simply no longer developed from the moment when they fell out of favour (which in many cases was as early as the 19th century). Until very recently, many active tournament players, upon reading a book

on – for example – the Italian Game, probably had the impression of entering a museum. A museum of opening theory, where every display case shows how openings *used* to be looked at in a very, very distant past.

But during the 1990s this situation changed rather suddenly. With the aid of that new tool the computer, many ancient openings were examined afresh with the result that some of them have been written off again (this time perhaps for good), but some have been restored to something of their former glory. In fact, we are still in the middle of this process today. Some of the old variations are still waiting for their turn.

Something that has not changed though is the major subdivision between 3...♗c5 and 3...♘f6. Even in the 21st century, these are the critical tests of 3 ♗c4. Anyone playing either of these moves has to be aware of the fact that he is provoking a sharp reaction. Some knowledge of the old (and the new!) variations is certainly to be recommended.

For those who do not trust themselves with these lines, there is **3...♗e7** 4 d4 d6. This is the old **Hungarian Defence**, which is not encumbered with a lot of theory.

Giuoco Piano: 3...♗c5

3	...	♗c5 *(D)*

When choosing this move, Black has to be aware of a wide variety of responses by White.

The classical reply is **4 c3**, preparing 5 d4. Ironically it is precisely this straightforward, logical variation that nowadays most closely resembles a museum artefact.

4 b4, the **Evans Gambit**, appeared to be destined for a similar fate, but this remarkable and in the eyes of a modern player probably highly dubious pawn sacrifice experienced a true renaissance in the 1990s, when even world champion Garry Kasparov adopted it.

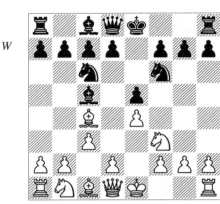

Then there is **4 ♘c3 ♘f6 5 d3** (or **4 d3 ♘f6 5 ♘c3**), equally ancient but much more solid and therefore always moderately popular though never a big hit. This is called the **Giuoco Pianissimo** (meaning 'Very Quiet Game'), clearly indicating that this is not 'the way of the despiser of material'.

A modern variation on this theme is to combine d3 with c3. This idea may look innocent, but it is in fact quite venomous. It was this line that was responsible for a first revival of the Italian Game during the 1980s. It can be played in a large number of move-orders. I shall take **4 d3** as the starting point, although **4 0-0** and **4 c3** are perfectly sound and equally popular alternatives.

3...♗c5 4 c3

4   c3   ♘f6 (D)

The most aggressive reply. In the days when 4 c3 was thought to be a dangerous line, **4...♗b6** or **4...♕e7** 5 d4 ♗b6 was sometimes played, but Black does not need to be that timid. It is perhaps noteworthy though that 4...♕e7 should not be played with the idea of meeting 5 d4 with 5...exd4. After 6 0-0! dxc3 7 ♘xc3 Black has won a pawn, but at too high a price. White has a very dangerous lead in development.

5   d4

This is the classical move, but it has fallen out of grace by now. The modern treatment of 4 c3 consists in playing **5 d3** (see page 305) or **5 b4 ♗b6 6 d3**. In the latter case, the question is whether b4 is a useful extra step forward on the

queenside or if it only gives Black an extra opportunity for counterplay.

5   ...   exd4
6   cxd4!

If **6 e5**, then 6...d5! is both necessary and a very strong rejoinder. In fact, this important theme is a recurrent one throughout the Italian Game and many of the other 1 e4 e5 openings.

The pawn sacrifice **6 0-0**, analogous to the line 4...♕e7 5 d4 exd4 above, is less powerful here, though it certainly remains an option. It is simply that ...♘f6 is more useful than ...♕e7 in this type of position. This gives Black the opportunity of playing 6...♘xe4 7 cxd4 and now the very thematic 7...d5. In fact, this is one of those dormant old lines that a new computerized investigation might well turn upside down.

6   ...   ♗b4+ (D)

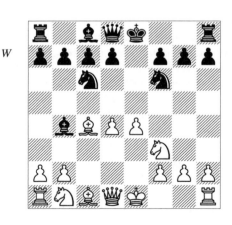

The story of this position is the story of chess in a nutshell. As early as the 16th century (and possibly even earlier) this was a hotly-debated position. At first the tone of these discussions was rather positive as regards to White's prospects, which is understandable if we realize that they concentrated on whether, after the double pawn sacrifice **7 ♘c3 ♘xe4 8 0-0 ♘xc3 9 bxc3 ♗xc3**, White's quickest way of demolishing the enemy position was 10 ♗a3 or 10 ♕b3.

But Black's defences were considerably strengthened when it was discovered first that 9...d5! is a much better move than 9...♗xc3 and second that 8...♗xc3 (instead of 8...♘xc3) is a major option for in that case 9 bxc3 d5! nips White's attack in the bud. But at that point the line was given a fresh impetus by the discovery of the truly astonishing 9 d5! *(D)*.

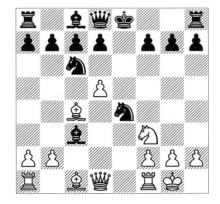

This position played a pivotal role in the Giuoco Piano during the greater part of the 19th and some of the 20th century. It was analysed in enormous depth, with subvariations which an opening manual as far back as 1938 already regretted to have to summarize in a mere three pages. To give the reader an impression: after 9...♗f6 10 ♖e1 ♘e7 11 ♖xe4 d6 12 ♗g5 ♗xg5 13 ♘xg5 0-0 (with 13...h6 an important alternative) the discussion focuses on the knight sacrifice 14 ♘xh7.

The more difficult it became to justify the ancient move 7 ♘c3, the more the alternative **7 ♗d2** *(D)* came to the fore as being both more modern and more reliable.

White does not sacrifice a pawn here, for 7...♘xe4 can now be very comfortably met by 8 ♗xb4 ♘xb4 9 ♗xf7+! ♔xf7 10 ♕b3+.

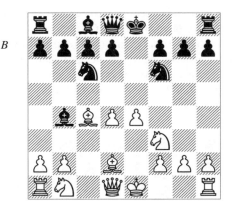

But although this meant that the classical treatment of the Giuoco Piano was saved, it also meant that its fate was sealed. For where once the greatest minds in the world of chess had delved into the inexhaustible riches of 7 ♘c3, modern-day students take note of the matter-of-fact statement that 7 ♗d2 ♗xd2+ 8 ♘bxd2 d5 9 exd5 ♘xd5 probably gives White little and move on to the next chapter.

Evans Gambit

4 b4 *(D)*

We now enter a world that must seem unreal, perhaps fairylike, to a modern chess-player. And this is hardly surprising for we are moving back more than a century and a half in time. Invented by Captain William Evans (1790-1872) and popularized by the famous matches between Labourdonnais and McDonnell in 1834, the Evans Gambit held the honorary title of 'queen of openings' for at least half a century. "This magnificent attacking game was invented to make man understand that chess is a gift from the gods" wrote Savielly Tartakower.

But even the Evans Gambit disappeared at the end of the 19th century, not so much for concrete reasons but rather as a natural result of the major changes in positional thinking of that era, when chess was transformed into the rational game we know today. Gone were the interest in and the intuitive understanding of the imaginative and opportunistic playing style that had marked chess in the 19th century and gone were the openings that expressed these ideals most clearly.

But it should not come as a big surprise that a full century later the Evans Gambit was rediscovered. In a time when traditional and dogmatic views are being challenged (and being overthrown in many cases) chess-players can be expected to be receptive to the beauty of the Evans Gambit once more.

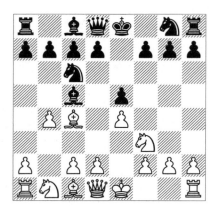

What then is this beauty?

By playing 4 b4, White offers a real gambit. He gives away a pawn, not intending to regain it quickly in one way or another, but to gain a tempo compared to the classical strategy of 4 c3 and 5 d4. It is the initiative that White is after, and he is working on the assumption that this initiative, once obtained, will more than compensate for the material deficit.

This is to a very large extent a matter of personal style and preference. Theory's task is to give an impartial evaluation of what is more important: initiative or material. But since these are basically incompatible factors, a truly objective assessment is very hard to come by.

4   ...   ♗xb4

Black can refuse the gambit by **4...♗b6**, but although this undoubtedly keeps the position simpler, it is by no means a refutation of 4 b4.

5   c3   ♗a5

Black's initial reaction was to play **5...♗c5**, after which 6 d4 exd4 7 0-0! was the standard continuation and highly characteristic of the dynamic way the Evans Gambit should be treated. The position after 7...d6 8 cxd4 ♗b6 was viewed as the Normal Position of the Evans Gambit throughout the 19th century. This is

where theoretical discussions had to start. Anderssen for one thought that White should play 9 d5 here, but first Morphy and later Chigorin considered 9 ♘c3 to be the critical line.

5...♗e7 6 d4 ♘a5 is a variation dating from and characteristic of the many years when the Evans Gambit was but a shadow of its former self. The idea is to meet 7 ♘xe5 with 7...♘xc4 8 ♘xc4 d5, simplifying the position and producing a type of position which is easily manageable and more or less equal. A handy line to have ready for those who are unlikely ever to face an Evans Gambit, but who do need to know something about it. But the false security offered by such a line was cruelly exposed by Garry Kasparov, when in 1995 he played, in the true spirit of the Evans, 7 ♗e2 exd4 8 ♕xd4. White refuses to win back the sacrificed pawn for so miserable a price and continues to play for the initiative.

We now return to 5...♗a5 (D):

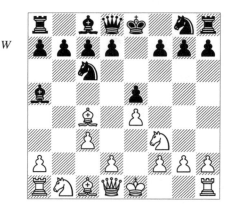

6   d4

The difference between 5...♗c5 and 5...♗a5 is that Black does not need to take on d4 now. Even so, it remains attractive to grab another pawn with **6...exd4** 7 0-0 and this was in fact one of the Gambit's main lines in the 19th century. The consistent follow-up 7...dxc3 in particular was very heavily analysed in those days.

With the rise of modern, positional chess the more solid **6...d6** came to the fore. Instead of taking an extra one or two pawns, Black is returning one (7 dxe5 dxe5 8 ♕xd8+ ♘xd8 9 ♘xe5). Here too, the spirit of the Evans Gambit dictates a more aggressive course, viz. 7 ♕b3. This too has been the subject of very deep investigations.

Nowadays, both moves are topical once more. Ancient theoretical views are being critically examined with surprising results. Anyone who is not averse to a little theoretical homework, and who has a flair for tactical play, might well have some real fun with the Evans Gambit.

Giuoco Pianissimo

4	♘c3	♘f6
5	d3	

If we compare this with the Evans Gambit, this no-nonsense set-up looks very tame indeed. But if White is determined to make the most of it, this variation offers plenty of scope.

5	...	d6

In every symmetrical position White has one weapon only: it is his move. He should play aggressively and force his opponent onto the defensive. There is only one move really which meets this requirement.

6	♗g5 (D)	

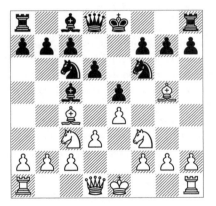

This is the starting point of this variation. Black has to find an answer to the threat of 7 ♘d5.

The most obvious solution is to play **6...h6**. Black is hoping for 7 ♗h4, when he will be able to break the pin against his knight by playing ...g5 at a moment of his own choosing. A drawback of this method is that it does not contribute

to a fast development. White can seek the initiative with 7 ♗xf6 ♕xf6 8 ♘d5 ♕d8 9 c3 followed by d4.

6...♘a5 is a sharper move. Nowadays White usually responds with the quiet 7 ♗b3, possibly followed by d4, but the older and more complicated main lines 7 ♘d5 and 7 ♗xf6 ♕xf6 8 ♘d5 ♕d8 9 b4 are still worthy of study.

3...♗c5 4 d3

4	d3	♘f6 (D)

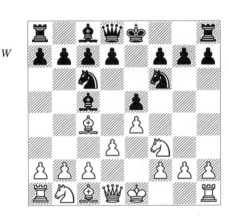

5	c3	

Naturally, 5 ♘c3 is the Giuoco Pianissimo again. With 5 c3 we are making a huge leap forward in time. Utterly neglected in antiquity, the idea of playing d3 and c3 became amazingly popular around 1980. It started with a few pioneers and some surprise victories, then came a phase of general curiosity which always follows success and then suddenly almost every 1 e4 player started using it. Almost overnight, this variation became *the* alternative to the Ruy Lopez. In fact the great attraction of this line is that White *is* virtually playing a Ruy Lopez, for the idea of playing d3 and c3 is a cautious yet fully realistic option in most lines of the Ruy Lopez and it does not really make a great difference whether White's bishop is on b5, a4 or c4. The positional aspects and the characteristic plans remain the same. In one variation there is even a direct transposition (see the line 3...♘f6 4 d3 ♗e7 on page 311).

5	...	a6

The most subtle reply. Black creates a square at a7 for his bishop, which will have to retreat anyway after a future b4 or d4. It goes without saying that the more down-to-earth moves **5...0-0** and **5...d6** are also quite playable.

<pre>
    6   0-0   ♗a7
    7   ♘bd2   d6
    8   ♗b3
</pre>

By now Black was threatening 8...♘a5 to exchange the white bishop.

<pre>
    8   ...   0-0 (D)
</pre>

Move-order is an extremely loose affair in this variation but the positional ideas and problems are perfectly clear.

The first important question is whether White is going to allow the pin ...♗g4 or if he prefers **9 h3**.

The same goes for Black. Should he prevent ♗g5 after a move like **9 ♘c4** or not? If he does not, opting, for instance, for the quiet developing move 9...♗e6, the next question is how to react to 10 ♗g5. The classical but double-edged method is to reply 10...h6 11 ♗h4 g5, when after 12 ♗g3 Black will want to establish firm control over the kingside with a manoeuvre like ...♘e7-g6-f4, but in the meantime White will try to break open the centre and occupy f5 with a knight.

Another positional problem that both players will have to solve is whether offering an exchange of bishops with ♗e3 or ...♗e6 makes sense, and if the answer is yes, should the recapture on e3 or e6 be made with a piece (rook or knight) or with the f-pawn? In the latter

case, after 9 ♘c4 h6 10 ♗e3 ♗xe3 11 fxe3, for instance, the open f-file may be useful, but White's pawn-formation has lost its flexibility.

Then there is the question of an advance in the centre, d4 for White and ...d5 for Black. Whoever gets this in first without any concrete problems is likely to obtain the initiative.

Finally, **9 ♖e1** followed by ♘f1-g3/e3 is a very natural manoeuvre, which again may be more or less copied by Black with ...♘e7-g6.

Two Knights Defence: 3...♘f6

<pre>
    3   ...   ♘f6 (D)
</pre>

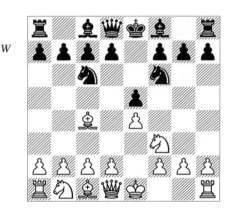

This move is more aggressive than 3...♗c5, since the knight is attacking e4. But it is also a tremendous provocation, for why on earth should White not respond with **4 ♘g5**, attacking f7?

We shall be looking at this move shortly. In fact, 3...♘f6 is a pawn sacrifice and 4 ♘g5 is the way to accept it, but there are great complications involved and not everyone will feel at home in this line.

White can also continue in a more 'normal' way and the most 'normal' thing to do is perhaps **4 d4**, a move which combines motifs from the Italian with the Scotch Opening. This variation, leading to an immediate struggle in the centre, has been heavily analysed. Although in some lines play becomes very complicated indeed, there are also a few lines where the tension is resolved rather quickly with a somewhat shallow middlegame lying ahead. For this reason 4 d4 is not seen very often in tournaments of the highest level any more.

The modern approach is **4 d3**, just as it is against 3...♗c5. White opts for a slow positional struggle, not for flashy tactical lines.

4 0-0, the move which is White's most dangerous reply to 3...♘f6 in the Ruy Lopez, is less to the point, the difference being that Black can simply play 4...♘xe4, when both 5 d4 and 5 ♖e1 (or 5 ♕e2) are countered by 5...d5, protecting the knight *and* attacking the bishop.

4 ♘c3 also shows up a negative side to 3 ♗c4, for far from defending e4, this move is actually an invitation to take it! After the standard combination 4...♘xe4! 5 ♘xe4 d5, followed, for instance, by 6 ♗d3 dxe4 7 ♗xe4 ♗d6, Black can be very satisfied with the result of the opening. He is able to develop his pieces freely and, with a pawn on e5, his central position is solid.

3...♘f6 4 ♘g5

4   ♘g5 *(D)*

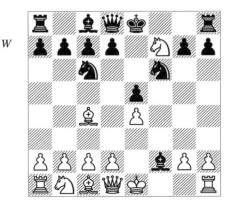

From this position, some of the most mysterious opening variations in chess take their cue.

4   ...   d5

This move may seem self-evident, almost forced really, but it is not, for Black has the most astonishing option of playing **4...♗c5**. This is the **Traxler** (or **Wilkes-Barre**) **Variation**, a rare bird in the tournament arena but the subject of fierce theoretical arguments among theoreticians for well over a century now. The

idea is twofold. If **5 ♗xf7+**, Black calmly replies 5...♔e7, judging (or hoping) that, after 6 ♗d5 ♖f8, for instance, his lead in development will compensate for the missing pawn. If this is already quite a show of optimism and boldness, it is nothing compared to what happens after **5 ♘xf7**, for in that case Black ignites an unparalleled display of fireworks with 5...♗xf2+! *(D)*.

There are two points justifying this sacrifice: **6 ♔xf2** is met by 6...♘xe4+ 7 ♔g1 ♕h4 8 g3 ♘xg3! and **6 ♔f1** by 6...♕e7 7 ♘xh8 d5 8 exd5 ♘d4 threatening 9...♗g4. In both cases Black's material deficit is almost too large to be measured, but the force of his attack is enough to chill one's blood.

Whether the Traxler will survive the test of new, computerized analysis is moot though. Black is aiming very high indeed and the slightest hiccup in one of the many variations may turn out to be a death warrant. But as an example of what can be achieved by imagination and courage, the Traxler deserves a very honourable mention indeed, even if it were to end up in a museum display case.

5   exd5

Now if Black has played 4...d5 with the intention of simply taking back on d5, he is in for a nasty surprise. As long ago as 1600 it was already common knowledge that **5...♘xd5** really invites White to offer a very dangerous knight sacrifice: **6 ♘xf7!?** ♔xf7 7 ♕f3+. It is true that a forced win for White has never been found against the only possible reply 7...♔e6, but one and a half centuries later it was established that the preliminary move **6 d4!** *(D)* is even stronger.

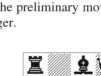

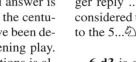

If 6...♘xd4 7 c3 Black simply loses a piece, while 6...exd4 7 0-0 gives White a terrific attack along the e-file. As a sample line, 7...♗e7 8 ♘xf7! ♚xf7 9 ♕h5+ ♚e6? loses to 10 ♖e1+.

Does this mean then that 4...d5 or even 3...♘f6 is just plain bad? Some players will say 'yes it is', but the official theoretical answer is somewhat different. In the course of the centuries, no fewer than three methods have been developed to try to justify Black's opening play. The positional outline of these variations is always the same: White's d5-pawn is liquidated in one way or another, leaving Black with full control over the centre. Black will also have a lead in development, for White's queenside is as yet fully undeveloped and both his c4-bishop and his g5-knight will be chased away.

But whether these lines really offer full compensation for the missing pawn is as unclear today as it was one or two hundred years ago. In the end, pawn sacrifices of this type are always a matter of taste. The materialistic type will always prefer White, while those with a hankering for the initiative will be inclined to favour Black.

5   ...   ♘a5

This has always been Black's most popular move, but **5...♘d4** and even the amazing **5...b5** have also had their followers over the years.

5...♘d4 is based on the highly imaginative idea 6 c3 b5! 7 ♗f1 ♘xd5 *(D)*.

Black need not be afraid of **8 cxd4** ♕xg5 9 ♗xb5+ ♚d8 and the quieter **8 ♘e4** ♘e6 9

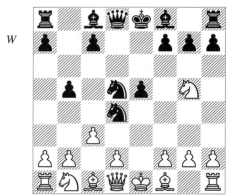

♗xb5+ ♗d7 also offers him a solid lead in development.

Playing **5...b5** immediately is a refinement of the same idea. Paradoxically, **6 ♗xb5** ♕xd5 gives Black the initiative while the highly unlikely retreat **6 ♗f1** is the real fighting option, for if now 6...♕xd5 White has the powerful reply 7 ♘c3 (and only then 8 ♗xb5) and 6...♘xd5 is answered by 7 ♗xb5, when Black can no longer reply ...♕d5. Black's strongest moves are considered to be 6...♘d4 (when 7 c3 transposes to the 5...♘d4 variation) and 6...h6.

6   ♗b5+

6 d3 is an alternative of long standing, the principled reply being 6...h6 7 ♘f3 e4.

6   ...   c6
7   dxc6   bxc6
8   ♗e2   h6 *(D)*

The dividends of 4 ♘g5 have been reaped, but now the price has to be paid. The knight has no safe retreat.

This is the main starting position of the 5...♞a5 variation.

9 ♞f3 is the classical move. Black will continue to harass the knight with 9...e4 10 ♞e5 and now, for example, 10...♝d6.

9 ♞h3 leaves the knight standing rather offside, but has the advantage of allowing White to develop his queenside more quickly and to stabilize his central position with d3.

3...♞f6 4 d4

    4   d4 *(D)*

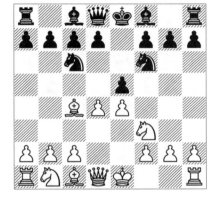

This move is based on a perception of the opening problems which is very different from 4 ♞g5. If the latter move can be summarized as simply accepting the pawn sacrifice inherent in 3...♞f6, 4 d4 is exactly the opposite: White sacrifices a pawn himself. His aim is quick development and an open centre. He is hoping to obtain the initiative rather than gain material.

This used to be an important variation, especially during the 19th century, but nowadays any well-informed player will have little difficulty in neutralizing the dangers. As a result, 4 d4 has lost much of its former charm.

    4   ...   exd4

In case of **4...♞xe4 5 dxe5**, White can be satisfied. Thanks to the position of White's bishop on c4, Black is unable to play ...d5 and White is threatening to win immediately with 6 ♛d5.

    5   0-0 *(D)*

The classical move, dating back to the glory days of the 4 d4 variation. White is daring his

opponent either to take yet another pawn, on e4, or else to secure the pawn he has already won.

The seemingly very aggressive **5 e5** is in fact more cautious. Black's traditional reply is 5...d5, when after 6 ♝b5 ♞e4 7 ♞xd4 ♝d7 8 ♝xc6 bxc6 9 0-0 White has regained his pawn with approximately equal chances. In recent years the more provocative 5...♞g4 has become increasingly popular.

The simple recapture, **5 ♞xd4**, is not a serious option, for it allows Black to take on e4 without any problems.

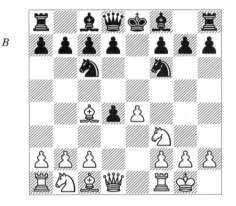

The main lines in this position are **5...♝c5** and **5...♞xe4**, but Black is not forced to play so sharply. A solid reply like **5...d6** 6 ♞xd4 ♝e7 7 ♞c3 0-0 is perfectly legitimate, although this is of course slightly passive. In fact, the position strongly resembles a Ruy Lopez Steinitz Variation (see page 272).

3...♞f6 4 d4 exd4 5 0-0 ♝c5

    5   ...   ♝c5

It was mainly this move which attracted all the attention in the 19th century. Black provokes a sharp reaction, which is known as the **Max Lange Attack**.

    6   e5 *(D)*

    6   ...   d5

Against 5 e5 (with the bishop still at f8) this was the solid option and 5...♞g4 the more provocative one. Here it is exactly the other way round. **6...♞g4** is the cautious move. By lashing

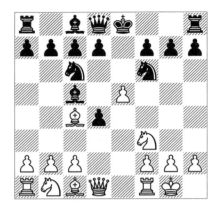

out with 6...d5, Black is really playing for all or nothing.

7	exf6	dxc4
8	♖e1+	♗e6
9	♘g5	

This introduces the main line of the Max Lange. **9 fxg7** is an alternative.

9	...	♕d5
10	♘c3	

Would not most of us just love to play a move like this?

10	...	♕f5
11	♘ce4 *(D)*	

The great theoretical battle starts here. Has White really achieved anything with his aggressive opening play or can Black breathe freely, having carefully ducked a few blows?

Despite tremendous analytical effort (especially in the 19th and early 20th century) this remains an open question. Opening manuals usually assess the position as 'unclear', which means they just do not know. Personally, I think that the variation 4 d4 and 5 0-0 would be tremendously popular if it were not for Black's alternative on move five that we are about to discuss.

3...♘f6 4 d4 exd4 5 0-0 ♘xe4

5	...	♘xe4

Superficially, this looks riskier than 5...♗c5, but it is this very move which allows Black to look to the future with confidence. By eliminating White's e-pawn, Black drastically reduces his opponent's firepower.

6	♖e1	d5 *(D)*

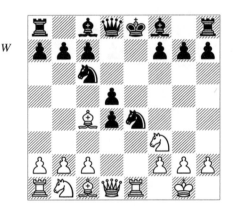

We have seen several instances of Black combining defence and attack with this move, delaying White's attack. This is the first time we have come across a position where there is no need for White to withdraw the bishop.

7	♗xd5

This move may cause some momentary confusion when first seen. Is this really possible? But once we get the point, we may wonder whether it is perhaps an idea to turn the moves around and play the even more spectacular **7 ♘c3**. This is the **Canal Variation**, one of those ancient Italian lines that have been hidden in a museum for many decades. After 7...dxc3 8 ♗xd5, both 8...f5 9 ♘g5 ♗d6 and 8...♗e6 favour Black.

7	...	♕xd5
8	♘c3 *(D)*	

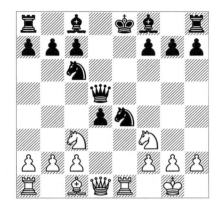

This move, which takes advantage of two different pins, justifies White's opening play. Probably because it is such fun to play a move like this, the variation has always been fairly popular at club level. But opening theory holds a chilly view on this line. After **8...♕a5 9 ♘xe4 ♗e6 10 ♘eg5 0-0-0 11 ♘xe6 fxe6 12 ♖xe6**, for instance, White has regained all of the material sacrificed, but he has given away the initiative he once had, and Black has nothing to worry about.

4 d3

> **4   d3**

This is the twin brother of 3...♗c5 4 d3 (see page 305), to which **4...♗c5** now transposes. But Black has a perfectly sound alternative.

> **4   ...   ♗e7**

The bishop will be less active on e7 (compared to the c5-square) for the time being, but on the other hand Black does not now have to worry about the consequences of d4 or b4. He can concentrate on a straightforward development of his pieces.

> **5   0-0   0-0** *(D)*

This position is critical. It is quite clear what White's general idea is, but there is the difficult problem of move-order. If Black plays the modest ...d6, White will want to reply c3 and ♘bd2, much the same as in the d3 lines of the Ruy Lopez. But in this position, Black still has the trump card ...d5 up his sleeve. This makes the situation delicate and theoretically interesting.

6 c3 is the nice and straightforward method, but unfortunately this move is precisely what

makes 6...d5 so attractive, because in the rather open position which arises after 7 exd5 ♘xd5 the weakening of White's d3-pawn is a telling factor. For example, the plausible 8 ♖e1 may be met by 8...♗g4 9 h3 ♗h5. If 10 g4 ♗g6 11 ♘xe5 ♘xe5 12 ♖xe5, Black has 12...♘b6!, subtly putting his finger on the weak spot.

For this reason, **6 ♖e1** is often played. This prevents ...d5, but White will now have to take care that his king's bishop does not get exchanged after 6...d6, threatening 7...♘a5. In this position a remarkable transposition to a line of the Ruy Lopez is hidden: after 7 c3 ♘a5 8 ♗b5 a6 9 ♗a4 b5 10 ♗c2 c5 we have the same position as after 3 ♗b5 a6 4 ♗a4 ♘f6 5 0-0 ♗e7 6 ♖e1 b5 7 ♗b3 d6 8 c3 0-0 and now 9 d3 (instead of 9 h3 – see page 288) 9...♘a5 10 ♗c2 c5. I have not mentioned this as a separate variation in the chapter on the Ruy Lopez, but it is in fact fairly often played by people wishing to avoid the heavily-analysed 9 h3 lines.

This clearly shows how delicate a task evaluating the position after 5...0-0 has become. In fact White has a third option, which is to play **6 ♗b3**. With his pawn still on c2, White is happy to allow 6...d5 and if 6...d6 he will play 7 c3, taking the game into well-known territory. With the bishop already on b3, White will meet 7...♘a5 with 8 ♗c2, without having to waste time on ♗c4-b5-a4-c2. It is interesting though that the truly bold meet 7 c3 with 7...d5 regardless of having played 6...d6 one move before. Obviously, they feel that the weakening of d3 compensates for the loss of tempo involved in ...d6-d5, a decidedly unorthodox point of view.

Scotch Opening

1	e4	e5
2	♘f3	♘c6
3	d4 *(D)*	

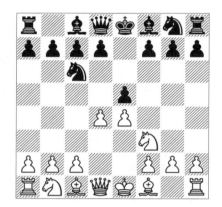

In the previous two chapters, we have seen several methods for White to seek an advantage in the centre, most of them based on long-term planning and very often involving c3 in preparation of d4. By playing 3 d4 straightaway, White chooses a different approach: clear, uncomplicated and above all direct. White creates a half-open centre where he can count on a spatial advantage and easy development for all his pieces. It may also be counted as an advantage that White determines the character of the opening (and probably the middlegame too) himself, unlike the Ruy Lopez where he has to be prepared for a great number of widely different variations.

The downside of this carefree approach is that it also clears the view for the opponent. Black enjoys similarly easy development and he is still free to adapt his plans exactly to the type of position that White has now created. This is a marked advantage over some lines of the Ruy Lopez where Black has already walled in his dark-squared bishop with ...d6 before White plays d4, for instance in the Steinitz Variation (3 ♗b5 d6 4 d4).

3	...	exd4
4	♘xd4	

The history of the Scotch is an interesting one. It became popular after a correspondence match between chess clubs from Edinburgh and London, which lasted from 1824 to 1828 and gave the opening its name. But this popularity was based on **4 ♗c4** (nowadays referred to as the **Scotch Gambit**), an approach which is considered fairly harmless if Black calmly replies 4...♘f6, transposing to the 4 d4 line of the Two Knights Defence that we discussed in the previous chapter (see page 309). Simply recapturing on d4 was thought to be harmless and it even had the reputation of being a 'drawing weapon' for a very long time. It was thought to show a lack of interest in maintaining the required tension in the position. But in 1990 the Scotch received a tremendous boost when Garry Kasparov used it to good effect in a match for the world championship against Anatoly Karpov. Almost overnight, the Scotch was transformed from a dusty museum piece into a dynamic modern opening. It is now seen as White's most important alternative to the Ruy Lopez.

White has a third option in **4 c3**, the **Göring Gambit**. This opening has always lived on the outskirts of opening theory, in the twilight zone where distrust and scepticism meet with fanaticism and where things are hardly ever seen in a clear light. It is a real gambit where White dares his opponent to capture one or even two pawns while he develops his pieces quickly and aggressively. By playing **4...dxc3** 5 ♘xc3 (5 ♗c4 is an option) followed, for instance, by 5...♗b4 6 ♗c4 d6 Black accepts the challenge, but eager devotees of the Göring also have to take the unsentimental **4...d5** into account. After 5 exd5 ♕xd5 6 cxd4 White suddenly faces a situation which differs greatly from what he was (perhaps) expecting. In a rather rigid position, the question is now a positional one: is White's isolated queen's pawn going to be weak or strong?

We now return to 4 ♘xd4 *(D)*:

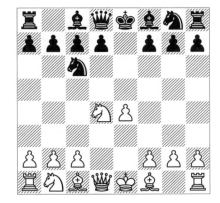

There are two main lines in this position, both aimed at obtaining active counterplay against White's central position: **4...♗c5** and **4...♘f6**.

Of the alternatives, **4...♕h4** is the most noteworthy, mainly because it may come as a great shock to one who is unprepared. This looks very aggressive, but in fact what is required to play such a move with any degree of success is mainly good defensive skills. White is practically forced to sacrifice his e-pawn (which implies that the Scotch is really a gambit!), yet by doing so he obtains a truly dangerous initiative. An important starting point for this variation arises after 5 ♘c3 ♗b4 6 ♗e2 ♕xe4 7 ♘b5. If, for example, 7...♗xc3+ 8 bxc3 ♔d8 9 0-0 Black has won a pawn, but with his king in the middle of the board he faces a difficult defensive task.

4...♗c5

4 ... ♗c5

This is the older of the two main lines. White has a wide variety of possible replies. There was a time when only **5 ♗e3** was thought to be correct, but nowadays **5 ♘xc6** is at least as important, with **5 ♘b3** a solid third option.

5 ♘f5 is played less often, although there seems to be no clear reason why this should be so. In the course of well over a century, both the sharp replies 5...d6 and 5...d5 (based on the

idea 6 ♘xg7+ ♔f8 7 ♘h5 ♕h4 8 ♘g3 ♘f6 and Black takes over the initiative) and the more cautious 5...♕f6 and 5...g6 have been tried.

4...♗c5 5 ♗e3

5 ♗e3

The classical reply. It is an attractive move for White if only because he is now threatening to win a piece by 6 ♘xc6, which means that Black is not free to continue his development with moves like 5...♘f6 or 5...♘ge7. On the other hand, Black has a vicious reply:

5 ... ♕f6

All of a sudden it is White who has to be careful.

6 c3

It is a pity for White to have to play this move, for he would of course have liked to reserve this square for his queen's knight, but the only alternative is to play the ultra-sharp **6 ♘b5 ♗xe3 7 fxe3** and there are few players who trust this. White needs to be prepared for the complications of 7...♕h4+ 8 g3 ♕xe4 *and* he has to value his attacking chances after 7...♕d8 or 8...♕d8 enough not to worry about his ruined pawn-structure.

6 ... ♘ge7 *(D)*

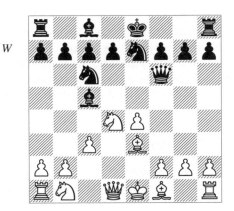

For a long time this was thought to be a very comfortable position for Black. After a neutral developing move like **7 ♗e2**, Black can indeed rest assured, for he then has the opportunity of lashing out with 7...d5, eliminating White's e-pawn and equalizing very easily. Other moves, like **7 g3** or **7 ♘c2**, are solid but hardly promising for White.

But in 1991 the 4...♗c5 variation was transformed by the sudden reappearance of **7 ♗c4** *(D)* on the scene.

This was a move that had been dismissed as early as the 19th century, with opening manuals reducing it to a mere footnote saying "7...♘e5 8 ♗e2 ♕g6 9 0-0 d5 is very good for Black", or even omitted it altogether. But now it turned out that 10 ♗h5! is a very strong continuation of the above variation, for after 10...♕xe4 11 ♘d2 Black is in great trouble. No other ways of casually refuting 7 ♗c4 were found, and a true hype was launched, which put not just 7 ♗c4, but also the Scotch Opening as a whole, on the agenda of almost every top player. Theory of this line has been completely rewritten and now contains many a sharp variation, full of pawn sacrifices and other materially unbalanced positions.

4...♗c5 5 ♘xc6

5   ♘xc6

Around 1994, the world had more or less recovered from the 7 ♗c4 shock when a new problem arose. After 5 ♗e3 had been transformed from a rather slack move into a dangerous attacking weapon, it turned out that 5 ♘xc6 was also not the innocent move it had been thought for years.

But in this case the problems are of a purely positional nature. Within a few years, theoretical assessments of certain characteristic positions changed dramatically.

5   ...   ♕f6

This surprising move had been the reason why 5 ♘xc6 was never taken very seriously. It is not that Black is intending to recapture on c6 with the queen (for c6 would not be a good square), but by threatening mate on f2 Black forces his opponent to make an 'awkward' move. There is no comfortable way of protecting f2. He must either advance wildly with **6 f4** or put his queen on an 'awkward' square. It needed a player of the calibre of World Champion Garry Kasparov to assure the chess world that this is not a problem for White:

6   ♕d2 *(D)*

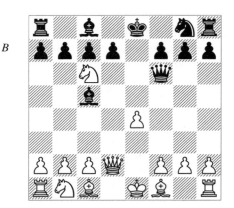

White's idea is very simple. He wants to demonstrate that after **6...dxc6** (which was always regarded as the best way to recapture) Black will experience long-term problems, especially in the endgame. White plays 7 ♘c3, intending to meet the natural developing move 7...♘e7 with 8 ♕f4, inviting an exchange of queens. This approach turned out to contain a good deal more venom than had been thought. Black has plenty of open files for his pieces but it is not so easy to create active play and White's pawn-majority on the kingside is patiently waiting to move forward. Little by little, alternative responses for Black were investigated, starting with the question of how to recapture on c6.

Interest in **6...♕xc6** has never been great. Both Black's queen and his bishop are liable to be harassed, for instance by 7 ♗d3 ♘e7 8 0-0 0-0 9 b4 ♗d4 10 c3 ♗b6 11 c4.

6...bxc6 on the other hand has become more and more popular. Black accepts a position which is a little cramped at first, but is very solid. 7 ♗d3 ♘e7 8 0-0 0-0 9 ♘c3 d5 is a plausible continuation.

4...♗c5 5 ♘b3

5 ♘b3

White avoids complications.

5 ... ♗b6

This is of course the natural reply, but it also allows White to show the main point of his knight retreat.

6 a4 a6

6...a5 would be met in the same way.

7 ♘c3 *(D)*

White continues to harass the black bishop. He intends 8 ♘d5, when 9 ♘xb6 is a very real positional threat, now that Black can no longer take back on b6 with the a-pawn.

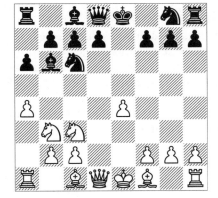

Black has tried all sorts of moves in this position. The most aggressive option is to play **7...♕f6**, but this has the drawback of inviting an equally sharp reply, viz. 8 ♕e2 ♘ge7 9 ♘d5 ♘xd5 10 exd5+ ♘e7 and now 11 a5 ♗a7 12 h4 threatening 13 ♗g5.

7...d6 is the more solid move. Black simply accepts the loss of tempo entailed in 8 ♘d5 ♗a7 and intends to exchange or chase away the knight with ...♗e6 or ...♘f6. After 9 ♗e3 ♗xe3 10 ♘xe3 the position is rather static.

4...♘f6

4 ... ♘f6 *(D)*

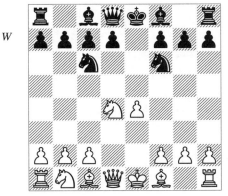

White now faces a very concrete problem. How is he to protect e4 without hampering the natural flow of his active piece development?

The simplest answer is to play **5 ♘c3**, but this rather invites Black to continue the attack against e4 by playing 5...♗b4 and cannot be seen as a permanent solution. Still, this is a classical variation, called the **Scotch Four Knights Game**.

5 ♘xc6 is a much more radical approach. White questions the soundness of Black's previous move, for he intends to meet 5...bxc6 with 6 e5, taking over the initiative. This is the **Mieses Variation**. It is one of the oldest yet one of the most hotly debated variations of the Scotch today. Some highly unorthodox and very complicated positions are likely to arise.

Scotch Four Knights Game

5 ♘c3

This position is equally relevant to the Four Knights Game, where it is reached via 3 ♘c3 ♘f6 4 d4 exd4 5 ♘xd4.

5 ... ♗b4 *(D)*

The classical reply. Now White has nothing better than to take on c6 after all.

6 ♘xc6 bxc6

7 ♗d3

7 e5 ♕e7 8 ♕e2, analogous to the Mieses Variation, is not nearly as strong in this case

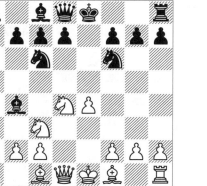

because after 8...♞d5 White cannot continue 9 c4.

| **7** | **...** | **d5** |

Thanks to his two previous moves, Black can now afford to make this aggressive step forward. **8 e5** is not a dangerous reply in view of 8...♞g4 9 ♗f4 f6, and so White has little choice: he will have to accept the elimination of his central stronghold.

| **8** | **exd5** | **cxd5** |
| **9** | **0-0** | **0-0** |

Black has achieved a great deal. He can develop his pieces freely and instead of facing a dominant white pawn on e4, he has a central pawn-majority himself. But White still has one trump card up his sleeve and this is a rather formidable one:

| **10** | **♗g5 (D)** | |

By thus pinning Black's king's knight, White makes it clear that there is also a downside to Black's aggressive opening play. 11 ♗xf6 is threatened, so Black has to protect d5.

This is the most important starting position of the Scotch Four Knights Game. **10...♗e6** and **10...c6** are the main lines.

In both cases Black has to be prepared for 11 ♕f3, confronting Black (again) with the possibility of ♗xf6 and initiating a potentially dangerous concentration of attacking forces against Black's king. The variation **10...c6** 11 ♕f3 ♗e7 12 ♖ae1 h6 13 ♗xh6!? gxh6 14 ♕e3 is illustrative of the situation's volatility. This position has been studied for well over a century and the conclusion is that 14...d4! 15 ♕xh6 ♕d6! forces White to take a draw by perpetual check, an

assessment which has saddled the Scotch Four Knights Game with the stigma of being a drawish opening. This is doing this ancient opening a terrible injustice! There is plenty of scope for both sides to deviate from the above variation.

Black also has to take the manoeuvre ♞e2 into account. Especially if Black plays **10...♗e6**, this looks rather inviting, with 11 ♞e2 ♗e7 12 ♞d4 as a plausible continuation, but also after 10...c6 there is no reason why White has to avoid 11 ♞e2.

A modern variation on this theme is to play ♞a4, for instance after 10...c6, when 11 ♞a4 signals White's intention to concentrate his forces on the queenside rather than against Black's king. He may start a frontal attack against Black's centre with c4, but c3 followed by b4 is also an option.

Mieses Variation

| **5** | **♞xc6** | **bxc6** |
| **6** | **e5** | |

The quiet continuation **6 ♗d3** offers White no better chances after 6...d5 than the Scotch Four Knights Game does. By playing 6 e5, White really sets the position on fire. This variation became tremendously popular when Garry Kasparov revitalized it in 1990.

| **6** | **...** | **♕e7** |

From a purely positional point of view, this is of course an awkward move, as the queen blocks the way for the bishop. But the strength of the move is that it forces White to do exactly the same! The alternatives **6...♘e4** and **6...♘d5** only appear safer. In reality they give White far too much freedom to utilize his spatial advantage.

> 7 **♕e2** **♘d5**
> 8 **c4** *(D)*

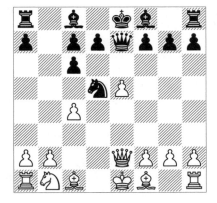

B

This is the critical position of the Mieses Variation and quite possibly of the entire Scotch Opening. White wants to chase the knight away from d5 and develop his pieces as aggressively as possible. Black has set his sights on attacking e5. The character of the middlegame will be determined by the method he chooses for doing so.

8...♗a6 is the sharpest option. For a long time this move was even thought to be self-evident. Black's motto here is 'Never move backwards until forced to do so!'. This attitude leads to great complications. A few of the problems that have to be solved:

a) After 9 b3 0-0-0 10 g3 ♖e8 11 ♗b2 f6 12 ♗g2 fxe5, is Black happy with the extra pawn or will he suffer from the chaotic state of his piece development?

b) Which side stands to gain from the wild variation 9 b3 ♕h4 10 a3 ♗c5 11 g3 ♗xf2+?

Both 12 ♔xf2 ♕d4+ and 12 ♕xf2 ♕e4+ cost White a rook, but will Black manage to bring his queen to safety after 12 ♕xf2 ♕e4+ 13 ♔d1 ♕xh1 14 ♘d2?

These are just a few of the many important variations, but they give one a good impression of the kind of very difficult positional assessments that lie ahead if Black chooses the ambitious 8...♗a6.

In the course of the 1990s, it gradually became clear that Black might as well try **8...♘b6** *(D)*.

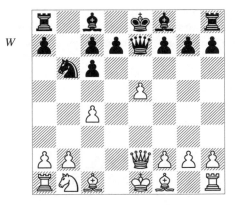

W

In many cases an advance of the a-pawn will come in handy, for instance after **9 ♘d2**: 9...a5 10 g3 ♕e6 11 b3 a4. And ...♗a6 remains an option. If **9 ♘c3**, for example, 9...♕e6 10 ♕e4 ♗a6, with the idea of answering 11 b3 with 11...♗b4 12 ♗d2 ♗xc3 13 ♗xc3 d5, is critical.

The Mieses Variation demands great versatility from both players: accurate calculations, a feeling for dynamic positions with unbalanced material, but also subtle positional judgement. What should one think, for instance, of the endgame that arises if in the last-mentioned variation Black plays 10...d5 11 exd6 cxd6 (instead of 10...♗a6)?

Four Knights Game

1	e4	e5
2	♘f3	♘c6
3	♘c3 (D)	

Compared to 3 ♗b5, 3 ♗c4 and 3 d4, this is a neutral, almost a waiting move. Black is not immediately put under pressure, so one would expect there to be a large choice of possible replies now. Strangely enough, this turns out not to be the case and it is precisely this aspect, the fact that Black does not have a wide range of replies, which makes this an attractive opening for White. To begin with, there is just one response to 3 ♘c3 which theory unreservedly approves of.

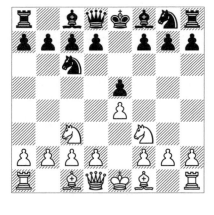

3	...	♘f6

With this move, we have reached the Four Knights Game, so named for obvious reasons.

There are alternatives, naturally, but none of them comes without certain problems. The following lines are known collectively by the equally logical name of the **Three Knights Game**.

The seemingly natural **3...♗c5**, for instance, runs into 4 ♘xe5!, a standard combination which we have already seen in the Two Knights Defence (with colours reversed: 3 ♗c4 ♘f6 4 ♘c3 ♘xe4). Both 4...♘xe5 5 d4 and 4...♗xf2+

5 ♔xf2 ♘xe5 6 d4 offer White splendid prospects of central domination and fast piece development.

3...♗b4 may be playable, but it certainly looks strange to provoke the aggressive and sound reply 4 ♘d5 like this.

3...d6 4 d4 is just a passive version of the Scotch.

3...g6 is probably Black's best bet if he does not want to play 3...♘f6 for some reason, but even this move has never really caught on. After 4 d4 exd4 5 ♘xd4 ♗g7 6 ♗e3 Black's chances are somewhere in between 3...♘f6 4 d4 exd4 5 ♘xd4 ♗b4 (see page 315), where Black exerts serious pressure against White's centre, and 3...d6 4 d4 exd4 5 ♘xd4, where Black remains passive (for the time being). Black's bishop is undoubtedly well-placed on g7, but White's freedom of movement is considerably greater than if the bishop were on b4.

We now return to 3...♘f6 (D):

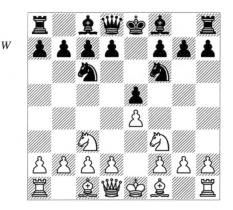

Like all 1 e4 e5 openings, the Four Knights Game is a very old opening, dating back at least to the 16th century. But it was only when modern, positional chess took over from the old romantic school that its merits were fully appreciated. In the early 20th century, the Four

Knights Game was very popular indeed. This heyday was followed by a long period of neglect, when it began to be associated in people's minds with ideas of safety, avoiding risks and avoiding a fight altogether. Playing 3 ♘c3 even began to be seen as a tacit draw offer.

But around 1990, this sad period of slow decay came to an abrupt halt. Many variations were injected with fresh ideas and renewed enthusiasm, and it was again played at the highest level of tournament chess. The Four Knights Game is now completely accepted once more as an opening which is indeed safe, but not at all devoid of tension or attacking power. White has plenty of means to try to make things difficult for his opponent, if he so desires.

4   ♗b5

The classical move in this position. White adopts the idea of the Ruy Lopez, hoping that the addition of ♘c3 and ...♘f6 will be in his favour.

4 d4 is an equally natural move. This leads to the Scotch Four Knights Game after 4...exd4 5 ♘xd4 (see page 315), but White has a surprising and very aggressive (and risky!) alternative in 5 ♘d5 *(D)*, avoiding the disagreeable pin 5 ♘xd4 ♗b4 in rather a drastic fashion.

This is the **Belgrade Gambit**. White is hoping to tempt Black into the complications of **5...♘xe4** 6 ♕e2 f5 7 ♘g5. This is very treacherous ground indeed, with 7...d3 8 cxd3 ♘d4 9 ♕h5+ g6 10 ♕h4 as an intimidating main line. After many decades of practical tests and analysis, theory still does not know what to think of

this. But it is important to know that Black is not forced to enter these complications. The simple developing move **5...♗e7** is a perfectly sound alternative.

4 g3 is a relatively new variation. It was inspired by the recent success of a similar line in the Vienna Opening (see page 342) and is a perfect example of the modern interpretation of the Four Knights Game. If Black replies by doing what White has just refused to do, viz. taking the initiative in the centre by 4...d5 5 exd5 ♘xd5, the situation is very similar to the 3...g6 line, but the extra tempo (♘f3) makes White's position much more promising than Black's in the analogous situation. For this reason, many players prefer quieter moves like 4...♗b4 or 4...♗c5, keeping the centre closed. Either way, the 4 g3 variation usually leads to some fierce fighting in the middlegame and is a far cry from what was once thought to be a drawish opening.

If White is thinking of developing his bishop to c4, he should prefer to do so a move earlier, for **4 ♗c4** runs into 4...♘xe4!, a trap we have already noted in the chapter on the Italian Game (see page 307).

We now return to 4 ♗b5 *(D)*:

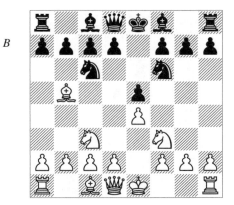

One major difference from the Ruy Lopez is that Black cannot get away so easily with **4...a6**, for 5 ♗xc6 dxc6 6 ♘xe5 is then a highly realistic option. It is true that Black regains the pawn by playing 6...♘xe4 7 ♘xe4 ♕d4, but after the simple 8 0-0 ♕xe5 9 ♖e1 or 9 d4 White has a very comfortable lead in development.

4...d6 too, though playable, is hardly a test of the soundness of the Four Knights Game: after 5 d4 we find ourselves in the Ruy Lopez Steinitz Variation (see page 272).

This means that Black has to play more aggressively. Two main lines have been developed over the years, both with a character of their own: the symmetrical **4...♗b4** and the sharp **4...♘d4**.

4...♗b4

4	...	♗b4

After this move there is not much sense in taking on c6 and e5, for Black can do the same on c3 and e4. Nor is **5 ♘d5** to be feared because of 5...♘xd5 6 exd5 e4!, which is in fact a standard tactic to note. It plays a major part in the 4...♘d4 line.

5	0-0	0-0
6	d3	d6
7	♗g5 *(D)*	

This is the crucial position of the 4...♗b4 variation. No matter how innocent the previous moves may seem, this is a truly interesting and tense situation.

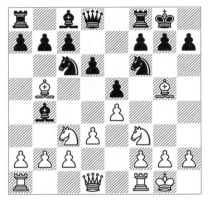

White is threatening 8 ♘d5. If Black has no wish to try something risky like **7...♗g4** or **7...♘e7**, he should eliminate White's queen's knight by **7...♗xc3**. This exchange changes the character of the position considerably. After 8 bxc3 White has increased his control over the centre squares, which means that he can play d4 at his leisure, without having to worry about

...exd4 any more, since that would only provide White with a very powerful central formation after cxd4. This again means that Black will probably have to remain passive in the centre. On the other hand, having doubled c-pawns means that White will not be able to create any inroads on the queenside by means of pawn-breaks. The standard plan of playing d4-d5 followed by c4, b4 and c5 is no longer feasible.

The result is that play is likely to become slow and based on long-term planning and will require patience and good positional skills from both players. Both sides will be searching for a weak spot in the opponent's armour. A classical continuation is 8...♕e7 9 ♖e1 ♘d8 10 d4 ♘e6 (a standard unpinning manoeuvre) 11 ♗c1 (the bishop has fulfilled its job at g5 and now retreats; 11 ♗h4 would allow 11...♘f4) and now, for instance, 11...c5. This is in fact a cunning way to protect e5: if 12 dxe5 dxe5 13 ♘xe5?? ♘c7! White loses a piece.

4...♘d4

4	...	♘d4 *(D)*

This aggressive move was responsible for the gradual disappearance of the Four Knights Game around 1920. Players on the white side became discouraged, doubts were raised as to the correctness of 4 ♗b5 and after a while everybody went back to playing the 'regular' Ruy Lopez again: 3 ♗b5. It took seventy years for this deadlock to be broken. When at the end of the 20th century a fresh interest in other moves than 3 ♗b5 took hold of the chess world, this variation too was re-examined and found to be far more interesting than had been thought.

Black sacrifices a pawn for the initiative. That is most certainly a reasonable proposition, but exactly *how* reasonable? Is the initiative worth *more* than a pawn? Is it *almost* worth a pawn? Is it just enough? It is these delicate assessments which become ever more subtle and ever more accurate when a variation gets analysed ever more deeply. In fact, this discussion has not come to an end yet (and is perhaps unlikely ever to do so), but what has become perfectly clear is that here a small part of opening theory which was thought to be dead has fully come back to life again.

In the position after 4...♘d4, several moves have been tried.

To begin with, **5 ♘xe5** needs to be examined. It is obvious that Black regains the pawn if he just plays 5...♕e7 6 f4 ♘xb5 7 ♘xb5 d6, but it is less clear how the position after 8 ♘f3 ♕xe4+ 9 ♔f2 should be evaluated. Is Black's queen in trouble or not?

5 ♘xd4 exd4 6 e5 is a very different idea. White offers a pawn himself, hoping to obtain a strong initiative after 6...dxc3 7 exf6, when 7...cxd2+ 8 ♗xd2 ♕xf6 9 0-0 allows White a tremendous lead in development. Unfortunately Black neutralizes this idea pretty easily by playing 7...♕xf6 8 dxc3 ♕e5+, forcing his opponent either to offer an exchange of queens (9 ♕e2) or to retreat the bishop (9 ♗e2).

But the really critical test of 4...♘d4 is thought to be a calm retreat of the bishop, thus keeping up the pressure on Black's position. There are two ways of accomplishing this. One is **5 ♗c4**, but by far the most popular move is the Ruy Lopez-oriented...

5   ♗a4 (D)

White allows his opponent to solve the problem of how to protect e5 very simply with 5...♘xf3+, relying on the small yet tangible lead in development that he enjoys after 6 ♕xf3. Most 4...♘d4 players are unlikely to go in for this rather tame line, for the whole point of this variation is that the dominant position of his knight provides Black with the chance of obtaining the initiative, even at the cost of a pawn.

B

5   ...   ♗c5

This is the move that gave White a real headache in the early decades of the 20th century. Black continues to develop his pieces aggressively without minding the loss of his e-pawn. It is also the move at which rehabilitation work of some seventy years later first took aim. Nowadays players are not so sure any more whether Black's compensation is fully adequate.

This uncertainty has caused a search for alternatives and has led to the rediscovery of **5...c6**. The idea is to meet 6 ♘xe5 with 6...d6 7 ♘f3 ♗g4, when the pin against his king's knight is very annoying for White. Analysis of this new line is still in full swing.

6   ♘xe5   0-0

Black's play may seem almost too casual: he simply continues to develop his pieces without worrying about material or the fact that White now forces back some of his most actively posted pieces with 7 ♘d3 ♗b6 8 e5 ♘e8. But the crux of the matter is that White's queenside is difficult to develop and this problem is only aggravated by these moves, for it is now not just Black's d4-knight, but also his own d3-knight which is blocking White's d-pawn and thereby causing all the congestion. Black will open the centre with ...d6 and if White is not careful this may cause real trouble for him. But of course it is in the accuracy of solving these problems that theory has made progress. Nowadays, among many options, 9 ♘d5, freeing the way for c3, has become the main line. It is the starting move for some very thoroughly analysed variations.

Petroff Defence

1	e4	e5
2	♘f3	♘f6 (D)

By playing this move, Black approaches the position in a way which can be described as the diametric opposite of 2...♘c6. Instead of defending his e-pawn, Black copies his opponent and attacks e4. This may seem more aggressive, but the idea is in fact to keep the position (relatively) simple and straightforward.

In case both e-pawns disappear, the remaining pawn-formation will be symmetrical. Anyone hoping to achieve an opening advantage from such a position should basically focus on two stratagems. In the first place, both players will be trying to develop their pieces as quickly and as aggressively as possible, a strategy which often involves pawn sacrifices. Secondly, one needs good technique and a lot of patience to make the most of every positional advantage that happens to come one's way, no matter how insignificant it may seem.

The Petroff was a popular opening in the 19th century, but then fell into disgrace (getting stigmatized as a drawish opening, quite unjustly so) until it was resurrected around 1980. Among the present top grandmasters, there is almost no one who does not play the Petroff at

least occasionally. In fact, this opening is probably much more popular among the world's best players than at club level – a paradoxical situation if one considers that the Petroff usually produces fairly simple positions strategically. Would it not seem that 'simple' positions are for 'simple' players? Apparently not. Indeed, rather the opposite may be true. It is precisely the so-called simple positions which are the most difficult ones, as a single error can condemn a player to grim defence. Handling these positions accurately takes a very strong player indeed, with exceedingly subtle positional feeling and good all-round intuition.

The Petroff Defence owes its name to Alexander Petroff (1794-1867) who analysed this opening together with Carl Jaenisch (1813-72) in the first half of the 19th century. It is also known as the **Russian Defence**.

There are two main lines, **3 ♘xe5** and **3 d4**.

If White prefers not to part with his e-pawn, he should play **3 ♘c3**, transposing to the Four Knights Game if Black replies 3...♘c6. There is, however, the alternative 3...♗b4 (which might be said to be more in the spirit of 2...♘f6), when after 4 ♘xe5 0-0 it is probably unwise to protect the e-pawn with 5 d3, for this allows Black to play 5...d5! with a strong initiative. The main line here is 5 ♗e2 ♖e8 6 ♘d3 ♗xc3 7 dxc3 ♘xe4 8 0-0. Instead, **3 d3** is simply not aggressive enough to worry Black. This is the sort of move which signals a willingness to leave opening theory behind, rather than make a contribution to it.

3 ♘xe5

3	♘xe5 (D)	
3	...	d6

Without this little move, the Petroff would not be a full-grown opening. It is the great merit of Jaenisch and Petroff to have clarified the

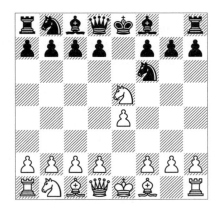

enormous difference between 3...d6 and the two moves that had 'dominated' the scene until then: **3...♘xe4** and **3...♕e7**.

It is true that **3...♘xe4?!** does not immediately lose after 4 ♕e2 thanks to 4...♕e7! 5 ♕xe4 d6, yet this can only be called a dubious pawn sacrifice at best (White simply continues 6 d4). **3...♕e7?!**, on the other hand, does regain the pawn, but leaves the queen terribly exposed after 4 ♘f3 or 4 d4 d6 5 ♘f3 ♕xe4+ 6 ♗e2, giving White plenty of opportunity for building up a comfortable lead in development. If there were nothing better for Black than either of these moves, 2...♘f6 would never have become more than a footnote. The strength of 3...d6 is precisely that it allows Black to regain the pawn in a perfectly natural way. First he chases away White's knight from e5, and then he plays 4...♘xe4. So simple!

4   ♘f3

The only real attempt to throw a spanner in Black's plan is to sacrifice a knight in the romantic style that belongs to the 19th century: **4 ♘xf7**. Bluffers, charlatans and grandmasters have tried this kill-or-cure remedy, yet – although it has been known since the times of Jaenisch and Petroff – until recently no decent opening manual would do much more than mention its existence, probably because no one knew what to think of it.

This is a true sacrifice. White is looking to obtain a long-term initiative, based on his menacing pawn-centre and the insecure position of Black's king after 4...♔xf7 5 d4. If 5...♘xe4? White regains the piece with 6 ♕h5+ ♔e7 (or

6...g6 7 ♕d5+) 7 ♕e2. It is not clear how Black should best defend himself. 5...g6, 5...c5 and 5...♕e8 have all been played at some time or another. What *is* clear, however, is that the impact of 4 ♘xf7 is mainly a psychological one. Will Black be intimidated or upset that he did not get his nice, quiet Petroff middlegame? Does White really believe in his chances? Does he have the mentality to be successful with a truly grand scheme like this?

4   ...   ♘xe4 *(D)*

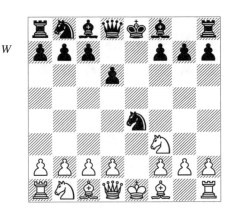

Having first inserted 3...d6, Black can now safely take on e4 without having to worry about **5 ♕e2**. After 5...♕e7 6 d3 ♘f6 nothing worse than an exchange of queens can happen to him.

But if we look at the position from White's perspective, it becomes clear that he *has* to attack the e4-knight in some way. How?

The simplest method is to play **5 d3**, but this does not really pose any problems to Black. He just replies 5...♘f6 and has nothing to worry about.

The developing move **5 ♘c3** is equally straightforward but contains a lot more venom. After 5...♘xc3 White plays 6 dxc3 and has at least opened another central file for his rooks, albeit at the cost of doubled pawns, which takes away some of the flexibility in his position. This is quite a popular alternative today, but the main line is still unchallenged:

5   d4

With this classical move, White refuses to make any compromise on optimal piece development. He will play 6 ♗d3 and leave it to his opponent to decide whether the knight should retreat or if Black should take advantage of the chance he is now given to consolidate the knight's position with ...d5. The latter option is the sharper and the more interesting theoretically.

5   ...   d5

If Black chooses the uncomplicated **5...♗e7** 6 ♗d3 ♘f6, his position is solid, but the initiative will be firmly in White's hands (for the time being at least).

6   ♗d3 *(D)*

This is one of the critical positions of the Petroff Defence. It is the starting point for several variations that have been studied thoroughly and over a very long period of time, but remain interesting and double-edged to this day.

The first sign that a fierce battle may be about to break out is the discovery that after **6...♗e7** 7 0-0 it is not the insipid 7...0-0, but the more aggressive 7...♘c6 (or **6...♘c6** 7 0-0 ♗e7) which constitutes the main line. This is an excellent way of anticipating the natural **8 ♖e1**, for Black now has the aggressive reply 8...♗g4, when **9 ♗xe4** dxe4 10 ♖xe4 ♗xf3 11 ♕xf3 (or 11 gxf3 f5) 11...♘xd4 offers White no advantage whatsoever. If White protects his d-pawn with **9 c3**, Black takes advantage of this lull in the fighting to play 9...f5. This aggressive advance is often unreliable because of a swift c4, opening the centre, or because of ♘e5, but both these moves are now less attractive because of the active positioning of Black's pieces and

because White has just played c3. Nevertheless, many attempts have been made to refute Black's set-up, mostly starting with 10 ♕b3, but up until now Black has managed to come up with an answer to everything.

For this reason, many players prefer to tackle the problem of 8...♗g4 in a totally different way: instead of 9 c3 they play **9 c4** or even **8 c4**. This very often leads to a position where White has an isolated queen's pawn and which – generally speaking – demands good positional understanding and a sharp eye for finesse and small advantages rather than a flair for tactical problems. One of the main lines goes 8 c4 ♘b4 9 ♗e2 0-0 and now either 10 ♘c3 ♗e6 or 10 a3 ♘c6. Alternatively, the more straightforward 9 cxd5 (instead of 9 ♗e2) 9...♘xd3 10 ♕xd3 ♕xd5 11 ♖e1 ♗f5 12 ♘c3 ♘xc3 13 ♕xc3 is also a line to be reckoned with. White loses no time moving his bishop from d3 and tries to make optimal use of the pin on the e-file.

The second option is to play **6...♗d6** *(D)*.

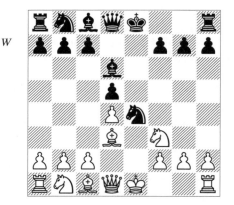

At first sight it may look as if the c4 plan is (even) stronger now than in the 6...♗e7 variation, but the point of 6...♗d6 is that Black now intends to meet this move with ...c6. The critical position arises after 7 0-0 0-0 8 c4 c6 and again play may easily become very sharp and complicated. What should one make of the rather wild continuation **9 ♖e1 ♗f5 10 ♕b3 ♘a6**, when 11 ♕xb7? is met by 11...♘b4 and 11 c5? by 11...♘axc5! 12 dxc5 ♘xc5, for instance? The perfectly sensible move **9 ♕c2** provokes an equally violent reaction, 9...♘a6, when Black is counting on 10 ♗xe4 dxe4 11 ♕xe4 ♘b4 (or 11...♖e8) to offer him sufficient compensation for the sacrificed pawn.

If White does not trust himself with these dangerous lines, he may want to choose the more rigid approach of **9 ♘c3** or **9 cxd5** cxd5 10 ♘c3. Instead of trying to undermine Black's e4-knight, White simply exchanges it off. Without this central stronghold, Black becomes vulnerable to an attack on the kingside. After 9 cxd5 cxd5 10 ♘c3 ♘xc3 11 bxc3, for instance, 11...♘c6 12 ♘g5 is already quite dangerous for Black. Pinning the knight with 11...♗g4 is more circumspect, but this too may lead to great complications after 12 ♖b1.

3 d4

3   d4 *(D)*

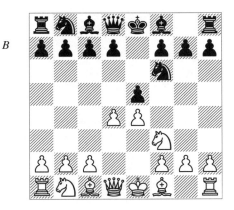

Once one has come to the conclusion that there is no such thing as a simple refutation of the Petroff after 3 ♘xe5, it becomes natural to start looking for alternatives. With 3 d4, White basically approaches the position in the same way as with the Scotch. But whereas 3 d4 against 2...♘c6 is hugely different from, say, 3 ♗b5 (meaning that 3 d4 can easily unsettle an opponent who was expecting 3 ♗b5), 3 d4 against 2...♘f6 is only marginally different from 3 ♘xe5 and is not likely to cause Black much psychological distress.

3   ...   ♘xe4 *(D)*

This is by far the most popular move nowadays. Until about 1970, **3...exd4** was regarded

as at least equally important, but this is now preferred only by those who want to avoid the complications of the thoroughly-analysed main lines. After 4 e5 ♘e4 5 ♕xd4 d5 6 exd6 ♘xd6 and now, for example, 7 ♘c3 ♘c6 8 ♕f4 Black must be very careful not to allow White's tiny lead in development to grow into a dangerous initiative.

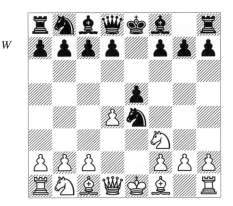

4   ♗d3 *(D)*

4 dxe5 is possible of course, but the idea of 3 d4 is primarily to arrive at the same type of position as 3 ♘xe5 via 4 ♗d3 d5 5 ♘xe5. The only difference is that after 3 ♘xe5 d6 4 ♘f3 ♘xe4 5 d4 d5 6 ♗d3 White's king's knight is on f3, whereas in the 3 d4 variation it is on e5.

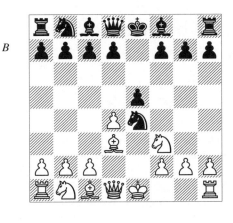

4   ...   d5

No wonder then that the chess world was so taken aback when in 1993 the brilliant Russian Yakov Murei came up with the fantastic alternative **4...♘c6**, which potentially uproots the whole 3 d4 variation. If 5 ♗xe4, Black regains the piece with 5...d5 6 ♗d3 e4 and even the ingenious 5 d5 fails to refute 4...♘c6, for Black has 5...♘c5 (or 5...♘f6) 6 dxc6 e4, again winning back the sacrificed piece.

Nevertheless, after an initial wave of popularity, Murei's move has failed to replace 4...d5 as the main line. A refutation has never been found, but once the consequences of 4...♘c6 were thoroughly analysed, it became clear that White is not denied his rightful chances of obtaining a 'normal' opening advantage. He may try, for instance, to prove that his slightly better pawn configuration after 5 d5 ♘c5 6 dxc6 e4 7 cxb7 ♗xb7 8 ♗e2 exf3 9 ♗xf3 is worth something, or he may try 5 dxe5 d5 6 exd6 ♘xd6 7 0-0, when his pieces are slightly more actively placed. Winning a pawn with 5 ♗xe4 d5 6 ♗xh7 seems less advisable. After 6...♖xh7 7 dxe5 ♗g4 Black has a nice, easy and harmonious development of his pieces to look forward to.

5   ♘xe5 (D)

White has achieved his aim. This position is almost identical to the main starting position of the 3 ♘xe5 variation, the only difference being that White's knight is on e5 instead of f3. But does this really improve White's chances? The answer to this question has been swinging gently from yes to no for more than a century and a half.

The two main lines start with **5...♗d6** and **5...♘d7**.

In case of **5...♗d6**, White's most ambitious plan is to play 6 0-0 0-0 7 c4, aiming to undermine the e4-knight. There are several possible replies, of which 7...♗xe5 8 dxe5 ♘c6 is believed to be the most critical. Black is daring White to play 9 cxd5 ♕xd5 10 ♕c2, which leads, after 10...♘b4 11 ♗xe4 ♘xc2 12 ♗xd5 (D), to a mysterious endgame. Black stands to gain an exchange on a1, but the big question is whether he will be able to extricate his knight, or, to put it perhaps more accurately: at what price will he be able to do so?

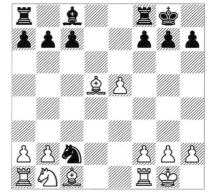

To give just a first impression of the complications: it is not the obvious 12...♘xa1 which is the main line (for this would allow White to cut off the knight's retreat with 13 ♗e4), but 12...♗f5. White then sacrifices a pawn with 13 g4 in order to achieve his objective anyway, but after 13...♗xg4 (if 13...♗g6 14 f4 the black bishop gets into trouble) 14 ♗e4 ♘xa1 15 ♗f4 Black will try to drive the bishop away from e4 again: 15...f5. And we have not even started yet! This variation has been analysed in enormous depth. The serious analytical work only **begins** in the position after 16 ♗d5+ ♔h8 17 ♖c1 (keeping the knight locked up in the corner).

This overload of theoretical baggage has caused 5...♗d6 to become a somewhat esoteric variation, not readily accessible to the uninitiated. In practice, therefore, attention centres on **5...♘d7 (D)** nowadays.

This is a fairly provocative move, for both the sacrifice 6 ♘xf7 and the materialistic 6 ♕e2

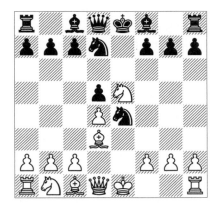

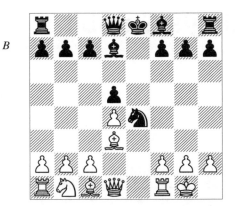

now seem very dangerous. But it turns out that Black's position cannot be overrun so easily. After **6 ♘xf7**, if Black plays simply 6...♔xf7 7 ♕h5+ ♔e7 White has nothing better than a draw by repetition with 8 ♕e2 (threatening 9 f3) 8...♔f7 9 ♕h5+, etc. Besides, Black has the ambitious 6...♕e7. And the second problem, **6 ♕e2**, is solved with the laconic 6...♘xe5 7 ♗xe4 dxe4 8 ♕xe4 ♗e6 9 ♕xe5 ♕d7. Black's lead in development and the pair of bishops turn out to be ample compensation for the lost pawn.

Therefore the usual reply to 5...♘d7 is the no-nonsense **6 ♘xd7 ♗xd7 7 0-0** *(D)*.

Surprisingly though, even here dangerous complications are lurking beneath the surface. For many years **7...♕h4** 8 c4 0-0-0 was a hotly

debated main line. Black intends to play 9...♗d6, which in case of 9 cxd5 ♗d6 10 g3 (10 h3? ♗xh3! is a catastrophe for White) 10...♘xg3 11 hxg3 ♗xg3 12 fxg3 ♕xg3+ leads to a draw by perpetual check. For this reason 9 c5 is the main line and the starting point for a rich complex of variations.

Nowadays the natural **7...♗d6** is the more popular move. This implies a pawn sacrifice, for after 8 c4 c6 9 cxd5 cxd5 10 ♕h5 Black has nothing better than to play 10...0-0. After 11 ♕xd5 ♗c6 Black's harmonious piece development promises to be sufficient compensation for the pawn. Another tactical justification for 7...♗d6 lies in the fact that 8 ♖e1 (or 9 ♖e1 or 10 ♖e1) allows an immediate draw by perpetual: 8...♗xh2+! 9 ♔xh2 ♕h4+ 10 ♔g1 ♕xf2+.

King's Gambit

1	e4	e5
2	f4 *(D)*	

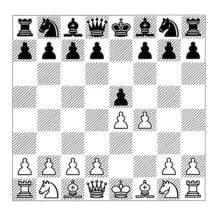

The King's Gambit is without a doubt the most fascinating of all openings. Surrounded by an aura of mystery, courage and heroism, it is this classical opening which (within the limits of the game of chess) comes closest to the eternal myth of the hero who leaves all earthly possessions behind and sets off in search of the Holy Grail. For it is not just technical competence that is required to play this opening (i.e. tactical genius), but first and foremost an absolute refusal to compromise and an attitude of total commitment. After all, White does not just sacrifice a pawn. He is opening the e1-h4 and g1-a7 diagonals, which means that he is actually sacrificing part of the natural protection of his king. His aim in doing so is to conquer the centre, to mobilize his forces quickly and to obtain the initiative, whatever the cost.

Born in an era beyond remembrance, when not just perception and positional understanding were completely unlike ours today but even the laws of the game were different, the King's Gambit has been a witness to the evolution of the game of chess from its humblest beginnings. It started with a recommendation dating

back to prehistoric times to follow up the opening moves 1 e4 e5 2 f4 exf4 3 d4 ♕h4+ 4 g3 fxg3 with the remarkable 5 ♔e1-g2, a very strong move indeed, but alas, no longer feasible under the present laws of chess.

The King's Gambit had its heyday in the early 19th century when, together with the Italian Game, it was the most popular of all openings. It was tailor-made for this, the golden age of romantic chess, when tactically-oriented play prevailed.

With the rise of modern, positional chess, the King's Gambit inevitably receded into the background, but there it has always kept a special place. Although the motives of the old masters were no longer understood, the force behind their favourite opening remained and was made palpable on rare occasions by courageous solitary chess-players who combined 19th century tactical genius with 20th century positional insight.

As deep into the 20th century as 1938 (when the world of chess had long become rationalized) the famous series of opening books by world champion Max Euwe could still open its chapter on the King's Gambit with the lyrical introduction "In the midst of the Open Games *[meaning the 1 e4 e5 openings – PvdS]* there rises, proudly and unweathered by the passage of time, the mighty fortress of the King's Gambit".

In a way, these words are still valid today. Somehow or other, the King's Gambit seems to elude rational judgement. Countless refutations of 2 f4 have been claimed, but each and every time the opening has survived the onslaught. It remains a source of inspiration to those who have courage and imagination. And even those who do not dare to play it, can learn a great deal from the wealth of variations this opening has to offer. There is only one theme here, yet it is an eternal one, the theme that no chess-player can avoid: the battle between the initiative and a material advantage.

The most prominent of these variations start with **2...exf4**, the **King's Gambit Accepted**, but several other moves have also grown into full-blown variations, most notably **2...d5**, the **Falkbeer Counter-Gambit**, and **2...♗c5**, the principal form of the **King's Gambit Declined**.

It is also useful to be acquainted with three lesser-known, yet venomous reactions to 2 f4, which I shall just briefly mention here:

2...♘c6 3 ♘f3 f5!? is a bold attempt to turn the tables on White.

2...♕f6 is equally ambitious and highly provocative. If possible, Black wants to capture on f4 not with the e-pawn but with the queen, thus accepting White's pawn sacrifice, yet without yielding his own central stronghold at e5.

2...♕h4+ 3 g3 ♕e7 is perhaps the most original of Black's options. Black draws the opponent's g-pawn forward with the paradoxical intention of taking on f4 only when that pawn is protected! If 4 fxe5, the idea is to play 4...d6! 5 exd6 ♕xe4+. It is more in the spirit of the King's Gambit to sacrifice a pawn with 4 ♘f3 exf4 5 ♘c3 or 4 ♘c3 exf4 5 d4.

The reader may have noticed that 3 fxe5 is not an option in any of these variations, since this would allow the devastating reply 3...♕h4+. This explains why there is no need for Black to protect his e-pawn with the passive **2...d6**. Then after 3 ♘f3, lines like 3...♘c6 4 ♗b5 or 3...♘d7 4 d4 allow White to obtain a good position 'for free'. The only testing move is 3...exf4, with a Fischer Defence (see page 330).

King's Gambit Accepted

2	...	exf4
3	♘f3	

It seems self-evident to play this move. Is not f3 the ideal square for the king's knight and is not 3...♕h4+ very efficiently prevented this way?

But the 'mighty fortress of the King's Gambit' was not built on trivial reasoning like this. Imagination, courage and a never-ending search for the limits of what is humanly possible were

equally important building materials, to say the least.

The position after 2...exf4 is a perfect example. No matter how strong and logical a move 3 ♘f3 may be, an intense search for alternatives has been made. By playing **3 ♗c4**, or – even more radical – **3 ♘c3** or **3 d4**, White allows his opponent to play 3...♕h4+, with the intent of proving this move to be a loss of time. White is confident that the gain of tempo by ♘f3, chasing the queen away from h4, will compensate fully for the loss of the right to castle.

Of course, it takes a truly admirable self-confidence to play a move like **3 ♘c3** and calmly meet 3...♕h4+ with 4 ♔e2 as if this was the most natural thing in the world, expecting the king to be able to take care of himself. But it says something about the underlying strength of this idea that only a really sharp reaction with 4...d5 5 ♘xd5 ♗g4+ 6 ♘f3 ♗d6 (or even 6...♘c6) is supposed to be adequate.

Compared to this, **3 ♗c4** *(D)*, almost looks tame.

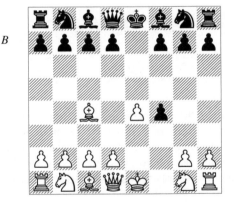

This is the **Bishop's Gambit**, considered a fully acceptable alternative to 3 ♘f3. After this bishop move, White can meet **3...♕h4+** civilly with 4 ♔f1. Here too, **4...d5** (or 3...d5 4 ♗xd5 ♕h4+) is a major option. Black sacrifices his d-pawn in order to open files and diagonals, giving his pieces plenty of scope, and opening the way for a solid protection of his f4-pawn after 5 ♗xd5 ♗d6. **4...g5** is a much riskier way of doing so. Here a strange echo can be heard of the prehistoric variation that was mentioned in the introduction to this chapter: after 5 d4 ♗g7 6 ♘c3 ♘e7 the bold 7 g3! fxg3 8 ♔g2! gets Black's queen into serious trouble.

A solid alternative is to omit 3...♕h4+ and prepare ...d5 without sacrificing a pawn. **3...♘f6** 4 ♘c3 c6, with the idea to play 5...d5 (*and the cunning threat of 5...b5 6 ♗b3 b4!*) is a widely respected variation. It is characteristic of this type of position that Black is not prevented from playing 5...d5 by 5 ♕e2. After the further 6 exd5+ ♗e7 Black simply continues his development, White's material gain is of little significance and White's queen is vulnerable to attack.

We now return to the position after 3 ♘f3 (*D*):

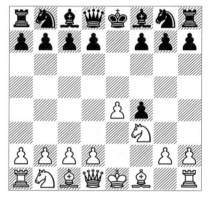

This is the departing point for some highly dissimilar variations. It is up to Black to determine the character of the upcoming middlegame and he should do so decisively, or else White will simply play 4 d4 and 5 ♗xf4 and be very happy with the result of the opening.

The oldest move known to theory, called the **Classical Variation**, is **3...g5**. Although it bears the stamp of the romantic spirit of the King's Gambit's heyday, this is still the main line even today. It is a principled attempt to refute the King's Gambit completely.

On the other side of the spectrum we find **3...d5**, the **Modern Variation**. This move was never seriously investigated until far into the 20th century, when players began to look for a logical, purely positional treatment of the opening. Black concentrates on the struggle

for supremacy in the centre and avoids weakening pawn moves (like ...g5).

Most of the alternatives (and there are quite a few of them!) can be classified somewhere in between these two extremes. Black is usually trying either to combine them or to refine one of them.

For instance, **3...h6** the **Becker Defence**, is a subtle attempt to carry out a ...g5 plan, without having to worry about the implications of 3...g5 4 h4 g4 5 ♘e5. After 3...h6 4 d4 Black plays 4...g5 (*D*).

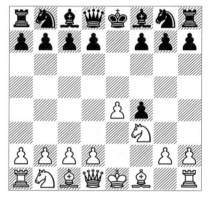

Having already played ...h6, he is now in a position to meet 5 h4 with 5...♗g7, holding on to his g5-pawn and thus indirectly to f4 as well. This means that White will have to look for alternative ways of breaking up Black's pawnchain on the kingside. The radical g3 plays a crucial part in this variation. White can either 'simply' play 5 g3 fxg3 6 hxg3 or 5 ♘c3 ♗g7 6 g3, when after 6...fxg3 both 7 hxg3 and 7 h4!? have been tried. In all of these lines White makes no attempt to regain his pawn. He is purely playing for the initiative, quite in the spirit of the King's Gambit.

3...d6 is based on a similar idea, for here too Black is preparing to play ...g5 under more favourable circumstances. This is the **Fischer Defence**. After 4 d4 g5 5 h4 Black has no objection to playing 5...g4, having eliminated the response ♘e5. Practice has shown, however, that even having to play the unorthodox 6 ♘g1 (*D*) does not really diminish White's attacking chances.

After 6...♝h6 7 ♘c3 c6 8 ♘ge2 ♛f6, for instance, it is 9 g3! again which allows White either to break open the kingside (9...fxg3 10 ♘xg3) or to immobilize Black's pawns and obtain a stronghold at f4 (9...f3 10 ♘f4).

A completely different approach to the opening underlies **3...♝e7**, the **Cunningham Gambit**. Black intends to force White's king away from e1 with 4...♝h4+, a motif we already know from the Bishop's Gambit. Now, anyone who remembers that a master of the King's Gambit does not flinch from playing 3 ♝c4 ♛h4+ 4 ♚f1, will understand that the prospect of having to play 3 ♘f3 ♝e7 4 ♝c4 ♝h4+ 5 ♚f1 holds very little terror indeed in the eyes of such a person. But there is a deeper and more modern aspect to the Cunningham which must be noted: after 4 ♝c4 Black can simply play 4...♘f6, meeting 5 e5 with 5...♘g4 6 0-0 d5 7 exd6 ♛xd6. This is in fact a subtle variation on the theme of 3...d5, the Modern Variation.

The same goes for **3...♘e7**, a move which hardly has a past (quite exceptional in the King's Gambit), but is very likely to have a future. It has become fairly popular in a very short period of time. The idea is to meet 4 d4 with 4...d5 (protecting f4 with 4...♘g6 is risky after 5 h4) 5 ♘c3 dxe4 6 ♘xe4 ♘d5. Black has reached a position akin to the Modern Variation, having avoided the theoretical obstacles that lie in the way of the immediate 3...d5.

Classical Variation

3   ...   g5 (D)

This move is as old as the King's Gambit itself. Without any qualms about weakening his own position, Black rushes forward to combine the defence of f4 with an attack of his own. He is threatening 4...g4 and, if the knight moves, 5...♛h4+.

4   h4

This may look like a wild move, but it is in fact perfectly solid. White defuses the threat of 4...g4 and ingeniously forces Black to go ahead with his plan regardless, only now it will be on White's terms. That is why White does not wait for Black to play ...♝g7, which would allow him to support his g5-pawn with ...h6. Now, the boot is on the other foot. But is it really?

Another idea is to play the aggressive developing move **4 ♝c4**. This too does not exactly prevent Black from playing **4...g4**, only the idea is a little different. Instead of safeguarding his knight, White is planning to sacrifice it with the nonchalant 5 0-0. This is the **Polerio Gambit** (also known as the **Muzio Gambit**), one of the very oldest theoretical variations of this ancient opening. White raises the stakes from a pawn to a piece. Today's chess-players will be so unaccustomed to the extremely high level of intensity of this approach that they will probably blink and not understand what has hit them. So utterly estranged have we become from this sort of gambit play that we just cannot believe it! And yet, no refutation has ever been found. Let us look at the starting position, which arises after 5...gxf3 6 ♛xf3 (D).

Once this was called 'the classical position of the King's Gambit'. To offer the reader a

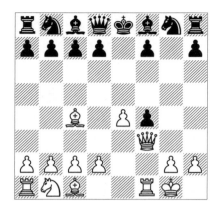

B

brief glimpse of what is possible here (but then what does the term 'possible' mean really?) I shall outline just a few of the many variations:

The most critical move is **6...₩f6**, which White meets with the pawn sacrifice 7 e5!? ₩xe5. Although White can hardly be accused of having taken it easy so far, he now goes completely berserk: to begin with, there is the variation **8 ♗xf7+!?** ♚xf7 9 d4, sacrificing another piece *and* his remaining centre pawn just to speed up the development of his remaining pieces to the utmost. After 9...₩xd4+ 10 ♗e3!, followed, for instance, by 10...₩f6 11 ♗xf4, Black finds himself facing a ferocious onslaught on his king. Compared to this, the alternative **8 d3**, with the possible continuation 8...♘h6 9 ♘c3 ♘e7 10 ♗d2 ♘bc6 11 ♖ae1 ₩f5 12 ♘d5, looks almost unnaturally self-restrained. Both these lines have been minutely investigated, especially in the late 19th century. In fact, a book published as late as 1910 was devoted solely(!) to the latter variation, or to be precise to the position arising after the further moves 12...♚d8 13 ₩e2 (with the idea 13...♘xd5 14 ♗xd5 ₩xd5 15 ♗c3!).

6...₩e7 is also a perfectly plausible move. Again, White slams on the accelerator by 7 ₩xf4!, planning to meet 7...₩c5+ with 8 d4 ₩xd4+ 9 ♗e3 ₩xc4 10 ₩e5+ and 11 ₩xh8.

But quite apart from the question what these variations are still worth today, the reason for the Polerio Gambit having undergone a process of fossilization has been the practical consideration that there is no need for Black to let himself be drawn into this strange world. By choosing the

solid **4...♗g7** (instead of 4...g4) Black keeps things simple and clear, emphasizing normal development rather than further material gains. After **5 h4** he plays 5...h6 6 d4 d6, meeting 7 c3, for example, with 7...♘c6 8 ₩b3 ₩e7. White's sharpest attempt is a plan that we have seen in the Becker Defence (3...h6): **5 0-0** d6 6 d4 h6 7 c3 ♘c6 and now 8 g3. Although Black's play in this variation so far may be called solid, it is clear that there is no question of this position being boring. After 8...g4 9 ♘h4 f3 10 ♘d2 a piece sacrifice on f3, clearing the way to Black's king, is in the air.

4   ...   g4 *(D)*

If **4...gxh4** 5 d4, White easily regains both pawns and obtains the initiative for free.

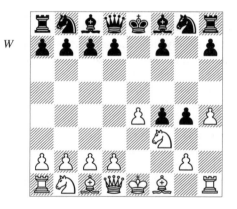

W

5   ♘e5

Nearly all variations of the King's Gambit bear romantic names of legendary chess-players from a distant past. 5 ♘e5 is the **Kieseritzky Gambit**.

A remarkable alternative is to play **5 ♘g5**, the **Allgaier Gambit**. White does not force the opponent into anything, yet he kindly invites him to win a piece by replying 5...h6. The idea is simply that Black's king gets drawn out of his comfort zone after 6 ♘xf7 ♚xf7. Again, I offer just a few variations to give the reader an idea of what is going on here. The obvious continuation **7 ₩xg4** is not sufficiently incisive to justify the piece sacrifice, for Black has a very easy way to develop his kingside pieces in 7...♘f6 8 ₩xf4 ♗d6. Equally, **7 ♗c4+** is not as powerful as it looks, since Black will be only too happy to open the c8-h3 diagonal for his bishop with 7...d5! 8 ♗xd5+ ♔g7. The main line starts with the neutral developing move **7 d4**. A possible (but not forced) reply to this is 7...f3, with the idea of meeting 8 gxf3 with 8...d5, trying to disorganize (and if possible slow down) White's attacking machinery.

We now return to 5 ♘e5 (D):

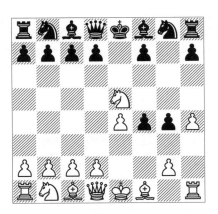

B

This is the basic position of the Kieseritzky Gambit. Many moves for Black have been suggested, tried and discarded here. More in particular, playing for material gains with moves like **5...h5** or **5...♗e7** meet with strong disapproval in the books. 5...h5 6 ♗c4 ♖h7 7 d4 plays into White's hands, as does 5...♗e7 6 ♗c4 ♗xh4+ 7 ♔f1.

Neutralizing White's initiative has to be Black's top priority and he does well not to worry about his extra pawn. **5...♘f6** is the traditional main line. Against **6 ♗c4** Black wants to play 6...d5 7 exd5 ♗d6 (or 7...♗g7). This leads, after 8 d4, to one of the crucial positions of the Kieseritzky Gambit. The material balance has been restored, but the positional balance is difficult to evaluate. Black has yielded his opponent an advantage in the centre but only to form a threatening and coherent pawn-front on the kingside. A characteristic continuation is 8...♘h5 9 0-0! ♕xh4 10 ♕e1! ♕xe1 11 ♖xe1 0-0 12 ♘c3. Notwithstanding the exchange of queens, the position remains tense. **6 d4** is a likely alternative. White allows his knight to be pushed back by 6...d6 *and* he gives away his e4-pawn, but after 7 ♘d3 ♘xe4 8 ♗xf4 White's

position is intrinsically sound. This is a real test for the Classical Variation. Black is a pawn up, but his kingside has been weakened. White has no concrete threats yet in due course an attack along the f-file is to be expected. In the meantime White has a space advantage and a beautiful square for his pieces at f4.

The alternative **5...d6** is no less ancient, yet this move has only recently risen to the fore. Even more so than 5...♘f6, this move is an attempt to wrest the initiative from White. The idea is to meet 6 ♘xg4 with 6...♘f6, when the variations 7 ♘xf6+ ♕xf6 8 ♘c3 c6 (or even 8...♘c6 9 ♘d5 ♕g6, hoping for 10 ♘xc7+?? ♔d8 11 ♘xa8 ♕g3+ 12 ♔e2 and now either 12...♘d4# or 12...♗g4# is mate) 9 ♗e2 ♖g8 and 7 ♘f2 ♖g8 8 d4 ♗h6 indicate only too clearly what Black is after. He is hoping to utilize the open g-file, bring his pieces quickly into play and use his f4-pawn to cramp the enemy kingside.

Modern Variation

3   ...   d5

Throughout the 20th century, this move was recommended in chess literature as a simple way of maintaining a positional balance. This assessment should perhaps be slightly modified. It is true that the opening problems are relatively simple in this line and that modern chess-players will probably feel more at home here than in a large section of the Classical Variation, but this is not necessarily to Black's advantage; it is a purely practical consideration. If Black has a superior understanding of the opening or if he is simply the better player, yes, he is almost certain to obtain a good position very easily. But if the opposite is true, he is equally likely to obtain a bad position. As in every other variation, there will be a struggle here, a struggle for the initiative and for domination of the centre.

4   exd5

In case of **4 e5** the classical move 4...g5 would now be much stronger than on the previous move since after 5 h4 g4 White will be unable to play 6 ♘e5.

4   ...   ♘f6 (D)

This variation is somewhat similar to the Scandinavian Defence (1 e4 d5). Black wants to recapture with the knight. If **4...♛xd5**, White is given a valuable extra tempo for his development: 5 ♘c3.

This is the starting point of the Modern Variation. Black's last move is based on the assumption that protecting the d5-pawn with **5 c4** is ineffective because of 5...c6, when 6 dxc6? (6 d4 is correct) 6...♘xc6 7 d4 ♗g4 gives Black a beautiful, fast and aggressive way of developing his pieces.

5 ♗b5+ is a much subtler way of provoking ...c6. After 5...c6 6 dxc6 ♘xc6 7 d4 ♗d6 8 0-0 0-0 9 ♘bd2 (intending to play ♘c4 and c3) a characteristic sort of position has arisen. Black's opening strategy has succeeded so far in that he has developed his pieces fairly quickly and managed to hang on to f4. It is around this pawn that the ensuing struggle will now revolve. Will White be able to capture it, using, for instance, the manoeuvre ♘c4-e5 to cut off the d6-bishop from its defence, or will Black be able to use the f4-pawn for aggressive operations like ...♘d5-e3 or ...♘e7-d5-e3?

This was the traditional main line of 3...d5 until around 1990 many players began to doubt whether it is really necessary to provoke ...c6 (giving White the opportunity to restore the material balance with dxc6). Nowadays it is **5 ♗c4** which is thought of as the main line. White lets his opponent play ...♘xd5 and is banking on fast development (again!). In short, he sacrifices a pawn *again*, which – theoretically at

least – is more in the spirit of the King's Gambit than the older moves 5 c4 and 5 ♗b5+. After 5 ♗c4 ♘xd5, the most important variations start with 6 0-0 ♗e7 7 d4 and 6 ♗xd5 ♛xd5 7 ♘c3.

Falkbeer Counter-Gambit

2   ...   d5

This move was already mentioned in our oldest sources on the King's Gambit, but, being judged primarily on the recapture on d5 with the queen, it received little attention at the time.

3   exd5 *(D)*

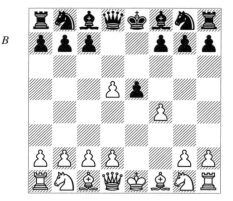

Now **3...♛xd5** offers White a tempo for free and looks unpromising after, for instance, 4 ♘c3 ♛e6 5 fxe5 ♛xe5+ 6 ♗e2 followed by 7 d4 or 7 ♘f3.

It was not until Ernst Falkbeer (1819-85) published a theoretical article in 1850, exploring the merits of the much more ambitious **3...e4**, that 2...d5 began to be appreciated. In the following century, it turned out that there is another way of justifying 2...d5: **3...c6**. In both cases Black ignores White's initial pawn sacrifice and sacrifices a pawn himself, a radical way of trying to turn the tables on White. We shall examine these two lines below.

A fourth option (and a perfectly valid one) is to play **3...exf4**. After 4 ♘f3 this leads to the Modern Variation. The point of this move-order is that Black avoids the Bishop's Gambit (3 ♗c4).

3...e4

3	...	e4

Falkbeer's move. In the same way as in the Albin Counter-Gambit (1 d4 d5 2 c4 e5 3 dxe5 d4; see page 50) Black boldly occupies the centre. White's second move, 2 f4, intended to open the f-file, now works against him: the pawn is not overly useful on f4 and White is vulnerable on the h4-e1 and a7-g1 diagonals.

If White does not tread carefully, Black will strengthen his e4-pawn and push White onto the defensive.

4	d3

White takes the bull by the horns. Now the straightforward **4...♕xd5** is not sufficiently powerful, for White takes over the initiative again by playing 5 ♕e2 ♘f6 6 ♘c3 ♗b4 7 ♗d2 ♗xc3 8 ♗xc3.

4	...	♘f6
5	dxe4	♘xe4 (D)

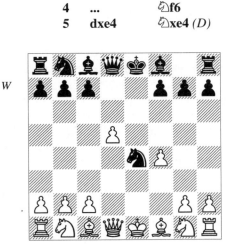

This position has been considered crucial for the 'old' Falkbeer Counter-Gambit for a long time now. There can be no doubt about Black having 'some' initiative for the pawn, but in spite of this 3...e4 seems to have lost its popularity. The reason for this decline must be that the general assessment 'some' becomes 'not quite enough' when minutely investigated. What was once a romantic and chivalrous way of meeting the King's Gambit has boiled down to a highly rational examination of the variation **6 ♘f3 ♗c5 7 ♕e2 ♗f5 8 ♘c3 ♕e7 9 ♗e3 ♗xe3 10 ♕xe3 ♘xc3 11 ♕xe7+ ♔xe7 12 bxc3**. In

this endgame Black will no doubt regain his pawn (he can do so immediately by taking on c2), but mainly owing to the vulnerable position of his king at e7, White is likely to retain the initiative.

3...c6

3	...	c6 (D)

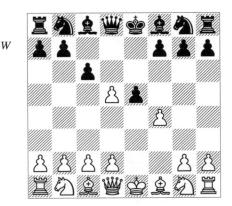

This move was proposed early in the 20th century by Aron Nimzowitsch, but never received full recognition until about 1985, when it suddenly became all the rage. Nowadays, this is one of the main replies to the King's Gambit. It is a more modern interpretation of the Falkbeer than 3...e4, and closely related to the Modern Variation (2...exf4 3 ♘f3 d5).

Taking advantage of the e5-pawn still being immune from capture because of 4...♕h4+, Black offers two different pawn sacrifices himself, for White can either simply play **4 dxc6** or the more sophisticated **4 ♕e2**. In both cases, Black is happy with the small lead in development that he enjoys after 4 dxc6 ♘xc6 or 4 ♕e2 cxd5 5 ♕xe5+ ♗e7 (when 6 ♕xg7?? loses the queen to 6...♗f6 7 ♕g3 ♗h4).

It is also important that White cannot simply play the developing move **4 ♘f3**, because that would make the advance 4...e4 really attractive. It is another knight move that has become the main line:

4	♘c3

If now **4...cxd5** then 5 fxe5 *is* possible. It is true that after 5...d4 6 ♘e4 ♕d5 7 d3 (or 7 ♗d3)

Black regains his pawn, but this is likely to yield the initiative to White.

4   ...   exf4

This move is much more ambitious, threatening 5...♕h4+ again.

5   ♘f3   ♗d6

It is odd that Black should play ...c6 in this line and then consistently refuse to play ...cxd5 in the next few moves. One could easily be led to believe that there is no deeper idea behind this line than to provoke dxc6. But Black has a very good reason for postponing ...cxd5: after **5...cxd5** 6 d4 it is difficult to defend f4 (6...♗d6 allows 7 ♘xd5 and 6...g5? fails to 7 h4 or 7 ♕e2+!) and just like in the Modern Variation it is defending this very pawn that is Black's primary aim in this variation.

6   d4   ♘e7 (D)

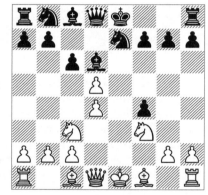

This is the basic position of the 'modern' Falkbeer Counter-Gambit. A very similar type of struggle to the Modern Variation is developing. Will White be able to capture on f4, or will this pawn remain a thorn in White's side?

King's Gambit Declined

2   ...   ♗c5

For centuries now, this move has been a safe haven for those who do not feel at ease in the jungle of the 'real' King's Gambit. Black refuses to be provoked by 2 f4 but he also refuses

to be intimidated (and play 2...d6). By placing his king's bishop on the a7-g1 diagonal, he makes a genuine effort to show up a darker side to the move 2 f4, yet at the same time he keeps play within the 'normal' range of 1 e4 e5 positions.

3   ♘f3   d6 (D)

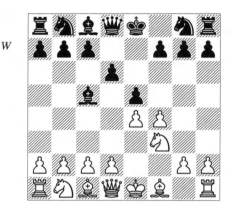

In this position White faces an important choice, one which is partly a matter of style and partly a question of sober analysis.

The most plausible plan is probably to play **4 c3**, intending to meet 4...♘f6 with 5 d4, gaining a tempo *and* closing the a7-g1 diagonal to the bishop, so that castling kingside becomes possible. The crucial question is whether Black can then make a breach in White's broad pawn-centre. Critical, for instance, is 5...exd4 6 cxd4 ♗b4+ 7 ♗d2 ♗xd2+ 8 ♘bxd2 ♕e7 and also the sharp 4...f5 is a real test for 4 c3. Theory has (as usual) not been able to reach a final verdict on these lines.

The alternative is simply to keep on developing pieces, starting with **4 ♘c3**. White does not worry about the problem of how to castle, and concentrates on other matters. After 4...♘f6 5 ♗c4 ♘c6 6 d3 ♗g4, for example, there is 7 ♘a4, eliminating the bishop. If Black plays 6...a6 (creating a7 as a retreat-square), then 7 f5 is a possibility. White bottles up Black's queen's bishop and prepares an attack on the kingside based on the advance g4-g5.

Other 1 e4 e5 Openings

1 e4 e5 *(D)*

Due to its long and interesting history, the theory of 1 e4 e5 has become rather fragmented. Several second- and third-move options for both White and Black have been given a name and a place of their own in the great body of opening theory. We have seen the most important of these in the previous six chapters and will now turn our attention to the remaining ones.

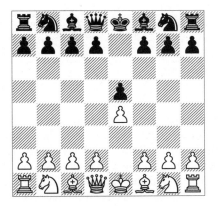

W

2 ♘f3 is White's most popular move in this position and **2...♘c6** is Black's most popular reply. The lion's share of 1 e4 e5 theory is based on this position, most of it starting with the four moves we have already looked at: **3 ♗b5, 3 ♗c4, 3 d4** and **3 ♘c3**.

Naturally, everyone is free to prefer a calm little move like **3 ♗e2, 3 d3** or **3 g3**, but this implies saying goodbye to the world of opening theory, for there has never been any 'official' interest in any of these moves. The only alternative that does have its niche alongside the Big Four is **3 c3**, the **Ponziani Opening**. White prepares d4 by making cxd4 possible should Black play ...exd4. This is a motif we know from the Ruy Lopez and the Italian Game.

As an alternative to 2...♘c6, we have so far only investigated **2...♘f6**, the Petroff Defence.

There are two other possibilities, admittedly of somewhat lower theoretical rank (from a modern point of view, that is), but which are playable nevertheless. These are **2...d6**, the **Philidor Defence**, and **2...f5**, the **Latvian Gambit**.

The **Damiano Defence, 2...f6?**, also deserves a mention (but no more than that), not because of any inherent merit of the move (there is none – even the apparent idea, which is to protect e5, is illusory for White is actually invited to start hacking away with 3 ♘xe5! fxe5 4 ♕h5+), but as a tragic case of totally misguided name-giving: Pedro Damiano, a Portuguese player living in the 16th century, did not recommend this move; he strongly disapproved of it. And for this sensible judgement he got his name attached to it!

Turning back to the position after 1 e4 e5, the next question is whether there are any alternatives to **2 ♘f3** and **2 f4**, the two moves we have looked at so far.

Indeed there are. **2 ♘c3** is the **Vienna Game** and **2 ♗c4** is the **Bishop's Opening**. These are respectable openings with a long history. And we conclude this chapter with **2 d4**, the **Centre Game**, where White opens the centre immediately.

Ponziani Opening

2 ♘f3 ♘c6
3 c3 *(D)*

This opening, named after Domenico Ponziani (1719-96), enjoyed a certain amount of popularity in the 19th century, but it came to be completely overshadowed by the Ruy Lopez, where White carries out the same plan in more favourable circumstances.

Because White does not put any pressure on the enemy position first (as with 3 ♗b5), Black is given the opportunity to react aggressively to c3, for instance with **3...d5**. This move is in fact

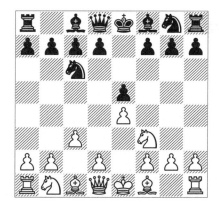

not often played, probably because 1 e4 e5 players who only get to face the Ponziani once or twice in their careers are not usually well-prepared for it and are a little worried about the critical reply 4 ♕a4. Besides, there is the simple and solid alternative **3...♘f6**. If we compare this position to the Ruy Lopez (for example, 3 ♗b5 a6 4 ♗a4 ♘f6 5 0-0 ♗e7 6 ♖e1 b5 7 ♗b3 d6 8 c3, where White has protected his e-pawn before he even embarks on the c3 plan) the Ponziani hardly creates a favourable impression. Nevertheless, even after 3 c3 there is still room for White to try to achieve an opening advantage and for this reason the Ponziani has never died out. After 4 d4 ♘xe4, for instance, 5 d5 may give White some spatial advantage. Whether this is of any importance after, say, 5...♘e7 6 ♘xe5 ♘g6 is another matter.

Philidor Defence

    2   ♘f3   d6

This opening deserves our attention if only because it bears the name of one of the most famous chess-players of all time, André Philidor (1726-95).

Philidor did not like to obstruct his pawns and for this reason he preferred 2...d6 to 2...♘c6. He was very consistent in his views for he also considered 2 ♘f3 a mistake which begged for severe punishment with 2...d6 3 d4 f5. Although this radical view never found a great following and the chess world went back to 2...♘c6 *en masse* after him, the Philidor Defence itself retained its special place in the world of opening

theory. In fact, the adaptability of this opening is truly astonishing. Throughout the centuries a new interpretation of the Philidor has always been found whenever new positional views demanded this. A theoretical overview of the variations of the Philidor is very much a display of how opening theory has changed over the years.

    3   d4 *(D)*

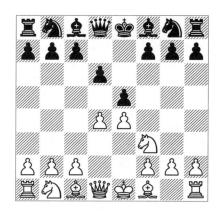

The oldest move in this position is **3...f5**, the choice of Philidor himself. Black attacks White's central position without fear of overextending himself. This variation was considered a highly crucial one until deep into the 19th century. Especially the position that arises after 4 dxe5 fxe4 5 ♘g5 d5 6 e6 was hotly debated (and still is) and the piece sacrifice 4 ♘c3 fxe4 5 ♘xe4 d5 6 ♘xe5 dxe4 7 ♕h5+ also greatly occupied the masters of old. In fact, a clear refutation of 3...f5 has never been found, but the trust, the basic trust required to play a very sharp move like this, has just deteriorated over the years.

With the rise of modern positional chess in the latter part of the 19th century, a more heavy-handed, more defensively orientated approach to the Philidor rose to the fore: **3...♘d7**. Black protects his e-pawn without exposing his queen's knight at c6 to a pin (♗b5) or a direct attack (d5). This is a choice in favour of a slightly compressed yet very solid position.

But it soon became clear that this admirable plan meets with great practical difficulties, for if White plays 4 ♗c4 Black needs to be very careful indeed. The unsuspecting 4...♘gf6?, for instance, is severely punished by 5 dxe5 dxe5 6 ♘g5 and 4...♗e7? 5 dxe5 ♘xe5 (5...dxe5? 6 ♕d5 is even worse) 6 ♘xe5 dxe5 7 ♕h5 is also quite unsatisfactory. The only way to survive these hazards is 4...c6 5 0-0 ♗e7, but even then 6 dxe5 dxe5 7 ♘g5! ♗xg5 8 ♕h5 g6 9 ♕xg5 disrupts Black's opening plan. But although the latter variation is thought to be somewhat annoying for Black, it is by no means a refutation of 3...♘d7.

Still, a subtle refinement of Black's idea was found in **3...♘f6**. But even this is not as rock solid as Black would like because of 4 dxe5, when after 4...♘xe4 the aggressive 5 ♕d5 ♘c5 6 ♗g5 is a realistic attempt to turn a tiny lead in development into a tangible initiative.

What Black is really hoping to achieve with either 3...♘d7 or 3...♘f6 is the position after **3...♘f6 4 ♘c3 ♘bd7**. Play might continue 5 ♗c4 (the traditional move, but the extraordinary 5 g4!? has been popular in recent years) 5...♗e7 6 0-0 0-0 (D), when we arrive at what surely is *the* fundamental Philidor position.

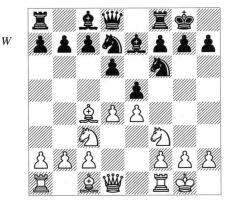

W

White has more space but it is very difficult to launch an attack against Black's fortress. After 7 ♖e1 c6 8 a4, for instance, Black can solve the problem of finding a proper way to develop his queen's bishop with 8...b6 followed by 9...♗b7.

And remarkably enough, despite the objections to both 3...♘d7 and 3...♘f6 outlined above, this remains a topical variation, for it so happens that there is a third route to the diagrammed position, or perhaps I should say: a

detour. By playing 1...d6 2 d4 ♘f6 3 ♘c3 e5 4 ♘f3 ♘bd7 Black reaches the Philidor Defence via the back door. Apparently then, in order to reach this classical 1 e4 e5 position, Black needs to abandon 1...e5! Unavoidably there are some pitfalls and complications even to this detour (though nothing as serious as with 3...♘d7 and 3...♘f6). We shall examine them in the chapter on the Pirc Defence (see page 453).

Finally, the most modern interpretation of the Philidor is to play **3...exd4**. This solution to the problem of how to protect e5 is as radical as it is simple, yet it was thought to be too passive for a very long time. But general considerations like this (which tend to become dogmatic) do not seem to impress today's players. On the contrary, it makes them want to take a closer look at the variation involved. After 4 ♘xd4 Black continues 4...♘f6 5 ♘c3 ♗e7. White has a spatial advantage but Black's position is very flexible. After 6 ♗e2 0-0 7 0-0, for instance, he can either adopt a wait-and-see attitude with 7...♖e8 and 8...♗f8, or he can open hostilities on the queenside with ...a6 and ...b5 or even ...c5. A counter-thrust in the centre, ...d5, is also hovering over the position.

Latvian Gambit

    2   ♘f3   **f5** (D)

This rowdy pawn sacrifice is one of the very few openings that **never** get a neutral qualification, not even in the most careful of opening books. The Latvian knows only two categories of chess-players: those who are for it (a handful of enthusiastic fans) and those who are against (the rest of the world). It is very old (it was mentioned by Greco as far back as 1669, and indeed is sometimes called the Greco Counter-Gambit) but has always had to live on the fringes of opening theory.

And what a nerve: Black not only leaves e5 unprotected but even puts another pawn *en prise* as well!

The point of 2...f5 is of course to meet **3 exf5** with 3...e4, attacking the f3-knight. It is significant for the extraordinarily weak positional foundation of the Latvian Gambit that

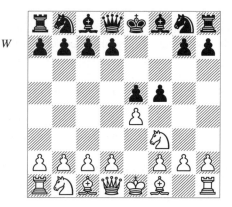

even this is a dubious line. 4 ②e5 ②f6 5 ♗e2, for instance, is pretty dangerous for Black.

But naturally, allowing White to play **3 ②xe5** is even more perilous, for this brings up the threat of 4 ♕h5+. The idea is to play 3...♕f6 first, neutralizing this threat, and then restore the material balance by taking on e4. Admittedly, this solves Black's immediate problems, but whether Black has much to be satisfied about in the long run, say after 4 d4 d6 5 ②c4 fxe4 or 4 ②c4 fxe4, is another matter. White has a considerable lead in development and Black has to be careful to avoid pitfalls like 4 ②c4 fxe4 5 ②c3 ♕g6 6 d3 exd3? (6...♗b4 is a better move) 7 ♗xd3 ♕xg2?? 8 ♕h5+, when White is already winning.

What is required to play the Latvian Gambit with any degree of success is a sharp eye for tactics and a mental attitude of total contempt for whatever theory has to say about it.

Vienna Game

2   ②c3 *(D)*

When compared to 2 ②f3 and 2 f4, this is a quiet move. White does not attack anything, nor does he put pressure on his opponent in any way. But it is a perfectly useful developing move and White gives no guarantee whatsoever that he will not become aggressive at a later stage (which may be as early as the next move).

The Vienna Game gained its independence in the second half of the 19th century, a time when players were still thinking along the lines of the King's Gambit (though not playing it as

often as they used to do): 2 ②c3 was seen as a sensible preparation for 3 f4.

About a century later, attention shifted to a quieter approach: 3 ♗c4, a line that Bent Larsen used to be successful with in the 1950s and 1960s.

3 g3 is perfectly playable as well, and this gained popularity later still, around the turn of the millennium.

It is for these three plans that Black now has to brace himself. He also needs to anticipate a possible change of tack by his opponent, who can still play 3 ②f3 and then perhaps 4 d4. **2...♗c5**, for instance, has to be judged by the implications of 3 ②f3 d6 (if 3...②c6 then 4 ②xe5!; see page 318) 4 d4 exd4 5 ②xd4. We are touching upon the bedrock of the entire Vienna Game here, for it was a theoretical discussion of the merits of 2...♗c5 around 1850 that sparked off interest in 2 ②c3 in the first place. Naturally it was not the prosaic 3 ②f3 that excited the masters of old. What occupied *them* was the question of whether on 3 ②a4 Black can successfully sacrifice a piece with 3...♗xf2+ 4 ♔xf2 ♕h4+.

Nowadays **2...②f6** and **2...②c6** are the main lines, each with a very specific point of its own.

2...②f6

2   ...   ②f6 *(D)*

From this position start the main lines of the Vienna Game: **3 f4**, **3 ♗c4** and **3 g3**.

Naturally, **3 ②f3** is also a perfectly good move, but this takes us back to the Petroff

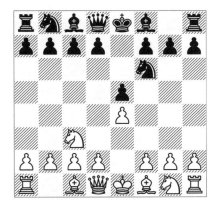 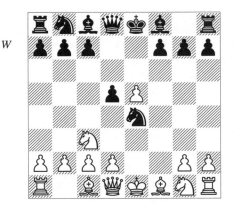

Defence (see page 322), or to the Four Knights Game in case Black plays 3...♘c6 (see page 318).

2...♘f6 3 f4

3   f4

At first sight, this sharp move may look more dangerous for Black now than a move earlier, since **3...exf4?** is very strongly met by 4 e5. But those who have already acquainted themselves with the dos and don'ts of the King's Gambit will immediately recognize that this is the perfect opportunity for Black to react in the spirit of the Falkbeer Counter-Gambit:

3   ...   d5

Now **4 exd5** can be met by 4...e4, directly transposing to the Falkbeer Counter-Gambit, yet in a relatively favourable version for Black, for after 2 f4 d5 3 exd5 e4 (see page 335), 4 d3 is thought to be more accurate than 4 ♘c3 since in the latter case, after 4...♘f6 (and this is the position we are dealing with here) 5 d3, Black has the powerful 5...♗b4. Another possibility for Black is to play the Modern Variation-inspired 4...exf4, while the simple 4...♘xd5 is not a bad move either.

But then the critical reply to 3...d5 is not 4 exd5...

4   fxe5   ♘xe4 (D)

This brings about the crucial position of the 3 f4 variation.

In the long run White may well get attacking chances on the kingside thanks to the half-open f-file and his outpost at e5. But for the time

being Black, with easy development to look forward to (beautiful open diagonals for both bishops), has little to worry about. Both players' immediate concern will be Black's e4-knight: White needs to eliminate this aggressor, but how should he tackle this problem without compromising his own development? If **5 ♘xe4** dxe4, the e4-pawn causes even more problems.

A more subtle solution is to play **5 d3** although this is a slight concession for after 5...♘xc3 6 bxc3 Black has 6...d4, which prevents White from supporting his e5-pawn by playing 7 d4. The sharp 5...♕h4+ is not to be feared for after 6 g3 ♘xg3 7 ♘f3 ♕h5 8 ♘xd5 the damage to Black's position is at least as serious as the damage to White's.

5 ♘f3 is also a main line. White eliminates 5...♕h4+ and intends to undermine the e4-knight while developing healthily with 6 d4 and 7 ♗d3. Laudable as this plan is, it is hardly dangerous for Black, since he has 5...♗e7 6 d4 0-0 7 ♗d3 f5 8 exf6 ♗xf6!, when taking twice on e4 loses a piece to 10...♖e8.

2...♘f6 3 ♗c4

3   ♗c4

This move is very similar to 2 ♘c3 in outlook. White prevents ...d5 and prepares f4. Black now faces an important choice.

3   ...   ♘c6

I give this move as the main line here, because the position that arises if White now plays 4 d3 is of vital importance for several move-orders. But for a sober judgement of the specific move-order that we are dealing with here, the sharp **3...♘xe4** is at least as important as 3...♘c6. We have seen this motif – the sacrifice of a knight at e4 (or e5) followed by the fork ...d5 (or d4) winning back the piece immediately – in several forms by now. This time the implications are fairly unique, for it is not the one-dimensional 4 ♘xe4 d5 nor 4 ♗xf7+ ♔xf7 5 ♘xe4 d5 that theory is interested in (these lines would only serve to justify 3...♘xe4), but the very dangerous 4 ♕h5!. Black is forced to respond 4...♘d6, when White, instead of going for the meek 5 ♕xe5+ ♕e7, plays 5 ♗b3!, sacrificing a pawn. The idea is to meet 5...♘c6 (5...♗e7 is simpler and safer, but less challenging) with 6 ♘b5, when 6...g6 7 ♕f3 f5 8 ♕d5 ♕e7 9 ♘xc7+ ♔d8 10 ♘xa8 b6 (D) takes us to the starting position of what is sometimes called the **Frankenstein-Dracula Variation**.

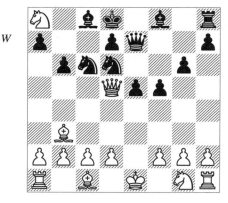

W

White has won a rook, but Black is well on his way to getting at least a knight back with 11...♗b7. The result will be an exceptionally complicated situation where Black has a huge lead in development and White's queen is in trouble. Theory has as yet failed to come up with a conclusive judgement in spite of many pages of published analysis. For anyone who loves to play (or just to analyse) chaotic positions, this is a treat.

4   d3 (D)

This position often arises via 2...♘c6 (3 ♗c4 ♘f6 4 d3) or via 2 ♗c4 (2...♘f6 3 d3 ♘c6 4 ♘c3), move-orders that side-step the tricky 3...♘xe4 problem.

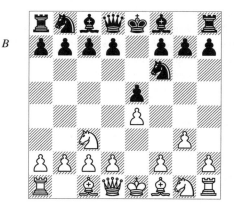

B

Just like a move earlier, Black now has **4...♗c5**, inviting a transposition to the King's Gambit Declined with 5 f4. He can also discourage 5 f4 by playing **4...♗b4**, when 5 f4 runs into the powerful 5...d5.

The most drastic way of giving this variation a face of its own, however, is to play **4...♘a5**, seizing the opportunity to eliminate the white bishop. The most critical reply is probably 5 ♘ge2 ♘xc4 6 dxc4. White gets a firm grasp on the crucial d5-square to compensate for the disappearance of his bishop. This is a rather slow sort of position, where it is not easy for either player to create a breach in the enemy fortress.

2...♘f6 3 g3

3   g3 (D)

B

For a long time, this little move was regarded as just one of the many uninteresting ways of relinquishing the fight for a serious opening advantage. After all, Black can now play **3...d5** and doesn't that mean that he is simply taking over the initiative? But when the variation was first thoroughly investigated, around 1990, things turned out to be not quite as straightforward as that. For after 4 exd5 ♘xd5 5 ♗g2, and now, for instance, 5...♘xc3 6 bxc3 ♘c6 7 ♘f3 ♗c5 8 0-0 0-0 9 ♖e1, there are several ways of attacking Black's central formation: a well-timed d4 for instance, or the more prudent d3 in combination with ♘d2, opening the diagonal for the g2-bishop.

And if Black prepares ...d5 with **3...c6**, he is rather inviting his opponent to take the initiative in the centre himself with 4 d4 exd4 5 ♕xd4, now that 5...♘c6 is no longer possible.

Naturally, Black does not have to try to refute 3 g3. There is no objection at all to playing something simple like **3...♗c5** 4 ♗g2 ♘c6, keeping the centre closed for the time being. Both sides will be able to complete their development in peace. Here too the plan to play f4 – the main theme of the Vienna Game – after due preparation of course, remains crucial.

2...♘c6

2 ... ♘c6 (D)

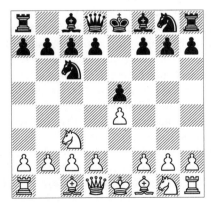

This move is usually played with the intention of meeting the advance of White's f-pawn in a way which is very different from 2...♘f6 3 f4 d5 as outlined above.

3 f4

If White prefers one of the other standard plans, the difference between 2...♘c6 and 2...♘f6 is less significant and may even be reduced to zero.

After **3 ♗c4 ♘f6**, for instance, we find ourselves on familiar ground. But playing 2...♘c6 does of course mean that there is no possibility of meeting 3 ♗c4 with 3...♘xe4.

In case of **3 g3**, Black's choice is also limited compared to the sister variation 2...♘f6 3 g3. There is of course nothing wrong with something like 3...♗c5 4 ♗g2 ♘f6 (this position is identical to the one arising after 2...♘f6 3 g3 ♗c5 4 ♗g2 ♘c6), but 3...d5 and 3...c6 are no longer feasible.

3 ♘f3 transposes to the Three Knights Game (see page 318).

3 ... exf4

Black accepts the gambit and in so doing creates a type of middlegame which is similar to the King's Gambit Accepted. But the only difference from the position after 2 f4 exf4 (the extra moves ♘c3 and ...♘c6) has more significance than one might think.

4 ♘f3

Much more than in the comparable position after 2 f4 exf4, the fearless d4 is a major option here. In fact **4 d4** was very popular in the 19th century and is named the **Steinitz Gambit**, after the first world champion. It must be admitted though that the reputation of this bold gambit has declined and that it will probably take a new Steinitz to reinvigorate White's chances after 4...♕h4+ 5 ♔e2 d6 6 ♘f3 ♗g4.

4 ... g5 (D)

The advantage (from White's point of view) of ♘c3 and ...♘c6 having been played is that Black does not have as wide a choice as after 2 f4 exf4 3 ♘f3, for he has to act quickly to prevent White from playing 5 d4 followed by 6 d5, and 4...d5 is not an option.

The disadvantage is that Black does not really *need* an alternative to ...g5. Since White cannot play the relatively solid Kieseritzky Gambit (solid in King's Gambit terms that is: 2 f4 exf4 3 ♘f3 g5 4 h4 g4 5 ♘e5) he has no alternative but to muster all the courage and audacity that he can find and go all-out for the 19th century approach: no holds barred.

W

5   h4

5 d4 is a major alternative. If then 5...g4, the situation is similar to the Polerio Gambit (see page 331). White sacrifices a piece with 6 ♗c4 and hopes to obtain more than enough compensation after 6...gxf3 in the shape of a lead in development, an attack and... mate. Just a little example, to get a first glimpse of the dangers of this sort of position: if 7 0-0? fxg2? Black is destroyed by 8 ♗xf7+ ♔xf7 9 ♕h5+ ♔g7 10 ♕g4+ ♔f7 11 ♖xf4+ ♘f6 12 ♘d5. However, modern theory indicates that 7 0-0? is refuted by 7...♘xd4! 8 ♗xf4 (8 ♕xd4? ♕g5!) 8...♗c5!, and that White should try 7 ♕xf3. This fearsome gambit, which nobody has the courage (or the foolishness) to play any more, is called the **Pierce Gambit**.

5   ...   g4
6   ♘g5

A comparison between this and the Classical Variation of the King's Gambit reveals a necessity for White to use only the sharpest and riskiest weapons which the King's Gambit armoury has to offer. We find ourselves in Allgaier Gambit territory here (see page 332). By playing **6...h6**, Black forces his opponent to sacrifice a piece: after 7 ♘xf7 ♔xf7 8 d4 the main lines are 8...d5 and 8...f3.

Like the Pierce Gambit, this variation (called the **Hamppe-Allgaier Gambit**) is not very popular any more. Chess-players of the 21st century have become estranged from this wild, reckless sort of gambit play. But for anyone interested in just learning something about the delicate balance between the initiative and a material

advantage, a closer scrutiny of old variations such as these can be highly recommended.

Bishop's Opening

2   ♗c4 *(D)*

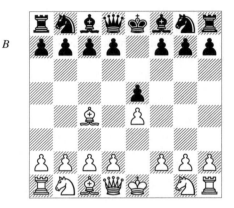

B

This is an ancient move and one that was preferred by Philidor to 2 ♘f3. Before the rise of the Ruy Lopez, c4 was considered the best square for White's king's bishop anyway, so why not play ♗c4 at once? In those days, the Bishop's Opening was a complicated theoretical affair, consisting of a maze of intricate variations. But most of these were firmly rooted in the strategic and tactical concepts of that era and are almost invisible today.

And yet quite recently this has become a popular opening again, mainly because of the revaluation of the very quiet set-up based on 3 d3. In fact, the Bishop's Opening has undergone the same transformation as the Italian: from an 'old-fashioned' opening full of fireworks to a modern, positionally well-founded alternative to the Ruy Lopez. And compared to the Italian Game, 2 ♗c4 has the added advantage of avoiding the Petroff Defence, a perhaps inconspicuous point but one that is much appreciated by many 1 e4 players nowadays.

2   ...   ♘f6

To give the reader a faint idea of how antique theory of the Bishop's Opening looked like: 2...♘f6 used to be called the Berlin Defence, while **2...♗c5** is (or was?) the Classical Variation. White would then often continue 3 c3 ♘f6

4 d4 exd4 5 e5, the Pratt Variation, but the truly fearless would of course prefer the McDonnell Gambit: 3 b4 ♗xb4 4 f4. Other moves, like **2...b5** or **2...f5** (the Calabrian Counter-Gambit) also used to have a prominent place in the books but have now completely disappeared.

3   d3 *(D)*

With this modest little move starts the modern interpretation of the Bishop's Opening. 150 years ago it was **3 d4** that was considered critical and in fact this is one of the very few elements of the 'old Bishop's Opening' that is still relevant today. White is planning to meet 3...exd4 with 4 ♘f3, when 4...♘c6 transposes to a line of the Two Knights Defence (see page 309) and 4...♘xe4 is the starting point of the **Urusov Gambit**. I think a modern player will find the position after 5 ♕xd4 ♘f6 6 ♗g5 ♗e7 7 ♘c3 c6 8 0-0-0 d5 9 ♖he1 no less fascinating than did Prince Urusov in 1857.

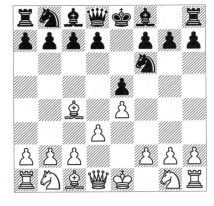

3   ...   c6

A principled move. Black intends to play ...d5, achieving two aims: to gain a tempo by attacking the bishop and to take the initiative in the centre. The immediate **3...d5** is less suited to these purposes, for after 4 exd5 ♘xd5 5 ♘f3 ♘c6 6 0-0 ♗e7 7 ♖e1 it is White who profits more from the opening of the centre.

Naturally, this line is crawling with transpositions to both the Italian and the Vienna Game and each player will have to make use of these possibilities according to his own insight and preferences. After **3...♘c6**, for instance, White has a choice between 4 ♘c3, transposing to a

position from the Vienna that we have just seen, and 4 ♘f3, transposing to the Two Knights Defence (see page 311). But the moment is ill-chosen to try to transpose to a King's Gambit, since 4 f4 gives Black a (relatively) comfortable game after 4...exf4 5 ♗xf4 d5!.

If **3...♗c5**, White has the same choice, but this move is often played specifically with the idea of replacing ...♘c6 with a ...c6 set-up in case White continues 4 ♘f3 d6 5 c3. Play might continue 5...♗b6 6 ♘bd2 0-0 7 0-0 c6 8 ♗b3 ♖e8 9 ♖e1 ♗e6 10 ♗c2 h6 11 h3 ♘bd7, for instance. The mere fact that this opening has been impregnated with subtle considerations like this is a clear sign of how seriously the d3 and c3 plan is taken nowadays. I have elaborated on this trend in the chapter on the Italian Game and what I have said there goes for the Bishop's Opening as well.

4   ♘f3   d5
5   ♗b3 *(D)*

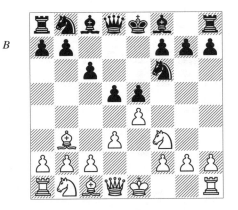

The history of this position nicely illustrates how opening theory works. It started as a footnote to 3 d4, judging 3 d3 (and consequently this position) to be 'perfectly harmless for Black'. Influenced by this comforting assessment, even the obviously inferior **5...dxe4** 6 ♘g5! (the very point of White's opening play) was dismissed with a curt '6...♗e6 and chances are equal'. And this was in a highly respected opening encyclopedia published in 1974! It was not until a few pioneers took up this line in the 1970s that a sensible body of variations began to take shape and **5...♗d6** became the main line. The idea of White's set-up then becomes clear for he continues 6 ♘c3!, immediately putting pressure on Black's pawn-centre and forcing Black to make a far-reaching decision. If **6...d4** 7 ♘e2, the diagonal of White's b3-bishop is opened again and White is given an opportunity for active play with moves like c3 and ♘g3-f5. It is safer and more popular to play **6...dxe4**, when 7 ♘g5 0-0 8 ♘cxe4 ♘xe4 9 ♘xe4 produces an open position where Black has a firm hold on the centre and White has free and easy development for his pieces. In some cases, an attack against Black's king with ♕h5 and ♘g5 may be a dangerous option.

To disrupt this plan, it was popular to insert **5...♗b4+** (with the idea 6 c3 ♗d6) for some time, but this now seems to be thought a little over-subtle, for this move is hardly ever played any more.

Centre Game

2   d4   exd4 *(D)*

W

3   ♕xd4

The double pawn sacrifice **3 c3** dxc3 4 ♗c4 cxb2 5 ♗xb2 was popular around 1900 and is called the **Danish Gambit**. Elaborate variations were developed, yet interest dwindled when it became clear that Black has a very simple and solid defence in 3...d5. After 4 exd5 ♕xd5 5 cxd4 ♘c6 6 ♘f3 a position is reached which we know from the Scotch. See page 312, where I

gave a similar description of (and prescription for) the related Göring Gambit.

Another possibility is to play **3 ♘f3**. It seems odd to play the moves d4 and ♘f3 in this order, giving Black a choice between the Scotch Opening (3...♘c6) and a line of the Petroff Defence (3...♘f6) *and* allowing some other moves (like 3...♗c5 and 3...♗b4+) as well. Nevertheless, this is becoming more and more popular these days. The idea is to circumvent one of the main variations of the Petroff: after 3 ♘f3 ♘f6 Black has missed out on the popular line 2 ♘f3 ♘f6 3 d4 ♘xe4 and has been tricked into the alternative line 3 d4 exd4 (see page 325) instead.

3   ...   ♘c6
4   ♕e3 *(D)*

B

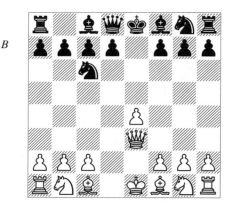

White has opted for the central pawn-formation which is typical of the Scotch. The only difference is the somewhat vulnerable position of his queen at e3 and the free development tempo ...♘c6 that Black has just cashed in. Still, White's opening play is not entirely unfounded. After, say, **4...♘f6** 5 ♘c3 ♗b4 6 ♗d2 0-0, thanks to his queen having been already developed, White has the aggressive option of castling queenside. After 7 0-0-0 ♖e8 he should not be frightened by the frontal attack against his e-pawn and continue in attacking style with 8 ♗c4 or 8 ♕g3. Protecting e4 with 8 f3 is less advisable for this allows Black to take the initiative with 8...d5!.

French Defence

1   e4   e6 *(D)*

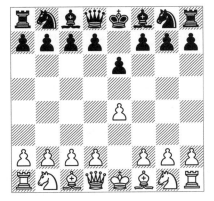

This perhaps slightly timid-looking move is in fact a clear signal that Black has different priorities from a classical 1...e5 player. He changes the course of the opening immediately.

Black allows his opponent to form what is called 'the ideal pawn-centre' by playing 2 d4 and thereby voluntarily accepts a more cramped position than 1...e5 would give. This may look like a disadvantage but the great benefit of this plan is that White is not given any targets. There is no black pawn at e5 begging to be attacked and the a2-g8 diagonal, so often Black's Achilles' Heel in the 1 e4 e5 openings, is firmly closed: there will be no white bishop leering at f7 in the French Defence!

So the concession Black makes in terms of space is compensated for by improved security. But it is not passivity that marks Black's outlook on life in the French Defence. On the contrary, his plan is to play 2...d5, attacking White's e4-pawn, and it is very likely that ...c5 will soon follow, (probably) attacking a white pawn on d4 in similar fashion. This strategy can easily lead to a violent confrontation in the centre and with a little bit of luck (or is it bad

luck?) this may result in truly unfathomable complications, which would have delighted the old masters of the 1 e4 e5 gambits! In fact, 1...e6, although known much earlier, first rose to the fore in the first half of the 19th century, probably as a reaction to the flood of fearsome gambit openings that washed over the classical 1...e5 in those days, like the King's Gambit and the Evans. After a famous correspondence match between the cities of London and Paris in 1834, where the French team played 1...e6, the name French Defence was coined and a new defence to 1 e4 was given a place on the map.

Nowadays the French is a popular reply to 1 e4 at all levels. It is certainly useful to be at least roughly acquainted with some of the sharper variations, but generally a good positional understanding is more important than ready theoretical knowledge. Usually the result of the opening will be a strategically dynamic middlegame, in which positional considerations and long-term planning are likely to dominate. But below the surface there is often a volcano of tactical violence boiling, waiting to erupt at any moment.

2   d4

This is without a doubt White's most natural move, but it stands to reason that there are alternative possibilities.

An important one is **2 d3**. White anticipates his opponent's plan: he wants to be able to recapture on e4 with a pawn. This avoids such immediate skirmishing in the centre as may be expected from 2 d4 and stabilizes White's central position. By continuing after **2...d5** with 3 ♘d2 *(D)*, White avoids an exchange of queens and initiates a plan of development that is based on the King's Indian Defence: ♘f3, g3 and ♗g2.

This is called the **King's Indian Attack**, a set-up that we have already met in the Réti

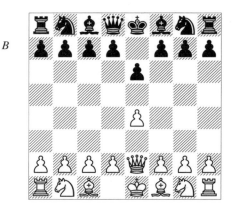

Opening. In fact, if play continues **3...♘f6** 4 ♘gf3 ♗e7 5 g3 0-0 6 ♗g2 c5 7 0-0, we reach a position that was mentioned in the chapter on the Réti Opening as resulting from 1 ♘f3 d5 2 g3 ♘f6 3 ♗g2 e6 4 0-0 ♗e7 5 d3 0-0 6 ♘bd2 c5 7 e4.

Naturally, by playing a move like 2 d3, White leaves his opponent a free hand and Black has many options beside the above. Some of the most popular ones are to play **3...c5** 4 ♘gf3 ♘c6 5 g3 and now 5...♗d6 6 ♗g2 ♘ge7 or 5...g6 6 ♗g2 ♗g7 7 0-0 ♘ge7. In both cases Black makes the crucial e5 advance more difficult for White to achieve than if he plays 5...♘f6. Another frequently played move is the Sicilian option: **2...c5**.

Most of these lines cannot really be said to belong exclusively to the French Defence. They are of at least equal importance to the flank openings (the Réti and 1 g3) and to the Sicilian Defence, especially the variation 1 e4 c5 2 ♘f3 e6, where 3 d3 is a very popular option (see page 420). The King's Indian Attack is really a sort of unguided missile that roams free throughout the world of opening theory. It is a plan of development not tied to any particular move-order and more effective in some situations than in others. After 1...e5 it has practically no significance to speak of, but as a way of combating the French, where Black has already committed himself to an ...e6 plan, it is relatively well-suited.

Another popular option is the very odd **2 ♕e2** *(D)*, a move that Chigorin (1850-1908) used to be fond of.

It looks barbaric to prevent a recapture on d5 with the e-pawn after 2...d5 3 exd5 in such a primitive way, but in fact White is again preparing for a King's Indian Attack, a scheme of development in which the move ♕e2 fits rather well. If 2...c5 3 ♘f3 ♘c6 4 g3 g6 5 ♗g2 ♗g7 6 0-0 ♘ge7 7 d3 0-0 8 c3, for instance, a position is reached that will look perfectly ordinary to most King's Indian Attackers.

These two moves (2 d3 and 2 ♕e2) steer the game in a direction that is totally different from the main route 2 d4. Another possibility is to accept this main route as a guiding principle but to travel in that direction on a parallel road, not on the main road itself. Such a variation is **2 ♘f3** d5 3 ♘c3 (or **2 ♘c3** d5 3 ♘f3, depending on how White intends to react to the Sicilian diversion 2...c5). While avoiding for the moment the real main lines of the French, White still takes advantage of their existence for in some cases he will certainly want to transpose. Thus, after 3...d4 4 ♘e2 play takes on a wholly un-French character, but after 3...dxe4 4 ♘xe4 ♘d7 5 d4 we find ourselves in a very ordinary Rubinstein Variation (see page 354). The most common reply is 3...♘f6, a move which illustrates the pluses and minuses of this 'parallel variation' rather nicely: after 4 e5 ♘fd7 5 d4 c5 White has indeed circumvented enormous chunks of theory from the main lines, but what he has ended up with is a fairly innocuous sideline of the Steinitz Variation (see page 356).

2 ♘f3 may also be played with a totally different idea, namely to meet 2...d5 with 3 e5, intending to gambit a pawn if Black continues 3...c5: 4 b4!?. This is a bold yet positionally well-founded sacrifice. After 4...cxb4 5 a3 bxa3 6 d4, White has diverted Black's c-pawn from attacking his own pawn on d4 and in so doing has strengthened his centre considerably.

The idea of anticipating 2...d5 by playing **2 c4**, which – as we shall see in the next chapter – occupies such a prominent position in the Caro-Kann Defence, is harmless against the French. After 3 exd5 exd5 4 cxd5 ♘f6 5 ♗b5+ (analogous to the Caro-Kann) Black calmly replies 5...♘bd7 6 ♘c3 ♗e7 and, after 7 d4 0-0 8 ♘f3 ♘b6 for instance, regains the pawn at his leisure. 2...c5 reaches a type of position we know from the Symmetrical English, and is also not bad. After 3 ♘c3 ♘c6 4 g3 g6 5 ♗g2 ♗g7 we have reached a position from the Botvinnik Variation (1 c4 c5 2 ♘c3 ♘c6 3 g3 g6 4 ♗g2 ♗g7 5 e4 e6).

2 ... d5 (D)

This is the real starting point of the French. It is also the first crisis in the opening battle, for White now has to make a fundamental decision with far-reaching consequences. He has several options of dealing with the threat against his e-pawn and every single one of them will to a great extent define the character of the forthcoming middlegame.

By playing **3 exd5** White resolves the tension immediately. This is the **Exchange Variation**, which was regarded as a drawing weapon for a very long time until Garry Kasparov rehabilitated the line in 1991.

Equally drastic but otherwise totally different is **3 e5**, the **Advance Variation**. This line too has gained considerably in popularity of late and is now almost on a par with the real main lines of the French, **3 ♘c3** and **3 ♘d2**. Oddly enough, the former of these does not have a name, even though it is the starting move for the sharpest and most crucial variations of the entire French Defence. The latter, **3 ♘d2**, is called **Tarrasch Variation**.

There are hardly any alternatives to these four moves. **3 ♗d3** is possible but the position after 3...dxe4 4 ♗xe4 ♘f6 5 ♗d3 c5 is considerably more comfortable for Black than the comparable Rubinstein Variation (see page 353) and **3 f3** makes little sense, for after 3...dxe4 it impossible to reply 4 fxe4 in view of 4...♕h4+.

Exchange Variation

3 exd5

This is undoubtedly the simplest solution to the problems raised by 2...d5, but the status of this variation is a singularly unusual one. In the middle of the 19th century, 3 exd5 was a favourite with Paul Morphy (1837-84), and in the early 1990s it was a speciality of Garry Kasparov. These are two of the very best chess-players the world has ever seen. But in the century and a half between those giants, the line was looked upon as a boring drawing variation. How to explain this glaring contrast?

3 ... exd5 (D)

The answer lies in the specific type of pawn-structure resulting from this obvious reply.

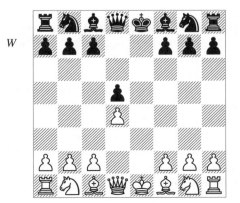

We know this symmetrical pawn-formation from the Petroff Defence. Although the position of a black knight on e4 and (in the 3 d4 variation) a white knight on e5 adds some extra tension to the Petroff (in particular the uncertainty whether these knights are well-placed), the situation is basically the same. Whoever wants to be successful in a position like this has to have a highly-developed intuitive sense of the initiative and extremely good technical skills. In short, he has to be able, like Moses, to beat water out of a rock. This was a talent that both Morphy and Kasparov were gifted with to an unusual degree, but for the ordinary mortal things are different. It must be admitted, therefore, that most people who choose the Exchange Variation as White are simply out for safety and in many cases – let us not beat about the bush – for an easy draw.

Both Morphy and Kasparov preferred the sturdy developing move **4 ♘f3** *(D)* in this position.

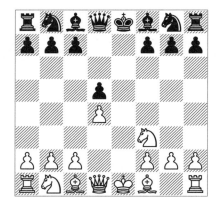

Morphy in particular was often successful with the symmetrical continuation **4...♘f6** 5 ♗d3 ♗d6 6 0-0 0-0. After 7 ♘c3 c6 8 ♗g5 he had just that little bit of an edge to put the screws on and make his opponents nervous. Nearly one and a half centuries later, it fell to Kasparov to demonstrate that other moves than 4...♘f6 do not yield Black easy equality either.

He introduced, for instance, after **4...♗g4** 5 h3 ♗h5, the subtle 6 ♕e2+ based on the idea that after 6...♕e7 7 ♗e3 ♘c6 8 ♘c3 0-0-0 9 0-0-0 Black's position suffers worse from the disorganization caused by the two queens standing on e2 and e7 than White's, for White can develop his king's bishop harmoniously at g2 by playing g4.

If instead **4...♘c6** 5 ♗b5 ♗d6, the moment is well-suited for the aggressive 6 c4 and the same goes for the immediate **4...♗d6** 5 c4. Both cxd5 and c5 can be nasty for Black, while 5...dxc4 6 ♗xc4 transposes to a line of the Queen's Gambit Accepted (1 d4 d5 2 c4 dxc4 3 e3 e5 4 ♗xc4 exd4 5 exd4 ♗d6 6 ♘f3; see page 40), which not every 'French' player will be happy with.

At any rate, these lines are more powerful than the immediate **4 c4**. This move is also sometimes played, but it hardly sets the opponent any problems after 4...♘f6 5 ♘c3 ♗e7 or 5...♗b4. Once theory really starts to dig into a line, such minimal differences (as between 4 c4 and 4 ♘f3 ♗d6 5 c4) often turn out to be quite serious.

Throughout the 20th century, most opening books gave **4 ♗d3** and even the symmetrical 4...♗d6 5 ♘e2 ♘e7 as the main line. This is based on defensive thinking: both players are worried about the possible pins ♗g5 and ...♗g4 respectively, so they decline to develop their knights at their most aggressive squares f3 or f6.

Advance Variation

3　e5 *(D)*

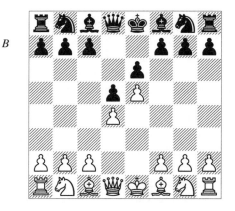

This move is of a totally different calibre from 3 exd5. White closes the centre and creates a spatial advantage for himself on the kingside. Long-term planning is likely to dominate the opening phase and indeed the rest of the game. Considerations of fast and efficient piece development become subordinate to finding the right plan and anticipating the enemy's movements.

The Advance Variation is very old and was quite important in the 19th century, but it fell into disrepute until Nimzowitsch revitalized it around 1910. Nevertheless, despite his efforts the line was often seen as a somewhat indolent way of playing and as a mere ploy to avoid the great main lines of the French. But towards the end of the 20th century this attitude changed. More and more top players began to take an interest in 3 e5 and its variations began to be explored deeper and with more precision and sharpness. I think it is fair to say that due to these efforts the Advance Variation has now become one of the main lines of the French.

3   ...   c5 *(D)*

It immediately becomes clear that 3 e5 is not a move aimed at fast development, for it can be said with only a slight amount of exaggeration that Black is now taking the initiative. He attacks d4 and has plenty of opportunity to become aggressive on the queenside. In fact this is exactly why, from time to time, theory has considered the Advance Variation to be inferior. But the crucial question is: how does Black's short-term initiative compare to White's long-term prospects? This is where theory has changed its mind again and again in the past (and is likely to keep on doing so in the future).

4   c3   ♘c6

A major strategic motif characteristic of this type of closed position comes to the fore if Black plays **4...♕b6 5 ♘f3 ♗d7**. The idea is to exchange bishops with 6...♗b5, very desirable from a purely positional or static point of view. White has two options. He can simply allow Black to carry out his plan and make the best of it (after all, White does retain his spatial advantage) or he can play the sharp 6 ♗e2 ♗b5 7 c4!?, seeking to open the position. This variation is thought to be theoretically critical. After 7...♗xc4 8 ♗xc4 dxc4 9 d5, for instance, dynamic considerations suddenly dominate the game, making static considerations like the exchange of bishops less important.

5   ♘f3 *(D)*

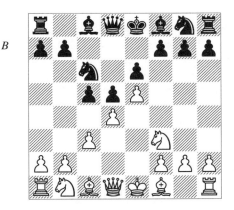

5   ...   ♕b6 *(D)*

The classical approach. Black continues to attack d4, while keeping b2 covered as well, making it difficult for White to develop his queen's bishop. Naturally, in the wave of popularity that has swept the Advance Variation during the past two decades, a thorough search has been made for possible alternatives at practically every turn. This has resulted in **5...♗d7** becoming a major option. This is a flexible move, keeping ...♕b6 in reserve. If 6 a3 c4, for instance, the manoeuvre ...♘ge7-c8-b6 may be a better way of using the b6-square and if Black has an ...f6 plan in mind (6 a3 f6 or 6 a3 c4 7 ♗e2 f6, for example), it may also be quite unnecessary to play ...♕b6. If 6 ♗e2, Black may play 6...♕b6 again but 6...♘ge7, in order to put the knight either on f5 (attacking d4 again) or on g6 (where it supports the advance ...f6 and thus indirectly attacks e5) is a useful alternative.

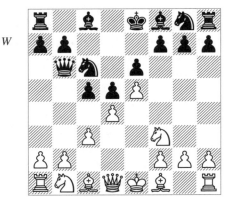

This is the most important starting position of the Advance Variation. It is also a good illustration of the strategic, long-term thinking that typifies this variation, for **6 &d3**, White's most natural developing move, although not *impossible* (for 6...cxd4 7 cxd4 &xd4?? 8 &xd4 &xd4?? loses the queen to 9 &b5+), does have a serious disadvantage: after 7...&d7 (instead of 7...&xd4??) White either has to lose a tempo with 8 &e2 or 8 &c2 or gambit a pawn with 8 0-0.

For this reason, **6 &e2** has become the more usual move, but of course this is in fact a (minor) concession, for the bishop is slightly less aggressive on e2. To make this perhaps somewhat abstract argument more concrete: Black might intensify the attack against d4 with 6...cxd4 7 cxd4 &h6 (or 7...&ge7), followed by 8...&f5, now that there is no bishop at d3 to eliminate this knight.

But the most popular move and probably the most critical test of 5...&b6 is **6 a3** *(D)*.

This may look rather slow and humble at first sight, but it is in fact the opening move of a very ambitious plan. White is going to challenge Black's domination of the queenside by playing b4, attacking c5, relieving the pressure against b2, creating a new square for the queen's bishop at b2 and gaining back space, all at the same time. All these features become tangible

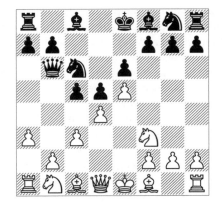

in the variation **6...&h6** 7 b4 cxd4 8 cxd4 &f5 9 &b2 &e7, when White can finally develop his king's bishop at the desired square with 10 &d3, making &xf5 a realistic prospect. This is in fact a topical and hotly contested line. Black might, for instance, strike back on the queenside with 10...a5.

Other moves, like **6...a5** and **6...&d7**, are also undergoing very serious examination indeed, but Black's most important move is the radical **6...c4** *(D)*.

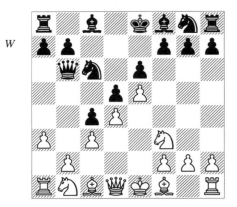

Black relinquishes the pressure against d4 and redirects his attention to the new Achilles' Heel in White's position: the b3-square. Not only is White unable to play 7 b3 cxb3 8 axb3 now that his pawn is no longer on a2 (as he certainly would in case of 6 &e2 c4 for instance), but he is also facing the positional threat of ...&a5-b3. It is true that by playing 7 &bd2 White prevents this rather easily but this bottles up his entire queenside for after 7...♞a5 the threat of ...♞b3 is permanent and the knight will not be able to leave d2 at will. This all means that a heavy positional struggle lies ahead, not just strategically but tactically as well. White may, for instance, decide to persevere in his plan of challenging Black's domination of the queenside and venture b4 as a pawn sacrifice. After 8 b4 cxb3 9 ♗b2 followed by 10 c4, a sharp fight for the initiative is likely to ensue. And if White simply develops his kingside instead, Black may play ...f6 sooner or later, which is again likely to trigger some very unclear complications.

3 ♞c3

3   ♞c3 *(D)*

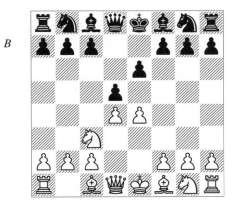

With this serene developing move, White pushes the problems back where they belong: on the opponent's doorstep. Instead of determining the central pawn-formation immediately, White simply waits for things to come.

In choosing a reply, Black must again carefully consider the consequences of both e5 and – to a lesser extent – exd5. The obvious solution to this problem is to cut the Gordian Knot at once by playing **3...dxe4**. This is the **Rubinstein Variation** and it is certainly the simplest of Black's options in this position.

The consequences of **3...♞f6** are rather more difficult to evaluate. White is challenged to play e5 with an attractive gain of tempo (as compared to 3 e5). This is usually called the **Classical Variation** these days. It was the unchallenged

main line of the French until another possibility rose to the fore around 1930: **3...♗b4**, the **Winawer Variation**. This is a highly complex line which, having driven generations of 3 ♞c3 players to despair, has now been tamed to some degree, but still constitutes the sharpest and most critical reply to 3 ♞c3.

In the shadow of these main lines there are a few other moves, of which **3...♞c6** is the most generally accepted. Instead of attacking e4, Black is aiming his guns at d4, but the idea is the same as what motivates 3...♞f6 and 3...♗b4: to force White to make a decision. After 4 ♞f3 ♞f6 5 e5 ♞e4, 6 ♗d3 ♗b4 7 ♗d2 has developed into the main line here, with the ambitious 6 ♞e2 a dangerous runner-up.

Rubinstein Variation

3   ...   dxe4

This interpretation of the French Defence first became fashionable around 1900. It was a controversial one from the start. Lasker and Rubinstein liked the move and often played it, but Tarrasch for one never had a kind word for it. Then when 3...♗b4 started to become popular, the Rubinstein Variation faded into the background and for almost the rest of the 20th century it was invariably given the epithet 'passive' in the books. The truth is that there was simply no interest in it. Nobody took the trouble to re-examine it properly for more than half a century. When this finally did happen in the 1990s, the long rest turned out to have done the Rubinstein a world of good. Below layers of dust lay a lively and resourceful variation, which became one of the most popular defences to 1 e4 almost overnight and which must be held partly responsible for the rise of interest in the Advance Variation.

4   ♞xe4 *(D)*

Having given up his stronghold in the centre, the pawn on d5, Black has chosen a type of middlegame which is very different from everything we have seen so far. White has more space and excellent opportunities for active piece development. Black has a position without any weaknesses and the strategic prospect of playing ...c5, eliminating White's remaining

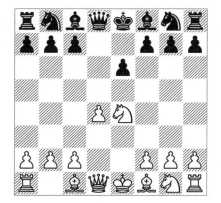

centre pawn. But first he has to find a way to develop his pieces.

4   ...   ♘d7

This is the classical method, preparing to continue ...♘gf6 and then recapture with the other knight if White plays ♘xf6+. Another idea is to develop the queen's bishop first. The straightforward **4...b6** has never had a good reputation because it allows White to force ...c6 by playing either 5 ♕f3 (threatening 6 ♘f6+) or 5 ♘f3 ♗b7 6 ♗b5+, obstructing the h1-a8 diagonal. But **4...♗d7** is thought to be a very reliable move and this is often played nowadays. A critical position is reached after 5 ♘f3 ♗c6 6 ♗d3 ♘d7 7 0-0 ♘gf6. In order to prevent exchanges on a grand scale, White usually retreats his knight to g3 or d2. In this variation Black often plays ...♗xf3 followed by ...c6 instead of the classical ...c5. This promises him a slightly passive (so the old epithet was not completely wrong!) but very solid position.

5   ♘f3   ♘gf6 (D)

One major difference from the 4...♗d7 variation is that 6 ♘g3 is now not very strong because this allows Black to play 6...c5 without any problems. This advance of the black c-pawn is the crux of the opening struggle. Will White be able to stop it, and, if the answer is negative, how should he anticipate it?

Thanks to the enormous popularity the Rubinstein has been enjoying of late, several possibilities have been tested intensively and at the very highest level. White's main trump is fast development, which enables him to go for some aggressive options. What makes this variation

so interesting is that Black does not need to fear this aggression. Notwithstanding the many dangers that lie in store for him, Black is almost always able to carry out his plan: to play ...c5.

6   ♘xf6+

The main alternative is **6 ♗g5**, when a position arises which is also (and in fact much more often) reached via the related Burn Variation (3...♘f6 4 ♗g5 dxe4; see page 357). It is sometimes said that the idea of the Burn Variation is to wait for White to play ♗g5 before taking on e4 and that this slight difference favours Black, but this is far from certain.

The big difference between 6 ♘xf6+ and 6 ♗g5 is that after 6 ♗g5 Black renews the problem by playing 6...♗e7 and that now 7 ♘xf6+ can be met by 7...♗xf6, when after 8 ♗xf6 ♕xf6 Black not only has the prospect of playing ...c5 but of ...e5 as well. It is very difficult for White to capitalize on his spatial advantage in this line. Attempts to improve on this are 8 ♕d2 and 8 h4 on the white side and 6...h6 7 ♗h4 ♗e7 (instead of the immediate 6...♗e7) by Black.

6   ...   ♘xf6 (D)

Again White has to make a decision: should he play the temptingly active **7 ♗g5** or does this move only provoke a further exchange of pieces? And again this is a position of equal importance for the Burn and the Rubinstein Variation. After 7...c5 the situation is critical. White has tried a variety of moves, of which 8 ♗b5+ is the most direct. After 8...♗d7 9 ♗xd7+ ♕xd7, practice has shown that Black does not have to worry about getting his f-pawns doubled by 10

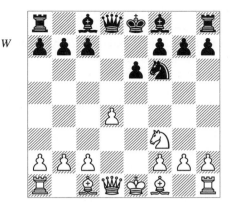

&xf6 gxf6. 10 ♕e2, intending to castle queen-side, is an option.

Since it is unclear who actually benefits from the pin ♗g5, other moves are at least equally critical, especially for the move-order of the Rubinstein Variation (it is only after 7 ♗g5 that the roads of the Burn and the Rubinstein inter-sect).

7 ♗d3 is White's most popular move. He al-lows Black to play 7...c5 and after 8 dxc5 ♗xc5 he has a choice between castling kingside (when play might continue 9 0-0 0-0 10 ♗g5 b6 11 ♕e2 ♗b7 12 ♖ad1) and castling queenside (starting with 9 ♕e2 0-0 10 ♗g5 or 10 ♗d2).

The alternative **7 c3** c5 8 ♘e5, preparing 9 ♗b5+, also has to be taken into account. Al-most a century ago, Capablanca even played **7 ♘e5** immediately.

Classical Variation

> **3 ... ♘f6 (D)**

Before the rise of the Winawer Variation, this was by far the most important line of the French. So normal was it to play 3...♘f6 in this position that it did not even occur to anyone to 'claim' the move and give it a name, except that it was sometimes called the 'normal' defence. But dur-ing the heyday of the Winawer, 3...♘f6 fell into disuse until it was rediscovered in the 1980s. Nowadays 3...♘f6 and 3...♗b4 are thought to be of equal importance and the old 'normal de-fence' has been named the **Classical Variation**.

The most obvious reply to 3...♘f6 is **4 e5**, the **Steinitz Variation**. It is this line in particular

that has profited from the recent wave of atten-tion 3...♘f6 has been receiving. Theory of this line has become immensely more detailed and complex.

Yet **4 ♗g5**, by far the most usual move in the first half of the 20th century, remains an impor-tant option. This is the starting point of three old, but highly topical variations.

The same cannot be said about **4 exd5**. Once it was thought that the inclusion of ♘c3 and ...♘f6 (as compared to the Exchange Variation, 3 exd5) would favour White, but this has turned out to be overoptimistic. After 4...exd5 5 ♗g5 ♗e7 6 ♗d3 ♘c6 Black has no problems to speak of.

Steinitz Variation

> **4 e5 ♘fd7 (D)**

This is to all practical purposes the starting point of the Steinitz Variation, although the rather speculative **4...♘e4** 5 ♘xe4 dxe4 (in-tending 6...c5) is also played occasionally.

A superficial comparison of the position after 4...♘fd7 with the Advance Variation would sug-gest that Black has not at all done well. He has made two moves with his king's knight as a re-sult of which this piece is now standing on what must look like an unfortunate square: d7. But if we take a closer look, things turn out to be not so simple. In fact there is a striking parallel with the Classical Variation of the King's Indian Defence 1 d4 ♘f6 2 c4 g6 3 ♘c3 ♗g7 4 e4 d6 5 ♘f3 0-0 6 ♗e2 e5 7 0-0 ♘c6 8 d5 ♘e7 (see page 107). Black is ready to attack d4 with ...c5 (just as he is

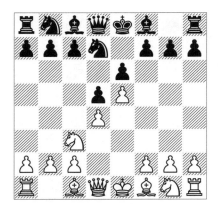

ready to pounce on e4 with ...f5 in the King's Indian), when c5 and b6 are likely to become excellent squares for the d7-knight and White's e5-pawn may come under attack. Besides, c3 is not necessarily a very good square for White's knight, for it obstructs the characteristic c3.

5 f4

White firmly protects e5 and makes it clear where his future lies: on the kingside. In the long run the advance f5 will become an option.

Just how very different a mind-set is required in closed positions as compared to the open type of position usually resulting from 1 e4 e5 openings is nicely illustrated by two alternatives: 5 ♘f3 and 5 ♘ce2.

5 ♘f3 may look like a perfectly natural and healthy developing move, but the strategic downside of it is that after 5...c5 followed by 6...♘c6, White's e5-pawn becomes vulnerable. If White adapts his play to this potential danger, there is certainly no cause for alarm: by playing 6 dxc5 ♘c6 7 ♗f4 he keeps everything well under control. But in this case Black will eliminate White's remaining centre pawn with 7...♗xc5 8 ♗d3 f6, when 9 exf6 ♘xf6 10 0-0 0-0 leads to a position where most of the tension has been resolved.

In striking contrast to 5 ♘f3, **5 ♘ce2** looks ugly and unnatural, but strategically this is a much more ambitious move (which is not to say that it is necessarily better!). White frees the way for his c-pawn so as to answer 5...c5 with 6 c3, thus preserving his stronghold at d4. After 6...♘c6 he will continue 7 f4, keeping his entire central pawn-formation intact. This variation is

likely to produce a heavy battle, for Black can be expected to strike back with all his might. There is, for instance, the move 7...b5, gaining space on the queenside, or there is 7...♕b6 to put maximum pressure on both d4 and b2. In some cases Black plays ...g5, while ...f6 and ...fxe5 to create counterplay along the f-file is also a likely option.

5 f4 could be called the middle way. While allowing his d-pawn to be exchanged, White strengthens e5 and continues to develop his pieces in a harmonious way.

5	...	c5
6	♘f3	♘c6
7	♗e3 (D)	

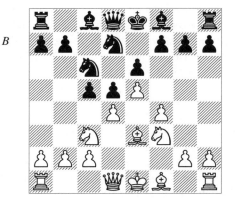

Starting from this position, some widely differing variations have been developed over the past two or three decades.

For many years, **7...♕b6** was regarded as the critical test of White's set-up. Black is attacking b2 and preparing 8...cxd4 9 ♘xd4 ♗c5 at the same time. This sharp move has to be judged on the merits of 8 ♘a4 ♕a5+ 9 c3 and more in particular on the consequences of the piece sacrifice 9...cxd4 10 b4 ♘xb4!? 11 cxb4 ♗xb4+ 12 ♗d2 ♗xd2+ 13 ♘xd2. At first Black's chances in this position, where he has three pawns for the piece and White's two knights are far from ideally placed, were viewed rather optimistically. But once theory began to dig deeper and deeper with more of the world's very best players taking an interest, enthusiasm for Black's prospects cooled off, even though a clear refutation has never been found.

A variation on this theme is to play **7...cxd4** 8 ♘xd4 and only then **8...♕b6** (D).

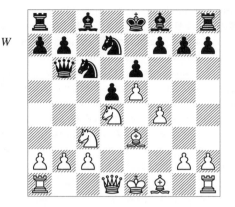

Now **9 ♘a4 ♕a5+** 10 c3 ♘xd4 is of little use to White since 11 ♗xd4? b5 drops a piece while the zwischenzug 11 b4 can be met by 11...♗xb4 12 cxb4 ♕xb4+ 13 ♗d2 ♕e7. The pawn sacrifice **9 ♕d2 ♕xb2** 10 ♖b1 ♕a3, and now, for instance, 11 ♗b5, is a critical line. While Black's position is both solid and resilient, White's lead in development is undeniably huge. This is an ideal variation for those who love to analyse their openings deeply and accurately at home.

A more common interpretation of this line is to follow 7...cxd4 8 ♘xd4 up with **8...♗c5**. While preparing ...♕b6, Black does not commit himself to this sharp move. Yet after the natural reply 9 ♕d2 Black has to lay his cards on the table. One option is to go for a mass-exchange of pieces with **9...♗xd4** 10 ♗xd4 ♘xd4 11 ♕xd4 ♕b6 12 ♕xb6 ♘xb6 and hope that Black's fortress will be strong enough to withstand the long siege that is to be expected. This is in fact playing for a draw rather blatantly and the name **Vacuum Cleaner Variation** is highly appropriate. The alternative is to initiate a sharp battle by simply castling into White's natural attacking zone, the kingside (**9...0-0**), and start looking for counterplay on the other side of the board. A characteristic and hotly debated sample variation is 10 0-0-0 a6 11 h4 ♘xd4 12 ♗xd4 b5 13 ♖h3 b4 14 ♘a4 ♗xd4 15 ♕xd4 and now, for instance, 15...f6!?.

The immediate **7...a6** is also played quite often. After 8 ♕d2 Black then not only has

8...cxd4 9 ♘xd4 ♗c5, which is likely to transpose to the above line after 10 0-0-0 0-0, but he can also play 8...b5 at once. White's attacking chances on the kingside catch the eye, but Black's territorial gains on the queenside are equally impressive. This is a variation that can only lead to a very fierce battle.

4 ♗g5

4   ♗g5 (D)

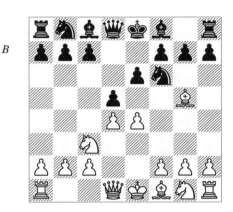

A move in the spirit of 3 ♘c3. In once more delaying the choice between e5 and exd5, White is again hoping to improve the circumstances for either of these moves. Now it is up to Black to choose between three wildly different variations, two of them rather obvious, but the third one not at all. The obvious ones are **4...dxe4**, the **Burn Variation**, and the calm developing move **4...♗e7**. The third is **4...♗b4**, the notorious **McCutcheon Variation**.

Burn Variation

4   ...   dxe4

As I mentioned in the section on the Rubinstein Variation (see page 353), this line is loosely based on the idea that taking on e4 is more accurate if White has already committed himself to ♗g5. But whether this is indeed so is quite unclear. In fact, many players who like this type of position have both the Rubinstein *and* the Burn Variation in their opening repertoire nowadays!

5   ♘xe4

If **5 ♗xf6**, an interesting aspect of this type of position is highlighted, which plays a more prominent role in the Burn than in the Rubinstein Variation. Instead of accepting the loss of time incurred by 5...♕xf6 6 ♘xe4 ♕d8, Black can very well play 5...gxf6, seeking to take the initiative immediately with 6 ♘xe4 f5 7 ♘g3 ♗g7 8 ♘f3 c5. The motif of recapturing on f6 with the g-pawn becomes more logical and powerful if White takes on f6 with the bishop, thus giving up the bishop-pair.

5   ...   ♗e7 (D)

This is the classical Burn move. **5...♘bd7** is a subtle alternative, which after 6 ♘f3 I have classified (rather randomly I must admit) as part of the Rubinstein Variation (see page 354).

White faces the same problem as in the Rubinstein Variation after 3...dxe4 4 ♘xe4 ♘d7 5 ♘f3 ♘gf6 6 ♗g5 ♗e7 (see page 354): what should he do with the e4-knight? As is so often the case, a minimal difference between two lines (the extra moves ♘f3 and ...♘bd7) causes the variations to be markedly different in character.

To begin with – and this is hardly sensational – **6 ♘xf6+** is unlikely to gain in strength now that Black can reply 6...♗xf6 7 ♗xf6 ♕xf6 8 ♘f3 0-0 and is probably able to find something better than ...♘d7 on his next move.

6   ♗xf6

Matters become more interesting after this move, which makes much more sense here than in the Rubinstein, where there is a knight on d7

to do the recapturing. If **6...♗xf6** White has consolidated the dominant position of his e4-knight. This will make it possible to prepare calmly for an attack on the kingside. 7 ♘f3 0-0 8 ♕d2 ♘d7 9 0-0-0 ♗e7 10 ♗d3 b6 11 h4 (or 11 ♘eg5) is a characteristic sample variation. Black has to be very careful here.

By playing **6...gxf6** (D) instead, Black introduces another dynamic factor. With his doubled f-pawns, he increases his control over the central squares, but of course he does create a few holes in his pawn-structure. This is the most difficult and the most controversial of the many ...gxf6 options that Black has in this variation.

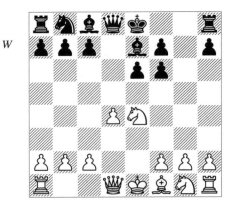

After the usual reply 7 ♘f3, White is better armed against **7...f5** than he is in the 5 ♗xf6 gxf6 line because after 8 ♘c3 ♗f6 Black has needed an extra move to put his king's bishop on the long diagonal. Nevertheless, this is an interesting option for Black and one which is played quite frequently.

The alternative **7...b6** is more cautious and is likely to lead to a heavy strategic battle. A typical (although by no means forced) continuation is 8 ♗c4 ♗b7 9 ♕e2 c6 10 0-0-0 ♘d7 11 ♔b1 ♕c7 12 ♖he1 0-0-0. Now 13 ♗a6 forces a useful exchange of bishops because the b7-bishop is an important defender of Black's king in this type of position. In many cases, Black will try to play ...f5 and ...♗f6 after all to activate his other bishop, but this plan has the drawback of making the e5-square accessible to White's knights. Another crucial element of the strategic make-up of the position is the advance d5.

In the long run White may try to force this central break with the help of c4.

Recently **7...a6** has also become popular. This is a bold and provocative variation on the theme of 7...b6. Apparently unafraid of giving the opponent more targets, Black wants to play 8...b5 and 9...♗b7, gaining space on the queenside.

4...♗e7

4 ... ♗e7 (D)

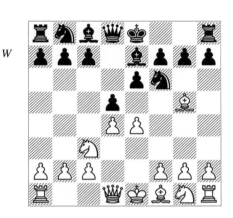

This is the classical reply to White's fourth move. White now finally has to decide what to do with his e-pawn unless he is prepared to give up his bishop-pair and play **5 ♗xf6**. This is unlikely to worry players with a natural preference for knights over bishops and in fact this very old variation (a favourite of the great Adolf Anderssen in the middle of the 19th century) is surprisingly similar to the hypermodern Trompowsky Attack (see page 171) but it is not popular at all.

5 e5

Just as on move four, taking on d5 is completely innocuous. After **5 exd5**, 5...exd5 leads to a position that was discussed under 4 exd5 and Black also has 5...♘xd5 6 ♗xe7 ♕xe7, solving his opening problems rather easily.

5 ... ♘fd7

5...♘e4 is an even more speculative sortie than was 4 e5 ♘e4 in the Steinitz Variation (see page 355). Nevertheless it is occasionally played, mainly as a surprise weapon. After 6

♗xe7, the lines starting with 6...♕xe7 7 ♘xe4 dxe4 8 ♕e2 b6!? or 6...♘xc3 7 ♕g4!? (more ambitious than 7 ♗xd8 ♘xd1 8 ♗xc7 ♘xb2 9 ♖b1) 7...♕xe7 8 ♕xg7 ♕b4!? 9 ♕xh8+ ♔d7 are sharp and critical. In the latter variation, White can try 10 ♘f3, when Black must avoid 10...♕xb2? 11 ♔d2!. However, 10...♘e4+ 11 ♔e2 ♘c6! (threatening 12...♘xd4+) 12 ♔e3 ♘xd4! is OK for Black.

6 ♗xe7

Natural as this move may be, it is not self-evident. However lazy or dull individual chess-players may be sometimes, opening theory as a whole certainly isn't and so in this position a double-edged pawn sacrifice has grown into a fully-fledged and popular alternative: **6 h4**, the **Chatard-Alekhine Attack**. White is out for more than just a positionally correct exchange of bishops; he wants an open h-file as well. Just how powerful White's attack really is after 6...♗xg5 7 hxg5 ♕xg5, and now 8 ♘h3 ♕e7 9 ♘f4, for instance, is not at all clear but in tournament practice most players prefer to decline the pawn sacrifice and go for solid moves like 6...c5 or 6...a6. After 6...c5 7 ♗xe7 Black (probably) has to recapture with the king because 7...♕xe7 runs into 8 ♘b5, but in a closed position like this it is not really a problem. 6...a6 is designed to eliminate this little quirk and can therefore be said to be more cautious.

6 ... ♕xe7 (D)

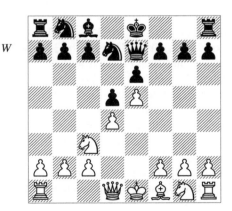

Until far into the 20th century, books on the French Defence tended to devote a large quantity of their pages to this position. It was called the basic position of the Classical Variation and every even remotely plausible move by White was treated as an independent variation and – in many books – given a name. But when 3...♗b4 expelled the classical 3...♘f6 from its dominant position, much of this ancient theory began gathering dust. Nobody was interested any more.

With the rehabilitation of the Classical French, the diagrammed position has resumed some of its former importance. It should be compared critically to the basic position of the Steinitz Variation (see page 356). A dogmatic comparison would suggest that the exchange of bishops must be to White's advantage, simply because it is his 'bad' bishop against Black's 'good' one that goes ('bad' meaning that the bishop is hampered in its activity by his own centre pawns fixed on squares of the same colour, and 'good' the opposite). In fact, this is what motivates many players to prefer 4 ♗g5 to 4 e5. They assume that they have now reached a favourable version of the Steinitz Variation. But this assessment is very complicated. There are other factors to be taken into account than just the colour of your bishop. Because of the exchange, Black's position – always a little cramped in the French – becomes freer and with the disappearance of White's dark-squared bishop a potentially dangerous threat to Black's kingside is eliminated.

The most important move by far in modern theory, just like in the Steinitz, is **7 f4**. A characteristic continuation would be 7...0-0 8 ♘f3 c5 9 ♕d2 ♘c6 10 dxc5 f6. Due to his greater freedom of movement (thanks to the exchange of bishops!), Black is in a position to break down White's entire pawn-centre. The downside to this plan is that it is precisely in the type of position resulting from these pawn exchanges, after 11 exf6 ♕xf6 12 g3 ♘xc5 for instance, that the absence of a dark-squared bishop is making itself felt the most, for White now has two potentially strong squares for his pieces at d4 and e5. But it remains to Black's credit that he enjoys relatively great freedom for his pieces. The light-squared bishop, for instance, often gets manoeuvred to g6 or h5 via d7 and e8.

McCutcheon Variation

4   ...   ♗b4 (D)

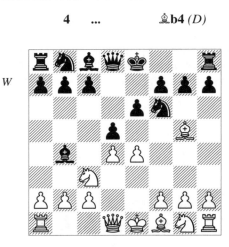

'Attack is the best form of defence' might be the motto of this variation. Black is trying to invert the dynamics of the position. Instead of civilly defending against the threat of e5, he makes an attempt to bend the consequences of that advance to his own advantage.

The McCutcheon Variation was very popular from about 1905 until 1925 even at the highest level. It then withdrew from the public eye and became a sort of ghost, appearing from time to time – always unexpectedly – to scare the living daylights out of an unsuspecting opponent and then disappear again. Any hope of finding comfort and solace in the books was always frustrated, for these had got stuck in the theoretical situation of 1925 and could offer little or no help to newer generations.

It was not until about 1990 that this situation finally began to change. More and more players started using the McCutcheon not just as a hit-and-run tactic but as a regular part of their opening repertoire. Inevitably, theory had to crawl out of the shadows where it had been hiding and much to everyone's surprise the McCutcheon appeared to tolerate the light of day very well. All variations that had appeared so elusive and phantom-like were nicely charted but not refuted. The strategic features were clarified yet without resolving the mystery and the inherent tension of the whole line. As a result, the McCutcheon now enjoys a healthy theoretical status, is widely popular, has retained something of its former mysterious aura *and* it remains controversial.

5   e5

The exchange **5 exd5** offers slightly better chances than it did a move earlier. Many players even avoid the symmetrical recapture 5...exd5 (though this is certainly playable) and prefer the more aggressive 5...♕xd5. The theoretical question then is whether after 6 ♗xf6 Black should just play 6...gxf6 (permitting White to 'rescue' his pawn-formation with 7 ♘e2) or if he should insert 6...♗xc3+.

Similar problems are raised if White plays **5 ♗d3**. A plausible continuation would be to play 5...dxe4 6 ♗xe4 ♘bd7 intending 7...h6 and (if necessary) 8...♘xf6. The position after 6 ♗xe4 also arises via the Winawer Variation (see page 363). It is one of only a very small number of actual links between these two variations which on the surface look so very alike.

5   ...   h6 *(D)*

Breaking the pin against the knight and avoiding the loss of a piece. White now faces a crucial decision.

6   ♗d2

This continuation has been the main line for decades.

Sustaining the pin with **6 ♗h4** is of little use for after 6...g5 7 ♗g3 ♘e4 Black is already taking over the initiative. The rather meek **6 ♗xf6** gxf6 also holds little promise for White.

But **6 exf6** is a serious alternative, even though White's position after 6...hxg5 7 fxg7

looks better than it actually is. After 7...♖g8 and now, for instance, 8 h4 gxh4 9 ♕h5 ♕f6, Black will collect the pawn at g7 and obtain a solid position.

6 ♗e3 is the sharpest move. White allows his opponent to play 6...♘e4, but avoids an exchange of his queen's bishop (as will be the case after 6 ♗d2). The critical continuation is 7 ♕g4 ♔f8 (or 7...g6) 8 a3. After 8...♗xc3+ 9 bxc3 Black can win a pawn at c3 either at once or after the preliminary (and highly thematic) 9...c5.

It is striking how difficult it is to evaluate the position in all of these variations. The McCutcheon almost always produces these murky, complicated middlegames where both sides are likely to persevere in their course of action but always run the risk of totally underestimating the opponent's chances.

6   ...   ♗xc3 *(D)*

Naturally **6...♘e4??** is now impossible due to 7 ♘xe4.

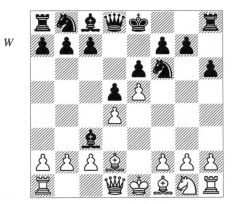

7   bxc3

This may look an odd follow-up to White's previous move. Why not play **7 ♗xc3**, keeping the pawn-structure intact? The answer is that this plan does not really work because after 7...♘e4 the consistent 8 ♗b4 runs into the treacherous 8...c5 9 dxc5 ♘xf2! 10 ♔xf2 ♕h4+. Another argument against 7 ♗xc3 is that by taking the bishop off the c1-h6 diagonal, White releases the pressure against Black's kingside. If he plays 8 ♕g4, for instance, Black can now simply castle or play 8...♕g5.

In spite of these objections, 7 ♗xc3 *is* occasionally played but it is definitely not the main line.

7　...　♘e4

So far everything is running smoothly for Black. His e4-knight is well-placed and after a 'normal' move like **8 ♗d3**, he has a very natural way of starting an attack on the queenside in 8...♘xd2 9 ♕xd2 c5, which will compensate him for White's space advantage on the kingside. If we compare this to the Winawer Variation (of which this position is reminiscent) Black has a comparatively easy game.

8　♕g4 (D)

However, this aggressive move shows up a drawback of Black's opening play. Unlike after 7 ♗xc3, Black has no easy way of protecting g7 for 8...0-0?? fails to 9 ♗xh6. He will have to make a concession.

8　...　g6

This has been the most popular choice, but **8...♔f8** also has its supporters. Which of these moves is better is truly difficult to say. By playing 8...♔f8, Black gives priority to the solidity of his pawn-structure. If 8...g6, it is the greater mobility of his pieces that he is interested in. A sample continuation after 8...♔f8: 9 ♗d3 ♘xd2 10 ♔xd2 c5 (exchanging queens with 10...♕g5+ 11 ♕xg5 hxg5 is not as good as it looks, for White can quickly seize the initiative on the kingside with 12 ♖f1 or even 12 f4 gxf4 13 ♖f1) and after **11 ♘f3 ♘c6** 12 h4 Black can start an attack on the queenside with 12...c4 followed by ...b5-b4. White will have to counterattack on

the kingside, for instance with h5 followed by ♖h3-g3. Just to illustrate how subtle and far-reaching even the slightest decision in this line can be: it could be an improvement for White to play **11 h4** straightaway, preserving the option of playing ♘e2/h3-f4 instead of ♘f3.

9　♗d3

White is prepared to move his king to d2, a courageous decision. In fact, even after 9 ♘f3 c5 10 ♗d3 ♘xd2 recapturing with the king is standard. It is undeniable that White's king is vulnerable in the middle of the board, but the fact that his knight and rooks will be able to move freely proves ample compensation.

9　...　♘xd2
10　♔xd2　c5 (D)

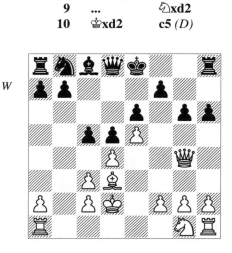

This is one of the most critical positions of the McCutcheon Variation. A battle on two fronts is in the offing. White will attack on the kingside and Black on the queenside. For White, an h4-h5 plan seems indicated, while the queen manoeuvre ♕f4-f6 may also be useful and in some cases even a piece sacrifice on g6 (♗xg6) is a possibility. Black has all sorts of options on the queenside, mainly based on ...cxd4 at some point. The slower plan of playing ...c4 is usually combined with 8...♔f8 because this move gives White less of a target on the kingside so Black does not have to hurry his own plans.

11 h4 is a characteristic continuation. Black then has the straightforward 11...♘c6 in order to meet 12 ♕f4 with 12...cxd4 13 cxd4 ♕a5+ 14 c3 (or 14 ♔e3) and now 14...b6 followed by ...♗a6 or 14...b5 intending ...b4. Another possibility is first to provide some cover for the kingside, most notably the f6-square, by playing 11...♗d7 and meeting 12 ♕f4 by 12...♗c6 13 ♘f3 ♘d7. In this case White may switch plans and play 12 h5 g5 13 f4, opening some files on the kingside as quickly as possible.

Winawer Variation

3   ...   ♗b4 *(D)*

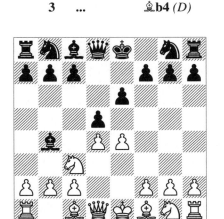

W

To a great many players, this move is the jewel in the crown of the French Defence. In a manner very similar to the Nimzo-Indian Defence, Black proposes to exchange bishop for knight and in so doing raises the uneasy question of how to evaluate the accompanying disturbance of White's pawn-structure. This introduces an element of tension and makes for a highly delicate positional equilibrium. As a result there will be chances for both sides, rather than White simply trying to create, and Black trying to neutralize, a small opening advantage.

It should not therefore come as a surprise that the Winawer has always been a variation for the real fighters, for those who are not interested in stability but in dynamics. It is also an opening for the optimists, who are more interested in their own chances than in those of their opponents. And finally it is an opening for the courageous, for it is a matter not of ignoring the opponent's chances and hoping for the best, but of not being afraid of them.

The similarity with the Nimzo-Indian is not a coincidence for they share the same originator.

Although 3...♗b4 was a well-known variation as far back as the 19th century and is usually attributed to Simon Winawer, who played it in 1867 against Steinitz, it was Aron Nimzowitsch (1886-1935) who turned the move into a coherent and meaningful opening system and in many countries it bears his name rather than Winawer's.

As is the case with 3...♘f6, Black is attacking e4, but he avoids both the pin ♗g5 and the loss of time involved in 3...♘f6 4 e5 ♘fd7. Those are important pluses. Are there any minuses?

In the days of Steinitz and Winawer, the answer to this question was sought in the symmetrical pawn-structure resulting from **4 exd5** exd5. The essence of their reasoning was that the bishop is no longer useful at b4 and that an exchange on c3 is no longer appealing. Nimzowitsch's great merit in this matter is to have demonstrated that this judgement is incorrect, or at least far too categorical. After 5 ♗d3 ♘c6 6 ♘e2 ♘ge7 7 0-0 ♗f5, for instance, Black has nothing to complain about.

This change of judgement suddenly left White with a serious problem. For if 4 exd5 holds no promise, what is he to play? A counterattack against g7 looks plausible but it is pretty clear that the blunt **4 ♕g4** is rather double-edged at best if Black boldly replies 4...♘f6 5 ♕xg7 ♖g8. Later the consequences of 4 ♕g4 were analysed in greater detail, together with the related lines **4 a3 ♗xc3+** 5 bxc3 dxe4 6 ♕g4 and **4 ♗d2** dxe4 5 ♕g4. These variations have obtained their place in the books, but although these are interesting attempts they have never managed to pose a serious threat to 3...♗b4.

4 ♗d3 and **4 ♘e2** produce a much quieter type of game, but neither of these moves pretends to be a refutation of 3...♗b4. They just try to avoid things getting out of hand.

4 ♗d3 leads, after 4...dxe4 5 ♗xe4 ♘f6 6 ♗g5, to a position that also arises from the McCutcheon (see page 361) and is obviously related to the Rubinstein Variation.

4 ♘e2 produces the same type of position after 4...dxe4 5 a3 if play now continues 5...♗e7 6 ♘xe4. Hanging on to the extra pawn with 5...♗xc3+ 6 ♘xc3 f5 is a possibility but this undoubtedly gives up the initiative (White might continue 7 f3) and is seen as rather risky. A more cautious way of making 5...♗xc3+ playable is just to forget about 6...f5 and play 6...♘c6 instead.

All of these possibilities have grown into fully-fledged variations over the years, but there is only one move that is seen, by friend and foe alike, as *the* critical test of 3...♗b4:

4 e5 (D)

After Nimzowitsch's defusing of the old 4 exd5, it was thought for some time that 3...♗b4 is actually an extremely solid defence to 3 ♘c3 for even if 4 exd5 was not a great move, there simply did not seem to be anything better. Even as late as 1941, the authoritative *Theory of Chess Openings* by Max Euwe judged "maintaining the tension in the centre to be best for White" only to admit immediately that a convincing way of doing so is sadly lacking.

Advancing the e-pawn to e5 was of course not an unknown idea but it was seen as too slow since after 4...c5 Black is virtually a move ahead on the comparable situation in the Classical Variation (3...♘f6 4 e5 ♘fd7). The implications of the critical 5 a3 were also seen in a negative light. However, after many years of uncertainty it finally turned out that precisely here, in the most distrusted part of the 3...♗b4 complex, the key lay hidden: the only way to put 3...♗b4 truly and fundamentally to the test.

4 ... c5

A principled reply but not the only one. No less a player than Nimzowitsch himself experimented with a much slower but strategically profound plan, that may be introduced by **4...b6** and **4...♕d7** alike and that has remained a major alternative to 4...c5 ever since.

Black aims to play ...♗a6 with the idea of exchanging his queen's bishop, always a problem child in the French Defence (and sometimes ironically nicknamed the French bishop), for White's king's bishop, a radical *and* a very sound solution to this problem. The drawback of this approach is that White is given a free hand, but since this variation is far from easy to play this may turn out (in practice) to be actually a disadvantage! Many a game with this line has seen White not knowing what to do with his freedom and just getting himself in trouble.

An important issue in this type of position is what both players think of the exchange on c3. If Black plays 4...b6, he has to be aware of the fact that the reply 5 ♕g4 will force him to take back his third move and play 5...♗f8 (unless he is prepared to make a major positional concession with 5...♔f8 or 5...g6). Fortunately, because of the extremely slow nature of the position, Black can afford this loss of time. Even after the more neutral 5 a3, there are those who play 5...♗f8 anyway, instead of the much more natural 5...♗xc3+.

There are also quite a number of players who prefer 4...♕d7. This move may look rather weird at first sight, but the idea is to meet 5 ♕g4 with 5...f5, which is perfectly sound, although it is not at all certain whether after 6 ♕g3 the change of pawn-structure benefits Black in the long run (for he can no longer attack White's central formation with ...f6).

Then there are those who wish to avoid a doubling of pawns (or at least do not wish to encourage it unduly). These players usually prefer 5 ♗d2 against either 4...b6 or 4...♕d7. The main long-term plan is to move the knight from c3 and go for b3 and c4, taking the initiative on the queenside, thus 'punishing' Black for not doing so himself (by playing ...c5).

Both 4...b6 and 4...♕d7 require a good positional understanding of the situation rather than a knowledge of variations. In fact, there practically aren't any! A few examples of how the game *might* develop:

a) **4...b6** and now:

a1) **5 ♕g4 ♗f8 6 ♗g5 ♕d7** and now **7 f4 ♗a6** or **7 ♗b5 c6 8 ♗a4**. The latter variation has the drawback of leaving the bishop stranded on a4 but it does avoid exchanging it for Black's queen's bishop.

a2) **5 a3 ♗xc3+ 6 bxc3 ♕d7** (this position can also be reached via 4...♕d7 5 a3 ♗xc3+ 6 bxc3 b6) **7 ♕g4 f5 8 ♕g3 ♗a6 9 ♗xa6 ♘xa6 10 ♘e2 0-0-0** with chances for both sides. Black has the satisfying prospect of moving his knight to c4 (...♘b8-c6-a5-c4), while White may either try to break open the queenside with a4-a5 and c4 (the violent option) or increase the pressure on the kingside with moves like h4-h5-h6 or g4 (the patient option).

b) **4...♕d7 5 ♗d2 b6 6 ♘f3 ♗a6 7 ♗xa6 ♘xa6 8 ♕e2 ♘b8 9 0-0 ♘e7 10 ♘d1 ♗xd2 11 ♕xd2 0-0 12 ♘e3**.

The same plan may be introduced by **4...♘e7**, when after 5 a3 ♗xc3+ 6 bxc3 Black can transpose to the main line with 6...c5 but he also has 6...b6. Here too 7 ♕g4 is the critical reply. Black can defend g7 by simply playing 7...0-0 but after 8 ♗g5 his king is not safe. The most important starting position of this line arises after 7...♘g6 8 h4 h5.

We now return to 4...c5 *(D)*:

W

5   a3

Modern opening books hardly comment on this move. At the very most it is said to be 'the most principled reply' or something to that effect. And yet there have been times when it was called 'old-fashioned', 'inadvisable' or 'of dubious value'!

White invests a whole tempo in persuading Black to make an exchange of pieces whose consequences are as yet totally unclear. Who benefits? This is indeed a decision that can only be made if you are absolutely sure of what you are doing or ... if theory presents it as being self-evident.

In fact, by playing 5 a3 White crosses the last border that still separated him from what is now thought of as the heart of the Winawer Variation. This type of position is difficult to play and almost impossible to understand.

Other moves are less committal, simpler, most certainly playable, but far less threatening to Black.

Even **5 ♕g4**, which is an aggressive move, is not really dangerous for Black since after 5...♘e7 the straightforward 6 ♕xg7 ♖g8 7 ♕xh7 is dubious due to 7...cxd4 8 a3 ♕a5, when White is forced to seek refuge in the murky exchange sacrifice 9 axb4 ♕xa1 10 ♘ce2. A more reliable move is 6 dxc5, but this makes the position of White's queen on g4 rather questionable.

5 dxc5 immediately or **5 ♘f3 ♘e7 6 dxc5** is also sometimes played, but if White is really looking for a solid option, he usually goes for **5 ♗d2**. The point of this move is that 5...cxd4?! is dubious due to 6 ♘b5, when after 6...♗xd2+ 7 ♕xd2 White gets his pawn back without any trouble and the threat of ♘d6+ will force Black to give up castling. But by simply playing 5...♘e7, Black takes most of the sting out of this set-up.

We now return to 5 a3 *(D)*:

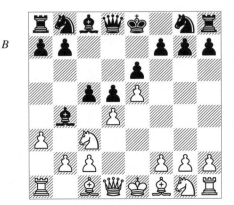
B

5   ...   ♗xc3+

Both this and **5...cxd4** were regarded as favourable for Black as 'recently' as the 1930s. But in the course of that decade it slowly began to dawn on the chess world that if White intends to achieve something against the Winawer he **has** to play these positions and – more importantly perhaps – that this is not quite so impossible as used to be thought. The first victim of this budding new insight was the variation 5...cxd4. This used to be judged primarily on the merits of 6 axb4 dxc3 7 bxc3 ♕c7, but when it transpired that White can easily afford a pawn sacrifice and play 7 ♘f3 or 7 ♕g4, enthusiasm for this approach quickly disappeared.

A third option for Black is to retreat the bishop: **5...♗a5**. Ironically, this move was regarded with great scepticism in the early days, after Alekhine had shown in 1924 that White gets excellent attacking chances with the pawn sacrifice 6 b4 cxb4 7 ♘b5!. But the variation came to life when it was discovered that Black should play the positionally much more consistent 6...cxd4! instead of the greedy 6...cxb4. This leads to the same ultra-sharp type of position that we are about to see in the 5...♗xc3+ variation if play continues **7 ♕g4 ♘e7 8 bxa5 dxc3 9 ♕xg7 ♖g8 10 ♕xh7** *(D)*.

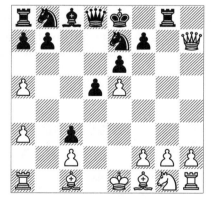

After 10...♘bc6 11 f4 ♕xa5 12 ♘f3 ♗d7 13 ♖b1 0-0-0 14 ♕d3, for instance, any aggressive, tactically oriented player (regardless of the colour he is playing) will probably get the feeling that this must be paradise. With hardly any positional footing for either side and major

parts of both White's and Black's position destroyed, it is almost impossible to judge who has the better chances, or, to put it more accurately, theory changes its mind about this all the time. White will try to round up the c3-pawn and his h-pawn is a powerful long-term trump card. But his Achilles' Heel is the insecure position of his king, which Black will try to attack with operations like ...d4, ...♘f5, ...♘ce7 and ...♗c6.

If **7 ♘b5** (instead of 7 ♕g4) a somewhat quieter game is likely to result, although even here the position is hard to judge. A critical position arises after **7...♗c7 8 f4**. White will regain his pawn quite easily, but Black can try to take advantage of his opponent's somewhat airy queenside pawn-formation with a move like 8...a5.

6   bxc3 *(D)*

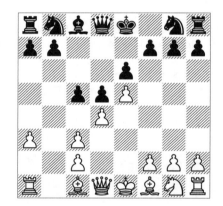

Thanks to the pawn that has appeared on c3, White has got his d-pawn firmly covered, just like in the Advance Variation (3 e5 c5 4 c3). But there are two major differences.

First, there is the exchange of knight for bishop. This has left Black vulnerable on the dark squares, but what does this really mean? We have already seen that White has the option of attacking g7, but we have also noticed that this is not always dangerous for Black. It is also clear that White's dark-squared bishop *might* become very powerful, for instance if it is put on the a3-f8 diagonal with a4 and ♗a3, but it is equally clear that it *might* become totally paralysed if this plan does not work and the bishop gets hemmed in by its own pawns.

Secondly, there are the doubled pawns. They make White's position rather static and vulnerable, for Black may attempt to attack both c-pawns *and* White's a-pawn. But in the meantime White will have a very useful open file on the queenside so that he does not necessarily have to remain passive on that wing. If Black castles queenside, for instance, as he often does in this line, advancing White's a-pawn or doubling rooks on the b-file may become quite dangerous.

So who benefits from these two positional factors is impossible to say. The real question is: who will use them the more skilfully? This is precisely what makes the Winawer such an exciting variation.

The first assessments of this position, dating from the 1920s, were not exactly friendly to White, but they were also decidedly one-dimensional. It was thought that Black has good prospects on the queenside if he follows a plan based on ...c4, to be played either immediately or after the preliminary moves 6...♘e7 7 ♘f3 ♘bc6 8 ♗e2 ♕a5 9 ♗d2. When it slowly became clear that in the meantime White's prospects on the opposite wing are at least as good, this assessment was modified. It became clear that Black does well to be flexible: he can play ...c4 if the circumstances are right, but in many cases ...cxd4 with the idea of using the c-file as a base for attack is more promising, and a counterattack on the kingside with ...f6 is also an idea to be kept in mind. Thus the whole variation gradually changed into an extremely complicated opening system, making high demands on both players.

By the end of the 1980s, the Winawer was again transformed when the uncompromising 7 ♕g4 began to be analysed with ever-greater precision and relentless tenacity. The image of the Winawer shifted as the somewhat noncommittal general considerations such as I just mentioned were brushed aside and replaced by highly concrete ways of coping with White's queen sortie. From this crisis, the cold-blooded reply 7...0-0 has emerged as an essentially new interpretation of this line.

6   ...   ♘e7

There is hardly a trace of the old move **6...c4** left in modern Winawer theory. The positional

drawbacks of this move leap to the (modern) eye: not only does 7 ♕g4 force Black to make a major concession with 7...g6 or 7...♔f8 (which is unnecessary after 6...♘e7) but with Black opening the a3-f8 diagonal so soon, the plan to play a4 followed by ♗a3 becomes very attractive indeed.

Nevertheless this ancient idea has not been completely abandoned; it has merely been refined. The modern and more subtle version of 6...c4 is to play **6...♕a5** 7 ♗d2 ♕a4, blocking White's a-pawn first and preparing to close the queenside with 8...c4 (after 8 ♕b1 for instance).

Another major option is to play **6...♕c7**, with the idea of meeting 7 ♕g4 with 7...f5. The question then is whether this change in pawn-formation favours Black or White after 8 ♕g3 cxd4 9 cxd4 ♘e7 10 ♗d2 0-0 11 ♗d3 for instance. The immediate 7...cxd4? does not work because after 8 ♕xg7! ♕xc3+ 9 ♔d1 ♕xa1 10 ♕xh8 ♔f8 11 ♗d3 Black's king is in far greater danger than White's.

We now return to 6...♘e7 (D):

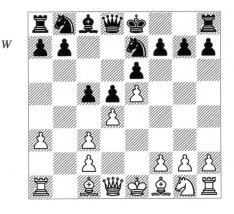

7   ♕g4

This aggressive approach has driven Black to despair at several moments in the life of the Winawer. Mikhail Botvinnik, one of its greatest champions ever, even gave up on 6...♘e7 after a disastrous loss to C.H.O'D.Alexander in 1946. When he lost two games with 6...♕c7 as well, both to Mikhail Tal in 1960 and 1961, things were looking very black for the Winawer. But the variation recovered from both of these blows and 7 ♕g4 even seemed to fade away shortly afterwards, possibly on the general grounds of just being too complicated and unsafe for most people. After all, sharp attacking variations are all very well to look at, but as long as they are not properly analysed – *and* these analyses laid down in books – actually playing them can be dangerously double-edged.

The present 7 ♕g4 wave seems to be headed in a different direction. Although at first Black's defensive barriers looked like they were going to be mercilessly demolished, the Winawer has again shown astounding resilience. But if nothing else, this time 7 ♕g4 seems to have taken a firm hold on the status of being the main line.

This development has considerably reduced the importance of the quiet, positional approach that dominated the image of the Winawer for decades (in between the peaks of 7 ♕g4). There does not seem to be a lot of interest any more in the subtle implications of **7 ♘f3** and **7 a4**. Quite a change! For instance, in the 1970s the question of whether, after 7 ♘f3 ♗d7 8 a4 ♕a5, White should play 9 ♗d2 or 9 ♕d2, was highly topical. 9 ♗d2 seems more natural, but 9 ♕d2 has the advantage of reserving the right to play ♗a3. 7 ♘f3 ♕c7 (this position also arises via 6...♕c7 7 ♘f3 ♘e7) 8 a4 b6 was another important variation in those days (and in a way it still is, but it catches the limelight far less often now than it did before). Black intends to play ...♗a6, exchanging his queen's bishop, a universal theme in the French Defence. White may want to thwart this plan at the cost of a tempo by playing 9 ♗b5+ ♗d7 10 ♗d3.

More recently and in the wake of 7 ♕g4, the alternative **7 h4** has risen to (some) prominence. This is in fact an alternative way of starting an attack on the kingside right away.

We now return to 7 ♕g4 *(D)*:

The story of this position began with the cautious assessment that, if nothing better, Black can safely guard his g-pawn by playing **7...♘f5** and that perhaps the sharp **7...♕c7** is playable. If, after three quarters of a century, we replace 7...♘f5 by **7...0-0**, this assessment is still the same. But on what oceans of games, analyses and theoretical publications it is now based!

To give just an idea of the progress opening theory has made here: once it was the position

B

after **7...♕c7** 8 ♕xg7 ♖g8 9 ♕xh7 cxd4 (or alternatively **7...cxd4** 8 ♕xg7 ♖g8 9 ♕xh7 ♕c7) that was considered the starting point for the sharp option. Nowadays we have to add at least the further moves 10 ♘e2 ♘bc6 11 f4 ♗d7 12 ♕d3 (if 12 cxd4 then Black has 12...♘xd4!) 12...dxc3 before theory 'really' starts. White has two ways of taking on c3. In both cases, Black will try to prove that the many open files for his rooks and the insecure position of White's king provide ample compensation for his slight material deficit. One thing that has not changed is that it is still totally unclear who has the better chances. What *is* clear, though, is that this is a wonderful variation for lovers of sharp, complicated and uncompromising play *and* for lovers of the most thorough opening preparation.

The safer option is of course to protect the g-pawn. The old **7...♘f5** lost most of its former glory in the 1960s when it was found that the endgame arising from 8 ♗d3 h5 9 ♕f4 cxd4 10 cxd4 ♕h4 11 ♕xh4 ♘xh4 12 ♗g5 is not easy for Black. But two decades later the bold **7...0-0** has turned out to be an excellent successor to 7...♘f5. It looks risky to castle 'into it' and it really *is* dangerous, but if Black plays with great accuracy (or if he knows his theory well enough) he need not fear the danger. The modern main line is to play 8 ♗d3, intending to meet **8...c4** with 9 ♗h6! ♘g6 10 ♗xg6 fxg6 11 ♗g5. In this rather static position Black seems to have a solid game but since he can hardly undertake anything, White can build an attack on the kingside at his leisure, starting with h4-h5. Therefore it has become more usual to play

8...❹bc6, which admittedly leads to the same type of position after 9 ♕h5 ❹g6 10 ❹f3 ♕c7 11 ♗e3 c4 12 ♗xg6 fxg6 13 ♕g4, but with two extra tempi this should now be playable for Black. Nevertheless, this remains an important option for White. Another possibility is to play **8...f5** with the reply 9 exf6 ♖xf6 10 ♗g5 ♖f7 11 ♕h5 g6 12 ♕d1 being the critical test. In all of these lines a heavy positional struggle lies ahead.

Tarrasch Variation

3 ❹d2 *(D)*

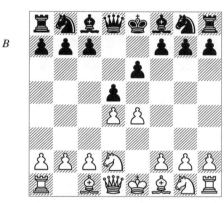

This alternative to 3 ❹c3 was first recommended by Siegbert Tarrasch (1862-1934), though he later came to condemn it. Nevertheless, his name remained attached to this move that did not really prosper until long after Tarrasch's era.

White avoids the pin ...♗b4. He is also well-placed to deal with the closed type of position that arises from **3...❹f6** 4 e5, perhaps even better than after 3 ❹c3, since with the knight on d2, it will be easy to protect d4 with c3. But these pluses come with a price tag. The drawbacks of 3 ❹d2 (as compared to 3 ❹c3) are obvious: White has far less control over the central squares d4 and d5 and his queen's bishop is hemmed in.

The great main lines of the Tarrasch are the radical reply **3...c5** and the more traditional **3...❹f6**, which in spite of what was said above has turned out to be eminently playable.

Three other moves have also grown into fully-fledged variations, but since they are not as popular as the two main lines I shall only deal with them briefly:

3...a6 is a far from obvious move, but Black can afford it because 3 ❹d2 is such a slow move itself. The idea is to play ...c5 without being disturbed by ♗b5(+), which is an important move in the 3...c5 variation. After 4 ❹gf3 c5, the pawn exchange 5 exd5 exd5 leads to a position from the 3...c5 4 exd5 exd5 line, with Black having circumvented 5 ♗b5+. If White wants to achieve more than this transposition (or if he just wants something different) he should probably try 5 dxc5 ♗xc5 6 ♗d3. By avoiding the pawn exchange on d5, White restricts the scope of Black's queen's bishop.

3...❹c6 *(D)*, insulting as it may be to the classical mind (after all, Black is blocking his own c-pawn, which definitely wants to move forward in a 'classical' French Defence), is in fact a well-considered attempt to show up the dark side of 3 ❹d2.

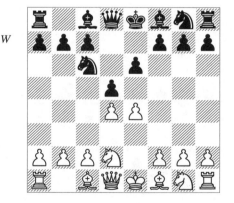

The idea is to meet **4 c3** with 4...e5, not exactly an everyday occurrence in the French! The deeper point is that the alternative **4 ❹gf3**, though superficially a natural move, is in fact a slight concession because (as we are about to see in the 3...❹f6 line) the moves ❹d2 and ❹gf3 do not necessarily go well together in the French. Black replies 4...❹f6 5 e5 ❹d7, switching to more classical means of attacking White's centre: he will play ...f6 or ...c5. Even the very slow ...♘b8 followed by ...b6 and ...♗a6 is a realistic option in some cases.

3...♗e7 is almost equally unorthodox, yet this move has become fairly popular in recent years. Black is subtly waiting for White (again!) to play 4 ♘gf3, when he will 'normalize' the position with 4...♘f6 5 e5 or 5 ♗d3 c5 6 e5 ♘fd7. In a closed variation of the Tarrasch like this, White's queen's knight often wants to move on to f3. With the king's knight on f3, the characteristic scheme of development ♘e2 and ♘f3 is no longer feasible.

Naturally, for those who want to play a Rubinstein Variation, 3 ♘d2 presents no problems. By playing **3...dxe4** the difference between 3 ♘c3 and 3 ♘d2 is swept aside without a murmur.

All of these lines usually lead to much quieter and more straightforward play than 3 ♘c3, although there are some sharp and chaotic lines here too, if both players choose to enter them. But overall, the Tarrasch has always been a favourite with those players who wish to avoid the complexities of the Winawer and who prefer a sober, sterner game.

3 ♘d2 c5

3   ...   c5 (D)

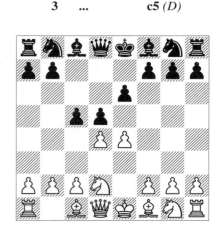

This advance against White's pawn-centre, hardly playable against 3 ♘c3, is the classical answer to 3 ♘d2. Black takes advantage of the fact that the pressure against d5 has decreased by attacking d4.

4   exd5

One could say that this move is a belated way of playing the Exchange Variation, but in fact there is hardly any connection with 3 exd5, for having played ...c5 Black has fundamentally altered the character of the position. If now **4...exd5**, play will usually revolve around the well-defined theme of the isolated queen's pawn (arising after an exchange of pawns on c5 or d4). If **4...♛xd5**, the central pawn-structure is the same as in the Rubinstein Variation.

3 ♘d2 c5 4 exd5 exd5

4   ...   exd5 (D)

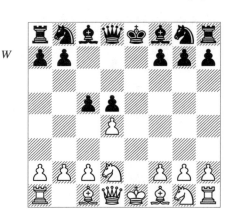

5   ♘gf3

This move is in fact a striking example of the way opening theory is always looking for the very, very best move (a self-perpetuating search really). Instead of immediately isolating Black's d-pawn (by playing **5 dxc5**), White is trying to get the same type of position in a slightly more favourable version. So instead of giving his opponent a free developing move (5...♗xc5) he waits, preferably until the bishop moves to d6 or e7.

Another idea is to try to disrupt Black's development by playing **5 ♗b5+**. The point of this move is that after the natural reply 5...♗d7 (or 5...♘c6) 6 ♛e2+ ♗e7 7 dxc5 Black cannot recapture on c5. This may lead to sharp play if White decides to hang on to his extra pawn but it usually boils down to an 'ordinary' isolated queen's pawn position in the end, for instance after 7...♘f6 8 ♘b3 0-0 9 ♘f3 ♖e8 10 ♗e3 a6 and now 11 ♗xd7 ♘bxd7 or 11 ♗d3 ♗a4 followed by 12...♘bd7.

A more cautious reply is to play 6...♕e7 instead of 6...♗e7, keeping c5 protected. But this confronts us with a more subtle problem of a positional nature: is it wise to exchange queens in a position where you are supposed to create active piece-play to compensate for the weakness of your isolated pawn? Most opening books deem this to be 'slightly better for White', but I would say it is really a matter of taste. A rather dry, technical sort of position is reached where some players will feel ill at ease while others may be perfectly comfortable.

We now return to 5 ♘gf3 *(D)*:

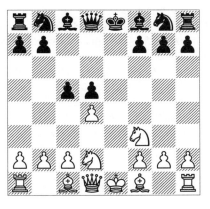

5   ...   ♘c6

Black could try to 'punish' White for not playing 5 dxc5 by pushing his c-pawn, but this has never been overly popular. After **5...c4** 6 b3, Black cannot hang on to his pawn-chain since 6...b5 runs into 7 a4, when the 'consistent' 7...a6 is impossible.

It is far more common to prepare this advance by first playing **5...a6**. If White still refuses to capture on c5, ...c4 will follow. The critical variations are 6 dxc5 ♗xc5 7 ♘b3 ♗a7 and 6 ♗e2 c4. In the latter case 7 b3 can now be safely countered with 7...b5. The position after 5...a6 can also arise via 3...a6 4 ♘gf3 c5 5 exd5 exd5.

Finally, **5...♘f6**, avoiding the pin by ♗b5, is also important. After 6 ♗b5+ ♗d7, 7 ♕e2+ resembles the variation 5 ♗b5+, while 7 ♗xd7+

♘bxd7 8 0-0 ♗e7 9 dxc5 ♘xc5 is a little easier for Black than the 5...♘c6 line thanks to the disappearance of the two light-squared bishops.

6	**♗b5**	**♗d6**
7	**dxc5**	**♗xc5**
8	**0-0**	**♘e7**
9	**♘b3**	**♗d6** *(D)*

The choice between this move and **9...♗b6** is a difficult one. In the latter case, 10 ♖e1 0-0 11 ♗e3 aiming to exchange bishops, is a sound strategy.

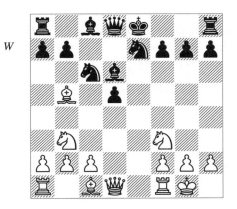

This is one of the critical positions of the Tarrasch Variation. White will lay siege to Black's d5-pawn, or at the very least try to take maximum advantage of the blockading square d4. Black can freely develop his pieces, quite an achievement in the French, and will seek active counterplay.

3 ♘d2 c5 4 exd5 ♕xd5

4   ...   ♕xd5 *(D)*

This leads to a sort of position which is rather different from the 4...exd5 line. Just like in the Rubinstein Variation, Black permits his opponent to develop his pieces freely, but he provides him with no targets.

5   ♘gf3

Again the rule of thumb of opening theory is never to choose the path of least resistance. Rather than playing **5 dxc5 ♗xc5**, giving away a development tempo for free, White allows the opponent to take on d4, intending to recapture

the pawn without losing time, in the swing of his piece development.

5   ...   cxd4
6   ♗c4   ♕d6

This is the unchallenged main line, but the ultra-solid **6...♕d8** is also played from time to time.

7   0-0

A somewhat sharper option which became popular in the 1990s is to play **7 ♕e2 ♘f6 8 ♘b3 ♘c6 9 ♗g5** and **10 0-0-0**.

7   ...   ♘f6
8   ♘b3   ♘c6
9   ♘bxd4   ♘xd4
10   ♘xd4 *(D)*

10 ♕xd4 is a cautious alternative. White is working on the assumption that an exchange of queens will be to his advantage, simply because Black's queen is actively placed on d6 and White's at d1 is not. Whether this is indeed the case is moot. After 10...♕xd4 11 ♘xd4 ♗d7 12 ♗f4 ♖c8, for instance, the positional tension has been reduced and it has become much easier for Black to find a safe place for his king.

The position after 10 ♘xd4 is the main starting point of the 4...♕xd5 variation. At first Black was satisfied with the solid but unpretentious **10...♗e7** followed by 11...0-0. With more and more players taking an interest in this line, ambitious moves like **10...♗d7** and **10...a6** also came under scrutiny. Black can then continue aggressively with ...♕c7 and ...♗d6 and perhaps even castle queenside. It goes without saying that this can lead to a very fierce battle. After 10...a6 11 ♖e1 ♕c7 12 ♗b3 ♗d6, for

instance, the meek 13 h3 is unlikely to worry Black, but after 13 ♘f5!? ♗xh2+ 14 ♔h1 0-0 15 ♘xg7! no one knows what is going on. The point of White's last move is 15...♔xg7 16 ♕d4 with a terrible attack, yet the cold-blooded zwischenzug 15...♖d8 appears to keep Black's chances alive.

Instead of 12...♗d6 there is the slightly less provocative (and still quite sharp) 12...♗d7. Play might continue 13 ♗g5 0-0-0 14 ♕f3, when rather than worry about defending f6, Black should probably lash out with 14...♗d6 again.

3 ♘d2 ♘f6

3   ...   ♘f6

For a long time it used to be thought that this move is asking for trouble, for at first glance the position after 4 e5 ♘fd7 looks better for White than the similar 3 ♘c3 ♘f6 4 e5 ♘fd7. But on closer inspection, the position of the knight on d2 turns out to have some disadvantages as well.

4   e5   ♘fd7 *(D)*

Just like after 3 ♘c3 ♘f6 4 e5 Black can also play **4...♘e4** here, which after 5 ♘xe4 dxe4 boils down to the same position (see page 355).

5   ♗d3

As always in positions with a (more or less) fixed pawn-centre, both sides have to think strategically. Every decision is likely to have far-reaching consequences which cannot easily be corrected.

The plausible developing move **5 ♘gf3**, for instance, runs into the problem that after 5...c5

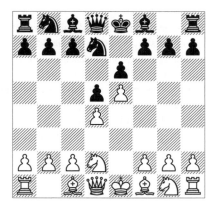

6 c3 ♘c6 7 ♗d3 ♕b6 White lacks a comfortable way of defending d4, a typical problem of 3 ♘d2. This does not necessarily mean that 5 ♘gf3 is a mistake, for the pawn sacrifice 8 0-0 cxd4 9 cxd4 ♘xd4 10 ♘xd4 ♕xd4 11 ♘f3 ♕b6 12 ♕a4 offers White a lead in development and many open files for his pieces, but it does make this variation 'for specialists only'.

5 f4 is of a different calibre altogether. White provides some extra cover for his e5-pawn and makes a first move forward on the kingside. After 5...c5 6 c3 ♘c6 the idea is to play 7 ♘df3 *(D)*, for the seemingly natural 7 ♘gf3 again runs into 7...♕b6.

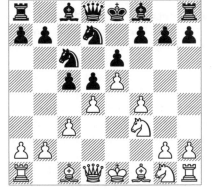

This full-scale consolidation of White's centre is closely related to the variation 3 ♘c3 ♘f6 4 e5 ♘fd7 5 ♘ce2 c5 6 c3 ♘c6 7 f4 (see page 356) and needs to be countered with force and conviction. In many lines, Black will attack White's centre with ...f6 and even ...g5 and in

some cases he will try to harass White's king. For instance after (7 ♘df3) 7...♕b6 **8 g3** cxd4 9 cxd4 ♗b4+ White is forced to go for the bold 10 ♔f2, when 10...f6 11 ♔g2 g5 is a fully realistic possibility. Some players anticipate this plan by playing **8 h4** (instead of 8 g3), but this leads to great complications as well after 8...cxd4 9 cxd4 ♗b4+ 10 ♔f2 f6. In many games Black has been successful with a knight sacrifice on e5 at some point, just to wipe out White's centre pawns and expose his king. In fact, this is one of the sharpest variations of the entire Tarrasch.

The neutral **5 c3** is often played, but this only delays the moment of truth, for after 5...c5 White will have to cut the Gordian Knot and choose between 6 ♗d3, 6 f4 and 6 ♘gf3 after all.

| 5 | ... | c5 |
| 6 | c3 *(D)* | |

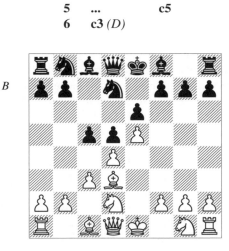

| 6 | ... | ♘c6 |

An alternative plan is to play **6...b6**, followed by ...♗a6. Looking at the position from a purely static perspective, this exchange of the light-squared bishop (which we have come to know in this chapter as highly characteristic of this type of position) is excellent for Black. But if we take the dynamics of the situation into account, this manoeuvre is far less impressive since White will make use of the time granted to him to strengthen his hold on the kingside, for instance with 7 ♘e2 ♗a6 8 ♗xa6 ♘xa6 9 0-0 ♘c7 10 ♘f4 or 7 ♘h3 ♗a6 8 ♗xa6 ♘xa6 9 ♕g4. Assuredly, this is an interesting variation, but only for those players who enjoy patiently nurturing long-term aspirations and who do not mind having to defend for a while.

> **7   ♘e2   cxd4**
> **8   cxd4 (D)**

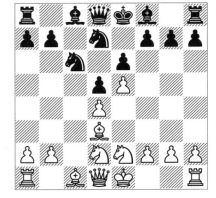

Now White is well-prepared for **8...♛b6** since he can reply 9 ♘f3, smoothly defending the d4-pawn, a major difference from the 5 ♘gf3 variation. This used to be the main line of the 3...♘f6 variation, continuing with 9...f6 10 exf6 ♘xf6 11 0-0 ♗d6 (and, for instance, 12 ♘c3).

However, the preparatory move 8...♛b6 is not strictly necessary for this plan. Nowadays most players prefer the immediate...

> **8   ...   f6**

In the early days of this line, White would sometimes try to punish this move with **9 ♘f4**, but this idea never aroused much enthusiasm. After 9...♘xd4 10 ♛h5+ ♚e7 11 exf6+ ♘xf6 12 ♘g6+ hxg6 13 ♛xh8 ♚f7 followed by 14...e5 White has won an exchange but lost his hold on the centre. Still, this remains an enterprising option which may be attractive to those who do not relish the heavy positional problems of the main line and who prefer something more concrete and tactical.

> **9   exf6   ♘xf6**

Black has eliminated the enemy outpost at e5, thus changing the character of the opening considerably. The position has become fairly open (by French standards that is) so that both sides can develop their pieces pretty comfortably. Even the passive queen's bishop will have reasonable prospects at d7. The deciding factor will be Black's backward pawn on e6 in combination with the blockading square e5. Will White somehow be able to take advantage of this? Will Black perhaps be able to play ...e5 at some point? These questions are not easy to answer, but they do determine the further course of the opening.

> **10   0-0   ♗d6**
> **11   ♘f3 (D)**

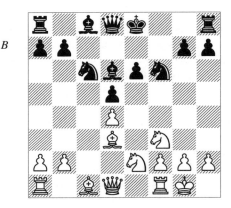

This is to all practical purposes the starting point of this variation. Black now has to take a decision with far-reaching consequences: to allow his opponent to play 12 ♗f4 or not? In itself this would be a positionally attractive exchange of bishops for White as it would increase his control over e5. That is why it seems obvious that Black should reply **11...♛c7**. If then 12 g3, Black has at least provoked a small but significant weakening of White's kingside pawn-structure. But White has a subtle alternative in 12 ♗g5, planning to achieve the desired exchange of bishops via another route: ♗h4-g3.

In fact it is not at all clear that it is necessary to stop 12 ♗f4. After **11...0-0** 12 ♗f4, for instance, Black may try to take over the initiative by lashing out with 12...♗xf4 13 ♘xf4 ♘e4. For a correct evaluation of this line it is vital to work out the consequences of the exchange sacrifice 14 ♘e2 ♖xf3!? 15 gxf3 ♘g5.

Caro-Kann Defence

1 e4 c6 *(D)*

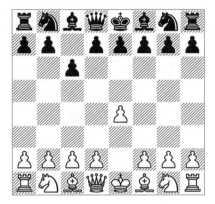

Though no less ancient than the French, this move had to wait until far into the 19th century before it received any form of recognition. In fact, it was not until Capablanca and Nimzowitsch started playing 1...c6 in the 1920s and 1930s that it was accepted as a serious opening. And even then it was often given the derogatory (and completely undeserved) epithet 'drawish opening' until the final breakthrough in the 1980s. With more and more top players using the Caro-Kann, old prejudices disappeared and 1...c6 finally became what it is today: one of the most important and popular replies to 1 e4.

Just like in the French Defence, Black is planning to play 2...d5, attacking White's e-pawn. He is using the c-pawn rather than the e-pawn to support this central advance because he wants to keep the c8-h3 diagonal open for his bishop. And no matter how closely related the starting moves 1...e6 and 1...c6 may be, this tiny difference immediately causes a fundamental divergence.

2 d4

There are a number of alternatives, but the only ones that are accepted as fully satisfactory are **2 d3**, **2 ♘c3** d5 3 ♘f3 (or **2 ♘f3** d5 3 ♘c3) and **2 c4**.

By playing **2 d3** d5 3 ♘d2 *(D)*, White introduces the **King's Indian Attack**, just like 2 d3 in the French (see page 347).

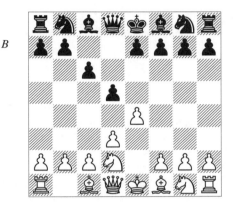

But there is a major difference between the position after 1 e4 e6 2 d3 d5 3 ♘d2 and the one arising after 1...c6 2 d3 d5 3 ♘d2: Black now has the chance to take even fuller control over the centre by playing either 3...e5 or 3...g6 4 ♘gf3 ♗g7 5 g3 e5. A characteristic situation arises after 3...e5 4 ♘gf3 ♗d6 5 g3 ♘f6 6 ♗g2 0-0 7 0-0 ♖e8. It could be said that White has declined to use his 'prerogative' and has decided to take the black pieces instead, for this is in fact a position from the Modern Defence (1 e4 g6) with colours reversed (see page 462). But of course there is always the extra tempo for White and although it is far from clear how important this factor really is, it does make this variation sufficiently attractive for many players. And it should be noted that this is a line that requires little theoretical knowledge!

2 ♘c3 d5 3 ♘f3 *(D)* (or **2 ♘f3** d5 3 ♘c3) is another set-up the Caro-Kann shares with the French (see page 348), but its importance is far greater in the Caro-Kann. In fact, this line (prosaically called the **Two Knights Variation**) used to be more popular than 2 d4 during the 1940s and 1950s. It is still a frequent guest in modern tournaments.

B

It is attractive for two reasons. Firstly, **3...d4** is not as strong as in the French Defence since after 4 ♘e2 Black has to lose a tempo with 4...c5 (the same goes for 3...♘f6 4 e5 ♘fd7 5 d4, when Black will have to play 5...e6 and 6...c5). Secondly, after **3...dxe4** 4 ♘xe4 the 'standard' 4...♗f5 is not as self-evident as one would expect because after 5 ♘g3 ♗g6 6 h4 h6 (parallel to 2 d4 d5 3 ♘c3 dxe4 4 ♘xe4 ♗f5; see page 382) White quickly seizes the initiative with 7 ♘e5!. If 7...♗h7, the powerful 8 ♕h5 would even force Black to bury his own bishop with 8...g6.

Black's most popular defence to the Two Knights Variation is **3...♗g4**. After the critical reply 4 h3, this either leads to a fierce tactical battle following **4...♗h5** 5 exd5 cxd5 6 ♗b5+ ♘c6 7 g4 ♗g6 8 ♘e5 or to a rather closed King's Indian Attack type of position starting with **4...♗xf3** 5 ♕xf3; e.g., 5...e6 6 g3 ♘f6 7 ♗g2.

2 c4 too is far more than just a way of avoiding the main lines. This move is intended as a subtle refinement on the Panov Attack (a dangerous enough line in its own right!): 2 d4 d5 3 exd5 cxd5 4 c4 (see page 378). Just like in the Two Knights Variation, the idea behind delaying d4 is to make it more difficult for Black to develop his pieces. White wants to meet the natural **2...d5** with a double exchange of pawns

on d5, 3 exd5 cxd5 4 cxd5, an important motif in the Panov and intended to be doubly dangerous now that it comes in an accelerated version. The straightforward **4...♕xd5** is not very attractive because of 5 ♘c3 (although players who are not inclined to worry about subtleties like a loss of tempo in the opening may in fact find this to be quite playable).

The real problem is that the 'ideal' **4...♘f6** *(D)* (intending to take back on d5 much more 'cleanly' with the knight) is also problematic.

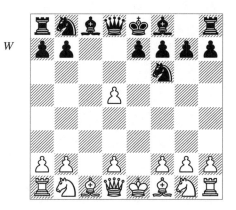

W

White has two destabilizing checks, 5 ♕a4+ and 5 ♗b5+, to prevent an immediate recapture on d5. One critical line starts with **5 ♗b5+** ♘bd7 (5...♗d7 is answered by 6 ♗c4) 6 ♘c3. The question then is whether Black should quietly develop his kingside starting with 6...g6, or if he should break the pin with 6...a6. But even the simple **5 ♘c3** ♘xd5 6 ♘f3 is a subtle test of 4...♘f6. White uses the time gained by delaying d4 for an ultra-fast development of his pieces (while retaining the option of transposing to a Panov proper by playing d4 at a moment of his own choosing). The underlying relatedness of all opening theory is made clearly visible here. Against the Panov proper, 4...♘f6 5 ♘c3 e6 is one of Black's best replies (see page 379). If then 6 ♘f3, Black has a choice between the solid 6...♗e7 and the aggressive 6...♗b4, both transposing to a line of the Queen's Gambit Declined if play continues 7 cxd5 ♘xd5 (the Semi-Tarrasch; see page 19). By playing 2 c4 d5 3 exd5 cxd5 4 cxd5 ♘f6 5 ♘c3 ♘xd5 6 ♘f3, White very cleverly eliminates the latter option, for if Black now chooses 6...e6, then after 7 ♗c4 (instead of 7 d4) the 'aggressive 7...♗b4' no longer makes any sense, so Black is reduced to the 'solid' option 7...♗e7. This may look like hair-splitting, yet such expert and intricate juggling with openings and variations forms an essential part of modern opening theory.

The fact that 2 c4 is a variation *par excellence* for players with a wide range of opening knowledge is further underlined by Black's main alternative **2...e5**, which after 3 ♘f3 d6 4 d4 ♘d7 5 ♘c3 ♘gf6, takes us straight into an Old Indian Defence (see page 160)!

2 ... d5 (D)

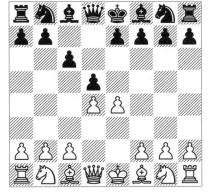

In this position White (again) has a range of options which *look* similar to the French Defence, but the consequences are rather different.

The exchange option, for instance, **3 exd5**, does not produce a symmetrical pawn-structure like it does in the French. Remarkably, this is not called the **Exchange Variation** (yet), for that name is reserved for the position after 3...cxd5, *if* White does *not* continue 4 c4. If he does, we call it the **Panov Attack**.

3 e5 is called the **Advance Variation**, as in the French, but because Black can reply 3...♗f5 he experiences far fewer problems, or so it seems at first sight. In fact, the Advance Variation was thought to be inferior for this reason until in 1982 the whole variation, including this assessment, was overhauled and theory suddenly took a few giant steps forward. Nowadays, 3 e5 is one of the most popular ways of tackling the Caro-Kann.

Nevertheless (and again: just like in the French) maintaining the tension in the centre is still thought of as the most critical test of Black's opening. In this case, though, it is almost irrelevant whether this is done by **3 ♘c3** or by **3 ♘d2** for in both cases 3...dxe4 is the standard reply. This is in fact a major difference between the French and the Caro-Kann Defences. The many alternatives to 3...dxe4 that Black has in the French are conspicuously absent in the Caro-Kann. If a player chooses 1...e6, it does not necessarily follow that he is fond of 3...dxe4 positions. But if someone plays the Caro-Kann, then that is precisely what he is aiming for.

Exchange Variation

3 exd5 cxd5

White now has two fundamentally different plans to choose from. He can either continue the fight for domination of the centre by lashing out with **4 c4** (this is the **Panov Attack**, which we shall deal with next) or he can interpret the position as a Queen's Gambit Declined Exchange Variation (see page 22) with colours reversed.

4 ♗d3

With that in mind, this is a very nice move, making it much more difficult for the opponent to develop his queen's bishop than in the 'real' Queen's Gambit. This then is the Caro-Kann **Exchange Variation**.

4 ... ♘c6 (D)

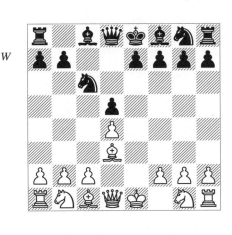

5 c3

This is more ambitious than the plain developing move **5 ♘f3**, which allows Black to play 5...♗g4. White is not giving away any presents, however small.

5   ...   ♘f6
6   ♗f4

Seen in the light of the previous note, it may look inconsistent that this is the main line rather than **6 h3**, but there are other factors besides the development of Black's queen's bishop to be taken into account. 6 h3 has the definite drawback of not contributing anything to White's development and by countering with 6...e5 7 dxe5 ♘xe5 Black might 'punish' his opponent for his slow play. This position is very similar to a typical 3...c5 4 exd5 exd5 French Tarrasch Variation (see page 370), but Black's better development should make this position relatively easy for him.

By playing 6 ♗f4, White admittedly allows ...♗g4, but with the clear intention of putting this move to a severe test. After all, though an active enough developing move in itself, it leaves Black's queenside rather vulnerable, in particular the b7-pawn.

6   ...   ♗g4

If Black restricts himself to playing **6...e6**, thus condemning his queen's bishop to passivity, White can be happy with the result of the opening. By taking up the gauntlet, Black makes it clear that he too is not giving any presents.

7   ♕b3 (D)

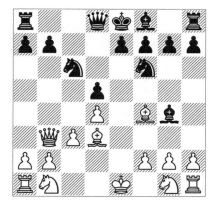

This is the most important starting position of the Exchange Variation. If Black 'simply' covers

his b-pawn by playing **7...♕d7** or **7...♕c8**, White will continue 8 ♘d2 e6 9 ♘gf3, which leads to a strategically clearly defined position. White's prospects are on the kingside, where he will try to start an attack based on a well-timed ♘e5. Black's prospects consist basically of a long-term plan of attack on the queenside with ...b5-b4.

7...♘a5 8 ♕a4+ ♗d7 9 ♕c2 is the most controversial option. White has succeeded in chasing Black's bishop away from g4, but in doing so he has created another option for Black: to play 9...♕b6 preparing an exchange of bishops with 10...♗b5.

Panov Attack

3   exd5   cxd5
4   c4

The Panov Attack occupies a special place within the Caro-Kann for White is in fact playing a sort of Queen's Gambit (1 d4 d5 2 c4). Rather than acquiesce to Black's occupation of d5, White fiercely attacks this central outpost: a veritable 1 d4 strategy. It makes the Panov a place where individual differences between 1 e4 and 1 d4 fall away and where these two great opening moves meet.

4   ...   ♘f6
5   ♘c3 (D)

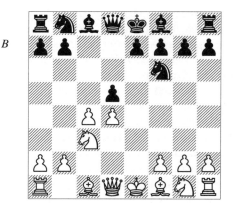

What White would really like to see now is his opponent simply (or lazily) taking on c4, either in this position or on one of his next few moves. After **5...dxc4** 6 ♗xc4 e6 7 ♘f3, for instance, the position closely resembles a similarly 'lazy' line of the Queen's Gambit Accepted (see page 44). In both cases, Black handles the opening in a way which is aimed at avoiding subtleties and complications. This is a legitimate way of playing, but opening theory itself does exactly the opposite. Its motto is always to look for something *even* more accurate, *even* more subtle or *even* better. This critical attitude has produced three main lines in this position: **5...g6**, **5...♘c6** and **5...e6**. In all three cases, White will need to act energetically if he is to obtain any sort of opening advantage at all. In other words: White will have to continue in true Panov style.

If **5...g6**, the sharp **6 ♕b3** is critical. Since taking on c4 is now really unattractive (after 6...dxc4 7 ♗xc4 e6 8 d5 Black is in serious trouble) Black is practically forced to sacrifice a pawn by 6...♗g7 7 cxd5 0-0. When studying this position, two questions need to be answered. First, will Black be able to recapture the pawn with a manoeuvre like ...♘bd7-b6xd5, or will White manage to protect his extra pawn, for instance with ♗e2-f3 and ♗g5xf6? Second, will the extra pawn be of any use to White if it takes almost an entire army to defend it? A somewhat more lucid version of this plan is to play **6 cxd5**. If then Black does not recapture, and plays simply 6...♗g7, White will have a few extra options like 7 ♗c4 and 7 ♗b5+. If Black does recapture, with 6...♘xd5, the idea is to play either 7 ♕b3 or 7 ♗c4, attacking the d5-knight. It is an intriguing question whether the position after, say, 7 ♕b3 ♘b6 8 d5!? ♗g7 9 ♗e3 0-0 10 ♖d1 offers White better chances than the 6 ♕b3 line. Precisely because White does *not* have an extra pawn (no doubled pawns on the d-file), his advanced post at d5 is easier to defend and for this reason possibly more effective.

By playing **5...♘c6** (D), Black immediately attacks d4, thus restricting his opponent's freedom of movement.

If **6 ♘f3** Black continues in similar fashion with 6...♗g4. This controversial variation has to be judged by the consequences of the sharp continuation 7 cxd5 ♘xd5 8 ♕b3 ♗xf3 9 gxf3. White is fighting for the initiative at the cost of his pawn-formation. If 9...♘xd4? 10 ♗b5+!

Black loses a piece, but the outcome of 9...e6 10 ♕xb7 ♘xd4 11 ♗b5+ ♘xb5 12 ♕c6+! ♔e7 13 ♕xb5 or 9...♘b6 10 d5 ♘d4 (or 10 ♗e3 e6 11 0-0-0) is far less easy to judge. White can avoid these problems by choosing **6 ♗g5**, only to run into others (of course!). For instance, after almost a century of changing assessments it is still not clear how strong, after the natural continuation 6...e6 7 ♘f3 ♗e7, the aggressive 8 c5 really is. Besides, Black has a number of sharp alternatives, most notably 6...♕a5 (based on 7 ♗xf6 exf6 8 cxd5 ♗b4!), the odd-looking but surprisingly effective 6...♗e6 and 6...dxc4 (here this previously 'lazy' capture is quite a critical line due to the attack on White's d4-pawn).

With **5...e6**, Black does not hurry to put pressure on his opponent's pawn-centre. He simply strengthens his grip on d5 and prepares to develop his kingside. This is where all boundaries between 1 e4 and 1 d4 theory evaporate. After 6 ♘f3 Black has a choice between 6...♗e7 and 6...♗b4. In both cases 7 cxd5 ♘xd5, transposing to a variation of the Queen's Gambit Declined (see page 20), is the usual continuation. But there is yet another surprising transposition: after 6...♗b4 7 ♗d3 dxc4 8 ♗xc4 0-0 9 0-0 a fundamental position of the Nimzo-Indian Defence (see page 70) has arisen.

Advance Variation

3   e5 *(D)*

Strange as it may sound, theory of the Advance Variation is practically brand new. For

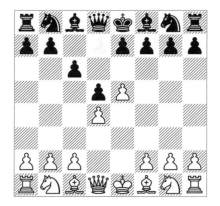

decades nobody was interested, since 3 e5 was not taken seriously. The old theoretical 'assessment' can be summarized as follows: "Black plays 3...♗f5 and since he has developed his queen's bishop outside his pawn-chain he now has an improved version of the Advance French. Black will play ...e6, probably ...c5 at some point and he has solved 'the problem of the French bishop', period." Sometimes the variation 4 ♗d3 ♗xd3 5 ♕xd3 was added to show how little promise this line holds for White.

Today, this view of the Advance Variation has changed beyond recognition.

3   ...   ♗f5

Black has also experimented quite successfully with **3...c5**, but some expertise is needed here to avoid ending up a tempo down compared to an Advance French.

But 3...♗f5 remains the most popular and sharpest line. White now has a far wider choice than older theory suggested. Far from simply exchanging Black's queen's bishop, for instance, it is now considered great sport to invent new ways of using this bishop as a target:

4 ♘c3 is the sharpest variation. White waits for Black to play 4...e6, cutting off the bishop's retreat, and then attacks with 5 g4 ♗g6 6 ♘ge2 *(D)*.

The idea is to play 7 ♘f4 followed by 8 h4 or 7 h4 immediately. If Black creates a much-needed square for his bishop with ...h6 or ...h5, White exchanges on g6, leaving Black (after ...fxg6) with a weakness at g6. This simple plan, which became popular in 1982, has proved

to be remarkably effective. Black has all sorts of ways to defend himself, but the threats looming over his position require great accuracy in defence.

But perhaps even more remarkable than the proven soundness of this attacking line was the discovery that even a very quiet set-up holds out promise of an opening advantage. To play 4 ♗d3 is to misunderstand this idea completely, but the simple **4 ♘f3**, for instance (a move which before 1990 did not even get a mention in the books), is very sound indeed. After 4...e6 5 ♗e2 c5 6 0-0 ♘c6 7 c3 cxd4 8 cxd4 ♘ge7 9 ♘c3 ♘c8 10 ♗e3 ♘b6 11 ♖c1 Black certainly has a solid position, but there is nothing wrong with White's 'normal' space advantage in a position of this type and the 'active' position of Black's f5-bishop does not trouble him at all.

A subtle variation on this theme, and one of the most recent additions to White's armoury, is to play **4 ♗e3**, with the idea of first developing the queenside (4...e6 5 ♘d2), retaining the option of playing f4 and even c4 in some cases.

The immediate **4 c4** is also not bad. Rather than wait for Black to play ...c5, White takes the initiative on the queenside himself. If Black exchanges pawns on c4, he will get a beautiful square at d5 for his knights, but White will obtain e4 and c4 for his own pieces.

Many players prefer to preface this plan with an advance on the kingside: **4 h4**. Black cannot reply 4...e6? because of 5 g4 ♗g6 6 h5 and after 4...h5 5 c4 Black's h-pawn may become a target.

3 ♘c3 / 3 ♘d2

3 ♘c3/d2

In contrast to the situation in the French (1 e4 e6 2 d4 d5) there is hardly any difference between these two knight moves. In both cases 3...dxe4 is by far the most usual reply, when 4 ♘xe4 reconnects the two roads.

The main difference between 3 ♘c3 and 3 ♘d2 lies in the possibility of Black playing **3...g6** instead of 3...dxe4. Fianchettoing the king's bishop makes the opening a close relative of the Modern Defence, 1...g6 (see page 462), which became a popular reply to 1 e4 in the 1960s and influenced several other openings, inspiring (among others) this variation of the Caro-Kann. Until then, the sturdy 3 ♘c3 had been the self-evident way of preparing for the equally self-evident 3...dxe4, but when all of a sudden 3...g6 required some attention as well, it seemed a good idea to take another look at the alternative knight move 3 ♘d2. And it is true that in this case 3...g6 loses some of its bite for c3 will protect d4 very firmly and put a major obstacle in the diagonal of the bishop about to appear at g7. For this reason 3 ♘d2 became all the rage in the 1970s and 1980s.

But the huge process of change the Caro-Kann has gone through since then has reduced any 'fear' of 3...g6 to something resembling a child's fancy. Nowadays White is facing much harder theoretical problems! In fact, anyone playing 3 ♘c3 today may even be quietly *hoping* for his opponent to take the game away from the major theoretical battles by playing 3...g6.

Theory of these lines concentrates mainly on **3 ♘c3 g6 4 ♘f3 ♗g7 5 h3**, reaching a position that will (briefly) be mentioned in the section on 1 e4 g6 (see page 463). About the sister variation **3 ♘d2 g6**, theory has little to say. White usually continues 4 ♘gf3 ♗g7 5 h3 or 5 c3, when sooner or later Black exchanges pawns on e4 after all, bringing about the characteristic pawn-formation of the Caro-Kann, but without any theoretical do's and don'ts to go with it.

3 ... dxe4
4 ♘xe4 *(D)*

No matter how interesting and important all the previous variations may be, it is not until

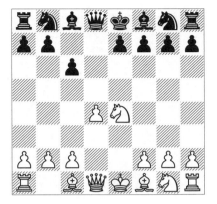

this point that we enter the true heartland of the Caro-Kann. In a way that is perhaps less obtrusive, but every bit as principled as the Panov Attack or the Advance Variation, White is challenging the correctness of 1...c6. For in this position Black has to prove that having a pawn on c6 rather than e6 (as in the Rubinstein Variation of the French) is useful.

The classical method of doing so is **4...♗f5**, which is not surprisingly called the **Classical Variation**. The main alternative, less obvious but profound and very popular nowadays, is to play **4...♘d7**.

4...♘f6 is more direct than either of these main lines, but far less popular. This move is in fact the starting point for *two* variations, for after the critical reply 5 ♘xf6+ Black has two ways of recapturing, both of them sound but very different in character:

5...exf6 has never been what you could call a popular line, but it occupies an important little place in opening theory all the same. It is solid and fairly simple strategically, but it must be admitted that Black is making a positional sacrifice of some sort. In exchange for obtaining open files, free development for all of his pieces and a safe place for his king (supposing that Black castles kingside) Black accepts a doubling of pawns which may eventually boil down to a virtual pawn sacrifice. For if White manages to obtain a passed pawn on the queenside, Black will have nothing to show for it on the kingside. This line is clearly a matter of taste.

5...gxf6 *(D)* is almost the exact opposite of the straightforwardness of 5...exf6.

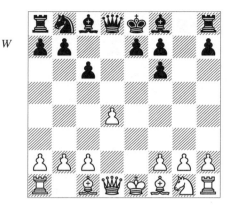

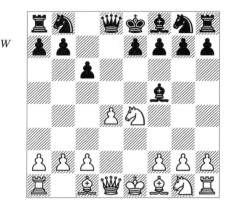

By recapturing with the g-pawn, Black is not aiming for clarity, but for darkness. He is not trying to get his pieces healthily and easily developed in a position with clear positional landmarks; he is heading for a position where both sides have no idea what is going on. Or, to put it more positively, Black is playing for **flexibility**. He will probably try to get his queen's bishop developed at f5 or g4, he will usually play ...e6 (but sometimes ...e5, or – at a later stage – ...e6-e5), but where the other bishop will go, or which side he will castle, is completely unclear. There are hardly any well-defined variations to speak of. A plan based on 6 c3 ♗f5 7 ♘f3 followed by g3, ♗g2 and 0-0 is probably the most common nowadays (and considered quite difficult for Black), but any number of other set-ups is possible. This is perhaps an ideal opening system for players with great self-confidence, good intuition and little or no taste for theoretical knowledge, but at the very highest level (where not only self-confidence but confidence in the actual openings you play *must* be a hundred percent) this variation, which used to be fairly popular in the 1960s and 1970s, has become a rare bird.

Classical Variation

4   ...   ♗f5 (D)

This simple, powerful move is the rock on which the Caro-Kann was built. Black utilizes the one big difference from the Rubinstein Variation of the French without delay: he develops the queen's bishop 'outside the pawn-chain'.

5   ♘g3

A move which is both defensive and counterattacking. The contours of the opening struggle are beginning to show: White does not simply take it for granted that Black's bishop is going to be actively placed. He will attack the bishop and do his utmost to try to make Black regret that he ever developed it.

5 ♘c5 is the only other more or less popular move in this position. It is usually played to avoid the long theoretical main line. The pawn sacrifice **5 ♗d3 ♕xd4** is almost never played.

5   ...   ♗g6
6   h4

The simple developing move **6 ♘f3** is less ambitious, though certainly not bad. After 6...♘d7 both 7 ♗c4 and 7 ♗d3 are played. In contrast to the situation in the main line (where h4 and ...h6 have been inserted), Black is not forced to take on d3 after 7 ♗d3. He has the excellent alternative of letting the opponent take on g6 himself and recapturing with the h-pawn.

Instead of these bishop moves, White also has the option of returning to the main line with 7 h4. Although the ♘h3-f4 manoeuvre is no longer possible (see below), the reply 7...h5 (rather than 7...h6) is almost never played. The true Caro-Kann player prefers yielding a little bit of space to giving up control over an important square like g5.

A more subtle plan is introduced with **6 ♘1e2**, or **6 ♗c4** followed by 7 ♘1e2. White wants to put a knight on f4, perhaps to take on g6 in some positions but more importantly to prepare h4 when the reaction ...h6 will no longer be an option. If after ♘f4xg6, Black has to take back with the f-pawn, his pawn-formation on the kingside is ruined. A possible answer to 6 ♘1e2 is 6...e6 7 ♘f4 ♗d6 in order to meet 8 h4 with 8...♕c7, undermining the f4-knight. If 6 ♗c4, the reply 6...e6 7 ♘1e2 ♘f6 is considered critical. White then not only has 8 ♘f4 but also 8 0-0 ♗d6 9 f4. The idea is to play 10 f5 and start an attack on the kingside.

6   ...   h6

6...h5 may look rather good at first glance, but 7 ♘h3 followed by 8 ♘f4 will quickly show up its drawbacks.

7   ♘f3 *(D)*

There is nothing wrong with the immediate **7 h5** but there is no need to hurry with this advance either. By playing 7 ♘f3 first, White is toying with the threat of 8 ♘e5.

7   ...   ♘d7

The classical reply to 7 ♘f3, preventing 8 ♘e5. However, around 2000 two other moves came into fashion that not only challenged this line of reasoning but even attempted to radically turn it around: **7...e6** and **7...♘f6**. It does not seem logical that Black should voluntarily lose a tempo with 8 ♘e5 ♗h7, but the idea is then to exchange White's proud knight with ...♘bd7. If this plan succeeds, it is indeed doubtful if 8 ♘e5 was such a good idea after all. Another argument in favour of these 'new' moves is that Black will have a few extra options (as compared to 7...♘d7) if White refrains from 8 ♘e5 and simply continues 8 h5 ♗h7 9 ♗d3. For instance, if 7...♘f6 8 h5 ♗h7 9 ♗d3 ♗xd3

10 ♕xd3 e6 11 ♗f4 Black now has the useful 11...♗d6.

8   h5   ♗h7
9   ♗d3

Having chased the black bishop for four moves on end, White now forces an exchange, thus gaining a 'free' developing move for his queen. Yet the outcome of the opening battle remains undecided, for it is still unclear who benefits from the action so far.

9   ...   ♗xd3
10   ♕xd3 *(D)*

Black now has three options, all of them equally logical, practically interchangeable even (in many cases they simply transpose), yet all with a peculiarity of their own.

By playing **10...♕c7** Black (probably) prepares castling queenside, something which was once seen as self-evident, but since the 1980s and 1990s, when the idea of castling kingside reached maturity, any such self-evidence has disappeared. If Black *does* want to castle queenside then it is of course perfectly reasonable to play 10...♕c7, but if he does not (or if he wants to keep both options open) this queen move is not strictly necessary and either **10...♘gf6** or **10...e6** may well be more accurate. We shall take the latter as our main line.

10   ...   e6 *(D)*

For White, the question which side to castle is not an issue. With his h-pawn as far advanced as h5 and with the spatial advantage this advance has yielded on the kingside, it is obvious that he should direct his attacking forces to that

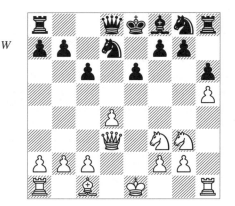

W

side of the board and bring his king in safety on the opposite wing. But White faces a more subtle problem: where to develop the queen's bishop? The choice is normally between d2 and f4.

11   &d2

The third option, **11 &e3**, has been held in contempt by opening books and players alike throughout the ages, presumably because of the opportunity that Black is given to eliminate the bishop with ...&f6-g4.

11 &d2 and **11 &f4** are about equally popular. Of these two moves, the same can be said as about Black's choice of three moves on the previous turn: they are almost interchangeable and yet they are also unique. Interchangeable especially if Black decides to castle queenside. Unique mainly if he does not. In the days when queenside castling was still the self-evident main line, both 11 &d2 **c7** and 11 &f4 **a5+** 12 &d2 **c7** were played to reach the same position. Though both of these lines are still played today, the criteria for deciding between 11 &d2 and 11 &f4 have changed. To begin with, White has to consider which square is best for the bishop in case Black castles kingside, for in that case the variations do not converge. Most players seem to prefer f4, but this again has the drawback of inviting a few unorthodox alternatives that are not available after 11 &d2 and which have served very well against 11 &f4. For instance, after 11 &f4 **a5+** 12 &d2 the surprising 12...&b4!? 13 c3 &e7 has been played. With the black queen at a5, White is prevented from castling queenside. The immediate 11...&b4+

12 c3 &e7 is another option. Black assumes that the extra move c3 is a slight weakening of White's queenside, an extremely subtle line of thinking and very difficult to judge.

11   ...   &gf6
12   0-0-0 *(D)*

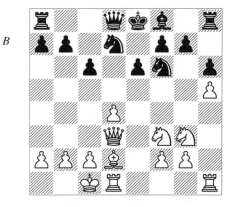

B

Now Black is at a crossroads: which way should he castle?

The old and respectable (*and* still very much alive!) plan is to play **12...&c7** followed by castling queenside (of course, if Black wants to play this versus 11 &f4, he needs to have inserted a check on a5, viz. 11...&a5+ 12 &d2 &c7, as mentioned above). White has tried a variety of replies, of which 13 &e4 0-0-0 14 g3 with the idea of playing 15 &f4 has been the undisputed main line ever since the 1980s. A characteristic follow-up is 14...&xe4 15 &xe4 &d6 (to stop 16 &f4) 16 c4 (intending to chase the bishop away from d6 by playing 17 c5) 16...c5. This leads to a lively battle for control over the centre after either 17 d5 or 17 &c3.

The modern (and still highly controversial) choice is to play **12...&e7** followed by castling kingside. Here too, White has a variety of possible replies. Black's play is very provocative and an assault on the kingside is likely to be imminent, though what exactly White should play is not clear. The manoeuvres &e2 (preparing &e5) and &e4 (freeing the way for an advance of the g-pawn – and not to g3 this time but to g4!), are likely to be vital elements of his plan, but the difference between 11 &d2 and 11 &f4

becomes tangible here. Two examples of what *might* happen in either case:

a) With the bishop on d2, 13 ♕e2 0-0 14 ♔b1 c5 is a popular line. In this position the improbable pawn sacrifice 15 d5!? has been tried, in order to add just that little bit of extra bite to White's attack that seems to be lacking after the 'regular' 15 dxc5 ♗xc5. If 15...♘xd5, White simply plays 16 ♘e4 followed by 17 g4 and if 15...exd5 the idea is to start hacking away at Black's kingside with 16 ♗xh6!? gxh6 17 ♘f5.

b) With the bishop on f4, it is 13 ♔b1 0-0 14 ♘e4 that has received most of the attention. White intends simply to play 15 ♘xf6+, forcing his opponent to choose between allowing g4 (by replying 15...♗xf6) or allowing ♘e5 (if he plays 15...♘xf6).

4...♘d7

4	...	♘d7 *(D)*

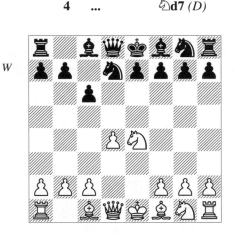

Superficially, this move does not seem to make any sense. Isn't the whole idea of the Caro-Kann to develop the queen's bishop? But a closer inspection of the position reveals that far from giving up on this plan, Black is in fact refining it. His idea is to play ...♘gf6 first (and in a way so as to be able to recapture on f6 with the other knight, hence 4...♘d7) and *then* develop the bishop. He thus not only pre-empts the usual harassment of his bishop (as in the Classical Variation), but he also obtains the option of playing ...♗g4, a development which in many cases is even more effective than ...♗f5.

In short: this is a profound and perfectly healthy strategic idea.

It is not a coincidence then that 4...♘d7 has become at least as popular and perhaps even more important than the classical 4...♗f5. Nevertheless, the success of 4...♘d7 is of recent origin. Before Anatoly Karpov started playing it on a regular basis in 1987, it was often thought (totally undeservedly) to be 'just a little too passive'. But as a result of Karpov's success, many of the world's top players have now adopted 4...♘d7. Theory of this opening system (which sadly lacks any widely accepted name) has been enriched with a huge number of sharp and original variations.

White will have to do a little more than just merrily develop his pieces if he wants to fight for the initiative in this position (as he should if he intends to be taken seriously by opening theory). After **5 ♘f3 ♘gf6 6 ♘xf6+ ♘xf6**, Black can be satisfied with the result of the opening after 7 ♗d3 ♗g4 or 7 ♗c4 ♗f5 (7...♗g4? would now be a mistake because of 8 ♗xf7+! ♔xf7 9 ♘e5+), for instance. Positionally more to the point is 7 ♘e5, in order to prevent 7...♗g4. But White's most promising way to add real depth to the game is 6 ♘g3 (instead of 6 ♘xf6+). By refusing to exchange on f6, White makes it more difficult for Black to liberate his queen's bishop. But the price that he pays is the loss of time involved in ♘g3 (for this is not a developing move) and the relatively passive position of his knight at g3. This was in fact the main line of 4...♘d7 until the 1960s, but it has now faded into the background. Practice has shown that Black has the excellent option of switching to the standard plan of the Rubinstein Variation of the French Defence (see page 353) by playing 6...e6 7 ♗d3 c5. Although strictly speaking White is a tempo up compared to a sideline of the Rubinstein (because of the loss of time involved in ...c6-c5), he has fewer and less dangerous possibilities of hindering Black's further development than in the standard Rubinstein because his own loss of time with his knight is at least as serious.

As a result, this line is now considered fairly harmless, but it does have the merit of illustrating a theme that is crucial to the 4...♘d7 variation: the idea of forcing or provoking Black to play ...e6, encapsulating his queen's bishop. This cannot be called a goal in itself, for the fate of the 5 ♘f3 line clearly shows that Black can well afford to play ...e6 if the circumstances are right. The question is: can White do any better than 5 ♘f3?

The answer to this question is sought mostly in **5 ♗c4**, intending to meet 5...♘gf6 with 6 ♘g5, and in the immediate **5 ♘g5**, when White can reply to 5...♘gf6 with 6 ♗d3, with plans based on some surprising tactical points.

5 ♗d3 intends to meet 5...♘gf6 with 6 ♘g5, and is thus the somewhat more conventional-looking sister variation of 5 ♘g5. However, it is less popular because of the reply 5...♘df6, which leaves White short of an effective and aggressive continuation. If White adopts the 5 ♘g5 move-order instead, then he can meet 5...♘df6 by 6 ♘1f3 or 6 ♗c4 (see 5 ♗c4 ♘df6 below).

Those who fancy a good opening trap may feel tempted to continue **5 ♕e2**, hoping that Black will fall for 5...♘gf6?? 6 ♘d6#. However, if Black prefers the more sensible 5...♘df6, White's queen will not be particularly well-placed on e2.

4...♘d7 5 ♗c4

5   ♗c4 *(D)*

Combining natural development with a clear plan: to attack f7.

5   ...   ♘gf6

The alternative **5...♘df6** (keeping the c8-h3 diagonal open) – although certainly playable – is not as strong in this position as it is after 5 ♗d3 or 5 ♕e2, for it has the drawback that after 6 ♘g5 further concessions are needed: unless Black plays 6...e6 after all, he will have to go for 6...♘d5 or 6...♘h6, neither of them particularly good-looking moves.

6   ♘g5   e6

White has achieved what he set out for: Black's queen's bishop is locked up inside his own pawn-chain. Now he faces a problem himself: what to do with the floating knight?

7   ♕e2

An important move. By threatening 8 ♘xf7 (8...♔xf7 9 ♕xe6+ ♔g6 10 ♗d3+ ♔h5 11 ♕h3#) White forces his opponent to make another defensive move.

7   ...   ♘b6 *(D)*

Superficially this may look like an attractive reply to White's previous move. Black wards off the threat of 8 ♘xf7 (for the e6-pawn is now protected) while at the same time attacking White's bishop *and* the d4-pawn. But at a deeper level this move (again) constitutes a slight concession to White's aggressive opening play: now that the route for his queen's bishop to f5 or g4 has been blocked off, Black's would have liked to fianchetto his queen's bishop. Putting a knight on b6 hardly fits into this plan.

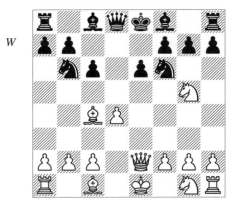

This is the main starting position of the 5 ♗c4 variation. White has a choice between two more or less equivalent moves: **8 ♗b3** and **8 ♗d3**. In both cases taking on d4 by 8...♕xd4 is extremely risky, because of the reply 9 ♘1f3 followed by 10 ♘e5. But after the more positionally oriented 8...h6, White has problems with the coordination of his knights and this really is the crucial point of the entire variation: White has managed to force a few positional concessions from his opponent, but do these outweigh the time he has had to invest? It stands to reason that Black has to react quickly though, for if White is given the chance to play ♘1f3 (allowing the other knight to drop back to e4) his problems are solved.

The critical variations as regards **8 ♗b3** start with 8...h6 9 ♘5f3 (if 9 ♘e4 Black can now safely take on d4) and now either 9...c5 immediately or 9...a5 first with the idea of playing ...c5 a little later (for instance, 10 a3 a4 11 ♗a2 c5).

Against **8 ♗d3** the main line goes 8...h6 9 ♘5f3 c5 10 dxc5 ♗xc5 11 ♘e5 ♘bd7 12 ♘gf3 ♕c7. Black is challenging White's control over e5 and frees the way for a natural plan of development: ...0-0, ...b6 and ...♗b7.

4...♘d7 5 ♘g5

5 ♘g5 *(D)*

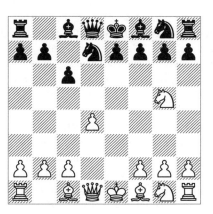

This most unusual knight move caused a veritable revolution in the 4...♘d7 variation between 1987 and 1989. For in its disguise as a blunt, perhaps even rather stupid, attacking move, 5 ♘g5 is actually a wonderfully subtle refinement of the idea behind 5 ♗c4. It stands to reason then that Black had great difficulties

coming to terms with this line. Having to dodge a few heavy blows first and then still being forced to play with great accuracy for several moves in order to avoid falling into a passive position, this is not an easy task. And though by now the worst of the storm is over, it is clear that 5 ♘g5 has come to stay. Today, in the early years of the 21st century, it is this very move that must be considered the real main line of the 4...♘d7 variation.

5 ... ♘gf6 *(D)*

The first point of 5 ♘g5 comes to light if Black unsuspectingly replies **5...h6?!**: if you did not see 6 ♘e6! coming (as Black) you will be greatly relieved to find that you do not have to resign on the spot. But all the same, after 6...♕a5+ 7 ♗d2 ♕b6 8 ♗d3 the damage to Black's position is bad enough. The knight on e6 is still taboo: 8...fxe6?? 9 ♕h5+ ♔d8 10 ♗a5 costs Black his queen.

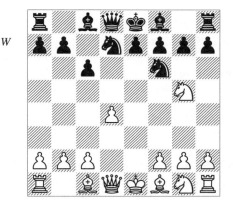

6 ♗d3

This is the deeper idea behind 5 ♘g5. It appears that White does not need to play **6 ♗c4** (transposing to 5 ♗c4 ♘gf6 6 ♘g5) to force his opponent to play 6...e6, for even after 6 ♗d3 there is simply nothing better.

6 ... e6

6...h6 again runs into the powerful 7 ♘e6!, when after 7...♕a5+ 8 ♗d2 ♕b6 not only 9 ♘xf8 but even the laconic 9 ♘f3 can be played. After 9...fxe6 10 ♗g6+ ♔d8 11 0-0 Black is a piece up, but his position is totally disorganized.

The alternative **6...♘b6** avoids any such problems, but without attacking a bishop on c4, this move is of course not quite so incisive, though certainly not bad. After 7 ♘1f3 ♗g4 8 h3 ♗xf3 9 ♘xf3 Black has solved the problem of his queen's bishop, but White can be satisfied with the harmonious development of his pieces.

7 ♘1f3 (D)

7 ... ♗d6

Black still has to tread carefully. **7...h6**, for instance, *may* be playable now, but Black has to be prepared for a complicated defensive task if White decides to sacrifice a piece for the initiative with 8 ♘xe6 (which is one of the main ideas behind the whole 5 ♘g5 line). Both 8...fxe6 9 ♗g6+ ♔e7 10 0-0 and 8...♕e7 9 0-0 fxe6 10 ♗g6+ ♔d8 lead to a position which is very difficult to judge (and to play!). Black's king cannot be brought into safety easily.

8 ♕e2 h6

Now that Black has made sure his position won't get disrupted by a piece sacrifice on e6, he can finally afford to play this move. Ironically, it is the seemingly more cautious **8...0-0** that gets punished by 9 ♘xe6 now (after 9...fxe6 10 ♕xe6+ ♔h8 11 ♕xd6 White has simply won two pawns).

9 ♘e4

Sacrificing on e6 is now less attractive because after **9 ♘xe6** fxe6 10 ♗g6+ ♔e7 11 0-0 ♘f8 Black's defensive lines remain relatively well-organized. By dropping the knight back to e4, White relinquishes any ideas of a blitzkrieg and it looks as if Black has weathered the storm. But now the second and perhaps the most difficult phase of the opening battle begins.

9 ... ♘xe4
10 ♕xe4 (D)

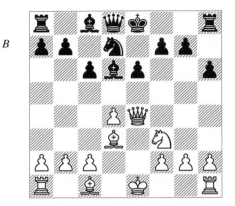

This is the great starting position of the 5 ♘g5 line. Just as in the 5 ♗c4 variation, White has prevented the development of Black's queen's bishop via the c8-h3 diagonal, albeit at the cost of a couple of tempi (♘e4-g5-e4). The question now is whether Black will be able to execute the alternative plan of developing the bishop on b7, preferably in combination with the powerful advance ...c5.

The most plausible method of doing so is to play **10...♘f6** and after 11 ♕e2 continue with 11...b6 12 ♗d2 ♗b7 13 0-0-0 ♕c7, but a drawback of this straightforward and thematic play is that White is given firm control over e5; e.g., 14 ♘e5 0-0-0 15 f4. To avoid this, the subtle **10...♕c7** is often played. While retaining control over e5, Black prepares ...b6 (or ...c5, depending on White's reaction). The weak link in this plan is Black's g7-pawn. After the sharp reply 11 ♕g4 Black has nothing better than 11...♔f8, giving up the right to castle. The next question is: does this really matter? After 12 0-0 c5 a fierce battle is in the offing.

Sicilian Defence

| 1 | e4 | c5 *(D)* |

W

If one opening could serve as a metaphor for the huge progress our understanding of chess has made in the course of the 20th century, from classical, in tune with clear, albeit static positional features to modern, complex and highly dynamic, there is only one candidate: the Sicilian Defence.

The name dates back to the 17th century, the first serious experiments and theoretical observations to the 19th, but it was not until the 20th century that 1...c5 slowly developed into that magical tool for the great and terrible demolition of the hegemony of both 1...e5 and of the entire classical school of thought of which that move is a product.

Like 1...e5, 1...c5 prevents the formation of an ideal pawn-centre with 2 d4, but without giving White the typical targets of the 1 e4 e5 openings: the e5-pawn and the a2-g8 diagonal with the vulnerable spot at f7. Nor does Black initiate any immediate skirmishing in the centre, as he expressly does both with 1...e5 and with the Caro-Kann and the French. This may sound a little passive, bent on avoiding a fight, and as a matter of fact this is exactly what people thought of the Sicilian Defence in the 19th

century. But it is precisely *this* assessment which has changed dramatically. From a marginal phenomenon, the Sicilian grew into the most combative and aggressive reply to 1 e4 and it has been the most popular opening outright for many a decade now. It has turned out to possess a latent power and flexibility that has been the source of a wealth of new ideas and it is no exaggeration to say that 1...c5 has become *the* crucial test of 1 e4. Players who do not feel comfortable with it will have to switch to another opening move. But for those who do manage to master the Sicilian, be it with White or with Black (and preferably both, of course) it is a mighty weapon indeed.

In fact, by playing 1...c5 Black chooses the same strategy that underlies 1 c4 and 1 ♘f3: he does not immediately occupy any central squares, but intends to control them from the flank with such moves as ...♘c6, ...g6 and ...♗g7. He then has the option of striking back at a later stage, for instance with ...d5, but he is under no obligation to do so, for with a pawn on c5, Black also has a natural plan of attack on the queenside: ...a6 followed by ...b5.

This strategy calls for a clear answer from White. His range of options may be roughly divided into three categories:

Plan A: White leaves the c5-pawn alone, calmly plays d3 at some point and contents himself with his stronghold at e4 and the potential attacking chances on the kingside that go with it.

Plan B: White plays c3, preparing an 'ideal' pawn-centre with d4 after all.

Plan C: White plays d4 without c3 and recaptures on d4 with a piece.

Plan C will normally produce a position where White has a spatial advantage and where (behind the broad back of the e4-pawn) he has every chance of developing his pieces easily and aggressively. It is this plan that has been perceived from the first as the critical test of 1...c5. It is also precisely this type of position that has undergone the greatest shift in assessment: from passive (for Black) to highly dynamic and with a multitude of possible plans (for both sides). It is in this soil that all the main lines of the Sicilian Defence are rooted, lines which have become so huge and complex that they could justifiably be regarded as independent openings. In fact, an experienced player hardly talks about 'the Sicilian', but about 'the Najdorf' or 'the Sveshnikov' (etc.) instead. And yet all these opening systems are very closely related. There are countless transpositional possibilities and for a thorough understanding of any single variation, a basic knowledge of some of the others is extremely useful.

Because of this interconnectedness of all variations and because many characteristic plans can be carried out in various ways, any form of systemization (such as I have attempted here) only makes sense to a very limited extent.

We shall start with what I have termed Plan A, the most important implementation of which is **2 ♘c3**, the **Closed Sicilian**.

2 f4, **2 g3** and **2 d3** are variations on this idea. There is quite a lot of theory on these moves (as there is on all subvariations of the Sicilian), but the general consensus is that these lines are relatively less threatening to Black. The first two can even be called (respectably) marginal. Both against **2 f4** and against **2 g3** Black has the immediate 2...d5, a counterblow that 2 ♘c3 is intended to prevent. After 2 g3 d5 3 exd5 ♕xd5 it is unfortunate for White that his h1-rook is under attack, while after 2 f4 d5 3 exd5 Black can afford to play 3...♘f6 since defending the pawn with 4 c4 leaves some nasty holes in White's pawn-structure that can be exposed with 4...e6 5 dxe6 ♗xe6.

With **2 d3** we enter the world of the **King's Indian Attack**. As we have seen in several earlier chapters, other gates to this world are situated in the Réti Opening, the French Defence (see page 347) and the Caro-Kann (see page 375). It has a most distinctive atmosphere and a charm of its own which is so captivating to some players that they play it almost regardless

of what the opponent is doing. Others are a little more judicious and play it only when the circumstances are really favourable. Just by way of an example: instead of the immediate 2 d3 White might prefer 2 ♘f3 and continue with 3 d3 only if Black chooses 2...e6, and not against other moves. The variation 2 d3 is interwoven with the Closed Sicilian. After 2...♘c6 3 g3 g6 4 ♗g2 ♗g7, for instance, 5 ♘f3 produces what you could call a 'pure' King's Indian Attack, 5 ♘c3 transposes to the Closed Sicilian and 5 f4 is a subtle attempt to improve on both moves. If 5 f4 e6 6 ♘f3 ♘ge7 7 0-0 0-0, White can still transpose with 8 ♘c3 but he also has the option of 8 c3, preparing the central advance d4.

This takes us to what I have termed Plan B: c3 followed by d4, a plan which can be carried out in many different versions. White might play 2 ♘f3, for instance, and continue with 3 c3 or not, depending on Black's reply, an option we shall examine more closely when discussing 2 ♘f3. But the simplest *and* the most important method of implementing this plan lies in **2 c3**, the **Alapin Variation**.

We then arrive at the main body of theory of the Sicilian: Plan C.

For this, **2 ♘f3** forms the logical introduction and by far the largest part of this chapter will be devoted to variations starting with this move.

A remarkable variation on this theme (or perhaps it is a hybrid between methods B and C is **2 d4**. The idea of this move is not to meet 2...cxd4 with 3 ♕xd4 (which would merely give Black the developing move 3...♘c6 for free) but with 3 c3. This is the **Morra Gambit**, a strange way of turning things upside down: instead of playing c3 to prepare d4 White plays d4 to prepare c3! Black can transpose to the Alapin Variation with 3...d5 4 exd5 ♕xd5 or 3...♘f6 4 e5 ♘d5 if he likes, but the critical test of this gambit is of course to accept it and play 3...dxc3. This brings us, after 4 ♘xc3 *(D)*, to the starting position of this line.

The differences from the position after the 'ordinary' move 2 ♘c3 are few but their impact is considerable. White's c- and d-pawns have disappeared and so has Black's c-pawn. This opening of files changes the character of the

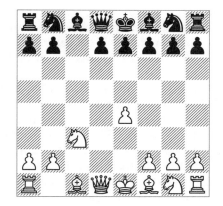

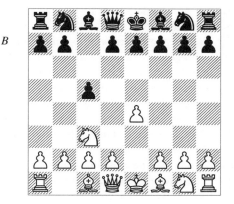

position enormously. White is ready to develop his bishops aggressively while Black will have to make several pawn moves to do the same. The Morra Gambit is perhaps best described as a radical method of exposing 1...c5 as a non-developing move. Nevertheless, this is a variation 'for specialists only'. White undoubtedly has the initiative, but is this enough for a pawn? Black's position is flexible and contains no weaknesses. Possible continuations after 4...♘c6 5 ♘f3 are 5...d6 6 ♗c4 e6 7 0-0 ♘f6 and 5...e6 6 ♗c4 a6 7 0-0 ♘ge7, amongst many others.

Naturally, there remain a few options that do not fit into my (or any) systemization of plans. The most remarkable of these is probably **2 b4**, the **Wing Gambit**. White eliminates Black's c5-pawn and is hoping, after 2...cxb4 3 a3, to obtain both a strong pawn-centre (with pawns on e4 and d4) and a quick development of his queenside. 3...d5 is a good reply.

A slow-motion version of this idea (but more radical for this very reason!) is to play **2 a3**, preparing 3 b4.

And finally, those who like 1 e4 but hate the Sicilian might try **2 c4**, turning the opening into a rough version of the Symmetrical English. If play continues 2...♘c6 3 ♘c3 g6 4 g3 ♗g7 5 ♗g2 the roughness is smoothed out and we have reached a Botvinnik Variation (see page 201).

Closed Sicilian

2   ♘c3 (*D*)

Once upon a time, in the days when opening theory, even of the Sicilian Defence, was clear and simple, this move was the introduction to the nicely compact plan g3, ♗g2 and d3, followed by ♘ge2 (or f4 and ♘f3) and 0-0. White hardly needed to take any notice of what his opponent was doing in the meantime, Black knew what he was up against, and everybody was happy.

Naturally, such an attitude is still perfectly legitimate today, but it has long lost the self-evidence it once had. Modern opening theory is always digging deeper and is always looking for new directions, but it is also constantly searching for ways to outfox the opponent. For this purpose, juggling move-orders is a perfect tool. Almost everyone who plays the Sicilian (as Black) restricts his preparation against the main line 2 ♘f3 [d6/e6/♘c6] 3 d4 cxd4 4 ♘xd4 to one or two variations. As we are about to see, these variations are primarily defined by Black's second and fourth moves. By playing 2 ♘c3 rather than the standard 2 ♘f3, the modern well-informed and flexible player forces his opponent to be on his guard not just for 3 g3, the classical Closed Sicilian, but also for a change of direction with 3 ♘f3 and 4 d4. If Black does not want to be tricked into a variation he does not know very well (regardless of how sound that variation might be in itself) he has to consider his reply to 2 ♘c3 very carefully.

2   ...   ♘c6

This move used to be axiomatic, but nowadays this is a highly technical matter. What main line would Black like to play and what does he want to avoid at all cost?

For instance, someone who is aiming for a Najdorf or a Dragon Variation is more likely to play **2...d6**. If then **3 ♘f3** he can simply reply 3...♘f6, when after 4 d4 cxd4 5 ♘xd4, 5...a6 or 5...g6 respectively will reach the desired result, while in case of 3 g3 the reply 3...♘c6 4 ♗g2 g6 5 d3 ♗g7 transposes to a standard position of the Closed Sicilian that is also reached via 2...♘c6 and which we shall be looking at shortly.

But there are two alternatives that a 2...d6 player has to take into account: **3 ♘ge2** and **3 f4**. The former repeats the dilemma of the previous move: White is waiting for Black to show his hand before he decides to continue 4 d4 or 4 g3. The idea behind 3 f4 is rather different. White develops his bishop to c4 or b5 and plays d3. This is called the **Grand Prix Attack**. It *may* be a very aggressive strategy, for in some cases White continues f5, sacrificing a pawn to start an attack against the ever-vulnerable f7-square. A sample line (albeit an important one): 3 f4 ♘c6 4 ♘f3 g6 **5 ♗c4 ♗g7** 6 0-0 e6 *(D)*.

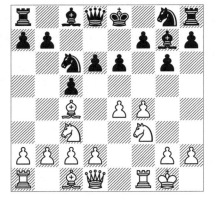

7 f5!? (simply 7 d3 ♘ge7 8 ♕e1 is also not bad), intending to meet both 7...exf5 and 7...gxf5 with the astonishingly calm 8 d3. Black has to be careful. If 7...gxf5 8 d3 ♘ge7, for instance, 9 ♘g5 followed by 10 ♕h5 might well get him into trouble very quickly.

Playing **5 ♗b5** (instead of 5 ♗c4) embarks upon a different plan altogether. White vaguely threatens to exchange on c6. This 'Nimzo-Indian' motif is quite important in the Sicilian

Defence. It is one of White's best options of keeping the position closed without relinquishing his ambitions to obtain the initiative.

If **2...g6** there is also 3 f4 to consider, besides the 'standard' 3 ♘f3 and 3 g3.

By playing **2...e6**, Black makes it clear that he is thinking in a different direction. Both 3 g3 and 3 f4 can now be met by a counter-thrust in the centre: 3...d5. And if 3 ♘f3 (making 3...d5 decidedly less attractive because of the firm reply 4 exd5 exd5 5 d4), Black will choose between 3...♘c6, 3...a6 or 3...d6, with a Taimanov, a Paulsen or a Scheveningen Variation in mind respectively. It is true that White has a plausible alternative to 4 d4 cxd4 5 ♘xd4 against any of these three moves, but nothing that will greatly worry Black. If 3...♘c6, he might consider 4 ♗b5 (reaching the same position as after 2...♘c6 3 ♘f3 e6 4 ♗b5); if 3...a6 White could play 4 g3 (analogous to 2...a6 3 g3 below) and if 3...d6, there is the option of playing 4 d4 cxd4 5 ♕xd4 ♘c6 6 ♗b5 (compare this to the variation 2 ♘f3 d6 3 d4 cxd4 4 ♕xd4; see page 435).

Black even has a fourth option against 3 ♘f3, which is to reply 3...♘f6, inviting a transposition to the risky Nimzowitsch Variation by 4 e5 ♘d5 (see page 401).

Probably Black's most adventurous second move is **2...a6**. Against 3 g3 the aggressive 3...b5 4 ♗g2 ♗b7 looks quite acceptable and against 3 ♘f3 Black can either play 3...e6 or 3...d6, inviting a transposition to a main line, or remain in (relatively) unexplored territory with 3...b5 4 d4 cxd4 5 ♘xd4 ♗b7.

We now return to 2...♘c6 *(D)*:

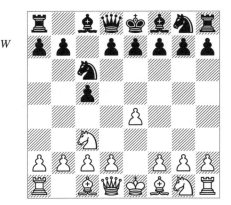

In this position White has all the options that we have just seen against Black's alternative second moves, and one extra.

The classical move, opting for a standard Closed Sicilian, is **3 g3**. The modern option is to play **3 ♘f3**. These are the main lines that we shall look into in rather more detail below.

Then there are the 'regular' alternatives **3 f4** and **3 ♘ge2** and finally there is **3 ♗b5**, a recent idea.

3 f4 may be combined with either ♗c4 or ♗b5 as in the 2...d6 3 f4 version (see page 392). ♗b5 is especially useful if Black plays ...d5, for instance in case of **3...e6** 4 ♘f3 d5 5 ♗b5. **3...g6** 4 ♘f3 ♗g7 is a little more solid for Black than in the 2...d6 3 f4 line.

A perfect illustration of the growing popularity of ♗b5 as a reply to ...♘c6 in countless different versions is the emergence of the variation **3 ♗b5**. Until very recently it was unheard of to play this move in a position where there is no objection to the aggressive reply ...♘d4. Nowadays White simply retreats the bishop (3...♘d4 4 ♗c4) and calmly continues with ♘f3 and ♘xd4.

By playing **3 ♘ge2**, White delays the moment to commit himself either for or against g3 for as long as he can. It is also a way of preparing for the possible reply 3...e5, which is a major option in case of 3 ♘f3 (see page 395), for White can now take full possession of the d5-square with 4 ♘d5 and 5 ♘ec3. But whether this manoeuvre is really something for Black to be afraid of is a moot point.

2 ♘c3 ♘c6 3 g3

3 g3

Superficially, this set-up is closely related to the King's Indian Attack, where White plays ♘f3, g3, ♗g2, d3 and (usually) ♘bd2. But with a knight on c3 and the diagonal of White's g2-bishop unobstructed by a knight at f3, it is far more difficult for Black to start operations in the centre based on ...d5. This gives the Closed Sicilian a decidedly different flavour.

3	...	g6
4	♗g2	♗g7
5	d3	d6

The decisive factor in this variation is the position of Black's e-pawn. 5...d6 is the most flexible move. Until the 1950s, **5...e6** was thought of as the main line, but then it was discovered that a plan based on ...e5 is often more solid, especially if White chooses a plan with 6 ♗e3 and 7 ♕d2. White intends to play ♗h6, undermining both Black's control over the centre and the safety of his kingside by the exchange of dark-squared bishops. This also enhances the prospects of a plan to advance in the centre after all: ♘d1 (or ♘ce2) followed by c3 and d4.

6 f4 (D)

If now **6 ♗e3**, Black plays 6...e5. The same applies to the oldest move in this position: **6 ♘ge2**.

By playing 6 f4, White concentrates his forces more fully on the kingside. Ever since Boris Spassky successfully used this idea in the 1960s, it has been the main line.

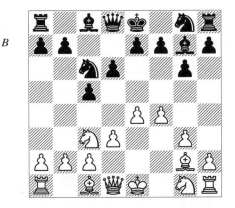

B

Black now faces a fundamental choice.

6...♘f6 is a healthy developing move, but it is also a provocation, for this move is practically begging to be 'punished' by g4-g5, an advance that White would like to play in any case. But in the meantime Black advances on the queenside. This usually results in a full-scale battle with chances for both sides; for instance, 7 ♘f3 0-0 8 0-0 ♖b8 9 h3 b5 and now 10 g4 b4 11 ♘e2 a5 12 f5, or – a little more subtle – 10 a3 a5 11 ♗e3.

Those who would rather concentrate on the centre will prefer **6...e5**, the same plan as is recommended against 6 ♗e3 and 6 ♘ge2. If White continues 'as expected' with 7 ♘f3, Black obtains a solid position by 7...♘ge7 8 0-0 0-0 9 ♗e3 ♘d4. The critical move is probably the unorthodox 7 ♘h3. White keeps both the f-file and the d1-h5 diagonal open and this generates some dangerous attacking chances. After 7...♘ge7 8 0-0 0-0, for instance, there is the energetic pawn sacrifice 9 f5!? gxf5 10 ♕h5.

Now that White has committed himself to a f4 plan, Black's most solid option is perhaps to switch to **6...e6**. This creates the opportunity to play ...f5 (as a reply to g4 for instance) blocking the enemy advance on the kingside. Again, there is one line out of the many possibilities that is particularly sharp and critical: 7 ♘f3 ♘ge7 8 0-0 0-0 9 ♗e3 (intending 10 d4) 9...♘d4 10 e5!?. This is in effect a pawn sacrifice for after 10...♘ef5 11 ♗f2 ♘xf3+ 12 ♕xf3 ♘d4 White will have to play 13 ♕d1, when Black can simply take his e-pawn. The idea is to meet 13...dxe5 14 fxe5 ♗xe5 with 15 ♘e4. White is threatening 16 c3, winning back the pawn and obtaining the upper hand in the centre. Black can try to take the initiative himself by 15...f5 16 ♘xc5 f4.

2 ♘c3 ♘c6 3 ♘f3

3 ♘f3 (D)

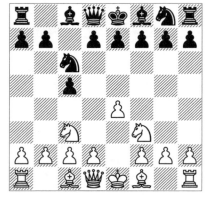

This position also arises (and indeed more often!) via 2 ♘f3 ♘c6 3 ♘c3. Black will have to select a reply which is compatible with the

variation he has in mind against the 'threatened' 4 d4.

For those who play the Accelerated Dragon, the choice is easy. All they have to do is play **3...g6** and wait for 4 d4 cxd4 5 ♘xd4, and their favourite variation arises. The alternative 4 ♗b5 is unlikely to worry them, for although not bad, this is definitely less threatening to Black than a regular Rossolimo Variation (2 ♘f3 ♘c6 3 ♗b5 g6) now that White has committed himself to ♘c3 at such an early stage.

The same applies to **3...e6**. Anyone who is not worried about playing one of the main lines arising from 4 d4 cxd4 5 ♘xd4 can safely play this move. 4 ♗b5 is a somewhat inflexible version of the analogous line 2 ♘f3 ♘c6 3 ♗b5 e6 (see page 402).

Again due to the early ♘c3, the option of playing 4 ♗b5 against **3...d6** is comparatively harmless. If 4 d4 cxd4 5 ♘xd4 instead, Black has three main lines to choose from: 5...g6 leads either to the Dragon Variation or the Accelerated Dragon after 6 ♗e3 ♗g7 7 ♗c4 ♘f6, 5...e6 (probably) to a Scheveningen Variation and after 5...♘f6 we have reached the starting position of the Classical Variation.

But things are more complicated if Black plays **3...♘f6** (D).

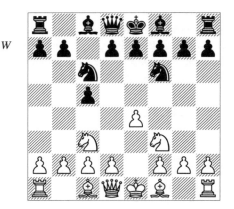

If one's repertoire against the main line of the Sicilian includes *only* the Sveshnikov Variation (and this again only in the version 2 ♘f3 ♘c6 3 d4 cxd4 4 ♘xd4 ♘f6 5 ♘c3 e5), this move is the only one that 'fits'. Unfortunately, it is precisely here that **4 ♗b5** is a fully-fledged alternative to 4 d4, mainly because **4...♘d4** runs into the sharp 5 e5. Now that the Sveshnikov has become one of *the* most important variations of the Sicilian, it is only logical that all the sidelines are also being turned upside down and this is one of White's most popular options of avoiding the Sveshnikov proper. **4...♕c7** is a spirited reply. Black prepares to play ...♘d4 after all (after 5 0-0 ♘d4, for instance, 6 e5? is now bad because of 6...♘xf3+ winning a pawn).

Black's most important alternative, and the only way to turn 2 ♘c3 ♘c6 3 ♘f3 into an independent variation (and consequently the only attempt at exposing White's opening play as 'dawdling'), is to play **3...e5**, radically preventing d4. This used to be thought inferior because of the hole in Black's pawn-formation at d5, but assessment of this positional feature has changed. If Black proceeds with the necessary caution, White's control over d5 should not unduly bother him and his chances should not be worse than in comparable variations like the Stonewall Variation of the Dutch Defence (see page 177). After 4 ♗c4 ♗e7 (not 4...♘f6?? 5 ♘g5) 5 d3 d6 **6 0-0 ♘f6** Black's position is sound. White would like to open the f-file to increase the pressure against Black's kingside, but a variation like 7 ♘g5 0-0 8 f4 exf4 9 ♗xf4 h6 10 ♘f3 ♗e6 is not overly dangerous for Black. A more subtle plan is to play **6 ♘d2** (instead of 6 0-0), intending not only to free the way for the f-pawn but also to play ♘f1-e3. However, this allows Black to get rid of his least active piece with 6...♗g5 followed by ...♗xd2 (or ...♗xc1, in case White plays 7 ♘f1).

Alapin Variation

2 c3 (D)

It could be argued that this is the only move to take 1...c5 seriously. White does not tiptoe around the c5-pawn, nor does he break the symmetry by playing 2 ♘f3 and 3 d4. He simply accepts the fact that Black has prevented 2 d4 and is now taking steps to carry out this plan anyway. Stubbornness or common sense?

Ironically, it is also the only move to suffer from the same defect as 1...c5 itself: it is not a

developing move. Quite the contrary in fact, for White voluntarily makes the c3-square inaccessible to his queen's knight.

This is really the Alapin Variation in a nutshell. White's plan is to build up a strong pawn-centre and for this he is taking a certain slowness of piece development in his stride. If Black wants to expose a possible downside to this plan, he will have to act quickly and decisively. It is hardly surprising then, that the main lines start with **2...d5** and **2...♘f6**.

2...e6 is a solid option, but Black has to be aware of the fact that after 3 d4 d5, 4 e5 transposes to the Advance Variation of the French (see page 351) and that 4 exd5 exd5 leads to a type of play which is very similar to the 3...c5 4 exd5 exd5 variation of the Tarrasch French (see page 370). Not bad, but very un-Sicilian-like.

The fianchetto **2...g6** allows an even more surprising transposition. Black calmly invites 3 d4 only to react very sharply: 3...cxd4 4 cxd4 d5. If then 5 e5 ♘c6 6 ♘c3 ♗g7 Black hopes to make good use of the open c8-h3 diagonal (e.g. by playing 7 ♘f3 ♗g4!) and if 5 exd5 ♘f6 6 ♘c3 we suddenly find ourselves in a Panov Attack Caro-Kann (see page 379).

A third alternative, and one that may seem obvious to someone who has just studied 2 ♘c3 ♘c6 3 ♘f3 e5, is to play **2...e5**. The only difference is that after 3 ♘f3 ♘c6 4 ♗c4 there is a pawn on c3 instead of a knight. Nevertheless, this is not a popular line for Black, perhaps because the permanent threat of White playing d4 makes the position unusually tense.

Finally, there is the less obvious but extremely tricky **2...d6**, waiting for White to play 3 d4 before lashing out with 3...♘f6 *(D)*.

Black seems to be asking for trouble here. First, what about 4 dxc5? Second, doesn't White simply achieve his strategic aim by just playing 4 ♗d3? It is the first of these lines where most of the venom is hidden. For Black is not intending to meet **4 dxc5** meekly with 4...dxc5 5 ♕xd8+ ♔xd8 hoping to be able to survive in a joyless endgame, nor is he intending to blunder a piece with 4...♘xe4?? 5 ♕a4+. He intends to play the simple but very surprising 4...♘c6. If White then defends his e-pawn with 5 f3 he is in for another surprise: 5...d5!?. Black ignores the c5-pawn and calmly continues to batter e4. His trump card is his lead in development, while the weakening of White's kingside (f3), however slight, may also make itself felt. After 6 exd5 ♘xd5 7 ♗c4 e6, for instance, there is the annoying threat of 8...♕h4+.

In practice, many players prefer **4 ♗d3**. Black's main idea in that case is to intensify the attack against d4 by playing ...e5, either at once (4...e5) or at a later stage, perhaps after first fianchettoing his king's bishop with 4...cxd4 5 cxd4 g6 6 ♘c3 ♗g7.

The bulk of these variations (and of 2...d5 and 2...♘f6 theory as well) is fairly young. The Alapin Variation was really viewed as an innocuous little thing until about 1980 and theory is just beginning to come to terms with it. It has now been extensively analysed, however, so Sicilian players need to be well prepared for 2 c3.

2 c3 d5

2	...	d5

A logical reaction to 2 c3 since – unlike in the Scandinavian Defence (1 e4 d5; see page 465) – after the exchange on d5 White does not have the free developing move ♘c3 at his disposal.

3	exd5	♕xd5
4	d4 *(D)*	

In the multitude of variations starting from this position, the driving force behind all opening theory is clearly discernible: the never-ending search for good, better, best.

For Black *could* be satisfied now with a simple reply like **4...cxd4** 5 cxd4 ♘c6 6 ♘f3 e6 7 ♘c3 ♕d6 8 ♗c4 ♘f6 9 0-0 ♗e7, which gives him a perfectly reasonable version of a typical middlegame we have seen in many an earlier chapter: the isolated white pawn on d4 against a black pawn at e6.

But chess-players are never satisfied with simple solutions and are always looking for better, better still and better again. And usually there is a good reason for this, for with a variation like the above one, Black not only makes life easy for himself but for his opponent as well: White gets the chance to play all his optimal developing moves for free.

So any serious theoretical investigation of this position should start with an attempt to bring about the same type of position in a slightly more favourable version. For example: Black could play **4...♘f6 5 ♘f3 e6**, delaying

...cxd4 until White has developed at least one of his minor pieces in a sub-optimal way, i.e. less aggressively than in the above variation with 4...cxd4. This could be a move like ♗e2 or ♘bd2. And even ♗e3 may be seen as a concession on White's part, however small. In fact, this line constitutes one of Black's safest options. After 6 ♗e3 cxd4 7 cxd4 ♘c6 8 ♘c3 ♕d6 the forthcoming middlegame is likely to develop along familiar lines: White has a space advantage and latent attacking chances on the kingside. Black has a wonderful square for his pieces at d5 and prospects of besieging White's d4-pawn.

Apart from this classical treatment of the opening, theory has investigated a number of more aggressive options as well. In the first place, Black may want to eliminate *all* the centre pawns and steer for a drawish position by playing **4...cxd4 5 cxd4 e5** *(D)*.

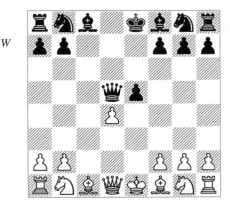

But this line has never been popular, possibly because the endgame after 6 ♘f3 exd4 7 ♕xd4 ♕xd4 8 ♘xd4 is undeniably a little better for White (because of his tiny lead in development) or perhaps because for anyone who has the courage to play the Sicilian, a sudden switch to playing for a draw like this is just out of character.

A more popular version of this idea is to play **4...cxd4 5 cxd4 ♘c6 6 ♘f3** and only now 6...e5 (the same position is reached via 6...♘c6 instead of 6...exd4 in the previous variation). The idea is to meet 7 dxe5 with 7...♕xd1+ 8 ♔xd1 ♗g4 and 7 ♘c3 with 7...♗b4 8 ♗d2 ♗xc3 9

♗xc3 e4. In both cases Black is hoping to obtain the initiative.

Another plausible method is to play ...♗g4 at some point, for instance **4...♘f6 5 ♘f3 ♗g4** *(D)*.

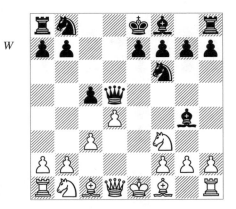

This line hinges on the 'threat' of exchanging pawns on d4 in the best possible circumstances (and on White trying to avoid or even refute this). Positional assessments are often very delicate and controversial. A possible continuation is 6 ♗e2 e6 7 h3 ♗h5 8 0-0 ♘c6 9 ♗e3 cxd4 10 cxd4.

2 c3 ♘f6

2 ... ♘f6 *(D)*

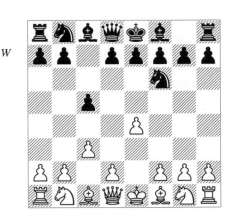

A provocative move and, just like 2...d5, a pointed attempt at exposing the drawbacks of 2 c3. The first problem for White is that he cannot protect his e-pawn with 3 ♘c3.

3   e5   ♘d5
4   d4

White can also play **4 ♘f3**, delaying d4 until he feels it is the best moment for this advance.

4   ...   cxd4 (D)

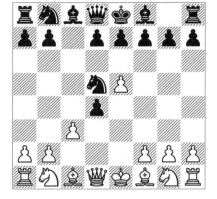

Unlike the comparable Alekhine Defence (1 e4 ♘f6; see page 447), here White's options for establishing a broad pawn-centre are rather limited.

5   ♘f3

This subtle move has gradually pushed the old main line, the obvious **5 cxd4**, into the background. In many cases these moves transpose but there is one important difference. After 5 cxd4 d6 6 ♘f3 ♘c6 White would like to play 7 ♗c4. Black then has 7...e6 or 7...dxe5 to protect his d5-knight, but the critical move is the counterattack 7...♘b6. For many years *the* great debate in the 2...♘f6 variation was about the position arising after 8 ♗b5 dxe5 9 ♘xe5 ♗d7, but around 1980 the discussion died down. Solid defences were constructed against all attempts to obtain an opening advantage for White. A change of direction was needed and 5 ♘f3 became the new main line.

5 ♕xd4 is also possible of course. This line has a long-standing reputation of being safe but not overly aggressive. White changes his strategy: instead of aiming for a strong pawn-centre (which is what 2 c3 is all about) he goes for open files and diagonals and speedy piece development. The basic position of this line arises after 5...e6 6 ♘f3 ♘c6 7 ♕e4. Black can eliminate White's last remaining centre pawn

in classical fashion by playing 7...d6 or he may want to play the more adventurous 7...f5.

We now return to 5 ♘f3 (D):

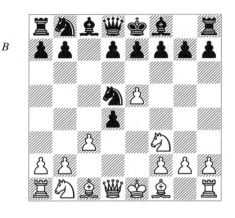

5   ...   ♘c6

This is the crucial test of 5 ♘f3, for with this move Black attempts to transpose into the 'old' main line as given above. For the same reason **5...d6** may also be played (6 ♗c4 ♘b6 7 ♗b3 ♘c6 transposes to the 5...♘c6 line) but this is rather less popular, perhaps because of the alternative recapture 6 ♕xd4 now being slightly more favourable than a move earlier.

The alternative **5...e6** leads to a very different sort of game. This position (or rather the position after 6 cxd4) is often reached via 2 ♘f3 e6 3 c3 and is therefore quite important. White has consolidated his central pawn-formation. The advanced position of his e-pawn guarantees a spatial advantage and promises latent chances on the kingside, but the dominant position of Black's d5-knight makes it difficult to build up an actual attack. Two main lines have sprung up from this position: the classical 6...d6 and the modern 6...b6.

If **6...d6** there are – roughly speaking – three possible schemes of development for White. One is 7 ♗c4 and there is also 7 a3 followed by 8 ♗d3 (the immediate 7 ♗d3 runs into 7...♘b4), both placing the king's bishop on an attractive square. On c4 it puts pressure on Black's powerful knight, while on d3 it is pointed at h7, making many an opponent nervous at the prospect of castling kingside. The third and most radical option is to play 7 ♘c3. At the cost of a weakening of his pawn-structure (after 7...♘xc3 8 bxc3 the c3-pawn will become a target), White eliminates the black knight.

6...b6 not only prepares ...♗b7 but also opens the way for a possible exchange of bishops with ...♗a6 as well. In this case 7 ♘c3 is the unchallenged main line. The position after 7...♘xc3 8 bxc3 ♛c7 9 ♗d2 is critical. One important option for Black is to start attacking White's e-pawn after all, with 9...d6 10 ♗d3 ♘d7.

6   ♗c4 *(D)*

This is the point of 5 ♘f3. It is also the most aggressive move in this position. **6 cxd4** transposes back to the variations that White could have reached a move earlier by playing 5 cxd4.

6   ...   ♘b6

Again, this counterattack is the theoretically critical reply. It is less aggressive, though certainly not bad, to play **6...e6**, when 7 cxd4 d6 transposes to the variation 5...e6 6 cxd4 d6 7 ♗c4 as discussed above, with the (minimal) difference that Black has already committed himself to a ...♘c6 plan.

7   ♗b3

The purpose of White's opening play becomes clear. In contrast to the variation 5 cxd4 d6 6 ♘f3 ♘c6 7 ♗c4 ♘b6, he makes no attempt to take advantage of the pin against the c6-knight by playing ♗b5, but instead keeps his bishop aimed at the most vulnerable spot in Black's position: f7. This strategy involves first of all a pawn sacrifice, albeit one that is almost never accepted: **7...dxc3** 8 ♘xc3, when White's lead in development is probably *too* threatening.

7   ...   d5

Secondly, White has to have an answer to this solid move.

8   exd6

This would also be the reply to **7...d6**.

8   ...   ♛xd6 *(D)*

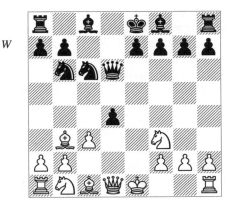

This is the great starting point of this variation. Most of the attention goes to **9 0-0**. Taking on c3 is still not attractive for Black. After 9...dxc3 10 ♛xd6 exd6 11 ♘xc3 he is lagging behind in development while his extra pawn on d6 is just a flimsy little thing in any case. Black has a much more powerful move in 9...♗e6, making use of the opportunity to eliminate White's dangerous b3-bishop. After 10 ♗xe6 ♛xe6 11 ♘xd4 ♘xd4 12 ♛xd4 White has got his pawn back but his lead in development has diminished. It is more aggressive to play 10 ♘a3 and after 10...dxc3 to sacrifice another pawn with 11 ♛e2.

The immediate **9 ♘a3** is a variation on this theme. 9...♗e6 now has the obvious drawback of granting White a free developing move in the form of 10 ♘b5. The alternative is 9...dxc3, when again 10 ♛e2 is critical and very controversial indeed.

2 ♘f3

2   ♘f3 *(D)*

At all times, this approach has been considered the most promising for White – as a refutation of the Sicilian even, but that was a very long time ago. White intends to play 3 d4, opening the d-file and taking charge of the centre, not with two pawns on e4 and d4 as in the Alapin but with a pawn and a knight and – most importantly – with beautiful open lines and natural squares for all pieces. Looking at the position from this perspective, one might well bow and say 'thank you' to 1...c5 and look to the future with great confidence.

But as I already described earlier in this chapter, it is precisely here, in this type of position, that the great transformation of the Sicilian Defence has taken place. The compactness of Black's position, his flexible pawn-formation, the latent central pawn-majority (two pawns against one), the open c-file which forms the base for an amazing wealth of possible counterplay on the queenside: these are factors that may look inconspicuous at first sight but which will inexorably come to light when the position is examined more closely. Many an individual chess-player has gone through this learning process and so has the world of chess in its entirety.

And precisely because White's prospects are so very different from Black's, the inherent tension is enormous. A lot of self-confidence *and* confidence in one's position is required from both sides. In almost any 'Sicilian' position, one side is bound to think he has the advantage. In fact, very often *both* players will think so! And play will always be sharp; there simply is no other way to play the Sicilian. This makes the Sicilian an attractive but also very difficult opening. It is also a highly complex opening with a multitude of variations, all with an idea, a name and a great body of theoretical knowledge of their own yet at the same time all very similar to each other. Some variations are so closely interwoven that it is almost incomprehensible why theory recommends move A in this line and move B in the other.

In the position after 2 ♘f3, Black faces a far-reaching decision. How should he anticipate the expected 3 d4? This decision will determine which variation eventually materializes, though some variations can be reached via several move-orders.

And Black should not forget that although White is preparing to play 3 d4, he has not so far committed himself. So, however Black chooses

B

to anticipate 3 d4, it must be compatible with his ideas of meeting alternative moves. Most of these are not quite so sharp as 3 d4, but some of them are not bad at all and have to be taken seriously.

Black's major options are **2...♘c6, 2...e6** and **2...d6**. All the main lines of the Sicilian are introduced with one of these moves and are based on play continuing 3 d4 cxd4 4 ♘xd4. All three of these moves offer White a specific choice of options.

From the remaining nineteen legal moves in this position, there are three 'minor' options to be aware of: **2...g6, 2...a6** and **2...♘f6**.

2...g6 is an alternative route to the Accelerated Dragon (3 d4 cxd4 4 ♘xd4 ♘c6, or 4...♗g7 followed by 5...♘c6). By avoiding the far more popular 2...♘c6, Black steers clear of the Rossolimo Variation (2...♘c6 3 ♗b5), but he has to be prepared for some other lines, most notably 4 ♕xd4 and 3 c3. The latter option is closely related to the variation 2 c3 g6 (see page 395) and may easily transpose if play continues 3...♗g7 4 d4 cxd4 5 cxd4 d5.

The seemingly aimless little move **2...a6** has a most remarkable theoretical status. On the one hand it must be regarded (strange as it may sound) as *the* way of discouraging White from playing 3 d4. On the other hand, it is practically useless if White continues 3 c3. The idea is to meet 3 d4 with 3...cxd4 4 ♘xd4 ♘f6 5 ♘c3 e5, what you could call an 'improved' Najdorf Variation ('improved' because unlike in the Najdorf proper, Black can develop his king's bishop at c5 or b4). The problem is that White in his turn may play an 'improved' Alapin Variation with 3 c3, when ...a6 comes suspiciously close to being just a loss of tempo.

2...♘f6 is a highly provocative move that strikes a balance between 2 c3 ♘f6 and the Alekhine Defence (1 e4 ♘f6). It is called the **Nimzowitsch Variation**. Compared to the Alekhine Defence, this line has the advantage of not allowing White to form a broad pawn-centre after 3 e5 ♘d5 thanks to the pawn on c5. But 4 ♘c3 shows up the drawback: **4...♘xc3** 5 dxc3 is now better for White than the comparable line in the Alekhine (1 e4 ♘f6 2 e5 ♘d5 3 ♘c3 ♘xc3 4 dxc3; see page 448), thanks to... the c5-pawn, which makes the liberating move ...d6 decidedly less attractive. After 5...d6 6 exd6 exd6 Black has only saddled himself with a weak pawn while giving his opponent full control over d5. For this reason it is not 4...♘xc3 but **4...e6** which takes us to the basic position of the Nimzowitsch Variation, which arises after 5 ♘xd5 exd5 6 d4 (D):

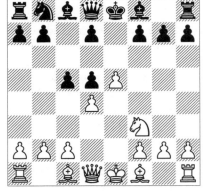

White is threatening to win a pawn with 7 dxc5 ♗xc5 8 ♕xd5. Black's answer to this problem is both simple and bold: he takes no notice of the threat and continues 6...♘c6, sacrificing a pawn in return for fast development. After 7 dxc5 ♗xc5 8 ♕xd5, **8...♕b6** leaves White no easy way of protecting f2, but he does have a dangerous way of *not* defending it: 9 ♗c4! ♗xf2+ 10 ♔e2 0-0 11 ♖f1. Most players prefer not to test this variation and play **8...d6**, opening another diagonal before lashing out: 9 exd6 ♕b6, when 10 ♗c4 ♗xf2+ 11 ♔e2 can

be met by 11...0-0 12 ♖d1 ♗e6. On the other hand, White now has an easy way of protecting f2, namely 10 ♕e4+ ♗e6 11 ♕h4. This variation hinges on the question of whether after 11...♗xd6 Black has enough compensation for the missing pawn.

2 ♘f3 ♘c6

2 ... ♘c6 (D)

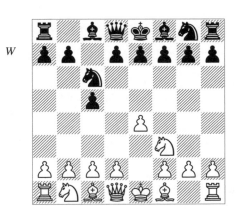

Of all the possible moves at Black's disposal, this one is perhaps the most natural. Black develops a piece and prepares 3...♘f6, as yet without committing himself to any particular pawn-formation.

But looking more deeply into the problem and looking ahead at the position after 3 d4 cxd4 4 ♘xd4, we have to be a little more critical. No matter how flexible Black's pawn-phalanx may be, certain main lines of the Sicilian are already beyond his reach. 2...♘c6 is not a neutral move, as none of Black's second-move options are. Anyone playing 2...♘c6 does so (or so one would hope) with some particular main line in mind.

3 d4

Naturally, White can play anything he likes here, but there is one move that truly deserves to be called the king of the minor variations: **3 ♗b5 (D)**, the **Rossolimo Variation**.

This move is popular at all levels with players who have no wish to expose themselves to the breakneck pace of the main lines (3 d4). White continues developing his kingside and only then

does he plan to undertake any sort of action in the centre. Depending on Black's reply, this may either be aggressive with d4 (possibly prefaced by c3) or very calm, with d3 for instance. The latent 'threat' of ♗xc6 adds a certain positional tension to the game, which not every Sicilian player will be happy with. For one thing, it is not always easy to decide whether taking on c6 is actually a good idea. It is also very often completely unclear whether Black should recapture with his b- or his d-pawn. The exchange on c6 is most certainly the central theme of the Rossolimo Variation.

After Black's most popular reply **3...g6**, there is a major division of minds. The classical approach is to play 4 0-0 and after 4...♗g7 to continue either with 5 c3 or the more flexible 5 ♖e1, but nowadays 4 ♗xc6 is a very popular alternative. If then 4...bxc6 White continues in classical fashion with 5 0-0 ♗g7 6 c3 followed by d4. If 4...dxc6 on the other hand (when the open d-file makes this plan less promising for White), a simple yet dangerous alternative plan has emerged, consisting in 5 d3 ♗g7 6 h3 ♘f6 7 ♘c3 0-0 8 ♗e3 followed by 9 ♕d2, ♗h6 and possibly even 0-0-0.

The same division occurs if Black plays **3...e6**, preparing ...♘ge7 and then ...a6 (thus actually encouraging White to take on c6!). At first this variation revolved around the question of whether after 4 0-0 ♘ge7 White should immediately open the centre (with 5 ♖e1 a6 6 ♗xc6 ♘xc6 7 d4 cxd4 8 ♘xd4 for instance), banking on his lead in development, or whether he should play 6 ♗f1 (instead of 6 ♗xc6),

planning to continue with c3 and d4, or 5 c3 a6 6 ♗a4 b5 7 ♗c2 with the same idea. But this line has also become infiltrated with the new idea of 4 ♗xc6 and this is a fully accepted option nowadays. After 4...bxc6 5 d3 ♘e7 (now with ...♘g6 in mind) the bold 6 ♘g5 is often played, freeing the way for f4.

Perhaps as a reaction against these popular 4 ♗xc6 lines, **3...d6** (D) has recently come to the fore.

At first this move looks illogical, for Black is actually pinning his own knight, but the idea is to prepare the harmonious unpinning move 4...♗d7. This line is also relevant to the variation 2...d6 3 ♗b5+, where interest in 3...♘c6 has grown considerably of late. After **4 ♗xc6+** bxc6 5 0-0 Black has two possibilities of hindering the crucial advance d4: 5...e5 and 5...♗g4. Although these are interesting enough lines, most players have so far preferred the classical **4 0-0** in this case. After 4...♗d7 5 ♖e1 Black then has to decide whether he will risk the loss of tempo involved in playing 5...a6, unafraid of 6 ♗xc6 ♗xc6 7 d4 cxd4 8 ♘xd4 (analogous to the variation 3...e6 4 0-0 ♘ge7 5 ♖e1 a6, given above) or whether he will first develop another piece with 5...♘f6, waiting for White to spend a tempo himself on 6 c3. In the latter case, 6...a6 forces White to take a similarly fundamental decision. For some time the pawn sacrifice 7 ♗xc6 ♗xc6 8 d4 was all the rage, but then the excitement died down and White started playing the more restrained 7 ♗f1, with Black usually replying 7...♗g4, again with the idea of hindering White's plan of playing d4.

From White's remaining options of avoiding the main lines, the following deserve at least a brief mention: **3 c3** is neither better nor worse than 2 c3 and often transposes; **3 d3** has a similar degree of compatibility with 2 d3; and **3 ♘c3** is a popular way of avoiding a Sveshnikov Variation – I have classified this a subvariation of 2 ♘c3 in this book (see page 394).

If White wants to play a c4 set-up, he should have done so a move earlier, for now **3 c4** leaves White's f3-knight blocking the vital advance f4 in case Black replies 3...e5.

> **3 ... cxd4**
> **4 ♘xd4 (D)**

This position is one of three main gates to the heart of the Sicilian Defence (the others are the analogous positions with 2...d6 and 2...e6 instead of 2...♘c6). Now, what options does Black have?

The first move that comes to mind is the sturdy **4...♘f6**. This leads, after the natural reply **5 ♘c3** (5 ♘xc6 bxc6 6 e5?? fails to 6...♕a5+), to a position where Black again has several options. **5...d6** (this position is also reached by 2...d6 3 d4 cxd4 4 ♘xd4 ♘f6 5 ♘c3 ♘c6) is the starting point of the **Classical Variation**, although its main lines have different names (the Richter-Rauzer and Sozin Attacks) by which they are better known.

The use of names for these lines is somewhat vague in any case, for **5...e6**, a variation that may also be reached via 2...e6, is known as the

Four Knights Variation, but is mainly used as a cunning route to the Sveshnikov.

More resolute than these two little pawn moves (but also more compromising) is the powerful thrust **5...e5**. For a long time this was called the **Pelikan Variation**, but is generally known nowadays as the **Sveshnikov Variation** (even if Sveshnikov himself has called it the Cheliabinsk Variation). Black immediately fixes the pawn-formation in the centre. Moreover, he does so in a way which at first sight looks rather dubious. Once upon a time this was regarded as a clumsy minor variation and in fact it was not really understood until the 1970s. Now it has conquered the world, for this is one of *the* most important variations of the Sicilian Defence.

Finally there is **5...♕b6**, which leads, after 6 ♘b3, to a position that will be briefly discussed in the short paragraph on 4...♕b6 below.

One set-up that is conspicuously absent from this list is the idea of a kingside fianchetto. Anyone having this formation in mind is likely to concentrate on the Dragon Variation (2...d6 3 d4 cxd4 4 ♘xd4 ♘f6 5 ♘c3 g6). Of course, there are ways of combining the development of the king's bishop at g7 with 2...♘c6, but Black has to be careful here. In fact, the oldest variation based on this theme was **4...♘f6 5 ♘c3 g6**, but this is hardly ever played nowadays because White has the annoying 6 ♘xc6, when both 6...dxc6 7 ♕xd8+ ♔xd8 8 ♗c4 and 6...bxc6 7 e5 ♘g8 8 ♗c4 are unattractive for Black. There is, however, a fully viable successor to this 'Primeval Dragon': **4...g6**, the **Accelerated Dragon**.

Another way of developing the king's bishop is via the a3-f8 diagonal. This plan was first implemented in the Four Knights Variation, but a subtle variation on this idea is to play **4...e6** (without the preliminary 4...♘f6 5 ♘c3). This is the **Taimanov Variation**. Since this variation is closely related to the Paulsen (or Kan) Variation (2...e6 3 d4 cxd4 4 ♘xd4 a6) and is in any case more often reached via 2...e6 in practice, I have chosen to include it in the section on 2...e6.

These are the variations that we shall go into a little deeper. There are three other moves for Black which have also made their mark, but which cannot really be included with the main lines. I shall just outline them very briefly:

The first is **4...♕c7**. This is in fact a paradoxical way of aiming for the Taimanov Variation, which now arises if White replies 5 ♘c3, as Black then plays 5...e6. The idea is to make the aggressive 5 ♘b5 less attractive for White by... inviting it. The point becomes clear in the position after 5...♕b8: Black is not faced with the threat of ♘d6+ (as he would be after 4...e6 5 ♘b5) so he does not have to play ...d6, closing the diagonal for his king's bishop. Should White continue 6 c4, Black can play 6...♘f6 7 ♘5c3 and now 7...e6 or 7...b6 8 ♗e2 ♗b7 9 0-0 e6. He has retained the option of playing ...♗c5 or ...♗b4, while in some cases even ...d5 is possible.

4...♕b6 is also one of those elusive variations which are played, accepted and written about in theoretical manuals, but without ever becoming a truly main line. Black chases the knight away from its dominant position on d4 at the price of a loss of tempo (for ...♕c7 will in due course be inevitable). This usually leads to a Scheveningen-type position, for instance after 5 ♘b3 ♘f6 6 ♘c3 (this position can also be reached via 4...♘f6 5 ♘c3 ♕b6 6 ♘b3) 6...e6 7 ♗e3 ♕c7. The aggressive plan of playing f4 and ♕f3 followed by the advance g4-g5 is critical.

Finally, there is **4...e5**, a variation on the theme of the Sveshnikov. Remarkably, this is both one of the oldest *and* the youngest variations of the Sicilian.

The old (but not old-fashioned) interpretation is to meet 5 ♘b5 with **5...a6** *(D)*, an approach based on tactical ideas.

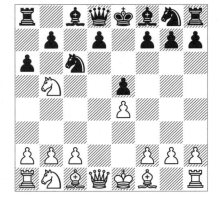

At first sight, the many holes in Black's pawn-chain after 6 ♘d6+ ♗xd6 7 ♕xd6 look truly horrendous but these are compensated for (to a certain extent at least) by Black's lead in development after 7...♕f6. If **8 ♕xf6** ♘xf6 9 ♘c3, the liberating 9...d5 becomes possible (10 exd5 ♘b4 wins back the pawn), while 9...♘b4 seems to be playable as well. Things become rather more complicated if White avoids the exchange of queens. After **8 ♕d1** ♕g6 9 ♘c3 ♘ge7, for instance, the advance ...d5 is again hovering over the position.

The modern approach is purely positional: **5...d6** *(D)*.

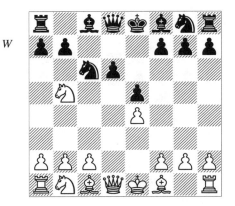

This line is of interest to players who are looking for the typical middlegame of a Sveshnikov Variation but without having to acquire the enormous theoretical knowledge which this variation nowadays demands from its devotees. If **6 ♘1c3** a6 (6...♘f6 transposes to the 'real' Sveshnikov) 7 ♘a3 b5 8 ♘d5, instead of playing 8...♘f6 (which again transposes to the Sveshnikov proper after 9 ♗g5) Black may try 8...♘ge7 or even 8...♘ce7.

6 c4 is a critical test of this line. White strengthens his grip on d5 and prevents ...b5. Nevertheless, there are quite a number of players who like to play this position as Black. The most important point in Black's favour is the manoeuvre ...♗e7-g5, activating or exchanging his 'bad' bishop. 6...♗e7 7 ♘1c3 a6 8 ♘a3 ♗e6 9 ♗e2 ♗g5 is a likely continuation. This variation leads to a strategic rather than a tactical battle.

Classical Variation

4	...	♘f6
5	♘c3	d6 *(D)*

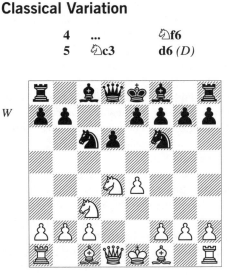

In the early decades of the 20th century, the heyday of austere classical chess, this position was *the* starting point of the Sicilian. What was investigated was whether this opening could stand up to the then modern, strictly positional dogmas, as contrasted with the old-fashioned, highly tactically coloured opening variations of the 19th century (like the variation 4...e5 5 ♘b5 a6 that we have just seen). That this – later called the Classical – variation was accepted is understandable. Black is playing healthy – classical – developing moves and avoids compromising his position in any way. And even though the world of chess, together with the Sicilian, has changed beyond recognition since those days, the Classical Sicilian remains one of the soundest and most important interpretations of this opening.

Now, how should we look at this position?

The first, almost self-evident, main line was **6 ♗e2**. Theoretical debate started with the question of whether Black should then reply **6...e6**, the **Scheveningen Variation**, or **6...g6**, the **Dragon Variation**.

In the early 20th century, **6...e6** was the most popular choice, until in a tournament at the Dutch town of Scheveningen in 1923, the Hungarian grandmaster Geza Maroczy beat the future world champion Max Euwe in a very impressive game that continued 7 0-0 ♗e7 8 ♔h1 0-0 9 f4 ♕c7 10 ♘b3 a6 11 a4. In those days it was thought to be essential for Black to make either the advance ...b5 or the manoeuvre ...♘a5(e5)-c4, in order to obtain active play on the queenside. Until then, an early ♗e3 was usually played, but by delaying this move (thus avoiding 8 ♗e3 a6 9 a4 ♕c7 10 ♘b3 ♘e5 11 f4 ♘c4 – with an attack against the e3-bishop! – for instance) Maroczy frustrated this plan. Such was the impression his treatment of the opening created, that the ...e6 plan was named after Scheveningen (which is really odd considering it was given a thorough beating there!) and – more importantly perhaps – that it disappeared into the background, until it was rehabilitated many years later (see page 427).

6...g6 became the new main line and this plan held up very well for many years, which – in hindsight – is not so strange because, as we shall see on page 445, the ♗e2 plan is not exactly the sharpest way to treat a Dragon.

Then in the 1940s another weapon was added to Black's arsenal: **6...e5** *(D)*, the **Boleslavsky Variation**.

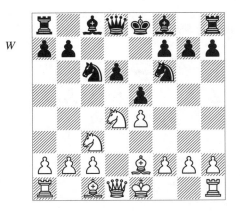

After 7 ♘b3 ♗e7 8 0-0 0-0 9 ♗e3 ♗e6, Black is ready to play ...d5. If 9 f4, trying to stop this plan, he switches to active play on the queenside with 9...a5 10 a4 ♘b4. That Black could afford to create a hole in his pawn-chain at d5 without any visible concrete compensation to show for it was a revolutionary discovery in those days, one which left many traces in other variations of the Sicilian, for instance in the Najdorf.

So halfway through the 20th century things were looking rather good for Black. But then the tide turned. It was becoming obvious that White needed something more incisive than 6 ♗e2, something that would restrict Black in his freedom of movement. Very slowly, assessments of 'Sicilian' positions began to change. From being based on general and somewhat rigid positional ideas, they became more concrete, paying more attention to the exact characteristics of each and every position. Variations became more precise, more dynamic, more daring. The old move 6 ♗e2 did not completely disappear (for there is nothing wrong with it) but it was no longer seen as a real test of the Classical Sicilian.

Two new variations emerged, which pushed 6 ♗e2 aside: 6 ♗g5, the **Richter-Rauzer Attack**, and 6 ♗c4, the **Sozin Attack**. We shall take a closer look at them.

Richter-Rauzer Attack

6   ♗g5 (D)

This is often called simply the Rauzer Attack, reflecting the fact that the modern handling of this line, with ♕d2 and 0-0-0, was devised by Vsevolod Rauzer.

The fact that 6 ♗g5 is more aggressive and forcing than 6 ♗e2 can be felt immediately:

6...g6?! is far less attractive now that White has the reply 7 ♗xf6 to ruin Black's pawn-structure. White is also much better armed to counter Boleslavsky's move, for if now **6...e5?!** then after 7 ♗xf6, 7...♕xf6? 8 ♘d5 ♕d8? 9

♘b5 is disastrous for Black, while 7...gxf6 8 ♘f5 is an inferior version of what we now call a Sveshnikov Variation because the vital advance ...f5 has been prevented.

This means that by playing 6 ♗g5 White more or less forces his opponent into a ...e6 plan (although there are in fact a few alternatives, like **6...♗d7**, for instance, anticipating 7 ♕d2, when Black intends to create swift counterplay on the queenside with 7...♖c8 8 0-0-0 ♘xd4 9 ♕xd4 ♕a5).

6   ...   e6

But after this move, more complicated problems arise and the first doubts as to the strength of 6 ♗g5 begin to creep in. Is g5 really such a good square for the bishop if Black neutralizes the pin against his knight so easily by playing ...♗e7? Were White to continue indifferently, with 7 ♗e2 ♗e7 8 0-0 0-0 for example, perhaps the bishop *would* rather stand on e3, for 9 f4?? is now very bad on account of 9...♕b6.

7   ♕d2 (D)

By playing this move, White lays his cards on the table: he intends to castle queenside. This has two concrete advantages: the kingside is kept free for attacking operations, and Black's d6-pawn comes under pressure.

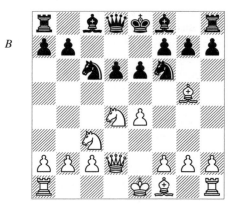

A great number of methods has been developed for Black to come to terms with the problems of this position. In the first place, Black has to find an answer to moves like ♘db5 and f4, especially in combination with e5 and ♗xf6. Exchanging on f6 is an important theme in the Richter-Rauzer Attack. In many cases it is very difficult to evaluate the resulting position when Black takes back with his g-pawn (which is often forced). This results in a complex type of position, which is fairly unique to the Richter-Rauzer. Black's kingside pawn-formation is somewhat rigid and White may well try to attack it by playing f4-f5. On the other hand, the doubled f-pawns give Black greater control over the centre *and* he has the pair of bishops, two factors that may be to his advantage in the long run, for instance if he manages to play ...d5. Some players are very fond of this pawn-structure, others are allergic to it and others again allow it only if they consider the circumstances to be truly favourable.

For instance, only the real die-hard ...gxf6 fan will go for this type of position immediately by playing **7...h6** 8 ♗xf6 gxf6 (if 8...♕xf6? 9 ♘db5 ♕d8 10 0-0-0 Black simply loses his d-pawn). It is not that there is a concrete problem with this – in fact, after 9 0-0-0 a6 10 f4 ♗d7 the position strongly resembles a main line that we are about to see – but the 'moderate' ...gxf6 player simply does not like to give the tempo ...h6 away for free.

Far more usual is **7...a6**, a useful move preventing ♘db5 and preparing ...b5 (in the long run). After the consistent reply 8 0-0-0 *(D)*, Black has several options:

8...h6 really makes sense now, for taking on f6 is not a problem for Black now that he can simply recapture with the queen. Nor is 9 ♗h4 ♘xe4! very promising for White. The main lines therefore are 9 ♗e3 and 9 ♗f4.

By playing **9 ♗e3** White simply accepts that his bishop has had to retreat. After 9...♗d7 or 9...♗e7, he will concentrate his attention on gaining space on the kingside with 10 f3 followed by g4.

9 ♗f4, on the other hand, attacks d6 and forces Black to defend rather ingeniously with 9...♗d7 (9...e5? fails to 10 ♘xc6 bxc6 11 ♗xe5), indirectly protecting the d-pawn for after 10 ♘xc6 ♗xc6 White's e-pawn is attacked and 11 f3 can be met by 11...d5.

Both these lines are well investigated and lead to a sharp fight.

A popular alternative is to play **8...♗d7**, when 9 f4 *(D)* is the normal reply.

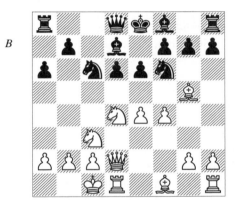

If then **9...h6**, the retreat 10 ♗h4 is OK since 10...♘xe4 can be met stoically with 11 ♕e1, which promises White a dangerous initiative after 11...♘f6 12 ♘f5. But the real point of 9...h6 is to play 10...g5!?, a spectacular way of breaking the pin on the f6-knight. Now the boot is on the other foot, for after 11 fxg5 ♘g4 it is White's g5-pawn that is pinned, making it difficult for White to consolidate his extra pawn. In the meantime Black has obtained a beautiful square for his knight at e5. This too is a controversial and fascinating variation that is hotly debated.

But Black may also choose simply to continue developing his pieces and play **9...♗e7** (instead of 9...h6). After 10 ♘f3 b5 there is again a parting of the ways. White has the sharp 11 e5 (to which 11...b4 is the recommended reply) and the positional 11 ♗xf6, when 11...gxf6 brings about that typical Richter-Rauzer pawn-formation again. 12 f5 ♕b6 13 g3 0-0-0 is a characteristic follow-up. White could start putting e6 under pressure with a manoeuvre like ♗h3 and ♘e2-f4, but he has to be careful all the time not to allow his opponent to take over the initiative by playing ...d5.

9...b5 10 ♗xf6 gxf6 is another way of bringing about this typical Richter-Rauzer pawn-formation. The alternative recapture, 10...♕xf6, is not quite impossible here, but it is rather risky because of 11 e5! dxe5 12 ♘dxb5, attacking d7.

Black may also try to do without ...a6, for the time being at least. In fact, the simple **7...♗e7** 8 0-0-0 0-0 is both the oldest and the most classical of Black's options. The Achilles' Heel of this line is d6 of course, but it turns out not to be easy for White actually to take advantage of the vulnerability of this little pawn. If **9 ♘db5**, for instance, 9...♕a5! 10 ♗xf6 ♗xf6 11 ♘xd6 ♖d8 is a strong reply. The powerful f6-bishop and the nasty pin on the d-file are sufficient compensation for the pawn. The main lines start with 9 ♘b3 and 9 f4.

9 ♘b3 is a more subtle version of 9 ♘db5. While introducing the possibility of playing ♗xf6, White does not commit himself. He also prepares an assault against Black's king with f3 and g4. Black has a defence against these threats in 9...♕b6 10 f3 (if 10 ♗xf6 ♗xf6 11 ♕xd6 Black can restore the material balance by taking on f2) 10...♖d8, covering d6 and introducing the counter-threat of ...d5. Other moves that have been tried include 9...a5 (to meet 10 ♗xf6 with a pawn sacrifice: 10...♗xf6 11 ♕xd6 ♕xd6 12 ♖xd6 a4 followed by 13...a3) and 9...a6 (to counter 10 ♗xf6 'simply' with 10...gxf6).

Against **9 f4** *(D)* Black again has several options.

First there is the radical attempt to transform the situation in the centre by means of the surprising counterattack ...e5. The most subtle version of this plan starts with **9...h6**. If White now plays **10 ♗xf6**, the idea is to sacrifice a pawn with 10...♗xf6. Both 11 ♘xc6 bxc6 12 ♕xd6 ♕b6 and 11 ♘db5 e5! (with the nasty point 12 f5?? ♗g5) offer Black sufficient counterplay. The critical variation is **10 ♗h4**, which allows both 10...♘xe4 (when White is satisfied with a

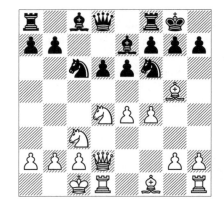

slightly better endgame: 11 ♗xe7 ♘xd2 12 ♗xd8 ♘xf1 13 ♘xc6 bxc6 14 ♗e7 ♖e8 15 ♖hxf1 ♖xe7 16 ♖xd6) and – more importantly – 10...e5. After 11 ♘f5 ♗xf5 12 exf5 exf4 the point of the inclusion of 9...h6 is revealed: White cannot recapture on f4 with the bishop. If 13 ♕xf4 instead, Black has the bold reply 13...d5 since 14 ♗xf6? ♗xf6 15 ♘xd5 (again) loses the queen to 15...♗g5.

A second main line is **9...♘xd4** 10 ♕xd4 ♕a5. Just to illustrate in how much detail this line has been analysed: if White chooses the healthy developing move 11 ♗c4, there is no need for Black to reply with the timid 11...♖d8. He can play the unperturbed developing move 11...♗d7 instead, for 12 e5 is met by 12...dxe5 13 fxe5 ♗c6, when 14 exf6 runs into 14...♕xg5+. If 14 ♗d2 ♘d7 15 ♘d5, Black defends with 15...♕d8 16 ♘xe7+ ♕xe7. In the resulting position, White has attacking chances against Black's king but Black's pieces are well-placed and his position is without obvious weaknesses.

Sozin Attack

6   ♗c4 *(D)*

Like 6 ♗g5, this move is specifically directed against **6...g6** and **6...e5**. **6...g6?!** is met by 7 ♘xc6 bxc6 8 e5! with the nasty point 8...dxe5?? 9 ♗xf7+ winning the queen. There are no such tactical objections to **6...e5?!** but the positional drawbacks of this move as compared to 6 ♗e2 e5 are clear enough: the white bishop is perfectly placed on c4, where it is aimed at the crucial squares d5 and f7.

B

W

Nevertheless, until the 1950s 6 ♗c4 was not a popular move. The reason for this was that c4 was not thought to be a good square for White's bishop after Black's most natural reply:

6 ... e6 *(D)*

Nowadays the aggressive **6...♕b6** is considered as much of a test of 6 ♗c4 as this quiet pawn move. In fact, this is probably the best of the many ...♕b6 variations that lie hidden in various corners of the Sicilian, since after chasing away White's knight there is the further prospect of chasing the bishop as well. After 7 ♘b3 e6 8 ♗e3 ♕c7 9 ♗d3, for instance, White has lost a full tempo on the 4...♕b6 variation that I gave on page 404. White really has to play imaginatively here. After 7 ♘b3 e6, for example, both 8 ♗f4 and 8 ♗g5 have been tried (instead of the perhaps slightly too routine 8 ♗e3) and an even more subtle idea is to play 7 ♘db5, planning to meet 7...a6 with 8 ♗e3 ♕a5 9 ♘d4. The resolute 7 ♘xc6 bxc6 8 0-0 is also quite logical. White makes no attempt to attack Black's queen but simply develops his pieces as fast as he can.

In the position after 6...e6, White has to justify his previous move, for if he plays without a clear plan Black will have plenty of ways to take advantage of the position of the bishop on c4: ...♘a5, ...a6 and ...b5, ...♕c7, ...d5 and even the combination ...♘xe4 (with the idea that after ♘xe4 there is the fork ...d5, winning back a piece on either e4 or c4).

The great breakthrough of the Sozin Attack came in the 1950s when it was discovered that advancing the f-pawn by f4-f5 constitutes a sound and aggressive plan for White. This will attack e6 and if that pawn can be removed (by forcing Black to respond with ...exf5 or ...e5) White obtains a strong square at d5. Also, the alternative advance e5 (supported by f4 of course) can be quite dangerous. This plan became so popular that it infiltrated the Najdorf and Scheveningen Variations as well (as we shall see further on in this chapter). A few decades later, an even more aggressive plan by the Yugoslav grandmaster Velimirović gave the Sozin another impulse.

7 ♗e3 ♗e7
8 ♕e2

This is the starting move of the notorious **Velimirović Attack**. White intends to castle queenside and by preparing this with ♕e2 rather than ♕d2 (as in the Richter-Rauzer Attack) he simultaneously prevents ...♘g4 and prepares g4.

The most important remnant of the original Sozin plan is the variation **8 ♗b3** 0-0 9 0-0 a6 10 f4, with the position after the further moves 10...♘xd4 11 ♗xd4 b5 12 e5 dxe5 13 fxe5 ♘d7 14 ♘e4 ♗b7 15 ♘d6 ♗xd6 16 exd6 being the crucial starting point for theoretical discussions. White has the bishop-pair and a dangerous passed pawn on d6, but Black's pieces are harmoniously placed (especially if Black continues aggressively with 16...♕g5) and it is completely unclear which side has the better chances.

8 ... 0-0
9 0-0-0 a6
10 ♗b3 *(D)*

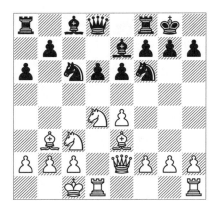

There are countless alternatives for Black on any of his previous moves, but this is the most important and also the most controversial basic position of the Velimirović Attack. White still has the option of playing f4 in combination with either f5 or e5, but – now that his king is safely tucked away on the queenside – the far more ambitious g4-g5 is a dangerous option.

10 ... Wc7

This is Black's main move here. White now has a choice between **11 g4** and **11 Ihg1**.

The immediate **11 g4** commits White to re-capture on d4 with the rook, for after 11...Dxd4, White loses a pawn if he plays 12 Axd4 e5. However, the position of the white rook after 12 Ixd4 is not as bad as it looks. There is, for instance, the prospect of a surprising switch to the kingside: 12...b5 13 g5 Dd7 and now 14 Wh5 with ideas of e5 and Ih4, while 14 f4 is another dangerous option.

Nonetheless, the preparatory move **11 Ihg1** is at least as important. After the further **11...b5** 12 g4 b4 White can spark off some impressive fireworks like 13 Dxc6 Wxc6 14 Dd5! exd5 15 g5! Dxe4 16 Axd5 or 13 g5 bxc3 14 gxf6 Axf6 15 Dxc6 Wxc6 16 Ah6. Even after the more cautious **11...Dd7** 12 g4 Dc5, Black is walking into a minefield. The reply 13 Df5!?, for instance, is already considered commonplace. White 'simply' intends to open the g-file after 13...exf5 14 gxf5 and obtain a beautiful square for his knight on d5. In fact, some hugely complex variations are only about to begin from this point! If Black 'calmly' replies 13...b5, he has to be aware of the spectacular continuation 14

Ad5!? Ab7 15 g5. Any attempt to say something sensible about this could only fail miserably so I shall remain silent, but this variation does give an idea of what it takes to play the Velimirović Attack. In comparison to such dazzling, science-fiction-like play, a line like **11...Dxd4** 12 Axd4 b5 13 g4 Dd7 14 g5 b4 15 Wh5! bxc3 16 Id3, threatening 17 Ih3, almost looks banal.

Summing up: while being tailor-made for the diligent student, preparing his openings to perfection in the quiet of his study, the Velimirović Attack is a pure kamikaze mission for one who goes about it unthinkingly.

Four Knights Variation

4	...	Df6
5	Dc3	e6 *(D)*

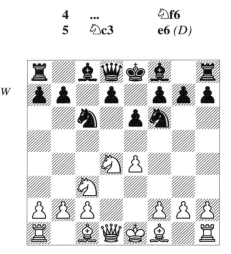

This line, which also arises via 2...e6, is older than the Classical Variation. Black keeps the a3-f8 diagonal open for his king's bishop, but has to accept a hole in his pawn-formation at d6.

A strong point of this plan is that it forces White to take some firm action, for against a routine move like **6 Ae2**, the aggressive 6...Ab4 is unpleasant. In fact, this practically forces White into the rather speculative pawn sacrifice 7 0-0 Axc3 8 bxc3 Dxe4, since attempts to protect e4 (such as 7 f3) run into the powerful 7...d5. Nor is the cautious **6 a3** the ideal solution, since 6...Wc7 and 6...d6 then transpose into relatively harmless sub-lines of the Taimanov and the Scheveningen Variations respectively.

White has to act vigorously. The obvious way of doing so is to try to find a way to take advantage of Black's principal weakness: the d6-square.

The first move that comes to mind is **6 ♘db5** *(D)*.

B

Black then has two options, the first being **6...♗b4**, which in its turn provokes two very different responses from White. In the first place, there is the ultra-sharp 7 ♗f4, with the position after 7...♘xe4 8 ♕f3 (or 8 ♘c7+ ♔f8 9 ♕f3) 8...d5 9 ♘c7+ ♔f8 10 0-0-0 ♗xc3 11 bxc3 as the crucial starting point. Secondly, there is the far more restrained 7 a3, with the position after 7...♗xc3+ 8 ♘xc3 d5! 9 exd5 exd5 10 ♗d3 0-0 11 0-0 d4 as the point of orientation. Black has taken advantage of the exchange on c3 to advance his d-pawn to a dominant position. This line is very old, yet still highly topical, for neither the mysteries of 7 ♗f4 nor the positional problems of 7 a3 have been solved.

But the Four Knights Variation can also be used as a means of entering the Sveshnikov Variation. After **6...d6** 7 ♗f4 e5 8 ♗g5 the same position is reached as after 5...e5 6 ♘db5 d6 7 ♗g5. This move-order is popular with players who prefer to avoid side-variations like 5...e5 6 ♘db5 d6 7 ♘d5 or who do not want to run into a Rossolimo Variation (2...♘c6 3 ♗b5). For this purpose, 2...e6 and the Four Knights Variation is the obvious shortcut.

But no shortcut is ever without its own little problems! Ever since the 1970s, **6 ♘xc6** has been a prominent alternative to 6 ♘db5. The critical position arises after 6...bxc6 7 e5! ♘d5 8 ♘e4 *(D)*.

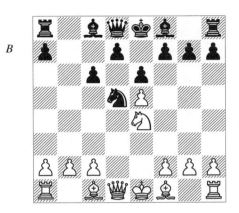

B

If Black does not make an effort here, White will play c4, chasing the knight away from d5 and obtaining a firm grasp on the centre. However, Black has several ways of trying to exploit his small lead in development. His most popular option is the subtle 8...♕c7 9 f4 ♕b6, when 10 c4 allows both 10...♘e3 and 10...♗b4+. This leads to sharp play, as is obvious from the fact that the main line of the latter variation starts with 11 ♔e2 f5.

Sveshnikov Variation

	4	...	♘f6
	5	♘c3	e5 *(D)*

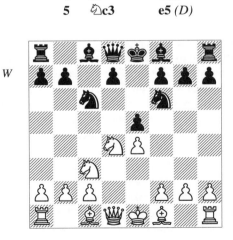

W

We have seen quite a lot of this opening by now, but it is only with this move that we are finally entering the Sicilian of the 21st century.

Long considered a fossil from the early 20th century, it was not until the 1970s that this move really started to attract attention owing to the stubborn attempts of the young Russian Evgeny Sveshnikov to turn it into a playable opening system. Influenced by his incessant analytical and practical efforts (and successes too!), around 1975 all former scepticism was swept aside and the Sveshnikov suddenly became all the rage. Everyone who was young in those days and not inhibited by dogma (or experience) threw themselves headlong into this new opening system that so very wonderfully (and mercilessly) flew in the face of 'old-fashioned' thinking. And that was only the beginning! For in the 1990s a generation appeared for whom the Sveshnikov was not something acquired or foreign. They were steeped in it ever since they were born. Players for whom nothing was more natural then to play the Sicilian in precisely this way began taking over the world of chess. Today, early in the 21st century, the Sveshnikov Variation is one of *the* most influential openings in the elite tournaments. It has become one of the great battlegrounds where world champions and their challengers meet.

This enormous popularity is the result of the sheer inexhaustible resilience of Black's position. Although the Sveshnikov can hardly be called solid, it is most certainly a variation where Black faces no greater dangers and is taking no greater risks than in many other lines of the Sicilian, while his chances of victory are unusually high. Experience of over thirty years now suggests that the harder White hits, the harder Black hits back. And yet White *has* to play sharply, for if he doesn't he has no prospect of obtaining any sort of opening advantage whatsoever. Both **6 ♘b3** and **6 ♘f3**, for instance, allow the aggressive 6...♗b4, while **6 ♘f5** runs into the powerful 6...d5!.

6   ♘db5   d6

The idea of allowing ♘d6+ which we saw in the 4...e5 variation (see page 404), has – in this version – faded into the background. After **6...a6** 7 ♘d6+ ♗xd6 8 ♕xd6 ♕e7 Black's position is simply a little less dynamic than in the

comparable version 4...e5 5 ♘b5 a6 6 ♘d6+ ♗xd6 7 ♕xd6 ♕f6. Only the subtle **6...h6**, to prevent ♗g5, is sporadically played.

7   ♗g5

This aggressive and natural move looks completely self-evident. White develops a minor piece, strengthens his grip on d5 and introduces the threat of ♗xf6, forcing Black to take back with the g-pawn, thus seemingly ruining his pawn-structure even further. But anyone taking a closer look at this variation will soon find out that such an evaluation is completely outdated. In fact the whole underlying point of the Sveshnikov is that doubled f-pawns are not a liability here, quite the contrary: they are a dangerous weapon!

To what extent this judgement is correct is of course the central question of the Sveshnikov. But in view of the complexity of this problem and the fact that the rather optimistic manoeuvre ♗g5xf6 often backfires, it is not surprising that alternatives have also been seriously investigated.

The most important of these is **7 ♘d5**, a move that is in every respect the exact opposite of 7 ♗g5. White uses his control over d5 only to bring about a radical change in the pawn-formation. After 7...♘xd5 8 exd5 he is banking on his queenside pawn-majority to be of more importance than Black's central advantage: 8...♘b8 9 c4 ♗e7 10 ♗d3 a6 11 ♘c3 0-0 12 0-0 f5 is a characteristic continuation.

The alternative **7 a4** is mainly an attempt to exorcise the hidden evil powers of the Sveshnikov. After 7...a6 8 ♘a3, the advance ...b5 is prevented and there is the positionally attractive prospect of playing ♘c4-e3, when White will have a firm grip on d5. The downside of this plan is that there is very little immediate danger for Black, who has plenty of opportunity to develop his pieces actively and comfortably himself, for instance with 8...♗e6 followed by 9...♖c8 and perhaps ...♘d4.

7   ...   a6 *(D)*
8   ♘a3

In the early years of the Sveshnikov (the 1970s), **8 ♗xf6** was often played in order to force Black to recapture with the g-pawn. But today this move has all but disappeared because:

a) After 8 ♘a3 the recapture ...gxf6 will be forced in the majority of cases anyway;

b) It is precisely this exchange that many players are keen to avoid *as White* these days, aiming for 8 ♘a3 b5 9 ♘d5 instead (see page 416); and

c) After 8 ♗xf6 gxf6 9 ♘a3 there is not just 9...b5 (which transposes), but also the immediate 9...f5 and even the amazing 9...d5!?, which – by the way – had been known long before the days of Sveshnikov and which is why the whole variation is still called the Pelikan in conservative circles.

8 ... b5

Without the preceding exchange of pieces on f6, there is far less point to **8...d5**, since after 9 ♘xd5 (if 9 exd5 Black has 9...♗xa3 10 bxa3 ♕a5) 9...♗xa3 10 bxa3 ♕a5+ White now has 11 ♗d2 as well as 11 ♕d2 ♕xd2+ 12 ♔xd2, in both cases taking advantage of his bishop not having been exchanged on f6.

Nor is there much point in playing the obvious but primitive move **8...♗e7?!**, for by playing 9 ♘c4 White easily renews the threat of taking on f6; then recapturing with the bishop will drop a pawn, while taking with the pawn will leave Black with his king's bishop badly placed at e7.

In fact, the only reasonably safe option for those wishing to avoid the enormous complications of 8...b5 is **8...♗e6**. 9 ♘c4 ♖c8 then brings about the same type of position as the already-discussed 7 a4 (with White of course relatively better off, not having played a4). Play is further determined by Black's reaction to 10

♗xf6. It is possible to reply 10...♕xf6 since 11 ♘xd6+ ♗xd6 12 ♕xd6 ♘d4 13 ♗d3 ♕g5 promises adequate compensation for the missing pawn, but on the other hand 11 ♘b6 ♖b8 12 ♘cd5 ♕d8 forces Black into a rather passive position. Recapturing with the pawn (10...gxf6) is more aggressive. 11 ♘e3 can then be met by 11...♗h6.

We now return to 8...b5 *(D)*:

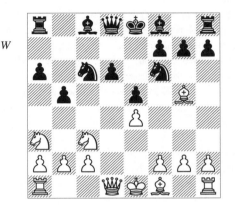

This is the true starting position of the Sveshnikov Variation. It seemed unbelievable at first that Black, having already played ...e5, can really afford to throw in 8...b5 as well, literally forcing White to occupy this splendid square at d5 that Black has gifted to him. Besides, there are a number of seductive options to try to punish ...b5 outright (like a piece sacrifice on b5, or c4 after White has played ♘d5). It is the great merit of Evgeny Sveshnikov to have demonstrated that Black can survive all these onslaughts and even come out on top sometimes! It turned out that Black's aggressive queenside advance is exactly what his position needs. White's king's knight is trapped at a3 and in many positions (especially if White plays c3 at a later stage) ...b4 is an excellent way of starting an attack on the queenside.

There are two main lines. The oldest, sharpest and still the most critical option is **9 ♗xf6**, while the more cautious alternative is **9 ♘d5**.

9 ♗xf6

9 ♗xf6 gxf6

The great transformation in positional thinking that was needed for the Sveshnikov to be understood and accepted was that taking back on f6 with the pawn was not an admission of weakness. Once it was seen that having *two* f-pawns to serve as battering-rams against White's central formation adds enormous power and dynamism to Black's position, the tide was ready to turn. In some variations, Black even makes use of the open g-file as an attacking base against White's king. That his own king's position is rather airy, to say the least, has hardly appeared noticeable in practice.

The more conventional recapture **9...♕xf6?!** only shows up the drawbacks of 8...b5: by playing 10 ♘d5 ♕d8 11 c4 White immediately opens fire against Black's queenside. If 11...b4 White has the powerful blow 12 ♕a4!; e.g., 12...♗d7?! (12...bxa3? 13 ♕xc6+ ♗d7 loses a rook to 14 ♕xa8! ♕xa8 15 ♘c7+) 13 ♘b5!, based on the same tactical point: 13...axb5 14 ♕xa8!.

      10   ♘d5 *(D)*

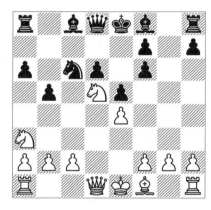

      10   ...   f5

The classical move, if that word is appropriate for a variation as young and unclassical as the Sveshnikov, but since about 1985 **10...♗g7** has shown itself to be a reliable alternative. The advance ...f5 is only postponed, not cancelled, and by developing the bishop first, Black defuses any sacrifices on b5 that White may have had in mind. If 11 ♗xb5? axb5 12 ♘xb5, for instance, Black brings his king into safety by simply castling. Moreover, Black can now play ...♘e7, an important manoeuvre strategically,

but not the best of moves *before* 10...♗g7, because of 10...♘e7?? 11 ♘xf6#!

The critical test of 10...♗g7 probably starts with **11 ♗d3 ♘e7 12 ♘xe7 ♕xe7**. Now 13 c4 allows Black to highlight a characteristic aspect of this line: far from meekly playing 13...bxc4 (making 14 ♘xc4 a wonderful present for White's knight) he strikes back at once with 13...f5!. If 14 cxb5 there is another surprise in store for White: 14...d5!. The critical line is 14 0-0 0-0 and now, for instance, 15 ♕f3 bxc4 16 ♘xc4 d5 17 exd5 e4 18 ♕e3 ♗b7.

The immediate **11 c4** also meets with a sharp reply: 11...f5 12 cxb5 ♘d4 with a highly explosive position.

A plan based on **11 c3** is more cautious. This leads, after 11...f5 12 exf5 ♗xf5, to a position that we shall come across later via 10...f5, when it arises following 11 exf5 ♗xf5 12 c3 ♗g7 or 11 c3 ♗g7 12 exf5 ♗xf5.

We now return to 10...f5 *(D)*:

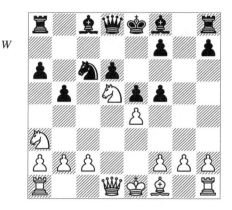

Starting from this position, a wealth of variations has been developed over the past 35 years or so.

First, there was the simple and unceremonious attempt to 'bash him flat' with **11 ♗xb5** axb5 12 ♘xb5. Black cannot reply 12...♕a5+ 13 c3 ♕xb5?? because of 14 ♘c7+, so he must either return material with 12...♖a7 or allow a white knight into the heart of his position at c7. The spectacular 12...♖a4 is generally regarded as the critical test of this idea. So far Black has been able to survive the resulting complications, which are almost unfathomable.

The alternative piece sacrifice, **11 ♘xb5** axb5 12 ♗xb5, has never been anywhere near as popular as 11 ♗xb5. Still, after 12...♗d7 (or 12...♗b7) 13 exf5 White has three pawns for the piece, so the material balance is not really disturbed. White's chances lie not so much in a direct attack against the enemy king, but in a (hoped-for) long-term positional domination.

Those who do not feel tempted by either of these sacrifices will want to concentrate on the strategic problem of how best to resolve the central tension. The simplest way of doing so is **11 exf5**, when Black will reply 11...♗xf5. In the early years of the Sveshnikov, this position was (again) seen mainly as an opportunity for White to refute the whole line with the sharp 12 ♕f3. But unlike 11 ♗xb5, this line disappeared very quickly when it was found that 12...♘d4! 13 ♘c7+ ♕xc7 14 ♕xa8+ ♔e7 15 c3 b4! 16 cxb4 ♕b6 gives Black the most wonderful compensation for the exchange. After that, attention finally turned to a more cautious approach and the solid 12 c3 became important. White intends to regroup his knight with ♘c2-e3/b4. This leads, after 12...♗g7, to a position that also arises via the surprising **11 c3**. This move is actually based on a trap: if 11...fxe4?, then the sacrifice 12 ♗xb5! axb5 13 ♘xb5 is much more convincing than on the previous move. After the more solid 11...♗g7 12 exf5 ♗xf5 (D) we arrive at the critical position:

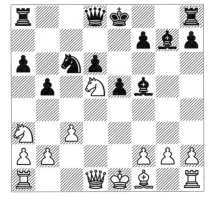

13 ♘c2 0-0 14 ♘ce3 ♗e6 15 ♗d3 f5 is a characteristic continuation. White has prospects of taking the initiative on the queenside with a4,

he has consolidated the position of his d5-knight and all of his remaining pieces are well-placed. Yet he is facing two intimidating pawns at e5 and f5, either of which might move forward at any moment with unforeseeable consequences.

The consequences of White most popular choice, **11 ♗d3**, are even more difficult to evaluate. This move strikes a balance between the savage piece sacrifices on b5 and the simple 11 exf5. While making a sound developing move, White leaves it to the opponent to resolve the tension in the centre. The immediate exchange 11...fxe4 12 ♗xe4 is unattractive, for this gives White an improved version of the 11 exf5 line, but after a few preparatory moves, taking on e4 in combination with ...f5 may well become a positional threat. The critical position arises after 11...♗e6 (D), intensifying the central tension even further.

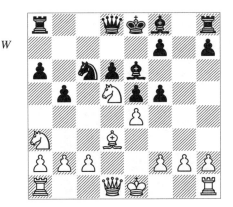

By taking aim at the d5-knight, Black not only prevents 12 exf5, but he also introduces the possibility of taking on d5, causing a change of scene whose consequences are very difficult to assess.

In the early days of the Sveshnikov, when players on the white side were still working on the assumption that they only had to make a few intimidating moves and Black's position would collapse of its own account, **12 ♕h5** ♗g7 13 c3 0-0 was usually played. This offers White the chance to play 14 exf5, for after 14...♗xd5 15 f6, mate is threatened at h7 and Black is forced to return the piece. In fact, the position which then arises after 15...e4 16 fxg7 ♖e8 is still topical today, but Black has been holding his own comfortably for well over thirty years now. Another important type of position arises if play continues 14 0-0 f4. After 15 ♖fd1 ♖b8 16 ♘c2 ♕d7, for instance, it is very difficult (but essential!) to evaluate properly the consequences of moves like ...f5 or ...♗xd5. In later years 12...♖g8 (instead of 12...♗g7) also turned out to be eminently playable, albeit equally hard to judge.

Another plan that has been an important weapon in White's arsenal right from the start, yet without ever causing the Sveshnikov to be refuted, is to attack the queenside with c4. One version of this idea is to play **12 0-0 ♗g7 13 ♕h5 f4 14 c4**. But more recently a whole new face was given to this line by the introduction of a new idea: instead of 12...♗g7, taking on d5 also turns out to be perfectly playable. In fact 12...♗xd5 13 exd5 ♘e7 is now one of *the* most hotly contested subvariations of the Sveshnikov.

9 ♘d5

9   ♘d5 (D)

By playing this move, White is trying to pacify the dark forces that seem to materialize inexplicably from Black's choice of the Sveshnikov Variation. White wants to keep the position simple and controllable, reducing the prospect of immense complications to a small, but tangible positional advantage. But the Sveshnikov would not have become the super-variation it is today if this plan worked. It is true that play usually

calms down a little, but providing Black is acquainted with a few basic strategic concepts, he has little to worry about.

9   ...   ♗e7 (D)

9...♕a5+ is a remarkable way of inviting the opponent to repeat moves: 10 ♗d2 ♕d8 11 ♗g5 ♕a5+. This invitation is in fact fairly often accepted, though probably more from subjective than objective reasons. If White wants more than a short draw, he has a choice between the sharp 11 c4 and the quiet 11 ♘xf6+ ♕xf6 12 ♗d3.

10   ♗xf6

10 ♘xe7 is also not without venom. It looks illogical to exchange the wonderful knight on d5 for Black's passive bishop, but the point is to retain the bishop which is well-placed on g5. 10...♘xe7 is the most popular reply, indirectly attacking the e4-pawn. If 11 ♗d3, Black renews the threat with 11...♗b7, while after 11 ♗xf6 gxf6 we again have the explosive pawn-formation of the 9 ♗xf6 line. The sharp 12 c4 ♗b7 13 cxb5 ♗xe4 is a characteristic follow-up.

10   ...   ♗xf6

It would be a mistake to recapture with the pawn (compare 8...♗e7). As we have had every opportunity to see, in this type of position Black's king's bishop belongs at g7.

11   c3 (D)

This is the basic position of the 9 ♘d5 variation. White intends to manoeuvre his a3-knight to e3 or b4 (♘c2-e3/b4) and is likely to play a4 at some point, taking the initiative on

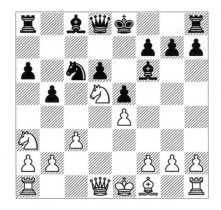

the queenside. A characteristic continuation is **11...0-0** 12 ♘c2 ♗g5 (this is a drawback of the ♗xf6 plan: Black's otherwise rather passive bishop finds the open c1-h6 diagonal) 13 a4. If Black were now to react somewhat sheepishly with 13...♖b8 14 axb5 axb5, he would simply be handing White another beautiful square for his knights at b4 *and* he will be tied down to the defence of b5. It is far better to play 13...bxa4 14 ♖xa4 a5. White still has a beautiful knight on d5 but Black has prospects of counterplay, both on the queenside (with ...♖b8) and on the kingside (with ...f5, possibly prefaced by ...g6).

Accelerated Dragon

<blockquote>

4 ... g6 *(D)*

</blockquote>

The name Accelerated Dragon sounds odd, but becomes understandable when viewed in its historical context. As I described in the introduction to the Classical Variation (see page 405), a century or so ago 4...♘f6 5 ♘c3 d6 6 ♗e2 g6 was the standard way of playing a ...g6 set-up. When everybody started to play 6 ♗g5 or 6 ♗c4 in order to make 6...g6 unattractive, many ...g6 devotees began looking for alternative ways of bringing about their favourite type of position. Since 4...♘f6 5 ♘c3 g6 is not really an option (see page 403), it is only logical to go back another move and play 4...g6 *and* to call this the Accelerated Dragon. It was not until much later that the move-order 2...d6 3 d4 cxd4 4 ♘xd4 ♘f6 5 ♘c3 g6 became popular. This even became *the* most popular way of fianchettoing the king's bishop. It also claimed the

name Dragon Variation, which used to be applied to any ...g6 set-up.

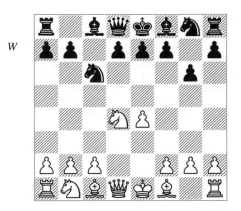

But the Accelerated Dragon is by no means an obsolete variation. After **5 ♘c3** Black may either 'return' to the Dragon Variation proper or play an independent variation. It is mainly **5 c4** that has been considered the critical test of 4...g6 ever since its introduction. White strengthens his grip on the centre and steers the game in a totally different direction. In fact this line, which has been named after Geza Maroczy (1870-1951), is much closer strategically to the English Opening than to most lines of the Sicilian Defence.

5 ♘c3

<blockquote>

5 ♘c3 ♗g7
6 ♗e3 ♘f6

</blockquote>

Black is not afraid of the aggressive **7 ♘xc6** bxc6 8 e5. He can either sacrifice a pawn for the initiative (and open files) with 8...♘d5 9 ♘xd5 cxd5 10 ♕xd5 ♖b8 or he can start an attack against e5 with 8...♘g8 9 f4 f6.

<blockquote>

7 ♗c4 *(D)*

</blockquote>

What makes this variation attractive to many players is the multitude of treacherous tactical explosives which lie hidden in this position. White has to be very careful indeed if he is to avoid stepping on these little mines, especially if he is bent on transposing to a main-line Dragon. Unfortunately there is no easy way of circumventing them (that is to say: not from the stern and lofty point of view of opening theory), since **7 ♗e2** 0-0 8 0-0 d6 leads only to a fairly innocuous subvariation of the Dragon (see page 445). Besides, Black has the aggressive (and highly characteristic) alternative idea 8...d5!?.

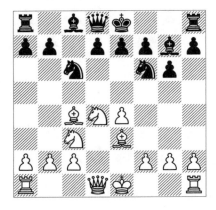

In this position there are two moves which leave White guessing whether Black is intending to transpose to a regular Dragon, and one move which immediately gives the variation a character of its own.

By playing **7...d6**, Black introduces the threat of 8...♘g4. Now, if White is keen on playing a main-line Dragon, 8 f3 is indicated (the alternative is to play 8 h3, but this transposes to a less critical line of the Dragon after 8...0-0; see page 445). If then 8...0-0 we do indeed have a Yugoslav Attack, but Black also has the double-edged option of 8...♕b6!?. This was a hotly-contested variation in the 1960s. Black is not only threatening 9...♕xb2, but 9...♘xe4 and 9...♘g4 as well. One of the critical lines is 9 ♘f5 ♕xb2 10 ♘xg7+ ♔f8 11 ♘d5 ♘xd5 12 ♗xd5 ♔xg7. Black has won a pawn but White has taken over the initiative.

Later **7...0-0** became the most common move. Again White has to be careful: 8 f3 ♕b6 is even more tricky now than in case of 7...d6 8 f3, and 8 ♕d2 is simply bad because of 8...♘g4. So if White wants to retain the possibility of a main-line Dragon he has to play 8 ♗b3. This works after **8...d6** 9 f3, but there are a few sharp alternatives to 8...d6, based on the knight jump ...♘g4 and the bold central advance ...d5. The most popular version is to start with **8...a5**, intending to meet **9 0-0** with 9...a4 10 ♘xa4

♘xe4 (although it is actually not at all clear who profits from this exchange). If White radically prevents the advance of the a-pawn with **9 a4**, then 9...♘g4 10 ♕xg4 ♘xd4 is much more powerful than on the previous move because a future ...♘xb3 will now have to be met by cxb3, weakening White's queenside pawn-structure. But the most surprising aspect of 8...a5 becomes visible if White plays the subtle **9 f3**, for in that case Black finally lashes out with 9...d5, radically opening the position. 10 exd5 is countered with 10...♘b4 11 ♘de2 a4 12 ♘xa4 ♘fxd5 and 10 ♗xd5 ♘xd5 11 exd5 with 11...♘b4 12 ♘de2 ♗f5 13 ♖c1 b5. In both cases Black obtains the initiative although it is really hard to make out whether this is sufficient compensation for the sacrificed pawn. Another tricky feature of Black's idea is highlighted after 10 ♗xd5 ♘xd5 11 ♘xd5 (and not the other way round: after 10 ♘xd5 ♘xd5 11 ♗xd5?? ♘xd4 12 ♗xd4 ♗xd4 13 ♕xd4 e6 White loses a piece) 11...f5, undermining White's centre from the other flank.

Finally there is **7...♕a5** *(D)*.

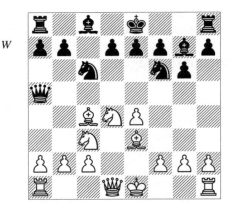

This move forces White to castle kingside, for both 8...♘xe4 and 8...♘g4 are nasty threats (for example: 8 f3 ♕b4 9 ♗b3 ♘xe4!). The only difference from what I have described above as "a less critical line of the Dragon" (7...d6 8 h3) is that Black has already committed himself to a ...♕a5 set-up (which – to complicate things even further – is actually not bad and even the preferred choice of quite a few players in the 7...d6 8 h3 variation!). The critical lines start with 8 0-0 0-0 and then either 9 ♘b3 ♕c7 10 f4 d6 11 ♗e2 or 9 ♗b3 d6 10 h3 ♗d7 11 f4.

Maroczy Bind

5 c4 (D)

For most players who are considering playing the Accelerated Dragon, this move will be the touchstone. A very specific (and rather un-Sicilian-like) type of position arises which not every player will feel comfortable with. Black's pawn-chain is strong and solid, but he has relatively little space for his pieces. He will have to attack White's central formation so as not to drift into a passive position. This requires not only a good strategic understanding of the situation but also a keen eye for every incidental tactical opportunity that might happen to come his way.

For White, the situation is very much the same. If he wants to be successful with a Maroczy Bind, patience and positional understanding are of the greatest importance, but he must also keep his eyes open for every even remotely possible attempt by his opponent to break the siege.

5 ... ♗g7

This natural move seems self-evident at first sight, yet there is a major alternative showing how predominant positional considerations are in this line. As a rule, the side that has less space (and consequently less manoeuvring room for his pieces) is well advised to exchange pieces

but this does not automatically make *every* exchange of pieces a good thing. In this position, for instance, playing **5...♘xd4** 6 ♕xd4 would be quite silly. The h8-rook is attacked and 6...♘f6 is strongly met with 7 e5. What *is* good though, is to play **5...♘f6** first and to take on d4 only after White has replied 6 ♘c3. After **6...♘xd4** 7 ♕xd4 d6 all doors are bolted and Black has the pleasant prospect of playing 8...♗g7 and 9...0-0, possibly followed by a juicy knight move attacking White's queen on d4.

Even more subtle (and more popular too) is to play **6...d6** instead of 6...♘xd4. This move-order makes it impossible for White to choose the aggressive set-up of 6...♘xd4 7 ♕xd4 d6 8 ♗g5 ♗g7 9 ♕d2 followed by ♗d3 (for after 6...d6 7 ♗g5 Black switches to 7...♗g7 – instead of taking on d4 – when White's d4-knight, left without the 'natural' support of his e3-bishop, comes under heavy pressure). An important starting point of this line arises after 6...d6 7 ♗e2 ♘xd4 8 ♕xd4 ♗g7. If 9 ♗e3, for instance, Black's standard development is 9...0-0 10 ♕d2 ♗e6 11 ♖c1 ♕a5 12 f3 ♖fc8 13 b3 a6, which is both efficient and aggressive. If 14 0-0 the advance 14...b5 will be possible. White's best chance according to theory is now to initiate exchanges himself with either 14 ♘d5 or (more subtly) 14 ♘a4. After 14 ♘a4 ♕xd2+ 15 ♔xd2 ♘d7 Black retains possibilities of active play though, either with ...b5 or with ...f5.

6 ♗e3

White can avoid the exchange on d4 by retreating the knight: **6 ♘c2** or **6 ♘b3**. Apart from the loss of tempo, this also leaves White slightly more vulnerable on the a1-h8 diagonal, yet in principle this is a sound idea, especially if White chooses 6 ♘c2. He is in fact playing the Rubinstein Variation of the Symmetrical English (see page 203) with colours reversed.

6 ... ♘f6

7 ♘c3 (D)

Again, the central (positional) issue is finding the right way of exchanging pieces. At first the surprising knight sortie **7...♘g4** was thought to be Black's best option. The critical position arises after 8 ♕xg4 ♘xd4 9 ♕d1. Black can consolidate his knight on d4 at the cost of his pawn-structure by playing 9...e5, but he also

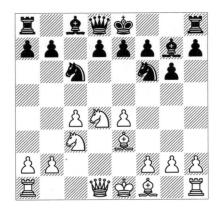

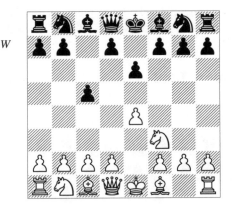

has the much more solid 9...♘e6 (or 9...♘c6). After 9...♘e6 10 ♖c1, Black can play 10...b6 11 ♗d3 ♗b7 12 0-0 0-0, for instance, when the advance ...f5 becomes crucial. Another characteristic plan is to play 10...♕a5 11 ♕d2 b6 12 ♗d3 ♗b7 13 0-0 g5, trying to gain control over the dark squares.

Starting in the 1980s, the simple developing move **7...0-0** became a popular alternative. This approach had long been considered too passive but on closer inspection this turns out not to be a problem at all. After 8 ♗e2 d6 9 0-0 Black has 9...♘xd4 10 ♗xd4 ♗d7 (or 9...♗d7 immediately) with the idea of putting the bishop on c6, where it keeps e4 under pressure. This is often followed up with ...♘d7-c5, for instance 11 ♕d2 ♗c6 12 f3 ♘d7. Black does not have to fear the exchange of his king's bishop in this position since 13 ♗xg7 ♔xg7 leaves White rather vulnerable on the light squares.

2 ♘f3 e6

2   ...   e6 (D)

In the 19th century, when the Sicilian Defence was only beginning to be taken seriously, this was the normal reply to 2 ♘f3. With the rise of 2...♘c6 and what was later to become the Classical Variation, 2...e6 faded into the background, but it is only natural that this did not last very long, since 2...e6 is a healthy move which fits perfectly into the 'modern' Sicilian as well.

3   d4

One of the advantages of 2...e6 is that there are no obvious alternatives to playing 3 d4 cxd4

4 ♘xd4. On the other hand, some of the 'standard options' are slightly more attractive – or perhaps we should say the timing is slightly better for them – now that Black has limited his range of possible replies, having already committed himself to a set-up with ...e6.

For instance, playing **3 d3** *(D)* here is the most popular way to reach the **King's Indian Attack** against the Sicilian Defence.

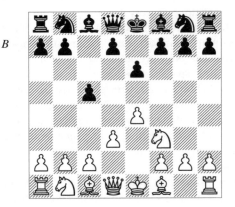

After **3...d5** 4 ♘bd2 a position arises that we have seen in the French Defence (see page 348). A more 'Sicilian' reply would be to play **3...♘c6** 4 g3 g6 5 ♗g2 ♗g7 6 0-0 ♘ge7. Theory regards 7 c3 0-0 8 d4 as the most critical test of this set-up. This is the same switch to Plan B that we have seen in the paragraph on 2 d3 at the start of this chapter (see page 390).

Similarly, Black now has fewer options against **3 c3** than he has against 2 c3. But there are some problems with this. If Black replies

3...♘f6, his choice of responses to 4 e5 ♘d5 5 d4 cxd4 6 cxd4 is indeed limited compared to 2 c3 ♘f6 (see page 398) and the same can be said about 3...d5 4 exd5 ♕xd5 5 d4 as compared to 2 c3 d5. But if Black chooses 4...exd5 instead of 4...♕xd5 in the latter variation, he is no worse off than after 2 c3 e6 3 d4 d5 4 exd5 exd5. And the most complicated problem arises if White tries to improve on this line by playing 4 e5 (instead of 4 exd5), hoping for a transposition to the Advance Variation of the French (4...♘c6 5 d4), for Black has an ambitious alternative frustrating this plan: 4...d4.

The position arising after **3 ♘c3** has been discussed in the coverage of 2 ♘c3 e6 3 ♘f3 (page 392).

If **3 c4** is met by the natural 3...♘c6 4 ♘c3 ♘f6, we arrive at a position that we have seen in the chapter on the Symmetrical English, where it arises via 1 c4 c5 2 ♘f3 ♘c6 3 ♘c3 ♘f6 4 e4 e6 (see page 208). Oddly enough, the straightforward follow-up 5 d4 cxd4 6 ♘xd4 takes us back into Sicilian territory, albeit an innocuous subvariation of the Taimanov (see page 422).

In fact, the only way to turn 2...e6 into a truly independent variation (without playing 3 d4 and within the limits of what opening theory finds acceptable) is to play **3 b3**. White tries to take advantage of 2...e6 in so far as the most logical reply to a b3 idea, a set-up with ...e5 to close the diagonal of the bishop that is about to appear at b2, is (more or less) ruled out now. But this variation is still in an experimental phase and theory has little to say on it.

3   ...   cxd4
4   ♘xd4 (D)

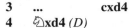

This position offers a very different range of options from the analogous situation after 2...♘c6, but there are some points of contact.

For instance, **4...♘c6** introduces the **Taimanov Variation**, which can also arise after 2...♘c6. On the other hand, **4...a6**, the **Paulsen** (or **Kan**) **Variation**, although very closely related to the Taimanov, is exclusive to 2...e6.

Another transposition to a 2...♘c6 line is offered by **4...♘f6**, when after 5 ♘c3 the Four Knights Variation (which I have included in the 2...♘c6 section) is only one move away: **5...♘c6**.

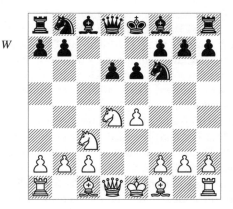

But one of the most important of all variations based on ...e6, perhaps even *the* most important and perhaps even the backbone of the entire Sicilian Defence, is the **Scheveningen Variation**, that arises after **5...d6** (D).

Not only is this a fundamental position (also accessible via 2...d6) in itself, but the whole Sicilian is literally steeped in shortcuts, secret paths and straightforward transpositions to one of the innumerable subvariations of this opening system. It is only a very slight exaggeration to say that whoever does not know the Scheveningen does not know the Sicilian Defence.

The Taimanov, the Paulsen and the Scheveningen are the great main lines in this position. There are also a few smaller variations, among which one is especially notable because it lies on the very edge of what is possible, both positionally and tactically: **4...♘f6 5 ♘c3 ♗b4** (D), the **Pin Variation**.

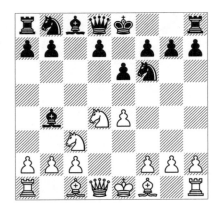

Black is aiming for the complicated position after 6 e5 ♘d5 7 ♗d2 ♘xc3 8 bxc3 ♗e7. White's queenside pawn-structure has been heavily damaged and Black can look to the future with confidence – if he makes it to the future! For in the meantime White has a lead in development, a space advantage and the initiative. 9 ♕g4 is critical and in particular the exchange sacrifice 9...0-0 10 ♗h6 g6. This is very much a variation 'for devotees only', but it can be most rewarding to give it a try, for most players on the white side are unlikely to be armed to the teeth for it.

4...♕b6 is one of the youngest variations in the Sicilian and practically unknown before 1990. The idea is to meet 5 ♘c3 with 5...♗c5, attacking the knight. 5 ♘b3 is rather more solid and is likely to transpose – after 5...♘c6 6 ♘c3 ♘f6 – to a position we know from the variation 2...♘c6 3 d4 cxd4 4 ♘xd4 ♕b6. There is plenty of room for new developments here.

A perhaps more plausible version of the same idea is to play **4...♗c5**, in order to meet 5 ♘c3 with 5...♕b6. *This* line is very old, but has been rediscovered by opening theory only very recently. The basic idea is known from the line of the Paulsen where Black plays 4...a6 5 ♗d3 ♗c5 (see page 426). If 5 ♘b3, Black replies 5...♗b6. After something like 6 ♘c3 ♘e7 there are prospects of opening a frontal attack against White's centre with either ...d5 or ...f5.

Taimanov Variation

4   ...   ♘c6 *(D)*

This subtle variation came into fashion during the 1960s and has remained very popular ever since. It is a great favourite with positionally-oriented players who see it as a means of escaping the ultra-sharp and deeply-analysed complexes of variations of the Najdorf and the Sveshnikov (for instance), without being shallow or boring (if it were possible to find such a line in the Sicilian!).

The christening of this line is rather vague. The Taimanov evolved from the much older Paulsen Variation and is often confused with it. Remarkably, Mark Taimanov himself, the Russian grandmaster who was the most responsible for the upsurge of this variation, spoke of 'my variation' only in those cases where Black develops his king's knight via e7!

5   ♘c3

The fundamental thesis of the Taimanov Variation (and of the Paulsen) is that Black considers it unnecessary to provoke 5 ♘c3 by playing 4...♘f6, because he is not afraid of the most plausible alternative to 5 ♘c3, a set-up with c4 (as we have seen in the Accelerated Dragon). Whether this is correct is still an open question. It is true that the straightforward **5 c4** is fairly harmless for this allows Black to retaliate immediately with 5...♘f6 6 ♘c3 (6 ♘xc6 bxc6 7 e5?? fails to 7...♕a5+) 6...♗b4. But White also has the preparatory move **5 ♘b5**, analogous to the Four Knights Variation, with the idea of playing 6 c4 only after Black has played 5...d6, closing the diagonal for his king's bishop. Evaluating this type of position, which we have come to know in the chapters on the English

Opening as the Hedgehog System, is difficult and in any case very much a matter of taste. There are some players who will *never* play the Taimanov because of this line and there are others who feel perfectly at home in it. In any case, White has made a concession to reach this type of position for he has had to play ♘b5 and he will have to 'lose' another move to get his knight into safety again (which is why hardly anyone ever plays 4...d6, giving White 5 c4 'for free'). The most important starting position of this line arises after 5...d6 **6 c4 ♘f6 7 ♘1c3 a6 8 ♘a3 ♗e7 9 ♗e2 0-0 10 0-0 b6 11 ♗e3 ♗b7** (D).

White has a spatial advantage, but Black's position is not only very solid, but also offers prospects of eventually lashing out with ...b5 or ...d5. It might be useful to study this variation in connection with the Hedgehog System of the Symmetrical English (see page 216).

White has an alternative in **6 ♗f4** (instead of 6 c4), a move we know from the Four Knights and the Sveshnikov Variations. The difference is that now after 6...e5 White cannot play 7 ♗g5 and has to drop the bishop back to e3 first (7 ♗e3) before 7...♘f6 8 ♗g5 becomes possible. Now that White has had to invest an extra tempo (♗e3-g5 instead of ♗g5 directly), this idea loses some of its bite.

> **5 ... ♕c7**

Here we get a first indication of the finesse and elasticity which characterize this variation. The a3-f8 diagonal is open, which means that Black *could* play **5...♗b4** or **5...♗c5**. But since neither of these aggressive moves would have

much of an impact at this stage, Black keeps them in reserve. Instead he chooses a piece deployment which leaves the opponent guessing where Black's king's bishop is going to reside (it might even go to d6 in some cases!), while all the time a 'simple' ...d6 remains a possibility. In fact, this is one of those cases where the Scheveningen Variation is sort of secretly present in the background of another variation. At any moment it might become visible, but even when it does not, it is still leaving its mark on the actual course of the opening. The ideal Taimanov player is someone who knows exactly which of the many Scheveningen subvariations he wants to play *and* who is a master of all weapons of the Taimanov.

Nevertheless, the immediate **5...d6** is a perfectly viable alternative. This is regarded as a reliable way of avoiding the dangerous Keres Attack (4...♘f6 5 ♘c3 d6 6 g4), but ever since White started to play 6 g4 even without a knight on f6, this shortcut has no longer been such a safe option.

By playing 5...♕c7, Black prepares 6...♘f6 (the immediate **5...♘f6** transposes to the Four Knights Variation). An alternative is to play **5...a6**, introducing the possibility of a quick ...b5 *and* preparing the delicate manoeuvre ...♘ge7 followed by ...♘xd4 and ...♘c6 (the immediate 5...♘ge7?! would run into 6 ♘db5). A characteristic variation is **6 ♗e2 ♘ge7 7 ♗e3 ♘xd4 8 ♕xd4 b5 9 0-0 ♘c6 10 ♕d2 ♗e7** (D).

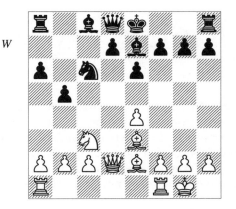

By eliminating White's d4-knight, Black has considerably reduced the pressure on his position, but having omitted the 'usual' attack against e4, he has also left White free to develop as he pleases. Black has a clear plan of action on the queenside with moves like ...♗b7, ...♖c8, ...♕c7 and ...♘a5-c4. White may want to make use of the weak point in Black's pawn-chain at d6, for instance by playing ♗f4-d6.

Illustrative of the relatively great room for original manoeuvring Black has in this line is the variation **7 0-0** (instead of 7 ♗e3) 7...♘xd4 8 ♕xd4 ♘c6 9 ♕d3 ♕c7 10 ♗g5 ♗d6!?, not only attacking h2 but with the unusual idea of centralizing the bishop by ...♗e5.

White has a straightforward attempt to show up a possible downside of 5...a6 in the simple **6 ♘xc6** bxc6 (6...dxc6 is unattractive because of 7 ♕xd8+ ♔xd8 8 ♗f4) 7 ♗d3. There are fanatic devotees of this plan who take on c6 a move earlier, yet this has never had the sanction of opening theory. But with Black having already played ...a6 – in this context a fairly useless move – ♘xc6 suddenly becomes more attractive.

We now return to 5...♕c7 *(D)*:

f4?? because of 8...♘xd4 9 ♕xd4 ♗c5. The logical preparation for this move is to play 8 ♗e3. Black then has 8...♗e7 9 f4 d6, transposing to the Scheveningen Variation, or he can play the much sharper 8...♗b4. The consequences of the latter move (inviting White, for instance, to play 9 ♘a4 with the idea of continuing 10 ♘xc6 and 11 ♘b6) have been the subject of thorough analysis for almost half a century by now.

Another option is to give the e-pawn some extra support. The oldest method of doing so is **6 g3** a6 7 ♗g2. This has the added advantage of making a direct transposition to the Scheveningen Variation not quite the perfect solution for Black, since, unlike against 6 ♗e2, a set-up with ...a6 and ...♕c7 is not considered one of Black's very best options against g3 in the Scheveningen (nor is it one of the very worst, to be honest). The critical response is the typical Taimanov idea of playing 7...♘f6 8 0-0 ♘xd4 9 ♕xd4 ♗c5. Black then continues ...d6, perhaps followed by ...e5. White has a slight lead in development, but Black's position is basically sound.

Another way to protect e4 is **6 ♗e3** a6 7 ♗d3 *(D)*.

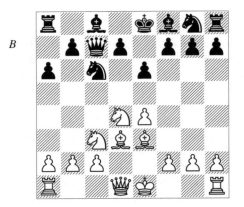

After 5...♕c7, taking on c6 (**6 ♘xc6**) is again relatively harmless because (unlike ...a6) ...♕c7 is a useful move in this type of position. Nor is **6 ♘db5** ♕b8 a major worry, though the sharp 7 ♗e3 a6 8 ♗b6 requires an accurate response. Therefore, White normally just develops his pieces.

The classical method is to play **6 ♗e2**, leading after 6...a6 7 0-0 ♘f6 to a classical starting position. White cannot play the aggressive 8

This position is of equal importance to the Taimanov *and* to the Paulsen Variation, where it arises via 4...a6 5 ♘c3 ♕c7 6 ♗d3 ♘c6 7 ♗e3. After 7...♘f6 8 0-0 Black has tried all the typical Taimanov weapons, such as 8...♗d6, 8...♘xd4 9 ♗xd4 ♗c5 and even 8...h5 (threatening 9...♘g4), but his most popular option is 8...♘e5 9 h3 ♗c5. This is often followed by

...b5 and ...♗b7. Black is developing his queenside before his kingside in order to take the initiative on that wing as soon as possible.

But the 21st century has brought changes to this respectable variation. Following the success of the English Attack against the Najdorf Variation, the idea of playing 6 ♗e3 a6 7 ♕d2 has also penetrated the Taimanov. White intends to castle queenside and wipe Black out on the kingside with a pawn-storm: f3 and g4, 'etc.'. This raw and aggressive approach has shown itself to be a severe test for the delicate touch of many a Taimanov specialist. 7...♘f6 8 0-0-0 ♗b4 seems a plausible reaction (threatening 9...♘xe4), but how to proceed after 9 f3 is far less obvious. Black has tried 9...♘e5, 9...♘a5 and 9...♘e7, all with the idea of making the prospect of ...♗xc3 more intimidating, sometimes in combination with ...d5. Theory of this line gets rewritten almost every day.

Paulsen Variation

4 ... a6 *(D)*

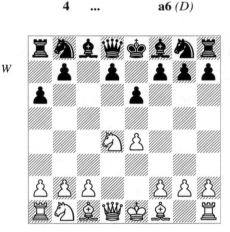

The Paulsen (or Kan) Variation was the main line of the Sicilian Defence in the 19th century, which makes it the oldest 'living' interpretation of this opening. It is the invention of Louis Paulsen (1833-91), who has been called the architect of the Sicilian Defence. Naturally, opening theory has come a long way since those days, but the Paulsen Variation has remained highly topical. Black does not yet commit himself to a square for his knights nor for his king's

bishop. In many cases he will first play ...♕c7 and ...b5 followed by ...♗b7. This flexibility appeals to the players who like to play the opening not overtly aggressively, but ready to pounce on his opponent if given the chance. One might call the Paulsen Variation the forerunner of the Hedgehog System that has been briefly mentioned in this chapter as part of the Taimanov Variation and is especially relevant to the Symmetrical English.

Since Black is playing in such reserved fashion, White can play just about anything he likes. But in this jungle of possibilities, a few main lines are clearly discernible nevertheless: **5 ♘c3** and **5 ♗d3**.

The principled **5 c4** is also of importance but, although better than against the Taimanov, this advance is still not considered all that dangerous for Black. After 5...♘f6 6 ♘c3 the straightforward 6...♗b4 7 ♗d3 ♘c6 used to be thought critical, although many players prefer 6...♕c7 these days. The latter move prevents 7 e5 and (again) leaves White guessing as to his opponent's intentions. Depending on White's reply, Black will either play ...♗b4 (against 7 ♗e2 for instance), or ...♗c5 (against 7 ♗d3), but in some cases he may delay such bishop moves even further and first develop his queenside with ...b6 and ...♗b7 (for instance if White plays 7 a3).

5 ♘c3

5 ♘c3 *(D)*

With this healthy and uncomplicated developing move, a position is reached that arises also via 2 ♘c3 e6 3 ♘f3 a6 4 d4 cxd4 5 ♘xd4 (see page 392) or via 2 ♘f3 e6 3 ♘c3, etc.

Black has at his disposal **5...♘c6** to transpose to the Taimanov Variation or **5...d6** to transpose to the Scheveningen, but the real Paulsen moves are the ultra-flexible **5...♕c7** and the immediate queenside advance **5...b5**.

By playing **5...♕c7** Black controls e5 and silently increases the pressure along the c-file. A transposition to either the Taimanov (with ...♘c6) or the Scheveningen Variation (with ...d6) remains possible, but there are many independent lines. If 6 ♗e2, for instance, the

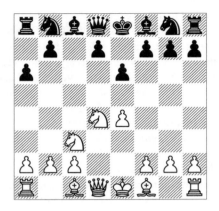

advance 6...b5 7 0-0 ♗b7 is slightly more incisive than on the previous move (5...b5) since with the bishop on e2, White's e-pawn is somewhat more vulnerable. If 6 g3 it is mainly 6...♗b4 that should concern White. If 6 ♗d3, a transposition to the Taimanov with 6...♘c6 7 ♗e3 (see page 424) is Black's most popular choice. Black does not have to worry about 7 ♘xc6 dxc6 in this case (compare 5 ♗d3 ♘c6 6 ♘xc6 dxc6 below) since the white knight is not optimally placed at c3 for this pawn-formation.

5...b5 is the most straightforward version of a plan that is available to Black in almost any position of the Paulsen or the Taimanov Variation. Black prepares to attack White's e4-pawn with ...♗b7 and ...b4. Protecting e4 with 6 ♗d3 is White's most plausible reply. A critical position arises if Black then continues 6...♕b6 7 ♗e3 ♗c5. Around 2000 it was discovered that this may lead to the most amazing complications if White plays the unbelievable 8 ♕g4!? ♗xd4 9 e5!. The point is 9...♗xe3 10 ♕xg7 ♗xf2+ 11 ♔f1, when, despite being two pieces up, Black's position is in grave danger of collapse.

5 ♗d3

5 ♗d3 (D)

In contrast to 5 ♘c3, which fixes the position of the knight (and the c-pawn!) while keeping all options for the king's bishop open, this move immediately fixes the position of the bishop and keeps several other options, most notably

that of playing c4, open. This implies that Black no longer has any 'easy' transpositions to the Taimanov or the Scheveningen. 5 ♗d3 detaches the Paulsen Variation from the complicated web of ...e6 systems and is therefore the only real attempt to show up its downside.

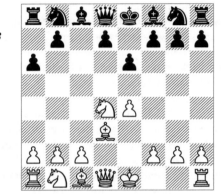

Oddly enough, however, this has inspired players on the black side to come up with a veritable arsenal of weapons to try to show up the drawbacks of 5 ♗d3. At first these were aimed at the now unprotected position of White's knight on d4. The simplest ways of doing so are **5...♘c6** and **5...♗c5**.

The critical test of **5...♘c6** is to take on c6: 6 ♘xc6. White is optimally placed to counter 6...bxc6 because after 7 0-0 d5 he can attack Black's centre with 8 c4. On the other hand, the situation is relatively favourable for Black to play 6...dxc6, because (unlike in the Taimanov Variation with 5 ♘c3 a6 6 ♘xc6) there is no queen exchange on d8 to destabilize the position of his king. Black is likely to play ...e5, when the symmetrical pawn-formation and the absence of immediate tactical problems demand a subtle positional understanding from both players.

5...♗c5 used to be played in combination with 6 ♘b3 ♗a7, when White's standard plan is to exchange Black's king's bishop. Theoretical discussions concentrated on variations like 7 ♕e2 ♘c6 8 ♗e3 ♗xe3 9 ♕xe3 d6 and on the question of whether White should castle queenside or kingside here. Nowadays 6...♗e7 is often played. Black is satisfied with having driven back the knight and leaves it up to his opponent to play a kind of Hedgehog (with c4) or an indefinable sort of Scheveningen Variation, for instance with 7 ♘c3 d6. This idea is comparable to the variations where Black plays ...♕b6 to chase White's knight back to b3 and then drops the queen back to c7, such as 2...♘c6 3 d4 cxd4 4 ♘xd4 ♕b6 (see page 404).

Then there are the more subtle ways of making use of White's unprotected knight on d4: **5...♘e7** and **5...g6**.

The idea of **5...♘e7** looks fairly straightforward, namely to play ...♘bc6 and be able to take back on c6 with the other knight. But it is in fact an extremely flexible move, for depending on White's reply, it may be (even) more useful to play ...♘ec6 and develop the other knight at d7.

5...g6 is the favourite of players with a strongly developed aesthetic sense (all pawns on a light square, the geometrical pattern), but it is also a powerful move. Black is planning to attack the d4-knight with 6...♗g7 and to prepare an all-out central attack with ...♘ge7 and ...d5. This would be quite unrealistic in most Sicilian Variations, but it makes good sense in this line because of the decrease of pressure along the d-file that is the result of White having played ♗d3.

But the most modern option is not to worry about attacking the d4-knight at all and to play – typically Paulsen – the very flexible **5...♘f6** 6 0-0 (6 e5? ♕a5+) 6...♕c7. This set-up has become especially popular with players who feel comfortable in a Hedgehog position (if c4 and ...d6 are played), but who want to keep the a3-f8 diagonal open just a little longer so that White still has to take moves like ...♘c6 and ...♗c5 into account. The immediate 7 c4, for instance, is met by 7...♘c6 8 ♘xc6 dxc6 followed by ...e5 and ...♗c5, emphasizing the hole in White's pawn-formation at d4. It is more cautious to play 7 ♕e2 first and only after 7...d6 to venture 8 c4.

Scheveningen Variation

4	...	♘f6
5	♘c3	d6 *(D)*

In the general introduction to the position after 4 ♘xd4 I have already attempted to make the reader aware of the enormous importance of the Scheveningen Variation. And by that I do not mean this particular position – although this certainly *is* an important starting point – but the pawn-formation ...e6 in combination with ...d6 in general, without White having played c4 and excluding a number of 'special cases' which cannot normally arise from this position. These we find mainly in the Richter-Rauzer and the Najdorf Variation.

The formation ...e6 and ...d6 evolved around 1900 from the older Paulsen Variation where Black – as we have just seen – starts by keeping the a3-f8 diagonal open for his bishop but often ends up playing ...d6 anyway. It looks passive to 'lock up' your own bishops behind pawns at e6 and d6, and indeed this is precisely how this formation was seen in the 19th century, but with the rise of classical positional chess, this perspective changed. It began to be appreciated that Black's position is very solid and that even without a bishop on b4 or c5, Black has plenty of opportunities to become aggressive on the queenside. More in particular, the plan of playing ...a6, ...♕c7 and ...♘c6-a5/e5-c4 at one point became so intimidating that the whole variation even began to be thought of as favourable for Black!

In the introduction to the Classical Variation (see page 405) I have already described how this process culminated (*and* came to a full stop!) in the tournament of Scheveningen in 1923, when Geza Maroczy so brilliantly defeated Max Euwe. The Scheveningen Variation deteriorated, the Dragon Variation rose to the fore and shortly afterwards the entire Classical Variation (of which both the Scheveningen and the Dragon were then seen as subvariations) trembled at the arrival of the Richter-Rauzer Attack.

But with the fast-growing interest in the Sicilian Defence as a whole, new paths were discovered, some of which turned out to lead back to... the Scheveningen. The Richter-Rauzer Attack was circumvented by delaying ...♘c6 (as in the move-order we are talking about here), improvements for Black were found against Maroczy's play and – perhaps most importantly – it was established that an immediate attack on the queenside is not Black's only option at all.

Then it was White's turn to start looking for alternatives to the classical ♗e2 (which later came to be called the Classical Scheveningen). New variations evolved, founded on new interpretations of the Sicilian Defence. The Scheveningen Variation was considerably enriched strategically and concrete variations became ever more complex.

Also, around the middle of the 20th century some other variations for Black were developed, like the Taimanov and the Najdorf Variation, that were partly based on a possible transposition to the Scheveningen. Gradually, a climate evolved where the Scheveningen Variation functioned as a sort of background to variations throughout the Sicilian Defence. It is not surprising then that the importance of a thorough understanding of the Scheveningen type of position and of the complex of variations that goes with it can hardly be overestimated.

But what exactly *is* this complex of variations? Strangely enough, this is not an easy question. Systematizing the Scheveningen is difficult for various reasons.

Firstly, this type of position is literally pervaded with move-order tricks and with extremely subtle nuances. Some characteristic plans may be executed in many different move-orders, all with pros and cons of their own.

Secondly, for many variations it is impossible to decide whether they should be classified as a Scheveningen or as some other system (a Najdorf for instance).

And finally, these positions are almost always of a type which centres on delicate positional assessments rather than concrete tactical problems (which in the end can always be more or less solved by patience, analytical prowess or a good computer).

All the characteristics summed up here are most prominent in the good old **6 ♗e2** variation, the **Classical Scheveningen**. This is where we shall start our survey.

Next, we shall turn our attention to the bold advance **6 g4**. This is the **Keres Attack**, which has been considered the most critical test of the Scheveningen since the 1980s. When this idea was introduced in 1943 by the brilliant Estonian grandmaster Paul Keres it was a revolutionary concept. Nowadays the plan of gaining space on the kingside by advancing the g-pawn is commonplace in many different variations of the Sicilian. The latest variation on this theme is 6 ♗e3 a6 7 ♕d2 in the Taimanov Variation (see page 425) and we have already seen the same plan executed on a grand scale in the Velimirović Attack.

But the more conventional **6 f4** remains an important touchstone of the Scheveningen as well. White prepares ♕f3 and (again) g4-g5.

These are the three main lines that we shall be looking at in somewhat more detail. The principal alternatives, which I shall just briefly outline here, are **6 g3**, **6 ♗c4** and **6 ♗e3**.

6 g3 is the start of a solid but unpretentious scheme of development, which requires little theoretical knowledge. Black's simplest reply is 6...♘c6 7 ♗g2 ♗d7 (parrying the threat of 8 ♘xc6 bxc6 9 e5) 8 0-0 ♗e7.

6 ♗c4 is the favourite of lovers of the Sozin Attack, to which a direct transposition is available with 6...♘c6 (see page 409) and of players who like the 6 ♗c4 variation against the Najdorf (6...a6; see page 439). Both of these lines could well be regarded as being part of the Scheveningen complex, but since in practice they usually arise via the Classical and the Najdorf Variations respectively I have decided to classify them as such. In the present move-order there is no need for Black to transpose to either of them (yet). 6...♗e7 is a perfectly good alternative.

6 ♗e3 confronts us with the same dilemma of classification. After 6...a6 we have a position that is 100% Scheveningen but which in practice arises far more often via the Najdorf and which I have decided to classify as such for precisely this reason (see page 442). The alternative 6...♘c6 transposes to the Sozin Attack after 7 ♗c4, but after 7 f4 it leads to the same position as 6 f4 ♘c6 7 ♗e3 (see page 433), while 7 ♗e2 is a Classical Scheveningen. However, nowadays 6 ♗e3 is mainly popular with players who are planning to continue along the lines of f3, ♕d2, 0-0-0 and g4, the **English Attack**. They are more likely to meet both 6...a6 and 6...♘c6 (and other moves like 6...♗e7) with 7 f3.

The moment is less well-chosen for **6 ♗g5**, the defining move of the Richter-Rauzer and a major variation of the Najdorf. After 6...♗e7, the Najdorf-oriented 7 f4 is not very good because of the tactical counterblow 7...h6 8 ♗h4 ♘xe4! 9 ♗xe7 ♘xc3. The Richter-Rauzer move 7 ♕d2 is relatively better, but after 7...a6 8 0-0-0 b5, for instance, the difference from the Richter-Rauzer Attack is to Black's advantage. White lacks the typical methods of attacking d6: ♘db5 or ♘xc6 in combination with ♗xf6.

Classical Scheveningen

6   ♗e2 *(D)*

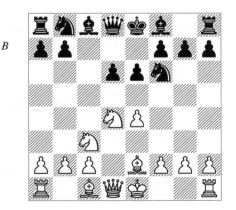

Almost all the main variations of the Sicilian Defence started out in life with the simple scheme of development based on ♗e2 and 0-0. It was only when it was realized that this does not *automatically* guarantee White an advantage that every variation was treated more sharply and with more regard for its own particular characteristics. I have already described how this process took place for the Classical Variation, which was the original starting point of the Scheveningen Variation in the first part of the 20th century (see page 405). However, it would be wrong to assume that this classical scheme of development is now outdated. In fact it runs though the entire Sicilian like a leitmotif and acts as a link between many different variations.

6   ...   ♗e7

Since both sides have been fairly reserved up to now, the position does not contain any concrete threats. As a result, there is no such thing as a forced move-order here; quite the contrary: both players have an almost unheard-of freedom of choice. Speaking very generally, it might be observed that a plan based on ...♗e7, ...♘c6 and ...a6 is the most common and that there are a number of standard positions connected with it, that can be reached in one way or another. In *this* position, apart from 6...♗e7, **6...♘c6** and **6...a6** are the most important moves to head for these standard positions. The position after 6...♘c6 often arises via the Classical Variation or via the Taimanov (4...♘c6 5 ♘c3 d6 6 ♗e2 ♘f6; see page 423), while the position after 6...a6 usually results from a Najdorf.

Naturally, there are also alternatives. Around 1940, a plan based on ...♘bd7 was called the 'Modern Scheveningen' and even upgraded to the 'Improved Scheveningen' some thirty years later, but despite these promising names this plan never managed to surpass the main line, which is based on ...♘c6. For example: 6...a6 7 0-0 ♘bd7 (the immediate 7...b5 is met by 8 ♗f3, with the awkward threat of 9 e5) and now either 8 f4 b5 9 ♗f3 ♗b7 or (more restrictively) 8 a4 b6 9 f4 ♗b7 10 ♗f3. The decision whether to stop ...b5 by playing a4 is one of the great dilemmas of the Classical Scheveningen. The more modern(!) version of this plan is to play 7...♕c7 (instead of 7...♘bd7). This move also prepares ...b5 (or ...b6 if White replies a4), but preserves the choice between ...♘c6 and ...♘bd7.

7   0-0   0-0
8   f4

Like his opponent, White also enjoys almost complete freedom of movement and instead of the text-move he might just as well play **8 ♗e3**, for instance. But the advance f4 in itself is an essential element of how this variation should be treated and this is what began to become clear in the days of Maroczy (see page 405). In fact, this is where the modern interpretation of the Sicilian Defence originated, for it was in this type of position that – after a period when it was thought *anything* would favour White, followed by a period when the startling discovery of ...a6, ...♕c7 and ...♘c6-a5-c4 seemed to swing the balance – the real strength of White's position was first understood: instead of hiding behind the e4-pawn, waiting for Black to do something on the queenside, White needs to be aggressive and hit Black with either e5, f4-f5 or g4-g5.

8 ... ♘c6

Naturally, the alternative **8...a6** is just as good, keeping the option of delaying ...♘c6 to a later stage or else putting the knight somewhere else altogether.

9 ♗e3 (D)

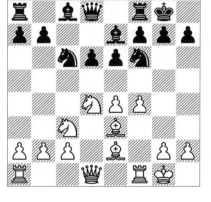

9 ... a6

I am adopting this move as the main line, not because it is the best or even the most popular move in this position (it probably isn't), but because the *plan* of ...a6 and ...♕c7 is very important indeed. Two other moves which are within the boundaries of this plan are **9...♗d7** and **9...♕c7**. A noteworthy alternative, based on a radically different interpretation of the position, is **9...e5**.

By playing **9...♗d7**, Black signals that he is not looking to start an immediate attack on the queenside. Instead, he is planning to exchange on d4 and play ...♗c6, a very natural and simple scheme of development and a sound way of keeping pressure on e4. Should White decide to pre-empt this plan by replying 10 ♘b3, Black may play 10...a6 11 a4 b6, heading for the same type of position that we are about to see in the 9...a6 line.

9...♕c7 is possible because Black need not fear 10 ♘db5 ♕b8. Otherwise, this line is very likely to transpose to 9...a6 10 a4 ♕c7.

9...e5, on the other hand, aims for simplification and an opening of the centre. The aggressive-looking 10 ♘f5 is not to be feared, for after 10...♗xf5 11 exf5 exf4 12 ♖xf4 d5 a position arises where White's pawn is not very well placed on f5, since it has left the vital squares e4 and e5 unprotected (making a manoeuvre like ...♗d6-e5 a realistic prospect for Black). Nor is 10 fxe5 dxe5 11 ♘f5 very dangerous after 11...♗xf5 12 ♖xf5 ♕xd1+ 13 ♖xd1 g6. White should be cautious with a pawn exchange at e5, for by doing so he solves the only structural problem of the Scheveningen formation: Black's space disadvantage. The most popular reply to 9...e5 is 10 ♘b3. Black can continue his plan of simplification with 10...exf4 11 ♗xf4 ♗e6 followed by ...d5 or he can play the more heavy-handed 10...a5.

10 a4

At the cost of a slight weakening of his queenside pawn-formation (the b4-square), White prevents ...b5. Allowing this advance but stopping further progress of the b-pawn with a3 is a major alternative. For instance, there is the plan of playing ♕e1-g3, starting with **10 ♕e1**. After 10...♘xd4 11 ♗xd4 b5 12 a3 ♗b7 13 ♕g3 Black cannot take on e4 because of mate at g7. Black has to make sure of his counterplay before White builds up too great a pressure on the kingside. 13...♗c6 14 ♗d3 ♕d7 15 ♖ae1 a5 followed by ...b4 is a characteristic continuation.

10 ... ♕c7

11 ♔h1 (D)

If **11 ♕e1**, Black has the characteristic reply 11...♘xd4 12 ♗xd4 e5, a variation on the theme of 9...e5. For this reason, most players prefer the more flexible text-move, in order to meet **11...♘xd4** with 12 ♕xd4 e5 13 ♕d3 (or 13 ♕d2) 13...exf4 14 ♗xf4.

B

This is one of those standard positions to which I was referring in the introduction. It is the starting point for an intricate maze of subtle and deeply studied variations.

Since the ...♘a5-c4 plan cannot readily be carried out yet (if **11...♘a5** White has the simple 12 ♕d3, for instance), the development of Black's queen's bishop is the real crux of this position. Apart from the already-mentioned 11...♘xd4, the obvious way of doing so is **11...♗d7** (for **11...b6?** runs into the powerful 12 ♘xc6 ♕xc6 13 e5 followed by ♗f3). But if White then retreats his knight by 12 ♘b3 to prevent the ...♘xd4 and ...♗c6 manoeuvre, we suddenly find ourselves in a type of position where the bishop would really like to be on b7, not d7. It is characteristic of the thoroughly strategic nature of the Scheveningen Variation that Black can now afford to play an extremely subtle waiting move, which is not really a waiting move:

11 ... ♖e8

Not only does Black delay the development of his queen's bishop, hoping that White will withdraw his knight voluntarily (in order then to meet **12 ♘b3** very comfortably with 12...b6 and ...♗b7), but by playing this mysterious rook move he also strengthens the effect of a possible ...e5. After **12 ♕e1 ♘xd4 13 ♗xd4 e5**, for instance, the potentially dangerous 14 fxe5

dxe5 15 ♕g3 is now parried with 15...♗d8, when both e5 and f6 remain protected.

White has tried a wide variety of moves anticipating 12...♗d7, 12...♘xd4 and 12...♘a5. **12 ♗f3** is what you might call a good solid move, while the much more recent pawn sacrifice **12 a5** is nothing less than a thunderbolt. The rather sensational idea is to meet 12...♘xa5 with yet another pawn sacrifice: 13 e5! dxe5 14 fxe5 ♕xe5 15 ♗f4 ♕c5 16 ♘a4 ♕a7 17 ♗c7, when Black's disorganized queenside is under heavy pressure.

Keres Attack

6 g4 *(D)*

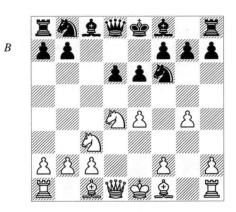

B

Few variations have had such an impact on the Sicilian Defence as this move. Instead of first developing his pieces and then looking around for a good plan, White immediately attacks, boldly and unreservedly. It took a long time for the chess world to grasp the enormous strength and significance of this idea, for it was not until around 1980 that this became a popular line (some forty years after its introduction). But when it *did* finally sink in, its effects were felt in even the remotest corner of the Sicilian. Many new variations, based on the advance g4, were developed (like the English Attack against the Najdorf) and lovers of the Scheveningen saw their wide, safe and comfortable avenue change into a narrow and dangerous mountain trail.

6 ... h6

Most players do not like to have their knight chased away from f6, but in fact there is no real consensus as to what Black should play. It appears to be very much a matter of taste.

The variation **6...a6** 7 g5 ᐦfd7 8 ᐦe3 b5, for instance, could be called making a virtue of necessity. While accepting the loss of space on the kingside, Black immediately counterattacks on the opposite wing, where the king's knight that has been driven away from f6 finds a new task. This is perhaps Black's sharpest way to react against the Keres Attack. 9 a3 ᐦb7 10 h4 ᐦe7 is possible, when the d7-knight may find gainful employment on b6 or c5.

Black retains a little more influence in the centre if he plays **6...ᐦc6** 7 g5 ᐦd7. If then 8 ᐦe3, many players like to play 8...ᐦe7 9 h4 0-0, seemingly castling 'into it'. But the point of this plan is that Black's king was not safe on e8 anyway and by castling he at least develops all of his pieces in a harmonious way, along the lines of 10 ᐦd2 a6 11 0-0-0 ᐦxd4 12 ᐦxd4 b5 followed by ...ᐦb7, for example. This variation too can lead to very sharp play.

We now return to 6...h6 (D):

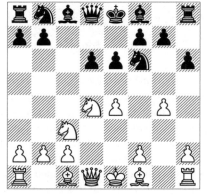

For a long time **7 g5** hxg5 8 ᐦxg5 was thought of as *the* main line in this position. White then has a bishop firmly anchored on g5 (he is in effect playing an improved version of 6 ᐦg5 – see page 429 – since Black can no longer reply ...h6), and as a result he is keeping the enemy position under pressure. On the other hand, the break-up of his kingside pawn-phalanx considerably weakens White's ability actually to *do*

something with this pressure. As a result, Black does not have to hurry so much looking for counterplay as he often does in other variations of the Sicilian Defence. For instance, Black can now afford to castle queenside, something which is unthinkable in most other variations since it usually is the queenside where Black has to become aggressive. After 8...ᐦc6 9 ᐦd2 ᐦb6 10 ᐦb3 a6 11 0-0-0 ᐦd7 12 h4 ᐦe7 13 ᐦe2 0-0-0 14 f4 ᐦb8, for instance, White will have to scrutinize the enemy defences for a possible weakness, while Black will be looking for a chance to counterattack in the centre with ...d5.

During the 1980s, players on the white side started looking for alternative methods, and it did not take long for **7 h4** to come to the fore as the new main line. White is planning to play ᐦg1 and only then g5, thus keeping his pawn-phalanx intact. Carried out in this way, the advance g5 costs more time but its impact is far greater than in the variations without 6...h6, for there is the immediate danger of the further advance g6 and with the h-file open (...hxg5, hxg5) castling kingside is no longer an option. Most players seem to agree that Black has to act fast before White gets his battering-ram in working order. After 7...ᐦc6 8 ᐦg1, one of the critical positions arises following 8...d5, but the surprising 8...h5 is played even more often. The point is to meet 9 g5 with the aggressive 9...ᐦg4 (rather than meekly retreating to d7). Ironically, 9 gxh5 ᐦxh5 brings about the same type of position as the 'old' main line 7 g5.

6 f4

6   f4 (D)

Until about 1980, when the Keres Attack took over, this variation was seen as *the* way of attacking the Scheveningen more fiercely and more directly than anything the Classical Scheveningen has to offer. White's intended scheme of development is ᐦf3, ᐦe3 and 0-0-0, when he can use either his e-, his f-, or his g-pawn as a bayonet to rip into Black's defences.

Like the Keres Attack, this is not an easy variation for Black to handle, although theory has certainly come to terms with it over the years. The counter-punch ...e5 in particular has

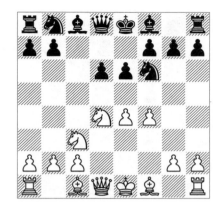

B

proven itself to be an excellent way of throwing sand in the enemy attacking machinery. One of the oldest versions of this idea becomes apparent after **6...♘c6** 7 ♗e3 ♗e7 8 ♕f3 0-0 9 0-0-0 ♕c7, with the idea of 'refuting' 10 g4 with 10...♘xd4 11 ♗xd4 e5 (this is extremely controversial because White continues unperturbed with 12 fxe5 dxe5 13 ♕g3!). Later the immediate 8...e5 (instead of 8...0-0) became popular, when 9 ♘xc6 bxc6 10 f5 is considered critical. The most recent variation is to play ...e5 even earlier: 7...e5.

Another, much more provocative, method is to counterattack immediately on the queenside. The best-known implementation of this strategy is **6...a6**, a variation that is often reached via the Najdorf. Black intends to meet 7 ♗e3 with 7...b5 8 ♕f3 ♗b7, attacking e4. After 9 ♗d3 ♘bd7 10 g4 b4 11 ♘ce2 ♘c5 12 ♘g3 a very sharp battle is in the making. If White plays 7 ♕f3 in order to meet 7...b5? very strongly with 8 e5!, Black can make preparations for this advance, either with 7...♕c7 (when e5 can always be parried by ...♗b7, for instance after 8 g4 b5), or more subtly with the by-now familiar manoeuvre 7...♕b6 8 ♘b3 ♕c7.

2 ♘f3 d6

2 ... d6 *(D)*

This reaction to 2 ♘f3 is specifically designed to cope with 3 d4 cxd4 4 ♘xd4, much more so than the alternatives 2...♘c6 and 2...e6. In the years when the Classical Variation was still predominant but players on the black side

began to feel annoyed at the new move 6 ♗g5 instead of 6 ♗e2, the alternative 2...d6 was 'discovered'. The idea is to be able to play – after 3 d4 cxd4 (or 3...♘f6 4 ♘c3 cxd4) 4 ♘xd4 ♘f6 5 ♘c3 – the fianchetto move 5...g6 immediately, thus reaching the Dragon Variation which until then used to be played via the Classical Variation, a route made inaccessible by 6 ♗g5 instead of 6 ♗e2 (see the introduction to the Classical Variation on page 405). Around 1940, 2...d6 was even called the 'Modern Variation'.

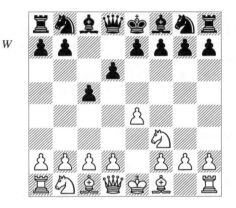

W

In the course of the stormy development the Sicilian has gone through since, the name disappeared but the move has remained. 2...d6 is extremely popular nowadays, not only among Dragon devotees, but also among those who want to play the Classical or the Scheveningen Variation and who prefer the 'side effects' of 2...d6 (the alternatives White has to 3 d4 cxd4 4 ♘xd4) to those of 2...♘c6 or 2...e6. Besides, 2...d6 is the (only!) introductory move to the Najdorf Variation, which in 1940 was hardly more than a footnote but has now become the most important variation of the Sicilian Defence.

What then are these side effects of 2...d6, and are they less damaging than those of the other two moves?

Well, in any case there are more of them. On any of the next three moves, White has a respectable deviation from the main road 3 d4 cxd4 4 ♘xd4 ♘f6 5 ♘c3.

3 d4

The 'standard' alternatives **3 ♘c3**, **3 d3**, **3 c4** and **3 c3** are nothing to worry the 2...d6 player.

3 ♘c3 (which was already discussed in the section on the Closed Sicilian; see page 392) can be met by 3...♘f6, **3 d3** is about as good or bad as 2 d3 (or 2 ♘f3 ♘c6 3 d3) and for **3 c4** the moment is not very well chosen because Black has two ways of preventing the crucial follow-up 4 d4: 3...e5 and 3...♗g4.

Things are more complicated with **3 c3**. This move also looks badly timed because Black can reply 3...♘f6 without having his knight chased away by 4 e5. On the other hand, now that Black has already played ...d6, he cannot take over the initiative in the centre with ...d5, like in the 2 c3 variations, at least not without losing a tempo. Besides, 4...♘xe4 is not a threat because of 5 ♕a4+. It is true that this prevents White from playing 4 d4 (for precisely this move *would* allow 4...♘xe4), but he may simply reply **4 ♗e2**, for instance. After a plausible continuation like 4...g6 5 0-0 ♗g7 6 ♖e1 0-0 7 ♗f1 White is ready to play d4, occupying the centre. Apart from 4 ♗e2, the somewhat surprising **4 ♗d3** (intending 5 ♗c2 followed by d4) and even the ultra-cautious **4 h3** have been played. None of these lines is an immediate attempt to go for the enemy's throat, but they are a godsend to many a player who does not trust himself with the hyper-sharp and ultra-theoretical Najdorf or Dragon Variations. Not overly sharp, not too difficult, requiring no theoretical knowledge to speak of, but perfectly sound and not what you would call spineless either.

The same could be said about what is undoubtedly the most important of the many 'side effects' of 2...d6: **3 ♗b5+** *(D)*.

This move aims for simplification and fast kingside development. It is also slightly more flexible than White's other third-move alternatives. For instance, after the plausible reply **3...♗d7** 4 ♗xd7+ ♕xd7 White has several standard plans to choose from: 5 c4 is now definitely more attractive than it was a couple of moves ago, as is the idea of playing c3 and d4. After 5 0-0 ♘c6 6 c3 ♘f6 White even has a choice between the cautious 7 ♕e2 (or 7 ♖e1) and the sharp 7 d4, sacrificing a pawn for the initiative, based on the idea of meeting 7...♘xe4

B

with 8 d5 followed by 9 ♖e1, with a considerable lead in development.

An ambitious alternative to 3...♗d7 is to play **3...♘d7**, hoping with a later ...a6 either to obtain the bishop-pair (if White takes on d7) or to chase away the bishop. However, neither of these 'results' is favourable in itself; it all depends on the exact circumstances. White simply carries on developing his pieces, for instance by playing 4 d4 ♘f6 5 ♘c3 cxd4 6 ♕xd4.

Finally, Black has **3...♘c6**, reaching a position that was discussed in the section on the Rossolimo Variation (see page 402).

3   ...   cxd4

Another distinguishing feature of 2...d6 is that it is the only second move where Black does not need to take on d4 at once. The zwischenzug **3...♘f6** even used to be the main line when 2...d6 was 'modern' (around 1940). In those days this was played in order to side-step the variation 3...cxd4 4 ♘xd4 ♘f6 5 f3. Nowadays, what makes 3...♘f6 the preferred choice of *some* players is that it makes it impossible for White to follow 4 ♘c3 cxd4 5 ♕xd4 ♘c6 6 ♗b5 ♗d7 7 ♗xc6 ♗xc6 up with a c4 formation, like in the analogous line 3...cxd4 4 ♕xd4 ♘c6 5 ♗b5 ♗d7 6 ♗xc6 ♗xc6.

If White refuses to make any of these concessions (minimal as they are) he may want to try to squeeze an advantage from 4 dxc5 ♘xe4. Most players, however, do not worry about these subtleties and simply reply 4 ♘c3 cxd4 5 ♘xd4.

4   ♘xd4

Another anomaly of 2...d6 is that it allows White to recapture on d4 with the queen, since after **4 ♕xd4 ♘c6**, instead of losing time with a queen move he can play **5 ♗b5**. This variation falls into the same category as 3 c3 and 3 ♗b5+. It is fairly popular with players who like their life a little quieter than is usual in the main lines of the Open Sicilian. Theory is uncomplicated and White simply gets a reasonable position. On the other hand, Black does not have to worry about any acute problems either. The main starting position arises after **5...♗d7 6 ♗xc6 ♗xc6** *(D)*.

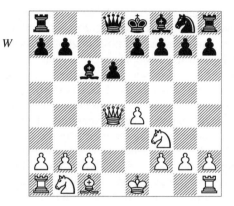

At the cost of his bishop-pair, White has maintained the speed of his development. He can now choose between the nimble **7 ♘c3 ♘f6 8 ♗g5 e6 9 0-0-0** (which comes close to resembling a main line) and the more heavy-handed **7 c4**, which rather resembles a Maroczy Bind.

> **4 ... ♘f6**

Another difference between 2...d6 and its rivals 2...e6 and 2...♘c6 is that any moves other than 4...♘f6 are highly unusual in this position.

4...e6 is unattractive in a situation where it allows White to play 5 c4 'for free', i.e. not having made any concessions, such as 5 ♘b5 in the (comparable) Taimanov Variation.

Nor are **4...g6** and **4...♘c6** 5 c4 g6 very popular, although theoretically there is nothing wrong with these moves. After 4...♘c6 5 c4 ♘f6 6 ♘c3 g6 (or 6...♘xd4 7 ♕xd4 g6) we are in the middle of a Maroczy Bind (see page 419).

> **5 ♘c3** *(D)*

At one time, **5 f3** was such a dreaded move in this position that 3...cxd4 was thought to be an inaccuracy. White avoids 5 ♘c3 because he

wants to play 6 c4. Around 1940, the c4 plan, which we have seen in several forms by now, was thought to be so powerful that any variation that allows White to play this move was seen as inferior. But 1940 is a long time ago. Nowadays this type of position is seen dispassionately as having its pros and cons and fears of 5 f3 have subsided, though it has remained a respectable option. Black may reply 5...♘c6 6 c4 g6 transposing to a Maroczy Bind and hoping that the very early f3 will restrict White in his choice of subvariations. Even 5...e6 or 5...♘c6 6 c4 e6 is playable now that White has opted for f3 so soon (which is, by the way, an excellent example of how finely tuned theoretical assessments can be, for it is less than half a page ago that I described 4...e6 5 c4 as being 'unattractive'). But the sharpest and theoretically most critical reply to 5 f3 is 5...e5, intending to meet 6 ♘b3 or 6 ♘f5 with 6...d5. Theory concentrates mainly on 6 ♗b5+.

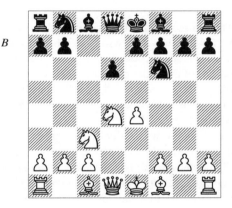

In this position, **5...e6** is a Scheveningen and **5...♘c6** a Classical Variation. I have assigned these lines to 2...e6 and 2...♘c6 respectively.

But this is also the starting point for two extremely important lines of the Sicilian Defence that we have not encountered via any other move-order: **5...a6** is the **Najdorf Variation** and **5...g6** is the **Dragon Variation**.

Other moves are rarely ever played. **5...e5**, which I have just recommended as the critical reply to 5 f3, is far less important here. In the position after 6 ♗b5+ ♘bd7 7 ♘f5, the developing move ♘c3 is of far greater use to White than the little pawn move f3. But this is not the fault of the ...e5 plan itself for, as we are about to see, this move plays a crucial role in the Najdorf Variation.

Najdorf Variation

5   ...   a6 *(D)*

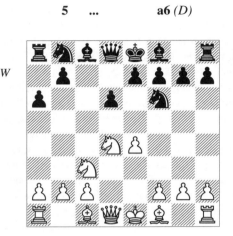

Anyone seeing this little, seemingly insipid move for the first time will find it hard to believe that 5...a6 introduces one of the sharpest variations of the entire range of chess openings. Unlike 5...e6, 5...♘c6 or 5...g6, it contributes nothing to Black's piece development. What does it do then?

The answer is not at all obvious, but to those who have read this chapter carefully it can hardly come as a surprise. Black is planning to meet **6 ♗e2**, the standard reply to *any* Sicilian variation in the first half of the 20th century, with 6...e5. In the wake of the Boleslavsky Variation (see page 405) in the 1940s the idea was born that an ...e5 plan might be viable even without ...♘c6. In fact, this makes Black's position more flexible, for in many cases d7 is a better square for Black's knight than c6. Besides, 5...a6 has the advantage of making b5 inaccessible to White's pieces and of preparing the ever-useful advance ...b5.

Under the inspiring leadership of the Polish-Argentinean grandmaster Miguel Najdorf (1910-97), this idea was tested and found to be excellent. During the 1950s and 1960s, 'the Najdorf' became a very popular line even at

the highest level. Its theoretical framework exploded, its subvariations grew sharper and sharper until finally refutations and refutations of refutations seemed to be coming quicker than lightning.

And this process has never really come to an end. The Najdorf is very much alive and kicking. It offers lovers of the Sicilian everything they are looking for from their favourite opening: aggression, resilience, the perfect combination of attack and defence.

One thing has changed though in almost three quarters of a century. Where 'Don Miguel' himself and his fellow pioneers needed no more than courage and positional understanding, present-day Najdorf adepts have to be prepared to work extremely hard at their opening, for in some subvariations Black is skirting the abyss so closely that a certain amount of ready knowledge has become indispensable. But for his opponent the situation is exactly the same!

The course of further developments is very much determined by White's next move. First we shall look at the classical (*and* evergreen!) **6 ♗e2**. White simply allows 6...e5 and continues to test the fundamental soundness of Black's plan. Positional subtleties abound in this line.

Next we shall turn our attention to **6 f4**. This move also allows 6...e5 but White is directing his attention emphatically to the kingside and in so doing creates a more dangerous and aggressive climate.

6 ♗c4 is sharper again. Just like in the Sozin Attack, White makes 6...e5 less attractive. But (again just like in the Sozin) the crucial question is whether White's bishop is not misplaced on c4 if Black switches to a Scheveningen type of position with 6...e6.

Then we shall look at **6 ♗g5**, the move that was seen for many decades as *the* ultimate test of the Najdorf Variation. It is this move in particular which has given rise to the most breathtaking complex of variations, richer in sacrifices, counter-sacrifices, destructive attacks and miraculous escapes than any other opening system.

Finally, we shall examine **6 ♗e3**, the newest star in the Sicilian firmament. This old move was given a new lease on life in the 1980s and

1990s, originally by a group of English players, which is why it came to be called the **English Attack**. White is preparing to play f3, ♕d2, 0-0-0 and g4, regardless of whether Black plays ...e6 or ...e5.

These are the five main lines that we shall be looking at in some more detail below. But it is only fair to say that practically every legal move has been tried in this position and that some of these moves are perfectly sound, quite important and well-researched theoretically. Nevertheless, within the enormous dimensions of the Najdorf they remain relatively 'small' and I shall just mention them briefly.

6 g3, for instance, is one of White's most solid replies. 6...e6 is a calm subvariation of the Scheveningen and after 6...e5 7 ♘de2 ♗e7 8 ♗g2 White has a firm grip on d5, be it in such a way that he cannot really do very much with it. But even here accuracy and fearlessness are essential requirements, as is illustrated by the variation 8...♘bd7 9 a4 b6 10 h3. White suddenly 'threatens' to become aggressive with 11 g4 and 12 ♘g3. By playing 10...h5, Black not only counters this plan, but he also threatens to take the initiative on the kingside himself by continuing ...h4.

Similarly, **6 a4**, **6 ♗d3** and **6 h3** (intending 7 g4) have grown into respectable side-variations. Nowadays, even **6 ♖g1** has become an acceptable option and **6 f3**, a move that was practically never played until very recently, has become an alternative route to the English Attack (preparing 7 ♗e3 and avoiding 6 ♗e3 ♘g4).

6 ♗e2

6   ♗e2 (D)

In the early days of the Najdorf Variation, this move was self-evident. But even today there are many players who like this variation because it offers the opponent just a bare minimum of targets for counterplay.

6   ...   e5

It is on this move that the mighty structure of the Najdorf was built. Just as in the Boleslavsky Variation, the knight has nothing better than retreating: 7 ♘db5 is of course out of the question while 7 ♘f5 invites the powerful reply 7...d5.

And yet 6...e5 is not the only way to justify 5...a6. Many lovers of the Classical Scheveningen play **6...e6**, preferring the Najdorf move-order to avoid the dreaded Keres Attack. Moves like **6...♘bd7**, **6...g6** and **6...♘c6** have also been played and are not bad. But **6...b5**, an almost prehistoric interpretation of 5...a6 which disappeared from the arena even before 6...e5 first surfaced, is less reputable. The problem is that 7 ♗f3! cannot be met by 7...♗b7 because of 8 e5!, while 7...e5 8 ♘f5 is now excellent for White.

7   ♘b3

With this move we have reached the most important starting point of this line. Thanks to his pawn on e5, Black has more space than he normally has in a Sicilian position and this makes it harder for White to organize a kingside attack. On the other hand, d5 is a potentially strong square for White's pieces. However, White's control over this square is not all that impressive. Contrary to the situation in the Sveshnikov Variation, White cannot straightforwardly occupy d5 by playing ♗g5xf6 followed by ♘d5, for Black will simply replace the one knight on f6 by the other (...♘bd7xf6), maintaining his influence in the centre.

Many games that are played from this position revolve around subtle positional problems, but in a Najdorf a sudden tactical explosion is never far away. Against **7...♗e6** (the oldest move in this position), for instance, White has the sharp reaction 8 f4 ♕c7 (in order to meet 9 f5 with 9...♗c4) 9 g4. For this reason, most players nowadays prefer...

7   ...   ♗e7

8   0-0   0-0 *(D)*

W

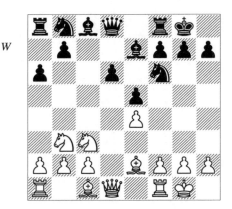

Getting to know this variation is not so much a matter of examining separate moves, but of grasping the strategic essence of the position. Several plans have been tried here.

At first White concentrated his attention on the queenside, starting with **9 a4**. The very logical idea is then to meet 9...♗e6 with 10 f4, not so much a display of kingside aggression as an attempt to gain control over d5 by playing f5, chasing back the enemy bishop. The standard reaction to this plan is to play 10...♕c7, enabling Black to meet **11 f5** with 11...♗c4. After 12 a5 ♘bd7 13 ♗e3 it may look as if White is getting on top in the battle for control over d5, but by playing 13...b5 14 axb6 ♘xb6 Black is just in time to create counterplay on the queenside. In order to avoid this problem, many players began to delay f5, playing **11 ♔h1 ♘bd7 12 ♗e3** instead. This gave rise to yet another characteristic type of position, since 12...exf4 13 ♖xf4 ♘e5 became the usual reply to this plan. By giving up his stronghold on e5, Black yields control over d4 and f4, but is rewarded for this by a mighty knight at e5.

This development in its turn made some players doubt the efficiency of the advance f4. During the 1980s it became all the rage to play **9 ♗e3 ♗e6 10 ♕d2**, creating a rather slow type of middlegame, where profound manoeuvring around d5 plays a predominant role. For example: 10...♘bd7 11 a4 ♖c8 12 a5 ♕c7 13 ♖fd1 ♕c6 14 ♗f3 ♖fe8 15 ♕e1 h6 16 ♘c1 with the idea ♘1a2-b4.

During the 1990s the f4 plan was rehabilitated, but now prefaced by **9 ♔h1**. The idea is that 9...♗e6 10 f4 exf4 11 ♗xf4 leaves White slightly better off than in the 9 a4 variation.

6 f4

6   f4

This is more aggressive than 6 ♗e2. White prepares the ♕f3, ♗e3 and 0-0-0 plan that we saw in the Scheveningen Variation. He can also retreat his knight to f3 without blocking his own f-pawn. Besides, the king's bishop might want to go to d3 or c4 instead of e2 on any of the next few moves *and* Black has to take the e5 advance into account.

6   ...   e5

Black has a large choice of moves in this position but basically there are three different plans, or rather pawn-formations: ...e6, ...e5 and ...g6. The latter two are often combined.

The immediate **6...e6** transposes to a very sharp subvariation of the Scheveningen (see page 433). This is actually Black's sharpest reply to 6 f4.

A set-up based on ...g6 can be reached in various ways. The straightforward **6...g6** is an option (*if* Black has an answer ready against 7 e5), but the preparatory moves **6...♘bd7** and **6...♕c7** are a little more cautious. Play might continue 6...♕c7 7 ♘f3 ♘bd7 8 ♗d3 g6 9 0-0 ♗g7.

7   ♘f3 *(D)*

B

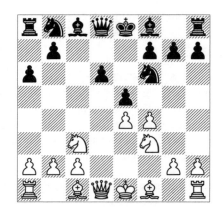

This is one of the most important and critical positions of the 6 f4 system. Thanks to his pawn on f4, White has the option of opening the f-file (with fxe5) to create attacking chances on the kingside at a moment of his own choosing, and in some cases f5 is a very useful alternative. On the other hand, Black may try to attack the e4-pawn, which can no longer be defended by f3. The standard means of doing so are the ...♘bd7-c5 manoeuvre, developing the queen's bishop on b7 and opening the e-file by playing ...exf4.

To begin with, Black has to protect e5. There are two methods of doing so, which differ only very slightly.

At first it was thought that Black needed to prevent the white king's bishop from coming to c4 by playing **7...♕c7**. After 8 a4 (to prevent Black's counterplay with ...b5) 8...♘bd7 9 ♗d3 g6 10 0-0 ♗g7 White then has 11 ♕e1, introducing a dangerous attacking scheme which is typical of any ...g6 variation, namely 11...0-0 12 fxe5 dxe5 13 ♕h4 followed by ♗h6 and ♘g5.

Later, **7...♘bd7** became the most popular move. After 8 a4 ♗e7, Black has a couple of sharp options if White ventures **9 ♗c4**. He can either play 9...0-0 10 0-0 exf4, intending to meet 11 ♗xf4 with 11...♕b6+ (there is the alternative of playing 10...♕b6+ 11 ♔h1 exf4), or he can play 9...♕a5, threatening 10...♘xe4 (and hoping for 10 0-0?? ♕c5+).

For these reasons, most players prefer to develop their king's bishop to d3 rather than c4 voluntarily, i.e. without being forced to do so by 7...♕c7. After **9 ♗d3** 0-0 10 0-0 Black again has the chance to stir up trouble with 10...exf4, intending to grab a pawn with 11 ♗xf4 ♕b6+ 12 ♔h1 ♕xb2, but this is double-edged and highly controversial. If Black prefers a somewhat safer course, he usually plays 10...♕c7 after all, or 10...♘c5 (based on the trap 11 fxe5 dxe5 12 ♘xe5?? ♕d4+).

6 ♗c4

6 ♗c4

This way of tackling the Najdorf became popular thanks to the excellent results Bobby Fischer had with it around 1960 and is often called the **Fischer Variation**. But when he started playing *against* it a few years later and was *again* very successful, its reputation dwindled. By the end of the 1980s, however, 6 ♗c4 was all the rage again and it has now definitely been accepted as a major variation even at the highest level.

Just as in the Sozin Attack (where Black has played ...♘c6 instead of ...a6), 6 ♗c4 makes the reply **6...e5** less attractive. Thanks to his increased control over d5, White can now not only play 7 ♘f5 but even 7 ♘de2, when the situation is more favourable for him than in, say, the variations 6 ♗e2 e5 7 ♘b3 or 6 g3 e5 7 ♘de2. Nor is **6...b5** something to worry about, for the situation remains largely unchanged after the simple retreat 7 ♗b3 (which after 7...e6 transposes to the line 6...e6 7 ♗b3 b5 – see below).

6 ... e6 (D)

The crucial question is whether White's bishop is well-placed or misplaced on c4 after this 'Scheveningen' reply.

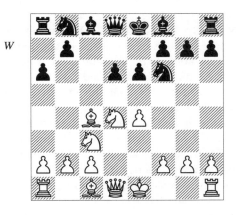

7 ♗b3

This seemingly timid little step backwards is in reality the introduction to an aggressive plan, or rather to a great many different plans, which I already listed in the section on the Sozin Attack. In the near future, White may try to blow up Black's central bastion at e6 with f4-f5, he may chase away Black's knight from f6 with f4 and e5 (which has the added advantage of opening the file – after ...dxe5 and fxe5 – creating dangerous attacking chances), or he may play ♗e3, ♕e2, 0-0-0 and g4, the basic scheme of the dangerous Velimirović Attack.

Especially with a view to discouraging the latter option, it seems obvious to reply **7...b5**. Black assumes a threatening pose on the queenside and creates the possibility of playing ...b4 and ...♘xe4, winning a pawn. During the 1960s and 1970s, the entire 6 ♗c4 variation revolved around this position and more in particular around the plan of 8 0-0 followed by 9 f4. But despite the most heroic analytical efforts to prove a forced win for White in the variation 8 0-0 ♗e7 **9 f4** ♗b7 10 e5 dxe5 11 fxe5, Black's defences were never overcome (11...♗c5! 12 ♗e3 ♘c6! 13 exf6 ♗xd4) and finally interest dwindled.

The reason why 6 ♗c4 came back into fashion around 1990 was the rise of the more restrained approach involving **9 ♕f3** (instead of 9 f4), which not only threatens 10 e5 but introduces the manoeuvre ♕g3, putting pressure on g7.

In order to avoid this new line, Black started looking for alternatives to what was until then the unquestioned main line, 7...b5.

Naturally, by playing **7...♘c6** Black can transpose to the Sozin Attack, but apparently this does not satisfy the ambitious Najdorf player, for the search continued.

7...♗e7 is an option, but this move receives very rough treatment with 8 g4.

Finally, it was **7...♘bd7** that turned out to be Black's main alternative to the old main line. Black puts his knight on c5 and forces White to act energetically. After 8 f4 ♘c5 a whole new complex of variations has been developed. White has tried 9 f5, 9 e5 dxe5 10 fxe5 ♘fd7 11 ♗f4, 9 ♕f3 and 9 0-0. That a pawn sacrifice is all in a day's work in this variation is clear enough from this list of options. After 9 0-0 ♘fxe4 10 ♘xe4 ♘xe4, for instance, White plays 11 f5 e5 12 ♕h5 and obtains a dangerous initiative.

6 ♗g5

6   ♗g5

This move is based on the same idea as the Richter-Rauzer Attack (which is still within Black's reach: **6...♘c6** transposes). While making the reply **6...e5** very unattractive (apart from

the solid 7 ♘f5, White even has the direct 7 ♗xf6 ♕xf6 8 ♘d5 to make life difficult for his opponent), White creates a certain positional tension by introducing the possibility of ♗xf6, the ramifications of which are hard to assess. But the crucial question (again) is how good or bad the position of White's bishop really is at g5 after the obvious reply:

6   ...   e6

If White now chooses the typical Richter-Rauzer plan of **7 ♕d2**, the reply 7...♗e7 brings about a position that we have seen as part of the Scheveningen Variation (see page 429) and which does not impress theory as very promising for White. This means, though it is still barely visible to the naked eye, that White has burned his bridges by playing 6 ♗g5. In order to justify this aggressive move, he *has to* continue aggressively.

At first, the appropriate way of doing so was thought to be **7 ♕f3**, but as early as the 1950s it was discovered that only by advancing his f-pawn can White put real pressure on the enemy position:

7   f4 *(D)*

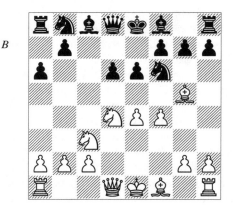

This position is the starting point for a great number of hair-raising variations, some of them analysed so deeply as to touch bottom with a forced mate or a draw by perpetual check, some of them extending into a difficult endgame. There is a really big chunk of theoretical knowledge waiting for the diligent student here with refinements and spectacular new finds being added almost daily.

There is little I can do within the limits set by this book but to outline the main structure and to give just an inkling of the actual variations and to leave less usual moves (like **7...♗d7**, or **7...♘c6**, which is based on the tactical point 8 ♘xc6 bxc6 9 e5 h6 10 ♗h4 g5 11 fxg5 ♘d5) aside.

7...♗e7 is the classical move, not with the idea of crazily castling straight into White's kingside attack but in order to continue after 8 ♕f3 with **8...♕c7** 9 0-0-0 ♘bd7, followed by ...b5 and ...♗b7. The reply 10 g4 has evolved as the main line in this position. If 10...b5, White wants to attack Black's central stronghold at e6 with 11 ♗xf6 ♘xf6 12 g5 ♘d7 13 f5. The fact that this allows Black to win a pawn on g5 (and with check!) does not worry White, who is counting on the open g-file as a future base of attack. Instead of playing 8...♕c7, Black can open the kingside himself with **8...h6** 9 ♗h4 g5!? 10 fxg5 ♘fd7. This is the **Gothenburg Variation**, obviously an extremely risky undertaking but – as yet – unrefuted.

Even at an early stage of the Najdorf Variation's history, attempts were made to accelerate the classical plan of playing ...b5. This started with the variations **7...♘bd7** and **7...♕c7** being developed. By economizing on ...♗e7, Black is hoping to be fast enough to defuse White's most dangerous plans, like the 10 g4 line given above. After 7...♘bd7 8 ♕f3 ♕c7 (8...b5 runs into 9 e5!) 9 0-0-0 b5, for instance, White has tried to raze Black's position to the ground in several ways, but – up to now – to no avail. A few examples: 10 e5 ♗b7 11 ♕h3 dxe5 12 ♘xe6 fxe6 13 ♕xe6+, or 10 ♗xb5 axb5 11 ♘dxb5 ♕b8 12 e5. And what should we think of 7...♕c7 8 ♕f3 b5 9 0-0-0 b4 and now 10 ♘d5!? or 10 e5 ♗b7 11 ♘cb5!? axb5 12 ♗xb5+ ♘bd7 13 ♕h3, threatening 14 ♘xe6 fxe6 15 ♕xe6+? And these are not coffee-house games, but products of thorough, deadly serious analysis!

But the culmination of this strategy is undoubtedly to play **7...b5** at once, without any form of preparation. This is the **Polugaevsky Variation**, a line that is so breathtakingly complicated that a remarkable discrepancy has evolved between theory and practice: there is a huge complex of deep theoretical analysis, but

there are very few games with this line. Polugaevsky (1934-95) himself described how he studied this variation several hours a day for half a year before he dared to play it for the first time.

If White cannot refute 7...b5, it is a wonderful move. After **8 ♕f3 ♗b7 9 0-0-0 ♘bd7 10 ♗d3 ♗e7**, for instance, Black has executed the classical 7...♗e7 plan by saving the move ...♕c7. The one and only critical reply must be the obvious **8 e5**. The answer to this move and the point of the Polugaevsky Variation is 8...dxe5 9 fxe5 ♕c7. Again, the aggressive 6 ♗g5 turns out to have its darker side as well, for if **10 exf6** Black regains the piece with 10...♕e5+. The far deeper point, and the real miracle of this variation, is that Black appears to be able to hold his own here, in spite of his enormous lag in development after, say, 11 ♗e2 ♕xg5 12 0-0. The second main line arises after **10 ♕e2 ♘fd7 11 0-0-0 (D)**.

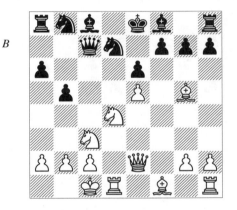

B

White's e5-pawn is taboo: if 11...♕xe5? 12 ♕xe5 ♘xe5, 13 ♘dxb5! is winning, while 11...♘xe5? allows 12 ♘dxb5! axb5 13 ♕xe5! ♕xe5 14 ♖d8#. The critical move is 11...♗b7. White then has several ways of going for his opponent's throat with a knight sacrifice on e6, starting, for instance, with 12 ♕h5 or 12 ♕g4, or even 12 ♘xe6 immediately. Yes, playing the Polugaevsky Variation requires a computer-like talent for calculating variations with flawless accuracy.

The same can be said of the last of Black's main defences to 7 f4: **7...♕b6 (D)**, the **Poisoned Pawn Variation**.

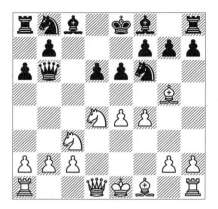

W

Every method of protecting b2 is a small concession. For instance, **8 ♘b3 ♘bd7 9 ♕f3 ♗e7 10 0-0-0 ♕c7** and with White's knight away from d4 there are far fewer attacking chances than in the comparable 7...♗e7 variation. That is why the critical reply is just to play **8 ♕d2**, allowing Black to reply 8...♕xb2 *(D)*.

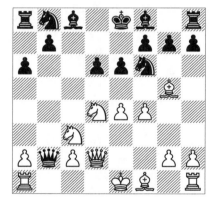

W

This leads, after 9 ♖b1 or 9 ♘b3 (threatening 10 a3 followed by 11 ♖a2) to a situation where White (again) has a huge lead in development and Black has an extra pawn *and* the superior queenside pawn-structure. It is in fact very attractive for White to sacrifice this pawn, while it is equally attractive for Black to take it. An ideal setting for a ferocious fight!

To show how wildly complicated this variation is, consider 9 ♖b1 ♕a3 10 f5 (other main lines are 10 ♗xf6, 10 ♗e2 and 10 e5, which has been very popular in recent top-level practice) 10...♘c6 11 fxe6 fxe6 12 ♘xc6 bxc6. Now

comes a second pawn sacrifice to speed things up: 13 e5 dxe5 14 ♗xf6 gxf6 15 ♘e4. This is the starting point for a terrific complex of variations, based on themes like 15...♗e7 16 ♗e2 h5 (to stop 17 ♗h5+) 17 ♖b3 ♕a4 18 ♘xf6+!? ♗xf6 19 c4 *(D)*.

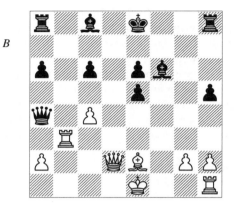

B

It seems incredible that White should have sufficient compensation for the great material sacrifices he has made, but Black's position is extremely uncoordinated and his king has no safe place anywhere on the board. According to the present state of opening theory, attack and defence are equally balanced, but... everyone is holding their breath for future developments.

English Attack

6   ♗e3

During the past thirty years or so, this move has spectacularly advanced from a mere footnote ('a very slow move indeed') to perhaps *the* new main line of the Najdorf Variation. This success story is based entirely on the strength of the plan f3, ♕d2, 0-0-0 and g4, which is in effect an adaptation of the Keres Attack to the specific circumstances of the Najdorf Variation. The g-pawn is used as a battering-ram against Black's kingside.

Three principled reactions have developed into the variations **6...e6**, **6...e5** and **6...♘g4**.

6 ♗e3 e6

6   ...   e6

This used to be an innocent invitation to transpose to an 'ordinary' line of the Scheveningen Variation with an 'ordinary' move like **7 ♗e2** or **7 f4**. Nowadays everyone behind the black pieces knows that he has to reckon first and foremost with a much sharper plan:

7 f3 (D)

White also has the even sharper **7 g4**. This move shows a willingness to sacrifice a whole piece for a transition to Keres-like territory, for after 7...e5 8 ♘f5 g6 the knight cannot move. White is hoping to obtain sufficient compensation after 9 g5 gxf5 10 exf5. A critical reply to this ferocious treatment of the opening is 10...d5, intending 11 gxf6 d4, with vast complications.

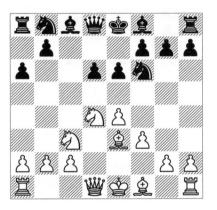

Black has to decide how to weather the storm of g4-g5. One of the major starting points of this line arises after **7...b5** 8 ♕d2 ♘bd7 9 g4 h6 10 0-0-0 ♗b7. One critical line is 11 h4 b4 and now 12 ♘a4 ♕a5 13 b3 ♘c5. The ultra-sharp alternative 12 ♘ce2 d5 13 ♗h3!? dxe4 14 g5 has also caused a few headaches. Instead of 9...h6, there is the option of playing 9...♘b6, vacating d7 for the other knight.

Paradoxically, it is slightly more solid to castle 'into it' and quickly mobilize the kingside by playing **7...♘c6** 8 ♕d2 ♗e7 9 g4 0-0 10 0-0-0 ♘xd4 11 ♗xd4 b5, analogous to 6...♘c6 against the Keres Attack (see page 432).

6 ♗e3 e5

6 ... e5

Like 6...e6, this move started out in life as a fairly quiet variation. Just as in the 6 ♗e2 line, White was merely intending to keep the black fury in check and was hoping, in some nice and quiet little way, to 'do something' with the d5-square in the distant future. Black, on the other hand, was satisfied with having diminished White's attacking chances on the kingside and was counting on obtaining some form of counterplay on the queenside, also in the distant future. In those days **7 ♘f3** was the usual move. This blocks the f-pawn, but White is hoping to develop his king's bishop actively on c4 (and have an escape-square ready at b3). But it turned out to be quite uncertain whether this strategy really promises White anything after the simple 7...♗e7 8 ♗c4 0-0 9 0-0 ♗e6. Another solid reply is 7...♕c7, preventing 8 ♗c4 altogether.

However, the real success story of 6 ♗e3 is built on another plan:

7 ♘b3

Just like in the 6...e6 variation, White intends to play f3, followed by g4. If he succeeds in driving the knight away from f6, the knight jump ♘d5 might well become very powerful indeed. Therefore it is useful for Black to put his queen's bishop on e6. The most important starting point of this line arises after the following moves:

7 ... ♗e6
8 f3 (D)

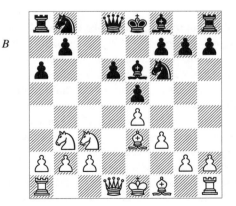

Black's 'normal' moves in this position are **8...♘bd7** and **8...♗e7**. After 8...♘bd7 9 g4 Black often does not stop to prevent g5 and counterattacks immediately with 9...b5 10 g5 b4 or 9...♘b6 10 g5 ♘h5.

A radical and unorthodox alternative is to nip the advance g4-g5 in the bud with **8...h5** or 8...♗e7 9 ♕d2 (9 g4 would be premature in this position because of 9...d5! 10 g5 d4) 9...h5.

6 ♗e3 ♘g4

| 6 | ... | ♘g4 |

This move came into fashion in the 1990s, after it became clear that it is more than just an impulsive reflex, for after White's natural reply, Black has a clear plan of action, daring of course but perfectly logical:

7	♗g5	h6
8	♗h4	g5
9	♗g3	♗g7 (D)

Black could be said to be playing an enlarged Dragon Variation. With his g-pawn on g5 rather than g6, his position is more threatening and aggressive, yet at the same time more vulnerable. White can attack his pawn-chain at once with h4 and the f5-square is a potential weakness (inviting White to play ♘f5, for instance).

White's main problem is the revitalizing of his queen's bishop, which has ended up in an offside position at g3. The obvious way of doing so is to play f3, followed by ♗f2, but the immediate **10 f3??** is a bad mistake because of 10...♘e3, when 11 ♕d2 ♗xd4 12 ♕xd4 ♘xc2+ costs White his queen. Speaking in general terms, one could say that White either has to solve this problem (i.e. find a way to play f3

anyway) or attack the weak points in the enemy position before Black has time to consolidate.

10 ♕d2, 10 ♗e2 and 10 h3 seem to have surfaced as the main lines. **10 ♕d2** is usually met by 10...♘c6 11 ♘b3 b5 12 f3 ♘ge5, **10 ♗e2** is answered with 10...h5, when 11 h4 and 11 ♗xg4 ♗xg4 12 f3 are both major lines, and **10 h3** is a move that keeps all options open. After 10...♘e5 both the quiet 11 f3 ♘bc6 12 ♗f2 and the aggressive 11 ♘f5 have been played.

Dragon Variation

| 5 | ... | g6 (D) |

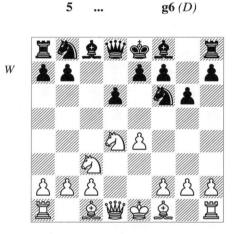

Finally, we arrive at the original point of 2...d6: to enable Black to fianchetto his king's bishop, the plan that had once worked so beautifully in the Classical Variation until that route got booby-trapped by the Richter-Rauzer and Sozin Attacks.

But the joy of those players who went through this transformation of the Sicilian in the middle of the 20th century was short-lived. For as early as the 1950s, it became clear that the new move-order, though it does indeed offer Black a rock-solid route *to* the Dragon Variation, also offers *White* a new and very dangerous weapon to fight it. Unlike the Classical Variation move-order, where White has already played ♗e2 before ...g6, 2...d6 gives White the opportunity to play ♗e3, f3, ♕d2 and 0-0-0, followed (in due course) by ♗h6 and h4-h5. This is the **Yugoslav Attack**. Though perhaps not really a refutation of Black's opening play, this plan radically changes what was meant as a dynamic positional idea into a razor-sharp and deeply analysed complex of variations.

6 ♗e3

This is the introductory move of the Yugoslav Attack, which has been the absolute main line of the Dragon Variation for well over half a century by now. But there are other moves, which may be important for players who, for whatever reason, do not want to be engaged in a theoretical duel.

To begin with, White can 'simply' play **6 ♗e2**. This is called the Classical Dragon nowadays and it brings us, after 6...♗g7 7 0-0 ♘c6 *(D)*, to the identical position that used to be reached via 6 ♗e2 g6 7 0-0 ♗g7 in the Classical Variation.

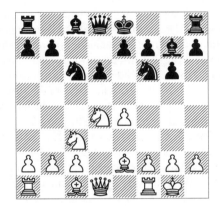

Now, after **8 ♗e3** 0-0, White would like to continue **9 f4**, but this move allows 9...♕b6, when the situation is difficult for White, who faces no fewer than three unpleasant threats: 10...♕xb2, 10...♘xe4 and 10...♘g4. For this reason, **9 ♘b3** is the usual move, which leads, after 9...♗e6 10 f4, to another critical position. The classical moves are 10...♕c8 (to prevent 11 f5 and if possible to simplify the position with ...♗g4) and 10...♘a5 (in order to meet 11 f5 with 11...♗c4).

A modern deviation from this line starts with **8 ♘b3** straightaway, with the idea of either developing the bishop more aggressively on g5 or of continuing with the restrained 9 ♖e1 and 10 ♗f1 to reinforce e4.

The immediate **6 f4** is one of the oldest weapons against the Dragon. The idea is to punish Black for his neglect of the centre with 6...♗g7 7 e5. Most players prefer to dampen White's enthusiasm a little by replying 6...♘c6 or 6...♘bd7.

White's most solid option is undoubtedly to play **6 g3**. By fianchettoing his king's bishop, White protects e4 and discourages any attempts to play ...d5. He is hoping that his spatial advantage will yield dividends in the distant middlegame, when ♘d5 may become a possibility. Interestingly, 6...♘c6 has turned out to be the main line here, with the idea of exchanging knights on d4: **7 ♗g2 ♘xd4 8 ♕xd4 ♗g7 9 0-0 0-0** followed by 10...♗e6 (threatening 11...♘d5), forcing White's queen to retreat. Should White want to avoid this, he will have to withdraw the knight from d4, for 7 ♗e3 is strongly met by 7...♘g4. After **7 ♘de2 ♗g7 8 ♗g2 0-0 9 0-0**, for instance, Black has 9...♖b8 followed by ...b5-b4, obtaining active play on the queenside.

6 ♗c4 *(D)* is a move with two faces.

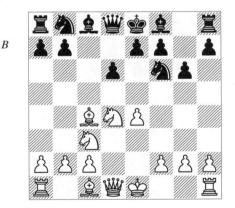

If it is intended as an alternative start of the Yugoslav Attack, White should be aware of the fact that after 6...♗g7 7 ♗e3 ♘c6, **8 f3** leads to a position from the Accelerated Dragon where Black has the treacherous 8...♕b6 (see page 418). But 6 ♗c4 may also be the start of a totally different plan. If **8 h3** instead, another subvariation from the Accelerated Dragon arises, albeit not (yet) an exact transposition: 2...♘c6 3 d4 cxd4 4 ♘xd4 g6 5 ♘c3 ♗g7 6

♗e3 ♘f6 7 ♗c4 ♕a5 (see page 418). Now that Black has not committed himself to ...♕a5, there are a few tactical problems for White: if after 8 h3 0-0 White plays 9 0-0, Black can reply 9...♘xe4 10 ♘xe4 d5 and if 9 ♗b3 there is 9...♘a5 to be taken into account. Remarkably though, in practice many players ignore these options and simply continue 9 0-0 ♗d7 10 ♗b3 ♖c8 or even 10...♕a5 after all.

6   ...   ♗g7

Unlike in the Najdorf Variation, **6...♘g4??** is not an option because of 7 ♗b5+ ♗d7 8 ♕xg4.

7   f3

Now if **7 ♗c4** the 'reflex action' 7...♘g4 *is* possible since 8 ♗b5+ can be met by 8...♔f8.

7   ...   ♘c6

8   ♕d2

This is by far the most popular move. The immediate **8 ♗c4** allows 8...♕b6 (as mentioned in the paragraph above on 6 ♗c4). It should be added though that many Dragon players do not trust this variation and simply continue 8...0-0 instead.

8   ...   0-0 *(D)*

This is the starting point of a sophisticated and deeply-analysed complex of variations. The first dividing line is drawn between **9 0-0-0** and **9 ♗c4**.

9 0-0-0 allows the counter-punch **9...d5**. It looks highly improbable that Black can really

afford this move, but the point is revealed if after 10 exd5 ♘xd5 11 ♘xc6 bxc6 White unsuspectingly takes the bait by **12 ♘xd5** cxd5 13 ♕xd5. After 13...♕c7! (based on 14 ♕xa8 ♗f5!) Black has lost a pawn but he has gained three vitally important open lines (the b- and c-files and the a1-h8 diagonal). Most players prefer the more circumspect **12 ♗d4**, trying to exchange the powerful g7-bishop. Just how complex the Dragon variation really is, is illustrated by the fact that after 12...e5 13 ♗c5 Black does not fear the loss of the exchange at f8 and calmly replies 13...♗e6.

Of course, there is no compelling need to venture 9...d5. The alternative **9...♘xd4** 10 ♗xd4 ♗e6 is the starting point of another multitude of very sharp variations.

The consequences of **9 ♗c4** are even more difficult to fathom. Almost every imaginable scheme of development has been tried against this move. Black's main task is to keep enough pressure on White's queenside to prevent him from devoting his full attention (and attacking power!) to the kingside. A standard follow-up is 9...♗d7 10 0-0-0, when the main line (if such a term is applicable to a continuously evolving universe like the Dragon Variation) goes **10...♖c8** 11 ♗b3 and after **11...♘e5** 12 h4, when the choice between 12...h5 and 12...♘c4 13 ♗xc4 ♖xc4 causes a major division of minds. Of late the relatively simple plan of playing **11...♘xd4** 12 ♗xd4 b5 has also become remarkably popular.

Another line that has been analysed down to the last detail over the years (but never really getting there!) is **10...♕a5**, planning to meet 11 ♗b3 with 11...♖fc8 to throw even more firing power into the queenside offensive. Just as an example, to give the reader a glimpse of what the daily life of a Dragon player looks like: this variation might continue 12 h4 ♘e5 13 h5 ♘xh5 14 ♗h6 ♗xh6 15 ♕xh6 ♖xc3 16 bxc3 ♖c8 17 ♘f5 ♗xf5 18 exf5 ♕xc3 19 fxg6 ♕a1+ 20 ♔d2 ♕c3+ 21 ♔c1, leading to a draw by perpetual check.

Alekhine Defence

1	e4	♘f6 *(D)*

This move used to be played sporadically during the 19th century, but never at top level and never without receiving slighting comments such as 'a curiosity' or worse. It was only when Alexander Alekhine (1892-1946) started to play 1...♘f6 in 1921 that the move *had* to be taken seriously, for an opening idea of the great Alekhine simply could not be cast aside with superficial and shallow commentary. "What I play is theory" was not one of his dictums for nothing.

And very soon this provocative move turned out to fit excellently into the then prevailing intellectual climate of critical investigation of all classical dogma. It has even been called "a striking example of the modern ideas, held by almost every great master in the first years after World War I". Contemporaries of Alekhine received his new move with great enthusiasm, and theory of the new opening flourished. After World War II this enthusiasm deteriorated, but in the 1960s and 1970s the fire was rekindled when a new generation of world-class players again used 1...♘f6 to challenge predominant (and rusty) views on opening theory.

	2	e5

One of the great attractions of the Alekhine Defence is that White has very little opportunity of steering the game in a different direction. The only serious alternative to 2 e5 is **2 ♘c3** (**2 d3** being really too tame to cause any theoretical development). But in the first place this move allows a transposition to the Vienna Game with 2...e5 and secondly White has to find an answer to the aggressive 2...d5. This variation has developed in two directions. White can either try **3 e5**, which can be met with 3...♘fd7, 3...♘e4 and even 3...d4, or **3 exd5 ♘xd5 4 ♗c4**. The latter variation was taken very seriously and analysed at top level in the days of Alekhine himself, but nowadays it is mostly a variation for the *avoiders* of main lines. Black has little difficulty obtaining a satisfactory position after 4...♘b6 5 ♗b3 ♘c6 or 4...e6 and the same can be said about White. Both sides are saving their energy for the upcoming middlegame.

2	...	♘d5 *(D)*

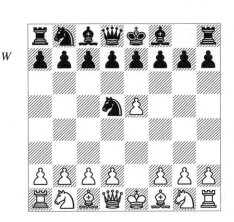

This is just as provocative a square for the knight as f6, and accepting the challenge by chasing the knight again with **3 c4 ♘b6 4 c5** must be regarded as a true test of Black's opening play. After 4...♘d5 both 5 ♘c3 and 5 ♗c4

are played. The sharpest option is to combine these moves and play 5 &c4 e6 6 ♘c3. White is hoping to obtain sufficient compensation for the pawn he is sacrificing, after 6...♘xc3 7 dxc3 &xc5 (7...♘c6 is the more cautious move) 8 ♕g4.

Another possibility is to play 3 ♘c3 ♘xc3 4 dxc3 (or 4 bxc3) at once. Again White is hoping to take advantage of the many open files and diagonals for a speedy development, but without the extra complication of the loose pawn at c5.

3   d4

This level-headed move is unchallenged as the main line. White keeps the option of playing c4 in reserve and does not make any unnecessary concessions. The crucial question is what to do after Black's thematic reply:

3   ...   d6 *(D)*

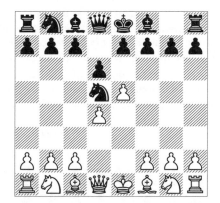

The positional tension is mounting. Does White have to allow his e-pawn to be exchanged and perhaps become a target for counterattack? Does he have to exchange on d6 himself, saying goodbye to the best part of his space advantage and its inherent potential attacking chances on the kingside?

There are no easy answers to these questions, nor is the Alekhine Defence an easy opening to play, either for Black or for White. To have arrived at this conclusion was sufficient for Alekhine and his fellow pioneers to justify 1...♘f6. And even today this will be all the encouragement and theoretical knowledge some players are likely to need.

But for those who *do* want to know more I shall continue a little further. There are three main lines for White. The sharpest option is to create as broad a pawn-centre as possible by playing **4 c4 ♘b6 5 f4**. This is the **Four Pawns Attack**. The most cautious is to take on d6. This is the **Exchange Variation**, which (for reasons that will be explained later) is most accurately reached via **4 c4 ♘b6 5 exd6**.

Between these two extremes of bravado and modesty lies the middle way of **4 ♘f3**. This simple, yet powerful developing move has been called the **Modern Variation** ever since the 1930s.

Four Pawns Attack

4   c4   ♘b6
5   f4 *(D)*

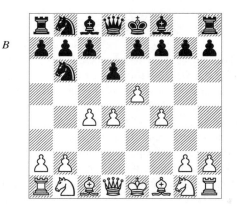

This uncompromising approach has brought White both glorious victories and crushing defeats. But more than anything else, it is the most heavily analysed of White's options. A certain ready knowledge of the variation complex is a primary requirement for both players.

5   ...   dxe5
6   fxe5   ♘c6

The most usual move, but some players prefer **6...c5**. Strategically this idea is totally correct (in the end Black will always have to attack White's central formation with either ...c5 or ...f6) and it contains a few enticing tactical points, but of course it is also extremely risky to offer White an even more threatening pawn-centre. The most important starting position arises after 7 d5 e6 (threatening 8...♕h4+ 9 g3 ♕e4+ so White has no time to play 8 d6) 8 ♘c3 exd5 9 cxd5 and now 9...c4 intending 10...♗b4.

7 ♗e3

The straightforward **7 ♘f3** allows the powerful reply 7...♗g4. After 7 ♗e3 Black has to develop the bishop to a slightly less active square.

7 ... ♗f5
8 ♘c3 e6
9 ♘f3 *(D)*

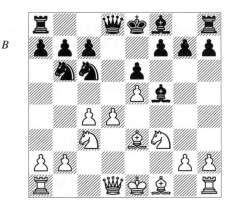

Black now has a great many options for putting pressure on White's centre. He can play **9...♗b4** in order to contain the threatened 10 d5. **9...♘b4**, intending 10 ♖c1 c5, is a possibility. Even with the loss of tempo (...♗f5-g4) **9...♗g4** is worth a try, the point being that the seemingly easy reply 10 ♗e2 ♗xf3 11 ♗xf3? fails to 11...♘xc4. **9...♕d7** with the idea ...0-0-0 or ...♖d8!? has been played.

But most of the attention has always gone to what is both the most modest and the most provocative move:

9 ... ♗e7

If White now simply continues his kingside development with **10 ♗e2** 0-0 11 0-0, Black attacks the centre with 11...f6, when after 12 exf6 ♗xf6 13 ♕d2 the strength of White's remaining centre pawns is more or less balanced by the pressure of Black's pieces *on* those pawns.

But the most critical move is **10 d5**. This can lead to truly chaotic situations. After 10...exd5 11 cxd5 ♘b4, the d5-pawn is attacked and

12...♘c2+ is threatened, but 12 ♘d4 parries the threats and attacks the f5-bishop. If now 12...♗d7 (12...♗g6 is strongly met by 13 ♗b5+) the *very* ambitious play 13 e6 fxe6 14 dxe6 ♗c6 15 ♕g4. White is prepared to sacrifice a whole rook for the initiative: 15...♗h4+ 16 g3 ♗xh1 17 0-0-0.

Exchange Variation

4 c4 ♘b6
5 exd6 *(D)*

An uncomplicated treatment of the opening. White is satisfied with an easy development for his pieces and makes no immediate effort to blow his opponent off the board.

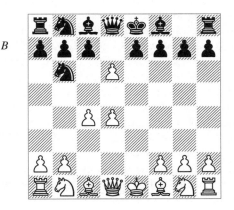

Black has three ways of recapturing on d6, but **5...♕xd6** is unattractive since 6 c5 forces Black to put his queen on a rather unfortunate square: e6. This is in fact why the Exchange Variation is usually prefaced by 4 c4. If 4 exd6 immediately, there is no objection whatsoever to 4...♕xd6, when 5 c4 can be met by 5...♘f6.

So the real choice is between **5...exd6** and **5...cxd6**. Both moves are about equally popular.

By playing **5...exd6**, Black creates the same symmetrical type of position that we have seen in the Petroff Defence and the Exchange Variation of the French, but with two small differences. Since Black's d-pawn is not on d5 (yet), his pawn-chain is more flexible and since White has already played c4 *his* pawn-chain is (paradoxically) both stronger and weaker for his pawns on c4 and d4 are in need of protection. Black normally picks on d4 first, for instance by playing ...♘c6 and ...♗e7-f6. Another characteristic plan is to play ...d5 at some point, either to open the d-file or to force White to play c5. A possible variation: 6 ♘c3 ♗e7 7 ♘f3 0-0 8 ♗e2 ♗g4 9 b3 (enabling White to take back on f3 with the bishop if necessary, without dropping c4) 9...♘c6 10 ♗e3 ♗f6 11 0-0 d5 12 c5 ♘c8 with the idea of continuing ...♘8e7-f5.

Intuitively, **5...cxd6** is perhaps the more Alekhine-like way of recapturing on d6, since this retains a good deal more of the positional tension. Black still has the option of attacking White's centre with ...d5, but ...e5 may also come in handy. On the other hand, White now has a queenside pawn-majority that offers him a clear long-term strategic perspective.

A straightforward (though by no means a forced) variation is **6 ♘f3** g6 7 ♗e2 ♗g7 8 0-0 0-0 9 ♘c3 ♘c6 10 ♗e3 ♗g4 11 b3 d5 12 c5 ♘c8 13 b4 (with the simple point 13...♘xb4?! 14 ♕b3, winning back the pawn at b7). But many players prefer to prevent ...♗g4, for instance by playing **6 ♘c3** g6 **7 h3** ♗g7 8 ♘f3. In this case, after 8...0-0 9 ♗e2 ♘c6 10 0-0 ♗f5 11 ♗e3, the even sharper 11...d5 12 c5 ♘c4 is critical. This position was hotly debated in the 1960s and 1970s. It is important to note that in both these lines, d5 as a reply to ...♘c6 is usually answered aggressively with ...♘a5. If, for instance, 11 d5?! instead of 11 ♗e3 in the latter variation, 11...♘a5! 12 ♘d2? (12 ♘d4 obtains some compensation) 12...♖c8 wins the c-pawn. Nowadays 6 ♘c3 g6 **7 ♗e3** ♗g7 8 ♖c1 is White's most popular plan, specifically designed to deal with this type of problem. By quickly putting his queen's rook on c1, White reinforces both the position of the c3-knight and his c-pawn so that he can freely play d5 or b3 if needed.

Modern Variation

4   ♘f3 *(D)*

White refuses to be tempted into playing the ambitious f4 and keeps both the exchange on d6 and the move c4 in reserve.

4   ...   ♗g4

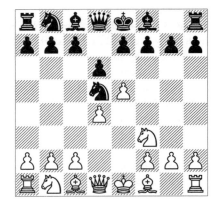

This natural and aggressive bishop move has always held the most prominent place in the books, but it would be a mistake to assume that other moves must be inferior or passive. In fact Black has a number of very interesting alternatives.

To begin with, the most obvious move is to take on e5: **4...dxe5**. This exchange used to be criticized on general grounds, for White's knight is invited to a very good square: 5 ♘xe5 *(D)* (5 dxe5 is far weaker since this would leave the e5-pawn *really* vulnerable after 5...♗g4).

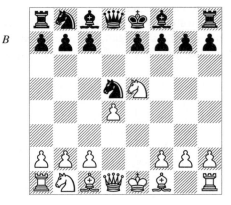

The first player to question this judgement was Bent Larsen, who in an important game against Mikhail Tal coolly continued **5...♘d7**, placing his (unprepared) opponent in a very awkward position. White either has to allow his actively posted knight to be exchanged or he has to try to annihilate his opponent with a knight sacrifice, 6 ♘xf7!? ♔xf7 7 ♕h5+ ♔e6.

The resulting position is extremely complicated. Most players assume that White must be winning somehow, but nobody is certain. Only a handful of specialists, mostly correspondence players, go in for this explosive variation.

Nevertheless, 4...dxe5 is also popular in the ordinary chess world for it has turned out that 5...♘d7 is not the only attempt at 'justification'. **5...g6** and **5...c6** in particular (intending to play ...♘d7 on the next move, when it will be much safer) are played quite often these days, with the latter being one of the main lines of the entire opening in modern practice. If in reply to 5...c6 White continues 6 c4, there is the nasty riposte 6...♘b4, threatening both 7...♗f5 and 7...♕xd4.

Another option is **4...♘c6**. This looks like a fairly blunt developing move, but it is in fact – as so often in the Alekhine – an outright provocation. If White continues (meekly) with 5 ♗e2, taking on e5 is fine for Black. This means that, unless White switches to the Exchange Variation (by playing 5 c4 ♘b6 6 exd6), he has no alternative but to go for an all-out fight, starting with the pawn sacrifice 5 c4 ♘b6 6 e6!?. Since 6...♗xe6? loses a piece to 7 d5, Black has to reply 6...fxe6. White then calmly continues 7 ♘c3, hoping that the extra pawn on e6 makes it harder for Black to develop his pieces. If 7...g6, for example, the advance 8 h4 is very dangerous. Black usually returns the gift by playing 7...e5 8 d5 ♘d4, giving his pieces some air.

The most important alternative to 4...♗g4 has traditionally been **4...g6** *(D)*.

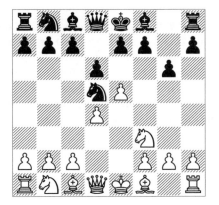

Without retaliating immediately, Black nonetheless increases the pressure against e5 by developing his king's bishop at g7. This line was also thought to be inadequate at first, mainly because of the sharp 5 ♘g5, threatening 6 ♕f3 and 6 ♘xf7, but it was rehabilitated when in the 1970s the calm reply 5...c6 (protecting the d5-knight and preparing to meet 6 ♕f3 with 6...f6) turned out to be perfectly OK for Black. This discovery freed the way for a much deeper investigation of 4...g6 and it soon became a very popular line. There is of course the possibility of transposing to the Exchange Variation with **5 c4 ♘b6 6 exd6**, or by taking on d6 at a later stage (for instance after 5 ♗e2 ♗g7 6 0-0 0-0), but sound as this may be from White's point of view, it does not constitute a refutation of 4...g6. The only really critical move is **5 ♗c4**. More in particular, the position after 5...♘b6 6 ♗b3 ♗g7 *(D)* is of vital importance.

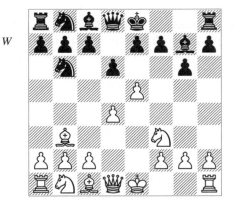

7 ♘g5 is White's sharpest option and **7 a4** the most subtle, but strangely it is the latter move which leads to the greatest complications if Black accepts the challenge and plays 7...dxe5. A starting(!) point of profound analysis is the position which then arises after 8 a5 ♘6d7 9 ♗xf7+ ♔xf7 10 ♘g5+ ♔g8 11 ♘e6 ♕e8 12 ♘xc7 ♕d8 13 ♘xa8 (13 ♘e6 is a draw by repetition) 13...exd4.

5   ♗e2

In this case **5 ♗c4** would be fairly pointless since Black can simply reply 5...e6 without having his queen's bishop bottled up at c8 (which would be a major positional drawback of 5...e6 in response to 4...g6 5 ♗c4). Nor is **5 h3** a particularly good idea for after 5...♗xf3 6 ♕xf3 dxe5 7 dxe5 e6 Black has every prospect of a harmonious piece development while White's e5-pawn is likely to become a target (...♘c6 or ...♘d7).

5   ...   e6

Now **5...dxe5** 6 ♘xe5 ♗xe2 7 ♕xe2 would just be stimulating White's development and the preliminary **5...♗xf3** lacks punch, for after 6 ♗xf3 the desired follow-up 6...dxe5 is refuted by 7 c4! ♘b6 8 ♗xb7. But the *motif* of an exchange on f3 is really important in this line, as is shown by the seemingly modest but very popular little move **5...c6**. Black intends to meet **6 0-0** with 6...♗xf3 7 ♗xf3 dxe5 8 dxe5 e6, when he is hoping to pressurize White's e-pawn with moves like ...♘d7, ...♕c7 and ...♘e7-g6. Players who do not fancy this prospect used to play **6 ♘g5** instead of 6 0-0. This leads, after 6...♗xe2 7 ♕xe2 dxe5 8 dxe5 e6 9 0-0, to the same pawn-formation but with a knight on g5 instead of a bishop on f3, which makes it easier for White to protect e5 and may increase White's attacking chances on the kingside (therefore Black tends to avoid this by playing 6...♗f5). Nowadays **6 c4** ♘b6 7 ♘bd2 is more popular. White prepares to recapture on f3 with the knight, while 7...dxe5 can now be met by 8 ♘xe5!, when 8...♗xe2 9 ♕xe2 ♕xd4 10 ♘df3 followed by 11 ♘g5 is very dangerous.

6   0-0   ♗e7

The most flexible move. **6...♘c6** has the drawback of inviting 7 c4 ♘b6 8 exd6 cxd6 9 d5.

7   c4   ♘b6 *(D)*

In this position the central question still is 'to take or not to take'. By playing **8 exd6** (or **8 h3 ♗h5 9 exd6**) White can bring about what looks like a favourable version of the Exchange Variation, for Black's king's bishop is not positioned on the beautiful a1-h8 diagonal, as it is, for instance, after 4 c4 ♘b6 5 exd6 cxd6 6 ♘f3 g6 (see page 450). But as it turns out, Black's

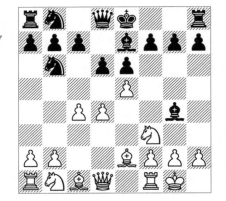

position is still very resilient. After **8 exd6** cxd6 9 ♘c3 0-0 10 ♗e3 the characteristic advance 10...d5 11 c5 creates strong counterplay if followed up with 11...♗xf3! 12 ♗xf3 ♘c4. After the further moves 13 ♗f4 ♘c6 (13...♘xb2 has a boomerang effect: 14 ♕b1 ♘c4 15 ♕xb7) 14 b3 ♘4a5 Black is ready to attack White's pawn-chain with ...♗f6 and ...b6.

For this reason, **8 ♘c3** or **8 h3 ♗h5 9 ♘c3** (White can allow himself the luxury of inserting 8 h3 because after 8...♗xf3 9 ♗xf3 the b7-pawn is under attack) has become the main line. After 8 h3 ♗h5 9 ♘c3 0-0 10 ♗e3 the moment is still not right for Black to take on f3 and e5, while **10...♘c6** (again) allows White to take the initiative with 11 exd6 cxd6 12 d5. Some Alekhine specialists have experimented with **10...a5**, but Black's most popular move remains **10...d5** with the idea of meeting 11 c5 with 11...♗xf3 12 ♗xf3 ♘c4 followed by ...b6. But after 1980 this variation has taken a different course. Instead of the obvious 12 ♗xf3, the seemingly very awkward 12 gxf3 became fashionable. Black cannot then reply with 12...♘c4 because of 13 ♗xc4 dxc4 14 ♕a4 winning a pawn, so he has to retreat. The resulting position (after 12...♘c8 13 f4 for instance) is very solid for Black *but* the initiative is firmly in White's hands (for the time being at least) and this is of course a most unusual situation in the Alekhine Defence!

Pirc Defence

1 e4 d6

So far removed is this opening from the world of classical positional principles that it was too modern even for the 'Hypermodern School', a movement in the 1920s that rebelled against the prevailing dogmas of that age and that produced, for instance, the Alekhine Defence.

Even as 'recently' as 1941, former world champion Max Euwe needed no more than a few lines in his standard work *De Theorie der Schaakopeningen* to dispose of 1...d6, which he could only see as a preparatory move for 2...e5, concluding that "further examination of this move is unnecessary".

It was not until the rise of the King's Indian Defence after World War II, that the ground was prepared for 1...d6 to flourish.

2 d4 ♞f6 (D)

With this move Vasja Pirc (1909-80) put a new opening on the map in the 1940s and 1950s, and it soon came to carry his name (although the Russians also attach the name of Anatoly Ufimtsev to this opening). In the two decades following his pioneering work, 'the Pirc' matured into a full-grown and popular defence to both 1 e4 and 1 d4.

Ironically though, after well over half a century the old **2...e5** has risen from the grave and is sometimes played nowadays, although the more common version of this idea is 2...♞f6 3 ♞c3 e5, which we shall be looking at shortly.

3 ♞c3

To a natural 1 e4 player, this move is probably self-evident. But theory of the Pirc Defence has evolved far enough for two alternatives to be treated as independent variations.

By playing **3 ♝d3**, White has a solid scheme of development in mind that is quite popular against 1...g6. He supports his d-pawn with c3 and completes his kingside development with ♞f3 and 0-0. This is not an attempt to refute the

Pirc, but it has the great merit of not offering Black any chances to strike hard against White's pawn-centre as in the main lines. After **3...g6 4 ♞f3 ♝g7 5 0-0 0-0 6 c3** a position is reached that is usually arrived at via 1 e4 g6 (see page 462). If this does not satisfy Black, he could try something a little more spicy, like **3...e5 4 c3** and now **4...♞c6** or even **4...d5!?**.

3 f3 (D) is a favourite with the 1 d4 players.

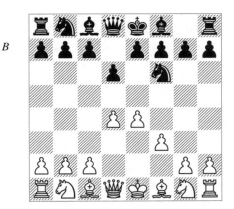

The idea is to continue with c4, transposing to the Sämisch Variation of the King's Indian Defence or something closely resembling this line. Thus, playing 3 f3 is really paying a great

compliment to 1...d6, for quite clearly White prefers a King's Indian to a Pirc! But a more down-to-earth explanation is that this variation probably arises most often via 1 d4, when after 1...d6 White does not like 2 c4 e5 (see page 191) so he plays 2 e4, but then after 2...♘f6 he prefers 3 f3 (followed by c4) to 3 ♘c3 because this move offers a 1 d4 player the chance to remain on familiar ground. After **3...g6** 4 c4 ♗g7 5 ♘c3 we have a King's Indian Sämisch (see page 97), while the alternative **3...e5** 4 d5 (or 4 ♘e2 followed by 5 c4) also gives White what he wants (in a strategic sense). The alternative 4 dxe5 is not bad either, by the way.

3...d5!? is a bold and radical attempt to alter the course of the opening. Black is counting on the move f3 being useless (or worse) in case of 4 exd5 ♘xd5 or 4 e5 ♘fd7 (even 4...♘g8 has been played) and above all play retains a distinct 1 e4 flavour. The typical pawn-formation of the French Defence, for instance, is not far away: 4 e5 ♘fd7 5 f4 e6 6 ♘f3 c5.

3   ...   g6

This is the defining move of the Pirc Defence. By developing his bishop at g7, Black creates the same sort of positional tension as in the King's Indian Defence. He does nothing to prevent White from building a strong pawn-centre, but he will soon start hacking away against it, either with ...e5, ...c5, ...♘c6 in combination with ...♗g4 or ...c6 and ...b5.

In general, play will not be as sharp and complicated as in the King's Indian. The extra move c4 makes White's pawn-formation even more threatening so for Black's counterattack to succeed it has to be even fiercer. Still, the Pirc Defence contains some sharp and dangerous variations.

But before we look at these, there are three alternative third moves for Black which demand our attention. For nowadays **3...e5**, **3...♘bd7** and **3...c6** have become almost as popular as 3...g6. All of them are fairly young (mostly born in the 1980s) and based on interpretations of this position that differ considerably from 3...g6. One could call them trespassers on the land of the Pirc.

3...e5 *(D)* is a move we have seen in the chapter 'Other 1 e4 e5 Openings', for this is a

popular move-order to reach the Philidor Defence (see page 339).

W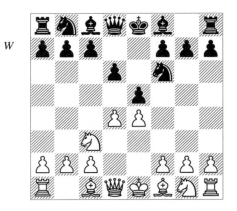

White has a major alternative to allowing this transposition (4 ♘f3 ♘bd7) in 4 dxe5. After 4...dxe5 5 ♕xd8+ ♔xd8 a queenless middlegame arises which looks a little better for White at first glance because Black's king has got stuck in the centre, but whether this theoretical advantage has any practical meaning is moot. The plausible 6 ♗c4 is met by the surprising 6...♗e6 7 ♗xe6 fxe6, when Black's doubled e-pawns are a little vulnerable naturally, but on the other hand they provide Black with a cast-iron grip on the centre.

However, since not every Philidor devotee feels at home in such a simplified, sober position, it is only natural that the alternative **3...♘bd7** has also become quite important. Again, if 4 ♘f3 e5 Black has achieved his goal. But unavoidably, even this subtle move-order has its problems. Black has to find an answer to 4 f4 e5 5 ♘f3 exd4 6 ♕xd4, for instance. This line offers White a space advantage and healthy open lines for his pieces. Remarkably, the most promising defence to this seems to consist in 6...♘c5 7 ♗e3 g6, aiming to put pressure on White's central fortress in the same way as... a 'proper' Pirc.

Finally, there is the somewhat mysterious little move **3...c6**, the **Czech Variation**, called after a group of Czech players who popularized this opening in the 1980s. This idea is of a different calibre altogether. Black is planning to meet 4 f4 with the powerful and unorthodox

4...♕a5. This move not only threatens 5...♘xe4 but also prepares the counter-punch ...e5. No matter how primitive this plan may look, it is not easy for White to come to terms with it. The main line runs 5 ♗d3 e5 6 ♘f3 ♗g4 and produces sharp play. Players who do not feel confident with this usually avoid 4 f4, but even then the opening is likely to run along unorthodox and challenging lines. If 4 ♘f3, for instance, Black has 4...♗g4, creating similar positional problems to the variation 1 d4 d6 2 ♘f3 ♗g4 3 e4 ♘f6 4 ♘c3 e6 (see page 192).

We now return to 3...g6 (D):

This is the real starting position of the Pirc Defence. By playing 2...♘f6, Black has forced his opponent to protect e4, but otherwise White is free to develop as he sees fit.

At first this liberal attitude was – of course – seen as a sign of weakness. Looking at the opening from such a lofty perspective, one is almost obliged to continue aggressively. Thus 4 f4 became the first main line of the Pirc.

However, it soon transpired that Black's position is not easily overrun by power play like this and White is in fact taking some chances himself if he persists in such an attitude. The second and far subtler test of the soundness of the Pirc is 4 ♘f3. White calmly develops his pieces. Does Black have an answer to this too?

Between these two extremes of fierce aggression and alert watchfulness, several other variations have been developed. We shall look into 4 ♗g5 and 4 g3 a little deeper. Other moves, like 4 ♗c4 ♗g7 5 ♕e2 (intending 6 e5)

have never really become popular (always with a few notable exceptions) and fall outside the scope of this book.

So the Pirc Defence was thoroughly examined, and it became a grown-up opening that began to be treated in a more businesslike manner. This culminated, towards the end of the 20th century, in a new system which combined many of the ideas behind the older variations and starts with 4 ♗e3. This method became so popular in such a short period of time that it is only a very slight exaggeration to call this the new main line of the Pirc Defence.

By playing 4 ♗e3, White does not yet commit himself to any particular pawn or piece formation. He can castle queenside or kingside, he can move his f-pawn to f4 or f3 or leave it on f2, and by playing ♕d2 White introduces the possibility of playing ♗h6 (which is also one of the ideas behind 4 ♗g5).

4 f4

4   f4

A gallant move, known as the **Austrian Attack**, throwing down the gauntlet at once. White is threatening to play 5 e5. Or is he?

4   ...   ♗g7

If this natural move were impossible, Black's opening play would have very little future. It is true that **5 e5** is a realistic option, but it is not a fundamental threat to the soundness of the Pirc. In fact 5 e5 is not even aggressive, but designed to simplify the position with **5...dxe5** 6 dxe5. White is hoping to obtain a slight advantage in the queenless middlegame thanks to his space advantage, but practice has shown that after 6...♕xd1+ 7 ♔xd1 ♘g4 8 ♔e1, for instance, Black will eliminate the enemy spearhead with ...f6 sooner or later. Taking back with the f-pawn is less promising than in other variations which we are about to see: after 6 fxe5 ♘d5 Black will find it relatively easy to attack White's centre with ...c5.

Instead of 5...dxe5, even the much sharper **5...♘fd7** has done very well in practice. Black retains the tension in the centre, preparing to strike back very powerfully with ...c5.

5   ♘f3 (D)

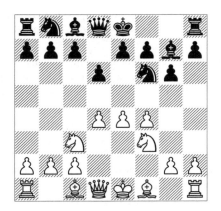

This is the crucial starting position of the Austrian Attack. There are two options for Black: he may want to complete his kingside development by playing **5...0-0** or he may prefer an immediate attack upon White's central formation with **5...c5**.

If **5...0-0** White again has the option of playing **6 e5** (with consequences very similar to 5 e5), but most players prefer one of three developing moves: **6 ♗e2, 6 ♗d3** or **6 ♗e3**.

The best reply to **6 ♗e2** is 6...c5 (or so theory will have it). If White tries to turn the opening into a sort of Benoni by playing 7 d5, Black's counterplay starting with 7...e6 runs like clockwork. The critical option therefore is to play 7 dxc5, when 7...♕a5! 8 0-0 (8 cxd6 ♘xe4 favours Black) 8...♕xc5+ 9 ♔h1 produces a Sicilian-type position. White will try to initiate a kingside attack with moves like f5 and ♕e1-h4. Black will either play the provocative 9...♘bd7 followed by ...a6 and ...b5 (resembling the 6 f4 variation of the Najdorf; see page 438) or he may choose the more solid 9...♘c6 in combination with ...♗g4 and/or ...♘b4.

To avoid 6...c5, many players prefer **6 ♗d3**, for now that e4 is protected White can simply meet 6...c5?! 7 dxc5 ♕a5? with 8 cxd6. Black has tried several other moves instead of 6...c5 and the main lines are 6...♘a6 and 6...♘c6.

6...♘a6 is aimed at achieving the advance ...c5 after all. After 7 0-0 c5 8 d5 a Benoni-like pawn-formation arises. This usually leads to a sharp middlegame with White attacking on the kingside (f5, ♕e1-h4) and Black on the queenside (...b5-b4).

6...♘c6 is slightly less provocative. If 7 0-0, Black intends to attack White's centre in a more 'conventional' way by means of 7...e5 or 7...♗g4. The critical move is 7 e5, for now that Black has put a knight on c6, he cannot easily counterattack with the thematic thrust ...c5. But there are other options. After 7...dxe5 8 fxe5 ♘h5!?, for instance, Black keeps d4 under pressure and prepares ...f6.

White's most recent attempt to win the struggle for domination in the centre is to play **6 ♗e3**. This move prepares ♕d2 and 0-0-0 and does not commit the king's bishop yet to any particular square. It is characteristic for the precision with which all these lines have been examined that it is yet another plan of counterattack that is considered Black's best chance here: 6...b6 with the twofold idea of playing ...♗b7 and ...c5.

The immediate **5...c5** *(D)* forestalls all these options.

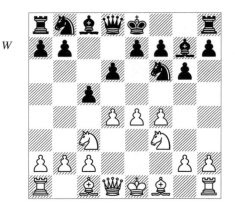

Black is aiming for the same Sicilian-like type of play that we saw in the 5...0-0 6 ♗e2 line, which arises after **6 dxc5 ♕a5 7 ♗d3 ♕xc5**. Now 8 ♕e2 0-0 9 ♗e3 ♕a5 produces a fundamental position. Again, 10...♗g4 in combination with 11...♘c6 is usually seen as Black's most solid plan.

A sharper reaction to 5...c5 is to play **6 ♗b5+**. The idea of this move is a very concrete one (as is often the case with these early checks), for there is something 'wrong' with every possible reply to it. If 6...♘bd7, for instance, the advance 7 e5 is much stronger than on the previous move (the immediate 6 e5 is met by 6...♘fd7). The main line runs 6...♗d7 7 e5 ♘g4, when the razor-sharp 8 e6 is probably White's most dangerous try. The point of this move is to meet **8...fxe6** with 9 ♘g5. This looks extremely menacing but several defensive possibilities have been discovered. There is a beautiful (though not forced) draw by repetition after 9...♗xb5 10 ♘xe6 ♗xd4! 11 ♘xd8 ♗f2+ 12 ♔d2 ♗e3+ 13 ♔e1 ♗f2+. Another complicated line is **8...♗xb5** 9 exf7+ ♔d7! (this is stronger than 9...♔xf7 10 ♘g5+) 10 ♘xb5 ♕a5+ 11 ♘c3 cxd4 12 ♘xd4. This position remains difficult to judge even though it has been analysed very deeply.

4 ♘f3

4   ♘f3

This move poses problems of a more positional nature. We have seen that against a set-up based on f4 Black has two fundamentally sound plans, ...e5 and ...c5, even though the tactical implications are often highly complicated. But if Black chooses either of these plans against 4 ♘f3, will he not end up in a rather dreary version of an 1...e5 or 1...c5 opening?

4   ...   ♗g7 (D)

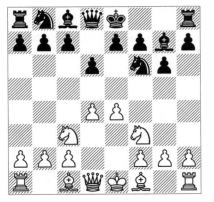

W

5   ♗e2

This modest but sound developing move is often called the **Classical Variation** (or **Classical Pirc**). The seemingly more aggressive **5 ♗c4** has the drawback of inviting 5...0-0 6 0-0 (6 ♕e2 is probably a better move) 6...♘xe4! 7 ♘xe4 d5,

breaking up White's ideal central formation. A more subtle (and indeed more highly regarded) alternative is to play **5 ♗e3** or **5 h3** 0-0 6 ♗e3, postponing the choice of a square for the king's bishop to a later moment. This line is closely connected with the variation 4 ♗e3, which will be dealt with at the end of this chapter.

5   ...   0-0
6   0-0 (D)

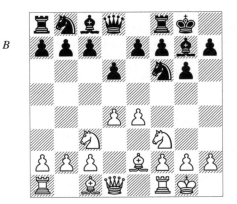

B

Now Black will have to show his hand. What chances does he see for himself in this position, where White has occupied the centre in such a solid, non-fanatical, sound and careful way?

Let us first take a look at what happens if Black plays either **6...e5** or **6...c5** straightaway.

As for **6...e5**, this move is conspicuous by its absence in both theory and practice. And yet there is no immediate objection to it! After 7 dxe5 dxe5 8 ♕xd8 ♖xd8 9 ♘xe5 Black regains the pawn with 9...♘xe4. The reason why this straightforward advance in the centre is obviously so unattractive to a Pirc player (in stark contrast to the comparable 5 ♘f3 variation against the King's Indian Defence; see page 102) must be of a temperamental nature. The sober (not to say barren) position after 9 ♗g5 can hardly be more than just 'slightly better for White', but its most prominent feature is a total lack of targets for counterplay. Black is restricted to a purely defensive role (for the time being at least), which is a big difference from the Exchange Variation of the King's Indian where there is a weak point in White's pawn-structure at d4.

6...c5 is a little more promising in this respect, for if now 7 dxc5 dxc5 8 ♕xd8 ♖xd8 Black has some potential counterchances based on ...♘c6-d4 or ...b6 and ...♗b7. But in this case the critical reply is likely to be 7 d5, transposing to the Schmid Benoni (see page 170).

If Black is happy with either of the above lines, his opening problems are solved. But especially for those who like to play ...e5, there remains an important question: are there any chances of successfully preparing this move?

6...♘bd7 is probably the first option that comes to mind. Unfortunately, this has the drawback of inviting the powerful reply 7 e5, because 7...dxe5? 8 dxe5 ♘g4 gets refuted by 9 e6!, when 9...fxe6? loses to 10 ♘g5. This means that the knight has to move backwards. After 7...♘e8 White supports his e-pawn with 8 ♗f4, when Black's position looks passive.

The alternative **6...♘c6** is more active, but it is also rather provocative of course, for Black is practically begging for 7 d5. The idea is then to continue 7...♘b8 or 7...♘b4 followed by either ...c6 or ...e6. At any rate, this variation creates a certain positional tension. It is therefore quite popular with the more ambitious among Pirc players.

Still, if this were all the Pirc had to offer, the picture would be rather dreary. Fortunately for Black, there are two other moves. Neither of them seems to contribute much to the preparation of ...e5 at first sight, but on closer inspection they both turn out to be extremely useful. These are the real main lines of the Classical Pirc: **6...♗g4** and **6...c6**.

By playing **6...♗g4** *(D)*, Black introduces the possibility of taking on f3, which weakens White's control over the central squares e5 and d4.

The main line is 7 ♗e3 ♘c6, when 8 d5 is answered by 8...♗xf3 9 ♗xf3 ♘e5 10 ♗e2 c6. Thanks to the exchange on f3, Black's development is running much more smoothly than after the immediate 6...♘c6. His piece coordination is also much better, now that one of his minor pieces has been exchanged. Another option for White is simply to play 8 ♕d2. This is a good moment for 8...e5, for although 9 dxe5 is still a realistic move, this exchange is now not as

unpleasant for Black as after 6...e5. The more robust alternative is to play 9 d5, when 9...♘e7 10 ♖ad1 (to prevent Black from nibbling away at White's central pawn-formation with 10...c6) leads to a King's Indian-like position with chances for both sides.

The calm **6...c6** prepares no fewer than three moves that in their turn are a preparation for ...e5: ...♘bd7, ...♕c7 and ...♕a5. This shows up the darker side of White's solid opening system, for he hardly has any means of *permanently* preventing or discouraging ...e5. White usually continues in such a way as to be able to meet ...e5 with dxe5, hoping that his pieces will be just that little bit more active than Black's in the resulting symmetrical pawn-formation. A concrete knowledge of variations is not a primary requirement in this line, but a subtle positional understanding is very useful.

4 ♗g5

4   ♗g5 *(D)*

This move, sometimes called the **Byrne Variation**, was popular in the 1970s, and then faded into the background, but it made a strong recovery at the turn of the century, in the wake of the fast-growing 4 ♗e3 system. On g5 the bishop is more aggressively placed than at e3, but it is also more vulnerable.

Naturally, 4...♗g7 is the first move that comes to mind in this position, but because White has the option of playing 5 ♕d2 and 6 ♗h6, exchanging dark-squared bishops, there has been a thorough search for possible alternatives.

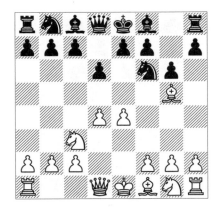

B

This has resulted in **4...c6** becoming a popular move. Black intends to meet 5 ♕d2 with 5...b5. Exchanging on f6 is almost never a problem for Black in this type of position, as long as he makes sure that he can follow up ...exf6 with ...f5, reopening the diagonal for his king's bishop.

But there is no unanimity whatsoever among theoreticians as regards to Black's best fourth move. Probably the classical **4...♗g7** is played slightly more often. Against 5 ♕d2 Black may choose 5...h6 6 ♗h4 g5 7 ♗g3 ♘h5, when the crucial question is who will benefit the most from a possible ...♘xg3. Another option is to play 5...c6 after all, not worrying about 6 ♗h6. I shall return to this subject in the section on 4 ♗e3. White's most popular reply, by the way, is the sharper 6 f4.

4 g3

4	g3

In view of the great importance of the g3 system against the King's Indian Defence, it seems obvious that this could be an interesting set-up against the Pirc as well. Strangely though, this is a relatively recent variation that was not even mentioned in most opening manuals before 1980.

White makes no effort to refute Black's opening play by violent means. By giving his e4-pawn a firm backing, he is hoping to defuse Black's expected counterattack. Thus White is in effect hoping – just like in the Classical Variation – to reduce the Pirc to a passive opening.

4	...	♗g7
5	♗g2	0-0
6	♘ge2 (D)	

This is a more harmonious development for the king's knight than **6 ♘f3**, although that move is certainly playable as well.

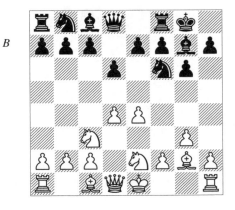

B

6	...	e5

There are other moves, such as **6...♘bd7** or **6...c6**, but unlike in the Classical Variation the immediate 6...e5 has no drawbacks, since there is no advantage to be gained from 7 dxe5. In principle, exchanging on e5 is not what White is after in the g3 system, nor is d5 the powerful option it is in comparable openings, such as the King's Indian Defence, where having a pawn on c4 strengthens White's queenside position. Quite the contrary, the idea of the g3 variation is to maintain the tension in the centre. With his e4-pawn firmly protected, White is working on the assumption that an exchange at d4 is not all that attractive for Black. But other forms of counterplay are not easy to find! So the opening battle revolves almost entirely around one theme: when is Black going to take on d4 and what follow-up does he have in mind?

Another characteristic of the g3 system is that a plan based on ...c5 is hard to achieve. **6...c5**, for instance, is not a problem for White, for after 7 dxc5 dxc5 (7...♕a5? makes no sense now that 8...♘xe4 is not a threat) 8 ♕xd8 ♖xd8 9 e5 or 9 ♗e3 the g2-bishop becomes very powerful.

7	h3 (D)

This subtle preventive move is more often played than **7 0-0**, since in that case 7...♘c6 cannot comfortably be met with 8 ♗e3 in view of 8...♘g4.

B

This is the most important starting point of the g3 system. Just as in the King's Indian Defence, Black now has a few solid options but also some astonishingly complicated ones. For instance, after **7...♘c6** 8 ♗e3 the straightforward 8...exd4 9 ♘xd4 ♗d7 10 0-0 ♖e8 11 ♖e1 ♕c8 is sometimes played. The point of this idea is to meet 12 ♔h2 with the absolutely uncompromising 12...♖e5!? 13 f4 ♖h5.

The alternative **7...c6** is more cautious. Black allows himself as much time for delaying ...exd4 as he can find. After 8 a4 (to prevent 8...b5) 8...a5 9 0-0 Black develops his queenside with 9...♘a6 10 ♗e3 ♘b4 11 ♕d2 ♗e6, preparing both ...♗c4 and the counter-thrust ...d5.

4 ♗e3

4   ♗e3 (D)

Until the late 1980s, White usually prefaced this move with **4 f3**, to prevent 4...♘g4. This now seems to have become obsolete for two reasons. First of all, there never was that much point in playing 4...♘g4 anyway, since White simply replies 5 ♗g5 without really being disturbed in his piece development. The second and far deeper reason is that the whole idea behind 4 ♗e3 has been completely transformed. From a one-dimensional (though not harmless!) attacking scheme, based on ♕d2, ♗h6, 0-0-0, f3, g4 and h4-h5, it has become an extremely subtle variation where – depending on Black's reaction

B

– White has a choice between a plan with f3, a plan with f4 or 'just' ♘f3 followed by ♗e2 (or ♗d3, or ♗c4) and 0-0, sometimes accompanied by h3, sometimes not. The latter option is in fact a variation on the idea of the Classical Pirc and is aimed at smothering Black's counterplay. 4 ♗e3 has come full circle.

Just as against 4 ♗g5, Black now faces a delicate choice. Does he simply continue **4...♗g7** or does he prefer **4...c6**, initiating queenside counterplay at once? The latter move has the undeniable advantage of saving a tempo if ♕d2 and ♗h6 can be met by ...♗f8xh6 instead of ...♗g7xh6. Postponing ...♗g7 has in fact become an art in itself in this variation. One of the main lines, for instance, goes (after 4...c6) 5 ♕d2 b5 6 ♗d3 (to protect e4 and allowing the queen's knight to regroup comfortably to e2 after ...b4) 6...♘bd7 7 ♘f3 e5. Here 5 h3 is a major alternative. The tactical point of this move is that, now that 6...♘g4 is no longer possible, 5...b5 runs into the powerful 6 e5. The strategic idea is to meet 5...♗g7 (or 5...♘bd7) with 6 f4.

The 'normal' **4...♗g7** again has the advantage of not yet committing Black to a plan with ...b5. Depending on further developments, Black could also lash out with ...c5 or ...e5. If 5 ♕d2, for instance, Black can reply 5...♘g4 6 ♗g5, when 6...c5!? is a serious option, while 6...h6 7 ♗h4 g5 8 ♗g3 e5 is also played. And yet, even here 5...c6 is the most popular move. Black is simply not afraid of ♗h6, as long as he has not castled kingside. If 6 ♗h6, Black plays 6...♗xh6 7 ♕xh6 ♕a5. Ironically perhaps, many players prefer the 'old-fashioned' 6 f3 in this case.

Other 1 e4 Openings

1 e4 *(D)*

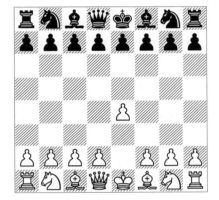

B

We have almost come to the end of our long and tiring journey through the world of chess openings. But for some the best part is yet to come! For in this final chapter we shall take a look at two openings that are both theoretically important *and* popular, even though they did not get a chapter of their own in this book (for which I offer my apologies). These are **1...g6**, an opening that has been given many names over the years, but is generally known as the **Modern Defence**, and **1...d5**, the **Scandinavian Defence**.

Furthermore, **1...♞c6** and **1...b6** should be mentioned, but on these moves I shall be brief:

1...♞c6 *(D)* is the **Nimzowitsch Defence**.

This is a very old opening, but it has never really come out of that dark and swampy area on the fringes of opening theory, where only the reckless and desperate ever venture. It *might* result in a difficult, unorthodox opening battle, but if Black does not know really well what he is doing he is likely to end up creating difficulties only for himself.

The relatively best charted line of this opening runs **2 d4 d5**, a variation on the idea of the Scandinavian. The point is that after 3 exd5

W

♕xd5 the d4-pawn is attacked so White cannot play 4 ♞c3. The main lines are 3 e5 and the pawn sacrifice 3 ♞c3 dxe4 (3...e6 transposes to a minor variation of the French; see page 353) 4 d5. Another interpretation of 1...♞c6 which is even more provocative is 2...e5.

Those who prefer to avoid these rather sharp variations usually play **2 ♞f3**, inviting Black to return to 'the civilized world' with 2...e5. It is of course more in the spirit of Black's adventurous first move to continue 2...d6 instead, in order to meet 3 d4 with 3...♞f6 4 ♞c3 ♝g4. This variation is closely related to 1 d4 d6 2 ♞f3 ♝g4 3 e4 ♞f6 4 ♞c3 e6 (see page 192) but with a knight on c6, the advance d5, which is the strategically correct plan anyway, becomes even more attractive.

Equally, **1...b6** has been known for a long time, yet for this move official recognition has been even less forthcoming. In fact, theoretical manuals for well over four centuries agree that this is a fairly passive opening move. Black allows his opponent to take up a strong central position for free, without any immediate prospects of counterplay. The difference between the position after 2 d4 ♝b7 on the one hand and the one after 1 e4 g6 2 d4 ♝g7 on the other is that in the latter case a counterattack with ...c5 is a realistic prospect, whereas the corresponding thrust ...f5 in the former case is not. Only after (1 e4 b6 2 d4 ♗b7) 3 ♗d3 is 3...f5 a possibility (based on tactical motifs), but the position arising after 4 exf5! ♗xg2 5 ♕h5+ g6 6 fxg6 is generally considered too dangerous for Black, so even this is hardly ever played. The normal move is 3...e6, when 4 ♘f3 c5 5 c3 allows White to consolidate his central position.

Modern Defence

1   ...   g6

In an earlier chapter I have already commented on this move, which is equally playable against 1 d4 and 1 e4 (see page 193). Black gives his opponent a free hand in the centre, but not without a reason. Just as in the Pirc – of which 1...g6 is in fact a more radical version – Black has a veritable arsenal of strategies at his disposal to strike against White's central formation with great force.

2   d4   ♗g7 (D)

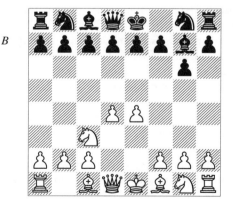

The most important difference between 1...d6 and 1...g6 is that 1...g6 allows **3 c4** (see page 194) transposing to the King's Indian Defence or a related 1 d4 opening.

Less drastic than such a shift from 1 e4 to 1 d4, but quite important nevertheless, is the difference that by playing 1...g6 rather than 1...d6 Black allows his opponent a set-up based on **3 c3**. In the Pirc this is normally impossible since playing 1...d6 and 2...♘f6 provokes ♘c3. Although, as we have seen, White may try to

adopt a c3 plan anyway by playing 3 ♗d3 instead of 3 ♘c3 – leaving the question just how dangerous this set-up actually is aside for the moment – there are a number of alternatives to 3...g6 in this case (see page 453). No such escape-route is available after 1...g6.

A major starting position of this line (which is also relevant to the opening 1 ♘f3 g6 2 e4; see page 249), arises after **3 c3 d6 4 ♘f3** (or **3 ♘f3** d6 4 c3) 4...♘f6 5 ♗d3 0-0 6 0-0. Black's classical plan is to prepare ...e5 by playing 6...♘c6 or 6...♘bd7. The main alternative, aimed at unbalancing the position rather than equalizing it, is 6...c5.

But it is obvious that, in an opening where White is given a free hand so emphatically, White *can* play anything he likes. For instance, a development of the king's bishop on c4 is much more popular here than in the Pirc (see page 455). After **3 ♘f3 d6 4 ♗c4 ♘f6** White has 5 ♕e2, threatening (or at least toying with the idea of) 6 e5.

3...c5 is an alternative reply to 3 ♘f3. This invites transpositions to various other openings. Both 4 ♘c3 cxd4 5 ♘xd4 ♘c6 and 4 c4 cxd4 5 ♘xd4 produce a variation of the Accelerated Dragon of the Sicilian Defence and 4 d5 is likely to lead to some variation of the Benoni or another. If White does not fancy these transpositions, he has two 'independent' alternatives, 4 dxc5 and 4 c3.

3   ♘c3 (D)

In spite of having a wealth of alternatives, this robust developing move is White's most popular choice (apart from 3 c4). White makes no attempt to refute 1...g6 and offers his opponent the chance to 'return' to a regular Pirc by playing 3...d6 and 4...♘f6. The question now is 'are there any other moves?'. In other words: what is the point of playing 1...g6 rather than 1...d6?

> **3   ...   d6**

There are two alternatives.

By playing **3...c5**, Black opens the door to the same transpositions that we saw after 3 ♘f3 c5. If 4 ♘f3 cxd4 5 ♘xd4 ♘c6 we have a Sicilian Defence and if 4 d5 it will be a Benoni. Theoretically, 4 dxc5 is perhaps the crucial move, or at any rate the hardest to judge. 4...♕a5 regains the pawn, but just exactly how dangerous is White's initiative after 5 ♗d2 ♕xc5 6 ♘d5?

3...c6 *(D)* looks slower than 3...c5, yet this is in fact a highly venomous move.

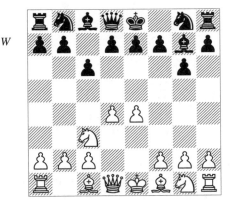

W

Black's idea is to meet **4 f4** – the old main line of the Pirc and superficially very attractive in this position as well – with 4...d5 5 e5 h5 (or 5...♘h6). Unlike the similar situation in the Advance Variation of the Caro-Kann, Black's first priority in this variation is to block White's kingside pawn-phalanx. If he succeeds, Black will eventually take the initiative on the queenside in classical fashion with ...c5. This strategy is likely to produce some heavyweight positional tussling, where a good general grasp of the position is much more important than concrete knowledge of variations. For example: 5...h5 6 ♗e3 ♘h6 7 ♘f3 ♗g4 8 h3 ♗xf3 9 ♕xf3 ♘f5 10 ♗f2 h4 11 ♗d3 e6. The kingside

is closed off for the time being. Everything now depends on which side will be the first or the more successful in getting his queenside moving: Black with ...c5 or White with c4?

Players who do not like or trust this variation usually prefer **4 ♘f3 d5 5 h3**. White prevents ...♗g4 and does not let himself be provoked into playing e5. This is a position which also arises via the Caro-Kann (1 e4 c6 2 d4 d5 3 ♘c3 g6 4 h3 ♗g7 5 ♘f3, for example) and which often leads – after an eventual ...dxe4 – to a typical Caro-Kann pawn-formation.

4 ♗c4 is another plausible move. It is true that this does not actually prevent 4...d5, for if 5 exd5 Black regains his pawn with 5...b5 6 ♗b3 b4 7 ♘ce2 cxd5, but most 3...c6 players do not seem to trust this line and prefer the less drastic 4...d6 instead. This produces a Pirc-like variation, where one of the theoretical issues is 5 ♕f3!? e6 6 ♘ge2.

We now return to 3...d6 *(D)*:

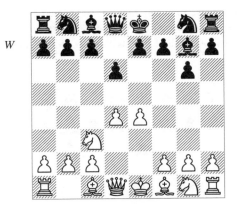

W

White now faces the same basic choice as in the starting position of the Pirc Defence. Does he go for the classical aggression of **4 f4**, the classical solidity of **4 ♘f3** or something in between? And what about the modern **4 ♗e3** and other moves that we have investigated in the Pirc? Are they stronger or weaker, now that Black has played ...♗g7 before ...♘f6?

Let us first examine the consequences of **4 f4**. Here there are three variations that have all been more or less accepted as playable (though all of them are regarded as riskier than a transposition to the Pirc with 4...♘f6).

The most closely related to a regular Pirc is probably **4...♘c6**. This is an obvious move, for 5 d5 can be countered with the excellent 5...♘d4. The more restrained reply 5 ♗e3 ♘f6 6 ♘f3 0-0 7 ♗e2 is probably critical.

4...c6 is a more profound move (which is not to say that it is better!). The idea is not just to be able to play ...b5 but also to prepare ...♕b6, increasing the pressure against d4 *and* against b2. This immediately produces some rather difficult strategic problems, for instance if play continues 5 ♘f3 ♗g4 6 ♗e3 ♕b6 7 ♕d2. It is clear that White does not have to worry about 7...♕xb2 8 ♖b1 ♕a3 9 ♖xb7, but what about 7...♗xf3 8 gxf3? And what if we continue this variation a little further with 8...♘d7 9 0-0-0 ♕a5, followed by an all-out attack on the queenside by Black with ...b5 and ...♘b6-c4 *and* an all-out attack on the kingside by White with e5, f5 or h4-h5?

Finally, **4...a6** is even more provocative. Here Black intends to combine ...b5 with ...♗b7, attacking e4; for instance, 5 ♘f3 b5 6 ♗d3 ♗b7.

Likewise, if White plays **4 ♘f3** *(D)*, there are some adventurous alternatives to a transposition to a Classical Pirc with **4...♘f6** (see page 457).

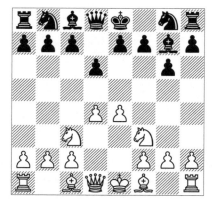

To begin with, **4...♗g4** seems logical, but although this is certainly a reasonable move it has never really caught on, probably because 5 ♗e3 ♘c6 6 ♗b5 neutralizes the pressure against d4, an option that is not available to White in the Classical Pirc.

4...c6 is more popular, now not with the idea of playing ...♕b6, but to continue ...b5, quite possibly in combination with ...♘f6. Black is hoping to reach the typical middlegame of the 6...c6 variation of the Classical Pirc in a slightly more favourable version. A subtle variation!

The most provocative move is **4...a6** again. Many opponents may find this rather phlegmatic treatment of the opening quite irritating, for Black is in effect practically ignoring classical principles (*and* his opponent!). After a seemingly simple and solid continuation like 5 ♗e2 b5 6 0-0 ♗b7 White still has to reckon with both ...b4 and ...♘bd7 followed by ...c5.

4 ♗e3 *(D)* also has to be studied in combination with its sister variation, 4 ♗e3 against the Pirc.

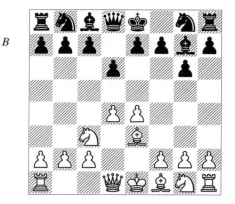

Black may of course immediately transpose with **4...♘f6**, but – analogous to postponing ...♗g7 in the Pirc – it seems logical to try postponing ...♘f6 in this case and developing the queenside first, with moves like **4...c6** 5 ♕d2 b5 or 5...♘d7. Again **4...a6** is a popular alternative, more so in fact than in any of the lines that we previously looked at. Here too, it is a certain psychological element, as well as the prospect of attacking the centre with 5 ♕d2 b5 6 f3 ♘d7 and ...c5, that makes this variation attractive.

Other fourth moves present a similar picture. Black always has the option of looking for something better than a transposition to the Pirc Defence, but it usually is very hard to tell if these alternatives really *are* better. Theory does not provide us with clear answers (something it is not very good at in any case). The ideal 1...g6 player is someone who does not need theoretical confirmation and who is always willing to extend the frontiers of his knowledge (and ours).

Scandinavian Defence

| 1 | ... | **d5** *(D)* |

Whereas 1...g6 gives White a free hand entirely, 1...d5 limits his choice to the utmost. These two openings are opposites in everything. While 1...g6 is probably the ultimate in flexibility, 1...d5 creates a very definite type of position at once. And whereas after 1...g6 the battle often takes a long time to get properly started, after 1...d5 there is a crisis already.

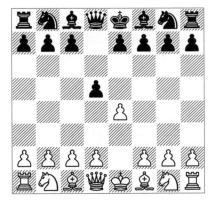

W

For all practical purposes, Black is making a mockery of the Caro-Kann and the French Defence. Why take the trouble to play 1...c6 or 1...e6 if you can play 1...d5 at once? But things are not that simple of course, or these two venerable openings would not have got a chapter of their own in this book and the Scandinavian would not have been squeezed in at the end. Theory has a very different view of the matter.

| 2 | **exd5** |

The great thing about the Scandinavian is that White cannot very well avoid this pawn exchange, for **2 e5 &f5 3 d4 e6** would produce an Advance Variation of the Caro-Kann with a beautiful extra move for Black, who has economized on ...c6.

The great drawback is that Black will have to take back on d5 and that – now that there is no

pawn on e6 or c6 to do the dirty work – this will have to be done either by the queen (**2...豐xd5**) or the knight (**2...♘f6**). Either way this will take up some time, which boils down to the fact that while Black is busy recapturing on d5, White will move his d-pawn to d4 and start developing his pieces.

But undeniably the strategic goal of 1...d5, the elimination of White's e4-pawn, has been achieved. It is not easy to weigh these two factors against each other, the disappearance of e4 on the one hand and the appearance of a pawn at d4 on the other. Theory has always been rather sceptical about the Scandinavian, but there have always been staunch supporters, great champions and exciting variations.

2...豐xd5

| 2 | ... | **豐xd5** |
| 3 | **♘c3** |

The classical and most logical move. White immediately accepts the free developing move to which 2...豐xd5 entitles him. But the alternative **3 ♘f3** is also not bad and perhaps rather frustrating to a player who was looking forward to the well-analysed 3 ♘c3 variations. White gives priority to his kingside development and cashes the free tempo afterwards. Depending on Black's reaction this may be done with ♘c3 or c4, for instance after **3...♘f6 4 d4 &g4 5 &e2 e6**.

| 3 | ... | **豐a5** |

The classical reply. Retreating the queen to d8 or d6 (**3...豐d8** or **3...豐d6**) is less compromising (for the queen is not safe at a5) but also less aggressive, though the latter move has also become quite popular of late.

| 4 | **d4** |

A powerful and consistent move, yet it reveals the point behind 3...豐a5: the c3-knight is now pinned.

| 4 | ... | **♘f6** |

There was a time when **4...e5** was seen as best on the grounds of a game Morphy-Anderssen from 1858. Having eliminated White's e-pawn, Black now gets rid of *all* the centre pawns. But the price of this 'achievement' is high, for it is precisely in an open, symmetrical position like this that White's lead in development becomes a telling factor. After 5 dxe5 ♕xe5+ 6 ♗e2 followed by 7 ♘f3 or simply 5 ♘f3, Black has far from solved his opening problems.

5   ♘f3 (D)

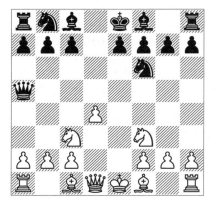

This is the main starting position of the 2...♕xd5 variation. The pawn-formation is identical to the one in those variations of the French and the Caro-Kann where Black exchanges pawns on e4, but the manoeuvre ...♕a5 gives the position a definite flavour of its own. There is little chance for Black to attack d4 directly, but he does have the opportunity of developing his queen's bishop actively. The variations roughly divide into those where Black plays ...♗g4 and those where he plays ...♗f5. Apart from the immediate **5...♗g4** and **5...♗f5**, there is also **5...c6**, a move that is often necessary in any case to prepare an escape-route for the queen. This allows Black to postpone the decision whether to play ...♗g4 or ...♗f5 until the next move.

The ...♗g4 lines are usually the sharpest, especially if Black, after **5...♗g4** 6 h3, for instance, does not exchange on f3 but maintains the pin on the f3-knight by playing 6...♗h5. The energetic but double-edged 7 g4 ♗g6 8 ♘e5, with the idea of continuing h4-h5, is critical. Likewise, **5...c6** 6 ♗c4 ♗g4 7 h3 ♗h5 8 g4 (or 8 ♗d2 e6 9 ♘d5 ♕d8 10 ♘xf6+) 8...♗g6 9 ♘e5 produces some lively complications.

A ...♗f5 set-up is less provocative. After **5...♗f5** 6 ♗c4 c6 (or **5...c6** 6 ♗c4 ♗f5) 7 ♗d2

e6 a critical position is reached. The great complexity of this variation is illustrated by the fact that the simple developing move 8 0-0 is almost never played. Much more popular are the sharp 8 ♕e2, the subtle 8 ♘e4 followed by 9 ♘g3 and the sobering 8 ♘d5 ♕d8 9 ♘xf6+, when 9...♕xf6 is met by 10 ♕e2. Without worrying about his c-pawn (10...♗xc2), White prepares both queenside castling and the strategically important d5 breakthrough.

2...♘f6

2   ...   ♘f6 (D)

Black would rather give away a pawn than a tempo by 2...♕xd5 3 ♘c3. Still, an eventual recapture on d5 cannot be avoided and even after ...♘xd5 White has the prospect of playing c4 at an opportune moment. But the big question is whether this advance builds up a strong or a vulnerable pawn-centre. It is around this positional problem that the 2...♘f6 variation revolves.

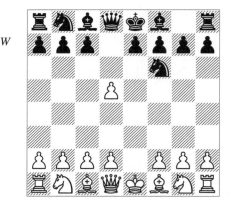

3   d4

This sensible move is the most common reply to 2...♘f6. Accepting the pawn sacrifice with **3 c4** c6 4 dxc6 is generally viewed as not very promising, since it is obvious that 4...♘xc6 5 d3 e5 offers Black sufficient compensation. He has a lead in development and White has seriously compromised his pawn-formation with holes at d3 and d4. Instead of 4 dxc6, however, there is the sound option of transposing to the Panov or the 2 c4 variation of the Caro-Kann with 4 d4 or 4 ♘c3 cxd5 5 cxd5 respectively (see pages 378 and 376). Some die-hard Scandinavian fans avoid these transpositions by playing 3...e6 instead of 3...c6, thus inviting their opponents not just to win a pawn but to build up a broad pawn-centre as well with 4 dxe6 ♗xe6 5 d4. This may lead to dangerous complications after 5...♗b4+ 6 ♗d2 ♕e7! 7 ♗xb4 ♕xb4+ 8 ♕d2 ♘c6!. A more cautious reply is 5 ♘f3 ♘c6 6 ♗e2 (instead of 5 d4).

3 ♗b5+ *(D)* is a more subtle approach, keeping the extra pawn at least a little bit longer.

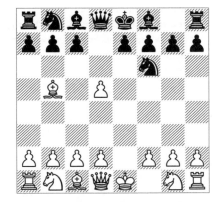

After the obvious reply 3...♗d7, White has a choice between the complications of 4 ♗c4 ♗g4 5 f3 ♗f5 and the simple 4 ♗e2 ♘xd5 5 d4. With Black's queen's bishop on d7 instead of c8, the pressure against d4 is weakened, which makes the ...g6 formation less effective. But 5...♗f5 is quite solid and likely to transpose to the 'regular' 4...♗f5 variation with 6 ♘f3.

The latter variation may look a little oversubtle for a fierce opening like the Scandinavian Defence, but it would be a mistake to think that a few simple and straightforward developing moves suffice to give White an opening advantage. A certain minimum of subtlety is required even here. The blunt **3 ♘c3**, for instance, transposes to a fairly harmless variation of the Alekhine Defence (see page 447).

In view of the fiery complications that we shall see in the next note, the cunning move-order **3 ♘f3**, with d4 to follow later, has been gaining ground in recent practice. 3...♗g4 can then be met by 4 ♗b5+.

3   ...   ♘xd5

It seems incredible but ever since around 1990 Black has had a serious alternative to this almost self-evident move: he can play **3...♗g4** *(D)*.

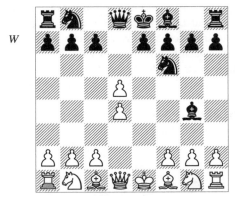

This wild new variation is based on two ideas, one extremely sober and one that completely sweeps away every rational or positional argument.

Firstly, Black wants to meet **4 ♘f3** with 4...♕xd5 after all, this time with the explicit idea of meeting 5 ♗e2 (for instance) with 5...♘c6 6 ♘c3 ♕h5 followed by castling queenside, a plan that was not available in the regular 2...♕xd5 variation. The modest **4 ♗e2** can be treated in the same way: 4...♗xe2 5 ♕xe2 ♕xd5 6 ♘f3 e6 followed by ...♘c6 and ...0-0-0.

Secondly, if White chooses the more ambitious **4 f3 ♗f5 5 c4** Black sets the board on fire (almost literally so!) with the double pawn sacrifice 5...e6! 6 dxe6 ♘c6!, the same motif as in the 3 c4 e6 variation. The sparkling activity of Black's pieces and the annoying weakening f3, which not only obstructs the much-needed developing move ♘f3 but makes White vulnerable on the e-file as well (something that becomes painfully clear after 7 exf7+? ♔xf7 8 ♗e3 ♗b4+ 9 ♘c3 ♖e8) combine to make the position very difficult to handle for White and perfect for an aggressive and dynamic Scandinavian player.

4   ♘f3 *(D)*

This cautious move is played slightly more often than the impetuous **4 c4**, but both moves have their pros and cons, and theory does not appear to have any preference for either move. It is important to note though that 4 c4 ♘b6 5 ♘c3 allows Black to seize the initiative with the pawn sacrifice 5...e5!? 6 dxe5 ♕xd1+ 7 ♔xd1 ♘c6 8 f4 ♗e6, which offers Black a marked lead in development. White may play 5 ♘f3 instead of 5 ♘c3, which after 5...g6 or 5...♗g4 transposes to the variations 4 ♘f3 g6 or 4 ♘f3 ♗g4 below (though with White having already committed himself to a c4 strategy). It is precisely to avoid these variations that 5 ♘c3 would be the obvious move (if it were not for 5...e5), for 5 ♘c3 eliminates the option 5...♗g4, while 5...g6 now allows 6 c5 ♘d5 7 ♗c4 with strong pressure against d5.

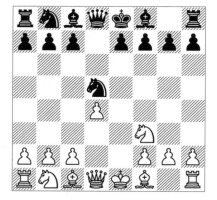

B

In this position there are two main lines, **4...g6** and **4...♗g4**, while a third move, **4...♗f5** is also played fairly often.

4...g6 is a real provocation to play c4, for although it is obvious that Black's g7-bishop will then become very powerful and that White's pawn-centre *might* be at risk, White's prospects of consolidating that centre and obtaining an opening advantage as a result look good. This variation is almost certain to produce a sharp fight. Some of the critical lines arise from **5 c4** ♘b6 6 ♘c3 ♗g7 7 ♗e2 0-0 8 0-0 and now either 8...♘c6 9 d5 ♘e5 or 8...♗g4. Sharpest of all is to play 7 h3 (instead of 7 ♗e2) 7...0-0 8 ♗e3 ♘c6 9 ♕d2, when after 9...e5 10 d5 ♘e7 11 g4 (stopping 11...♘f5) 11...f5 12 0-0-0 fxg4

13 ♘g5 White has consolidated his central formation but lost a pawn on the kingside.

The more cautious approach is not to play c4 at all. After **5 ♗e2 ♗g7 6 0-0 0-0 7 ♖e1**, for instance, the position resembles some of the calmer variations of the Alekhine Defence, like 4 ♘f3 dxe5 5 ♘xe5 g6 (see page 451). Black is not under any immediate pressure, but neither is White.

4...♗g4 is equally logical and perhaps a little more solid than 4...g6, since Black is not giving his opponent any targets. After 5 ♗e2 e6 6 0-0 ♘c6 7 c4 ♘b6 a problem arises which is highly characteristic of this variation: White's pawns on d4 and c4 are both threatened by the imminent ...♗xf3. Although there are several ways to do something about this (8 b3, for instance, with the idea of meeting 8...♗xf3 with 9 ♗xf3 ♘xd4 10 ♗xb7, regaining the pawn), there are many players who prefer to treat this variation either much more aggressively (with 5 h3 ♗h5 6 g4 ♗g6 7 ♘e5, for instance) or more conservatively (by omitting c4).

4...♗f5 *(D)* is the least provocative move.

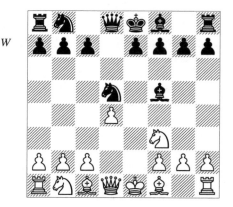

W

White can either proceed in classical fashion with 5 ♗e2 e6 6 0-0 (and after 6...♗e7 start wondering whether 7 c4 is going to be met by 7...♘b4), he can simplify the position with 5 ♗d3, or he can play 5 ♘h4. The latter option in particular is a step into uncharted territory and can be said to mark the end of our journey through the world of opening theory.

Index of Named Opening Lines

Index of Variations

Chapter Guide

Queen's Gambit Declined

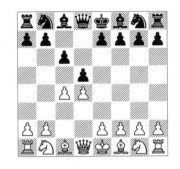

4...♗b7 *78* 5 ♗g2 ♗e7 6 0-0 *80*
4...♗a6 *81* 5 b3 ♗b4+ *82*
4 a3 *84*
4...♗b7 *84* 5 ♘c3 d5 *84*
4...♗a6 *85* 5 ♕c2 ♗b7 6 ♘c3 c5 7 e4 *86*
4 ♘c3 *86* 4...♗b4 5 ♗g5 ♗b7 6 e3 h6 7 ♗h4 *87*
4 e3 *87* 4...♗b7 5 ♗d3 *88*

Bogo-Indian Defence

1 d4 ♘f6 2 c4 e6 3 ♘f3 ♗b4+ *89*
4 ♗d2 *89*
4 ♘bd2 *91*

King's Indian Defence

1 d4 ♘f6 2 c4 g6 (without ...d5) *93*
3 ♘c3 *94* 3...♗g7 4 e4 d6 *94*

W

5 f4 *95* 5...0-0 6 ♘f3 *95*
  6...c5 *95* 7 dxc5 ♕a5 *95*
  6...♘a6 *96*
5 f3 *97* 5...0-0 6 ♗e3 *98*
5 ♘f3 *101* 5...0-0 6 ♗e2 *101* 6...e5 *102*
  7 dxe5 *103* 7...dxe5 8 ♕xd8 ♖xd8 9 ♗g5 *103*
  7 d5 *103* 7...a5 8 ♗g5 h6 9 ♗h4 ♘a6 *104*
  7 0-0 *104*

B

  7...exd4 *105* 8 ♘xd4 ♖e8 9 f3 *105*
  7...♘bd7 *105*
  7...♘c6 *106* 8 d5 ♘e7 *107*
  7...♘a6 *109*

7 ♗e3 *110* 7...♘g4 8 ♗g5 f6 9 ♗h4 *111*
5 ♗e2 0-0 6 ♗g5 *111*
  6...c5 *111* 7 d5 *111*
  6...h6 *113*
  6...♘bd7 *113* 7 ♕d2 e5 8 d5 ♘c5 9 f3 a5 *113*
  6...♘a6 *113*
3 g3 *114* 3...♗g7 4 ♗g2 0-0 5 ♘c3 d6 6 ♘f3 *114*
  6...♘bd7 *115* 7 0-0 e5 8 e4 *115*
  6...♘c6 *116* **7 0-0** *116*
    7...e5 *117*
    7...a6 *117* 8 d5 ♘a5 9 ♘d2 c5 *118*
  6...c5 *118* 7 0-0 ♘c6 8 dxc5 dxc5 *119*
  6...♘c6 *119* 7 0-0 ♕a5 8 h3 *120*

Grünfeld Defence

1 d4 ♘f6 2 c4 g6 (with ...d5) *121*
3 ♘c3 d5 *121*

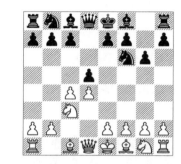

W

4 cxd5 *121* 4...♘xd5 5 e4 ♘xc3 6 bxc3 ♗g7 *121*
  7 ♘f3 *122* 7...c5 *122*
    8 ♗e3 *122* 8...♕a5 9 ♕d2 ♘c6 10 ♖c1 *123*
    8 ♖b1 *124* 8...0-0 9 ♗e2 *124*
      9...♘c6 *125*
      9...cxd4 *126*
  7 ♗c4 *126* 7...c5 8 ♘e2 ♘c6 9 ♗e3 0-0 *126*
4 ♗g5 *127* 4...♘e4 5 ♗f4 *128*
4 ♗f4 *129* 4...♗g7 *129*
  5 e3 *129* 5...c5 6 dxc5 ♕a5 *130*
  5 ♘f3 *131* 5...0-0 *131*
4 ♘f3 *131* 4...♗g7 5 ♕b3 dxc4 6 ♕xc4 0-0 *131*
7 e4 *132*

B

Benoni and Benko

Other 1 d4 ♘f6 Openings

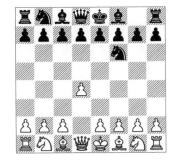

Dutch Defence

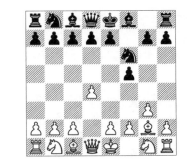

Other 1 d4 Openings

1...g6 *193* **2 c4 ♗g7** *194* **3 e4 d6 4 ♘c3** *195*
   4...♘c6 *195*
   4...e5 *196* **5 ♘f3 exd4 6 ♘xd4 ♘c6** *197*

Symmetrical English

<u>**1 c4 c5**</u> *199*

W

2 ♘c3 *199*
   2...♘c6 *199* **3 g3 g6 4 ♗g2 ♗g7** *200*
   2...♘f6 *202* **3 g3 d5 4 cxd5 ♘xd5 5 ♗g2** *203*
2 ♘f3 *204*
   2...♘c6 *204*
      3 d4 *204* **3...cxd4 4 ♘xd4 ♘f6 5 ♘c3** *204*
      3 ♘c3 *207* **3...♘f6 4 g3** *208*
        4...d5 *209* **5 cxd5 ♘xd5 6 ♗g2** *209*
        4...g6 *210* **5 ♗g2 ♗g7 6 d4 cxd4 7 ♘xd4 0-0** *210*
   2...♘f6 *211*

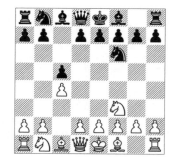

W

   3 d4 *212* **3...cxd4 4 ♘xd4 e6 5 g3** *213*
   3 ♘c3 *214*
      3...d5 *214* **4 cxd5 ♘xd5** *214*
      3...e6 *216* **4 g3 b6 5 ♗g2 ♗b7 6 0-0 ♗e7** *216*
        7 d4 *216* **7...cxd4 8 ♕xd4 d6** *217*
        7 ♖e1 *218* **7...d6 8 e4 a6 9 d4** *219*
   3 g3 *220* **3...b6 4 ♗g2 ♗b7 5 0-0 g6 6 ♘c3** *221*

Reversed Sicilian

<u>**1 c4 e5**</u> *222* **2 ♘c3** *222*
2...♘c6 *223* **3 g3 g6 4 ♗g2 ♗g7** *223*
2...♘f6 *224* **3 ♘f3 ♘c6** *225*

4 d4 *226*
4 e3 *226* **4...♗b4 5 ♕c2** *227*
4 g3 *227*

B

   4...d5 *228* **5 cxd5 ♘xd5 6 ♗g2 ♘b6 7 0-0** *228*
   4...♗b4 *230* **5 ♗g2 0-0 6 0-0 e4** *230*
   4...♗c5 *231* **5 ♗g2 d6 6 0-0 0-0** *231*
   4...♘d4 *232* **5 ♗g2 ♘xf3+ 6 ♗xf3 ♗b4** *232*

1 c4 ♘f6 and Other English Lines

<u>**1 c4**</u> *233* <u>**1...♘f6**</u> *233*
2 ♘c3 *235*
   2...e6 *235*
      3 e4 *235*
        3...d5 *236* **4 e5 d4 5 exf6 dxc3 6 bxc3 ♕xf6** *236*
        3...c5 *237* **4 e5 ♘g8** *237*
      3 ♘f3 *237*
        3...♗b4 *238* **4 ♕c2 0-0 5 a3 ♗xc3 6 ♕xc3** *239*
        3...b6 *239* **4 e4 ♗b7 5 ♗d3** *240*
   2...g6 *240*
   2...d5 *241* **3 cxd5 ♘xd5 4 g3 g6 5 ♗g2** *242*
2 ♘f3 *243*
   2...e6 *243* **3 g3 d5** *243*
   2...g6 *244* **3 ♘c3 d5 4 cxd5 ♘xd5** *245*
   2...b6 *246* **3 g3 ♗b7 4 ♗g2** *247*

Réti Opening

<u>**1 ♘f3**</u> *248*

B

1...d5 *249*

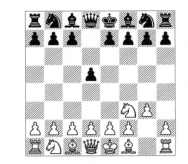

B

Other Flank Openings

Ruy Lopez

B

B

Italian Game

B

Scotch Opening

1 e4 e5 2 ♘f3 ♘c6 3 d4 *312* **3...exd4 4 ♘xd4** *312*

B

4...♗c5 *313*
  5 ♗e3 *313* 5...♕f6 6 c3 ♘ge7 *313*
  5 ♘xc6 *314* 5...♕f6 6 ♕d2 *314*
  5 ♘b3 *315* 5...♗b6 6 a4 a6 7 ♘c3 *315*
4...♘f6 *315*
  5 ♘c3 *315*
  5 ♘xc6 *316* 5...bxc6 6 e5 ♕e7 7 ♕e2 ♘d5 *317*

Four Knights Game

1 e4 e5 2 ♘f3 ♘c6 3 ♘c3 *318* **3...♘f6 4 ♗b5** *319*

B

4...♗b4 *320* 5 0-0 0-0 6 d3 d6 7 ♗g5 *320*
4...♘d4 *320* 5 ♗a4 ♗c5 6 ♘xe5 0-0 *321*

Petroff Defence

1 e4 e5 2 ♘f3 ♘f6 *322*
3 ♘xe5 *322* 3...d6 4 ♘f3 ♘xe4 5 d4 *323*
3 d4 *325* 3...♘xe4 4 ♗d3 *325* 4...d5 5 ♘xe5 *326*

King's Gambit

1 e4 e5 2 f4 *328*
2...exf4 3 ♘f3 *329*
  3...g5 *331* 4 h4 g4 5 ♘e5 *332*
  3...d5 *333* 4 exd5 ♘f6 *333*
2...d5 *334* **3 exd5** *334*

3...e4 *335* 4 d3 ♘f6 5 dxe4 ♘xe4 *335*
3...c6 *335* 4 ♘c3 exf4 5 ♘f3 ♗d6 6 d4 ♘e7 *336*
2...♗c5 *336* 3 ♘f3 d6 *336*

Other 1 e4 e5 Openings

1 e4 e5 *337*
2 ♘f3 ♘c6 3 c3 *337*
2 ♘f3 d6 *338* 3 d4 *338*
2 ♘f3 f5 *339*
2 ♘c3 *340*
  2...♘f6 *340*
    3 f4 *341* 3...d5 4 fxe5 ♘xe4 *341*
    3 ♗c4 *341* 3...♘c6 4 d3 *342*
    3 g3 *342*
  2...♘c6 *343* 3 f4 exf4 4 ♘f3 g5 5 h4 g4 6 ♘g5 *344*
2 ♗c4 *344* 2...♘f6 3 d3 c6 4 ♘f3 d5 5 ♗b3 *345*
2 d4 *346* 2...exd4 3 ♕xd4 ♘c6 4 ♕e3 *346*

French Defence

1 e4 e6 *347* **2 d4 d5** *349*

W

3 exd5 *349* 3...exd5 *349*
3 e5 *350* 3...c5 4 c3 ♘c6 5 ♘f3 ♕b6 *351*
3 ♘c3 *353*
  3...dxe4 *353*
  3...♘f6 *355*
    4 e5 *355* 4...♘fd7 5 f4 c5 6 ♘f3 ♘c6 7 ♗e3 *356*
    4 ♗g5 *357*
      4...dxe4 *357* 5 ♘xe4 ♗e7 6 ♗xf6 *358*
      4...♗e7 *359* 5 e5 ♘fd7 6 ♗xe7 ♕xe7 *359*
      4...♗b4 *360* 5 e5 h6 6 ♗d2 ♗xc3 7 bxc3 *361*
  3...♗b4 *363* 4 e5 c5 *364* 5 a3 *365*
3 ♘d2 *369*
  3...c5 *370* **4 exd5** *370*
    4...exd5 *370*
    4...♕xd5 *371*
  3...♘f6 *372* 4 e5 ♘fd7 5 ♗d3 c5 6 c3 ♘c6 *373*

Caro-Kann Defence

1 e4 c6 *375* **2 d4 d5** *377*
3 exd5 cxd5 4 ♗d3 *377*

Sicilian Defence

1 e4 c5 *389*

Alekhine Defence

Pirc Defence

Other 1 e4 Openings

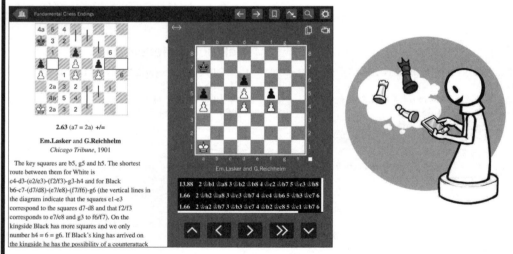